CHURCHILL: WARRIOR

CHURCHILL: WARRIOR

How a Military Life Guided Winston's Finest Hours

BRIAN LAVERY

CASEMATE

Oxford & Philadelphia

Published in Great Britain and the United States of America in 2017 by
CASEMATE PUBLISHERS
The Old Music Hall, 106–108 Cowley Road, Oxford OX4 1JE, UK
and
1950 Lawrence Road, Havertown, PA 19083, US

Hardcover Edition: ISBN 978-1-91086-022-9
Digital Edition: ISBN 978-1-61200-567-6

A CIP record for this book is available from the British Library

—

Printed and bound in the United Kingdom by TJ International Ltd
Typeset in India by Lapiz Digital Services, Chennai

For a complete list of Casemate titles, please contact:

CASEMATE PUBLISHERS (UK)
Telephone (01865) 241249
Email: casemate-uk@casematepublishers.co.uk
www.casematepublishers.co.uk

CASEMATE PUBLISHERS (US)
Telephone (610) 853-9131
Fax (610) 853-9146
Email: casemate@casematepublishers.com
www.casematepublishers.com

Contents

Acknowledgements

Thanks are due to John Lee for suggesting the book in its present form and encouraging me with it; and to Deborah Blake for editing it sympathetically. Also to the staffs of the London Library, Churchill Archives Centre, Imperial War Museum, National Maritime Museum, British Library, Public Record Office of Northern Ireland, and the National Archives at Kew.

Introduction

Monday 28 April 1941 was a relatively ordinary day during the extraordinary years of the Second World War. The British Prime Minister had spent the weekend in the country retreat at Chequers. General Sir Alan Brooke, the commander-in-chief of home forces, thought Churchill was in 'great form' after a broadcast to the nation. Though he was kept up until 3.30 am, he wrote to Churchill that 'These informal talks are of the very greatest help to me,'[1] though in later times he would be less happy about the Prime Minister's late hours. Meanwhile Churchill was driven 40 miles, partly though the blitzed streets of London, back to Downing Street to begin his day's work. He drafted a long memo on the situation in the Middle East, looking at the prospects there now that Greece had been evacuated, and considered the possibilities of war with Japan, which he thought unlikely for the moment. He produced another memo on the use of fighter aircraft fired by catapult from merchant ships to drive off enemy reconnaissance aircraft, to be presented to the Battle of the Atlantic Committee which he chaired. In a separate memo he asked about plans for the evacuation of Egypt if the enemy advance continued there. Another memo queried what had happened about his order of last summer to train 5,000 parachute troops, though that was reduced to 500. He had heard that the Italians had shot Free French prisoners of war and wanted to consider the question of reprisals. He suggested that the navy should resume the blockade of enemy-held ports in Tripoli and asked about plans to defend Crete, where it was believed the enemy was planning an airborne attack. He wrote to the Foreign Secretary telling him not to discourage direct questions from President Roosevelt, for United States support was crucial to his plans; and Lord Halifax was also to consult with the Ministry for Economic Warfare about an Italian presence in Iraq. He followed up a previous telegram to the commander-in-chief in the Mediterranean about general policy.

Every one of these memos was personal to Churchill. His secretary, John Colville, later wrote that by 1943 'it was possible to imitate his style fairly closely on matters which were not of supreme importance and I reached the stage where I could draft most of his shorter compositions without his correcting them'.[2] But there was no suggestion that was happening in 1941. There was never any doubt that Churchill's own thoughts were being conveyed in the memos, and he was not dependent on expert advisers in producing them.

All this was done before or after a long lunch followed by his usual afternoon nap. Then in the evening he chaired a meeting of the War Cabinet in which he agreed to have an open debate in the House of Commons on the progress of the war, and offered to begin it himself. He commented on unexpectedly low figures for shipping losses, which paradoxically should not be published as they might give ammunition to American isolationists who would argue that US support was not needed. He thought that American journalists were not being fed enough news, which gave the Germans an advantage. He wanted to warn the puppet Vichy government in France that they should not allow German troops in their colonies, and foresaw friendly neutrality from Turkey. He discussed the evacuation from Greece in some detail, and thought that its success was a matter for congratulation. But still his day was not done, for at 9.30 that evening he took the chair at a meeting of the Defence Committee of the War Cabinet, attended by the heads of the armed services as well as politicians. He wanted the army to fight for every inch in Egypt now that the Germans were fighting there as well as the far less effective Italians. He was told that tanks were the key to desert warfare, and current British types were unsuitable. He queried the efficiency of the air force in the region and was reassured by the Chief of Air Staff. It was clear that Churchill had views on every aspect of the war on land, sea and in the air, as well as its effect on neutral and friendly countries.

It was not just his work rate and his self-confidence which allowed Churchill to dominate the war effort. He had a unique and intimate inside knowledge of all three services which allowed him to assess their real needs – a crucial task when money, material resources, and especially manpower, were reaching their limits. No defence minister in modern times has faced such severe problems. No one else has ever been able to balance the needs of the services in such a way – most of the ministers came from outside with little service experience, while for those trained in a service career it is almost impossible to gain inside knowledge without a bias in favour of one service or another. But Churchill's knowledge of the three services was almost perfectly balanced by his experiences since he first joined the army in 1893. He made his share of mistakes as a war leader, but this balance served him, his cause and his country well.

This book looks at how Churchill gained his unique insight into war strategy and administration, and the impact this had on his thinking and leadership. The final part deals with the effect of these experiences on his wartime leadership – not just the direct references to the past, which are relatively few, but how they gave him the knowledge and confidence to deal with advisers who were usually vastly more knowledgeable and experienced within their own fields. It is not intended as a history of the Second World War, or even of Churchill's role in it, but as a demonstration of how his past experiences affected his conduct and decision, and how much his personal opinions and interventions affected policy.

It may be difficult to believe there is a gap in Churchill studies, but this book is intended to fill one. His most extensive biographies have been written by political historians who do not always stress the importance of the military dimension in his life. Military histories of the period often focus on specific issues. For example, there are many books on naval history before 1914, but they usually deal with specific aspects – technology, ship design, strategy, gunnery, aviation, administration and so on – and these works do not always appreciate the full range of Churchill's activity. His administration of the Admiralty from

1911–14 is overshadowed by the Fisher reforms which went before it, and the dramatic events of his own later career, but this book will contend that it was one of the most important periods in his life, and that his reforms, had war not intervened, would have seemed as important as those of Fisher, and often more successful.

Military historians are also sceptical about Churchill's influence, not understanding the depth of his knowledge and his hunger to acquire it. He alienated many people over the years with his overbearing manner, his combative style, his political misjudgements, especially during the 1920s, and his violent opposition to left-wing causes such as the Russian Revolution and the General Strike. All this is reflected in history and in hostile biographies. There is no doubt that he made his share of mistakes, though these have been exaggerated because in his early days he lacked the politician's ability to sidestep blame, particularly in the case of the Dardanelles. This book attempts to produce a balanced view, and it will show that his many insights helped to create the tools for fighting the Second World War, and equipped him mentally to conduct it.

Throughout most of his life Churchill would pursue three careers, as warrior, wordsmith and politician. He was a warrior rather than a mere soldier, for he was never likely to become a cog in the military machine but was always an independent force. If he ever became 'cannon fodder' it was not because he was driven to it by the intransigence of generals, but because of his own bravery, which bordered on recklessness. As a wordsmith he wrote as well as he spoke, though usually with a great deal of preparation – his doctor Charles Wilson wrote later: 'Without that feeling for words, he might have made little enough of his life.'[3]

The three careers often supported one another. His role as a war correspondent allowed him to see a greater variety of war than any of his contemporary officers, while his training and experience as a soldier gave him insight into topography and tactics. Lecturing to the Royal United Services Institute in 1901, Churchill suggested that official war correspondents might be found among the junior officers – 'trustworthy and clever, with a good military education and a nice literary style'; one might almost suspect that he was looking for a role for himself, except that by that time he had been elected to parliament. He started his political career on the crest of his South African adventures, but throughout it he would deploy his broad knowledge of military affairs. Whilst his combative style would prove valuable in war, it would often be disastrous in peace.

His military upbringing was reflected in his parliamentary career. One commentator wrote in 1908, after Churchill had spent some years as a Liberal member.

> ... the whole spirit of his politics is military. It is impossible to think of him except in terms of actual warfare. The smell of powder is about his path, and whenever he appears one seems to hear the crack of musketry and to feel the hot breath of battle. To his impetuous swiftness he joins the gift of calculating strategy. His eye takes in the whole field, and his skirmishes are not mere exploits of reckless adventure, but are governed by the purpose of the main battle.[4]

Besides his role in the legislature, Churchill was part of the executive for the most important parts of his life. He was immensely proud of the way in which British politicians maintained their supervision over the military. Though he was referring to Lloyd George and his intervention with the Admiralty in 1917 to defeat the U-boat, Churchill's comments of 1932 also referred to his own attitudes and self-confidence:

> ... we British politicians ... were powerful people, feeling they owed their positions to no man's favour. They asked all kinds of questions. They did not always take 'No' for an answer. They did not accept the facts and figures put before them by their experts as necessarily unshakable. They were not under moral awe of professional authority, if it did not seem reasonable to the lay mind. They were not above obtaining secretly the opinions of the junior officers concerned with the problem, and of using these views to cross-examine and confute the naval chiefs.[5]

His experience as a warrior complemented his role as an administrator. One of his best-known biographers wrote in 2001: 'Churchill's position after 1914 ... turned on his vastly greater knowledge of naval and military commanders than that possessed by any of his ministerial colleagues – except for Kitchener'.[6] But it was far more than that; already he had deep knowledge of the customs, material and practices of both services. Eventually he would spread this to include the air force. In March 1926 he wrote of his 'unequalled experience of all three fighting departments'.[7] This experience and knowledge had been 'bought not taught', as he told Neville Chamberlain at the start of the Second World War.[8] His research assistant Maurice Ashley claimed that 'much of his conduct as prime minister and minister of defence in the war of 1939–1945 was powerfully influenced by what he had learned not only in taking part in the previous world war but also in writing about it'.[9] When he took office as Prime Minister during the fateful month of May 1940, as he recalled later, 'I felt as if I was walking with destiny, and that my past life had been but a preparation for this hour and for this trial. ... I thought I knew a good deal about it all, and I was sure I should not fail.'[10] His military experience was an essential part of this preparation.

PART I

Preparing for War

CHAPTER I

Becoming a Soldier

Winston Leonard Spencer-Churchill was born on 30 November 1874, in a room just off the Great Hall of Blenheim Palace, his grandfather's home. The Palace was hung with tapestries of the military victories of their great common ancestor, John Churchill, 1st Duke of Marlborough (1650–1722), but they probably did not make more than a subliminal impression on the infant. His first recorded military experience, and his oldest memory, was of a parade of riflemen in Dublin where his father Lord Randolph was secretary to the Viceroy. He even claims to have remembered and understood the phrase 'and with a withering volley he shattered the enemy's line' – a considerable feat for a five-year-old.[1] He wrote later, 'From very early youth I had brooded about soldiers and war ...'.[2] He was back among the Marlborough tapestries at Blenheim in 1882 at the age of seven when his mother sent him a present of soldiers and a castle,[3] and they must have seemed appropriate in a huge and magnificent house built as a reward for military victory. By 1882 Winston had 'such wonderful toys; a real steam engine, a magic lantern, and a collection of soldiers already nearly a thousand strong'.[4] In 1885 his brother Jack was sent a box of soldiers representing the Nile expedition which led to the death of General Gordon at Khartoum that year, and the two were building their miniature armies. Most model soldiers were made in Germany at that time, particularly by Georg Heyde of Dresden who cast 'semi-solid' and 'solid' figures in lead in a great variety of periods and nationalities – it was just before William Britain of London entered the field in 1893 with much lighter and cheaper 'hollow cast' soldiers, bringing in a golden age for the collector.[5] But so far military affairs had played only a small part in Winston's life and he was far more concerned with his difficulties at school, where he failed dismally to understand the key subject of Latin.

Around the time of Winston's entrance to Harrow School in 1888, his father made a 'formal visit of inspection' to his model soldiers. He now had nearly 1,500, all to the same scale and organised with precocious military understanding into an infantry division and a cavalry brigade supported by 18 field guns plus fortress pieces. It was lacking in 'what every army is always short of – transport' until a family friend provided funds to make up the deficiency. Winston knew how to rig the battles against his brother Jack, who was only allowed 'coloured' troops without artillery. Lord Randolph spent 20 minutes studying the 'impressive scene' – a comparatively long time for him to be with his children – and then asked Winston if he would like to go into the army. The boy naively thought that it would be 'splendid to command an army' and that his father has discerned some military genius in him, so he gave an enthusiastic 'yes' – but Lord Randolph had merely decided that he was not clever enough to go to the bar.[6] Nevertheless, as Churchill wrote later, 'the toy soldiers turned the current of my life. Henceforward all my education was directed to passing into Sandhurst and afterwards to the technical details of the profession of arms. Anything else I had to pick up for myself.'[7]

That meant training with Harrow School's rifle corps in his spare time, and eventually joining the army class there. In June 1888 he wrote to his father: 'I am getting on very successfully in the corps especially in the shooting. We use the full sized Martini-Henry rifle and cartridges, the same as the Army. The rifles kick a good deal ...'.[8] Late in October, 'The Rifle Corps had a grand sham fight yesterday which Mamma saw. Harrow versus Haileybury and Cambridge. Harrow won – we defended the town successfully for two hours.'[9] There was an even grander affair in March 1889 when the corps went to Aldershot to join 1,300 other public schoolboys and 11,000 regulars. The mock battle 'was great fun. The noise was tremendous. There were four batteries of guns on the field and a Maxim, and several Nordenfelts. We were defeated because we were inferior in numbers and not from any want of courage.'[10]

But these were merely pleasant interludes in the daily grind of study. In September 1889 J. E. C. Welldon, the headmaster, told Lord Randolph that Winston's mathematics were not good enough for the engineers and artillery in the Royal Military College at Woolwich, so he would be trained to pass into the other college at Sandhurst with a view to joining the cavalry or infantry.[11] At the end of the month Winston reported: 'I have joined the "Army class". It is rather a bore as it spoils your half holiday: however we do French and geometrical drawing which are the two things most necessary for the army' – or at least for passing the entrance examinations.[12] He did well in English composition, which boded well for his career as a writer and orator. For the dreaded subject of Latin, he formed an alliance with an older boy to do each other's homework until he was almost caught out in an oral examination.[13]

As to the army class,

> It consisted of boys of the middle and higher forms of the school and of very different ages, all of whom were being prepared either for the Sandhurst or the Woolwich examination. We were withdrawn from the ordinary movement of the school from form to form. In consequence I got no promotion, or very little, and remained quite low down upon the School List, though working alongside boys nearly all in the Fifth Form. Officially I never got out of the Lower School, so I never had the privilege of having a fag of my own.[14]

For the entrance examination to Sandhurst, he chose French and chemistry alongside the compulsory subjects of mathematics, English and Latin. He was strong in English and chemistry but needed at least one other subject to gain entry, and mathematics seemed the most likely. At his first attempt he had gained only 500 marks out of 2,500 for the subject. Special coaching by one of the Harrow masters brought him up to nearly 2,000 at the second try, but nevertheless he failed overall. Like many other potential officers he was then sent to a 'crammer' to be prepared specifically for the third attempt. It was run by Captain James in the Cromwell Road in London. 'It was said that no one who was not a congenital idiot could avoid passing thence into the Army. ... They knew with almost Papal Infallibility the sort of questions which that sort of person would be bound on the average to ask on any of the selected subjects.' It was a 'renowned system of intensive poultry-farming'.[15] However his natural bravery turned to foolhardiness when he failed to leap across a chine or ravine near Bournemouth, and he spent several months recovering from his injuries. Eventually he qualified for a cavalry cadetship at Sandhurst, though his marks were not high enough for the infantry, much to the disgust of his father.

Gentleman-Cadet Churchill arrived in the mock-Georgian splendour of the Royal Military College Sandhurst at the beginning of September 1893, to spend the first three days 'being measured for the uniform and finding one's way about – the latter no easy task in so huge a building'. He found a discipline which was far stricter than at Harrow: 'No excuse is ever taken – not even the plea of "didn't know" after the first few hours: and of course no such thing as unpunctuality or untidiness is tolerated', and his first conduct report stated 'Good, but unpunctual.'[16] In general he liked the life but had to get away at weekends – in April 1894 he wrote that he could not endure two Sundays running in the place.[17] He had the greatest pleasure in riding, claiming that 'no-one ever came to grief – except honourable grief – through riding horses. No hour of life is lost that is spent in the saddle.'[18] With the help of private lessons he became one of the best riders in the college, in December 1894 he took part in a gruelling college competition in which he jumped with and without stirrups and with his hands behind his back. He came second with 199 marks out of 200.[19]

On to the more academic side, he ordered several books, including the works of Prince Kraft zu Hohenlohe-Ingelfingen, lauding the Germany army and its performance in the war of 1866 against Austria and in 1870–71 against France. Kraft still assumed troops would fight in line, and only made a brief mention of the 'mitrailleuse', the primitive machine-gun used by the French. Though he was a gunner himself, Kraft asserted that 'Cavalry, like artillery, can only expect to obtain the best results, if it remains always convinced that it is only an auxiliary to the infantry. The infantry is the army, and makes use of cavalry and artillery. The cavalry must work for the infantry, and can learn only by close union with the infantry what services the latter will require from it …'.[20] Its main service was reconnaissance ahead of the infantry, for the days of the great cavalry charge were over. But Kraft was only thinking about European armies, not the less sophisticated forces in the overseas empires. Another source was Colonel Edward Hamley's *Operations of War*, first published in 1866 and again in 1878 and 1900. As well as the Napoleonic Wars it drew heavily on the more recent experiences of the American Civil War when rifles became standard for the first time. It began by claiming that the 'very numerous' readers of military history saw it as a romance, whereas he applied an encyclopaedic knowledge of battles past to study war scientifically. As well as citing the work nearly half a century later,[21] Churchill perhaps learned something about how to present the subject on paper, and Hamley's use of maps, 'containing all that is wanted and no more', was almost as well-contrived and extensive as Churchill's own in his later writings.

According to the syllabus approved by Major-General Edward Clive in 1888, the course at Sandhurst consisted of seven subjects. Gymnastics was to be done 'As laid down in the regulations' while Drill was not described at all. Churchill wrote later: 'From nine to ten there is drill, and the broad square in front of the College resounds with the cautions of the manual firing and bayonet exercises, and those more violent forms of exertion which come under the heading of "Physical Drill".' He remained very weak in both these subjects, but was happier when they were 'varied by a combined attack, with long lines of skirmishers, supports and reserves, upon the fir-woods beyond the cricket pavilion, terminating in a wild bayonet charge and frantic cheers'.[22] Fortification was a major subject and was one of Churchill's best, surprising for one who always looked to the offensive. The standard textbook was written by Colonel G. Phillips and first published in 1877. It was by no means confined to the formal and permanent stoneworks such as those that had been built around the Royal Dockyards in the 1860s, and it was far more prescient than Kraft about the role of machine-guns, even the relatively primitive models of the time. 'The Gatling … is capable of delivering a continuous stream of bullets at the rate of 400 per minute. Its fire is equal to that of about 22 rifles, and nearly equal to that of two 9-pdr guns up to 1,200 yards. The Gatling gun as a weapon for defensive positions is of great value.'[23] It was a warning of things to come.

'Military topography' began with map-reading but went on to drawing and sketching, which was essential in the days before photography became common. It may have contributed to Churchill's later skill as an artist, but for the moment he did not enjoy it: 'We have been doing a lot of sketching – maps etc. out of doors and it is very hot and uncomfortable work.'[24] It was not his best subject, in the final examination he had 471 marks out of 600. 'Elements of Tactics' was probably closer to his heart. Lectures were still based on those delivered by Francis Clery in 1872–75, and his textbook *Minor Tactics* was recommended for the course. Unlike Kraft, Clery used many examples from the Napoleonic Wars as well as from Germany's more recent conflicts, though he showed little interest in the American Civil War and touched only briefly on campaigns on the North-West Frontier of India. He was ambivalent about the role of cavalry. On the one hand, 'The power of cavalry lies in the impetus derived from motion. Accordingly, its action should under all circumstances be offensive. It should therefore never await an attack, should if possible forestall one, but in all cases should advance to meet it.' This must have seemed very attractive to Churchill, but Clery also wrote, 'Modern Warfare has reduced the role of cavalry on a battle field to very insignificant proportions. It has ceased to be used in great masses, or rather the attempts to use it in this manner have had as yet scarcely satisfactory results.'[25] Churchill did well in tactics, gaining 263 marks out of 300 in his final examinations. 'Military law' consisted largely of court martial procedure, while 'Military administration' dealt mainly with enlistment and payment of the men, with a conclusion on the logistics of supporting an army in the field. Churchill did quite well in these subjects, which perhaps befits a future government minister. In January 1895 he passed out of Sandhurst as 20th out of 130 in his class.

He was now qualified for an infantry regiment. His father had railed constantly against his extravagance and wanted to put him into the 60th Rifles, one of the most prestigious regiments apart from the Guards and under the colonelcy of the Duke of Cambridge, commander-in-chief of the army and a cousin of the Queen. In such a unit Lord Randolph would not have to bear the great expense of horses and uniforms – an infantry subaltern could be equipped for about £200, a cavalry officer might need £600–£1,000 for two chargers and elaborate uniforms.[26] A pattern book of 1894 describes the Hussar tunic: 'On each side of the breast six loops of gold chain gimp, forming three eyes at the top, passing under a netted cap at the waist, and ending with an Austrian knot reaching the bottom of the skirt; with a tracing of gold braid all round the gimp.' In addition an officer needed blue trousers, pantaloons for mounted duties and for evening levees, 'undress' or less formal frock and trousers, a blue and a serge patrol jacket, a stable jacket, a mess waistcoat, a cloak and a cape.[27]

With his love of riding it is not surprising that Winston was determined to join the cavalry, and he cultivated the friendship of Lieutenant-Colonel John Brabazon of the 4th Hussars stationed at Aldershot nearby. He visited them at the end of April 1894:

> In those days the mess of a regiment presented an impressive spectacle to a youthful eye. Twenty or thirty officers all magnificently attired in blue and gold, assembled round a table upon which shone the plate and trophies gathered by the regiment in two hundred years of sport and campaigning. It was like a state banquet. In an all-pervading air of glitter, affluence, ceremony, and veiled discipline, an excellent and lengthy dinner was served to the strains of the regimental string band.[28]

In May 1894 he wrote to his mother: 'How I wish I was going into the 4th instead of those old Rifles.'[29] He had already produced arguments in favour of the cavalry, which might have made his father question his belief that he would never make a good lawyer – promotion was quicker in the cavalry than the infantry, especially the 60th Rifles which was slowest of all; a commission would be obtained much sooner in the cavalry; the Hussars were going to India soon and if he joined quickly he would perhaps have six or seven others junior to him when the regiment was augmented before going overseas; cavalry regiments were generally taken good care of in India, whereas the infantry 'have to take what they can get'; and horses could be kept cheaper in the cavalry as the government would provide stabling and forage. He added some 'sentimental advantages' which perhaps appealed more to his mother than his stern father. These included the uniform, the interest of a life among horses, the 'advantages of riding over walking and of joining a regiment where he knew some of the officers'.[30] Lord Randolph Churchill died in January 1895. It is not clear if he approved of Winston's transfer to the cavalry before he died, or Winston relied on the acceptance of his more pliable mother. In any case, she wrote to the Duke of Cambridge to arrange his change of regiment.

★

The army consisted of four main elements, infantry, cavalry, artillery and engineers. Churchill was not eligible to serve in the last two because he had trained at Sandhurst rather than Woolwich. The infantry was dominated by the Cardwell System, set up in the 1870s. Each regiment had a local base and would recruit its men largely from that area, inspiring great loyalty among the troops and pride in the local population. Churchill always approved of this, writing in 1897 that the soldier's bravery came out of loyalty to 'something smaller and more intimate' than the nation, to 'the regiment, whatever it is called – "The Gordons", "The Buffs", "The Queen's".'[31] A regiment had two regular battalions, one serving overseas in the empire and the other at the depot for training and home defence, so they were not expected to serve together. In addition there was a part-time militia battalion and later several battalions of territorials, and these could be augmented in a major war, when up to 60 battalions might be raised. The system was less strong in the cavalry, where a regiment had only one regular battalion and its local associations were wider and vaguer; but the identity was just as strong. The colonel of the regiment was an honorary post, usually given to members of the royal family, local aristocrats or distinguished officers who had served in the regiment – Churchill would hold several such colonelcies in his later life. The battalion was led by a lieutenant-colonel, the commanding officer who set much of its tone.

Churchill's whole career depended on the development of the rifled gun for use on land, at sea and to a certain extent in the air. The infantryman's standard weapon now had an accurate range of up to 2,000 yards instead of 100 yards for a smooth-bore musket. Moreover with repeating rifles the volume of fire was greatly increased even before the machine-gun was taken into account. After using the Martini Henry with a .45 inch round which had strained Winston's shoulder in 1888, the British army reduced the calibre to .303 inches with the Lee-Metford, introduced just as Churchill entered the army class at Harrow. A shortened and improved version, the Short Magazine Lee-Enfield or SMLE, entered service in 1902 as Churchill began his political career, and in various marks it would remain the standard infantry weapon for more than half a century – when the Churchill government decided to replace it with the Belgian FN in 1954, he had to defend the rejection of a British weapon in an acrimonious debate.[32] Like nearly all rifles of the age it was 'repeating' rather than 'automatic' like a machine-gun. This meant that the bolt had to be opened and closed with every round, but the Lee-Enfield had a ten-round magazine, twice the size of its German rival. the Mauser. As to machine-guns, the navy had first used the Gatling and Nordenfelt in 1880 as a means to fight off torpedo boats, but the great breakthrough came when Hiram Maxim's gun reached the army in 1891 – it used the waste gases from the explosions to reload, eliminating the need to turn a handle. Despite the predictions in 'Phillips on Fortification', the full value of the machine-gun was not appreciated until 1914. After adopting the British name of Vickers, it became the standard heavy machine-gun for the army through two world wars and the main forward-firing gun of the air services.

As to artillery, rifled breech-loading guns came in from the 1880s, and in 1904, after failures during the Boer War, the British Army adopted the 18-pounder quick-firing field gun which could fire up to 20 explosive rounds per minute over more than four miles. Land forces could use much larger guns for fortress, siege and coastal artillery, but there were problems with moving and supplying them before motor vehicles became common. This was not a problem at sea where improved shells vied with new types of steel armour plate for several decades late in the century. Ships could already carry 12-inch guns firing 710 lb shells by 1900. But meanwhile Churchill's own arm, the cavalry, saw no improvements apart from better rifles, and it would soon find itself squeezed out to the fringes of the battle. From being the heroes of the massed battlefield charge of old, they were turning into a reconnaissance force or, worse still, mounted infantry, which most of the officers feared as it would devalue their long training and greatly reduce their status.

★

Churchill joined the 4th Hussars at Hounslow on 18 February 1895, and by April he was fitting all too well into the enclosed world of the officers' mess. He was implicated in the characteristic bullying of the day – in this case it was serious enough to attract attention in press and parliament. Already a young officer named Hodge had been dumped in a horse trough and forced out of the regiment. His successor, Allan Bruce, had been a colleague and rival of Churchill at Sandhurst. He was invited to a dinner at the Nimrod Club in London by a group of subalterns. Churchill, acting as their spokesman, 'informed Mr Bruce ... that he was not wanted in the regiment'. He was told that his allowance of £500 per year was not enough to support him, which was disingenuous as Churchill's was only £300 – but he had aristocratic connections. Bruce refused at first but was eventually forced out. His father campaigned on his behalf, but went too far in accusing Churchill of 'acts of gross immorality of the Oscar Wilde type' and had to pay £400 damages. There was another scandal when Churchill took part in a horse race, the 4th Hussars Challenge Cup, under the name of Mr Spencer. It was eventually found that one of the horses was a 'ringer'; the race was declared null and void by the National Hunt Committee, and all the horses which took part were perpetually disqualified. No action was taken against the participants, but the anti-military elements in the press made full use of the scandal, and Churchill's role was dubious to say the least.[33]

Reading Kraft had perhaps warned Churchill about the rigorous training needed in modern cavalry.

> Formerly it was sufficient to have a strong arm, a good sword, and the courage of a good rider on a good horse in order to be an excellent cavalry soldier. These are now only elementary matters of course; the improvement in firearms has so much increased the difficulties with which the cavalry have to struggle, with reference to their training and leading, that they daily require more energy and spirit, if these are to be overcome and the duties of the cavalry of the future are to be discharged.[34]

Churchill was never lacking in energy and spirit, but nevertheless the regimental training programme was formidable. He wrote:

> 75 per cent of the cavalry soldier's time was taken up with drill in preparation for shock tactics. ... It is quite true that he had a carbine, but that was only intended for bye-days. In every drill season, and at every inspection, regular, machine-like drill was what was required. ... And there is no doubt that they did it very excellently. Anyone who has led the directing troop of, let us say, the third squadron from the squadron of direction, in a long brigade advance, knows what an art troop-leading is, and what ceaseless practice and unremitting effort is required to obtain that accuracy of distance and alignment which is the proof of well-drilled, well-disciplined men. How beautiful it is too![35]

Regimental training tended to assume that the new officer knew little or nothing:

> ... the principle was that the newly-joined officer was given a recruit's training for the first six months. He rode and drilled afoot with the troopers and received exactly the same instruction and training. ... At the head of the file in the riding-school, or on the right of the squad on the Square, he had to try to set an example to the men. This was not a task always possible to discharge with conspicuous success. ... Many a time did I pick myself up shaken and sore from the riding-school tan and don again my little gold braided pork-pie cap ... with what appearance of dignity I could command, while twenty recruits grinned furtively but delightedly to see their officer suffering the same misfortunes which it was their lot so frequently to undergo.[36]

Despite this apparent equality on the training ground, the social gap between officers and men was immense. The pretext for the dismissal of the unfortunate Lieutenant Hodge was that he had visited the sergeants' mess to meet a veteran of the Crimean War. Churchill hardly mentions the rank and file in his autobiography – only that in the early days in India he often had 'a long day occupied mainly in scolding the troopers for forgetting to wear their pith helmets and thus risking their lives' and that there was a long-standing feud between the men of the 4th and 19th Hussars which did not extend to the officers.[37] As to the 'rankers' themselves, Sergeant S. Hallaway recalled his arrival: '... as Captain Kincaid and Mr Churchill walked over the squadron parade ground towards my stable I thought how odd he looked, his hair and gold lace forage cap the same colour'. He did not find the young officer easy to deal with.

> After a field day Mr Churchill would arrive at stables with rolls of foolscap and lots of lead pencils of all colours, and tackle me on the movements we had done at the exercise. We were nearly always short of stable men, and there were lots of spare horses to be attended to, so it was quite a hindrance to me. ... I was a busy man, and I had no time for tactics.[38]

But Churchill had plenty of time for tactics and other aspects of military science. At Sandhurst he had attended a course in the subject which was 'very interesting', and now he delivered an excellent lecture on musketry.[39]

CHAPTER 2

Wars and Words

As he awaited his regiment's move to India, Churchill decided to use his rather generous leave allowance to his mental and financial advantage. He was aware that in those days of peace, 'scarcely a captain, hardly ever a subaltern, could be found throughout Her Majesty's forces who had seen even the smallest kind of war. ... It seemed to my youthful mind that it must be a thrilling and immense experience to hear the whistle of bullets all round and to play at hazard from moment to moment with death and wounds.'[1] With his fellow subaltern Reginald Barnes he used contacts with the British Ambassador in Madrid to arrange a visit to Cuba where the natives were fighting the Spanish for their independence. The editor of the *Daily Graphic* commissioned him to write a series of letters from the conflict at a rate of five guineas each. He travelled by sea to New York and visited the American Sandhurst at West Point, but was shocked by the repressive treatment of the cadets: '... they have far less liberty than any private school boys in our country. I think such a state of things is positively disgraceful and young men of 24 or 25 who would resign their personal liberty to such an extent can never make good citizens or fine soldiers.'[2] He went by train to Florida and ship to Havana, which he thought was magnificent, then joined the army of Marshal Martinez Campos on a march to Sancti Spiritus, 'a very second-rate place and in the most unhealthy state'.[3] He soon saw that the great majority of the population supported the rebels and despaired of the country's future.

He heard plenty of 'the whistle of bullets all round', but it is doubtful if he did 'play at hazard from moment to moment with death and wounds' for the rebels' marksmanship was very poor.[4] Nevertheless a few shots did come close, and he now considered himself as having been under fire. Churchill saw the tactics of a guerrilla campaign – the word had been coined by the Spanish themselves during their 1808–14 insurrection against Napoleon:

> ... Maximo Gomez is encamped with 4,000 men a couple of leagues to the east, and early tomorrow we start after him. Whether he will accept battle is not certain, but if he does not want to fight the Spaniards have no means of making him do so, as the insurgents, mounted on their handy little country-bred ponies, knowing every inch of the ground, possessed of the most accurate information, and, unimpeded by any luggage, can easily defeat all attempts to force a battle.[5]

In general Churchill's comments on tactics were restrained, though the American journalist who claimed that he knew 'only the amount of strategy necessary for the duties of a second lieutenant' was perhaps being unfair.[6] He recognised that 'To describe ground shortly is always difficult, and to describe it at length is futile, as no-one ever takes the trouble to read the descriptions carefully', but his unhappy lessons in military topography had perhaps borne fruit, as can be seen in his descriptions. 'The road – if one may use such a term – lies sometimes along the bed of a watercourse and at others broadens out into a wide grass area. Frequently it is so traversed by morasses as to be quite impassable, and long detours have to be made across country. The intricate nature of the ground prevents anything like a thorough reconnaissance, and much has to be left to chance.'[7] His articles were a great success and launched his journalistic career. He remained fond of Cuba, smoking its cigars for the rest of his life and describing it as 'this large, rich beautiful island' in 1944.[8]

★

On arrival in India after a voyage on the SS *Britannia*, Churchill soon fell into the pattern of regimental life.

> Just before dawn, every morning, one was awakened by a dusky figure with a clammy hand adroitly lifting one's chin and applying a gleaming razor to a

lathered and defenceless throat. By six o'clock the regiment was on parade, and we rode to a wide plain and there drilled and manoeuvred for an hour and a half. We then returned to baths at the bungalow before the sun attained its fiercest ray. … the noonday asserted his tyrannical authority and long before eleven o'clock all the white men were in shelter. We nipped across to luncheon at half-past one in the blistering heat and then returned to sleep till five o'clock. Now the station begins to live again. It is the hour of Polo … for which we have been living all day long.[9]

After a game they 'returned to hot baths, rest, and at 8.30 dinner, to the strains of the regimental band and the clinking of ice in well-filled glasses' before going to bed at 10.30 or 11.[10] He soon became aware that the chances of action in his present post were small, and he was beginning to regret his lack of a university education. He wrote early in 1897: 'I find my literary tastes growing day by day – and if only I knew Latin and Greek I think I would leave the army and try to take my degree in history, philosophy and economics. But I cannot face parsing and Latin prose again.'[11] He read history and studied style, especially the classic historians Gibbon and Macaulay whose combination of historical narrative and beautifully balanced sentences made a deep impression on him.[12]

★

Churchill was on leave in England when he heard of an opportunity for active service, this time with the soldiers of his own country, and in a cause of which he had no doubts.[13] A revolt by Afghan tribes on the North-West Frontier of India was to be opposed by a large force of British and Indian troops. Civilisation, he wrote, 'is face to face with militant Mohammedanism'.[14] The expedition was to be commanded by another charismatic leader to match Colonel Brabazon, a man who was close to Churchill's ideal of a military hero:

Thirty-seven years of soldiering, of war in many lands, of sport of every kind, have steeled alike muscle and nerve. Sir Bindon Blood, himself … a keen polo player, is one of the few officers of high rank in the army, who recognise the advantages to soldiers of that splendid game. He has pursued all kinds of wild animals in varied jungles, has killed many pig with the spear and shot every species of Indian game, including thirty tigers to his own rifle.[15]

He was of a type 'which has not been, perhaps, possessed by any nation except the British, since the days when the Senate and the Roman people sent their proconsuls to all parts of the world'.[16] Churchill wrote to Blood asking for an appointment and interrupted his leave to sail back to India. With the help of his mother he arranged to have his reports published in the *Daily Telegraph* and the *Allahabad Pioneer*.

On the voyage out he was disappointed that no news awaited him at Port Said or Aden. On 17 August at Bangalore he was disappointed again, but soon he received a letter from Blood dated the 22nd. The general had already made up his staff and had no 'billet' for the moment, but he advised Churchill to come along as a press correspondent and he would find a military post for him at the first opportunity. 'Fincastle was arranged for in this way, and is now attached to the Guides *vice* an officer killed in action.'[17] Churchill therefore took the train north, a journey of five days, 'Nearly as far that is as across the Atlantic', and 'not a very pleasant experience'; but he was determined to take 'a good chance of seeing active service and securing a medal'.[18]

On arrival he wrote to Barnes: 'No fighting at present except firing into camp – à la Cuba – only on a smaller scale and no-one wounded since I have joined force.'[19] He saw similarities with Cuba in that it was difficult country with no obvious strategic points and a highly mobile guerrilla army with nothing to lose. It was very difficult for the regular forces to catch up with them, in which case they melted away.[20] Though the campaign would be almost forgotten today without Churchill's reports, he had no doubts about its importance. It was the most successful attempt so far to mobilise the frontier tribes.[21] A Jihad had been proclaimed, and to the tribesmen 'The combined allurements of plunder and paradise proved irresistible.'[22]

Soon he found himself in action, picked up a rifle from a wounded man and fired 40 shots, believing he killed four men. He produced the memorable comment: 'Nothing in life is so exhilarating as to be shot at without result.'[23] He was referring to the return of a patrol in which he had not taken part, but it is not misleading to suggest that it represented his own feelings for the rest of his life. When he published his account of the campaign he tried to make it impersonal, but to his mother, of all people, he wrote almost obsessively about being under fire and in danger. On 30 September there was 'another severe action ... I was under fire for five hours – but I did not get into the hottest corners. Our loss was 60 killed and five wounded – out of the poor 1,200 we can muster.'[24]

After an attack on 16 September he wrote frankly to his uncle Lord William Beresford, 'I daresay you have understood that their "retirement" was a rout; in this I was involved. The tribesmen got to within stone throwing distance. I fired nine shots from my revolver. The men were completely out of hand. The wounded were left to be cut up. We could do nothing.'[25] It was an extremely brutal war in which no quarter was given, the wounded were tortured and the dead mutilated, while medical facilities were special targets. As for the British, they destroyed the tanks which the tribesmen depended on for water in the summer. They used dum–dum bullets, and Churchill was strangely contradictory about the morality of this. In private he wrote that such bullets' 'shattering effects' were 'simply appalling'; he believed that 'no such bullet has ever been used on human beings before, but only on game ...',[26] but in his public writings he was prepared to justify and even praise it. The bullet was 'a wonderful and from the technical point of view a beautiful machine. On striking a bone this causes the bullet to "set up" or spread out, and then it tears and splinters everything before it, causing wounds which in the body must be generally mortal and in any limb necessitate amputation. ... I would observe that bullets are primarily intended to kill, and that these bullets do their duty most effectively, without causing any more pain to those struck by them.'[27] But to his mother he made the most startling claim, and we will never know how much it was tongue in cheek: 'Bullets – to a philosopher my dear Mamma – are not worth considering. Besides I am so conceited I do not believe the Gods would create so potent a being as myself for so prosaic an ending.'[28]

Already Churchill was beginning to find the essence of his tactics, to avoid the frontal assault if at all possible, whether in a skirmish in the mountains of India, or in a gigantic struggle to master Europe and the world. 'To capture the position by frontal assault would involve heavy loss. The enemy were strongly posted, and the troops would be exposed to heavy fire in advancing. On the other hand, if the ridge could once be captured, the destruction of the tribesmen was assured. ... Sir Bindon Blood ... determined to strike at the enemy's left, not only turning their flank, but cutting off their proper line of retreat.'[29] Despite the Sandhurst textbooks, he found some value in cavalry after a charge by the 13th Bengal Lancers at Shabkadar and by the Guides Cavalry and 11th Bengal Lancers during the relief of Chakara. But he complained that this was only for Indian regiments; British cavalry was too expensive to risk in action.[30] He entered the age-old debate about whether the sword or the lance was the best cavalry weapon and came down in favour of the latter, provided it was not allowed to sink too deep into its victim – otherwise the lance 'either gets broken or allows the enemy to wriggle up and strike the lancer'.[31]

Churchill saw the importance of transport, perhaps reflecting on his collection of model soldiers. 'I can well recall my amazement, when watching a camel convoy more than a mile and a half long, escorted by half a battalion of infantry. I was informed that it contained only two days' supplies for one brigade.'[32] The leather equipment worn by soldiers was excessively heavy and he suggested it should be replaced by web, or canvas. He saw the value of good signalling, by heliograph in this case. He deplored the short-service system now used by the army creating a prevalence of 21- or 22-year-old soldiers who could not compete with the long-serving Indian troops of perhaps 30.[33] But he did not let his own lack of years deter him from criticising his seniors.

He lauded the virtues of active service: 'From a military point of view, the perpetual frontier wars in one corner or other of the Empire are of the greatest value. This fact may one day be proved, should our soldiers ever be brought into contact with some peace-trained, conscript army, in anything like equal numbers.'[34] For officers, 'The ambition that a young officer entering the army ought to set before him, is to lead his own men in action. This ought to inspire his life, and animate his effort.'[35] Yet he never did command his own troops in action, and his whole life might be seen as a substitute for that. In this campaign, he admitted, 'I had no military command and only rode about trying to attract attention.'[36]

He was pleased with his articles in the *Telegraph* which clearly showed the influence of Gibbon and Macaulay. Two of the letters were 'the best things I have ever written ... There is not a single sentence out of balance or a word which is unnecessary.'[37] His old headmaster Welldon wrote that he possessed 'in a high degree the special correspondent's art of seizing the picturesque and interesting features of a campaign'.[38] The biggest disappointment was that they were published under the by-line 'By a young officer' – Churchill did not fear any retribution for openly commenting on military affairs well above his station, and he had hoped to use them to get his name known with a view to finding a parliamentary seat. Soon he had the idea of turning them into a book, realising that Captain Younghusband had made a large sum of money by publishing his letters on the Chitral campaign of 1895. He worked on it for five hours a day for two months and told his mother: 'I have broken up the D.T. letters completely – you will only recognise parts of them. Most is entirely rewritten.'[39] He worked the material into a book called *The History of the Malakand Field Force*, but unfortunately his mother made a poor choice of proof-reader and Winston was shocked to 'spend a miserable afternoon in reading the gross and fearful blunders which I suppose have got into the finished copies'.[40] The editor of the *United Service Magazine* wrote that he had 'seldom obtained so much pleasure, as well as useful information, from a military work'.[41] The *Athenaeum*'s reviewer wrote of Churchill as a literary phenomenon and said that the book needed 'only a little correction of each page to make its second edition a literary classic. As it stands, it suggests in style a volume by Disraeli revised by a mad printer's reader.'[42]

Blood honoured Churchill by mentioning him in dispatches. Ordered back to his regiment, he found himself involved in polo and soldiering and missed the excitement of the last two months, the best of his life so far.[43] He was ready to join another expedition, to Tirah, but the campaign ended before he could get there. He sailed home on leave again.

★

Churchill already had his eye on the campaign which was being prepared in British-occupied Egypt. The Conservative government under the

Marquis of Salisbury was determined to rectify the loss of Khartoum and the death of General Gordon, events which they attributed to the weakness of Gladstone's Liberal government in 1885. General Herbert Kitchener, the Sirdar or General of the Egyptian army, was to command a force of nearly 26,000 British and Egyptian troops to proceed up the River Nile by foot, rail and boat. Churchill was determined to become part of this, but his activities were attracting unfavourable notice. There were 'ill-informed and ill-disposed people' who 'began to develop an adverse and even a hostile attitude. They began to say things like this: "Who the devil is this fellow? How has he managed to get to these different campaigns? Why should he write for the papers and serve as an officer at the same time? Why should a subaltern praise or criticize his senior officers?"'[44] Kitchener shared these views; he believed that Churchill was merely making a convenience of the army to further his political prospects, and that the posts should go to those whose army career depended on them. Despite Lady Churchill's lobbying he flatly refused to have the young officer, who was campaigning for the Conservative Party at Bradford at the time. There was hope when the Prime Minster summoned Churchill and professed himself 'keenly interested' in *The Malakand Field Force*, which had given him a vivid picture of the fighting on the frontier.[45] Salisbury offered to have a word with Kitchener, who replied by return telegram that he already had all the officers he required. Sir Francis Jeune, a judge and family friend, pointed out that the composition of the British regiments was a matter for the War Office and not the Sirdar, and as a result Churchill was appointed supernumerary lieutenant in the 21st Lancers. He was to proceed at his own expense and there would be no compensation for death or wounds. He sailed in 'a filthy tramp – manned by these detestable French sailors'.[46] The *Morning Post* was to pay him £15 per letter, although Lady Jeune had promised Kitchener that he would not write.

By 2 August Churchill was in Abbasiya Barracks in Cairo where the officers 'paraded in the panoply of modern war – khaki uniforms, sun helmets, "Sam Browne" belts, revolvers, field glasses, and Stohwasser gaiters'. The soldiers were in '"Christmas tree order" with water-bottles, haversacks, canteen-straps, cloaks, swords, and carbines …'. They boarded a train with a great deal of 'kicking and squealing' from the Arab stallions, and then went by river to Luxor, where Churchill began to feel 'a very strange transformation scene ... When I think of the London streets – dinners, balls, etc. and the look on the Khaki soldiers – the great lumbering barges full of horses – the muddy river, and behind and beyond the palm trees and the sails of the Dahabiahs.'[47] As they proceeded south Churchill began his criticism of Kitchener for causing his troops to make long marches of up to 30 miles per day, killing horses and exhausting men. He found it difficult to fulfil his correspondent duties due to lack of time and exhaustion.[48]

At first he was not impressed with his regiment and wrote to his mother: 'The 21st Lancers are not on the whole a good business and I would much rather been [attached] to Egyptian cavalry staff – they hate all the number of [attached] officers and some of them take little pains to conceal their dislike.'[49] There was possible embarrassment as he was sent with a report to the Sirdar, whom he approached circuitously on his horse. Churchill saluted and Kitchener nodded but apparently did not recognise the young officer. Churchill described the situation and Kitchener asked how long he had before meeting the enemy. Churchill guessed at least an hour or an hour and a half, but after he parted he had to do rapid calculations to make sure that he was right. Battle was expected on 1 September, and a representative of the German General Staff joked rather heavily about it being the anniversary of their great victory over France: '*Our* great day and now *your* great day: Sedan and Soudan,' though some of the British officers suspected him of irony. Churchill watched as naval gunboats assaulted forts:

> Throughout the day the loud reports of their guns could be heard, and, looking from our position on the ridge, we could see the white vessels steaming slowly forward against the current. ... the forts, which mounted nearly fifty guns, replied vigorously; but the British aim was accurate and their fire crushing. The embrasures were smashed to bits and many of the Dervish guns dismounted. The rifle trenches which flanked the forts were swept by the Maxim guns.[50]

But the Battle of Omdurman on the banks of the Nile opposite Khartoum did not begin until the second of the month when his regiment lined up to charge the Dervishes. As Churchill described it,

'The trumpet sounded "Right wheel into line", and all the sixteen troops swung round towards the blue-black riflemen. Almost immediately the regiment broke into a gallop, and the 21st Lancers were committed to their first charge in war!'[51] They approached the enemy line diagonally and Churchill looked over his left shoulder to see what effect their fire was producing. Suddenly the task seemed much greater. 'Instead of the 150 riflemen who were still blazing I saw a line of nearly … 12 deep and a little less on our front of closely jammed spearmen.' He was undaunted and thought 'capital – the more the merrier'. After that, 'Opposite me they were about 4 deep. But they all fell (arse over tip) and we passed through without any sort of shock. One man in my troop fell. He was cut to pieces. … Then we emerged into a region of scattered men and personal combats.'[52] He wrote, 'I had been trained as a cavalry soldier to believe that if ever cavalry broke into a mass of infantry, the latter would be at their mercy.' But in this case a man on the ground was swinging his sword to hamstring Churchill's horse and he had to turn it rapidly, or he would have been in even greater danger. 'So long as you are all right, firmly in your saddle, your horse in hand, and well armed, lots of enemies will give you a wide berth. But as soon as you have lost a stirrup, have a rein cut, have dropped your weapon, are wounded, or your horse is wounded, this is the moment when from all quarters enemies rush upon you.'[53] He emptied all ten rounds of his Mauser pistol and claimed to have killed at least three men, though that figure does not stand examination. The Dervishes began to reform and after a few seconds two men aimed rifles at him so he galloped away to re-join the squadron which was reforming 150 yards away. He was relieved that he had survived 'without a hair of my horse or a stitch of my clothing being touched. Very few can say the same.' He recognised that this was perhaps 'the most dangerous two minutes I shall live to see'. He wanted his men to charge again but that was not ordered, instead 'the dismounted fire was more useful'. The battle was won and the Dervishes retreated. Churchill wrote: 'I was glad to have added the experience of a cavalry charge to my repertoire.'[54] It was the last the British army ever carried out, so it offered no lessons for the future. Indeed the historian of the British cavalry compared it with the Charge of the Light Brigade in that 'the most futile and inefficient part of the battle was the most extravagantly praised'.[55] The regiment had sacrificed 21 officers and men killed and 50 wounded out of just over 300, with the loss of 119 horses, and had inflicted 23 casualties on the enemy – though the Dervishes, with far greater numbers, could bear the loss more easily.

After the battle Churchill revised his opinion of the regiment, or at least the rank and file who had enlisted under the short service scheme. 'I never saw better men than the 21st Lancers. I don't mean to say I admired their discipline or their general training – both I thought inferior. But they were the 6 year British soldier type – and every man was an intelligent human being who knew his own mind. My faith in our race and blood was much strengthened.'[56] He was disgusted with Kitchener's conduct as the army entered Khartoum, defacing the Mahdi's tomb, allegedly using his skull as a trophy and killing the wounded.[57] But in the meantime, as he reported with some irony, 'the defeat and destruction of the Dervish army was so complete that the frugal Kitchener was able to dispense with the costly services of a British cavalry regiment',[58] and he started the journey home. Though his letters to the *Morning Post* had been very difficult to write on active service, he was pleased that they had been widely read.

He was in disfavour with the authorities after the battle and resigned his commission in 1899, after Kitchener made difficulties with his research for his book, *The River War*. 'I can live cheaper & earn more as a writer, special correspondent or journalist: and this work is moreover more congenial and more likely to assist me in pursuing the larger ends of life.'[59] Even in the privileged conditions enjoyed by late Victorian officers with aristocratic backgrounds, his position caused comment in the press. 'Can it be for the good of the service that young subalterns, however influentially connected and able they may be, should be allowed as Lieut Churchill is to go careering over the world, elbowing out men frequently much abler and more experienced ... than themselves?'[60]

Churchill returned to India and finished his time with the regiment with a polo match which he remembered more than 40 years later as his outstanding achievement. 'I served in this regiment before many of you were born. I once played in the polo team, the only time they won the

Cavalry Cup, by the way.'[61] A report by Robert Baden Powell, later the hero of Mafeking and founder of the Boy Scout Movement, suggests that the boisterousness of the young officers had not diminished. After his speech, '… one in authority arose and gave voice to the feelings of all when he said "Well, that is enough of Winston for this evening", and the orator was taken in hand by some lusty subalterns and placed underneath a sofa upon which two of the heaviest were then seated. It was not enough to silence him, he crawled out claiming "It is no use sitting upon me, I am India rubber."'[62]

CHAPTER 3

South African Springboard

South Africa had been settled by the Dutch East India Company from 1652 onwards, but the Cape of Good Hope was captured by the British for the second time in 1806, and retained. In 1835–37 large numbers of Boers or Dutch farmers went on their 'Great Trek' to the north after the British abolished slavery. They founded the republics of Transvaal and Orange Free State and fought successfully for their independence in 1880–81. Gold was discovered in the Transvaal in 1886 and this led to an influx of 'uitlanders' whose rights were severely restricted. In 1895 Dr Jameson, an associate of the colonial visionary Cecil Rhodes, launched a rash and unsuccessful raid into the Transvaal, which inflamed the Boers and caused European opinion to react against Britain. Relations got worse, and on 11 October 1899 a Boer ultimatum expired and the South African War, also known as the Second Boer War, began.

As usual Churchill was keen to get to the scene of the action and booked a passage in the liner *Dunnottar Castle* as a correspondent for the *Morning Post*. The ship left Southampton carrying the commander-in-chief General Sir Redvers Buller, to cries of 'Give it to the Boers!' and 'Bring back a piece of Kruger's whiskers!' while the crowd sang 'God Save the Queen' as the taciturn Buller waved from the bridge. Perhaps no war ever engaged the British public so much as this one. It was against people rather like them, it was reported daily by telegraph in the newly established popular press, and it had a major effect on Britain's relations with Europe. The next major war would be fought much closer to home and would deploy far more people, but in that case the reality was almost too horrible to report and grasp. In this one, Churchill and his contemporaries wrote extensively on the conflict, citizen armies were raised, and the public demonstrated their support vigorously in music halls and in the streets. There were some who questioned Britain's onslaught on two independent nations of European stock, including Churchill's future friend David Lloyd George, who had to be smuggled out of a hall in Birmingham disguised as a policeman after his speech caused a riot.

The voyage south was 'a nasty rough passage' and the roll of the ship prevented Churchill from writing very much, but he found that 'Sir R. Buller is very amiable and I do not doubt that he is well disposed towards me'.[1] Buller 'looked stolid' but 'said little, and what he said was obscure'.[2] The ship travelled at the Union Castle line's normal economic speed for a 14-day voyage, and there was no radio so there was no news of the progress of the war after they left Madeira. Eventually they met a tramp steamer whose crew held up a blackboard announcing that the Boers had been defeated, three battles had been fought and General Penn Symons had been killed. Apart from lamenting the loss of a popular officer, the officers and correspondents worried that it might all be over by the time they arrived.[3] They reached Cape Town on 31 October to find that the situation was far worse than they had expected. The Boers had launched offensives to the east and west, and the British had been defeated at Nicholson's Nek and were besieged in Ladysmith.

Yet again Churchill was in a different kind of war. Instead of the mountains of Cuba or the North-West Frontier, he was in the undulating hills of the Transvaal, intersected by mountain ranges; instead of the narrow Nile Valley he was in the wide veldt. The enemy too was very different. Churchill had learned very little about the Cuban rebels except that they had popular support and were poor shots. In contrast he came to know the Boers more intimately than he had hoped, which paradoxically led to friendships which would affect the course of British strategy in the future. Though their ancestors had often been in the country for a quarter of a millennium, and though they tended to be isolated from world events, the Boers were still Europeans in appearance, culture and attitudes. In contrast to the savage cruelty of the Pathans, they treated prisoners very well, much better than they treated the 'Kaffirs' or Africans. The Boer warrior was brave and resourceful, but not a fanatic like the Dervishes. He was an excellent marksman, knew the country intimately, had 'a beautiful seat' on his pony and rode 'recklessly and boldly over the most rocky ground'.[4] He was not organised in a regular army in European style, but in less formal units known as 'commandos'. Promotion was by merit rather than class and seniority, and Louis Botha, whom Churchill would come to know well, moved easily from political to military leader. And unlike the earlier opponents, the Boers had very efficient German-made artillery whereas the British army was short of heavy weapons and relied on naval guns landed from ships.

Soon Churchill was involved in a foray using an armoured railway train, which at the time he considered it to be 'a very useful means of reconnaissance' even if it was 'puny' compared with trains he had seen elsewhere.[5] In fact it was a most unsuitable vehicle, especially if not backed up by cavalry and on an operation which General Buller dismissed as 'inconceivable stupidity'. Later Churchill saw the essential absurdity: 'Nothing looks more formidable and impressive than an armoured train; but nothing is in fact more vulnerable and helpless. It was only necessary to blow up a bridge or culvert to leave the monster stranded, far from home and help.' Nevertheless he set out in the force under Captain Haldane, including two companies of infantry backed by a naval 6-pounder gun. Soon they were under fire from Boer artillery. It did not need the blowing up of a bridge or culvert, or even lifting the rails, to derail the train – the Boers did it by placing an obstruction on the line: '… suddenly there was a tremendous shock, and [Haldane] and I and all the soldiers in the truck were pitched head over heels on to its floor'.[6] Though he was now a civilian, Churchill cajoled the driver into moving the engine back and forward in an attempt to clear the track. He rallied the troops in defence until he was confronted by a Boer horseman whom he came to believe (probably mistakenly) was the future general Louis Botha. He had misplaced his Mauser pistol and had to surrender. He tried to ditch his cartridges of dum-dum bullets (recently banned by the Geneva Convention) but one clip was found in his possession. He claimed immunity from imprisonment as a war correspondent, but that was disingenuous as he had engaged in the fighting, and he risked being shot as an irregular combatant.

He was taken to Pretoria as a prisoner of war, a situation which did not suit his temperament and was at one of the lowest points in his life. Though it was 'the least unfortunate kind of imprisonment', he ruminated. 'You are in the power of the enemy. You owe your life to his humanity, and your daily bread to his compassion. ... Meanwhile the war is going on, great events are in progress, fine opportunities for action and adventure are slipping away. ... Hours crawl like paralytic centipedes. Nothing amuses you.'[7] It is not surprising that he tried to escape, plotting with Captain Haldane and another officer to overpower the guards in the State Model School where they were held. In an operation of 'desperate and magnificent audacity' they intended to release 2,000 men in the other ranks camp nearby and then take the Boer capital with its leaders, perhaps forcing an end to the war. That was vetoed by senior officers and remained a young man's dream. Instead the three officers plotted to get out by climbing the wall between the inadequate and casual sentries, but only Churchill got away before they were spotted – Haldane later maintained that he had acted selfishly in abandoning his comrades. He then made an almost incredible escape without food, equipment or a coherent plan. He hid among coal sacks in a goods train going to a colliery area, and on arrival at Witbank he was extremely fortunate in finding John Howard, an English mine manager, who with his colleagues and at risk to his own life hid Churchill in a rat-infested shaft. After a few days they concealed him among wool bales in a train to Delagoa Bay in neutral Portuguese East Africa, where he woke up the British consul to claim his freedom. He was now a popular hero and was shipped to Durban. There Buller granted him the rank of lieutenant in the South African Light Horse, the 'Cockyolibirds', despite orders that war correspondents were no longer to be allowed to hold military rank.

★

Churchill was still in his 'durance vile' when the British army had its 'Black Week' of 10–15 December 1899, when they were defeated at Stromberg, Magersfontein and most seriously under Sir Redvers Buller at Colenso. Though he was now superseded in overall command by the highly popular 'Bobs' Roberts, Buller pressed on, taking Churchill with him, and in January 1900 attempted to force a crossing of the winding Tugelo River to relieve the siege of Ladysmith. His men occupied Spion Kop, 'a rocky hill – almost a mountain – rising 1,400 feet above the river with a flat top about as large as Trafalgar Square'.[8] In the darkness and fog they did not realise that other peaks controlled by the Boers could dominate the position. Soon they were under bombardment by the German-made 'Long Tom' guns and facing a counterattack. They tried to dig in but the ground was rocky and the trenches were not deep enough. Churchill's South African Light Horse was kept inactive during this, but he decided to go on his own as a war correspondent. He and a companion climbed to the top of the hill, meeting the wounded and seeing the effects of shellfire for the first time.

> Men were staggering along alone, or supported by comrades, or crawling on hands and knees, or carried on stretchers. Corpses lay here and there. ... the splinters and fragments of shell had torn and mutilated in the most ghastly manner. I passed about two hundred while I was climbing up. There was moreover, a small but steady leakage of unwounded men of all corps. Some of these cursed and swore. Others were utterly exhausted and fell on the hillside in a stupor. Others again seemed drunk, though they had no liquor. Some were sleeping heavily. Fighting was still proceeding.[9]

He found that General Woodgate had been killed and Colonel Thorneycroft was now in command and refusing to surrender. Churchill went down to report the situation to General Warren, who decided to send reinforcements. Churchill returned in darkness to find the colonel was now 'exhausted morally and physically by the ordeal through which he had passed' and had already decided to retreat. Churchill concluded that he 'erred gravely in retiring against his orders from the position he had so nobly held by the sacrifice of his troops'. The defeat greatly affected Churchill and Spion Kop had such resonance with the British public that even to this day it is used as the name for the terraces in English football grounds.

Buller eventually resumed his advance into the Transvaal, and on 12 February Churchill's brother Jack was slightly wounded and taken to the hospital ship *Maine*, sponsored by their mother. After more fighting Churchill was able to report to the *Morning Post*, 'now at last success was a distinct possibility'. Churchill described the relief of Ladysmith on 28 February for his paper, though in fact he was not present, being several miles away with his regiment.[10] Heading for Johannesburg he waxed lyrical about the military formation: '... the Seventh and Eleventh Divisions, the Lancer Brigade, the corps troops, the heavy artillery and Hamilton's four brigades were all spread about the spacious plain, and made a strange picture; long brown columns of Infantry, black squares of batteries, sprays of Cavalry flung out far to the front and flanks, 30,000 fighting men together ...'. The reconnaissance balloon of the Royal engineers was 'like the pillar of cloud that led the host of Israel, ... full blown, on its travelling car'.[11] As the army advanced towards Pretoria, Churchill cycled ahead with a French mining engineer and was not the last war correspondent to enter a capital before the army. 'Johannesburg stretched about me on every side, silent, almost deserted. Groups of moody-looking people chatted at the street corners, and eyed us suspiciously. All the shops were shut. Most of the houses had their windows boarded up. The night was falling swiftly, and its shades intensified the gloom which seemed to hang over the town, on this the last day of its Republican existence.'[12]

Lecturing to the Royal United Services Institute in 1901, Churchill criticised the failure of artillery support during the war, though at other times he admitted that arm of the service was not his forte. From his experience as a message-carrier, he recounted 'the great difficulty in finding brigade and divisional commanders in the field' and suggested balloons to mark their position – not the 'great balloon' but 'a very convenient portable balloon abut a yard square' and perhaps 'with original designs painted on them'. He acknowledged that the traditional cavalry change was unthinkable in the circumstances, and smaller-scale attacks would be fatal. 'Why did not the cavalry gallop after the Boers and slash them to pieces with the sword? The only answer I can see is, that the Boers used to get off their horses, and shoot at the cavalry when they saw them approaching in the distance.' The sword should be rejected along with 'the mysterious rubbish with which their horses were encumbered – extra high-lows, hold-alls, shoe cases and such like'. But he rejected the idea the cavalry could only be used as mounted infantry. Instead he wanted them to be 'cavalry who could shoot', but they were held back by the standard Lee-Metford carbine, which was 'a poor weapon at the best'. They envied the longer rifles used by colonial and reserve troops and took them from the dead and wounded whenever they could. From 1902 the army would issue cavalry and infantry with the classic Short Magazine Lee Enfield which could be used equally effectively by both arms.[13]

That referred to the regular cavalry, who were intensively trained over three years, as Churchill had been, in horsemanship. The amateur soldiers of the yeomanry, who had volunteered for South African service in large numbers, were 'probably among the best fighting material in the world' but were only 'sham cavalry'. They did not ride well, and a Boer joked that 'they were chiefly occupied in holding their hats on'. They were not trained in scouting and reconnaissance and they could not look after their horses, with many deaths during the march from Bloemfontein to Pretoria.[14] Already the War Office was beginning to reorganise the yeomanry, as Churchill would find from personal experience.

★

Churchill now believed that 'Lord Roberts had laid the Boer republics low' – he did not know that guerrilla resistance would continue for two years and the British response would introduce the term 'concentration camp' to the language. He did however know that a general election was in prospect and that he would never have a better opportunity to enter parliament, his dramatic escape having made him a national hero. He therefore returned home to fight in what became known as the 'Khaki Election'. He was elected as Conservative member of parliament for Oldham.

Soon he began to disagree with the Conservative policy of 'imperial preference' instead of the more traditional one of free trade. He also found the Liberal Party more intellectually appealing. 'I found that Rosebery, Asquith and Grey and above all John Morley seemed to understand my point of view far better than my own chiefs. I was fascinated by the

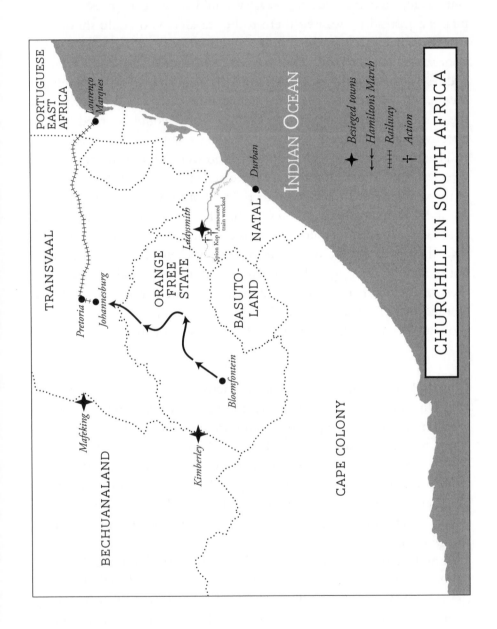

CHURCHILL IN SOUTH AFRICA

intellectual stature of these men and their broad and inspiring outlook upon public affairs …'.[15] In 1904 he took his seat on the opposition benches alongside his friend David Lloyd George. Early in 1906 the Liberals won a landslide victory and Churchill had his first government post as under-secretary for the colonies at the age of 31. In September 1908 he married Clementine Hozier, who was to provide a bedrock of stability and good sense for the rest of his life.

We tend to see the Edwardian and Georgian period of 1901–14 as an interval of calm and stability before the catastrophe of two world wars, but it did not look that way at the time. Apart from the gathering war clouds in Europe, the British Isles were racked by three great conflicts, with trade unionists, suffragettes and Irish nationalists, and Churchill was to be deeply involved with all three in different ways.

He continued part-time service with the Oxfordshire Yeomanry near his birthplace at Blenheim Palace, in which he reached the rank of major in 1905. The force was reorganised after the Boer War and by this time drills were taken far more seriously – but that did not prevent Churchill complaining to his wife after a field day in 1909:

> There were lots of soldiers and pseudo soldiers galloping about, and the eight regiments of yeomanry made a brave show. But the field day was not in my judgement well carried out …. These military men very often fail altogether to see how simple truths underlying the relationships of all armed forces, and how the levers of power can be used upon them.[16]

Churchill was first considered for the post of First Lord of the Admiralty in 1908 as Herbert Asquith was preparing to take up the premiership. He was tempted by the 'amenities and attractions' of 'the most pleasant & glittering post in the Ministry', but he was unwilling to displace his uncle, Lord Tweedmouth, from the post.[17] Instead he took charge of his own department as President of the Board of Trade, with a seat in the cabinet, where he set up the first labour exchanges. He became Home Secretary, one of the four 'great offices of state'. As always, Churchill gave his heart and soul to the role he was playing at the time. Even in this relatively peaceful job his combative side came out, most notably during the Siege of Sidney Street in January 1911, when he appeared to lead troops and police against a group of anarchists. But at the same

time he never lost his humanity, and campaigned for prison reform after
his own experiences in South Africa. He was obliged to deal with the
growing militancy of the suffragettes, which made him unpopular in
certain quarters, but at the same time he supported Lloyd George in
his setting up of national insurance, in his radical budget of 1909 and
the reform of the House of Lords. He was firmly identified with the
radical wing of the Liberal Party; Sir Frederick Milner wrote of him:
'The violence & bitterness of your language, and your extreme views
against your own class filled me with sorrow and dismay.'[18]

In 1906 Churchill was invited to witness the German army manoeuvres in Silesia. Despite animosity over the Boer War, Germany seemed
no more dangerous than France had done at many points in the last
century. The battleship *Dreadnought*, which would become the starting
gun for the great naval arms race, had not yet been launched. Kaiser
Wilhelm welcomed the young minister, who remarked on Queen
Victoria's grandson's 'unaffected and easy grace'. Churchill could not
help being impressed by the huge body of German troops: 'the infantry,
regiment by regiment, in line of battalion quarter columns, reminded
one more of the great Atlantic rollers than human formations'. But he
was less impressed by the tight formations in the manoeuvres themselves,
for he had 'carried away from the South African veldt a very lively
and modern sense of what rifle bullets could do' and also remembered
Omdurman, 'where we had shot down quite easily, with hardly any loss,
more than 11,000 Dervishes'. He concluded: 'On the effects of fire of
large numbers of guns we could only use our imagination. But where
the power of the magazine rifle was concerned we felt we possessed a
practical experience denied to the leaders of these trampling hordes.'[19]

He returned to watch the manoeuvres at Wurzburg in 1909, by which
time the arms race was well under way, the Kaiser was far less friendly,
and the German generals had clearly learned something.

> The absurdities of the Silesian manoeuvres were not repeated. The dense masses
> were rarely, if ever, seen. The artillery was not ranged in long lines, but dotted
> about wherever conveniencies of the ground suggested. The whole extent of the
> battlefield was far greater. The cavalry were hardly at all in evidence, and only
> on the distant flanks. The infantry advanced in successive skirmish lines, and
> machine-guns had begun to be a feature.[20]

The formations were still tighter than the British were now using, but showed some recognition of the conditions of modern warfare.[21] Perhaps they inspired Churchill's comments on his yeomanry exercises that year, for he never gave up his dream of leading an army in battle:

> Do you know I would greatly like to have some practice in the handling of large forces. I have much confidence in my judgement on things, when I see clearly, but on nothing do I seem to <u>feel</u> the truth more than in tactical combinations. It is a vain and foolish thing to say – but <u>you</u> will not laugh at it. I am sure I have the root of the matter in me – but never fear in this state of existence it will have a chance of flowering – in bright red blossom.[22]

Soon he would be involved more closely in the growing conflict with Germany.

CHAPTER 4

Ruling the Navy

Though he grew up during the great age of British sea power, there had never been any prospect of Winston Churchill becoming a regular naval officer. In his youth the only way was by entry to the training ship *Britannia* at the age of around thirteen. Entrance required skill in mathematics, at which Winston did not excel. It was not common for an eldest son to enter the navy: he was expected to take over the family estate eventually, and an army career was much easier to interrupt. His family had no naval tradition, and no great interest in yachting – though one wonders what might have happened if Winston had collected model ships rather than soldiers. And perhaps he regretted it when in 1932 he wrote of Admiral Sir Roger Keyes's memoirs of life as a young midshipman, 'When most of their contemporaries were still at their books he plays a part in skirmish and foray afloat and ashore in command of men who have real jobs to do.'[1]

But in 1896, as his army career began, he recognised the supreme role of the Royal Navy.

> I believe it is necessary for us to have an unequalled navy; a fleet strong enough to render us superior to a combination of any two powers and with ample margin for accidents. I would support taxation to almost any extent necessary to attain this end. With such a fleet an army does not become a necessity for defence. For offence an army corps or perhaps two would adequately carry out such enterprises in foreign countries – out of Europe – as might be expedient. The only other duty of the British army is to provide a training ground for our army of occupation here [in India].[2]

Churchill saw something of the navy during the Nile campaign, which relied heavily on naval transport and gun support. On the eve of Omdurman he watched naval gunboats successfully bombarding Dervish forts, which may have given him an exaggerated idea of the possibilities. He was delighted when Lieutenant Beatty, commander of one of the gunboats, offered him a bottle of champagne which he had to wade into the river to retrieve. Even in inland South Africa the notorious armoured train had carried a naval gun crew, while much of the British artillery was provided by guns landed from warships, including those of the cruiser *Terrible* under Captain Percy Scott.

In 1903, as a young Conservative MP, Churchill argued against having army estimates as high as naval estimates: 'There was one advantage we are possessed over other countries in Europe which enabled us to have a navy far greater and better than they could have ... and that was while all these powers had to depend upon a great army and to consider enormous land preparations for the defence of their frontiers, we, in this island, were able to concentrate the whole of our energies and strength upon the fleet.'[3]

As a Liberal government minister in 1908–9 Churchill was sceptical about increased naval expenditure. The government planned to build six new Dreadnoughts that year, based on a spurious estimate of German intentions. Churchill wanted only four: 'What Parliament will say to Navy Estimates of over 40 millions ... is a queer question to answer. ... A resolute effort *must* be made to curb Naval expenditure.' He regretted having turned down the post of First Lord in 1908, for now he knew 'what a tremendous part these warlike matters played in the inner life of a Liberal Cabinet'.[4] The Conservatives raised the catchy slogan, 'We want eight and we won't wait', but eventually there was a compromise in which four Dreadnoughts were laid down that year and four the next. Everything changed with the Agadir Crisis of 1911, when Churchill and Lloyd George realised that the threat of war with Germany was serious. As Home Secretary Churchill was an ex-officio member of the Committee of Imperial Defence which was intended, with limited success, to advise the Prime Minister on defence matters and bring the two services together. It was there, in August 1911, that he witnessed the display which would lead to his new appointment.

The army thought any war with Germany could best be conducted by sending a strong military force across the channel. Brigadier-General H. H. Wilson, the Director of Military Operations, produced a large-scale map and began to talk in some detail about how six divisions of the British army would be sent to back up France's 66 divisions against Germany's projected 84. It was a highly competent presentation, but the navy had its own ideas. The First Sea Lord, Admiral Sir Arthur Wilson, outlined a rival naval plan, stating that 'The policy of the Admiralty on the outbreak of war with Germany would be to blockade the whole of the German North Sea coast.' He suggested occupying the islands of Wangerooge and Schillinghorn for bases and destroying a fort at the entrance to the Weser. Wilson's proposal was not so much a plan as a succession of ideas, and none of them seemed very practicable. Churchill was incredulous and pointed out that it 'would appear to involve keeping the Fleet very close to the shore and would expose the ships to the fire of shore guns and torpedo attack'. Such an operation would keep the fleet tied to the troops who had been landed and the ships would be at great risk in these narrow waters.[5]

During the debate Churchill showed a great deal of strategic insight, though it would be years before the full extent of his prescience was evident. It was he who raised the question of whether the Germans might attack through Belgium. The soldiers eventually replied that the Belgian army was not negligible. Churchill was still proud of this foresight 25 years later, writing that he had 'predicted accurately the exact course on land of the first two months of a possible war between France and Germany, and that I even specified the twentieth day of mobilisation as the date by which the French armies would be in full retreat by the frontiers upon Paris, and the period after the fortieth day of mobilisation as that in which an effective counterstroke might be expected. These dates were in fact borne out almost to the day by the event.'[6] Even more striking was Churchill's comment that in the event of a defeat in France, the army could always retreat to the sea. Lloyd George added that it would be the end of the campaign, like

Sir John Moore's retreat to Corunna in 1808, when the army was successfully evacuated.

It was clear that the navy needed a general staff like the army's as represented by Brigadier Wilson. The First Lord of the Admiralty, McKenna, seemed to be under the thumb of his naval advisers, so a new political head was needed. The obvious person was Viscount Haldane, who had already had great success in reforming the army; but there was a feeling that the sailors would resist an imposition of army methods. Churchill was keen to do the job, he had been very impressive at the Committee of Imperial Defence, and he was possibly the only Liberal minister with any strategic vision. Thus Asquith made his decision to appoint him, during a visit to Archerfield in Scotland. Churchill was excited beyond measure and declined refreshment from the Prime Minister's daughter. 'I don't want tea – I don't want anything – anything in the world. Your father has just offered me the Admiralty.' She recalled: 'His whole life was invested with a new significance. He was tasting fulfilment. Never, before or since, have I seen him more completely and profoundly happy ... he interjected, "This is a big thing – the biggest thing that has come my way ... I shall pour into it everything I've got."'[7] He went to bed buzzing with thoughts about the 'peril of Britain, peace-loving, unthinking, unprepared' contrasted with 'mighty Germany, towering up in the splendour of her Imperial State'.[8]

★

The Royal Navy was still affected by the shake-up that Admiral Sir 'Jacky' Fisher had given it as First Sea Lord from 1904 until his retirement in 1910. He was a unique and extraordinary character, and some of that can be seen in his letters, written in forthright conversational style, full of underlinings and block capitals. But letters do not give the full flavour of the man; in his own view the written word could 'never convey the virtue of the soul. The *aroma* is not there,' and he regretted that print could not show his 'fist-shaking'. He had a vivid turn of phrase and is credited with originating 'Yours till hell freezes' and 'OMG'. He loved aphorisms and paradoxes, for example 'Never deny: Never explain: Never apologise' and '"Tact" is insulting a man without knowing it.'[9]

When he wrote, 'Favouritism is the secret of efficiency,' he possibly just meant that it was better to select by merit rather than seniority, or rotate offices as was common in the navy; but it was easy for his opponents to infer that he was highly partial in his selections. It did not help when he threatened his opponents in characteristic Biblical style: 'I'll make your wife a widow and your house a dunghill!' There were numerous examples of Fisher's treatment of those who did not please him. As a junior officer Barry Domvile had written a prize-winning article which conflicted with Fisher's views on big-gun ships. Fisher tried to have him removed from HMS *Dreadnought* and passed over for promotion, until the First Lord intervened.[10] Captain Wester Wemyss declined a plum appointment as Fisher's naval secretary because the price was 'absolute subserviency to his views'.[11] And Churchill wrote later: 'A deplorable schism was introduced into the Royal Navy, which spread to every squadron and to every ship.'[12]

As the professional rather than the political head of the navy, Fisher was nominally under the authority of his political master, but he reformed the Admiralty Board so that the naval members reported to him and he was the only channel for naval advice to the First Lord. He was brought in to increase efficiency, and did this by scrapping many older ships used to police the empire. He began to concentrate the fleet closer to home waters to meet the emerging threat from Germany (though that process was far from complete by the end of his term). With great dramatic flourish he built the *Dreadnought* in 1905–06, the first all-big-gun battleship which at a stroke made all the others obsolete. Arguably this accelerated the naval race which was beginning with Germany, in that, despite Britain's advantage in launching the first ship, her huge lead in older battleships was wiped out. But he much preferred the battlecruiser, almost as powerful as a Dreadnought but faster and less well armoured; and towards the end of his period in office he was beginning to see the submarine as the future of naval warfare. Most of the Fisher reforms were beginning to bear fruit just as Churchill took up the post in October 1911. It took years to build Dreadnought battleships and this was the first time that a full squadron of eight was available to exercise. It took even longer to train a naval officer, but the first products of the

Selborne Scheme, sponsored by Fisher, were reaching the fleet. There was plenty for Churchill to do.

Churchill and Fisher had been at odds during the 'we want eight' crisis of 1908–09, but they respected one another. Churchill recalled Fisher from his self-imposed exile in Switzerland as soon as he knew of his Admiralty appointment. They spent three days in Surrey, where the old admiral was 'a veritable volcano of knowledge and inspiration'. 'By the Sunday night the power of the man was so deeply borne in upon me, and I had almost made up my mind to ... place him at the head of the Naval Service.' He did not fear the outcry which would result, but Fisher's reinstatement would lead to a revival of the feuds. 'All the way up to London the next morning I was on the brink of saying, "Come and help me," and had he by a word seemed to wish to return, I would surely have spoken.'[13] He did not, but Churchill relied heavily on Fisher as an advisor. This relationship was disrupted when Churchill attempted to heal the schism by bringing back officers who had left under the old regime. These included Sir Reginald Custance, a clever man and implacable opponent of Fisher's reforms, who was to head an inquiry into officers training; Sir Hedworth Meux, a hero of the Boer War who was appointed commander-in-chief at Portsmouth; and Sir Berkeley Milne, a friend of the late King Edward VII who took command of the Mediterranean Fleet. Fisher was furious, writing that 'I consider you have betrayed the Navy in these three appointments' and 'this must be my last communication with you in any matter at all'.[14] But relations were soon restored during a Mediterranean cruise on the yacht *Enchantress*.

★

The Admiralty was not used to a civilian First Lord with Churchill's dynamism. Sir James Graham had initiated many reforms between 1832 and 1855, giving sailors regular engagements and putting them into uniform. Between 1885 and 1892, Lord George Hamilton had secured £21 million to build new ships, founded the Naval Intelligence Department, instituted annual manoeuvres and built barracks so that sailors could finally abandon the hulks in which they had lived between sea drafts. But the recent First Lords had been much less pro-active. Lord Selborne, in office from 1900–05, had given his name to the scheme for training officers, but the concept was pure Fisher. His successor was Lord Cawdor, who suffered from bad health during his nine-month term before the Conservatives lost the election. Lord Tweedmouth took office for the Liberals, but he was already suffering from an illness which would cause his death, and he was dominated by Fisher. Reginald McKenna was an effective politician and administrator, but like most civilians he knew little about the navy and was soon sucked into the naval arms race. He failed to protect Fisher over a scandal which caused his resignation, and he showed no sign of carrying out any reforms. His health too was declining. Churchill, on the other hand, was young and strong; he had total faith in his own ability and an enquiring mind which led him into every aspect of naval strategy and administration.

The department was headed by the Board of Admiralty. It was always a moot point whether the First Lord was merely its chairman or had executive authority in his own right, but Churchill naturally favoured the latter. The navy proper had 5,454 commissioned officers and 1,960 warrant officers, 96,670 petty officers and men, and 2,161 boys. The Admiralty also controlled 3,000 men of the Coastguard, who dealt with shipwrecks, smuggling and naval recruitment, among many other matters. It had a military force of just under 17,000 Royal Marines, making a total of 125,889 men in uniform at the beginning of 1912.[15] The Admiralty also controlled a huge civilian workforce of around 50,000, including 34,500 in the Royal Dockyards at home. In October 1911 the navy had ten of the latest Dreadnought battleships in service, plus 48 of the older type, now known as 'pre-Dreadnoughts'. It had seven battlecruisers plus 34 older armoured cruisers and 93 smaller cruisers of assorted types. There were 27 gunboats which had survived the Fisher reforms, and 112 torpedo boat destroyers, whose name was being shortened to destroyers. There were nine submarines in commission and a host of smaller craft.[16]

Oswyn Murray, a senior civil servant during Churchill's term, denied that the Admiralty was merely a 'congeries' – an unconnected mass. Certainly it had many departments which had often grown up almost by chance, but it had a unique sense of purpose in building and equipping the Royal Navy. Churchill liked to keep the same faces around him, and he brought his secretary Eddie Marsh from the Home Office. Discreetly homosexual in an age when the practice was severely persecuted, Marsh had an extremely rich life outside the office and was on good terms with many artistic and literary figures. He was the opposite of Churchill in many ways but devoted to him. His other private secretary was the far more austere James Masterton-Smith, who had been in the Admiralty since 1901 and knew its inner workings. The only uniformed member of the private office was the Naval Secretary to the First Lord, who according to Captain Chatfield, a future First Sea Lord, 'is, to the young captain, the power behind the throne. It is his personal responsibility to study the careers and records of all Flag officers and captains and to advise the First Sea Lord and the First Lord on the most suitable officers for the various appointments.'[17] Churchill favoured David Beatty, whose career had stalled; he had not spent enough time at sea for promotion from captain and even worse, he had declined an appointment as not being up to his expectations. But Churchill remembered him from the Nile campaign and was impressed that he had 'seen a lot of fighting on land with the army'. He was a hard-riding foxhunter, which Churchill believed was a good indication of character.[18] He became the youngest rear-admiral since Nelson. Beatty left late in 1912 to take command of the battlecruisers, but continued to correspond with Churchill and to criticise him behind his back. Meanwhile the First Lord selected Rear-Admiral Dudley de Chair, who reported of his master: 'We thought he considered himself more like Napoleon and Marlborough than any living man, and he appeared to have an immense amount of courage and initiative. He could be exceptionally charming and interesting. But at times, when crossed or corrected, he could be remarkably trying.'[19]

Beyond the private office, Churchill's most important colleagues were the sea lords. Sir Arthur Wilson, First Sea Lord since 1910, was a Fisher nominee and nearly 70. Known as 'Old' 'Ard' 'At' and 'Tug' to the lower deck, he was an estimable character and a very experienced seaman and tactician, but his memo rejecting the idea of a war staff was practically a resignation letter in the circumstances. His successor was Sir Francis Bridgeman, who had no Admiralty experience but was noted for his common sense. Churchill wrote that he was 'a fine sailor, with the full confidence of the service afloat, and with the aptitude for working with and through a staff well …'.[20] Fisher recommended Prince Louis of Battenberg but the Prime Minister objected that his German origins would make him unpopular. Instead Battenberg became Second Sea Lord in charge of personnel. Rear-Admiral Charles Briggs stayed on as Third Sea Lord and controller, the only naval member to keep his place. His principal responsibilities were 'Design of Materiél for the Fleet, including Ships and their Machinery, Armour, Naval Ordnance and Gun mountings, Aeroplanes and Airships and Docking facilities'.[21] The Fourth Sea Lord was Captain William Pakenham, in charge of the transport service naval stores.

Apart from the naval officers, the Board included the Civil Lord, a member of parliament who was responsible for the buildings of the navy and the civil service employees. George Lambert, a Liberal MP from Devon, had held the post since 1905, though the press had dismissed him as 'a farmer sent to sea'. There was also a parliamentary and financial secretary, who was in charge of estimates, accounts and the purchase and sale of ships. Thomas Macnamara was an educational reformer who was appointed to the Admiralty in 1908, and Churchill came to rely on him.[22] An additional civil lord was created to relieve the controller in handling shipbuilding contracts. The non-political post was offered to Sir Francis Hopwood, who wrote of Churchill: 'He is most tiresome to deal with & will I fear give trouble – as his father did – in any position to which he may be called.'[23] Nevertheless he accepted.

*

Churchill started work very quickly on the naval staff. Even before his formal appointment, he met Rear-Admiral Sir Charles Ottley, the secretary of the Committee of Imperial Defence, and Captain Ballard, who was regarded as '100% the ablest officer of his rank and standing now in the Service'. In the simpler days of the Napoleonic Wars, which had ended in 1815, or even during the Crimean War of 1854–56, war plans had been carried in the head of the commander. The stunning

Prussian military victory over France in 1870–71 had demonstrated the need for a general staff to plan and co-ordinate a modern war, using railways, telegraphs, repeating rifles and long-range artillery.

The existing naval staff was small and limited. According to Captain Herbert Richmond, 'The [department of naval intelligence] as it stands is merely a collector of notes on various subjects. It provides badly written and dull blue books with confidential written on them ...'.[24] If the title of the intelligence department over-stated its role in modern ears, that of the mobilisation department understated it. Its task was to co-ordinate the preparing of men and ships for ready use, though most of the detailed work was done by the Second Sea Lord's department and the staffs at the naval ports. What was lacking in all this was the 'brain' of the navy. As Ballard put it, the Admiralty was 'in the condition of a man with a powerful and healthy body but a weak intellect. ... his brain is not capable of ... anything better than a haphazard and feckless existence'.[25]

Four days after taking office Churchill adopted a paper by Ballard practically word for word. Within two days Sir Arthur Wilson had produced a rejoinder: 'The agitation for a Naval War Staff is an attempt to adapt to the Navy a system which was primarily designed for an army.' If it was decided to send an army abroad it was necessary to hire ships, load them with supplies and ammunition, produce maps and intelligence of the area of operations, find accommodation and carry out many other tasks. 'Ships, on the other hand, contain in themselves all that they require for war ... so that they are ready to move anywhere at the speed ordered as soon as they can get steam ready, and up to the limit of their coal capacity.'[26] As well as sealing his fate as First Sea Lord, Wilson's memorandum revealed his misunderstanding of the role of the staff, for the tasks he mentioned were purely administrative. He retired, to be replaced by the more complaisant Sir Francis Bridgeman.

Churchill wrote that the First Sea Lord was to be provided with 'a staff specially adapted to the purpose, and capable of preserving a continuous development in the study of war problems'. It was to be headed by 'an officer of distinguished attainments but of middle rank' because, as he told the King later, 'It is not intended that the Chief of Staff should compete in rank or authority with the First Sea Lord whose principal assistant he will be.'[27] The staff would prepare war plans and supply the First Sea Lord with information. They would report on vulnerable points in the coast, have an input in the design and armament of ships and would advise on the education and training of war staff officers. They would consider 'the concerted action of land and sea forces' but for themselves they were to work 'only in the domain of thought and not of action'.[28] There would be three departments – the existing department of naval intelligence (DNI) for 'war information'; the department of naval mobilisation or 'war arrangements' and the new department of naval operations or 'war plans'.

Churchill's main memorandum of 8 January 1912 began cleverly by incorporating Wilson's views on the differences between naval and land warfare, and much of it was intended to conciliate his opponents. 'The formation of a War Staff does not mean the setting up of new standards of professional merit or the opening of a road of advancement to a different class of officers. … all, or nearly all the elements of a War Staff at the Admiralty have been successively evolved in the practical working of everyday affairs …'. There was no need to alter the constitution of the navy which had been 'respected through centuries of naval supremacy by all ranks in the fleets'. Haldane thought this would 'mark a new and great departure in the history of the Navy'. To Lord Esher it was 'the most pregnant reform which has been carried out at the Admiralty since the days of Lord St Vincent'.[29] But when the war staff began work under Rear-Admiral Ernest Troubridge it numbered only 50, compared with 44 before the reorganisation, and it cost only £3,027 more per annum.[30]

The longer-term problem, the lack of suitably trained officers, was to be addressed through the war college at Portsmouth. During a discussion there Lieutenant Kenneth Dewar had suggested the training of junior staff officers but was put down by an admiral who 'asked in a friendly way, what the hell I meant by suggesting that Lieutenants should be trained to do the work of Admirals'. He did not dare offer the obvious reply that 'Admirals did not know their work because they had not studied it when their minds were fresh and susceptible to impression by self-education.' Then, according to Dewar, 'Mr. Churchill apparently took this view and early in January, the War College was ordered to make arrangements for the training of staff officers.'[31]

The president, Vice-Admiral Sir Henry Jackson, began to plan the course with Dewar at his elbow. Students were to drop their special-isations in gunnery, torpedo and so on, 'and to devote the time they would spend in perfecting their knowledge of their one pet subject, to studying the new work that lies before them'. The first object of the course was

> ... to develop mental faculties, such as powers of observation, accuracy in detail, appreciation of situations and of character, thoroughness in all work, tact in dealing with persons of all ranks and professions, powers of expressing wishes of their chiefs in clear, concise, and comprehensive terms, omitting all unnecessary detail ...

However Dewar was critical of the results of the first course which ended in January 1913: 'work was focussed on the routine duties of a junior staff officer. There was very little study of tactics or strategy'.[32]

Meanwhile in Whitehall, all was not well with the new staff. Its chief did not get on with Ballard, who had 'more brains in his little finger than Troubridge has in his great woolly head'. Troubridge went to sea, but Churchill was not happy with Ballard either: 'He has been there now nearly 2 years, and I have seen a great deal of his work. His abilities and power of expression are good, but I cannot feel that he sees deeply into the great problems with which he deals.'[33] When Troubridge left in May 1914 Churchill appointed Sir Henry Jackson, formerly of the war college and a leading pioneer of wireless telegraphy, but he was 'no personality' according to Asquith.

In September 1913 Churchill was 'not ... entirely satisfied with the views put forward by the War Staff'.[34] A committee under Admiral Slade only made small and detailed criticisms.[35] Churchill showed its report to General Haig in the War Office, who had '... an uncomfortable feeling that all is not well in the navy. It must surely be worth a good many bat-tleships to get matters right, but the recommendations of the Committee do not ... seem to be either sufficiently wholesale or altogether logical.'

Every naval officer should be asking himself 'What exactly does war mean – war on a large scale against a very efficient enemy? What exactly will my job be? And am I ready for it?'[36]

In April 1914 Churchill went back to the basics of naval training and asserted: 'As early as possible in his service the mind of the young officer must be turned to the broad principles of war by sea and land. His interest must be awakened.' He suggested that every lieutenant should do a two-month course on the broader issues. He proposed a major reorganisation of the staff in the light of two years' experience. The mobilisation division would be superseded; its duties were 'almost entirely administrative, and administration is foreign to the sphere of the War Staff'. The operations division should have four sections – war plans, coast defence, trade defence, and war mobilisation. He proposed a new war training division, largely to produce manuals and to prepare schemes for the annual manoeuvres. The intelligence division was to be divided into groups covering friendly countries, neutrals and hostile countries, in which case it would look at 'What they will probably do against us' and 'What would be the worst they could do against us.' It would contribute to strategic planning and operate in 'a large creative and imaginative sphere'. The three divisions were to be 'parts of one united organisation'. Major Ollivant, the military adviser, thought the paper contained 'in embryo everything that is necessary to give our Navy a thoroughly efficient War Staff and a system of war-thought education, organisation and training second to that of no European Army or Navy'. But there was opposition to the proposals, and no time to implement them before August 1914.[37]

The members of the naval staff claimed some success for their work, having suggested that 'in the event of a war with Germany the enemy's submarines might prove a serious menace to the movements of our fleets in the North Sea. Mr. Churchill was much impressed with this, but it was too novel an idea to meet with the approval of the Board.' Other 'elaborate and far-seeing plans were drawn up by the War Staff established by Mr. Churchill in 1912, ... these required the Board's concurrence before they could be adopted, and the Board, in general, being deep in the old grooves, regarded the new War Staff unsympathetically and turned down any War Staff submissions that savoured of advanced ideas.'[38]

There was no chance to produce an efficient staff system before the outbreak of war in August 1914, as Churchill recognised and Dewar agreed. 'Mr Churchill did invaluable work for the Navy during 1912–14 but his plans for a naval staff were interrupted by the outbreak of war before very much was accomplished in the way of reorganisation.'[39] Churchill had done no more than lay the foundations, and the idea of a naval staff was soon accepted. There was never any danger of it becoming an object of international fear like the German General Staff, despite the powerful and sometimes threatening presence of the Royal Navy in world affairs. Nor did it become an object of ridicule like the British army staff during the war of 1914–18.

CHAPTER 5

Strategy and Tactics

Across the North Sea, the new German navy had been built up by Alfred Friedrich von Tirpitz, benefiting from the country's first economic miracle when it began to rival Britain as a great industrial power. When Kaiser Wilhelm II came to the imperial throne in 1888 he was keen to establish Germany's position on the world stage. Tirpitz became State Secretary to the Reichmarineamt (Imperial Naval Office) with direct access to the Kaiser. Since the army was always the principal service in Germany, Tirpitz saw no hope of building a fleet as big as the British but adopted the 'risk theory'. If Britain fought a war with Germany, she would risk losing so many ships that her fleet would not be fit to take on another. This could not fail to attract attention in Britain and Tirpitz recognised there would be a dangerous period in which the British might decide to attack before Germany became strong. Germany had a fleet of 20 battleships by 1904, just before the building of the *Dreadnought* opened up the field, and also wrong-footed Tirpitz. His planning was long-term and rigid, for he used five-year programmes or Navy Laws to avoid interference from two opposite sides, the mercurial Kaiser and the anti-military elements in the Reichstag. The first German Dreadnought, the *Nassau*, was not ready until 1910. On the face of it she was inferior to the British model, with only 11-inch guns and old-fashioned reciprocating engines, but she had all the benefits of German engineering and the pace would soon hot up, with three more ships entering service that year, three in 1911, two in 1912 and four in 1913.

The expectations placed on naval power were enormous and there was huge public interest. The American strategist Alfred Thayer Mahan's classic 1890 work, *The Influence of Sea Power upon History*, was a worldwide success and helped persuade many nations that they needed stronger navies. Mahan's premises included the vital role of the sea as the most efficient means of transport and the concentration of force in the crucial area of operations. He believed that a large merchant marine went hand in hand with a strong navy, providing both a means of training seamen and a demand for trade protection. Paradoxically he also believed that attacks on merchant shipping, the '*guerre de course*' traditionally practised by the French, were futile. But the situation had changed over the last century. Railways now rivalled sea transport. Military and civilian navies were separate and trained their men in different ways. Britain was now far more dependent on imported food and raw materials and was vulnerable to war on her commerce, even before the submarine changed the picture. However the belief that a strong navy was essential to protect trade was fundamental to Tirpitz's plans – Germany now had the second strongest merchant fleet in the world, and deserved a navy to protect it.

The Navy League was founded in 1895 to foster interest in the Royal Navy. It claimed to be non-political and to operate with all classes and shades of opinion, including the working classes who were turning increasingly towards socialist and pacifist movements. Most of its members were Conservative, but at least 48 Liberal MPs were associated with it.[1] At the upper end of the social scale its members attended 'drawing room meetings' like one hosted by Lady Beaumont in Eaton Place in June 1912. Harold Feber was employed to deliver 'Lectures to Working Men' in the clubs of the North of England, while Marshall J. Pike held a series of street meetings in the London area. The league was moderate compared with the breakaway Imperial Defence League, which would not support the Liberal government in any circumstances. These groups, and the popular press led by Lord Northcliffe's *Daily Mail*, made sure that naval issues would never be far from the public eye. Any slackening in the naval race against Germany would lead to a quick and well-orchestrated public outcry.

From the other side, in December 1911 William Royle of the Manchester Liberals expressed the unease of the party faithful about the government's foreign policy and the hostility to Germany. He hoped that Churchill might do something to redress this, but complained: '... your voice which has been silent for months is very much missed in these anxious days when foreign affairs occupy so much of public opinion'. Churchill replied that policy was dictated by 'one conception, namely, national safety'. The expansion of the German navy was 'the main preoccupation in the minds of those responsible for the security of the country'. It was particularly dangerous because

> The union of a Navy of such great power with the largest Army in Europe will be a most sinister and disquieting fact, especially when we consider that these gigantic engines of destruction will not be wielded by ... a democratic Government, ... but a military and bureaucratic oligarchy supported by a powerful Junkers landlord class.

He offered only slight hope:

> I earnestly hope that with the new year better relations between England and Germany may begin; but I am not sanguine. If Germany were to slacken her preparations for Naval War by any substantial or definite step there would be an immediate *détente* in Europe, and the revulsion [reversion?] of feeling in Europe would be extraordinary.[2]

Churchill grasped at a half-chance for an honourable end to the race early in 1912. The German-born British banker Sir Ernest Cassel, a friend of the Churchill family, was in contact with Albert Ballin, the managing director of the Hamburg-America Line, who deplored wasteful competition even within his own shipping industry. He told the Kaiser that he had been 'successful in establishing complete concord amongst Germans, British, French, Italians, Austrians, and a whole series of small nations'.[3] He thought he could do the same for diplomatic relations. Churchill was invited to visit and deal directly with the Kaiser but thought it inappropriate. Unlike Churchill, Lord Haldane was mature and unlikely to inflame opinion by a rash statement. An alumnus of the University of Göttingen, he loved the old Germany of cobbled streets, though he was less at home in the new nation of industrialised efficiency. He got on well with the Kaiser and could visit the country without attracting too much notice.

In the meantime Churchill read that the Kaiser was promising increases in the army and navy. In Glasgow he made a speech stressing that British naval power was essentially defensive. 'The British Navy is a necessity to us and, from some points of view, the German Navy is more in the nature of a luxury.'[4] No doubt he meant it in the dictionary sense of 'something which is desirable but not indispensable', but it did not translate well into German, and inflamed opinion there.

On meeting the Kaiser, Haldane insisted that the British would like to reach an accommodation based on the present rate of German naval expansion. The Kaiser, however, insisted that the new naval law, the 'Novelle', which was about to be put before the Reichstag, must be taken into account. Haldane was given an advance copy of it, but he refused to comment before consulting experts, and gave it to Churchill on his return. The Novelle identified two 'serious defects' in German fleet organisation. First, a third of the conscripts left in the autumn every year and it took some time to replace them with a new entry – 'Owing to this, the readiness of the Battle Fleet for war is considerably impaired for a prolonged period.' Secondly, only 21 out of 58 capital ships were available until the reserve fleet could be made ready. But according to the new plan, 'Both these defects are to be removed, or at any rate considerably ameliorated, by the gradual formation of a third *active* squadron.' It was not explained how a third squadron would solve the problems of training a large number of conscripts every year.[5]

It is not clear what naval experts Churchill consulted, as the new naval staff was only three weeks old and the intelligence division was in the process of reorganisation. Possibly it was Churchill himself who noticed 'a serious and formidable provision' in the Novelle, for he drafted some 'observations' almost immediately. He took at face value the statement that both defects of the German organisation would be removed, and that three squadrons – eight battleships each plus a fleet flagship – would be ready for instant action without the need to call up reserves – in other words they could attack Britain without warning at any time. This gave the potential for the 'bolt from the blue' which had obsessed British strategists for some years.

At present, owing to the fact that in six winter months the 1st & 2nd squadrons of the High Sea Fleet are congested with recruits, there is a great relief to us from the strain to which we are put by German naval power. The addition of a 3rd squadron will make that strain continual throughout the year. The maintenance in full commission of 25 battleships which after the next 4 or 5 years will all be Dreadnoughts exposes us to constant danger which will only be warded off by vigilance approximating to war conditions.[6]

Churchill gave up any hope of reducing naval expenditure. In addition, the Germans had added three more battleships to their building programme over the next six years, which would have to be matched; and by 1915 the Kiel Canal would be enlarged to take Dreadnoughts. There would no longer be a 'safety signal' as key ships of the fleet were observed passing from the training ground in the Baltic to the North Sea. Underlying it all was the recognition that the attacking power can choose the timing of its assault. Despite its good intentions, the Ballin-Cassel initiative only made the situation worse.

★

Since 1889 British naval policy had been ruled by the two-power standard – the Royal Navy should be as large as the next two navies combined, plus 10 per cent. This had been promulgated when Britain was secure enough to enjoy 'splendid isolation' but had no clear enemy. There were various rising navies, including Russia, Italy, Japan and the United States, alongside the traditional rival of France. Germany did not figure until very near the end of the century but now she was a very definite naval rival, with huge and growing industrial and financial strength, with a mission to make its mark on the world and a virulent popular hostility to Britain. Meanwhile the two-power standard became increasingly irrelevant – the second biggest navy was now the United States, but an alliance between her and Germany was extremely unlikely. The idea of a 60 per cent superiority over Germany arose in 1909, when the McKenna/Fisher Admiralty used it to plan naval manning. Now it was to move into the public sphere and be proclaimed as the official basis of naval policy. Not only was it abandoning a cherished policy of more than 20 years, it was announcing officially that Germany was the main potential enemy, instead of a hypothetical alliance of smaller naval powers.

Churchill announced, 'We have no longer to contemplate ... the alliance, junction, and co-operation of two naval powers of approximately equal strength ... but we have had for some time to consider the growth and development of a very powerful homogenous navy, manned and trained by the greatest organising people of the world, ... and concentrated within easy distance of our shores.'[7] In addition, Churchill adopted the policy of 'two keels for one' – if the Germans built any more capital ships beyond what was already announced, the British would lay down twice as many in return, so they could never hope to win the naval race.

As it became more difficult to find ships for constant readiness, the Admiralty had to look elsewhere. The Mediterranean had a special place in the hearts of the English ruling classes. Italy was the fount of all good architecture and culture ever since the aristocratic grand tour of the eighteenth century. Wealthy families, including the Churchills, spent a good deal of time on the French Riviera. It was of great strategic importance in wars with France: Admiral Byng had been shot for losing the base on Minorca in 1756, Nelson had won his greatest victory at the Nile in 1798. The Mediterranean fleet was the largest and most prestigious in the navy for most of the nineteenth century. It included ten battleships when Churchill passed through the sea in 1896, and Fisher himself had held the command from 1899 to 1902. Britain held the naval bases of Gibraltar and Malta, the island of Cyprus, and ruled over Egypt. The strategic importance of the sea had been greatly increased by the building of the Suez Canal, and more than 28 million tons of shipping passed through it in 1912, 63 per cent of it British.[8] Though a war with France was no longer likely, Italy and Austria were both building Dreadnoughts and were members of the Triple Alliance with Germany. Any withdrawal from the Mediterranean was certain to be extremely controversial.

Nevertheless, in his speech on the naval estimates in 1912 Churchill announced a plan to move the Atlantic Fleet from Gibraltar to the south coast of England, and to remove the Mediterranean battle squadron from Malta to Gibraltar where it could face 'eastward or westward' as required. This caused an outcry. As Churchill wrote to Haldane, 'Of course if the Cabinet and the House of Commons like to build another fleet of Dreadnoughts for the Mediterranean the attitude of the Admiralty will be that of a cat to a dish of cream. But I do not look upon this as practical politics.'[9] The main purpose of the *Enchantress* voyage in the Mediterranean in the spring of 1912 was to meet with Churchill's old adversary Lord Kitchener on Malta. As consul-general and de facto ruler of Egypt, Kitchener produced a strong case against withdrawal, arguing that it would be fatal to Britain's prestige in the region. Under pressure, and without consulting the sea lords, Churchill agreed to keep two battlecruisers in the Mediterranean, based at Gibraltar. But the 'Malta compromise' did not satisfy the government at home and there was a meeting of the Committee for Imperial Defence. Churchill tried to argue that the Mediterranean could be held by 'flotilla defence' using destroyers and submarines, and this was supported by Fisher. McKenna, the displaced First Lord, asked if the same was not true for the North Sea. Churchill was not ready to abandon faith in the battleship and the argument between him and McKenna became very heated. Eventually it was agreed to keep a small battle fleet in the Mediterranean to a 'one-power standard', equal to the next strongest power in the area, excluding France. Churchill had lost a great deal of authority over the matter, and his actions satisfied neither his political colleagues nor the sea lords. But the affair did lead to improved naval relations with France, in the absence of a formal alliance.

★

It is tempting to believe that the Dreadnought age began with the launch of the great ship of that name in 1906 and it was only a matter of time before the Grand Fleet was formed, with its screen of cruisers and escort of destroyers; but reality was far more complex than that. For one thing, the new ships took some time to build, and moreover Fisher gave priority to the battlecruisers. It was late in 1911 before a full squadron of eight Dreadnoughts was available for exercise and manoeuvres. Fisher had tended to assume that the battleships would sail alone, with the battlecruisers ahead as a scouting force, eventually assisted by aircraft. He was moving towards the view that they would stay outside the North Sea, which would be uninhabitable by bigger ships due to destroyers and submarines. But his successors did not accept this and planned for a 'grand fleet of battle' inside the sea, shielded by cruisers and destroyers. Churchill tended to follow this.

By 1907 the Royal Navy's 'wet heater' torpedo had been developed and doubled the range to almost 10,000 yards – though the problems of aiming at such a range were not fully appreciated. This was likely to be copied by other navies, so the old fear of torpedo attack on the battle fleet was revived. To counter this, the battleships were to be screened by cruisers in the daytime and destroyers at night, while the latter would also launch torpedo attacks on the enemy line. The Germans already had such ships accompanying the battle fleet, and the Royal Navy began to design ships and adopt tactics to do it. It was very difficult to control such a fleet, and so far no realistic exercises had taken place. Battenburg, usually a reliable adviser, wrote in May 1912: '... no-one has any clear idea how the Commander-in-Chief, wherever he may be in the line, is to effectively command such a fleet'.[10]

It was highly unusual for a civilian First Lord of the Admiralty to take any interest in tactics, but Churchill had no hesitation in applying his military experience to the navy. The old idea of a close blockade of the enemy coast was now ruled out as highly dangerous in the age of the submarine, mine and torpedo, but Troubridge, the chief of staff, favoured a patrol line across the North Sea. Churchill quoted Napoleon: '... these long thin cordons of troops are good enough to stop smuggling, but ... one does not expect to see such follies'.[11] Troubridge protested to the First Sea Lord – how could the opinions of the established naval authorities be overruled by a civilian First Lord 'whose knowledge of fleets and their tactical limitations and possibilities is theoretical and not founded even on the smallest experience that may be expected even of a Lieutenant?'[12] The principle was to be tested in the annual manoeuvres of 1912. The aim, as Churchill told Asquith, was 'to test certain situations and dispositions possible in the initial phase of a potential war between Great Britain and Germany'.[13] The Red fleet, representing Germany, was commanded by Admiral Sir George Callaghan and based in the Thames estuary, controlling the land from Dover to Great Yarmouth. The Blue fleet, representing Britain, was to defend the country against an invasion or raid on commerce. Under Battenberg, it controlled the rest of the country except for a neutral zone between Yarmouth and Flamborough Head. Most of the ships were assembled at Spithead where Churchill watched exercises including submarine attack and aircraft launches. Red's objects were to land troops on the Blue coast and to interrupt Blue's trade by getting ships into the Atlantic, Blue was committed to operating a patrol line of four squadrons of cruisers running diagonally across the North Sea, from Yarmouth to the Naze of Norway. Red's forces were 'disappearing in and out of the fog bank like rabbits in and out of a furze bush' and slipped back and forward through the Blue line several times in poor visibility. The Red fleet began a mock landing operation, the battleships hoisting flags to turn themselves into troop transports, and landed a theoretical 28,000 men before two Blue battle squadrons turned up. Callaghan decided to leave the six pre-Dreadnoughts of the *Majestic* class to delay the enemy while the rest escaped, and the exercise ended.[14]

Churchill reported to the Prime Minister that the patrol line – or 'cordon' as he called it – it was a dismal failure: '... it is manifestly a serious misapplication of force and a waste of war power to utilise large armoured vessels in a service which, when necessary, could be undertaken by the lightest cruisers or by any small vessel fitted with wireless apparatus, supplemented in the future by aircraft'.[15]

The manoeuvres were notable in that the Blue fleet was controlled by wireless from the Admiralty in London for part of the time, with the first floor of Churchill's home in Admiralty House cleared out for a war room; he turned down a request for a dinner there on the grounds that 'the Naval War Staff is incessantly at work in the building during the manoeuvres, and the Admiralty staff are mobilised for work throughout the night'.[16] This was an extension of a system which had been set up by Fisher from 1908, on becoming aware that 'The advance of wireless telegraphy has been so great and so rapid ... that the Admiralty are compelled to assume the responsibility for the strategic movements of the fleet in a far more complete manner than was ever formerly practicable.'[17] That organisation was designed to control Fisher's battlecruisers as they chased enemy raiders across the oceans. Now it was adapted for the far narrower waters of the North Sea. This raised the question of

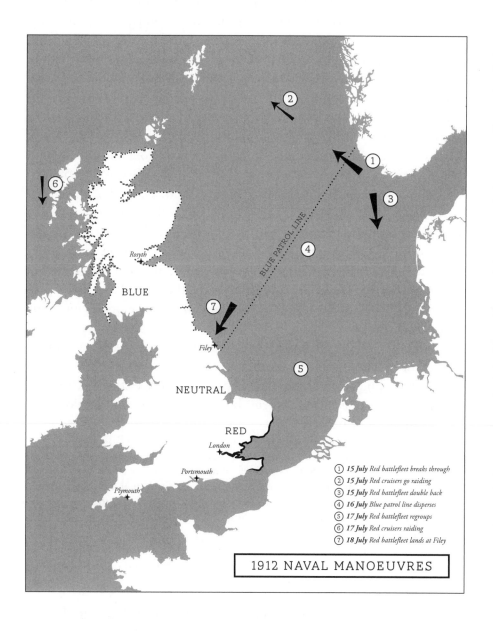

1912 NAVAL MANOEUVRES

1 *15 July* Red battlefleet breaks through
2 *15 July* Red cruisers go raiding
3 *15 July* Red battlefleet double back
4 *16 July* Blue patrol line disperses
5 *17 July* Red battlefleet regroups
6 *17 July* Red cruisers raiding
7 *18 July* Red battlefleet lands at Filey

the relative responsibilities of the Admiralty and the commander on the spot, which Churchill tried to define. 'Until warning telegram is despatched movements of the Blue Fleet should be regulated by Admiralty. Thereafter full discretion will rest with the Commander-in-Chief, but Admiralty will assist him with all their wireless telegraphy information, and the situation may arise which will entail a direct order.'[18] It was an issue which would dog the navy many years later.

Churchill drafted his own views on the manoeuvres, but Jackson, the new chief of staff, daringly pointed out that the memo, 'in its present form, bristles with controversial professional matter and contains information which, though probably of interest to the Public, is so well known to professional seamen as to partake of the nature of platitudes, and might even raise a smile of derision in the faces of the less seriously disposed officers who read it'.[19] But it was clearly established that a patrol line would not work. According to a modern historian, 'During the summer manoeuvres of 1912 ... Churchill ... was vindicated. Practical exercises had demonstrated beyond reasonable doubt that the Royal Navy had too few cruisers and destroyers to maintain an effective observation line across the North Sea.'[20]

Churchill regretted that a more aggressive policy was not possible: '... distant blockade was not adopted from choice, but from necessity. It implied no repudiation on the part of the Admiralty of the fundamental principle of aggressive naval strategy, but only a temporary abandonment of it in the face of unsolved practical difficulties.' Instead,

> ... by closing the exits from the North Sea into the Atlantic Ocean, German commerce would be almost completely cut off from the world. It was expected that the economic and financial pressure resulting from such a blockade would fatally injure the German power to carry on a war. It was hoped that this pressure would compel the German fleet to come out and fight, not in his own defended waters, but at a great numerical disadvantage in the open sea. ... we could continue meanwhile to enjoy full command of the seas without danger to our sea communications or to the movement of our armies, and ... the British Isles could be kept safe from invasion.[21]

The 1913 manoeuvres were similar, in that the Red fleet was charged with attacking Blue, which represented the United Kingdom. Aircraft would take part for the first time, including two seaplanes flown from the cruiser *Hermes*. Sir George Callaghan was to play the defending role this year, and Sir John Jellicoe took time off from his job as Second Sea Lord to command the attackers. Neither side was to be under Admiralty control, perhaps to test the naval staff system at sea. Army officers were invited on board the ship as observers. Visiting the *Enchantress* yacht in the Forth, Beatty complained tartly of 'a large party of naval experts, all except one amateurs', including General Sir John French, Colonel Seely (Churchill's counterpart in the War Office), and Major Ollivant, 'who apparently advises now on all naval strategy questions'. Beatty 'burst a bomb by pointing out that if Jellicoe did a certain thing, and he probably would, nothing the Blue C-in-C could do would stop him'.[22] Jellicoe apparently did, for he was able to mount three successive raids on the British coast. The 'war' was stopped at 8 pm on the 28th after five days for fear of giving useful information to the Germans.[23] The conflict resumed after three days and Jellicoe headed round the north of Scotland to raid Glasgow. Churchill joined the *Thunderer* in the Thames Estuary and sailed with her. On board, according to her captain, 'He used to wander about by himself and talk to the men and in case he got lost or got in difficulties I told a lieutenant to shadow him. I often heard the men taking about "the mate" and asked the commander who they meant. He said it was Churchill because of his Trinity House uniform.' Next morning the 'enemy' battlecruisers *Lion* and *Indefatigable* were sighted and chased. The Blue battle fleet was sighted at 5.17 in the afternoon and a tactical exercise was carried out before the manoeuvres ended formally at eight. At nine next morning a sea-boat was lowered to take Churchill to the destroyer *Swift*, to convey him to the shore.[24]

The army officers found much to criticise with the staff work: 'Hundreds of pages of printed and typed sheets were distributed before operations commenced. Many of these were of an instructional character, pointing out the manner in which officers should perform their ordinary duties ...'.[25] The conclusions were not optimistic – a daring enemy could do serious damage in raids on the British coast and get away with it.

★

The great fleet of Dreadnoughts and the thousands of highly trained men were useless unless their devastating guns could hit the target. Early in the century the rapid improvement in naval gunnery was reported in the popular papers, and a *Punch* cartoon of 1906 showed the Kaiser being astonished by the latest figures. Everything depended on the skills of the highly trained ratings, the gunlayers, who aimed each gun. Petty Officer Walter Grounds of HMS *Terrible*, for example, was a lower-deck hero. 'His shipmates had nothing but praise for ... his intense devotion to the science of shooting.'[26]

Gunnery was essential to the Dreadnought concept, which was based on a number of guns of identical calibre firing together so that the fall of shot could be 'spotted' and corrected. Sir Percy Scott, the maverick gunnery officer who had somehow prospered in the stifling atmosphere of the Victorian and Edwardian navy, soon noticed that the gunlayers in the *Dreadnought* could not aim forward at high speed due to spray, while the smoke from the funnels often interfered with the aftermost guns. His solution was to aim all the guns from a director set up high in the ship. Centralised control would also mean that all the guns were aimed in the same way, and were fired simultaneously by means of electricity. It would be much easier to spot and correct the fall of the shot in each salvo. This met with a good deal of opposition. The role of the gunlayer would be reduced to following a dial. It was believed that salvo firing would increase the time between shots, as it had to follow the slowest gun crew. 'Percy Scott's invention caused a great split among Naval Officers ... heated arguments everywhere in clubs and messes.'[27] Scott credited Churchill with allowing a trial of his system late in 1912. The *Thunderer* was fitted with the new gear and set against the *Orion*, the best gunnery ship under the conventional method. The *Thunderer* was able to fire 39 rounds with 13 hits on the target and 23 on the theoretical ship it represented. *Orion* only fired 27 rounds with a total of six hits. According to Commander Henry Oliver, 'After the result of the trials was known the differences between officers ceased and everyone wanted director firing.'[28] But it took time to get the new system in operation generally, and by August 1914 only a few ships had been fitted with it.

Churchill was marginally involved in another controversy about gunnery. Arthur Pollen, a businessman and inventor, was visiting Malta in 1900 when he was invited by his cousin, a naval lieutenant, to witness a firing exercise. He quickly saw that the maximum range used was 1,400 yards, while similar guns had been effective at 8,800 yards during the Boer War. He set about designing an aiming system for such ranges and even greater, using a manual computer which was input with various factors such as range, movement of the target, atmospheric conditions, wear of the barrels, and many others. By the time Churchill arrived at the Admiralty Pollen had already alienated the department by demanding excessive prices for his equipment, refusing to compromise and threatening to sell it to foreign powers. Nevertheless Churchill reversed policy and ordered a large number of his Argo Clocks, but soon balked at the price. Most of the navy was equipped with a system devised by Lieutenant Dreyer, and historians are still divided about whether it was inferior to the Pollen system.[29]

CHAPTER 6

Churchill at Work

It was notoriously difficult to get anything done in the Admiralty, where most business was conducted by dockets which passed from one department to another. According to the 'Official Procedure and Rules' of 1913,

> On receipt of a paper, the Branch or Department responsible makes, in the first instance, any preliminary references or inquiries which may be necessary for the proper consideration of the question involved, taking care to refer the paper to any other Branch or Department whose work may be affected. ... These references or inquiries are made on minute sheets enclosed within the docket, and the results then gathered together in the form of a submission on the docket sheet, with the addition of any advice which knowledge or experience can suggest.[1]

Unless the matter was given impetus by a member of the board, any decision could take some time. At the end of April 1912, for example, the Second Sea Lord's department drafted a scheme for the career structure of engineering officers trained under the Selborne scheme. It was sent round by Charles Walker, a civil servant in the secretary's department, on the 29th, and on 2 May the engineer-in-chief commented that there was good reason for the modification. The director of education concurred with a few small amendments and sent it on to Grahame Greene, the permanent secretary, who also agreed after small changes. Beatty looked at it on the 9th and passed it on to Churchill, who agreed to it on the 15th. It was sent to the printer for proofs the following day, but on the 20th it was back on Walker's desk – he asked if Sir Reginald Custance, conducting an enquiry into the training of officers, could have a copy. Beatty agreed on the First Lord's behalf, and the proof went to Oswyn Murray who approved and had it signed by Greene to give it the board's authority. It was finally sent to the printer on 15 June after a month and a half.

According to Barry Domvile, who served for a time in the intelligence branch, an officer might arrive in the Admiralty with the intention of carrying out reforms, but

> ... on arrival has found himself quickly absorbed in the machine; entangled in the meshes of department docket and minute, the factors which contribute to the fascinating Whitehall correspondence game. The avoidance of reaching a decision, that bugbear of officialdom, is the motive of the pleasant pastime: so the players pass the buck to someone else as long as they can, till the subject perishes of fatigue and inanition.[2]

Churchill would have to fight this inertia if he was to achieve anything. He soon established his authority over the Board of Admiralty, helped by the fact that its naval members changed regularly and were not always of strong character. Although his father had thought him too dim to be a barrister, he had developed advocacy skills which impressed and horrified Jellicoe.

> I admired very much his wonderful argumentative powers when putting a case before the Cabinet of the Committee of Imperial Defence. He surpassed in that direction the ablest of lawyers and would make a weak case appear exceeding strong. Whilst this gift was of great use to the Board, when we wanted the naval case well put to the Government, it became a positive danger when the First Lord started to exercise his powers of argument on his colleagues on the Board. Naval officers are not brought up to argue a case, and few of them can make a good show in this direction.[3]

After a disagreement over whether to train accountant officers as seamen, Churchill complained that Jellicoe 'was always trying to thwart him'. The admiral replied that he 'only did so when his proposals were of an impossible nature'.[4]

★

One of the primary duties of the First Lord of the Admiralty was to present the annual naval estimates to parliament. They did not come out of the blue, Sir Richard Vesey Hamilton wrote in 1896, '... the Navy Estimates must be largely based upon those of previous years. They are, in fact, those Estimates modified by the new conditions which have arisen.' At that time 'the chief condition modifying the Navy Estimates is the naval progress of foreign countries'.[5] That in effect meant maintaining the two-power standard. Though Churchill would substitute the 60 per cent superiority over Germany for the two-power standard, that remained substantially true, but there were two other factors – rising prices and wages, and technological change.

On 28 December Churchill wrote to the Chancellor: 'I think it is time I should let you know the way in which the Naval Estimates for 1912–13 are shaping themselves. ... The general cost of the whole Naval Establishment is increasing steadily from causes most of which are entirely beyond any sudden control.' The new ships coming off the stocks were bigger than the ones they replaced and needed more fuel for their much larger engines. Building work at Portsmouth and Rosyth was about to enter the most expensive phase. Ammunition for bigger guns was more expensive but the First Lord could not 'entertain any idea of allowing any depletion of our reserves of shot, shell and torpedoes' in view of the European situation.[6]

As always Churchill was well prepared when he rose to his feet on 18 March to present the estimates to the Commons. He began with a highly partisan point to rouse the benches behind him, claiming that naval expenditure was only possible because of sound finance, and in particular because of his friend Lloyd George's budget of 1909. The Conservatives laughed loudly; the 1909 budget had imposed taxes on the rich and caused a constitutional crisis. But Churchill soon turned the tables. Following on from his Glasgow speech, he identified Germany as the main enemy. He produced an apocalyptic vision of a battle of attrition in which both the main fleets fought to destruction, but the British had enough margin of superiority to win. 'It will always pay for the stronger naval power to lose ship for ship. The process of cancelling would conduct us, albeit by a ghastly road, to a certain victory, and to a condition, not of relative, but of absolute superiority.' He formally announced the 60 per cent standard. He outlined a new cruiser design, a class which had been neglected by Fisher, and raised the possibility of adopting oil instead of coal as the main fuel, though it was an issue which offered 'anxious and perplexing problems'. Mr A. H. Lee, the Conservative spokesman on naval affairs, rose to say that, apart for the reference to the 1909 budget, it was 'the first speech by a First Lord of the Admiralty since the present Government have been in office to which I have listened with pleasure'. Keir Hardie, the Labour leader, was one of the few to object in principle, that spending over £40 million per year was 'a great menace to our peace and national security'. Churchill's fellow cabinet minister Lewis Harcourt on the other hand thought it was 'certainly the ablest statement I have ever heard on Naval Policy' and might someday be known as the 'Churchill memorandum'. The newspapers were favourable and Charles à Court Repington, the influential military correspondent of *The Times*, wrote to Churchill to congratulate him on his 'masculine handling of naval policy'.[7]

Supplementary estimates were not unusual, especially in the circumstances of 1912. Haldane had been given the copy of the German Novelle in confidence by the Kaiser, and Churchill felt it could not be divulged until it was published on 22 March, four days after the British estimates went before parliament. Churchill later presented a supplementary estimate of £990,000 to the House, mostly to pay for an extra 1,500 men needed to cover the increased German preparedness.[8] He outlined the effect of the Novelle, explaining that 'nearly four-fifths of the German navy will be maintained in full permanent commission – that is to say, instantly and constantly ready for war'. He took the chance to outline other policies, including the expansion of the air arm, the manning of the fleet, the scheme for giving commissions to men of the lower deck, and the reform of naval punishments, but debate centred on the number of ships being built and the danger of war.

Preparation for the 1913–14 estimates had begun by October 1912. It was clear that the battle to reduce naval expenditure could not be won due to several long-term factors. Various loans were being repaid; the 'windfall' from Fisher's policy of scrapping old ships had gone, wages and prices were rising; the extra power needed for modern ships was costly – to raise the speed of a Dreadnought from 19 to

22 knots would add 50 per cent to the first cost of the engines, and the most recent Dreadnoughts cost 70 per cent more in annual fuel bills than the last pre-Dreadnoughts. The switch to oil fuel would cost more than £1.2 million, and aircraft would cost £100,000. It was pointed out that British naval expenditure had only increased by 29 per cent over ten years while Germany's naval budget had gone up by 125 per cent and Austria's by 284 per cent. On New Year's Day Churchill wrote:

> The Navy is passing through a phase not merely of expansion, but of swift and ceaseless development. It is in fact a vast scientific business of ever-growing range and complexity, stimulated and governed by inventions and improvements in every sphere of applied mechanics, forced without cessation to enter upon new paths of research and application, and fanned to the highest point by the rapid advance in every direction of rival Powers. ... There is no prospect of avoiding large and continuous increases in the Naval Estimates, unless the period of acute naval rivalries and rapid scientific expansion through which we are passing comes to an end.[9]

His letter to Lloyd George was more defensive, as he prepared him for an estimate of more than £43 million:

> Assenting to the foregoing figures as the basis of a financial arrangement will not relieve me of my duty to cut them down in all possible ways of detail, nor prejudge the Treasury examination of each specific item. On the other hand it is a work of immense difficulty to forecast the future and I can only say I have done my best and believe that the forecast will come true.[10]

Presenting the estimates to parliament, he mentioned the new fast battleships of the *Queen Elizabeth* class which would outclass everything else, but he also hinted that they might not reign supreme for ever:

> The public at large, in this and other countries, is accustomed to reckon in 'Dreadnoughts,' and in 'Dreadnoughts' alone, and these are the units which form the basis for all those intricate statistical calculations by which the newspapers of every complexion reach the conclusions which their editors desire. But the strength of navies cannot be reckoned only in 'Dreadnoughts' and the day may come when it may not be reckoned in 'Dreadnoughts' at all.

He was already thinking of the possibility of using submarines as the main means of defence, and he asked for the right to build other types of vessel as a substitute for battleships if the need arose. He ended with a rousing peroration:

> Is there any part of the world where the White Ensign does not revive associations of good feeling and fair play? Is there any part of your national life more healthy and more admirable than this great service of sacrifice and daring? Is there any small nation in Europe, any young people struggling to acquire or maintain its independence, which would not hear with rejoicing of a reinforcement of the British Fleet? Is there any Great Power which during these months of tension and anxiety has not been thankful that the influence of Britain in the European concert is a reality and not a shadow, and that she has been free and strong to work for that general peace, precious to all, and precious most of all to us?[11]

★

Churchill was the opposite of W. S. Gilbert's first lord in HMS *Pinafore*, who advised:

> Stick close to your desks and never go to sea
> And you all may be rulers of the Queen's navy.

He was a supreme advocate of hands-on management. Visits to ships and naval installations were an essential part of his style. His secretary Eddie Marsh reported: 'The sailors seem to like him very much – he has completely changed his character in some ways and has come out with a brand new set of perfect manners and a high standard of punctuality.' But Jellicoe was less happy about this: 'I noted that when visiting men-of-war his methods of obtaining information direct from the men, as he was in the habit of doing, were such as to tend to weaken discipline.' The most serious crisis came in November 1913, when Churchill visited the torpedo training base *Vernon*, and asked a lieutenant to send on his ideas. His captain refused to forward them to the commander-in-chief, so the lieutenant considered he had been ordered to send them direct to Churchill. The captain and C-in-C both complained to Jellicoe and it blew up into a full-scale row in which all four sea lords, including the usually pliable Battenberg, threatened to resign. Churchill was forced to back down for once.[12]

★

Churchill soon found that one of his privileges as First Lord – 'the sweetest of all the sweets of office' according to his friend Violet Asquith – was the use of the Admiralty yacht *Enchantress*. It was built by the famous Belfast firm of Harland and Wolff in 1903, but it had a serious stability problem – it was 'damnable at sea', as Fisher warned Churchill. The *Enchantress* employed a crew of just under 200 officers and men. The Lords of the Admiralty and other passengers lived near the centre of the ship, lavishly fitted out, partly because Harland and Wolff had been asked to improve the fittings as compensation for the ship's poor performance. The First Lord had a large suite just under the bridge, including a day cabin, sleeping cabin and bathroom. Perhaps following Fisher's advice, Churchill was quite cautions about his use of the *Enchantress* in the early days. He first joined her at Cowes on 5 November 1911 and made the short and sheltered passage to Portsmouth, where he visited the submarine depot and the dockyard. He was back a few days later and the *Enchantress* escorted the King and Queen out of the Harbour in HMS *Medina*, on the way to the Delhi Durbar. Again that month, he stayed on the ship during the launching of the new Dreadnought *Neptune* at Plymouth. He was using the ship mostly as a hotel, as one MP complained; but Churchill did not see any problem in that.[13]

His voyages soon became more ambitious. In March 1912 he risked seasickness by sailing from Portland to watch firing practice: 'The squadron of 4 ships all firing at once was most impressive, a stern & terrible picture of the wrath of man.'[14] There was 'a certain amount of motion' but Churchill had discovered the pill Mothersill, which he would continue to use for the next 30 years. In April he joined the *Enchantress* at Portsmouth, then sailed to Torbay, Paignton and Plymouth before returning, his first port-to-port voyage in the open sea in the yacht. Soon he was planning a much more extensive trip. On 22 May 1912 a train left London carrying Churchill, the Prime Minister, several government officials and their families. There was a 'train de luxe' to Paris where hot baths were available in the Ritz, then the journey south. The *Enchantress* was waiting at Genoa. They visited Napoleon's house on Elba, 'a disappointing shrine for W's pilgrim heart' and then cruised to Naples where they picked up 'that old rascal Fisher', as Beatty called him.[15] It was an opportunity for Churchill and Fisher to patch up their strained relationship. By the end of the trip, according to Violet Asquith, they were 'locked together in naval conclave. ... I'm sure they can't resist each other for long at close range.'[16]

Churchill landed at Malta and was joined by Lord Kitchener from the cruiser *Hampshire*. The First Lord reassured the people that the government would 'assign such a proportion of repair and refit work to the Dockyard as would keep it in a normal condition of activity and render it at all times capable of attending the needs in peace or war of any fleet or naval force cruising or operating in Malta'. But in fact the island played very little part in the government's plans to concentrate on the Atlantic and North Sea.[17] On 1 June the party went out to watch gunnery exercises, 'the best day of all', according to Violet Asquith. 'It was less like a sound than a thrilling shock to one's whole being. Every inch of one's body was shaken and vibrating from the soles of one's feet upwards.'[18] Asquith stayed with the ship for the voyage home, and the *Enchantress* finally arrived at Portsmouth on 10 June.[19] Churchill used the time to prepare a long memorandum on naval policy in the Mediterranean which he wrote soon after his return.

This emboldened Churchill to embark on more trips round the British coast. In June and July he visited bases in Ireland and Wales, leaving the ship at Pembroke to take the train to London. On 19 August he began a longer trip along the east coast, stopping off at Harwich where he found much was lacking in shore and recreation facilities for the flotillas based there.[20] He visited Yarmouth, Immingham, Grimsby, the Tyne and the new dockyard being built at Rosyth. At Cromarty ('incomparably the finest [harbour] on the East Coast of Great Britain') he landed and met Commander Munro who was drawing up plans for a new base.[21] He left the ship in Aberdeen but joined her again at Greenock a week later, to visit the Clyde shipyards. Off the remote island of Colonsay he witnessed the peace being broken by night gunnery practice from HMS *King Edward VII*. *Enchantress* sailed south to look at shipyards in Birkenhead and Barrow-in-Furness, where Sub-Lieutenant Cecil Talbot was not impressed with his attitude: 'He went round *E 6* first, making several impracticable suggestions on small details, and being very rude to Vickers directors about their lateness in delivery of boats.'[22]

Churchill carried on with his normal work during the voyages and wrote from the ship in May 1912, 'I have done some important things today – sacked Briggs, appointed Moore in his stead, & a new Commodore of Destroyers, & a new Director of Naval Ordnance. Generally I have cleared off a lot of difficulty & serious matters which were hanging and flapping week after week.' And in April 1913, 'the papers in files & bags and boxes come rolling in. One never seems to do more than keep abreast of them.'[23] David Beatty, who was never adequately grateful for the way in which Churchill had rescued his career, did not enjoy his time on board. In May 1912 in the Mediterranean he wrote: 'Oh dear! I am so tired and bored with the whole thing. … the party on board bores me to tears. Winston talks about nothing but the sea and the Navy and the wonderful things he is going to do. … I can bear it no longer …'.[24] Violet Asquith confirmed Churchill's obsession with all things naval and military:

> W. in glorious form though slightly over-concentrated on instruments of destruction. Blasting and shattering are now his *idées fixes*. As we leaned side by side against the taffrail, gliding past the lovely, smiling coast-line of the Adriatic, bathed in sun, and I remarked 'How perfect!' he startled me by his reply: 'Yes – range perfect – visibility perfect – if we had some six-inch guns on board how easily we could bombard …'.[25]

In May 1913 there was another summer cruise when the party embarked in Venice. There was little naval purpose this time, but Churchill was not able to relax. Visiting the palace of the Emperor Diocletian at Split, Violet remarked that there was something to be said for being a retired Roman Emperor, Churchill remarked sharply, 'Why retired? There's nothing to be said for retiring from anything.'[26]

★

By the end of that year Churchill was involved in a crisis over the rising naval estimates. Already in 1912 his friend Lloyd George, the Chancellor of the Exchequer, had claimed during a cabinet meeting that 'Bankruptcy is staring me in the face.' This time round there was a petition to the Prime Minister signed by five ministers questioning 'so enormous an increase in our naval expenditure' to a total of £53 million. Churchill regarded any letting up of the pace as reckless, but according to Sir Francis Hopwood he had painted himself into a corner, as 'he was fool enough to tell the world what his programme was going to be for about half a dozen years ahead. To this he is bound hand and foot.' But Hopwood saw that Lloyd George was 'only trying it on'. The Chancellor suggested that Churchill might agree to reduced budgets in years ahead, but the First Lord refused to countenance this. Instead he tried to find economies elsewhere but wrote graphically to Asquith: 'the sledge is bare of babies, and though the pack may crunch the driver's bones, the winter will not be ended'. The failure to secure Dreadnoughts funded by Canada came as a 'heavy blow', partly compensated by an offer of a *Queen Elizabeth* from Malaya. The stakes were high, the issue might split the government and it would lose much of its parliamentary legislation, but when it came to a crunch in February 1914, Churchill's opponents backed down when offered a few minor concessions. He wrote a few months later that if the estimates had been cut, 'There would also have been another First Lord of the Admiralty! And who can say – if such gaps were opened – there would not have been another government – which does not necessarily mean lower estimates.'[27]

CHAPTER 7

Personnel

The early training of naval officers had been reformed at the beginning of the century. It was still believed, as in Nelson's day, that a boy had to start at the age of about thirteen to adapt to naval ways. In the earlier age the boys had usually gone straight to sea, but under the Selborne Scheme of 1903 they would enter Osborne College on the Isle of Wight for two years from the age of thirteen. Contact with the sea was slight, and Queen Victoria's former home faced inland. After that, a boy would go to Dartmouth College in Devon, in a new building above the River Dart. Training under sail was abolished. Most important and controversial of all, engineer officers, who had been regarded as inferior tradesmen and mechanics, were to be trained alongside the executives, and not allocated to the branch until later. Since it took nine years to produce a fully-fledged lieutenant, the first fruits of the Selborne Scheme were just beginning to appear as Churchill joined the Admiralty.

In March 1912 Churchill appointed a committee to look into 'the education and training of naval officers of the Military Branch'. It was chaired by Admiral Sir Reginald Custance, a clever man and a long-standing opponent of Fisher. It soon found evidence of failure. Only boys between twelve years eight months and thirteen were eligible, a very narrow band which could easily be missed. Preparatory school masters protested at the upper limit and wanted it raised to at least thirteen and a half – the age when boys normally went on to public school, and any who left before that would miss out on the vital last part of their education, when they developed quickly and might have a chance to show leadership qualities.[1]

Limited numbers of boys applied for cadetships at Osborne. Many parents believed they needed a nomination from the First Lord, though that had been abolished. Some believed that under the Selborne Scheme the boys might be forced to become engineers against their will. Osborne was considered an unhealthy place, due to epidemics. The fees and expenses were high, and it would cost a parent around £93 per year.[2] As a result only about 175 applied for 70 places in an average year. All were invited to appear before an interview board, provided they met the minimum requirements, were of 'pure European descent' and could pass a medical. The Custance Committee found that 'boys of somewhat low ability' were sometimes selected 'due, not to any failure in the system of selection, but to an insufficient number of suitable candidates'.[3] According to the headmaster at Osborne, 'The average ability of the cadets is probably not very different from the average ability of boys of the same age and class. There is less conspicuous ability among them than is to be found at the leading public schools.' It was clear that the navy was not attracting the flower of the nation as much as it would have liked. Up to 10 per cent would be 'weeded' by the end of the first year at Osborne, but it was claimed that even this was becoming softer. The committee concerned 'tends to defer the final decision, and to put it off from term to term in the hope that the boy will improve. He hangs on until the last term, and then it is said "It is a great pity to weed out the boy just as he is going to Dartmouth; let us see how he gets on there."'[4]

The education at Osborne, Churchill thought, had 'a certain air of kindergarten', while the Dartmouth course was 'so ambitious for boys of that age as to provoke doubts that it is thorough'. He was no more satisfied with the boys themselves: 'A large proportion of the cadets are colourless, and a minority, perhaps as large as one-sixth, are not of good enough quality for the work they will be required to do or for the men they aspire to command.' He compared their education to tourists from the United States visiting India who 'tick off the places they have visited in the guide book ... and then after a month or six weeks, come away and think they know all about India'.[5]

The emphasis in engineering training was much deplored by the intellectuals who founded the *Naval Review* in 1913, and whose views Churchill largely shared. As Kenneth Dewar wrote, 'it is evident that no single mind can cover the whole field of modern naval technique: seamanship, navigation, engineering, gunnery, torpedo, submarines and aviation …'. His colleague Reginald Plunkett elaborated: '… continuous work with machinery militates against the development of certain faculties which are essential for command or staff work. Powers of reasoned criticism and balanced judgement are not developed in an engineroom … Nor can the eye of the seamen and tactician be trained below as it is on deck. … The requirements for the two branches are so widely different that all attempts at amalgamation can only be harmful …'.[6] But the system would survive for the moment and was only abolished in 1920 in what engineer officers regarded as 'the great betrayal'. Plunkett was probably right, the two professions need different mind and skill sets, but there was no reason to discriminate against the engineer in status and promotion prospects. Obviously he would not be able to take charge of ships and fleets but he could have executive authority over his own department, and should be eligible for higher administrative posts – a situation which was not attained until late in the twentieth century.

After two years at Dartmouth undergoing a general education with a mathematical bias, the boys were promoted to midshipman and went to sea, first in a training cruiser and then in the ships of the fleet. Midshipmen of an earlier age had stayed with one ship for as long as they were needed; the modern youths moved with bewildering speed, perhaps five or six ships in three years. Moreover there was no regular training programme. Some were given the opportunity to steer a great battleship like the *Dreadnought*, though that was not normally part of an officer's duties. Some took nominal charge of one of the ship's boats, but only the cleaning of it in the case of Sub-Lieutenant Tyrell, one of the first products of the Selborne Scheme. If they did take the boat to sea they were no more than passengers, while on the ship's deck they were only fit for duties as 'superior messengers', according to Commander Backhouse. Their navigation was even worse – they were careless in their calculations, a fatal flaw. They had 'no experience in acquiring the habit of command', while in gunnery they had learned a great deal about the construction of guns, but not enough in aiming and firing them. Many of them resented their duties in the engine room. They could not be allocated regular duties as they were liable to be called away for training and education. Worst of all, they were moved from one department to another as soon as they were beginning to learn. For example in boat work, 'after two months, when he has got fairly good at that, he is taken below and put on engineering, or at gunnery, or torpedo'.[7] Meanwhile the midshipman had to prepare for his written examinations for lieutenant, which would affect his future seniority. This soon came to dominate his thoughts to the neglect of his shipboard duties.

Churchill was not impressed with the standard of training or the type of youth produced:

> The selection of candidates at such a very immature age, the limited opportunities given to them and to their parents for embracing the naval profession, the lack of consideration shown to the interests of the private schools in the present system, apart altogether from questions of expense, tend to exclude at every stage large and valuable classes upon whom the Navy has a right to count, and from whom it is bound to draw if the service is to obtain the highest possible share in the general ability of the nation.[8]

Churchill was moving toward a far-reaching reform. There was an immediate crisis looming as the fleet expanded far faster than the officer corps. 'In adjusting the supply of Naval Officers to the requirements of the fleet the fundamental condition is that, while it takes only two years to build a battleship, it takes about nine years from the time at which a cadet enters Osborne to make a naval lieutenant.' During these nine years the great naval arms race with Germany had taken place, and at the same time the new air and submarine services demanded a much higher proportion of junior officers. To solve the looming officer shortage, and at the same time begin to remedy the defects of the training system, Churchill was 'strongly of the opinion that the public schools ought to have a chance and not be ruled out absolutely from the naval service'. He proposed to offer 20 commissions next year to 'candidates from the great public schools' after highly competitive selection interviews and examinations. With the class system of the time, it was assumed that only the so-called 'public schools' could produce the leaders needed. They would probably have served in the school's Rifle Corps or Officer Training Corps as Churchill had done. He foresaw a time when about 15 per cent of the officer corps would be recruited that way, with a further 15 per cent from the lower deck and the remaining 70 per cent from Osborne and Dartmouth.

In a paper of January 1914 Churchill mentioned 'a project for meeting the needs for the immediate increase in the number of lieutenants by temporary recourse as an emergency measure to a system of direct entry for a limited number, not exceeding 100 spread over 3 years, of suitable candidates from 17½ to 18½ years of age'. He clearly anticipated opposition from traditional officers, and noted that this was an 'experiment which is to be regarded as temporary and exceptional', but at the same time he opened up the possibility of future reform – it would 'afford a most valuable means of comparing our present system with those in force abroad'.[9] The scheme itself was temporary, but the officers' careers were to be permanent, and despite their late entry they were to have an equal chance of rising through the service. The 'Special Entry' scheme set up by Churchill continued in use through two world wars, and many officers considered its products better than those from Dartmouth. In the 1950s it became standard for naval cadets to enter at the age of eighteen after completing their normal education.

In 1914 Churchill made a minor change to the officer structure. Since 1877, lieutenants of more than eight years seniority had worn a thin gold stripe between the two thicker ones on their sleeves. Churchill's idea, which he referred to as 'my proposal', was to change the title of such officers to 'lieutenant-commander'. This had been used as a rank by the United States Navy since 1862, while in the Royal Navy senior lieutenants were often given the command of small vessels such as destroyers with the title of 'lieutenant and commander', 'lieutenant in command', or 'lieutenant commander'. Churchill wanted to use the last title as a substantive rank, which every officer would gain after eight years as a lieutenant. A few should be given the rank a year or two early, on the basis of 'distinguished or responsible service' as a 'valuable stimulant'.[10]

That did not meet the approval of the sea lords, but the substantive rank of lieutenant-commander was approved by Order-in-Council on 4 March 1914, with no mention of promotion by selection. Though its effect was moral rather than material, the rank of lieutenant-commander proved very useful in two world wars. In a battleship he would be a mere cog in a large machine, but in the growing numbers of destroyers or submarines he was likely to be the commanding officer, and the substantive rank and title gave him a little extra authority beyond mere seniority.

★

The gulf between officers and men had widened greatly during the a century of peace, and for most of the nineteenth century it was practically impossible for a member of the lower deck to rise to commissioned rank. There was no large middle-class element in the peacetime navy. According to a leading campaigner for lower-deck rights,

> At one end of service-life we have the officer recruited from that comparatively small class that is wealthy enough to spend £700 on a boy; at the other end we have the men recruited from the poorer artisan and labouring class. In between lies the pick of the nation. It will not send its sons on to the lower-deck because of the great limitation in the facilities for advancing; it cannot send its sons in as officers through lack of money.[11]

Many naval families were strongly opposed to lower-deck promotion. They had invested money and effort in getting their sons trained at Dartmouth, and did not want that devalued by opening up the ranks. Henry Capper, a middle-class rating who hoped for promotion, was told by the mother of a sub-lieutenant, 'The Navy belongs to us, and if you were to win the commissions you ask for it would be at the expense of our sons and nephews whose birthright it is.'[12] In 1913 one officer claimed that 'the general wish of the lower deck is to be officered by gentlemen of the upper and middle classes. ... they prefer that ... their officers should be men trained in the traditions of the "gentry".'[13] 'Clinker Knocker', a lower-deck rebel, found that upper-class officers were often amazingly tolerant of his escapades, but an ex-Engine Room Artificer was 'abhorred by the whole engine room department. ... We were fortunate to have real gentlemen by birth and breeding in higher positions than the senior [engineer], or it would have been harder for us.'[14]

The ancient rank of warrant officer was open to the lower deck, but that was declining in importance. The carpenter was no longer the man who kept the ship afloat, and his successor the warrant shipwright was far more dependent on dockyard facilities. The boatswain had less to do in the new sail-less ships, while his disciplinary role was largely taken over by the ship's police. The gunner was sandwiched between the gunnery lieutenant and the chief gunner's mate who was closer to the lower deck. The warrant officer's life was often a lonely one, and his position between the lower deck and the quarterdeck was awkward. Nevertheless it was warrant rank which provided the first opportunity for lower-deck commissions, albeit at a very late stage in a man's career when was too old to ever get beyond lieutenant. From 1903 a few selected chief warrant officers were commissioned as lieutenants.

Churchill began a major reform of this, introducing the 'mates' scheme in 1912. This would enable

> ... warrant officers, petty officers and seamen to reach the rank of commissioned officer at an early age. The candidates selected undergo courses of instruction at Portsmouth, and on passing are given the rank of Acting Mate. They then proceed to the Royal Naval College at Greenwich for four months' instruction in navigation, followed by two months' instruction in pilotage at the Navigation School at Portsmouth. On passing the examination at the termination of this course, they are confirmed as Mates and are embarked in sea-going ships for two years, at the end of which time they will be eligible for promotion to the rank of lieutenant. Their duties as lieutenants will be the same as those of other lieutenants, and they will be considered for promotion to commander with other lieutenants on their merits.[15]

Only 44 men had been commissioned as mates or acting mates by the spring of 1914. It was a small but important beginning.

★

Long service was regarded as the key for the non-commissioned members of the navy, known collectively as the lower deck after where they had lived in sailing ships. It was firmly (and probably mistakenly) believed that this made them far superior to their German counterparts, who were largely three-year conscripts. The largest branch was the seamen, who normally joined at the age of fifteen or sixteen, underwent a gruelling course in a hulk or a shore base, and then were promoted to ordinary seaman at the age of eighteen, to serve a minimum of twelve years as an adult. This might be modified in times of expansion, when men could sign on for five years with the fleet and seven in reserve. A young man was normally promoted to able seaman after a year and he could rise to leading seaman, to petty officer, and to chief petty officer, when he would change into a simplified version of the officers' uniform – though many men were never promoted and stayed on as 'three-badge ABs' wearing the maximum number of good-conduct stripes. Once qualified as an able seaman a man was eligible to undergo courses in gunnery, torpedo and physical training to increase his pay and promotion prospects. Signallers were selected from among the boy seamen and trained alongside them, while wireless telegraphy was a new branch.

The next largest group was the stokers, who were needed in great numbers for the hungry engines of the new Dreadnoughts and battlecruisers, until Churchill and Fisher converted them to oil and turned the stoker into a semi-skilled mechanic. Stokers were recruited as adults and had very different standards of discipline and cleanliness from seamen, so were kept apart on the mess decks. They often presented disciplinary problems, and many officers remembered a mutiny in the naval barracks at Portsmouth in 1906. Above them in the engineering branch were the engine room artificers, who had served an apprenticeship either inside or outside the navy and were the most privileged members of the lower deck, the equivalent of chief petty officers on completion of their training.

The Royal Marines were the next largest group, also recruited as adults but imbued with parade-ground discipline and fiercely proud of their corps. They might serve afloat as part of the crew, or on shore in battalions. They were divided into infantry with red full-dress army-style uniforms, and artillery in blue, who played a part in manning the ship's guns. Seamen and stokers wore the now traditional 'square rig' uniform of the seaman with round cap, square collar and bell-bottom trousers. Members of other branches, including stewards, cooks, writers (clerks) and sick berth attendants, wore blue jackets, collars and ties and peaked caps, and they too were kept separate from the other branches on board ship, to avoid both friction and conspiracy.

The lower deck had many grievances. It had not had a pay-rise for 60 years, sailors had to pay for their own uniforms, and promotion to commissioned officer was far more difficult than in the army. Though flogging was no longer used for adults, punishments were often degrading and out of proportion to the offence. Any attempt to form a trade union in the navy would be a serious breach of discipline, but lower-deck societies had started mainly as friendly societies intended to support members in illness or hardship. By 1910 there were 124 societies, each contributing to an annual petition to the Admiralty asking for better conditions. By 1912 the movement had spread to seamen and stokers. The societies only represented about 10 per cent of the lower deck, but they contributed to a feeling that naval discipline, like order in society in general, was about to break down. The *Daily Chronicle* reported that 'numbers of men, disappointed by all parties alike, have jumped from old-time naval conservatism to political views in advance of radicalism', while a lower-deck correspondent claimed in the *Portsmouth Evening News* that 'There is only one thing for the bluejackets to do, they must combine themselves with the trade union movement.'[16]

James Wood had joined the Royal Navy in 1878 at the age of fifteen, transferred to the coastguard in 1884 and resigned in 1897 to take up full-time journalism. He adopted the name of Lionel Yexley and edited a newspaper called *The Bluejacket*, then another called *The Fleet*, to campaign for better conditions. By 1912 he was in contact with Fisher and Churchill, who still had many of the instincts of a social reformer and was well aware of the lower deck's problems – he even suggested Yexley as a parliamentary candidate for Portsmouth in 1912.[17] Churchill raised the question of pay in parliament:

> ... outside the naval service everything has advanced, and the relative position of the bluejacket compared to the soldier, the policeman, the postman, the fireman, the railway man, the dockyard labourer – in fact, with everyone with whom he comes in contact at the great ports, has markedly declined. ... The concentration of the Fleet in Home Waters has diminished the sailor's opportunities of saving

money, and led him into constant expenditure. It has induced a greater proportion of marriages. The serious rise in prices of the last twelve years, amounting to 15 per cent, has increased the stringency of life in the dockyard towns. Owing to the movements of the Fleet, a large amount of railway travelling is necessary for the men to get to their families, and this alone is a new and heavy drain upon their resources. On the other hand, the service becomes more strenuous every year; the number of practices and exercises of all kinds continually increases, and the standards are raised.[18]

By this time the government was spending so much on new Dreadnoughts that there was very little left for the lower deck. Churchill had a certain amount of success, however, and Yexley was jubilant, claiming 'practically every cause of unrest … has been removed as far as legislation can remove them … to Mr Winston Churchill we must give the credit'.[19] But Churchill had not succeeded on the biggest issues, on marriage allowance, on payment for uniform or on pay – a rise of 3d per day for an able seaman after six years was recognised as a compromise, which was not enough to cover the rising cost of living.

CHAPTER 8

Matériel

Churchill took a serious and penetrating interest in ship design, often resolving the differences between different schools of thought. He enjoyed this, and the relevant chapter in *The World Crisis* is entitled 'The Romance of Design'. According to Sir Tennyson d'Eyncourt, who became Director of Naval Construction in 1912, 'Winston Churchill too was a keen exponent of progress in all things to do with the Navy, and his encouragement and interest were a never-failing inspiration and bulwark of support, though his own career had not given him the practical knowledge of ship design possessed by Lord Fisher.'[1] Churchill paid tribute to 'the manner in which the Royal Corps of Naval Constructors can juggle with these factors, and the facility with which the great chiefs and masters of battleship design … were able to speak on these matters were marvellous beyond belief'.[2] When Churchill came to office the head of the Corps was Sir Philip Watts, who started as an apprentice shipwright in Portsmouth Dockyard and was selected to study in the School of Naval Architecture in South Kensington. He worked with the pioneering naval architect William Froude and left the navy in 1885 to work in the Armstrong Yard at Elswick on the Tyne, where he gained experience on British and foreign warships. He came back in 1902 to succeed Sir William White as Director of Naval Construction. He designed the *Dreadnought*, the *Queen Elizabeth* class battleships and the cruiser *Arethusa* before retiring in 1912.

For his successor, Churchill took the unprecedented step of advertising outside the service. Eustace Tennyson d'Eyncourt was on the Tyne designing ships for the Brazilian Navy when it was suggested he might apply. At first he thought it was a joke, but he was summoned to an interview by Churchill. It was his first time in government service, but as he wrote: 'Perhaps it was not altogether the drawback it appeared to me than, as my genuine ignorance of Civil Service methods enabled me to pursue certain courses of action at times when an old government servant would have hesitated to take such a line.'[3] He was soon involved in the design of the *Revenge* class battleships and the C-class cruisers, and in developing underwater protection against torpedoes.

★

Since the original *Dreadnought* was launched in 1906, battleships had expanded from 18,000 tons to 23,000 and from the *Orion* class of 1910–12 they carried 13.5-inch guns instead of 12-inch, giving greater range and penetrating power. All the turrets were now mounted on the centre line and some were 'superimposed' above others, so that all could be fired at once in a full broadside. Churchill claimed the credit for initiating the next step. He quickly realised that the increase in calibre had increased the weight of each shell from 850 to 1,400 lbs. 'I immediately sought to go one size better. I mentioned this to Lord Fisher at Reigate, and he hurled himself into its advocacy with tremendous passion.' For he had concluded that 'Nothing less than a 15-inch gun could be looked at for all the battleships and battle-cruisers of the new programme. ... What was it that enabled Jack Johnson to knock out his opponents? It was the big punch.' Churchill went on, 'Enlarging the gun meant enlarging the ships, and enlarging the ships meant increasing the cost. Moreover, the redesign must cause no delay and the guns must be ready as soon as the turrets were ready.' He claimed that 'No such thing as a modern 15-inch gun existed' though in fact the Ordnance Board had begun to look at possible designs in February 1911.[4] In any case, he went on, 'I hardened my heart and took the plunge. The whole outfit of guns was ordered. forthwith.' He recognised that this was a great gamble, for if they did not work he would be subjected to enormous pressure, and he was relieved when an advance model, known for security reasons as 'the 14-inch experimental', was successfully tested at the Elswick works.

It was decided to arm the new ships with eight rather than ten main guns, as that would still provide a punch of 16,000 lbs rather than 14,000, and over a longer range. Though Fisher thoroughly supported Churchill with the increase, he opposed the idea of using 6-inch guns for defence against torpedo boats, perhaps reasoning that the old secondary armament of the pre-Dreadnoughts was creeping back. 'If you let these silly idiots frighten you into the 6-inch gun I shall be bitterly disappointed … Utterly silly.'[5] But the increased range of torpedoes meant that attackers had to be fought off at longer range, and the 6-inch guns were to prove themselves in battle.

Of course the guns were only the beginning. Churchill described the process in 'very unexpert language':

> You take the largest possible number of the best possible guns that can be fired in combination from one vessel as a single battery. You group them conveniently by pairs in turrets. You put the turrets so that there is the widest possible arc of fire for every gun and the least possible blast interference. This regulates the position of the turrets and the spacing between them. You draw a line around the arrangement of turrets thus arrived at, which gives you the deck of the ship. You then build a hull to carry this deck or great gun platform. It must be very big and very long. Next you see what room you have got inside this hull for engines to drive it, and from this and from the length you get the speed. Last of all you decide the armour.[6]

But Churchill wanted more than a 'great gun platform' for the 15-inch guns. He planned 'a division of ships fast enough to seize the advantageous position and yet as strong in gun power and armour as any battleship afloat' which would score 'almost with certainty an inestimable and a decisive advantage'. Tactical studies in the war college showed that a speed of 25 knots would be necessary for this, compared with 21 knots for most existing Dreadnoughts, while the battlecruisers 'had thin skins compared to the enemy's strongest battleships, which presumably would head his line'. There was only one way to achieve all these advantages. 'We could not get the power required to drive these ships at 25 knots except by use of oil fuel.'[7] The ships were designed by Sir Philip Watts and four of them were ordered, supplemented by one funded by the Federated Malay States. They were the famous *Queen Elizabeth* class, laid down from October 1912 to October 1913, and they were completed in 1915–16, to make a significant contribution during two world wars. Beatty, who did not always give Churchill the credit he deserved, wrote that 'the Q.E. is the *finest* fighting unit in the world'.[8]

★

Oil fuel offered great advantages as a means of heating the boilers of steam engines, compared with the more traditional coal. In Churchill's words, 'In equal ships oil gave a large excess of speed over coal. It enabled that speed to be attained with far greater rapidity. It gave 40 per cent greater radius of action for the same weight of coal. It enabled a fleet to re-fuel at sea with great facility.' Furthermore it could be pumped rather than shovelled so the gruelling operation of coaling, often done after an exhausting patrol, was avoided. Once it was on board the great army of stokers was no longer needed and their numbers could be cut by half, while the remainder became semi-skilled mechanics. Accommodation was less tight on board, and wages bills were reduced.

Against this there was the minor disadvantage that the coal no longer protected against shellfire, and the far greater one that it had to be obtained from abroad, and that storage facilities and large reserves would have to be built up almost from scratch. Destroyers and submarines already used oil, but battleships and cruisers had far larger engines. Churchill told the House of Commons in 1912: 'The adoption and supply of oil as a motive power raises anxious and perplexing problems … can we make sure of obtaining full supplies of oil in time of peace and of war? Can we accumulate and store a sufficient reserve of oil to meet our ever-growing requirements, and can we make that reserve properly protected against attack either by aeroplanes or sabotage?'[9] Moreover the world oil supplies were largely controlled by Standard Oil of New Jersey and by Royal Dutch Shell, partly owned by Germans and based in the Netherlands, which was vulnerable to German invasion.

The idea of oil fuel was not new and Fisher was pushing hard for it, though in 1904 his then First Lord had dismissed it on the grounds that 'oil does not exist in this world in sufficient quantities'.[10] And Fisher himself had a different agenda, believing that oil should be used to power diesel engines instead of steam boilers – though no diesel which was anything like big enough for a battleship would appear until much later. In December 1911 a departmental enquiry under Pakenham, the Fourth Sea Lord, was lukewarm about the prospects for oil, but Churchill went over his head and asked Fisher to chair a Royal Commission on the subject. He told Fisher: 'You have got to find the oil: to show how it can be stored cheaply: how it can be purchased regularly and cheaply; and with absolute certainty in war.'[11] Since Fisher was allowed a free hand in choosing the membership of the Commission, it is not surprising that the report concluded in 1913: 'The use of oil-fuel makes it possible in every type of war vessel to produce a ship which will fulfil given conditions of speed, armament, &c., on lesser dimensions and at smaller cost.'[12] On the question of supply, the Commission wanted to buy oil on the open market as it did coal, though of course it was far more international. Churchill had a different idea, to find and develop the country's own resources using the Anglo-Persian Oil Company which already had concessions in Iran and was building a refinery at Abadan. The British government invested heavily in APOC and acquired a controlling interest, hoping to guarantee the supply of oil. This was popular at the time: Conservatives saw the Admiralty taking decisive steps at last, while socialists were glad to see a form of nationalisation, and taking on the great oil giants. This was the origin of British Petroleum, and it was to involve much difficulty with the Iranian government over the decades, sometimes involving Churchill.

Meanwhile other practical difficulties were solved by building 5,000-ton oil tanks at the major naval ports. They were difficult to hide, and Churchill worried about their vulnerability to air attack and sabotage. By July 1914 the navy had large facilities at Sheerness and Portsmouth with capacity for 210,000 and 170,000 tons respectively, with other depots mainly on the east coast. A fleet of tankers was built up. In the navy itself, the change was welcomed by the sailors as more and more ships were completed to use oil, or were converted. Able Seaman George Saban reported: 'The seamen were free as soon as they had secured the oiler alongside … That was, I think, the biggest step forward in the service ever.'[13]

★

In the meantime, however, there was a backward step with the battleships of the 1913–14 programme. Pakenham and Lambert, the Civil Lord of the Admiralty, had dissented from the Royal Commission report and urged caution over oil supplies, claiming public opinion 'would crucify any Board that failed to make a certainty of plentiful oil supplies'.[14] The new ships, known as the R or *Revenge* class, retained the 15-inch guns but were smaller and cheaper and were to revert to a speed of 21½ knots, as the 'fast division' would only include the *Queen Elizabeths*. There were still doubts about oil fuel and they were to use a combination of coal and oil until that was changed in 1915 to oil alone.

Churchill disagreed with Fisher over his pet project, the battlecruisers. He wrote later: 'I do not believe in the wisdom of the battle-cruiser type. If it is worthwhile to spend far more than the price of your best battleship upon a fast heavily gunned vessel, it is better at the same time to give it the heaviest armour as well.'[15] In effect the new *Queen Elizabeth* class were to replace the battlecruisers, and no more were ordered during Churchill's peacetime administration. In the matter of smaller ships, Fisher firmly believed in his battlecruisers as a means of protecting British commerce, though he did not explain how a small number of expensive ships could cover the vast oceans. As a result there was a ten-year gap in building smaller cruisers, which had various functions, 'now scouting for the Battle Fleet; now convoying merchantmen; now fighting an action with another cruiser squadron; now showing the flag in distant or tropical oceans'.[16] In addition, it was becoming clear that they might have to fight off torpedo attack on the battle fleet, as the Germans were sending destroyers out with their battleships. Apart from the battlecruisers there were four different types of cruisers in service in 1911. Armoured cruisers were almost equivalent to pre-Dreadnought battleships and had guns of up to 9.2 inches. They were obsolescent, though many remained in service. Protected cruisers were just as big but had much lighter armour so their coal was distributed to help absorb shot. Scouts were intended to lead destroyer flotillas and had very light gun armament of 12-pounders or later 4-inch. The 'Towns' had been built more recently with 6-inch guns but were unarmoured and tended to be poor sailers.

Churchill soon concluded that 'We required a very large number of small fast vessels to protect the Battle Fleet from torpedo attack, to screen it and within certain limits to scout for it. After hearing many arguments, I proposed to the Board that we should concentrate on this type, to exclude all requirements of the distant seas, and to build vessels for attendance on the Battle Fleets in home waters and for that duty alone.'[17] Fisher was not helpful, claiming 'You are forced by the general consensus of opinion to have these useless warships ...'. He wanted fast battlecruisers, fast destroyers and fast submarines, for 'The first of all its necessities is SPEED ...'.[18] Nevertheless Churchill set up a committee of admirals to consider the cruiser question and two possibilities offered themselves – in effect a large destroyer based on the *Swift* of 1907, or a small cruiser based on the *Blonde* class of scouts of 1909–11. The admirals chose the latter, and Churchill justified it to Fisher: 'These vessels are intended primarily for service with the battle-fleet as destroyer-destroyers as well as scouts and patrols. In the last character they have many points of superiority over the Super-Swift: they have better observation platforms, stronger batteries, larger radius of action, and are much less likely to their lose speed in a sea-way. ... They are also cruisers and count as such: there is no flotilla they cannot break up, and no flotilla-cruiser they cannot go round.'[19] They had the unusual armament of six 4-inch guns firing forward and two 6-inch in the stern. As Churchill put it, 'When advancing to attack destroyers she could fire a large number of 32-lb shots, each sufficient to wound them grievously; when retreating from a larger cruiser she could strike back with her two 6-inch guns. I personally insisted upon the two 6-inch. The Navy would never recognise these vessels as cruisers if they did not carry metal of that weight.'[20] Described as 'light armoured cruisers', eight ships of the *Arethusa* class were built in 1912–15, followed by six of the improved version, the *Caroline* class, in 1914–15. Many more were added during the war and they proved very suitable for North Sea conditions, though rather cramped. Eventually most of them were fitted with the 6-inch armament. One of them, the *Caroline*, survives to this day.

Churchill described his philosophy for destroyers: 'Build slow destroyers! One might as well breed slow racehorses.' He 'gave directions to design the new flotilla to realize 35 knots speed without giving up anything in gun-power, torpedoes or seaworthiness'.[21] They were based on the existing L class but with increases in length and power, and the result was the M class. He wrote in 1917: 'The 1912–13 destroyer, for which I was responsible, lifted six or seven knots on its predecessor, attaining the immense speed of thirty-six or thirty-seven knots without the sacrifice either of gun-power or sea-keeping capacity. These boats, which are almost miniature cruisers, were designed to catch and hunt down the best destroyers of the German Navy in their own waters across the broad distances of the North Sea.'[22] They were none too soon: faster destroyers were needed to escort the battle fleet and make torpedo attacks, and the design became the basis for many more ordered during the war.

★

Apart from aircraft, the submarine was by far the most revolutionary factor in naval warfare when Churchill came to the Admiralty. Such vessels had been tried many times, most notably by Robert Fulton in the Napoleonic Wars and by the Confederates in the American Civil War. The Irish-American John P. Holland intended his early submarine as a challenge to British sea power, and had developed a successful craft by the 1890s. In 1900 the British Admiralty bought a vessel from the Electric Boat Company, which had acquired Holland's rights. Known as Holland 1, it entered service in 1901 and despite its loss development proceeded over the next decade. By 1911 the latest boats of the E-class had a speed of 15.25 knots on the surface and 9.75 knots underwater. They carried four 18-inch torpedoes and a crew of 31, and had a range of more than 3,000 miles on the surface at 10 knots. However, like all such craft of the day, they were 'submersibles' rather than true submarines, only able to stay underwater for limited periods.

Though the submarine was generally seen as a weapon by which a weaker naval power could threaten a stronger one, both Fisher and Churchill were enthusiastic about its use. Fisher saw it as a means of blockading the German battleships in port and defending the British coast against invasion, while Churchill believed it was the only kind of vessel, apart from battleships, that might 'directly determine the fate of a naval war', as he told the Prime Minister of Canada. Fisher wanted two classes of submarine, the coastal type to protect from invasion and the overseas type to blockade Germany. In a paper of August 1913 Churchill advocated a third, the 'ocean' or 'fleet' submarine: 'The ocean submarine (or submarine cruiser) must have sufficient speed to overhaul a battle fleet so as to make sure of being able to anticipate it at any point, to get head in order to dive and attack.' A minimum of 24 knots was needed on the surface, and such vessels would be accompanied by surface ships to guide them to the point of attack. The design was examined in Churchill's office in December, and the Director of Naval Construction 'expressed great confidence in the design and did not anticipate any great difficulty in controlling a vessel of this displacement'. But he clearly had doubts, remarking that 'if it failed as a submarine, it would still be a very formidable surface torpedo craft'. Commodore (submarines) pointed out that it would have three times the displacement of an E-class boat and was nearly twice as long, but 'no serious objection was raised by anyone present to the laying down of one experimental vessel – except that the money might be better spent'.[23] That was a good point, as it diverted funds away from the smaller boats which would prove more useful.

In the meantime Fisher had been commissioned to report on the future possibilities of submarines. He foresaw uses in fleet battle, in commerce defence and destruction, and coastal defence. He also raised the possibility that the Germans might sink merchant ships without warning – 'inhuman and barbarous' but a 'truly terrible' menace for British commerce and indeed survival, for 'no means can be suggested at present of meeting it except by reprisals'. Churchill was horrified and commented: 'If there were a nation vile enough to adopt systematically such methods, it would be justified and indeed necessary, to employ the extreme resources of science against them: to spread pestilence, poison the water of great cities, and, if convenient, proceed by the assassination of individuals.' Though he claimed these were 'unthinkable propositions' which 'marred' Fisher's paper, his extreme reaction suggests that he was fearful of the danger.[24]

However Churchill was with Fisher in agreeing that the submarine might supplant the battleship, and in March 1914 he told the House of Commons: 'The whole system of naval architecture and the methods of computing naval strengths are brought under review by the ever-growing power, radius and seaworthiness of the submarine ...'.[25] Historians are bitterly divided on whether Churchill and Fisher were on the verge of a revolution before they were interrupted by the war; but as always they were keen to put forward new ideas.

*

Churchill was always interested in the British Empire and the contribution it might make to naval power. He looked towards the quasi-independent dominions, especially Canada, Australia and New Zealand, which had total control over their own budgets but not over their foreign policy. There were several ways in which they could help: by forming their own navy for regional defence as Australia had done, or by providing ships and men for the main fleet in British waters. Churchill's big idea in 1912 was an Imperial Squadron of battlecruisers supplied by the three dominions plus cruisers from South Africa and India: 'Separately these navies are weak and even ridiculous. One Dreadnought, *et praeteria nihil*! But combined they might make a force which no European power could face without dispersing its own concentration & consequently releasing ours. ... In times of peace to move constantly from station to station spending 3 or 4 months in rotation in the waters of each Dominion ...'.[26] That proved impracticable, but New Zealand agreed to fund a battlecruiser for presentation to the Royal Navy. Later in the year Robert L. Borden, Prime Minister of Canada, suggested that the dominion might provide three Dreadnoughts, and Churchill offered to go to there to help muster support. He raised the possibility that an equal amount of money might be spent on submarines. He wrestled with the question whether the Dreadnoughts would be part of the ships needed for the 60 per cent superiority over Germany or additional to it, and for political reasons he had to maintain the latter, though he also argued that 'the three ships now under discussion in Canada are absolutely required from 1916 onwards for the whole world defence of the British empire, apart altogether from the needs of Great Britain in home waters'.[27] He was in the middle of the naval estimates crisis of 1913 when the Canadian parliament rejected the proposal; it was 'a heavy blow'.

CHAPTER 9

The Naval Air Service

The Wright Brothers made their first successful flight at Kitty Hawk Bay, North Carolina, on 17 December 1903. It established that the combination of the glider and the new internal combustion engine was possible, and that their system of lateral control, by warping the wings rather than moving the crew from side to side, was the way forward. That first flight was very short and they proceeded cautiously – it was nearly a year before they could stay in the air for more than five minutes. Europe only became fully aware of their achievement in the summer of 1908 when they demonstrated their machine near Le Mans. In London *The Times* reported: 'All present affirm that, after yesterday's experiment, there can be no doubt that the Wrights possess a machine capable of remaining an hour in the air and almost as manageable as if it were a small toy held in the hand.'[1] In Britain the three Short brothers had been making balloons, but soon realised where the future lay. They bought a licence to build six Wright flyers, and soon began to develop designs of their own.

Churchill had observed the Royal Engineers balloon in the march to Ladysmith but did not enquire deeply into its function. His interest in aeroplanes is first noted on 15 February 1909 when the Committee for Imperial Defence (CID) was informed that C. S. Rolls (one of the founders of Rolls Royce) had purchased a Wright biplane from the Shorts and was offering its services to the government for experiments. Churchill, then President of the Board of Trade, noted that 'there was a danger of these proposals being considered too amateurish. The problem of the use of aeroplanes was a most important one, and we should place ourselves in communication with Mr Wright himself, and avail ourselves of his knowledge.'[2] As Home Secretary in 1910, Churchill was concerned about international agreements on the use of the air. In particular, he wanted to retain the right to prevent aircraft from over-flying sensitive areas such as naval dockyards.[3] In May 1911 he attended a display of 'bombing' arranged by Claude Grahame-White when he dropped sandbags on mock targets in his airfield at Hendon.[4] Meanwhile in February 1911 a wealthy enthusiast, Frank McClean, offered the use of two aircraft for training naval pilots. Four officers were chosen out of 200 applicants and they were trained at Eastchurch, where McClean had a site which he let out to the Royal Aero Club. The first to qualify, in April 1911, was Lieutenant Charles Samson, quickly followed by Lieutenant Arthur Longmore. They were given the task of training another batch of pilots at Eastchurch.

Aside from this progress with heavier-than-air machines, Churchill came to the Admiralty just after naval aviation's first great setback. The airship R1 (popularly known as *Mayfly*) had been built by Vickers in Barrow in Furness with very little experience of airship design, and limited intelligence of the highly successful craft being built by Count von Zeppelin in Germany. On 24 September she was wrecked by a combination of structural weakness and crew inexperience in handling her as she was put into her shed. Her cost had doubled to £70,000, a large slice of the naval aviation budget. This was precisely the moment when heavier-than-air naval aviation reached the first stage of its gesta-tion. According to Longmore, 'By the end of October 1911, our flying education was sufficiently complete to turn our attention seriously to the business of applying the new science to the needs of the Navy.'[5] In April 1912, on the recommendation of the Committee of Imperial Defence attended by Churchill, the Royal Flying Corps was created as a joint-service organisation. There was to be a Central Flying School at Upavon in inland Wiltshire, where army and navy pilots would be trained to fly, an army wing, and a naval wing based at Eastchurch, which would concentrate on the purely maritime aspects of flying. A few weeks later

Churchill was able to set up the post of Director of the Air Department under the formidable Captain Murray F. Sueter. Two years older than Churchill, he was an intelligent, inventive and outspoken officer who had already worked on the development of mines, torpedoes and submarines before taking over as inspecting captain of airships in 1910. In his new post, he answered to no less than three separate Lords of the Admiralty on different matters, but Churchill later claimed that he had 'placed the Royal Naval Air Service under my personal administration, i.e. it was not administered by any of the Sea Lords of the Admiralty, but the Director of the Air Division received his instructions directly from myself'.

Churchill insisted that the air service should not grow out of the Royal Engineers Balloon Service, but be 'a new and separate organisation drawing from civilian, as well as naval and military sources'. He wanted to 'make aviation for war purposes the most honourable, as it is the most dangerous profession an Englishman can adopt'.[6] At this time he was in favour of a good deal of joint operation between the army and naval air services. In November 1911

> His view on the matter was that the principal part of the art of aviation was neither naval nor military. Before airmen could be useful either for naval or military purposes they must have mastered the art of flying. Once this had been accomplished it would be comparatively easy for airmen to acquire such special knowledge as would render them useful to the Navy or Army. Even without such special knowledge an airman would be of great value, for he could take an expert as passenger.

Lieutenant Samson was outspoken enough to challenge the last point. At present, 'the tendency was to employ aeroplanes without a passenger for naval purposes, owing to the sacrifice of petrol and the consequent reduction in the radius of action when a passenger was carried'.[7]

During his first year at the Admiralty Churchill was preoccupied with the problems of setting up a naval staff. When he presented his first naval estimates to parliament on 4 March 1912, there were only three lines on naval aviation, lacking in any detail: 'The development of aviation for naval purposes has been the subject of special attention, and all possible measures have been taken to procure an adequate and immediate supply of trained officers and mechanics.'[8] Already he was being urged on by Fisher: '*Aviation* supersedes small cruisers and intelligence vessels.'[9] But after so much money had been lost on the *Mayfly*, it was difficult to get more.

The naval wing tended to attract officers of independent disposition, who were only too glad to get away from the stifling atmosphere of the regular navy. At their head was the Director himself, Captain Murray Sueter, who soon became a tireless advocate of air power. Among the pilots, the first to qualify (by a few hours) was Lieutenant Charles Samson. At first the relationship between the two was not easy, however. According to Sueter:

> At first I did not understand Samson. He always reminded me of what one reads of Francis Drake. Until you knew him, a most difficult man to deal with. But once he saw that a Senior Officer was full out to help him in every possible way, he was a different person. No job was too difficult for him to undertake, and his men would follow him anywhere.[10]

It was officers like these who took most of the initiative in the development of naval air power, but Samson recognised that Churchill encouraged them. He and Murray Sueter were 'the two people responsible for anything the Navy did to help Naval Aviation'.[11]

When the first programme was drawn up for 'The Inspection of the Fleet by His Majesty the King at Weymouth' on 7–11 May 1912, there was no mention of aerial activity except a list of four in the 'Aeroplane "Flight"' – a term which Churchill claimed to have devised himself.[12] These were of some variety, a Short 'hydro-aeroplane', a French Deperdussin monoplane, a Short monoplane and a Short biplane, with the possibility that a French Nieuport might be added. They would be flown by the original naval pilots, Samson, Longmore, Reginald Gregory and Eugene Gerrard.

In the event much of the naval display was interrupted by bad weather, but the naval aviators, supported by civilian pioneers such as Claude Grahame-White, were undaunted. Pencil notes were added to a surviving copy of the programme, it is not clear whether before or after the event. As the King arrived his yacht was to be 'met by aeroplanes, who signal approach to fleet'. As the Red and Blue fleets selected for the annual manoeuvres rendezvoused, there would be 'Aeroplanes probably in attendance.' On the final day there would be an 'aeroplane display – tracking torpedoes etc.'.[13] On 8 May Gregory dropped a 300-lb weight representing a bomb near the Royal Yacht and raised the possibility of attacking warships. The civilians gave a 'dazzling display' while Grahame-White photographed the battleship *Neptune* and it was reproduced in the newspapers. Samson flew the Short 'hydro-aeroplane' off from the bay, the first public demonstration of such a take-off.

The highlight was planned for 9 May. Samson had already taken off from a system of rails on the battleship *Africa* at anchor off Sheerness, following the American pioneer Eugene Ely. Now he was to carry out the first take-off from a moving ship, the *Hibernia*. The King was said to fear that he might crash into the water ahead of the ship, but when the battleship steamed at 10½ knots across the bay Samson was able to use the wind to get in the air in 45 feet, less than half the distance he had needed on the *Africa*. He landed in an airfield nearby, having demonstrated what would become the standard method of launching in the future. The display was largely improvised by the aviators themselves and attracted a great deal of attention in the press. Churchill was present and was perhaps influenced by it. Lord Rothschild wrote to him of 'the great effect produced on your guests at the Naval Review by everything they saw'.[14] In August Churchill was still complaining: 'I am much surprised to get a third refusal from the treasury on the subject of the Air Department at the Admiralty.' He would 'not be responsible for the conduct of Admiralty business unless this most vital aspect of naval aeronautics received the attention and study it deserves'.[15] But soon this would begin to change.

★

In October 1913, after two years at the Admiralty, Churchill turned his full attention to the role of naval air power. He saw four main tasks – scouting from a ship at sea, fighting enemy aircraft and airships to protect the fleet, protecting vulnerable points on the British coast, and patrolling the coast. He proposed three types of aircraft. The 'overseas fighting machine' was intended to operate from a ship and was to be fitted with floats and folding wings for stowage. It could be used to attack the 'vulnerable points' of the enemy on shore, such as docks and magazines, though for the moment 'promiscuous attack' should be ruled out. It would depend on its speed to escape from enemy fighters, though that tended to contradict the use of floats. It would also defend the fleet against reconnaissance by enemy airships, perhaps by dropping explosive charges or fireballs on them from a height of 2,000 feet. The 'home service fighting machine' was to defend vulnerable points such as oil tanks and magazines. It did not need the burden of floats, but would carry a passenger who would operate a hand gun, plus the bombs or fireballs as the main offensive weapon against airships. The third type, the 'sea scouting machine', was for use by the fleet at sea. They might be carried by specially equipped ships, or individually by battleships. Speed could be sacrificed to long range, and they too would need floats and folding wings.[16]

As early as December 1911, Churchill was convinced that 'real, young and capable men, who have already done so much for the new arm', should be 'placed effectually at the head of the new Corps of Airmen'. This aim would always conflict with conventional naval opinion, which deplored temporary rank or accelerated promotion, and high rank should only be attained by long years of effort.[17] But the new service could not be set up without some senior officers, and they did not necessarily have any experience of flying: 'It seems unlikely that senior officers will be required for or suited to the work of pilots ...'.[18] Such men did not always accept the open discussion that Churchill encouraged. After the cruiser *Hermes* was fitted with an aircraft for the 1913 naval manoeuvres, her captain, G. W. Vivian, was technically in command of all naval air personnel. Vivian did not understand that his role was purely nominal. When Churchill held a meeting on board the *Enchantress*, Lieutenant Seddon complained about conditions in his new base on the Isle of Grain, and was encouraged to put it in writing for the First Lord. When he did so, Vivian was incensed and complained. Churchill decided to terminate his appointment as soon as the commission of the *Hermes* ended in a few months' time.[19] Likewise Captain Godfrey Paine of the Central Flying School was by-passed, because it was believed he had 'a very poor opinion of the Naval Wing'. He was not really a member of it, but a naval officer on secondment to the Central Flying School, and he should be left there.[20]

The biggest problem was likely to be with the middle levels, the squadron and flight commanders who would lead their men in the air and on the ground. Seniority as a naval lieutenant was no guarantee of suitability in the flying role. In January 1914 Pakenham and Sueter made two proposals for rank structure which Churchill rejected. One alternative would make it possible for 'a very young and junior officer in the Navy to be advanced to be a Squadron Commander in the flying service' so that he would have 'substantive rank and authority over officers of the regular naval service four, five, and six years his senior'. This would 'not be assented to by the Second Sea Lord, and would be very much disliked in the service afloat' – a level of opposition which even Churchill did not want to take on. The other proposal was for officers simply to retain their rank in general service while attached to the flying branch, which had equally severe problems. 'It condemns an officer of junior naval rank to remain permanently at the bottom of his flying grade, and no matter how long he has been flying or how high his qualifications he will be automatically superseded by officers of senior naval rank in the same flying grade, not matter how temporary their connection with the flying service may be.'[21]

In July 1914, therefore, a system of officer ranks was set up especially for the RNAS, in an attempt to by-pass the rules of naval seniority. New entrants from civilian life would be probationary flight-sub-lieutenants. A flight lieutenant was equivalent to a sub-lieutenant RN, a flight commander to a full lieutenant with at least four years seniority. A squadron commander who was not actually in command would be equivalent to a senior lieutenant, or a lieutenant commander if senior enough; a squadron commander in command would have the relative rank of lieutenant commander. Above that in the senior ranks were six wing commanders, including Samson. The highest rank of wing captain was held by Sueter. Promotion would be by selection only, a policy which Churchill supported fully. Officers could expect to serve for four years in the air service, for Churchill believed that 'we ought not to expect at present that any officer, however young, will continue to fly an aeroplane for more than from three to five years'.[22] After that an officer might revert to general service, unless he was offered a post in the higher command.[23]

Churchill was aware that this was less favourable than the army system, for 'The [War Office] give temporary military rank effective for all purposes, even outside the Flying Corps to military flying officers proportioned to their flying grades, involving in most cases an advance of a distinct grade. Thus an Army Captain who is promoted Squadron Commander in the Flying Corps is made an Army Major *for all purposes* on the day of his promotion in the Flying Corps, and so on.' The navy scheme was 'far more modest' in that the higher rank had no effect outside the flying service.[24] Possibly this is what caused Sueter to notice that 'some of the Air Officers are not in complete agreement with the new scheme for the Royal Naval Air Service'. He issued a memo pointing out that officers who had 'a personal bias towards a policy which has definitely been rejected' should buckle under or leave the service.[25]

The 1914 scheme also allowed for candidates to enter from civil life. Churchill had considered this in August 1913, and commented: '… it is necessary to authorise and organise the direct entry of civilian flyers into the Naval Air Wing. The maximum age should, I think, be higher than 22. I apprehend the numbers will not be forthcoming unless the ages is raised to, say, 24.' They would serve for up to ten years after which they would be entitled to a pension or lump sum, or in some cases transfer to the regular navy.[26] In May 1914 he outlined his ideas further:

> It is essential that all persons joining the naval wing should receive the groundings of a good military training. Flying should only form a portion of their work, and periods of flying should alternate with other forms of instruction. For the present I must regard the Central Flying School as the best means of weeding those who are not likely to make good flying officers. But thereafter, during their first year of training, the probationers should be at least three months at marine headquarters, and three months either attached to the Nore Defence destroyer flotillas or in larger ships, as may be found convenient.[27]

This was substantially adopted in the July 1914 order, though it was soon to be overtaken by events.

In 1914 Churchill concluded that naval airmen should wear 'Naval uniform with an eagle instead of an anchor on buttons, cap badges, epaulettes, and sword belt clasps, with an eagle over the curl on the sleeve.'[28] According to Sueter,

> Mr. Churchill wanted an eagle for a badge to be worn on the sleeve of the coat to distinguish the naval airmen. An artist was sent for and he produced a design like a goose. But Mrs. Sueter had a gold eagle brooch of French Imperial design that she had purchased in Paris. I took this eagle brooch to the Admiralty to show to Mr. Churchill and Admiral Prince Louis of Battenburg. They much preferred it to the goose design of the artist and adopted it for the badge of the Royal Naval Air Service.[29]

The eagle was to be worn at all times. On one hand it showed that the wearer was a brave pilot. On the other hand, as Churchill put it, 'The flying badge (which must always be worn) excludes them from all executive command outside the RF service.'[30]

By the beginning of 1913, Churchill was much less enthusiastic about a joint service air arm.

> [He] had originally been strongly in favour of a joint Naval and Military Air Service, but the lines of development of flying machines in the two Services were divergent. Naval effort was now concentrated on the Hydro-Aeroplane. ... The development did not concern the Army, which required machines to alight on the land. ... Observation on land was also quite different to observation on the sea. Except, therefore, in experimental work, he did not think the Navy profited in any way by co-operation with the Army in this Service.[31]

However, with his inter-service instincts, Churchill soon became a strong advocate of close links between the naval and military wings. In June 1914 he affirmed that he 'had always looked on the Naval and Military Wings as branches of one great service' — which might be taken to anticipate the eventual formation of the Royal Air Force.[32] But less than a week later an order on the organisation of the Naval Air Service referred to it as 'part of the Military Branch of the Royal Navy'. This has been taken to mean a move towards separation, but seen in context it was merely stating Churchill's own policy, that all flying officers, including those seconded from the engineer and paymaster branches, should be considered part of the 'military' or 'executive' branch of the navy.

This is confirmed by the next sentence, in which it was stated that this would not allow them to take command of ships, which was reserved for those on full careers in the military branch. The document went on to refer to 'The Royal Naval Air Service, forming the Naval Wing of the Royal Flying Corps'.[33]

Churchill claimed that he flew for the first time a few months after taking office, which might explain a letter from his cousin the Duke of Marlborough dated March 1913, in which he suggested he end his 'journeys in the air' and that he owed it to his friends and family 'to desist from a practice or pastime ... which is fraught with so much danger to life'.[34] One of his first instructors was Lieutenant Spenser Grey, whom he consulted on aircraft control.[35] On 6 October 1913, as the *Enchantress* visited the naval air station at Cromarty, Lieutenant Longmore took him up in a Borel seaplane. 'It was one of those perfect autumn evenings and from 5,000 feet we had the most beautiful view right across the hills and mountains of Scotland, with their wonderful colour effects. We both enjoyed it immensely.'[36] Years later Churchill described early flying in terms he would not have used to his wife at the time.

> One sat in a wicker chair with a footrail and a clear view of the earth beneath. In front was a vertical rudder, on the movements of which the flight depended. Behind was the engine, of about 50 or 60 horse-power. Accidents were frequent, and often fatal. The modern generation of aviators take it for granted that the engine will go on running. In those days it was only two or three to one against it cutting out in an hour's flight. The rule was to fly as high as possible, and always have a gliding line to some practicable landing-place. One hated flying over extensive woods. As for the sea, it was a gamble with life, the odds being somewhat in one's favour.[37]

On 23 October he visited Eastchurch with some friends and dignitaries, most of whom were 'aethereal virgins' who had not flown before. Samson took him up on a visit to the new station at the Isle of Grain, where 'we found another large flock of sea planes in the highest state of activity'. The Astra Torres airship landed and Churchill was flown round the Medway in her, with a group of generals. He was allowed to steer the ship for an hour. He wrote to his wife: 'It was as good as one of the old days in the S. African war, & I have lived entirely in the moment, with no care for all those tiresome party politics ...'.[38] But Clementine was not impressed and wrote back: 'please be kind and don't fly any more just now'.[39]

Churchill made light of this and was tempted again at the end of November during a visit to the Sheerness area. He began to go beyond mere 'journeys in the air' and started to learn to fly. At Eastchurch 17 naval aircraft were set out for him plus three private machines. He wrote: 'Down here with twenty machines in the air at once and thousands of flights made without mishap, it is not possible to look upon it as a very serious risk. Do not be vexed with me.'[40] So far the accident record of the Naval Air Service had been very good. Captain Gilbert Wildman-Lushington of the Royal Marines had been one of the officers chosen for the first flying course but had had to drop out through illness and joined a later course. According to Lushington, 'I started Winston off on his instruction about 12.15 & he got so bitten with it, I could hardly get him out of the machine, in fact except for about ¾ hour for lunch we were in the machine till about 3.30. He showed great promise, & is coming down again for further instruction and practice.'[41] He flew in the same Short biplane in which Samson had flown from the deck of the *Hibernia* ship in the previous year, though the aircraft had been modified since.

Though he clearly enjoyed the flight, Churchill was not happy about the operation of the controls. He wrote to Lushington:

> I wish you would clear up the question of the steering control and let me know what was the real difficulty I had in making the rudder act. Probably I was pushing against myself, though I am not quite sure about this. It may be that they are very stiff and hard to work. Certainly the feeling I had was that I was being repeatedly over-ridden, and I thought you were controlling the steering the whole time.[42]

Lushington felt that he had done himself 'quite a lot of good' during his first flight with Churchill, and investigated the matter. He flew no 2 from the passenger seat and found that the rudders were unbalanced and slightly heavy but that was 'a good fault for an instructional machine, as the pupil is not so likely to get into difficulties'. Churchill had been pushing against himself, which was a common fault. 'These little faults rectify themselves in time, and as you continue with your instruction, other little errors will continually be arising which you will find out for yourself. ... as an instructor, I prefer the pupil to find out these difficulties himself.'[43]

As the official manual explained, '... the most difficult part of flying is not the act of keeping the machine upright in the air, but that of getting into the air and getting back to the ground again'.[44] Even an experienced pilot like Lushington could fall foul of this, and soon after replying to Churchill he crashed and was killed while coming in to land at Eastchurch. Churchill wrote to his fiancée: 'To be killed instantly without pain or fear in the necessary service of the country when one is quite happy and life is full of success & hope, cannot be reckoned the worst of fortune. But to some who are left behind the loss is terrible.'[45]

The accident inspired more criticism of Churchill's risk-taking. In April 1914 there was a narrow escape when an engine failed and his aircraft had to land near Clacton Pier.[46] He flew again 'in good & careful hands & under perfect conditions' during a visit to the Central Flying School in May, but the accident toll was mounting, and at the beginning of June Clementine was again troubled: 'Dearest I cannot help knowing that you are going to fly as you go to Sheerness & it fills me with anxiety. I know nothing will stop you from doing it so I will not weary you with tedious entreaties, but don't forget that I am thinking about you all the time & so, do it as little, & as moderately as you can, & only with the *very best* Pilot.' She was pregnant at the time and finally got through to Winston, who agreed not to fly any more, 'at any rate until you have recovered from your kitten: & by then perhaps the risks may have been greatly reduced'. It was a great wrench to him, for he was about to take his pilot's certificate. 'I only needed a couple of calm mornings; and I am confident of my ability to achieve it very respectably.' He went on to sum up his flying career so far.

> ... I know a good deal about this fascinating new art. I can manage a machine with ease in the air, and even with high winds, & only a little more practice in landings would have enabled me to go up with reasonable safety alone. I have been up nearly 140 times, with many pilots, & all kinds of machines, so I know the difficulties and dangers of the air – well enough to appreciate them, & to understand all the questions of policy which will arise in the near future.[47]

Certainly his experiences gave Churchill detailed opinions on aircraft control which some might consider to be micro-management. Two days before giving up flying he had written to Sueter:

> The engine controls of the new Maurice Farman are a good example of what to avoid in this class of work. They are awkward, flimsy, inconveniently shaped, and ill-secured to the fuselage. The switch is also cheap and common in the last degree. No-one would put such fittings in a motor car costing £1,000.[48]

One might ask why, after 140 flights, he had not yet learned to fly properly or even gone solo. According to the future Chief of Air Staff, Hugh Trenchard, who saw him flying occasionally at Upavon (and who was never a very good pilot himself), 'He seemed altogether too impatient for a good pupil, and I could sympathise. He would arrive unexpectedly, usually without pyjamas or even a handkerchief, see what he wanted to see, and stay the night – or what was left of it when he'd finished talking.'[49]

CHAPTER 10

The Aircraft

In November 1912, as Churchill began to turn his attention to aviation, the naval wing of the Royal Flying Corps had seven biplanes, five monoplanes and eight seaplanes in service – each with its own characteristics and often with a nickname. There was a Bleriot monoplane, similar to the one which had made the historic flight across the English Channel in 1909, known as 'the birdling', which was repaired several times after crashes, including one caused by Samson trying to avoid some sheep when landing.[1] One of McClean's original machines was an early Short biplane known as 'the Dud' which unsurprisingly was not used for long. Another Short aircraft, known as the 'Triple Twin' used two engines to power three propellers in an attempt to provide slipstream over all the control surfaces. Another, with a simpler twin-engined layout, was known as the Tandem-Twin, the 'Gnome Sandwich' because the crew was placed between the engines, or the 'Vacuum Cleaner' because it allegedly had the ability 'to pull hairs out of a fur coat'. Another was known as the 'Field Kitchen' because of the excessive heat from its engines; and the twin-engined Short monoplane was named 'Double-dirty' because the crew was sprayed with castor oil.[2]

Very little had yet been fixed about the future of aviation. Lighter-than-air craft, known as airships or dirigibles, had been developed in France and, more worryingly, Germany, but British progress came to a halt with the wrecking of *Mayfly*. In December 1911 Churchill announced that he 'would want a lot of converting before he would acquiesce in a policy of building dirigibles'.[3] It was becoming clear that there were many ways in which aircraft could operate over the seas, even if their ranges were short. They might use floats or boat-like hulls to land on the water, though that could only be done in smooth seas. They could be launched from ships, though as yet there was no way of landing them back on board. They might also be launched from barges towed behind ships. Balloons could be tethered to ships for spotting and reconnaissance, or kites could be towed behind them. All these would be tried by the Naval Air Service.

Heavier-than-air craft came in many shapes, though not in a great variety of sizes so far. The biplane was the most common, with one wing braced against the other for strength. The monoplane was regarded as weaker, and after an accident they were banned for a time by the army but not the navy, which caused some tension between the two wings of the Royal Flying Corps. There were triplanes, much favoured by A. V. Roe, the founder of the famous firm Avro, in his early days, though craft with more wings than that never became common. The monoplane was generally in decline; there were only four of them on the books of the Naval Air Service by August 1914.

Even within the biplane category, there was a great deal of variation. Many of the early aircraft had the 'pusher' layout, with the engine behind the pilot and the propeller behind that, rather like the arrangement of a ship. Others had the 'tractor' layout, with the engine and propeller ahead, where it operated in 'cleaner' air. The most prolific builders of naval aircraft were Short Brothers, particularly Horace Short, whom Churchill met in October 1913. 'The Mr Short who makes the bi-planes has got a deformed head 4 times as big as any other head you have ever seen in the world – outside pantomime. He is a good man, but terrible to look at.'[4] Horace tended to favour the pusher layout in the early days, partly because the pilots and passengers were less subject to the slipstream of the propeller.[5]

The Wright Brothers had first taken to the air lying prone on the centre of the wing, but soon adopted a sitting position. Pilot and passengers remained exposed to the elements in the early stages. The Short S38 was a pusher biplane which originally had the open layout. It was the second aircraft to be purchased by the Naval Air Service, rather than lent to it, and it was given the number T2 or later no 2. In December 1911 it was fitted with three air bags to give an amphibious element, and Samson descended on the River Medway with it. The next month Samson flew it from the *Africa*, and in May from the *Hibernia*. After that it was converted to have the pilot and passenger (or pupil) enclosed in a nacelle.[6] Churchill would fly in it several times. Tractor aircraft adopted the 'fuselage' instead, rather longer and extending all the way from the propeller to the tailplane and rudder. The Wright brothers had used an elevator mounted ahead of the pilot, and that was still fitted in the Maurice Farman Longhorn employed by the navy; but the fact that it got its name from this feature suggests that it was becoming rather quaint by 1911. Its sister design, the Maurice Farman Shorthorn, had the elevator behind.

The next question was whether aircraft should take off and alight from the land or the sea, and that was one that was to tax the Naval Air Service for the whole of its existence. Floatplanes had already been tried in France and the USA before November 1911, just as Churchill arrived at the Admiralty, when Commander Oliver Schwann of the airship service carried out experiments at Barrow-in-Furness, financed by himself and his fellow officers and backed informally by Sueter. They used an Avro biplane, typically underpowered with a 30–35 horsepower engine and fitted experimentally with seven different designs of float. They were reasonably successful in the calm waters of Cavendish Dock, but Samson was cautious about their value. 'It is necessary to remember that it is the high sea that is to be dealt with, where water without any motion is seldom found, and not the enclosed waters where these experiments were naturally carried out. ... the possibility of an aeroplane rising from the water by means of hydroplanes in anything but a dead calm sea appears extremely remote.'[7]

Floatplanes and flying boats were originally known as 'hydro-aero-planes', and in 1913 Sir Alan Burgoyne MP asked if they could be 'given an official and less ponderous designation?' He suggested 'navyplane', but on 17 July 1913 Churchill told the House of Commons: 'We have decided to call the naval hydroplane a *seaplane*, and the ordinary aeroplane or school machine, which we use in the Navy, simply a plane, which is, I think, an effective method.'[8]

It was suggested that the seaplane should be the main province of the naval wing, as the landplane would be of the army wing. Churchill had announced in January 1913 that 'Naval effort was now concentrated on the Hydro-aeroplane',[9] but in June 1914 he modified this considerably: '... the Naval Wing must have a certain small proportion of aeroplanes in addition to their sea-planes in order to be able to avail themselves of the most convenient and efficient form of flying machine.' He did not contemplate 'large aeroplane operations', but landplanes were needed 'to undertake their share of the protection of vulnerable points near the coast'. There were many days when aeroplanes could go up and seaplanes could not. Conversely, it was agreed that 'the Army would require a small proportion of seaplanes for experimental purposes and for the defence of fortresses in the same way that the Navy required a certain number of aeroplanes'.[10]

By 1914 the tractor layout was becoming the most common, for it allowed the fuselage to be tapered aft of the pilot and avoided the drag-producing struts and wires that were necessary to support the rudder and tailplane in a pusher layout. The main problem was that as yet there was no way of mounting a machine-gun to fire forward without damaging the propeller. Churchill tended to be sceptical about the value of guns in aircraft in any case. Against airships, the aeroplane would always suffer from her opponent being a far steadier gun platform, while it would be 'wholly incongruous to place a cannon (except for experimental purposes) in so light and frail a craft as an aeroplane'. Of the three types of aeroplane he recommended, only the sea scouting machine and the land fighting machine would be equipped with a 'passenger and hand gun', presumably a pistol, for defence against enemy aircraft. A reconstructed Short biplane, RNAS no 66, was fitted with a Maxim gun towards the end of 1913 and used for trials at Eastchurch under Lieutenant Clark-Hall. He advised that two machines of each squadron should be fitted, but by August 1914 only four of the navy's aircraft had machine-guns, including an early example of the Vickers Gunbus developed for the army, with a pusher layout and the first effective British fighter aircraft. Another gun-carrying aircraft was on order from Sopwith, and one from A. V. Roe.

The Short brothers were innovative but their aircraft tended to have an unspectacular performance. Thomas Sopwith was another highly inventive designer of naval aircraft and often they were the fastest of the day. Sueter regarded him as 'the "stand-by" of the Royal Naval Air Service, in many of the difficult air matters that came up for solution him to undertake'.[11] Churchill wrote to Sueter in December 1913: 'I should be glad of one of the Sopwith biplanes at Eastchurch could be fitted with dual controls of exact equality (ie without over-riding power), and if the engine switches, gauges, &c., were duplicated too. This machine would be useful for long-distance flying and enable one pilot to relieve the other.'[12] A much more detailed specification followed on the 21st, perhaps reflecting Churchill's mastery of technical detail, or more likely with the assistance of his current flying instructor, Lieutenant Spenser Grey. It was to have a 100 horse-power engine with a specific carburettor, self-starting gear, four hours of fuel, five specified instruments, a map case and safety belts.[13] Churchill visited the Sopwith factory at Kingston-on-Thames in February to see it being constructed. When finished it was known as the 'Sociable' because its side-by-side layout resembled a carriage of that name; the 'Tweenie' because it was between the single-seater layout of the Sopwith Tabloid on which it was based and the three-seater layout which was becoming common; or the 'Sopwith Churchill'. He flew in it from Hendon on 28 February.[14]

The Naval Air Service was working hard to solve the particular problems of naval aviation and exploit the opportunities it offered. In 1912 Churchill encouraged Horace Short to develop folding-wing aircraft for naval use. This had borne fruit by November 1913, when Churchill inspected 22 machines at Eastchurch, including Short seaplanes in which the wings could be folded from the cockpit.[15] Sueter was a torpedo officer and he considered dropping one from an aircraft as early as 1908, but 'the aeroplane could hardly carry a passenger and a few hours' fuel'.[16] He revived the idea on a visit to Germany in 1912, but it was still difficult to find an aero engine powerful enough for the job, until the Sunbeam Company developed one of low weight and comparatively high horsepower. Longmore conducted experiments at Calshot, and in July 1914 Churchill visited and ordered them to be speeded up. Longmore replied that if he could retain the services of a Short seaplane powered with a 160 horse power Gnome engine, he could launch a 14-inch torpedo weighing 900 pounds, which was agreed. On 28 July Longmore 'took *121* out with torpedo and managed to get off the water and fire it successfully; torpedo made a good run'.[17] But he had to admit that it was a stunt; a machine that could carry a torpedo and navigator over a long range still lay in the future.

Despite his negative views on the naval staff, Sir Arthur Wilson could be far-sighted. Dismissing airships as a naval weapon in December 1912, he commented that for reconnaissance of enemy ports 'the only way of doing it is to provide a suitable ship from which *aeroplanes* could work'. He suggested an obsolescent cruiser with the main mast removed and 'a light hurricane deck built above all other obstructions from a few feet beyond the stern to the after funnel'. If this was not long enough, the funnel might be hinged and lowered.[18] Churchill also recognised the need for specialised aviation ships, commenting in February 1913: 'A ship is badly required for developing aeroplanes in ship work. A ship loaned to the Eastchurch School is no use; she must be attached to the school permanently for many months to carry out systematic experiments.'[19] Plans were made to take over a merchant ship but there was no money, so the cruiser *Hermes* was converted for the 1913 manoeuvres with a launching platform forward and a small hangar aft, carrying two seaplanes. She was a partial success in that her scouting proved useful, but the experiment also showed how easily aircraft could be damaged on landing in rough water, or being hoisted in and out. Meanwhile, at the request of Sueter, the Clydeside firm of William Beardmore carried out a sketch design of an aircraft-carrying ship with a flush deck and hangars on either side, though it was never executed.[20]

Churchill was initially sceptical about the future of the airship, and he admitted that for his first four or five months at the Admiralty he did not believe in them.[21] In April 1912, reacting to great advances by Count von Zeppelin with the support of the German government, he reported to the aerial navigation sub-committee of the CID that 'dirigible balloons in Germany had made great advances, and sheds for their accommodation are being constructed on the German North Sea Coast'.[22] He could now see the possibilities, both for the Germans to raid Britain with airships, and for their use in reconnaissance over the sea. On his recommendation the question was taken up afresh. Churchill returned to the subject in December, when he told the technical committee of the CID that 'the matter was urgent, both from the point of view of airships as auxiliaries to the Fleet and from that of defence against their attacks'. The country was not yet in peril, but dockyard facilities were defenceless against this form of attack. He was opposed by Sir Arthur Wilson who claimed he had 'gone very thoroughly into this question'. Once loaded up with fuel and crew, an airship could carry very little. Even if guns could not shoot them down, aeroplanes could. The Prime Minister concluded that the matter needed 'further elucidation'. The Admiralty took some time to carry this out, but during January Churchill was advised by Sueter, who remained an airship enthusiast despite the failure of the *Mayfly*. According to Sueter's account, 'The airmen kept pegging away for airships, and never took "no" for an answer, and in 1913 I obtained Admiralty approval to place an order through the Director of Contracts ... for an Astro-Torres airship of 350,000 cubic feet hydrogen gas capacity with the French Astra Co.'[23] A Parseval airship was ordered from Germany as Zeppelins could not be exported, and several more were to be built by Vickers. A tiny 35,000 cubic feet ship had been bought from the Welsh pioneer Ernest Willows and became HM Airship no 2. Meanwhile the army had made a small amount of progress, with four airships of increasing size built in the Royal Aircraft Factory at Farnborough. Late in 1913 it was agreed that they should be taken over by the navy, against the protest of Field-Marshal Lord Roberts.[24] As a result of doubts and delays, the navy had only seven airships in service in May 1914, with eight more on order.[25] Apart from one on order which would not materialise for more than two years, they were all non-rigid or semi-rigid. Unlike the Zeppelins they relied on gas pressure rather than an internal framework to keep their shape. They would collapse if their speed was too high, so they were relatively small and their performance was limited.

★

Only £50,000 was allocated to naval air in 1911, and £141,000 in the following year. In 1913 this rose to £321,000, and the question of setting up naval air stations, in addition to the one at Eastchurch, was considered. With the growing emphasis on the seaplane it was necessary to have bases with water access, and the Isle of Grain, on the opposite bank of the Medway from Eastchurch, was considered. In May 1913 a temporary base was set up at Cromarty in the North of Scotland by Lieutenant Longmore. Ownership of the land was in dispute. 'Since we were only to be there for the summer, the problem was solved by asking the permission of both parties.' Portable Bessonneau hangars were sent up: 'This particular pattern of tent could hold four or five aircraft of the period ...'. Floatplanes arrived by rail and ship and were erected by workmen and naval ratings. Longmore wrote that despite the distance from London, 'Winston was a constant visitor to our station.'[26]

By August 1913 there was a more ambitious plan to set up bases on eleven sites, all on the east coast of Scotland and England apart from Calshot near Southampton, which was to be used for instruction and experimental work. They were intended 'To provide suitable bases for the use of Naval hydro-aeroplanes co-operating with the Patrol Flotillas' and 'To provide ports of call and repair depots for Naval aircraft.'[27] It was proposed to use £20,000 for building sheds, or hangars, at Grain and Cromarty, because 'It has been found that the wood and fabric of aeroplanes deteriorates considerably unless good quality sheds are provided for these machines.'[28] But money was tight, as Sueter pointed out: 'every penny I could squeeze had to go in machines and sheds to house them'. It was decided to site the first stations where existing coastguard houses and buildings could be used – 'If a seaplane or aerodrome site was not ideal we were forced to take it because of the housing difficulty.'[29] Churchill was insistent that the Naval Air Service should 'gradually replace, as far as possible, the existing Coast-Guards, occupy their premises where required, and discharge their duties'. This would offer 'large economies' if it was fitted in with 'the disjointed claims of the Board of Trade, the Customs, and the Life-Boats'.[30] In June 1914 he refused to sanction extra men to carry out coastguard duties in some of the stations: 'This is contrary to the principle by which the Air Service should take over the duties of the Coast-Guard at these particular points.'[31]

No amount of economy could produce eleven air stations on the money available, and in November 1913 Churchill ordered the effort to be concentrated on a few.

> Although the establishment of seaplane bases along the south and east coasts is necessary on strategic grounds, and their erection must proceed without hindrance, I do not consider it desirable at present to man them all. Neither our personnel nor our machines are numerous enough for this, and the scattering of officers and seaplanes by detachments of twos or threes is not beneficial either to discipline or efficiency. The occupation of bases which are in an unfinished condition by officers and men leads to heavy expense by them and to considerable inconvenience. ... There should be a minimum of eight or ten officers at each occupied base. It is desirable that regular messes should be formed at which officers dine in uniform ....[32]

Effort was to be concentrated on a few bases for now. Calshot had been opened in March 1913, and Felixstowe and Yarmouth in April.

In December 1913 Churchill also wanted a new role for the navy's oldest air station: 'It appears to me that Eastchurch cannot continue to be only a flying school, and that it should certainly support a squadron of naval aeroplanes which shall have a definite value for war in connection with coast defence.'[33] By May he was putting this into more concrete terms. He wanted a squadron of ten machines for defence of the dockyard areas, Until this time naval air units had been referred to by the station in which they were based. Churchill began to use the term 'squadron' specifically to refer to a fighting unit: 'It is most important that a war squadron of ten fighting aeroplanes should be created at Eastchurch as quickly as possible, in order to assign a definite military value to the personnel assembled there, and to help provide to some extent for the aerial defence of the Chatham Dockyard, the

Chattenden magazines, and the oil-fuel tanks. ... In the first instance the squadron should consist of two flights of four machines each, with one in reserve.'[34] It was the first effort to create standardisation in such a disparate group of aircraft. 'They should all be identical in pattern, should all come from one maker, and should have their parts interchangeable.'[35] The term 'squadron' meant very different things to the army and navy. For the army it was sub-division of a cavalry regiment, of about 150 men, for the navy it was a group of up to eight battleships or cruisers commanded by a rear- or vice-admiral, with perhaps 10,000 men on board. Clearly the RNAS's squadron was closer to the army's than the navy's. The squadron of about twelve aircraft would remain the basic unit of British air power, though other nations used different measures – an issue which would cause Churchill some confusion in later years.

The Naval Air Service began to assemble for the Fleet Review at Spithead in July 1914. Twenty machines were allocated, plus up to twenty more in reserve. They included three Short Folders from the Isle of Grain, three or four more Shorts from Dundee, four Maurice Farmans from Felixstowe, Henry Farmans from Yarmouth, and a variety of craft including the Gunbus and 'bat-boats', or flying boats, from the local station at Calshot. Among the assembled fleet, the aircraft again provided one of the highlights. The *Western Daily Press* reported on the 20th:

> One of the greatest attractions proved to be the double row of waterplanes which lay on the surface between the submarines and the Portsmouth shore. During the afternoon the waterplanes rose one after the other, flying along by the beach and between the lines of the fleet. They then returned to Calshot. About six o'clock airship No. 3, which left Sheerness just before noon, arrived at Spithead, and flew over the anchorage, while the Gamma some hours later made a night flight over Spithead. At this time the fleet was playing its searchlights, and the powerful beams sweeping land and sky in all directions made a wonderfully effective sight.

It was three weeks since the heir to the Austro-Hungarian throne had been assassinated in Sarajevo, and a week after the Review the Austrians declared war on Serbia, triggering off a system of alliances which brought in Germany on the Austrian side and France and Russia against them. With no formal alliance with any of these powers, the British hesitated until a German ultimatum to Belgium united the country and war was declared on Germany on 4 August. Churchill believed he had done everything possible to get the fleet ready, and unlike his cabinet colleagues he relished the prospect. Margot Asquith, the Prime Minister's wife, noticed his enthusiasm later in the year: 'He is at his very best just now; when others are shrivelled with grief ... Winston is intrepid, valorous, passionately keen and sympathetic, longing to be in the trenches – dreaming of war, big, buoyant, happy, even. It is very extraordinary, he is a born soldier.'[36]

PART II

The Fortunes of War

CHAPTER II

The North Sea War

Aside from a few socialists, pacifists and sceptics, the war brought excitement and a sense of purpose to whole generations, especially those young enough to fight, as men who had been confirmed socialists a few days before queued up at the army recruiting offices. There was an atmosphere of hysteria, and no one was more affected than Winston Churchill. He wrote to his wife: 'Everything tends towards catastrophe and collapse. I am interested, geared-up and happy. Is it not horrible to be built like that? The preparations have a hideous fascination for me.'[1] This contrasted with the other members of the Liberal cabinet. Sir Edward Grey, the Foreign Secretary, famously looked out of his window and remarked: 'The lights are going out all over Europe; we shall not see them lit again in our generation.' The cabinet clearly needed a more militaristic composition, though for the moment there was no question of a coalition with the Conservatives. Instead, Churchill went to a meeting to find that his intellectual mentor Lord Morley had been replaced by his old adversary Lord Kitchener. Churchill recollected how they had clashed in Egypt and over the withdrawal from the Mediterranean, but were on much better terms now; he was glad about the appointment. 'Admiralty and War Office business were so interlaced that during the whole of the first ten months we were in almost daily personal confrontation.'[2]

At the lowest point in his political fortunes, while serving with the army in 1916, Churchill wrote to his wife that his part of the Western

Front would be 'watched with the vigilance that mobilised the fleet'.[3] And in 1918, soliciting the Prime Minister for a new appointment, he wrote that 'any claim I may be granted in the public good will always rest on the fact that "The Fleet was ready"'.[4] However the preparedness of the fleet in August 1914 was partly the result of a decision taken nearly a year earlier. 'In the autumn of 1913 ... I had sent the First Sea Lord a minute advising that for the purposes of economy we should omit the Grand Manoeuvres in the year 1914–15, and substitute a mobilization of the Third Fleet. ... without connection of any kind with the European situation, the Test Mobilization began on 15 July [1914].' One of the sailors wrote of the Fleet Review: '... the ships of the mightiest armada the world has ever seen, lying in the anchorage between the Isle of Wight and the mainland. Line upon line of battleships, cruisers, destroyers, torpedo-boats, submarines, depot ships, and auxiliaries, each class in perfect formation ready for His Majesty King George V to inspect.'[5]

It was Battenberg, the First Sea Lord, rather than Churchill himself who took the key decision to keep the reserve forces mobilised as war approached, though he had no legal basis for his actions. On 27 July 1914 Rear-Admiral Ballard of the naval staff was 'Sent for by 1st Sea Lord and informed that that he had decided to keep the patrol flotillas fully manned as a measure of precaution instead of reducing them to a second fleet basis as was to have been done.' The Admiralty announced: 'Orders have been given to the First Fleet, which is concentrated at Portland, not to disperse for manoeuvre leave for the present. All vessels of the Second Fleet are remaining at their home ports in proximity to their balance crews.' Later Churchill acknowledged to Battenberg that 'The first step which secured the timely concentration of the fleet was taken by you.'[6]

★

At the end of July 1914, as war with Germany seemed certain, the great fleet of 20 Dreadnought battleships, four battlecruisers, 21 cruisers and 42 destroyers was ordered to Scapa Flow in Orkney. In the expectation of battle, all wooden items were cast aside, including wardroom furniture and even pianos. A leader was needed for this great force. Sir

John Jellicoe had just given up the duties of Second Sea Lord and was about to become second-in-command of the main fleet when he had a conversation with Churchill and Battenberg during which, to his surprise, 'it was intimated to me that, in certain circumstances, I might be appointed commander-in-chief in succession to Sir George Callaghan'. He protested about this but had the impression 'that the change was not one that had been finally decided upon, but that it might take place'.[7]

Fisher had recommended Jellicoe many times to Churchill, asserting that 'He has the four Nelsonic attributes.'[8] It is difficult to know what he meant by this, Jellicoe was certainly a great administrator but his caution and centralisation were the opposite of Nelson's daring and delegation. Churchill of course did not always follow Fisher's recommendations, and he was well aware of Jellicoe's caution – it was already evident three weeks before the start of war when he questioned Churchill's belief that the British fleet was superior in quality. 'I think it will be conceded that the only fair method of comparison between ships is of displacement. It is prudent to assume that the German designers are not inferior to our own and therefore, if British ships of approximately the same displacement show a marked superiority over the German ships in, say, the weight of metal fired from a broadside, it is certain that they have some corresponding inferiority … much inferior protection on the side, for the gun positions, conning towers, internally against torpedo explosion …'.[9] Perhaps Churchill was influenced by Jellicoe's 'brilliant and daring' performance in the 1913 manoeuvres, but he would soon find out that daring in manoeuvres does not necessarily translate into daring in real war. And perhaps he remembered that Callaghan was 'getting too old to be out of bed for more than three nights running'.[10] However, if anyone could find a way to control the vast fleet with the limited means of signalling available, Jellicoe could – assuming that was the best way to win a battle.

Jellicoe protested in at least five telegrams on the journey north to join the fleet. Churchill replied: '… personal feeling cannot count now only what is best for us all …'.[11] Jellicoe superseded Callaghan at 8.30 am on 4 August. Mrs Churchill wrote: 'I don't want Lady Callaghan and Lady Bridgeman to form a league of retired officers' cats to abuse you. Poor old Lady Callaghan's grief will be intense but if you are good to him it will be softened; if he is still employed she will be comparatively silent.'[12] Though Churchill developed many criticisms of Jellicoe, he ultimately recognised his great responsibility. 'The standpoint of the Commander-in-Chief of the British Grand Fleet was unique. ... It might fall to him as to no other man ... to issue orders which in the space of two or three hours might nakedly decide who won the war. The destruction of the British Fleet was final. Jellicoe was the only man on either side who could lose the war in an afternoon.'[13] But this created a great paradox – the greatest naval force was cautiously led, while Churchill sought aggressive action on the fringes.

Churchill's ungrateful protégé, David Beatty, was already in command of the battlecruisers. Churchill perhaps saw him as a complement to Jellicoe, like a dashing cavalry commander under a staid commander-in-chief. According to Beatty's flag captain, Ernle Chatfield, 'Audacity was in his nature; it was impossible to think of his ever being "fussed" or put on the wrong leg; or even if he was, not speedily getting on to the right one again with entire sang-froid, to the embarrassment of others, perhaps, though not of himself ... No, he would go in with a dash and train his captains to be bold ...'.[14]

Churchill later wrote: 'It was no part of my duty to deal with the routine movements of the fleet and its squadrons, but only to exercise a general supervision. I kept my eyes and ears open for every indication that would be useful, and I had many and varied sources of information.'[15] That did not stop him having views and issuing orders when he thought it necessary. His role included allocating resources in ships, men and materials, helping to guide various different groups of ships by means of the War Room, and encouraging a more daring policy. The main strategy was to prevent Germany communicating with the rest of the world by blocking the exits to the North Sea.

The immediate means of achieving this would not be the battleships of the Grand Fleet but the cruisers and requisitioned armed merchant cruisers that would patrol the seas north of Scotland, examining all passing shipping. It was largely done by the 10th Cruiser Squadron which 'held the 800 mile stretch of grey sea from Orkney to Iceland. In those waters they intercepted thousands of ships taking succour to our enemies, and they did that in Arctic conditions, and mainly in the teeth of storm and blizzard ...'.[16] Nevertheless the Grand Fleet was an essential part of the scheme, otherwise the German High Seas Fleet could sweep away the cruisers and perhaps exit into the Atlantic to devastate British shipping. To prevent this, it was best to have it based to the north of Scotland, where additionally it was believed it would be comparatively safe from submarine or torpedo boat attack.

As the war started, there was a diversion when it was reported that the Germans had set up bases in neutral Norway. On 7 August the Third Cruiser squadron, supported by the First Battle Cruiser Squadron 60 miles to the east, searched the area and interrogated fishermen. The Admiralty eventually ordered that the Jellicoe and his squadron commanders were to 'take whatever steps he considered necessary to prevent the Germans using a Norwegian port as their base ... whilst instructing them to be particular not to offend the Norwegians, and to explain the situation to them if their harbours are entered'. But there was to be no such violation during this war.

Churchill worried about getting the army over to France between 9 and 22 August, 'a period of great anxiety to us'. The Admiralty suggested that the Germans might mount raids on the coast: 'Alternatively or simultaneously, they may attempt to rush the Straits and interrupt the passage of the army.'[17] It seemed unlikely that they would risk their battle fleet in such a dangerous operation, but a squadron attack could do a great deal of damage, and dispositions were made to prevent this. Orders to the fleet were usually given in the name of the Admiralty, but one issued on 12 August, at the crucial point of the army's crossing, had the stamp of Churchill's style: 'We cannot wholly exclude the chance of an attempt at landing during the week by a large scale of the high Seas Fleet. Extraordinary silence and inertia of the enemy may be prelude to serious enterprises ... You ought to be nearer the scene of decisive action as we originally contemplated, and now that you have shaken off the submarine menace, or as soon as you can do so, it would appear necessary to bring the fleet to the eastward of the Orkneys ... Cruiser sweeps to the east and south east should be made as convenient.'[18] Jellicoe was always reluctant to come south in view of the submarine menace and their limited range: 'My object will ... be to fight the fleet action in the Northern portion of the North Sea, which position is incidentally nearer our own bases ...'.[19] But despite the public expectations of a 'second Trafalgar', all was quiet in the North Sea in the first weeks of war.

As to battle tactics, Jellicoe was equally cautious. The enemy might try to draw the Grand Fleet into a submarine ambush, which would probably 'involve a refusal to comply with the enemy's tactics by moving in the invited direction. If, for instance, the enemy battle fleet were to turn away from the advancing fleet, I should assume that the intention was to lead us over mines and submarines, and should decline to be so drawn.' It was a sensitive point in view of the daring expected of naval officers, and Jellicoe was anxious 'to draw the attention of their Lordships to this point, since it might be deemed a refusal of battle, and, indeed, might possibly result in failure to bring the enemy to action as soon as is expected and hoped'. He realised that that would be 'absolutely repugnant' to the navy and worried about the 'odium' it might bring on him but wanted to cover himself. There is no sign that Churchill demurred at the time.[20]

★

Despite Churchill's proud claims that the fleet was ready, this was not true in one important respect. The naval bases were situated for a war with France, the main enemy for centuries. A new base at Rosyth in the Firth of Forth had been planned from 1903, but work was halted during the Fisher years. Churchill appointed a committee under Jellicoe to look into the matter, which concluded that 'It will be necessary to develop Rosyth in a full scale.'[21] However, it was already too late to be useful at the beginning of the war, and in any case there would be no protected anchorage outside for ships to exercise. Work was suspended in the belief that it would be a short war.

Scapa Flow in Orkney was well situated to block the northern exit from the North Sea – it was the hinge of the door which isolated Germany from the outside world. Fisher claimed later that he had 'discovered' it, but this was disputed by Captain Munro: 'It was a great pity that when he did "discover" it that he did not take in hand its construction into a defended naval harbour ...'.[22] On arrival there in 1914, Jellicoe was aware that nothing had been done to create a safe anchorage. 'I was always far more concerned with the safety of the Fleet when it was at anchor in Scapa Flow.'[23] On 1 September his worst fears seemed to be realised. A look-out in the cruiser *Falmouth* reported a periscope about 50 yards away and the ship's guns opened fire. The whole fleet was ordered to go to sea. But there was no German submarine in the area; the look-out had probably seen a pole caught in the wash of a destroyer. The fleet went to Loch Ewe and other Scottish and Irish bases, and Beatty wrote: '... we have no place to lay our heads. We are at Loch na Keal, Isle of Mull. My picket boats are at the entrance, the nets are run out, and the men are at the guns waiting for coal which has run low, but ready to move at a moment's notice.' He questioned, 'If we ever use the Scapa anchorage again ...'.[24]

Communication between the Admiralty and the Grand Fleet was mainly by telegram, but in September Churchill travelled more than 700 miles by train 'in great style – saloon with arm chairs etc.' according to Roger Keyes, to a conference at Loch Ewe. After getting off at Lochalsh they travelled by car in less comfort, crammed into the back seat while Keyes and Commodore Tyrwhitt of the Harwich Force of cruisers and destroyers took the opportunity to harangue Churchill about the government's Irish policy and his support for Lionel Yexley.[25] Tyrwhitt spotted a searchlight on the roof of a large house and suspicions were aroused, but investigation showed it was used for hunting.[26] When Churchill sat down with Jellicoe, his squadron commanders and his staff on board his flagship *Iron Duke* on the 17th, it was agreed that Churchill's pet projects, an attack on Heligoland and an expedition into the Baltic, would not be advisable for the moment. Allocations of the new light cruisers and destroyers were discussed, not to Jellicoe's advantage. The Loch was to be defended by destroyers rather than shore guns, and proposals on the resources needed to make Scapa safe were agreed to. There was 'much discussion but no decision' about the control of traffic in the North Sea, no decision again on whether to send ships north to monitor German traffic near Norwegian islands, and arrangements were made to ensure the passage of liners carrying Canadian troops for the Western Front. Submarines, cruisers and destroyers were to be deployed for reconnaissance of the Kattegat at the entrance to the Baltic, and then the 'general line of strategy' came up for discussion. It was agreed that cruiser squadrons should try to prevent minelaying and protect trade off the British coast while the sea to the east should be swept occasionally by battlecruisers and light cruisers. The battle fleet would remain in support in a northern position, and any move south would only be done with four days' notice.

Churchill knew that the fleet was too far from the North Sea and issued orders in familiar style. 'Every nerve must be strained to reconcile the Fleet to Scapa. Successive lines of submarine defences should be prepared, reinforced by contact mines as proposed by the Commander-in-Chief. Nothing should stand in the way of the equipment of this anchorage with every possible means of security. The First Lord and the First Sea Lord will receive a report of progress every third day until the work is completed ...'.[27] The Grand Fleet went back to Scapa early in November, though there were still gaps in the defences.

Jellicoe's fleet was adequate in numbers of battleships and battlecruisers at the beginning of the war, which is not surprising in view of the money and public attention that had been lavished on them in the last few years. A superiority of 20 to 16 was assumed, with greater gun power in the British ships. But despite Churchill's efforts since 1911, its supporting vessels were inadequate. Jellicoe wrote in November: '... the question of the relative strength of the High Seas Fleet and the fleet now with me cannot of course be decided without reference to the cruiser and destroyer strengths of the two fleets. It is my comparative weakness in these two essentials that counter-balances any battleship superiority.'[28] The cruiser squadrons were largely made up of older and slower ships, with very few of the new *Arethusas* and C class in service. The destroyer force was mostly ships of the H and L classes with speeds of around 30 knots. There was great competition for the services of the new and faster M class when they came into service late in 1914, and Jellicoe was not happy when they were allocated to the Harwich Force. He complained of 'the weakness of the torpedo boat destroyer flotillas immediately with the Grand Fleet as compared with the probable strength of this class of vessel of the High Seas Fleet'. The Germans, it seemed, had 88 of them; Jellicoe had only 33, and he worried that 'The menace of so large a number of torpedo boat destroyers attacking cannot ... be disregarded without the certainty of heavy losses in the battle line.'[29] His fears about the submarine were confirmed by the loss of the cruisers *Aboukir, Cressy* and *Hogue* on 22 September.

The Grand Fleet included the modern ships of the First Fleet. The Second and Third Fleets, largely manned by reservists, included the numerous pre-Dreadnought battleships and the older cruisers and slower destroyers. These provided most of the ships of the Channel Fleet. In the event of invasion, Churchill proposed that 'the Grand Fleet deals at its convenience with the High Seas Fleet as its prime and sole duty. The Channel Fleet and the flotillas deal first with the invaders and their escort, and thereafter at their earliest moment come under your [Jellicoe's] command for the main battle if it has not already been fought.'[30] Admiral Sir Lewis Bayly took command of the fleet; Henry Oliver of the Naval Intelligence Division wrote: '... at that time he did not believe in submarines, we heard he had been out exercising without TBDs [torpedo boat destroyers]'. Perhaps this was what made him more daring than other admirals. Fisher wrote: 'The busy Bayly wants to attack Borkum tomorrow!!! He certainly is full of ginger and a welcome change to the dismal Burney.'[31] This naturally attracted the notice of Churchill.

The Harwich Force was a very different group. It was based in the east coast port of that name. Technically a part of the Grand Fleet, it was a group of fast cruisers and destroyers intended to cover the southern portion of the North Sea and to join the main fleet if required, though Jellicoe was sceptical about this, and indeed it never happened. It was commanded by Commodore Reginald Tyrwhitt with his flag in the *Arethusa*, the prototype of the modern light cruiser. It was a highly active force and Fisher praised Tyrwhitt's habit of spending most of his time at sea, whereas his colleague Roger Keyes, he alleged, was always lobbying at the Admiralty.[32]

★

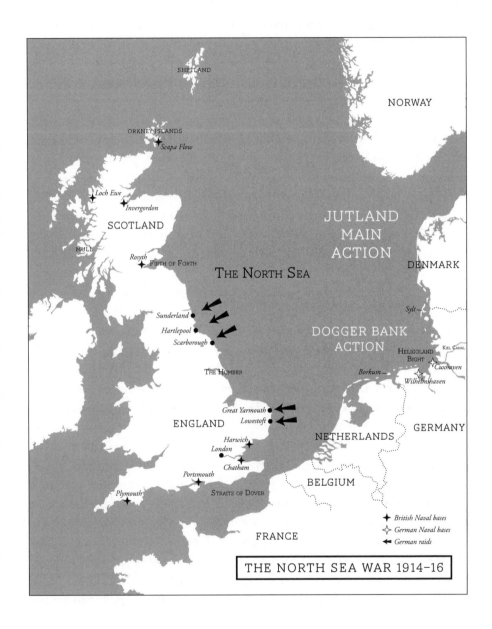

THE NORTH SEA WAR 1914–16

On 23 August Commodore Keyes, in command of the submarines, did indeed come to Churchill and suggest a 'well-organised drive' into the Heligoland Bight, which the Germans regarded as their home territory. Next day Churchill had a meeting with Keyes and Tyrwhitt of the Harwich Force and they worked out a plan to attack the enemy cruisers and destroyers which patrolled the Bight. They would be backed up by Beatty's battlecruisers. The operation took place on the 28th, but it was far from 'well-organised'. Due to bad staff work at the Admiralty the different forces had not been informed of one another's presence and it was fortunate that no casualties were caused by mistaken identification. Nevertheless three German light cruisers were sunk by the battlecruisers, while the British suffered only slight damage. Churchill had to admit that they had been lucky, but it was hailed as a victory at a time when the navy was still reeling from the escape of the *Goeben* and *Breslau* despite the efforts of the Mediterranean Fleet. and the armies were retreating in France. Lord Haldane wrote that it was a 'splendid piece of work' which was 'worthy of the inspiring spirit of their First Lord'.[33] But Churchill's claim that it caused the Kaiser to restrict the movements of the High Seas Fleet was probably exaggerated.[34]

Jellicoe was still reluctant to take his ships south and wrote to Churchill on 30 September: 'It is suicidal to forego our advantageous position in the big ships by risking them in waters infested by submarines. The result might quite easily be such a weakening of our battle fleet and battlecruiser strength as seriously to jeopardise the future of the country by giving the Germans the command of the open seas. ... We have not nearly sufficient cruisers to form the double line that is really necessary to stop all ships during short days and long nights. ... We must give up the idea ... of southerly battle fleet movements.' Churchill agreed: 'The main point is to secure the safety of the battle fleet during the long and indefinite period of waiting for a general action. ... It is not necessary, as manoeuvre experience has suggested, to traverse the waters of the North Sea with the battle fleet with any degree of frequency. Such movements should only be undertaken for some definite, grave and primary purpose.'[35] Fisher went further than Jellicoe after he returned to the Admiralty on 30 October: '*In my decided opinion your fleet and no big ship of your fleet should* EVER *be in the North Sea.* NEVER.'[36] It was largely Churchill's urging that caused the fleet to move out in occasional intelligence-led sweeps.

On 3 November the German battlecruisers bombarded Great Yarmouth on the Norfolk coast, hoping to create a public outcry which would force Jellicoe to split his fleet to protect the coast. Fisher and Churchill were in the War Room as soon as the news was received, asking what it meant. Was it the start of an invasion attempt, or a diversion from an operation elsewhere? The Grand Fleet was still on the west coast and the battlecruisers were at Cromarty in Scotland, so there was no possibility of intervention as the enemy withdrew. This led to increased pressure for Jellicoe to move his fleet south, and on 16 November the Admiralty drew his attention to 'The importance of preventing the enemy from making a serious attack on our coast and getting away without being engaged' which made it 'imperative to have a force nearer the probable points of attack than either Scapa Flow or Cromarty'.[37] The Battle Cruiser Fleet under Beatty was moved to the Firth of Forth where gunnery and tactical training were far more difficult than at Scapa, and this would eventually show in action. Nevertheless in January 1915 Churchill wanted Jellicoe to move his whole fleet there.[38] Beatty's fleet was to go to the Humber under the same scheme, but he argued strongly against it. 'On the subject of the change of bases I talked to the 1st Lord about it and I certainly thought I made it plain that I did not agree with putting the battle-cruisers in the Humber. First of all and lastly it is impossible, there is insufficient water' (large ships could leave for only three hours either side of high water, that is six hours out of twelve). He went on: 'I also think it would be a mistake to move the battle fleet to Rosyth. It no doubt could be made safe with extra craft and vigilance, but it seems to me it would be laying into enemy hands to bring within nearer reach our capital ships ... and take them away from a place where they can enjoy some measure of opportunity for gunnery practices.'[39] The Grand Fleet remained at Scapa until 1918, when extended submarine defences created a much larger safe area inside the Firth of Forth.

★

It was the use of wireless that allowed Churchill and the Admiralty to follow movements at sea and sometimes to influence them, but of course it had its downside – messages could be overheard by the enemy and give away the positions of ships, and sometimes they could be decoded. Fortunately for the allied cause, the Germans were very slow to take advantage of this, but the British were not. Early in the war Oliver set up 'directional stations' which could plot the positions of German ships by their radio signals. But of course the information had to be interpreted and supplemented by other sources. Reginald Hall had been an innovative captain of the battlecruiser *Queen Mary*, but his health could not stand the strain of war and he asked Battenberg and Churchill to get him an appointment as director of the intelligence division as Oliver moved on. He was 'very energetic and excitable and used to dash about a great deal and every month he would have to go to a farm in the west country for a few days' rest'. He established the highly secret Room 40 and, according to Oliver, 'the few who were allowed to know about it cut into staff duties and organisation very severely'.[40] In September the Russians captured a code book from the wreck of the cruiser *Magdeburg* and a Royal Navy ship was sent to pick it up. Churchill and Battenberg were delighted to receive 'these sea-stained priceless documents' and set up an organisation under Sir Alfred Ewing, the director of naval education, to interpret the signals. The Germans often changed their codes or sent false signals, but for the moment the source was invaluable.

On 14 December Wilson came to Churchill's room to tell him that intelligence indicated some kind of movement of the enemy battlecruisers in the North Sea, perhaps a raid on the British coast. The main German force was apparently not involved, so the Grand Fleet stayed well north. The battlecruisers, the powerful Second Battle Squadron under Sir George Warrender, the old ships of the Third Battle Squadron and the Harwich force were moved into position and there were high hopes of setting a trap. Churchill was in his bath on the morning of the 16th and was characteristically unembarrassed when an officer came in with a note from the War Room, saying that the German battlecruisers were bombarding Hartlepool. Churchill wrote: 'I jumped out of the bath with exclamations of joy (Hartlepool, Scarborough, forgive me)' but he omitted this last part from the published version of *The World Crisis*.[41] He was soon in the War Room where Fisher had just arrived and Oliver was marking positions on the map. The German ships ceased their bombardment at nine and the team 'went on tenter-hooks to breakfast'. Churchill hoped to destroy the German battlecruiser squadron, 'whose loss would fatally mutilate the whole German Navy and could never be repaired'. He went to a cabinet meeting where he was asked, 'What was the navy doing and what were they going to do?' In reply he produced a series of diagrams showing how the trap was planned to spring about noon – 'These disclosures fell on all with a sense of awe, and the committee adjourned till the afternoon.'[42]

By 12.30 Fisher 'did really think that our "day" had come'.[43] But in the North Sea there was one factor that interrupted plans and made the diagrams in the War Room unrealistic – poor visibility: '... ominous telegrams began to arrive. Warrender soon had horizons of only 7,000 yards, Beatty of only 6,000; some of the light cruisers nearer to the coast already mentioned 5,000, and later on 4,000 was signalled. ... The solemn faces of Fisher and Wilson betrayed no emotion, but one felt the fire burning within.' Churchill could not concentrate on his other work and at 1.30 Wilson stated, 'They seem to be getting away from us.' What the warlords did not know at the time was that two of Beatty's cruisers had made contact with the enemy but had been withdrawn due to a signalling error by the admiral's flag lieutenant, Ralph Seymour. In London, Churchill told the War Committee what was happening, then back in the Admiralty Wilson said 'in his most ordinary manner, "Well, there you are, they have got away. They must be about here by now,"' pointing to the map.[44]

Though there were no losses in battle, the Grand Fleet was suffering from attrition. The new Dreadnought *Audacious* had already been sunk by a mine on 27 October. The pre-Dreadnought *Formidable* was torpedoed off the coast of Devon early on New Year's Day 1915 and this time her consorts were ordered not to put themselves at risk by picking up survivors, so 600 out of 800 men were lost. Asquith blamed Admiral Bayly for not taking his squadron to safety during a filthy night and allowing the Start Point lighthouse to illuminate them.[45] Bayly was mystified when he was removed from command, but Churchill wrote to Jellicoe that he had 'outraged every principle of prudence and good seamanship without the slightest military object'.[46] With various ships under repair and additions to the German fleet, the margin of superiority had reached a low point. The Grand Fleet was made ready for action after an intercepted signal of 15 January suggested that the Germans would try to take advantage of this, but that was a false alarm. Then on the 23rd more movements were reported – the German battlecruisers were about to attack the soft target of British fishing boats on the Dogger Bank, believing they were gathering information on their movements. The Admiralty sent orders for the Grand Fleet to sail and for the Battle Cruiser Fleet and the Harwich Force to rendezvous 180 miles off Heligoland at seven next morning in the hope of interception. Churchill went to dinner with the French ambassador but could not talk about the impending event. 'One felt isolated from the distinguished company who gathered there, by a film of isolated knowledge and overwhelming inward preoc-cupation. ... battle at dawn. Battle for the first time in history between mighty Super-Dreadnought ships!'[47]

Churchill, Fisher, Wilson and Oliver were all in the War Room before dawn, in time to receive the signal that the enemy had been sighted. At 9.48 they received the signal from Beatty's flagship, the *Lion*: 'Am engaging enemy battle-cruisers. Range 16,000 yards.' His seven battlecruisers were up against four of the enemy, who retreated as soon as they saw the trap; but Beatty's ships were faster and were catching up. There was silence from the flagship for nearly an hour and a half as Beatty pursued, until there was a disturbing report that the *Lion* was knocked out – she had been hit by a shot from the *Derfflinger* and was unable to pursue. After that there was tragi-comedy as Beatty signalled to the other ships still in pursuit to 'attack the rear of the enemy' and 'course north east'. Unfortunately the incompetent Seymour had both signals hauled down at once and Admiral Moore, now in command of the pursuers, took this to mean 'attack the rear of the enemy – north east' which meant he chased the ill-conceived quasi-battlecruiser *Blucher* and sank her, letting the rest escape. It was put forward as a victory and Churchill found that it 'brought for the time being abruptly to an end the adverse movement against my administration of the Admiralty ...'.[48] Having seen real action and led by a charismatic commander, the Battle Cruiser Fleet was now by far the most glamorous part of the navy; its faults in training, gunnery and signals were ignored, by Churchill as much as anyone else.

By this time Churchill was preoccupied with his plans for the German islands, the Baltic and the Dardanelles, and relations with Jellicoe did not improve. 'To strengthen our naval forces by every conceivable means, to add every new vessel to the Grand Fleet and to remain in an attitude of inactive expectancy was the sum and substance of the naval policy advocated from this quarter.'[49] On the other side, Jellicoe complained about the 'constant slights' from the Admiralty.[50] But no major action developed in home waters in the next few months as both Churchill and the German navy pursued other strategies. Churchill hoped to replace Jellicoe with Beatty, but events prevented this.[51]

CHAPTER 12

Antwerp

Under the Schlieffen-Moltke Plan, the German army was to make a quick advance through Belgium into France, defeat the country as in 1870–71, and then use the railway system to switch the troops to the eastern front and defeat the slow but immensely powerful Russian 'steamroller'. But this did not work as planned: the Russians mobilised more quickly than expected and troops had to be withdrawn to cope with them. The tiny British army was immensely proud of its resistance at the Battle of Mons on 22 August, but the main event was the halting of the German advance on the River Marne, dangerously close to Paris, on 5–9 September, after which both sides began a 'race to the sea'. They failed to outflank one other and dug in with lines of trenches, which heralded the beginning of a long war. Meanwhile Lord Kitchener, the new Secretary of State for War, was raising great numbers of new battalions from the volunteers who had been swept up in the mood of the moment. Churchill approved of the numbers and in September told a recruiting rally, 'We must win this war, but the only sure way is to send Sir John French an army of at least a million men ...,'[1] but he deplored Kitchener's policy of ignoring the established organisation of the Territorial Army to form new 'K' or Kitchener battalions. The field marshal's face, which Churchill had first looked on during the Nile campaign 16 years before, gazed down from the famous poster 'Your Country needs you.'

Churchill first noticed the situation in Antwerp on 7 September, as the Battle of the Marne raged to the south and the German advance stalled. In their drive through Belgium the invaders had bypassed the coast and the port. In a memo to his fellow ministers, Churchill emphasised the importance of Antwerp, as after Brussels, the Belgian capital, fell: 'It preserves the life of the Belgian nation ... it safeguards a strategic point which, if captured, would be of the utmost menace.'[2] Antwerp was still accessible from Dunkirk and Lille by a corridor at least 13 miles wide. To save the city when the Germans eventually decided to attack, the allies needed to defend the lines of fortresses round it, and to secure access from the sea. Churchill was confident that the former was 'tolerably well provided for by the Belgian army', which could be reinforced if necessary by naval guns and territorial regiments. As to the second, sea access was only through Dutch waters, and they were anxious to maintain their neutrality in the face of German domination. Churchill went so far as to suggest that 'From a purely naval point of view, war with Holland would be better for us than neutrality', which allowed goods to be imported for Germany. He suggested that 'The obstruction of the Scheldt by Holland to any supplies, military or not military, troops or cannon needed for the defence of Antwerp, is a base and hostile act, which should be strenuously and fiercely challenged.' But since Britain had entered the war to defend the rights of neutral Belgium, this was not a point that could be pushed too far, and the Foreign Secretary declined to approach the Dutch on it.[3]

Churchill had not yet acquired his consuming interest in history, despite his prowess in the subject at school. Otherwise he might have noticed that a landsman aristocrat, Lord Howard of Effingham, had commanded the English forces against the Spanish Armada in 1588, over the heads of the great sailors Sir Francis Drake and Sir John Hawkins. He might have observed that James Duke of York, the Lord High Admiral and future King James II, had personally commanded the fleet against the Dutch in two wars in the 1660s and 70s. Even more to the point, in 1653 it was Cromwell's 'generals-at-sea' who reformed naval tactics and imposed the line of battle on the sea captains, with great success.

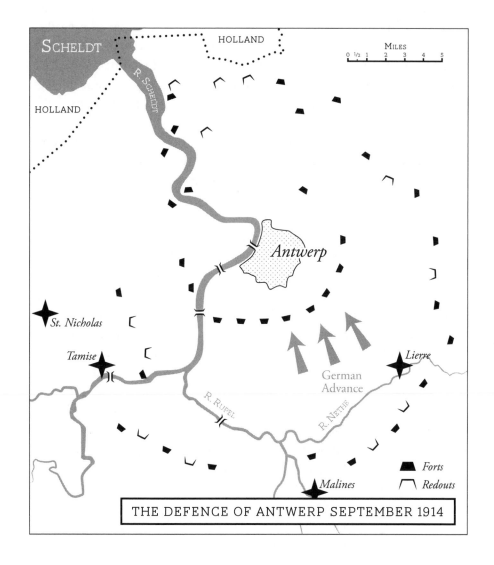

SCHELDT

HOLLAND

HOLLAND

R. SCHELDT

Antwerp

MILES
0 ½ 1 2 3 4 5

St. Nicholas

Tamise

Lierre

German
Advance

R. RUPEL

R. NETHE

Malines

Forts

Redouts

THE DEFENCE OF ANTWERP SEPTEMBER 1914

Indeed some years later Kenneth Dewar, a member of the naval staff and later an adviser on Churchill's *The World Crisis*, wrote that '... in the Dutch Wars, soldiers proved themselves better Admirals than their sailor contemporaries'.[4] Of course controlling a modern battle fleet was a highly technical business, but then so was managing a fleet of up to 100 sailing ships in the seventeenth century – the gentlemen officers relied heavily on the skills of the 'tarpaulin' captains and the sailing masters. As far as we know none of these thoughts went through Churchill's head at the time, or he might have been tempted to seek a more direct command of the fleet.

It was very different in land warfare, where he had real experience of an unusually wide variety, and a flexible mind which was rare in the army. And as new battalions were formed, Asquith noted: 'His mouth waters at the sight & thought of [Kitchener's] new armies. Are these "glittering commands" to be entrusted to "dug-out trash", bred on the obsolete tactics of 25 years ago ...'.[5] In the meantime he had the makings of his own private army. There were thousands of Royal Marines in barracks with no ships to be posted to, and they could be supplemented by recalled fleet reservists and the men of the Royal Naval Volunteer Reserve – amateur civilian sailors who were generally unwanted by the regular navy. With the fleet fully manned there was no need for amateurs, and Churchill ordered them to be assembled at Dover. He outlined his plan, which did not go down well with the men of the RNVR who had enlisted because they loved the sea and were not happy to be turned into soldiers. 'They said they had been cheated and made the only "conscripts" in all the British forces. They demanded to be sent to sea at once, or sent home with authority to join up with their home regiments and friends.' Their leader, the Marquis of Graham, had to placate them and get a promise from Churchill that they would go to sea as soon as possible.[6]

Major George Richardson was seconded to the Admiralty from the War Office, perhaps because his experience as an instructor in New Zealand's citizen army would be useful. Churchill told him that he had 'a large number of naval reservists who would not be required for the fleet and that he intended to organise them together with one brigade of marines as a division and that they would probably be required to go on service at an early date'. Richardson asked who was to command the division but got no answer. 'From various rumours and the attitude of the First Lord of the Admiralty I formed the idea that his personal ambitions prevented him from appointing an officer to command.' He too noted Churchill's extraordinary concern for detail: 'Winston Churchill, although in charge of the Navy in the greatest crisis of the Empire's history, was able to find time to discuss with the staff small details of uniform, kit, promotions and appointments of junior officers and even petty officers – in fact he sometimes dealt with matters which are normally decided by company commanders.'[7]

The Royal Marine Brigade under Brigadier-General Sir George Aston was sent to Ostend at the end of August under Churchill's orders to 'create a diversion, favourable to the Belgians, who are advancing from Antwerp', and to threaten the western flank of the German southern advance – they were to be 'ostentatious' and reconnaissance forces of cyclists were to be sent out to Bruges, Thourout and Dixmude.[8] They stayed for only a few days on an expedition which the Prime Minster compared to the that of Grand Old Duke of York. Churchill then decided to set up a base at Dunkirk, largely to oppose the Zeppelins and raid the enemy, and that was augmented after General Joffre of the French army requested a diversion. On 19 September the brigade embarked again, with the marines still wearing their blue uniforms until khaki was later issued to them. Kitchener allowed the Queen's Own Oxfordshire Hussars, including Churchill's brother, to provide cavalry support, though Asquith, whose son 'Oc' was with the unit, had no faith in their staying power and feared 'if they encounter Germans in any force, we shall see very few of them back again'.[9] In addition there were 97 London buses, which would be filled with troops and make 'daily demonstrations … in the direction of Ypres and Bailleul'[10] to impress the population. There were 400 naval and marine ratings under Commander Samson, with aircraft and armoured cars.

The First Lord sent Richardson to take charge of the logistics, overcoming difficulties that Churchill perhaps never understood. 'The establishing of a base is a very big business even for a small force as all the machinery in miniature of a big force is still necessary. … I had recently learned the requirements during my Staff College course but never anticipated that I would be placed in such a position and asked to set up a machine with no material or trained personnel to work with.' As an expert organiser he lamented that 'there was not time to organise a proper system of records and the officers were quite untrained in administration'.[11] The historically minded Richardson thought the plan was similar to Confederate tactics during the American Civil War, but Aston with his 'negative magnetism' was 'neither a [J. E. B.] Stuart nor a Stonewall Jackson'. Aston was taken ill and replaced by the more dynamic Major-General Archibald Paris. From Dunkirk the brigade sent a detachment to Lille and occupied Cassel to the south, from where Richardson heard the German bombardment of Antwerp 90 miles away.

Meanwhile the naval reservists and the amateurs of the RNVR were under training as soldiers in southern England. One of the officers was Rupert Brooke, the poet, a friend of Churchill's secretary Eddie Marsh. Another was George Cornwallis-West, recently divorced from Churchill's mother. He was only 16 days older than Winston, who had always opposed the marriage, and there was no warmth between stepfather and stepson. Cornwallis-West thought an efficient force might have been produced, given time, but 'One part of the training was sadly lacking and that was the musketry. Service rifles were not issued till about October 1st. Most of the men had fired a few rounds at a miniature range, but practically none had fired even a recruit's course on a service range.'[12] They were awakened during the night of 3–4 October, Captain Cunningham of the Indian Army by a fellow officer throwing pebbles at his window, Signalman J. C. Aird of the RNVR by 'unexpectedly and violently … loud banging on the tent wall' and a cry of 'Get up you beggars, start for France in five minutes.'[13]

Until now the Germans had merely been investing Antwerp from the south-east, using second line troops. On 29 September they began a mass artillery attack and soon demolished one fort. The Belgian Prime Minister and Minister of War told the British Ambassador that if the outer line of forts was carried the government and the field army would have to be evacuated, leaving only the garrison troops to defend the city. Kitchener offered to send newly formed divisions from home and the French would provide a territorial division and a marine brigade, but that would take ten days. Meanwhile on 1 October the Germans broke through the outer forts, forcing the Belgians to retreat to the line of the River Nèthe, seven miles outside the city. Churchill decided to use the half-trained naval brigades to reinforce Antwerp. As they went to embark at Dover, according to Cornwallis-West, they had 'no khaki, no slings to their rifles, no packs, mess-tins, water bottles, great-coats, ammunition pouches. Only a few naval volunteers had leather gear. The majority of the men carried their bayonets in their gaiters or in any odd place.' They were given long Lee-Metford rifles from ships' stocks. They were issued with coats, bottles and haversacks on board ship and at Dunkirk, but only one between two in some cases.[14]

Churchill was on a special train to Dover on the way to Dunkirk on the night of 2 October, when it was stopped and went back to London. He was taken to Kitchener's house where he met the Foreign Secretary and First Sea Lord. They had received an urgent telegram from the ambassador in Antwerp, telling them that the Belgian government was about to leave, and that the city could not be held for more than five or six days, if that. It was decided that 'someone in authority who knew the general situation should travel swiftly into the city and there ascertain what could be done on either side'. Churchill had already planned to go to Dunkirk, and Kitchener encouraged him to go on to Antwerp, while Battenberg promised to take responsibility for the Admiralty in his absence. Churchill left London on another special train at 2 am on the 3rd, and at Dunkirk he conferred with General Paris and summoned his staff officer – 'Richardson, I want you to motor to Antwerp today and make arrangements for the reception of the RM brigade.' Richardson replied, 'I hope you won't leave us there to be locked up.' Churchill asked why he put the question and was told, 'Because I was very surprised that the Germans had not completely invested Antwerp long ago.' The First Lord replied that 'we need not fear being left there too long, the government would look after that if it became necessary'.[15]

Churchill arrived in Antwerp on the following afternoon. Kitchener had advised his staff officer there not to raise hopes of British and French forces arriving soon,[16] but Churchill created a different impression, as one officer related in an intercepted telephone call: 'At exactly one o'clock a big grey motor car filled with British officers rolled up in front of St Antoine and out stepped a short stoop-shouldered boyish looking man in undress uniform of Lord of Admiralty. It was Winston Churchill come to save Belgium! Talk about climaxes on the stage. No playwright could have staged it better. At eleventh-hour and fifty-ninth minute, when a cloud of despondency overhangs land, and government is fleeing, up dashes young man in uniform! "Here I am!" he says "You needn't leave dear old home, everything will be arranged – Antwerp is saved!"'[17] Churchill went to meet the Belgian Prime Minister, and they agreed that the defence would be continued for at least ten more days, while the British would decide within three days whether they could send a substantial relief force – if not the Belgians would be free to retreat.

On his arrival back in Downing Street on the 5th, Asquith found a telegram from Churchill proposing to resign his office and take command of the military force. The Prime Minister was both horrified and amused, and he commented, 'W[inston] is an ex-Lieutenant of Hussars and would if his proposal had been accepted have been in command of two distinguished Major-Generals, not to mention the Brigadiers, Colonels etc., while the Navy was only contributing its little brigades.' Reluctantly he put the matter before the cabinet where it was received with 'a Homeric laugh' – though Kitchener of all people wrote in the margin of the telegram, 'I am quite prepared to give rank of lieutenant-general.' Asquith's reply was tactful, that Churchill could not be spared from the Admiralty.[18] Churchill was disappointed by this; many years later he told Field-Marshal Alexander that he had always wanted 'to command great victorious armies in battle – I thought I got near to it once, ... when I commanded those forces in Antwerp. I thought it was going to be my great opportunity.'[19] But for now he continued with his mission and telegraphed Kitchener early that afternoon: 'In view of the situation and developing German attack, it is my duty to remain here and continue my direction of affairs unless relieved by some person of consequence. If we can hold out for next three days, prospects will not

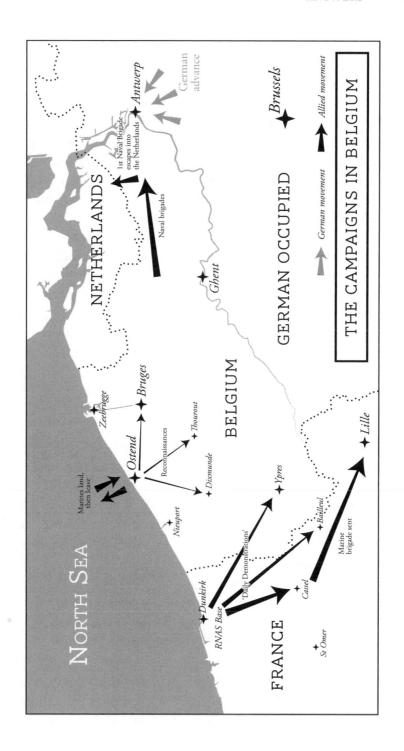

THE CAMPAIGNS IN BELGIUM

German movement

Allied movement

GERMAN OCCUPIED

Brussels

Ghent

Antwerp

German advance

1st Naval Brigade escapes into the Netherlands

Naval brigades

NETHERLANDS

BELGIUM

Bruges

Zeebrugge

Ostend

Thourout

Reconnaissances

Dixmunde

Marines land, then leave

Nieuport

Ypres

Bailleul

'Daily Demonstrations'

Marine brigade sent

Cassel

Lille

Dunkirk

RNAS Base

St Omer

NORTH SEA

FRANCE

be unfavourable. But Belgians require to be braced to their task, and my presence is necessary. Collapse on their part would be fatal.'[20]

Rear-Admiral Oliver of the naval staff had been ordered to go to Antwerp on 29 September to sink some German merchant ships which might be used in an invasion of England, and he became an adviser to the ambassador. Now he met Churchill and they went on a reconnaissance of the lines by car. They passed Belgian wounded in houses and taxis and refugees making their way to the city. They reached a long slope which was as far as cars could go, where they were observed by a German balloon and shelled. They reached a farmyard from which Belgian field artillery was withdrawing. Churchill insisted on seeing the Belgian trenches and was taken there by a staff officer while the others sheltered behind a hedge from a German aircraft. Next morning they drove through a wood to see the Royal Marine positions, where they were shelled again and saw a wounded sergeant getting first aid in a ditch. 'Here, for the first time, I saw German soldiers creeping forward from house to house or darting across the street.' The Marines fired with machine-guns from a balcony. 'The flashes and streams of flame pulsating from the mouth of the machine guns, lit up a warlike scene amid crashing reverberations and the whistle of bullets.' Then, in a typical Churchillian contrast, 'Twenty minutes in a motor car, and we were back in the warmth and light of one of the best hotels in Europe, with its perfectly appointed tables and attentive servants all proceeding as usual!'[21]

The German artillery had far greater range than the antiquated Belgian guns. Churchill had tried to send naval and army artillery to augment them, but most did not arrive on time, or no mountings were available for them. A naval armoured train with 4.7-inch guns was however available and this time it was used properly. Signalman Aird 'Found out afterwards that the Germans were baffled why their guns could not get the range. The train would have run out for two or so miles firing as it went creating havoc with one or two guns belonging to the German battery.' The marines went into position on the 4th to support the Belgians on the Nèthe line. The local inhabitants were enthusiastic and supported the troops, and Colour Sergeant Meatyard recorded that 'during our march to this position we were besieged with handfuls of fruit, pears being in abundance'.[22] This was fortunate, as feeding arrangements were tenuous. After that supplies were sent out to the battalions in buses but the marines did not have cookers or sufficient dixie cans, and the naval brigades, when they arrived, had nothing.

The marines attempted a counterattack, and on the afternoon of the 5th Churchill summarised the situation in a telegram to Kitchener.

> Attack has been pressed. Marines have stood well, with some loss, but, on the right a regiment has fallen back under shell fire, and some German infantry to the west of Lierre are across Nethe. General Paris has ordered four Belgian battalions and his reserve battalion to join another Belgian brigade to drive them back and reoccupy positions. This is now in progress. Every effort is being made to gain time.[23]

But still there was no news of the French reinforcements, or additional naval guns. On the morning of the 6th Churchill telegraphed, 'Where are our heavy guns and detachments?' That afternoon the main German attack on the Nèthe line began. Churchill had a long and busy day, his fourth of 'moving, thinking and acting', and got to bed at 2 am after meeting the Belgian ministers.

The Germans were crossing the river Nèthe as the men of the Naval Brigades finally arrived, and a decision had to be made about their deployment.

> The naval brigades had arrived and detrained and were now marching to their assigned positions in the line. But where was the line? It was one thing to put these partially trained and ill-equipped troops into a trench line, and quite another to involve them in the manoeuvres of a moving action. Solidly dug in with their rifles and plenty of ammunition, these ardent, determined men would not be easily dislodged. But they were not capable of manoeuvre. It seemed to me that they should take up an intermediate position until we knew what was happening on the front.[24]

According to Cornwallis-West, 'In the early morning of October 7th the naval brigade were ordered to occupy the entrenchments between the forts and redoubts of the second line of defence. ... These entrenchments had been made on old models and were practically useless against the German artillery, with the result that men already tired had to start again to dig themselves in.' But that was not easy; eventually they got about a thousand entrenching tools, but it was reported, 'I don't think the men did much with these except tire themselves out.' With the high water table it was impossible to dig trenches more than about a foot deep, which offered little protection. Signalman Aird and his comrades were sad to see some locals evacuate their home, but 'Their house was searched for suitable objects to make bomb proof shelters, doors, shutters, railings and the farmyard supplied shafts of timber. The barn was emptied of its straw to line the trenches.' Soon he was under fire for the first time: 'The whirr and ping of bullets never to be forgotten.' The forts themselves were occupied by the Belgians, but Cornwallis-West claimed they were out of date and little better than the trenches – 'They were practically shell traps and one big shell dropped in the middle would generally suffice to silence them.' He went on: 'No-one seemed to know who was in command. All were given to understand that General Paris, a distinguished Marine, was really so, but through the ubiquity of the First Lord of the Admiralty and the late Minister of War, it was not difficult to guess who was really directing the operations and who were responsible for the amateurish proceedings. The men were given a small entrenching tool as used in the Belgian army. Water was supplied to them in the trenches in bottles which had been requisitioned from the local brewery. If it were not so serious it would be laughable.'[25]

Churchill left Antwerp for Bruges on the evening of the 6th as the position deteriorated, and the Belgian government fled the next day. But still he exercised supervision. General Paris telegraphed from the new front line: 'The situation here is difficult. Forts 1 and 2 are being attacked. If either fall my flank is turned and I must act as prearranged.'[26] Churchill replied from the safety of the Admiralty: 'It is not understood how shelling of individual forts can affect the security of your lines so long as the intervals between the forts are obstinately defended, and the ruins of the forts occupied and entrenched after attack. … It is your duty, unless you receive further orders, to hold your position at all costs and to stand and repulse an infantry assault if one is delivered.'[27] But it was hopeless, and the naval brigade was ordered to evacuate the city a few hours later. The First Naval Brigade under Commodore Henderson was trapped by the German advance and crossed into Holland where they were interned for the duration of the war. Most of the others escaped, though some considered they had been very lucky. In all the losses amounted to 57 officers and men killed, 138 wounded, 1,479 interned and 936 taken prisoner.[28]

Sir Edward Grey, the Foreign Secretary, wrote to Clementine Churchill describing Winston as a hero, but others were far more critical. Lord Esher wrote: '… the Antwerp performance was appalling. I cannot believe any thinking soldier would have agreed to a plan which violated all principles of war. This, following the loss of three cruisers given away to the submarine does make me fear the possibilities of the future …'.[29]

Churchill summed up the battle as 'a case, until the Great War unknown, of an attacking force marching methodically without regular siege operations through a permanent fortress line behind advancing curtains of artillery fire. Fort after fort was wrecked by the two or three monster howitzers; and line after line of shallow trenches was cleared by the fire of field-guns; and following gingerly upon these iron footprints, German infantry, weak in numbers, raw in training, inferior in quality, wormed and waddled their way forward into "the second strongest fortress in Europe".'[30] After his return he met Asquith who wrote candidly: 'Having, as he says, "tasted blood" these last few days, he is beginning like a tiger to raven for more, and begs that sooner or later, and the sooner the better, he may be relieved of his present office and put in some kind of military command.' Asquith maintained that Churchill could not be spared from the Admiralty, to which Churchill protested that 'the naval part of the business is practically over, and our superiority will grow greater and greater every month', but he stayed in the job for the time being.[31]

Churchill did not admit that his intervention was a mistake. Within a week he wrote: 'The loss of Antwerp was a bitter pang to me. But you must not suppose that sentiment dictated our movements. The sudden and total collapse of the Belgian resistance, and the diversion of the promised French aid, were factors that destroyed a good and reasonable chance of saving the place – even at the last moment.'[32] But that did not absolve him of the charge of sending grossly under-trained and under-equipped men into action. Cornwallis-West was perhaps not free of bias when he wrote: 'Never was a better example given of the utter futility of sending out untrained and unequipped troops to take their part in the firing line against highly-trained masses of Germans.'[33] But Asquith too was horrified when he realised the extent of Churchill's mistakes, writing to Venetia Stanley:

> Strictly between ourselves, I can't tell you what I feel of the wicked folly of it all. The Marines of course are splendid troops and can go anywhere and do anything. But nothing can excuse Winston (who knew all the facts) from sending in the two other naval brigades. I was assured that all the recruits were being left behind, and that the main body at any rate consisted of seasoned naval reserve men. As a matter of fact only about ¼ were reservists, and the rest were a callow crowd of the rawest tyros, most of whom had never fired off a rifle, while none of them had ever handled an entrenching tool.[34]

Churchill, however, remained unrepentant, writing in 1923: 'I could not foresee that the mission I undertook would keep me away from the Admiralty for more than forty-eight hours, or that I should find myself involved in another set of special responsibilities outside the duties of the office which I held' – though if he was really planning to take command of the Royal Naval Division as Richardson and others suspected, that was disingenuous. On the strategic level, Churchill claimed that the resistance of the city had been prolonged by five days, and that was 'certainly advantageous to the allied cause'.[35] A more common opinion is that it was a rash and ill-planned venture which led many to question his judgement.

CHAPTER 13

Defence and Attack in the Air

With the great expansion of his activities by land and sea after the war started, Churchill gave up his attempts to learn to fly and had less direct interest in naval aviation, but he was nevertheless drawn towards it in ways that could not be predicted. The practice of launching aircraft from the bows of warships was not developed much further. *Hermes* had her ramp removed but was transporting two Short Folders when she was sunk by U-boat at the end of October. Churchill was 'very angry' that her captain had disobeyed orders and sailed in daylight.[1] Four cruisers of the Harwich Force operated with ramps but found that the North Sea winter was a far harsher environment than Weymouth Bay and the aircraft soon became unserviceable. In any case the ramp severely restricted the ship's main armament and the idea was not revived until 1917, when take-off platforms were fitted on top of gun turrets, which could be turned into the wind.

The idea of a specialist aircraft carrier began in a modest way, the 1914 naval estimates allowing for a converted merchant ship as a 'sea-plane carrying ship'. This was named *Ark Royal* and had her engines and superstructure aft, a very large hangar forward and a deck above for aircraft to take off. She was commissioned in December 1914, when her speed of 10 knots proved too slow for fleet work. On the outbreak of war the Admiralty took over three fast cross-Channel steamers, the *Empress, Riviera* and *Engadine*. They were fitted with canvas hangars aft, later replaced by more permanent structures. A much larger ship, the ex-Cunard *Campania* of 12,000 tons, was bought in November for service with the Grand Fleet and was ready by April 1915, but with her old machinery she found it difficult to keep up with the fleet. In addition, two German merchant ships were seized at Port Said on the outbreak of war and fitted to carry seaplanes to serve in the Middle East. But so far no one had found any way of landing an aircraft back on a ship, and that problem would only be solved by building 'flat top' aircraft carriers just as the war ended.

Experiments with other ways of handling aircraft continued, and on 26 October 1914 Churchill wrote to Sueter about launching from barges, showing his usual concern for detail:

> The failure yesterday was very disappointing. It is no use trying these enterprises with loaded machines. Either aeroplanes or seaplanes with wheels instead of floats must be used. Examine the following:
> Prepare six machines with means of floatation but detachable wheels. Choose three of the longest barges which can be found. Fit them with a trolley on rails actuated by an accelerating windlass. Choose a calm night; tow your barges with the machines on them up to the launching point. Make the attack, and alight on the water. Never mind wrecking the machines or, if pressed, scuttling the barge after it has served its purpose. Prepare two or three barges at once to allow for failure. You will be able by this means to carry much more explosive, and the machines would have something in hand for manoeuvring and climbing when making the attack.[2]

According to Churchill's account, the War Office had claimed sole responsibility for the air defence of the country before the war, even resisting a naval offer to use its aircraft when raiders were close to naval air stations. However when war started the army was so fully occupied in Belgium and France, both on land and in the air, that there were no resources available for home defence. On 25 August a Zeppelin attacked Antwerp, revealing German intent and capabilities, and the question became urgent. The War Office had provided only 33 guns for the air defence of London, but 28 of these were pom-poms which Churchill dismissed as useless – 'No shrapnel is available for them, and the shells provided do not burst on the fabric of a Zeppelin, and almost always fall back to earth as solid projectiles.'[3] There were 3-inch guns on Admiralty Arch, the Foreign Office and the Crown Estate Office in or near Whitehall. They were manned by soldiers of the Royal Garrison Artillery and controlled by telephone from the War Office.[4] At a cabinet meeting on 3 September Kitchener asked Churchill if the Admiralty would assume responsibility for the air defence of the country, and he quickly agreed. Though he had tended to underrate the airship as 'an enormous bladder of combustible and explosive gas', he realised that there was an immediate problem in that 'Aeroplane engines were not powerful enough to reach the great heights needed for the attack of Zeppelins in the short time available. Night flying had only just been born; the location of aircraft by sound was unknown; the network of telephones and observation points was non-existent. And here was the danger, certainly real and not easy to measure, literally on top of us.'[5]

Of course Churchill was not interested in purely passive defence, and he had already anticipated events. On 1 September he instructed Sueter:

> The largest possible force of naval aeroplanes should be stationed in Calais or Dunkirk. Reports have been received, and it is also extremely probable, that the Germans will attempt to attack London and other places by Zeppelin airships, of which it is said a considerable number exist. The close proximity of the French coast to England renders such an attack thoroughly feasible. The proper defence is a thorough and continual search of the country for 70 to 100 miles inland with a view to marking down any temporary airship bases, or replenishing airships before starting to attack.

Samson was to take charge, with Major Gerrard RM as second-in-command. It was proposed to use 30 or 40 aeroplanes which would operate from mobile bases 30 or 40 miles inland, supported by 50 or 60 armed motor cars.[6] Churchill visited the base at Dunkirk regularly, for example on 22 September when he 'inspected his mixed lot, and colloqued with the French governor and general'.[7] On 26 September he strayed further beyond his remit as First Lord by visiting 15 miles of the newly entrenched front lines, only 300 yards apart, with a fierce melee every night in which it was claimed three Germans were killed by rifle and bayonet to every Briton. After that he went on 'a visit to his own little army at Dunkirk'.[8] But the base was to play as large a part in other stories – the development of strategic bombing and of the armoured

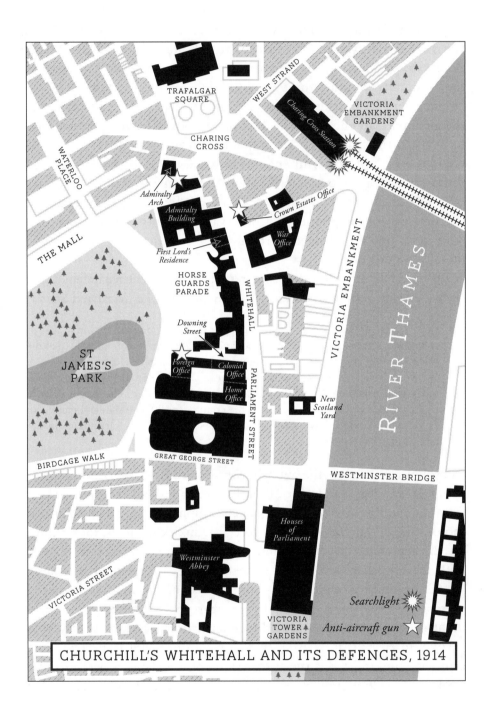

TRAFALGAR SQUARE

WEST STRAND

VICTORIA EMBANKMENT GARDENS

Charing Cross Station

CHARING CROSS

WATERLOO PLACE

Admiralty Arch

Admiralty Building

Crown Estates Office

First Lord's Residence

War Office

THE MALL

HORSE GUARDS PARADE

VICTORIA EMBANKMENT

WHITEHALL

RIVER THAMES

Downing Street

ST JAMES'S PARK

Foreign Office

Colonial Office

Home Office

New Scotland Yard

PARLIAMENT STREET

BIRDCAGE WALK

GREAT GEORGE STREET

WESTMINSTER BRIDGE

Houses of Parliament

Westminster Abbey

VICTORIA STREET

Searchlight

VICTORIA TOWER GARDENS

Anti-aircraft gun

CHURCHILL'S WHITEHALL AND ITS DEFENCES, 1914

vehicle, and the defence of Antwerp – as in the air defence of the homeland.

The whole of London could not be defended, only the 'most vital portion' from Buckingham Palace to Charing Cross Bridge, though that left out the docks and the highly explosive contents of the Royal Arsenal at Woolwich. Sueter was put in charge of the defences and the Admiralty took over the three guns, using pensioner naval gunlayers, while a volunteer Anti-Aircraft Corps of the RNVR was formed. Pairs of searchlights were placed on Charing Cross Station, Lambeth Bridge and Hyde Park Corner, positions where they would not interfere with the sighting of the guns. In the first instance they were manned by special constables, who were found to be 'men of education who quickly picked up their duties and compared very favourably with seamen crews' – though they had a tendency to complain about frequent changes of plan and lack of consultation.[9] A telephone control system was set up based in Admiralty Arch and modelled on the night defence system of a battleship.

Two experimental night flights were made over London by British airships. On 22 September one failed to find her way back to Wormwood Scrubs until she could see the lights of Golders Green underground station and follow the main roads at 300 feet. Four days later the second ship spent an hour over the city and 'formed a good target for the guns on every approach to the important area'.[10] A report suggested that 'Darkness is the best defence', and a 'dim-out' was introduced by order of the Home Office on 1 October. Illuminated signs were banned. It was not possible to turn all the gas street lights off in anticipation of a raid, but some were permanently extinguished while others were shielded from above. False lights were installed in parks, which were regarded as landmarks for the Zeppelins. Buildings of 'military value' were to be issued with special blinds to make them 'as dark as practicable'.[11] A ring of aerodromes was to be set up ten miles from the centre of the city, though for the moment there was no effective weapon for use against the Zeppelin; moreover 'On fire being opened [from the ground] there could be no discrimination by gunlayers between hostile and friendly aircraft, nor between airships and aeroplanes.' Additional guns were found from naval resources, and on 22 October Churchill reported to the cabinet that nine 3-inch, 43 6-pounder and four

3-pounders had already been mounted, with nearly 50 more on the way. Squadrons had been established at Eastchurch, Dover and Portsmouth, though with the difficulty in reaching height they would only be able to attack the airships on their return voyage. Those based at Hendon, however, would be able to attack them over London.[12]

Volunteer anti-aircraft corps were also set up in Dover and Sheffield. Henry Capper, a retired naval officer who had risen from the ranks, was asked to organise one. He got the services of a boatswain and 50 men from the sunken cruisers *Aboukir, Cressy* and *Hogue* and chose civilian volunteers from a list of 500 provided by the mayor. 'The corps was divided into three companies, each of two crews, the crews being on duty from sunset to dawn on alternate nights; the seamen having charge of the stations by day and augmenting the civilian crews at night.'[13]

The forward-firing aircraft machine-gun was not yet in use except on 'pusher' aircraft, but weapons had to be developed and on 2 October Churchill told d'Eyncourt and Sueter:

> The experiments with regard to projectiles for use against aircraft must be worked out on the most generous scale, eight or ten different lines being pursued simultaneously, the necessary funds being provided. It is perfectly useless in time of war to go through successively the whole series of experiments appropriate to a peace-time administration. Let me have a report on the projectiles available. We must have means of attacking Zeppelins, not only with shells from guns, but with incendiary bullets or grenades from aeroplanes.[14]

By the first day of 1915 Churchill was expecting a mass attack, as he told the War Council:

> Information from a trusty source has been received that the Germans intend to make an attack on London by airships on a great scale at any early opportunity. The Director of the Air department reports that there are approximately twenty airships which can reach London now from the Rhine, each carrying a ton of high explosives. They could traverse the English part of the journey, coming and going, in the dark hours. The weather hazards are considerable, but there is no known means of preventing the airships coming, and not much chance of punishing them on their return. The unavenged destruction of non-combatant life may therefore be very considerable.[15]

A week later he described the defences as they now stood. The ten aircraft at Dunkirk would prevent the building of airship bases in Belgium, though it was now possible that the Zeppelins could reach London without calling there. Sixty aircraft were now based in the triangle formed by London, Sheerness and Dover, armed with incendiary bullets which had been tested by experiments on balloons and were capable of destroying a Zeppelin; and Churchill believed that some aviators were even prepared to 'charge a Zeppelin', presumably in a suicide attack. There were now 76 guns within the triangle, and the pom-poms had an incendiary shell. But he was not optimistic. 'Notwithstanding these preparations, if the enemy thought it worthwhile to attack London merely for the purpose of inuring and terrorising the civil population and damaging property, there was no means of preventing it.'[16]

No mass attack developed, the Zeppelin offensive being hampered more by bad weather and poor navigation than any British countermeasures. Individual Taube aeroplanes had already bombed Dover at the end of 1914 with practically no effect. Two airships were planned to attack Humberside on 19–20 January but bombed East Anglia instead. There was a raid on 2–3 February and Churchill reported to the cabinet that 'the balance of evidence inclines to the conclusion that the invaders were airships and not aeroplanes; the damage to life and property was very slight'.[17] The first attempt to bomb London, on 26 February, had to turn back. A larger raid on 17 March was frustrated by fog and there was a lull until raids on Ipswich at the end of April and Southend in May. The RNAS failed to intercept another raid on 26–27 May as the aircraft could not climb fast enough. Finally on 30 May LZ38 dropped 120 small incendiary bombs across east London, killing seven people and burning out seven properties. Only one of fifteen aircraft which took off against the raider came into contact with it but did no damage, while searchlights and guns, concentrated in central London, had no effect. Churchill left the Admiralty at this point and the first success of any kind came on 17 June when Flight Sub-Lieutenant R. A. J. Warneford shot down LZ37 over Belgium and received the Victoria Cross. The attack on London intensified after that, but Churchill's amateur defences were still totally ineffective and largely misplaced. Command was taken over by the great gunnery expert Sir Percy Scott, and then the duty was transferred to the army's Royal Flying Corps. It was agreed that the RNAS would deal with the enemy over the sea and the RFC over the land – an unworkable arrangement which perhaps helped support the idea of 'the indivisibility of the air' which became an article of faith for post-war airmen.

The Zeppelin could be used only at night because its low speed and great bulk made it an easy target in daylight. Navigation was not nearly accurate enough for precision bombing on military targets, and they were far too few in numbers for a devastating attack. Their only real effect was psychological, which would become increasingly important as the performance of aircraft improved.

★

There was no question of direct retaliation for the Zeppelin raids on London. British airships were underdeveloped and would not be capable of such a task, even if they had not been needed for sea patrol. And Berlin was a far more difficult target, 400 miles from allied territory. However on 25 September Churchill wrote to Grey, the Foreign Secretary, after a Zeppelin dropped two bombs on Ostend, 'an open town of no military significance'. He wanted to 'teach the Germans the uselessness of such warfare' and proposed that the naval airmen should drop a equal quantity of bombs 'into Aix-la-Chapelle, or some other convenient German town'. Or, he asked half-jokingly, should it be in the proportion of 10 to 16, the same as the supposed superiority in Dreadnoughts? He would 'explain the reason and announce that this course will inevitably be followed in the future'. Care would be taken to hit military targets, and this was 'the only effective way of protecting civilians and non-combatants'. Grey replied that it was 'too soon to begin retaliating in kind' which would 'only put us on the same moral plane as they are' and that the Germans had more aircraft so it would be useless. Churchill had to agree, but thought 'soon it will come to it'.[18]

Part of Churchill's motive for the attempt to save Antwerp was to set up a base to bomb the Zeppelin facilities. He wrote on 7 September, 'We have already stationed six aeroplanes with superior pilots at Antwerp, and propose to increase their numbers to 15 or 20 as rapidly as possible. The duty of these aeroplanes will be to attack Zeppelins which approach the city (or better still, in their homes on the Rhine).'[19] As the bombardment of the city began on 8 October, the aircraft were taken out of their shed to avoid damage by splinters and placed in the middle of the aerodrome. Next morning the weather was misty but early in the afternoon Squadron-Commander Spenser Grey, Churchill's former flying instructor, and Flight-Lieutenant R. L. G. Marix took off to attack the Zeppelins in Cologne and Dusseldorf. Spenser Grey failed to find the sheds in thick mist and dropped two bombs on the main railway station instead. Marix arrived at Dusseldorf and found the airship shed. He dived on it and turned up after letting his bombs go at 600 feet. It was not clear if one or both bombs hit, but according to the official report '... the destruction was complete. The roof fell in within thirty seconds and flames 500 feet high were observed, indicating that an inflated Zeppelin must have been inside.' He had indeed destroyed Z9. It was a rare and perhaps lucky success, which may have caused over-optimism about the effects of bombing. Marix's Sopwith Tabloid was damaged by rifle and shell fire but he managed to fly to within 20 miles of Antwerp before his fuel ran out. He borrowed a bicycle, then used a car to get him back to Antwerp.[20] Churchill had both pilots awarded the DSO for 'their wonderful attacks'.[21]

A group of aircraft led by Squadron-Commander Noel Pemberton-Billing was sent to Belfort in eastern France, and on 21 November three of them took off to raid the Zeppelin factory at Friedrichshafen on Lake Constance. They dropped nine bombs on the sheds and the hydrogen factory, though one of the pilots was shot down and captured. Asquith reported that Winston was 'quite pleased ... a hydrogen factory wrecked, one Zeppelin probably destroyed, and two out of three aeroplanes safely back'.[22] However it was asserted that they had flown over Swiss territory to get there, which Churchill made light of: 'The international conference of 1910 reached no agreement on the subject of aeroplanes flying over neutral territory. ... no question can arise of breach of neutrality.'[23]

Another raid at the end of the year combined three strands of RNAS activity – shipboard aircraft, defeating the Zeppelin and strategic bombing. On Christmas Day, as British and German soldiers were fraternising on the Western Front, nine Short seaplanes were prepared on the carriers *Engadine, Empress* and *Riviera,* supported by the cruisers and destroyers of the Harwich Force. Only seven of them would take off, led by Squadron-Commander Cecil L'Estrange Malone, one of the first naval aviators, and the observers included Erskine Childers, whose novel *Riddle of the Sands,* set in these waters, had started the anti-German scare in 1903, but who also smuggled guns to Irish republicans. They were heading for the airship sheds at Cuxhaven, but failed to find them in fog and did very little damage. Four of the aircraft ditched but their crews were picked up. The ships offshore were attacked in turn by Zeppelins, the first air attack on British warships. Bombs were dropped, some landing close, but no damage was done. Churchill's secretary Eddie Marsh described the affair over lunch with the Prime Minister, who could see little to rejoice about. 'I am afraid that it was in essentials a coup manqué – out of seven seaplanes four are lost, and one very good officer. ... the only satisfactory thing I can see about the adventure is that it demonstrates the limitations of the Zeppelins, which fled like seagulls when they were fired at by our cruisers.'[24]

The Cuxhaven raid was not repeated, but by next spring Churchill had developed much grander ideas. Though he was pre-occupied with the Dardanelles affair by that time, on 3 April 1915 he pointed out to a committee of air officers 'the necessity of developing a very large fleet of aircraft, capable of delivering a sustained series of "smashing blows" on the enemy; more in the nature of a "bombardment" by ships than the present isolated "dashing exploits" of individual two or three aeroplanes dropping a few bombs only. The object to aim at was to harass the enemy and destroy his works as to effect very materially his ability to continue the war.' He went on to tell the War Council, 'The object now to be aimed at from June will not be reconnaissance and patrolling, but the attacking with bombs on the largest possible scale of military points on enemy territory. For this, the weight of explosives and numbers of machines are more necessary than skill of pilots or special fighting qualities in the machines. ... the carrying of 2 or 3 tons of explosives to a particular point of attack in a single night or day is the least we should aim at as an operation in the future.' He hoped to have a total of 1,000 aeroplanes and 300 seaplanes by the end of the year, and needed

300 more pilots to man them.[25] Murray Sueter had already asked for a 'Bloody paralyser' of a bomber, and the twin-engine Handley Page 0/400, crewed by four men and armed with up to 16 112lb bombs and five Lewis guns, was under development, though it did not fly until December 1915. It was the grandfather of the heavy bomber.

★

Two new aircraft types entered service with the RNAS in the early months of the war. The Avro 504 was a single or two-seater tractor biplane which later saw long service as a trainer. The Short 184 (so called from the serial number of the first one delivered to the RNAS) was an ungainly looking seaplane but the first effective torpedo bomber, whose 225 horsepower engine was just enough to lift her off the sea carrying an 18-inch torpedo. High performance was not particularly valued at the time. Aircraft were rarely armed with more than a pistol or a rifle and it was not until the summer of 1915, when the interrupter gear allowed the firing of a machine-gun through a propeller, that the 'Fokker scourge' made speed and manoeuvrability essential. In the meantime Samson's favourite aircraft at Dunkirk was no 50, a BE2a, an early example of a type which would be devastated by the Fokkers due to its inherent stability. Later in the Dardanelles campaign, Samson decreed that every pilot was to carry a pistol and each observer a rifle. However he did have the use of a few pusher biplanes which could mount forward-firing machine-guns, and he instructed his crews: 'Remember in a "pusher biplane", with a machine gun, you must always be a winner if he stops to fight.'[26] He thought the Avros were 'just so much waste money' and favoured the older Maurice Farmans which could 'do 75 mph, carry wireless and 1 100 lb bomb, therefore they can spot, reconnoitre or attack, whatever is wanted. They can also fight. Their only drawback is that they turn and wallow about in a wind.'[27]

The campaign in the Dardanelles found new uses for aircraft, and Fisher wrote to Jellicoe in April 1915: 'You MUST have aeroplanes and undoubtedly they can (*if you have a sufficient number*) defend you against the Zeppelins. You should write direct to First Lord and ask for them at once, before they are all sent to the Dardanelles, where they are now going by dozens!'[28]

Naval airships were rather slow in coming forward, but it was realised that large numbers could be useful in spotting the 'feather' made by the periscope of a submarine. It was Fisher rather than Churchill who sponsored a simple non-rigid or 'blimp' design using the spare envelope of a small training ship. Each had an aircraft fuselage – a BE2c, Maurice Farman or Armstrong Whitworth – slung underneath for the crew of two. In all 59 of them were built, with nearly 100 others of variant types, and they made a considerable contribution to the anti-submarine war, though only after Churchill had left office.

★

Expectations of naval air power had perhaps been raised too high by public demonstrations such as Samson's take off from the *Hibernia* and Marix's destruction of Z9. But the problems of naval aviation – of navigation, of bad weather, of landing on either the sea or on a deck and of carrying an effective armament – were a long way from solution. As a historian of the period put it:

> The elementary fact is that in 1914 the airplane and even the rigid airship were drastically inferior to the surface warship in every category of performance. The airplane had a radius of at best perhaps 150 miles, endurance of only a few hours, a payload of a few hundred pounds. It was mechanically erratic and unreliable, utterly at the mercy of the weather, and could not function at night. Its navigational accuracy, especially in overwater flight, was untested but unpromising. The seaplane suffered all these defects of the landplane and in addition could not function in the slightest of rough seas. Even the rigid airship was inferior to the cruiser in radius and endurance, and it, too, was subject to the whims of the weather.[29]

It did not help that Churchill and Sueter had cast their nets far too widely. On 6 June 1915, after Churchill's removal from the Admiralty, Asquith's private secretary wrote: 'The military wing is a success largely because it has been developed and trained as a branch of the army with military objects strictly in view. The naval wing is a failure because it has not been designed for naval objects with the result that it has degenerated into a crew of highly skilled but ill-disciplined privateersmen. What is wanted is to make the naval wing more "naval", not more "aerial".'[30] This was echoed by Admiral Jackson in the presence of Sueter: '... the

Air Service, owing to its enormous expansion had become unwieldy, discipline was bad, not unnaturally owing to the small percentage of the personnel used to discipline; the expenditure of money was enormous and he implied it had been wasteful.'[31] The new regime at the Admiralty was determined to impose discipline on the force. An Admiralty Weekly Order decreed that 'The Royal Naval Air Service is to be regarded in all respects as an integral part of the Royal Navy.' The first age of innovation was over.

CHAPTER 14

Armoured Car and Tank

The great futuristic writer H. G. Wells suggested an armoured vehicle in 1903 in his short story *The Land Ironclads*. It was 'the size of an ironclad cruiser' but he did not explain how it would be kept secret, or got to the battlefield. More realistically, it was mounted on Diplock's Pedrail, an existing system patented in 1903, using pads or feet attached to a large wheel by ball-and-socket joints. But in real life the development of the armoured car and tank was a remarkable story involving war on land, sea and air. It began bizarrely enough with the threat of German airship raids on London, and Churchill's response in setting up the air base at Dunkirk. Since the effective radius of action of an aircraft might be as little as 30 miles, he planned to seize advanced bases in the surrounding countryside, disputed between the two sides but patrolled by German lancers. He 'received accounts of the remarkable work done by a Belgian motor car hastily equipped with armour and a machine gun in shooting down and driving back the numerous Uhlans [lancers] with which the enemy was seeking to over-run the country'.[1] He wrote to Battenberg and Sueter on 5 September 1914:

> According to all accounts received, the Germans, in so far as they have penetrated this region, have done it simply by bluff. Small parties of Uhlans, taking advantage of the terror inspired by their atrocities in Belgium, have made their way freely about the country, and have imposed themselves upon the population. We require, in the first instance, 200 or 300 men with 50 or 60 motor cars, who can support and defend out advanced aerial bases.[2]

They were to be under the command of Charles Samson, whose buccaneering spirit proved ideal for the task. For two months a force of sailors, marines and civilian chauffeurs and mechanics fought a land and air war. His superior officer Sueter was given the job of providing the armoured vehicles, but in the meantime Samson improvised. They started with ordinary cars fitted with machine-guns, then added improvised armour plate from local blacksmiths, but ordinary iron was worse than useless as it tended to splinter. There was an armoured lorry covered with boiler plate which could not keep out fire at short range, and it was too slow to keep up with the cars. Talbot and Wolseley chassis were used but Samson reported that the Rolls Royce was the best vehicle, not because of its luxury interior but because it was by far the most reliable. Lord Annesley armoured his own car in a local garage but it was 'a very comic home-made affair' and bits tended to drop off. Naval armour plate was needed, but when the first cars fitted with it arrived from home it was found that only the driver and engine were protected. The unit, which had not been consulted, 'did not like the finished article at all'. It was also discovered that overhead protection was needed in this kind of fighting, and that a revolving turret offered the best solution, so a wooden mock-up was made. Samson also produced a Mercedes lorry which he claimed was a forerunner of the tank, with six machine-guns, a conning tower for the commander and a second steering wheel for it to be driven backwards; but he had to admit that it could not be operated away from the roads.

Churchill was enthusiastic about the unit and wanted seven or eight squadrons to be formed. He visited it on 20 September 1914 and was persuaded that raids might be used on the front. 'The cars alone could not achieve very much; but working with the support of artillery and infantry certain important points like railway bridges could be attacked and destroyed.'[3] But this campaign came to an end early in November as the 'race to the sea' resulted in trench warfare from the Alps to the North Sea and there was no scope for vehicles which could operate only on roads. Churchill was disappointed on 14 November when General Sir John French decided that the armoured cars were no longer needed, as 'Now the lines of battle in this theatre are continuous, there is no possibility of using the armoured cars in the manner originally intended.'[4] By December, based on the experience of Samson's unit, the Admiralty had produced the first three turreted Rolls Royce armoured cars, each with a machine-gun and a speed of 50 mph. It was a classic design which would serve throughout the war and even up to the Second World War.[5]

It was no longer possible to pass round the trenches, but Churchill still had ideas for a system to enable vehicles 'to traverse and pass over the trenches themselves'. Admiral Sir Reginald Bacon, now manager of Coventry Ordnance Works, was called on and produced a plan for a machine which would lay a bridge, pass over it and then lift it again. Perhaps it was an ancestor of the bridge-laying tanks of the Normandy invasion, but for the moment it was too clumsy and slow and could not cross a second line of trenches. Churchill ordered 30, but it was rejected by the War Office after trials and the order was cancelled. Colonel Swinton wrote: 'Mr. Churchill in *The World Crisis* refers to these machines as caterpillar tractors. They were, in fact, wheeled vehicles carrying a portable bridge; and their only resemblance to the Tank was that they were intended to perform part of the task performed by the Tank. They were not sufficiently successful in doing this to be adopted.'[6]

Meanwhile a different system had emerged. Lieutenant-Colonel Ernest Swinton of the Royal Engineers was appointed Official Correspondent on the Western Front after Kitchener banned newspaper reporters from the area. It was Churchill who recommended him for the post, having read his book, *The Defence of Duffer's Drift*, describing British tactics in the Boer War. It was not unlike the post Churchill had suggested to parliament in 1901, though in this case everything had to be censored by Kitchener himself.[7] Among other achievements, Swinton is believed to have been the first to apply the term 'no-man's-land' to the space between the trenches. He was unable to report the full horror of that desolate area due to censorship, but he began to look for ways to cross it. Just before the war he had been contacted by a mining engineer who wanted to find the best means of transport in remote regions. He recommended a vehicle he had found at Antwerp, 'an agricultural machine of American manufacture called the Holt Caterpillar Tractor, which had surprising powers of crossing country. ... it could traverse narrow trenches or holes in the ground and was so powerful that it could drag a five-furrow plough, set at the maximum depth, through marshy soil.'[8] By October, as the stalemate developed on the Western

Front, he began to see it as the basis for a means of attack. He reasoned that Kitchener himself would be too busy to give it full consideration, so he reported it to Sir Maurice Hankey, his former chief as secretary of the Committee for Imperial Defence, who 'had access to everyone, and was in a position of influence which enabled him to speak with the authority of the Prime Minister behind him and so obtain a hearing in a way no one else could'.[9]

Swinton saw Hankey on 20 October and suggested that the tractors should be 'obtained and modified, or redesigned, and converted into fighting machines'. Hankey was sympathetic and drafted a paper. Swinton then went to see the Prime Minister, but 'did not feel that Mr. Asquith appreciated the fundamental implications of what I told him, or the urgency of everything to do with the conduct of war – which indeed was something foreign to his whole upbringing, experience and temperament'. He was unable to see Kitchener before going back to France, and once there he failed to get any interest from the engineer-in-chief.

But unknown to Swinton, Churchill had received a copy of Hankey's paper when it was circulated to Cabinet members. On 5 January he wrote to the Prime Minister:

> It would be quite easy in a short time to fit up a number of steam tractors with small armoured shelters in which men and machine guns could be placed, which would be bullet-proof. Used at night they would not be affected by artillery fire to any extent. The caterpillar system would enable trenches to be crossed quite easily and the weight of the machine would destroy all wire entanglements. Forty or fifty of these machines, prepared secretly and brought into positions at nightfall, could advance quite certainly to the enemy's trenches, smashing away all the obstructions and sweeping the trenches with their machine gun fire and with grenades thrown out of the top. They would then make so many *points d'appui* [rallying points] for the British infantry to rush forward ....[10]

Asquith sent the letter to Kitchener, who referred it to the Master General of the Ordnance. 'Extremely severe' conditions of testing were laid down for a Holt tractor and as a result no further action was taken. Churchill was under great pressure of Admiralty business by this time, but on 18 January he sent a minute to Sueter asking him to make experiments with steam rollers which could smash enemy trenches. This too failed, but an approach came from yet another source.

Albert Stern was a banker who offered the services of his car to Churchill in December 1914. Too late for the Belgian campaign, he was commissioned in the RNVR and sent to the armoured car depot at Wormwood Scrubs, west of London. There he met Thomas Hetherington and the Duke of Westminster – for the armoured car force included many officers who supplied their own vehicles, and most of them were wealthy and sometimes titled. Hetherington, James Radley and Stern discussed the use of 'a landship with three big wheels, each as big as the Great Wheel at Earl's Court' – 40 feet in diameter. Hetherington got the Duke of Westminster to invite Churchill to dinner at Murray's Club, an event also attended by Stern. Churchill was delighted with the idea and referred it to Sueter.[11]

Though he was ill at the time, this initiative led Churchill to call a meeting in his bedroom at the Admiralty on 20 February in which he appointed the Landships Committee chaired by Sir Tennyson d'Eyncourt, the Director of Naval Construction. Churchill never claimed to have invented the tank; indeed he stated that 'There never was a moment when it was possible to say that a tank had been "invented". There never was a person about whom it could be said "this man invented the tank". But there was a moment when the actual manufacture of the first tanks was definitely sanctioned, and there was a moment when an effective machine was exactly designed as the direct outcome of this authorisation.'[12] The first moment was described by Colonel Swinton: 'Then it was that he took the first of two steps to ensure full consideration for a project upon which he had set his heart. On the 20th February, 1915, he formed a semi-technical committee under the Director of Naval Construction expressly to deal with it.'[13] Hetherington of the armoured car squadron was deputy chairman, Stern was secretary and Colonel Crompton provided engineering expertise. The committee had no accommodation so Stern rented an office unofficially. Squadron 20 of the Royal Naval Armoured Car Division was retained for experimental purposes while the others were dispersed to different fronts where they often proved very useful – the Duke of Westminster's went to Flanders then Western Egypt, others to the Dardanelles and German West Africa, and eventually to Russia.

The second of Churchill's key moments was again described by Swinton: 'Five weeks later, when this committee had brought matters to the executive stage of experiment necessitating the expenditure of money, he took the second step – one for which he deserves the gratitude of the Army and of the nation. He sanctioned the expenditure of £70,000 of public funds upon what was a speculative venture, not – be it noted – for the Service for which he was responsible, but for the Army.' Churchill wrote: 'I thus took personal responsibility for the expenditure of the public money involved, about £70,000. I did not invite the Board of Admiralty to share the responsibility with me. I did not inform the War Office, for I knew they would raise objections to my interference in their sphere, and I knew by this time that the Department of the Master General of the Ordnance was not very receptive of such ideas. Neither did I inform the Treasury.'[14] He ordered 18 vehicles, six of the wheel type and six caterpillar. A wooden mock-up of the former showed a very strange machine which would have been impossible to conceal once assembled. It was reported that the cross-country qualities would be good but it could not cross rivers, and would be destroyed by powerful artillery. As to the caterpillars, a report of June 1915 stated: 'These landships were at first designed to transport a trench-taking storming party of fifty men with machine guns and ammunition.' It was found that such vehicles could not be steered round the narrow lanes of France and it was proposed to split them in two halves and articulate them.[15]

Churchill left the Admiralty on 27 May as a result of the Dardanelles affair and a quarrel with Fisher, but continued in government as Chancellor of the Duchy of Lancaster. He was still involved and presided over a meeting on 8 June, while the new First Lord, Arthur Balfour, asked him to maintain his interest in the project.[16] By 23 June the Landships Committee was in possession of a Killen-Strait tractor which had two caterpillar tracks side by side and a smaller one ahead, two giant creeper-grip tractors which had arrived from America and were believed to be 'well suited for this work, and sufficiently substantial in construction to stand all the hard usage it is likely to receive other than absolute destruction by shell fire', and two Diplock experimental one-ton tractors, which used a 'Pedrail' system – not the one described by H. G. Wells but a later invention using a chain drive – but it had not been developed for larger vehicles. These were tested on its experimental ground at Burton-on-Trent.[17]

On 30 June the Killen-Strait tractor was demonstrated crossing barbed wire in front of Churchill and Lloyd George who was now the Minister of Munitions. It 'enlisted the interest of the latter – which he never lost – in the subject. As a result he agreed to take over from the Admiralty the responsibility for the supply of landships after that department should have produced a satisfactory machine. And it was on this date, as we have seen, that the Landships Committee first received definite instructions as to the direction in which it should work. Up till then it had been groping about in the dark, concentrating its efforts chiefly on the production of a vehicle to carry a number of men rather than on an engine manned by a minimum fighting crew to destroy machine guns …'.[18] Until now the vehicles had been known as 'landships' to the navy and 'machine-gun destroyers' to the army. It was suggested that the name should be changed for security reasons and the red herring of 'water carrier' was proposed. Stern commented: 'In government offices, committees and departments are always known by their initials. For this reason I, as secretary considered the proposed title totally unsuitable. In our search for a synonymous term, we changed the word "water carrier" to "tank".'[19]

It was July 1915 before Swinton discovered the Admiralty's work after a Major Glyn 'confirmed what he had heard rumoured vaguely before, namely, that the Admiralty had taken up the idea and that Mr Churchill had formed a technical committee to investigate and experiment the subject of "landships" and had been pressing the scheme for all it was worth with Admiralty money!'[20] This delay was possibly because, as Stern claimed, Churchill took care to keep the recalcitrant War Office out of the picture – 'On the 29th of June the War Office and the Admiralty at last joined forces, although this had been opposed by Mr Churchill since the start.'[21] Swinton wrote:

> And so it came about that we two, each independently and without the other's knowledge, were working in the same direction – one which we both felt to be vital to the nation's success. This surely was a malicious prank of fate, for had we been able to collaborate in that autumn of 1914 – Mr Churchill bringing to the

scheme his initiative, driving power, and all the weight attaching to his position as a Minister – it is possible that the benefit of this new weapon might have been bestowed on our Arms many months earlier than was actually the case – with what saving of life God alone knows.[22]

Swinton brought a much-needed army perspective to the work. In addition, according to Stern, 'With his keen sense of humour, his understanding of the value of propaganda, his intimate knowledge of the War Office and all its mysterious ways, and with his exceptional position as Deputy Secretary to the Committee of Imperial Defence, he was able to push forward our schemes and to cut short all sorts of red tape for us.'[23]

The big wheel and the Killen-Strait had proved to be dead ends. In August Stern viewed a model of the Tritton Trench-Crossing Machine, designed by an agricultural engineer in Lincoln and incorporating the Holt caterpillar as recommended by Swinton. The tests of this machine, nicknamed 'Little Willie', were discussed in the White Hart Inn in the city and the War Office requirements were considered – a production model should be able to cross a trench 5 ft wide and 4 ft 6 ins high. This would require a 60-foot wheel, or a caterpillar track of the right circumference. A machine was designed with the track going round a characteristic rhomboid shape. It was d'Eyncourt who suggested 6-pounder guns in sponsons as the main armament. On 3 December this tank, to be known as 'Mother', began trials at Lincoln.

Meanwhile Churchill left the government, but according to Swinton he 'had not forgotten his protégés, the landships. In November he had joined the Army in France, bearing, as he informs us, a good gift – "the conception of a battle and a victory". Having for several months had a similar conception myself, I can fully understand and sympathize with his feelings in this matter.'[24] But soon d'Eyncourt began to feel neglected, and he later wrote to Churchill: 'After losing the great advantage of your influence I had some difficulty steering the scheme past the rocks of opposition and the more insidious shoals of apathy which are frequented by red herrings, which cross the line of progress at frequent intervals.'[25]

On 26 January 1916 'Mother' was ready to be tested at Hatfield in the presence of government ministers. Churchill was now commanding a battalion on the Western Front, but d'Eyncourt wrote to him:

It is with great pleasure that I am now able to report to you on the success of the first landship (Tanks as we call them). The War Office have ordered one hundred on the pattern which underwent most successful trials recently. ... The official tests of trenches, etc., were nothing to it, and finally we showed them how it could cross a 9 feet gap after climbing a 4 feet 6 inches high perpendicular parapet. Wire entanglements it goes through like a rhinoceros through a field of corn. It carries two 6-pounder guns in sponsons (a *naval* touch) and about 300 rounds; also smaller machine-guns, and is proof against machine-gun fire. ... In appearance, it looks rather like a great antediluvian monster, especially when it comes out of boggy ground, which it traverses easily. The wheels behind form a rudder for steering a course, and also ease the shock over banks, etc., but are not absolutely necessary, as it can steer and turn in its own length with the independent tracks.[26]

Churchill wrote a letter to Asquith and sent it via Clementine. The Prime Minster replied: 'I have heard a great deal about the Caterpillar from those who have seen it on trial and we hope great things from it.'[27] They were not the same vehicles that Churchill had sponsored in 1914–15, but he deserves credit for starting the process off, and overseeing the elimination of unsuitable schemes until the most viable one was discovered.

CHAPTER 15

The Underwater War

Underwater warfare had been a dream of inventors for more than a century, with experimental and usually unsuccessful submarines. Mines, known at the time as torpedoes, were used by the Russians during the Crimean War, but the Great War was the first in which these weapons would play a vital role. Historically the British had tended not to encourage or develop mines, preferring to advocate freedom of the seas. The Germans got in first at the start of the war by laying fields off Lowestoft and in the Humber during August 1914. Churchill accused them of using them 'indiscriminately upon the ordinary trade routes' without 'any definite military scheme such as the closing of a military port'. He tried to turn it to advantage, he 'wanted to impress not only on British but on neutral shipping the vital importance of touching at British ports on entering the North Sea, in order to ascertain according to the latest information the routes and channels which the Admiralty are keeping swept ...'.[1] In a further statement on 2 November he accused the Germans of laying mines from supposedly neutral ships and declared the whole of the North Sea to be a military area.[2]

The *Audacious*, one of the new 13.5 inch super-Dreadnoughts, was sunk by a mine off the north coast of Ireland on 27 October 1914, an event which Churchill tried to keep secret.[3] He remained sceptical about mines and resisted 'the many unwise proposals which were pressed upon me ... to squander our small stock of mines'. He divided them into two types – 'Ambush mining', in which they were 'scattered about in small patches, or short lines in the neighbourhood of the enemy's ports or of the approach to your own ports or landing places on the chance of enemy ships running into them', and 'Blockade mining', which was not practicable unless superior force was maintained in the area.[4] The only British minelaying consisted of fields off the Goodwin Sands and Ostend laid early in October, but the latter had to be swept as British troops were sent into Zeebrugge soon afterwards. In view of the limited numbers available, Churchill was sceptical about 'scattering a few bouquets of mines from destroyers' and told Fisher that it was 'like saving a few lottery tickets. But it is no substitute for going to work'.[5] Fisher replied in January: 'The German policy of laying mines has resulted in denying our access to their harbours – has hampered our submarines in their attempts to penetrate into German waters – and we have lost the latest type of Dreadnought and many other war vessels and over 70 merchant vessels of various sizes.' In return the British had laid only the field off Ostend. Fisher advocated a strong offensive policy, though there were few minelayers and only 4,900 mines were currently available, plus more from Russia.[6] Soon controlled mines would be developed to protect the main harbours such as Scapa, operated electrically from a control station.

*

Regarding British submarines, Fisher complained about 'the undoubted German submarine superiority in design' which he attributed to Wilson's neglect during his time as First Sea Lord.[7] But as Churchill pointed out, 'The submarine is the only vessel of war which does not fight its like.' It would not have been an answer to the German submarine threat 'to have multiplied our submarines by four, nor should we have exposed Germany to an equal danger had we done so', for Germany was far less dependent on seaborne trade.[8] At the beginning of the war the British submarines were under Commodore Roger Keyes, whom Churchill protected from the slights of Fisher, eventually offering him a post as chief of staff to Admiral Carden in the Dardanelles campaign. Keyes was pleased to get away from 'a very wicked vindictive old man'.[9] He was replaced by the return of S. S. Hall, who had already served as Inspecting Captain of Submarines in 1907–10.

The C-class coastal boats patrolled off the bases, but in the event they had no contact with the enemy and their main use was in training crews. At first overseas submarines were intended to be employed with destroyers and cruisers, and Keyes often went out in the aptly named destroyer *Lurcher*, in which even a hardened sailor could be seasick. This was abandoned because of the difficulties of communication, and Commodore (S) became a shore job at Harwich, to Keyes's disgust. They had a few successes, such as the sinking of the cruiser *Hela* in September and the destroyer *S116* in October, but as Churchill put it, 'they suffered from one overwhelming disadvantage … viz a dearth of targets'.[10] Some were sent to the Baltic where they had more success, and some to the Mediterranean. Despite the difficulties, Churchill wrote to Fisher on 28 October: 'Please propose without delay the largest possible programme of submarine boats to be delivered in twelve to twenty-four months. … You should exert every effort of ingenuity and organisation to secure the utmost possible delivery.'[11]

★

Churchill outlined his own ideas for dealing with enemy boats to Asquith in October 1914, including 'enveloping and protecting "shoes"' round ships, 'a huge net-work of wire and nets, a "hencoop"' off the east coast where major warships would be safe, and a larger 'bird cage', further north. Asquith, who knew very little about the subject, was pleased: '… it is inventive and resourceful, and shows both originality and dash'. It helped justify having a civilian minster at the Admiralty when the War Office had Kitchener – 'I laugh at our idiotic outside critics who long for an expert instead of a civilian at the head of the Admiralty.'[12]

The initial German submarine assault was on warships as expected and the scout cruiser *Pathfinder* was sunk on 5 September, followed by a major tragedy. At the Loch Ewe conference on 17 September, Churchill heard an officer refer to 'the live bait squadron' and asked what he meant. It was a group of old cruisers patrolling the Broad Fourteens off the Dutch coast. He soon realised the danger (though at the time he was thinking of attack by surface ships) and ordered: 'The *Bacchantes* ought not to continue on this beat. The risk to such ships is not justified by any services they can render. The narrow seas, being the nearest point to the enemy, should be kept by a small number of good, modern ships' – presumably light cruisers which were fast enough to escape from trouble, or even battlecruisers which could fight almost anything on the surface. In fact he was not the first person in authority to spot the danger, Keyes had been urging their removal since August and Herbert Richmond of the naval staff was also suggesting a change, but it is not clear if they reported this to Churchill.[13] In any case, the First Lord's order to recall the cruisers was delayed and on 22 September *U-9* fired a torpedo into the *Aboukir* which caused her to capsize. Her consorts *Hogue* and *Cressy* chivalrously went to rescue the men and were themselves torpedoed, with the loss of 1,400 men. Churchill had recently made a speech describing the German fleet as being trapped like 'rats in a hole', but the King commented on 'what alas! happened today when the rats came out of their own accord and to our cost'. To Asquith it was 'some very bad news: the worst, I think, since war began'.[14]

The submarine war was still quite gentlemanly in the early stages. The first merchant ship to be sunk was the *Glitra* of Leith, on the way to Stavanger in neutral Norway. On 20 October *U-17* surfaced near her and gave the crew ten minutes to take to the boats before sinking her by gunfire. Then the submarine towed the boats towards the Norwegian coast until they were met by a pilot boat. The submarine war was raised to a very different level on 4 February 1915 when the German Admiralty declared: 'All the waters surrounding Great Britain and Ireland, including the whole of the English Channel, are hereby declared to be a war zone. From February 18 onwards every merchant vessel found in this war zone will be destroyed without it always being possible to avoid dangers to the crews and their passengers' – and neutrals would not be exempted. Churchill immediately identified this as a submarine attack and drafted a memorandum after consulting his cabinet colleagues. 'As it is not in the power of the German Admiralty to maintain any surface craft in these waters, this attack can only be delivered by submarine agency. ... the British government cannot recognise attacks by submarines on merchant ships as a legitimate means of warfare.'[15] Potentially this was the 'truly terrible' menace which Fisher had predicted.

It was not Churchill's central issue at the time; according to Asquith he was 'breast-high' with the Dardanelles.[16] Nor was it taken very seriously at first. The Germans had only 29 modern U-boats, so there were only about eight or nine at sea at any given time. To Asquith, it was 'the truly absurd "blockade of our seas and coasts"'.[17] After two weeks of the attack Churchill could still claim that in general the seas were 'practically safe'.[18] Indeed he welcomed the campaign as 'a means of embroiling the U.S. with Germany' and wanted to attract more neutral shipping to inflame the issue.[19] Later he wrote: 'On hundreds of ships proceeding weekly in and out of scores of harbours, this handful of marauders could make no serious impression. It was like hundreds of rabbits running across a ride, with only two or three one-eyed poachers to shoot them.'[20] It was decided to publish figures of losses to show how futile the German campaign was.

However, if the campaign intensified it could become serious, for as Fisher had written in 1913, there were 'no means ... of meeting it except by reprisals'. The main anti-submarine technique at the start of the war was a sweep fitted with floats and TNT charges which was towed by a group of destroyers in line abreast, hoping to catch any submarine that passed through.[21] The torpedo school HMS *Vernon* began to develop a depth charge in December 1914 after a request from Jellicoe, but a suitable hydrostatic pistol did not come along until 1916. It was found that the wake or 'feather' of a periscope could be seen from the air in calm conditions, but aeroplanes did not have enough endurance for extended patrols while there were still very few airships – the first of the Sea Scout Class was delivered on 18 March but lost in an accident two months later. Commander C. P. Ryan, a friend of Beatty's wife, was developing sound detection of submarines by means of the hydrophone in the Firth of Forth from the start of the war.[22] There was some progress by March 1915 but the system remained experimental.[23] There is no sign that Churchill paid much attention to this apart from a brief mention later.[24] In the meantime the Auxiliary Patrol of armed motor yachts, largely manned by members of the RNVR who had not been sent to fight on land, was augmented, and more merchant ships were to be armed. Churchill was bombarded with ideas from the public. Arthur Pollen, the disgruntled inventor of a fire control system, wanted tramp steamers to be fitted with concealed guns and to carry German prisoners between Le Havre and Dover – if the ship lost its gun battle with the submarine, 'there would at any rate be the consolation of drowning some German officers and men'.[25]

Sir Arthur Wilson rejected Churchill's ideas on how to make ships torpedo proof as this could not be done 'without at the same time greatly impairing their sea-going qualities, economy and speed'.[26] However the First Lord favoured two main solutions. The first was the use of indicator nets made of thin, strong wire, which were suspended from floats. If a submarine made contact a portion of the net would detach itself and foul it, while giving notice of the submarine's position by a buoy attached to the net. These were to be laid in an attempt to close the Straits of Dover to U-boats, as well as the North Channel, the main shipping route into Liverpool.

The second scheme was less passive. It was still the custom for U-boats to surface and sink merchant ships by gunfire, thus saving expensive torpedoes, and it was planned to take advantage of that. In September a small steamer carrying fruit and vegetables between Southampton and St Malo was fired on a by a U-boat. Admiral Sir Hedworth Meux, commander-in-chief at Portsmouth, heard about it and suggested to Churchill that a gun might be hidden under the fruit; that was done but it was never used. However it led to the idea of the Special Service Ship, or Q-ship. As described by Churchill, 'Early in February I gave directions for a number of vessels to be constructed or adapted for the purpose of trapping and ambushing German submarines …. These vessels carried concealed guns which by a pantomime trick of trap doors and shutters could suddenly come into action.'[27] In fact such ships had been in service since November without any success, but many more were to be fitted. Another deception was to have a submarine towed behind a small merchant ship. The crews were connected by telephone and if the surface ship was attacked the submarine would torpedo the enemy. This was a case of one submarine attacking another, contrary to Churchill's prediction.

Aggressive as ever, on 10 February 1915 Churchill issued orders to merchant ship masters that ' … any submarine which shows by her action that she is attempting to close or communicate with a merchant vessel should be treated as hostile … No British merchant vessel should ever tamely surrender to a submarine, but should do her utmost to escape.' If a submarine was seen straight ahead then the merchant ship was to 'steer for her at your utmost speed' and the submarine would probably dive. This became known as the 'ramming order', though that term was not used. One side-effect, according to Asquith, was that 'we have a whole flotilla of our own submarines, huddled together in Dover Harbour, & afraid to go out, lest they should be rammed or sunk by British merchant ships, which now go for every periscope that appears above the surface'. Captain Charles Fryatt of the Great Eastern Railway Company applied the order on 2 March when he escaped from a U-boat in the steamer *Wrexham*. On the 28th *U-33* surfaced in front of him in the *Brussels* and he did indeed steer for her at full speed, forcing her to submerge. In June 1916 he was captured and tried by the Germans as a *franc-tireur*, or unauthorised combatant, and shot.[28]

The anti-submarine measures had their first success on 4 March when *U-8* was entangled in the indicator nets in the Straits of Dover and sighted by a destroyer, which used her sweeps and forced her to surface. Her crew surrendered but Fisher wanted to try them for murder. The nets were effective as a deterrent and forced the U-boats to head round the north of Scotland, but this was the only time they played any part in a sinking or capture. Six days later the destroyer *Ariel* rammed the conning tower of *U-12* as she tried to dive and her consort *Attack* shelled her, forcing the submarine's crew to scuttle her. The most evocative success came on the 18th when *U-29*, which had sunk the three cruisers, was rammed and sunk by the battleship *Dreadnought*. But sinkings of merchant ships almost quadrupled to 84,000 tons in March, before dropping to half that in April.

The Cunard liner *Lusitania* left New York on 1 May carrying 1,965 passengers, despite German warnings that British ships in the war zone were liable to be sunk. On the 7th she was off the south coast of Ireland when she was sighted by Captain Walther Schwieger in *U-20*. He had been told to watch out for transports which might invade Schleswig-Holstein (though in fact they were being prepared for the Dardanelles) and at 1340 he fired a single torpedo at a range of 700 yards, causing a large explosion. The ship sank in 18 minutes. Only six of 48 lifeboats could be launched and 1,201 passengers were lost, including 128 Americans. At the time Churchill was absorbed in the biggest crisis of his career and Fisher would resign four days later;

but later Churchill wrote: 'Even in the first moments of realizing the tragedy and its horror, I understood the significance of the event. ... On two supreme occasions [the other was the invasion of Belgium] the German Imperial Government, quenching compunction, outfacing conscience, deliberately, with calculation, with sinister resolve, severed the underlying bonds which sustained the civilisation of the world and united even in their quarrels the human family.'[29] There was outcry in the United States, which forced a drastic reduction and then an end to the submarine campaign against merchant shipping. Conspiracy theories that the British government or Churchill had engineered the sinking do not hold much water. The ship was carrying a consignment of small arms ammunition and shrapnel shells weighing 173 tons, as Churchill admitted in 1923;[30] even if the Germans had known about that and used it as an excuse, sinking the ship would have been grossly disproportionate and would not have absolved them of a huge diplomatic blunder.

Churchill had left the Admiralty by the time the towed submarines had their first successes. On 23 June *U-40* was sunk by *C24* off Aberdeen, and *U-23* by *C27* off Fair Isle, but the project was soon abandoned after two of the submarines struck mines. Q-ships captured the popular imagination and several books were written about them. Their first success was on 5 June with the sinking of *U-14* off Peterhead. On the 24th *U-36* was sunk off the Hebrides by the gunfire of a decoy ship, *Prince Charles*. In all 215 Q-ships were commissioned and they sank eleven U-boats, but lost 20 of their own number. Later Churchill described the whole affair as 'The First Defeat of the U-Boats', but in fact it was not the naval campaign which called the onslaught to be called off but rather the Germans' lack of submarines and the irresistible pressure of the neutrals. In fact the campaign was quite misleading, and Churchill's favoured measures offered little for the future.

★

The Germans resumed their unrestricted submarine campaign in February 1917, gambling that even after an American declaration of war they could still force Britain out of the conflict before any large-scale American help arrived. This time they had more than 130 U-boats in service. The British had developed the depth charge and airships patrolled the seas, but Ryan's hydrophone was only effective for shore stations, not from ships. Out of office, Churchill watched from the sidelines as merchant shipping losses mounted to an unstainable 880,000 tons in April and Britain was in danger of starvation. The sea lords, now headed by Jellicoe, refused to adopt a system of convoy until it was forced on them by Lloyd George as Prime Minister. Contrary to the myth, Lloyd George probably did not take personal charge of an Admiralty meeting to enforce the change, but issued a decision of the War Cabinet which the Admiralty had already accepted by the time he visited the building the next day. But it was a momentous decision all the same. In overriding the considered advice of his service advisers, Lloyd George was committing an act in truly Churchillian fashion – except that Churchill was out of office. In fact it was more determined, and had much greater effect, than any single act of Churchill's before 1940, and it was carried out by a 'real' civilian politician, not a warrior in political office. Churchill was rather dismissive of it in 1927, perhaps because he was no longer in alliance with Lloyd George, perhaps because he was jealous. In *The World Crisis* he merely stated that 'The trial of the convoy system was urged upon the naval authorities by the Cabinet, and in this the Prime Minster took a decisive role.'[31] He was much more effusive in 1932 when he wrote an article for the *Daily Telegraph*, later incorporated in a book:

> On April 23 the War Cabinet debated the whole issue with their naval advisers. The results of the discussion were wholly unsatisfactory. On the 25th, therefore, the War Cabinet, sitting alone, resolved upon decisive action. It was agreed that the Prime Minister should personally visit the Admiralty 'to investigate all the means at present used in anti-submarine warfare, on the ground that recent inquiries had made it clear that there was not sufficient co-ordination in the present efforts to deal with the campaign'. The menace implied in this procedure was unmistakeable. No greater shock can be administered to a responsible department or military profession. The naval authorities realised that it was a case of 'act or go'.[32]

By next day the sea lords had agreed to institute convoys. Sinkings soon began to fall to manageable levels and the crisis, probably the worst that Britain faced during the war, was over.

CHAPTER 16

The Rest of the World

Before the war British shipbuilders such as Armstrong of Tyneside and Vickers of Barrow made a lucrative business out of building warships of all sizes for foreign nations. In August 1914 Armstrong was completing the *Almirante Latorre* for Chile, which was taken over and re-named *Canada* – perhaps to soften Churchill's disappointment in not getting three ships from the Dominion earlier in the year. This caused little controversy, in contrast to his other major takeover.

The *Reshadieh* at Vickers in Barrow was one of a pair ordered by Turkey in 1912, but one was cancelled. The *Sultan Osman I*, built in Armstrong's yard, was originally ordered by Brazil as the *Rio de Janeiro* and with 14 12-inch guns she was in some respects the most powerful battleship of her day. When rubber prices fell Brazil was unable to afford her and the uncompleted ship was sold to Turkey early in 1914. Churchill ordered: 'In case it many become necessary to acquire the Turkish battleships that are nearing completion in British yards, please formulate plans in detail showing exactly the administrative action involved in their acquisition and the prospective financial transactions.' Some years later he justified his actions: '… the Turkish ships were taken over, as our margin of superiority was so small that we could not afford to do without them. Still less could we afford to see them transferred to a potentially hostile power. Had these ships gone to Turkey and been manned by Germans they would have required three or four British Dreadnoughts to cover them and watch them. Thus we should have been five or six ships poorer in home waters, and the number of Dreadnoughts in the British and German fleets would have been within one or two of actual equality.'[1] But as Asquith wrote, 'The Turks are very angry – not unnaturally – at Winston's seizure of their battleships here.'[2] It caused a breach with Turkey which the Germans were determined to exploit.

The Germans had two major warships in the Mediterranean, the cruiser *Breslau* with 4.1-inch guns and a speed of 25 knots and the powerful battlecruiser *Goeben* with ten 11.1-inch guns and a speed of 25½ knots, under Admiral Souchon. The British commander-in-chief was Admiral Sir Berkeley Milne, whom Churchill had appointed in the face of Fisher's opposition. His second-in-command, and potential successor, was Rear-Admiral Ernest Troubridge, who had been found wanting as chief of staff at the Admiralty. The fleet, operating mainly from Malta, was the one which Churchill had tried to reduce in 1912.

In the early stages of the *Goeben* affair Churchill made it clear from his writings that he was personally controlling the ships in the Mediterranean, and his account in *The World Crisis* is peppered with the first person singular pronoun. This was appropriate as the situation hovered between peace and war with Germany, Austria-Hungary and possibly Italy, and any naval engagement might have huge political consequences. On 28 July 1914 he suggested to Battenberg that an additional battlecruiser should be sent to the Mediterranean, but there was no time. On the 30th he called for the war orders of the Mediterranean Command and discussed them with Battenberg. In view of the latest situation, the two of them drafted more specific instructions, in which they were 'completely in accord'. The position of Italy was uncertain, but she would probably be neutral. The commander-in-chief was not to engage with Austrian ships before it was known what Italy would do. War with Germany was highly likely and the first task of Milne's fleet was to help protect the large numbers of French troops to be brought over from her African colonies. If necessary he was to engage with 'individual fast German ships, particularly *Goeben*, which may interfere with that transportation'. But there was a note of caution at the end of the orders: 'Except in combination with the French as part of a general battle, do not at this stage be brought to action against superior forces. The speed of your squadrons is sufficient to enable you to choose your moment. You must husband your force at the outset and we shall hope later to reinforce the Mediterranean.' Churchill claimed that the orders were perfectly clear: 'So far as the English language may serve as a vehicle of thought, the words employed appear to express the intentions we had formed.' Of course he was an expert in using the English language 'as a vehicle of thought' but the orders do have their ambiguities, perhaps reflecting the aggressive style of Churchill in the first half and the more cautious approach of Battenberg in the second. Moreover, the claim that Milne's ships had sufficient speed would not prove to be true.[3]

★

On the evening of 2 August Churchill signalled to all commands that the situation was critical, to be ready for surprise attacks and to enter into communication with local French commanders, though Milne was unable to do this and did not inform the Admiralty of it. Next day Churchill and Battenberg signalled Milne, apparently dividing responsibility between Milne and Troubridge – two battlecruisers were to shadow the *Goeben* while Troubridge's cruisers were to watch the entrance to the Adriatic in case the Austrian fleet moved. At 1250 that day, 3 August, Churchill personally drafted a telegram to Milne: 'Watch on the mouth of the Adriatic should be maintained, but *Goeben* is your objective. Follow her, and shadow her wherever she goes and be ready to act on declaration of war, which appears to be probable and imminent.' Early in the morning of the 4th he was delighted with a signal reporting that the *Indomitable* and *Indefatigable* had sighted the enemy battlecruiser and were following her. He replied: 'Very Good. Hold her. War imminent.' She was to be 'prevented by force from interfering with French transports'. This was beyond Churchill's authority as war had not yet started, but Asquith and Grey appeared to acquiesce subject to the approval of the cabinet. That was not forthcoming, the British ultimatum to Germany did not expire until midnight GMT and at 2.05 in the afternoon Churchill had to signal cancelling the authorisation to engage the *Goeben*. Meanwhile Battenberg suggested British ships should respect Italian neutrality and that they should stay six miles off her coastline. Churchill agreed. At five

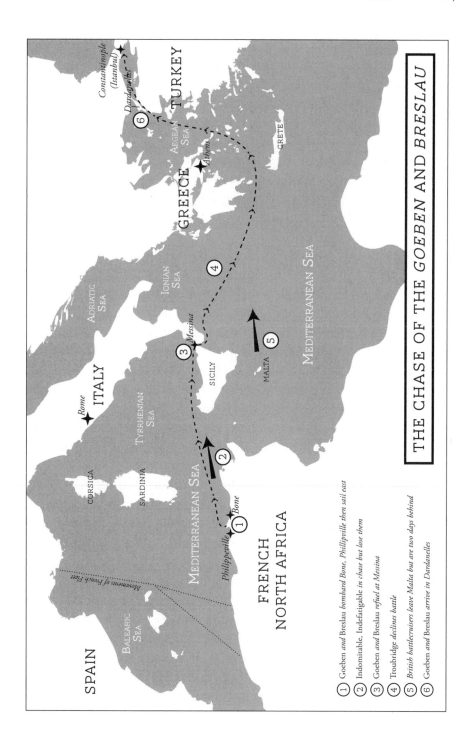

THE CHASE OF THE *GOEBEN* AND *BRESLAU*

SPAIN

BALEARIC
SEA

FRENCH
NORTH AFRICA

Movements of French Fleet

Philippeville

Bone

MEDITERRANEAN SEA

CORSICA

SARDINIA

Rome

ITALY

TYRRHENIAN
SEA

ADRIATIC
SEA

SICILY

Messina

IONIAN
SEA

MALTA

MEDITERRANEAN SEA

GREECE

Athens

AEGEAN
SEA

CRETE

TURKEY

*Constantinople
(Istanbul)*

Dardanelles

① Goeben and Breslau bombard Bone, Phillipville then sail east

② Indomitable, Indefatigable in chase but lose them

③ Goeben and Breslau refuel at Messina

④ Troubridge declines battle

⑤ British battlecruisers leave Malta but are two days behind

⑥ Goeben and Breslau arrive in Dardanelles

in the evening of that fateful day, Battenberg suggested that there was still time to sink the *Goeben* before nightfall, but Churchill was bound by the cabinet decision. In the night the *Goeben*, with her consort the cruiser *Breslau*, used darkness and their superior short-term speed to give the British battlecruisers the slip. They went to Messina on the north-east corner of Sicily to replenish their coal.[4]

Churchill remarked on the 'strange interlude' of calm in the hours before the war actually started, but by the 5th he had his hands full with other business, in particular arranging for the movement of the British army to France. Moreover, as he wrote later, 'the exceedingly prompt manner in which the *Goeben* had been found, although in the open sea, on the 4th had given the Admiralty the feeling that the Admiral on the spot had a grip of the situation and needed no further directions'.[5] Churchill was no longer in personal control of the pursuit of the *Goeben* and the new Admiralty staff system was not able to cope. Milne stationed two of his battlecruisers off the northern entrance to the Straits of Messina but sent the *Indomitable* west to Bizerta in French Tunisia to refuel, rather than Malta to the east. He felt his orders about remaining six miles off Italian territory prevented him from passing through the straits, so the southern exit was uncovered. As yet no one had any idea that the Germans might want to head east, rather than attack the French convoys to the west, and no one thought to ask Churchill's permission to change the order.

Admiral Souchon in the *Goeben* had instructions to deliver his ships to Turkey, and left Messina at 5 pm on August 6th with bands playing. He headed south and then eastwards, leaving the British heavy ships far behind. Now the only opposition was Troubridge's squadron of obsolescent cruisers off the mouth of the Adriatic. On hearing of the enemy movement he took the initiative and left his station to meet them. He made plans to put his ships across the *Goeben*'s bows, though his cruisers had only 9.2-inch guns against the battlecruiser's 11-inch, and he knew full well that 'a cruiser could not engage a battlecruiser with any prospect of success' and that 'The multiplication of cruisers had no bearing on this when the meeting was in the open sea.' He did not mention the possible effect of a torpedo attack by his destroyers. Early in the morning of the 8th his flag captain, Fawcet Wray, asked if he intended to go into action. Troubridge answered yes, adding, 'I know it is wrong, but I cannot have the name of the whole Mediterranean Squadron "stink".' Wray, a gunnery officer, went back later and found the admiral in the darkened chartroom. He had often pointed out that the effective range of the ageing 9.2-inch guns was 8,000 yards whereas the Goeben could be effective at twice that distance. An attack would lead to 'the suicide of the squadron'. Troubridge was also aware of the orders not to be 'brought to action against superior forces' and to 'husband' the fleet. He was in tears when he decided to abandon the attack, but neither officer had any other plan. The Goeben and Breslau were allowed to escape.[6]

Milne was some way behind with the main force, not pursuing very fast, and was diverted by a bizarre incident. An official telegram announcing the war with Austria had been drafted in advance and put on a desk, whose occupant then left it. The result was that 'a blameless and punctilious Admiralty clerk', according to Churchill, sent it out and Milne followed his orders and turned back towards the Adriatic. The cancelling signal was sent after a few hours, but there was confusion as it was not coded so Milne naturally queried it. The reply was equally confusing, reading 'With reference to the cancellation of telegram notifying war on Austria, situation is critical,' which caused the over-cautious Milne to hesitate yet again. There is no evidence that Churchill played any role in the error and it seems that he was busy elsewhere dealing with the army crossing to France; but it suggests that the Admiralty system did not work well when not supervised by the First Lord and the First Sea Lord. The German ships headed for Constantinople where they were welcomed ecstatically and incorporated in the Turkish navy as compensation for the loss of the Sultan Osman I and another ship, the Sultan Mehmet Rechad.

Milne's conduct was 'the subject of careful examination' by the Admiralty, but their lordships 'approved the measures taken by him in all respects'. Fisher could not resist a jab at his old enemy: 'I see the wording of the telegram to Sir B Milne should be "Haul down your flag and come on shore" (He ought never to have left the shore!!)'[7] Troubridge was recalled to face a court of enquiry, which cleared him;

but Hamilton, the Second Sea Lord, claimed that 'The Court has been entirely led off its track by a clever lawyer.'[8] Churchill wrote:

> ... if the *Goeben* and *Breslau* had become involved with an action, it is hard to believe that none of the sixteen British cruisers and destroyers which were available could have closed in upon them and attacked them with gun or torpedo. All the destroyers were capable of reaching the enemy and could have found their opportunity to attack. It would have been indeed a prodigious feat on the part of the Germans to dispose of so many antagonists.[9]

Troubridge, on reading this, wrote: 'How often Mr Churchill has said to me, "In politics one can never afford to admit that one has made a mistake".'[10] Captain Wray was not tried but heard that Churchill was saying 'poor Troubridge was wrangled by his flag captain for two hours and eventually was persuaded by him not to fight'.[11] Wray strongly resented rumours of his cowardice but sought an interview with Churchill in vain. Troubridge was lukewarm in his support, but Wray was eventually given the command of another cruiser.

★

Churchill described the scene outside European waters at the start of the war:

> On an August morning, behold the curious sight of a British Cabinet of respectable Liberal politicians sitting down deliberately and with malice aforethought to plan the seizure of the German colonies in every part of the world! ... our sea communications depended largely upon the prompt denial of these bases or refuges to the German cruisers; and further, with Belgium already largely overrun by the German armies, everyone felt that we must lose no time in taking hostages for her eventual liberation. Accordingly, with maps and pencils, the whole world was surveyed, six separate expeditions were approved in principle and remitted to the staffs for study and execution.[12]

Apart from in her colonies, Germany had five cruisers on the China Station, the *Königsberg* in the Indian Ocean and two more in the West Indies. Only five of them were able to leave harbour in the face of the British blockade, but they were to cause far more than their share of trouble. The *Königsberg* sank a small British cruiser and forced the adoption of a convoy system in the Indian Ocean to protect troop convoys

THE REST OF THE WORLD • 191

and regular trade, but was found and blockaded in German East Africa from the beginning of November, so that only two ships instead of six were needed to contain her.

When the war started Vice-Admiral Maximilian Graf von Spee, in command of the German East Asiatic Cruiser Squadron based in China, detached the light cruiser *Emden* to prey in the Indian Ocean where she carried out a heroic campaign, capturing 16 merchant ships and shelling the gas tanks at Madras. Up to 75 British and allied ships were needed to seek her out. Spee's squadron also included the powerful 8.2-inch gun cruisers *Scharnhorst* and *Gneisenau*, manned by fully trained professional sailors. After Japan declared war on Germany it was impossible to operate them in the western Pacific, so Spee moved his squadron eastward. It threatened Australian and New Zealand troop convoys, and expeditions to capture German islands in the region. Often it disappeared from the allied view for days at a time, and it raided Bora Bora and Papeete. By 4 October it was clear that the squadron was heading for the west coast of South America. The main British force in that area was a group of old cruisers under Rear-Admiral Sir Christopher Cradock, largely intended to raid German trade in the area.

The *Goeben* campaign was the first in history to be conducted over a long distance by radio, but this one was carried out at far greater ranges, and often well away from established British naval bases. Many messages between the Admiralty and Cradock's ships were sent via local British diplomats, for example three from 24 to 26 October via the consul at Punta Arenas in the Straits of Magellan, Chile. And at the end of the month Cradock signalled: 'Up to 4th November send telegrams for me to the British Consul, Coronel; then until further notice to British Consul-General, Valparaiso.'[13] All this could lead to delays but did not stop Churchill directing the campaign. On 11 October he received a signal from Cradock which suggested that the enemy force was concentrating for battle. He was concerned that previous instructions from the naval staff did not emphasise the need for British concentration and on the 12th wrote a reply on the back of Cradock's telegram – 'It would be best for the British ships to keep within supporting distance of one another …'. They would postpone a cruise along the west coast and were instructed that the *Scharnhorst* and *Gneisenau* were 'our quarry for the moment. Above all, we must not miss them.' Battenberg agreed, adding the word 'settled' to the telegram.[14] But concentration was not to be total, for Rear-Admiral Archibald Stoddart had a squadron off Montevideo, including the armoured cruiser *Defence*, which was separate from Cradock's command.

Cradock's ships were clearly inferior to the German force in many respects. The *Canopus* was an old battleship of 1897. Her four 12-inch guns were more than a match for the Germans' by weight, even if aged and in poor condition and with an inferior range, but with her speed of 18 knots (probably reduced in practice) she could not hope to catch them or keep up with the rest of the fleet. The armoured cruiser *Good Hope* had been launched in 1901, well before the Dreadnought revolution. Her two 9.2-inch guns were more powerful that the Germans' 8.2-inch, but their range was only slightly greater, and they could not be fired in a broadside, which would make it more difficult to correct the fall of shot. The *Monmouth* was from the same era, with fourteen 6-inch guns; only nine of them could be fired on a broadside, and at least two of these were mounted so low in barbettes that they could not be used in heavy seas. She had been rescued from scrapping at the start of war and was manned by a hastily assembled crew of reservists and recruits. The *Glasgow* of 1909 was a light cruiser from the transitional stage with a main armament of only two 6-inch guns, and poor stability which made them difficult to aim.

On the 26th Churchill received a rather disturbing signal that Cradock considered the *Canopus* too slow for his squadron and he was using her to escort colliers. The Admiralty was in flux at the time as Battenberg left, and Churchill later admitted that his response was weak – he minuted Oliver: 'This telegram is very obscure and I do not understand what Admiral Cradock intends and wishes.' Cradock replied that he would use the *Glasgow* and *Monmouth* to draw the German ships south onto the *Good Hope* and *Canopus*, and that they would 'keep within supporting distance of each other'. Churchill assumed that this meant that the *Glasgow* and *Monmouth* would be 40 or 50 miles ahead of the others and the larger ships would be able to close as soon as a battle started; but there was a growing worry in his mind, and on the 30th he expressed it to the newly reinstated Fisher: 'I said, "you don't suppose he would try to fight them without the *Canopus*?" He did not give any decided reply.' After more information on 2 November, Churchill, Fisher and Sturdee, the current chief of war staff, sent a message to Cradock the following evening, announcing the detachment of a cruiser from Stoddart's squadron.[15]

> *Defence* has been ordered to join your flag with all dispatch. *Glasgow* should find or keep in touch with the enemy. You should keep in touch with *Glasgow* concentrating the rest of your squadron including *Canopus*. It is important you should effect your junction with *Defence* at earliest possible moment subject to keeping in touch with the *Glasgow* and enemy.[16]

It was too late. At 7 in the morning of 4 November Churchill opened his dispatch box to find devastating news from the British consul at Valparaiso. He had learned via a Chilean admiral that 'German admiral states that on Sunday at sunset, in thick and wicked weather, his ships met *Good Hope*, *Glasgow*, *Monmouth* and *Otranto*. Action was joined, and *Monmouth* turned over and sank after about an hour's fighting. *Good Hope*, *Glasgow* and *Otranto* drew off into the darkness. *Good Hope* was on fire, an explosion was heard, and she is believed to have sunk.'[17] It was all true, and a disastrous defeat which did not go unnoticed in press and parliament. Since Cradock was killed in the action with most of his staff, we will never know what went through his mind. Perhaps he was aware of the fate of Troubridge, who had been castigated for failing to seek action against the *Goeben* and was just about to face a court of enquiry. Perhaps he noted the concluding words of Churchill's telegram of the 12th – 'above all we must not miss them'. Asquith commented, 'Poor Winston is in for a run of bad luck … Fancy their [the Germans] being able last Sunday to get together 5 excellent cruisers outside Valparaiso on the W. coast of S. America, to engage our squadron in battle, and sink two of our most useful cruisers … And all through sheer stupidity, for if the Admiral had followed his instructions he would never have met them with an inferior force.'[18] He was even franker to the King: 'The cabinet are of opinion that this incident, like the escape of the *Goeben*, the loss of the *Cressy* and her two sister cruisers, and that of the *Hermes* last week, is not creditable to the officers of the navy.'[19]

There was slightly better news from other seas. On 4 November, three days after the Battle of Coronel, the cruiser *Karlsruhe* sank in the Caribbean. The *Emden* was finally surprised by the Australian cruiser *Sydney* on the ninth and sunk. Churchill chivalrously recognised her crew had fought 'without offending against humanity or the laws of sea war' and ordered that her officers were to be allowed to keep their swords as a mark of respect.[20] But the defeat at Coronel opened up a number of 'unpleasant possibilities' that Spee's cruisers might 'turn back into the Pacific, and repeat the mystery tactics which had been so baffling to us. He might steam northwards up the West Coast of South America and make for the Panama Canal … He might come round to the East Coast and interrupt the main trade route.'[21] Fisher sprang into action at this point, for a long-range war against enemy raiders was just what his favourite ships had been designed for. Churchill wanted to send the battlecruiser *Invincible*, but the First Sea Lord 'was in a bolder mood. He would take two battlecruisers from the Grand Fleet for the South American Station. More than that, and much more questionable, he would take a third – the *Princess Royal* – for Halifax and later for the West Indies in case von Spee came through the Panama Canal.'[22] Jellicoe was ordered to fill the *Invincible* and *Inflexible* with coal and send them south, and he accepted this without protest despite a slender margin of superiority in the North Sea. But as Churchill wrote: 'Thus to compass the destruction of five warships, only two of which were armoured, it was necessary to employ nearly thirty, including twenty-one armoured ships …'.[23]

The two battlecruisers were sent to Plymouth to prepare for the long voyage and on 9 November Fisher came into Churchill's office with the message that the earliest date for completion was midnight on the 13th. Churchill sent the order: 'Ships are to sail on Wednesday 11th. They are needed for war service and dockyard arrangements must be made to conform. If necessary dockyard men should be sent away in the ships to return as opportunity may offer. You are held responsible for the speedy despatch of these ships in a thoroughly efficient condition.'[24] Sturdee left his post as chief of war staff to be replaced by Oliver, and took command of the force. But he did not do justice to the dockyard's haste, stopping to search merchant ships on the way south. They joined with

Stoddart's squadron and reached Port Stanley on the Falkland Islands on 7 December, to find *Canopus* defending the harbour. They were extremely lucky, Spee was indeed on the way to attack the islands and intelligence of British movements failed to reach him. But Churchill was concerned in the evening of the 8th when Oliver came into his room with a telegram announcing 'Admiral Spee arrived at daylight this morning with all his ships and is now in action with Admiral Sturdee's whole fleet, which was coaling.' The suggestion that Sturdee had been caught napping 'sent a shiver up my spine'; but two hours later the 'stern and sombre Oliver wore something which closely resembled a grin. "It's all right, sir; they are all at the bottom."'[25] And indeed all the German ships had been sunk except the cruiser *Dresden*.

The King wrote to Churchill: 'I am delighted at the good news. Sturdee has avenged poor Craddock & the loss of his ships. Please convey my hearty congratulations to Sturdee & his ships for this most opportune victory.'[26] Churchill was generous to Fisher and wrote to him in the admiral's own style: 'My dear – This is your show and your luck. I should only have sent one greyhound [battlecruiser?] this would have done the trick. But it was a sizzling coup. Let us have more victories together and confound all our foes abroad – And (don't forget) – at home.'[27] But Fisher himself was not satisfied that Sturdee had let the *Dresden* escape and quoted his hero: 'When Hardy told Nelson that 15 ships had struck their colours at Trafalgar he said "That won't do – we want the 20"! *and he got them before he died!*'[28]

The success at the Falklands was seen as a triumph for the battlecruiser concept, not least by Fisher himself. He also pointed out that they had saved the day at Heligoland Bight, and that more of them would have prevented the raids on Yarmouth and Scarborough. The four battleships ordered in the 1914 programme had been cancelled at the beginning of the war on the grounds that they would not be completed before the end of 1915. This was not a problem with the two ordered from the Royal Dockyards, but the private yards would demand compensation so the work was continued in a different form. Fisher conceived a plan to use the materials to build two new battlecruisers, the equivalent of the *Queen Elizabeth* class, with six 15-inch guns each. It was only with

Fisher's drive and determination, perhaps revived after four years of rest, that he could even think of getting them finished before the end of 1915. He was helped by the fact that the guns and turrets were already available, and that merchant shipbuilding had stopped, leaving space in the yards. Despite his efforts the two ships, *Repulse* and *Renown*, were not quite finished in time but were launched early in 1916. Churchill would come to know them both well, for very different reasons.

With the elimination of the threat on the high seas, it was possible to move increasing numbers of warships for another project, in the Eastern Mediterranean.

CHAPTER 17

Plans for Attack

From the very first days of the war Churchill was looking for ways to use the navy in an attacking role in the North Sea. Within five days of the start he had produced quite a detailed plan to occupy the Dutch islands and submitted it to Battenberg and Sturdee, the current chief of war staff. He intended to draw out the German destroyers and make them fight with their guns, which were lighter than those fitted to British destroyers. It would also give the short-range C-class submarines 'a part in the oversea warfare from which they are now excluded, and thus compensate to some extent for our deficiencies in numbers of big boats'. He was not worried about the violation of neutrality; the Germans would have to carry out 'a much more tangible violation of Dutch territory to respond'. It is difficult to see how that would have weighed much in the diplomatic balance and it was not explained what would have happened if the Dutch had declared war on Britain. No more was heard of it.[1] By 19 August he had written a memorandum suggesting an attack by aircraft or destroyers on the Kiel Canal which linked Germany with the Baltic. Perhaps inspired by Fisher, he hoped this would allow the British fleet to enter the Baltic even before the High Seas Fleet had been defeated, but he did not explain how an invasion of Britain could be prevented – perhaps he had 'flotilla defence' by submarines and destroyers in mind.[2] Again there was no immediate result as the situation in France and Belgium remained fluid, but more would be heard of the Baltic.

By chance the Admiralty acquired three vessels which mounted quite heavy guns and were suitable, in some respects at least, for inshore work. In 1912 Brazil had ordered three river gunboats for use on the Amazon, with a wide beam, very shallow draft and two six-inch guns in turrets. The country could not pay for them due to a fall in rubber prices and they were put up for sale by Armstrong's yard on Tyneside. As war approached Churchill was concerned about them falling into enemy hands and they were taken over along with the Turkish and other ships, at a cost of £155,000 each. It was soon found that they had their problems, their shallow draft of 4 ft 6 ins meant that they were blown sideways in a moderate wind, and their propellers were larger than the draft which meant they had to operate through a tunnel, which made it impossible to go astern until modifications were made. But they would soon find their uses in the shallow waters off Belgium.[3]

★

After the failure of Churchill's Antwerp enterprise, the way was open for the Germans to occupy most of the rest of Belgium and perhaps secure control of some of the ports on the English Channel. On 16 October, ten days after he left Antwerp, he wrote to Kitchener: 'Now that the operations extend up to the North Sea between Ostend and the advanced defences of Dunkirk, it would be important for the two allied navies to participate in these operations by supporting our left wing and acting with long-range guns on the German right wing.'[4] Rear-Admiral Horace Hood, recently Churchill's naval secretary, was in charge of the new Dover Command and was tasked with obstructing the enemy along the coast. He used the three ex-Brazilian ships, now known as monitors, and after being delayed for two days due to winds they entered the fray supported by cruisers and destroyers. Four German destroyers were sunk when they attacked the force. A U-boat fired a torpedo at one of the monitors, the *Severn*, but it passed under her shallow hull. It was often difficult for the monitors to see the targets beyond the sand dunes, but signalling systems were set up, and two captive balloons were sent out to direct the fire. One of them located an enemy battery but had to descend due to gunfire; it was set up again 5,000 yards further from the line. The enemy advance was stalled, but Churchill was still worried and wrote to Sir John French on 26 October:

> ... how damnable it will be if the enemy settles down for the winter along lines which comprise Calais, Dunkirk or Ostend, there will be continual alarms and greatly added difficulties. We must have him off the Belgian coast, even if we cannot recover Antwerp.
>
> I am getting old ships, with the heaviest guns ready, protected by barges with nets against submarines, so as to dispute the whole seaboard with him. On the 31st instant Revenge, four 13½ inch guns, will come into action if required, and I have a regular fleet of monitors and 'bomb ketches' now organised which they all say hit the Germans hard, and is getting stronger every day.[5]

The French and Belgian armies attempted a counterattack with naval support. As usual the telegrams from the Admiralty showed the First Lord's personal touch. On 27 October he directed Hood to 'husband ammunition till good targets show, but risks must be run and the Allies' left must be supported without fail by the Navy'. The Belgians wanted him to fire more rapidly, but shortage of ammunition was a major factor as ships used far more rounds in a shore bombardment than they would do in a naval battle. Churchill issued the rather ambiguous order: 'Save ammunition where possible, but don't lose any chance of hitting the enemy ... You have full discretion to go ahead.'[6] But the attack failed and the allies had to accept that Ostend was in German hands, though Dunkirk was saved.[7]

It is notoriously difficult to assess the real effects of shore bombardment, especially if the territory involved falls into the hands of the enemy. The official naval history claimed that 'It is scarcely too much to say that the naval assistance for which all three of the allied armies had called had turned the scale.'[8] The army history says very little, merely commenting that a German staff officer had reported that the ships 'furnished valuable support to the defence'. Nevertheless, 'Although shelled at long range from the sea by Admiral Hood's squadron, the German 5th Reserve Division ... nearest the coast, achieved the most success. It actually crossed the Dixmunde-Nieuport railway embankment, which formed the main Belgian line of defence, and secured possession of

Ramscappelle ... beyond.'[9] Churchill did not take sides on this issue in his book, *The World Crisis*, but merely reproduced telegrams between Hood and the Admiralty. But seeds had been sown about the possibilities of army-navy co-operation in coastal waters.

★

Charles M. Schwab of the Bethlehem Steel Company arrived from the United States in the liner *Olympic*, having seen the sinking of battleship *Audacious* off the north coast of Ireland. He reached the Admiralty on 3 November, at just the right moment: Churchill was looking for ways to take the offensive, while Fisher had just been installed as First Sea Lord and was receptive to new ideas. Among other business Schwab mentioned that he had four twin 14-inch turrets for Germany nearing completion, prevented from delivery by the British blockade. Churchill and Fisher snapped them up as it would bypass the usually protracted process of making new turrets, and they had ideas about how to use them while still staying within the deadline for the projected end of the war. D'Eyncourt, the Director of Naval Construction, began design work on two armoured monitors to be built in four months with a very light draft of 10 feet to operate inshore and protected by 'crinolines' or anti-torpedo bulges. He and his staff worked hard to produce a design by 17 November, but it was for a very ugly, unbalanced ship which horrified conventional naval architects. Because of the bulges resistance in the water would be very high, they would be very difficult to control and would be blown sideways like the Brazilian ships. Four ships were ordered, coded 'Styx' to conceal their function, and were ready by the middle of 1915.

The Brazilian ships were already known as monitors by the beginning of 1914. The name originated with the American Civil War ironclad, which her inventor John Ericson had intended as a 'monitor' or warning to other naval powers, She battled with the Confederate *Virginia* in 1862 and introduced the gun turret to the world's navies, but the concept had long since been left behind by naval development. It was now revived to mean a ship dominated by heavy guns, usually in a single turret, on the smallest practicable hull, protected as far as possible by armour and torpedo bulges, but ultimately cheap and expendable, unlike a battleship. The name also reflected the American origin of the guns, but when the Admiralty named the four ships after American commanders it was not appreciated as undermining their neutrality. They were re-named after historic British generals, perhaps reflecting their role with the army.

Meanwhile more monitors were ordered, in a programme which was largely controlled by the availability of guns and their mountings. On 11 December 1914 Churchill ordered eight more using spare 13.5 and 15-inch guns, but that proved impracticable as mountings would take too long to produce. Instead 12-inch guns were found in older pre-Dreadnoughts and were fitted in the *Lord Clive* class. However, two 15-inch turrets were freed because the new battlecruisers *Repulse* and *Renown* needed only three each, rather than four for the battleships they replaced. These were fitted in the *Marshal Soult* and *Marshal Ney*, named after Napoleon's commanders, but Churchill and Fisher made the mistake of using unreliable diesel engines. Early in 1915 Fisher turned his attention to smaller monitors using obsolete 9.2-inch guns and 6-inch guns which had to be removed from the *Queen Elizabeths* because their low positons in the hull made them impossible to use. In all 33 monitors were ordered during the Churchill-Fisher period, plus the three Brazilians and two Norwegian coast defence vessels; only two more would be built in the rest of the war.[10]

★

There were recurring plans to launch a land offensive along the Belgian coast, but it was complicated by the fact that the northern end of the great trench line was occupied by the French rather than the British. On 10 December Churchill pointed out that from the 14th onwards the tides would be suitable to support an army advance to Ostend, with a force including two pre-Dreadnoughts, the three monitors and six destroyers. After that the taking of Zeebrugge would eliminate a submarine base and 'add greatly to the safety of our ships'. But Sir John French could not muster French support in time and by the 18th it was too late: '... no ships can fire tomorrow. Monitors alone would be knocked out by the enemy's batteries. … It is not justifiable to expose *Majestic* to submarine risk unless to support a real movement in which every risk will be run and ample support provided.'[11] On 13 January the War Council (which had been established in November 1914 and included Asquith, Grey, Lloyd George, Kitchener and Churchill) discussed the Zeebrugge plan and Churchill agreed that 'the clearance of the coast would be a first class victory', but efforts were diverted elsewhere.[12]

As the stalemate on the Western Front was prolonged and the High Seas Fleet refused to come out, Churchill revived a plan to provoke the Germans. In the spring of 1913 Rear-Admiral Lewis Bayly had been given the task of planning an attack on the island of Borkum – the most westerly of the German Friesian islands and more than 20 miles from the German mainland, which would have made it difficult to use land-based artillery against the operation. Bayly had the help of Captain Arthur Leveson and Colonel George Aston who would later take initial command of the marines at Antwerp. They were given a room on the ground floor of the Admiralty building and had it cleared of sample naval uniforms. Bayly commissioned a plasticine model of the area including rivers, railways and canals, and invited Churchill and Grey the Foreign Secretary to stand on a table and view it.[13] Churchill showed the plan to Jellicoe as Second Sea Lord, but he 'expressed a view unfavourable to the report'. It was not the end of Jellicoe's opposition. On the eve of war he went on: 'After a consideration of the proposals for seizing Borkum or Sylt … I am not of the opinion that the advantages to be derived from the use of such a base are worth the cost in men and ships of capture. It is doubtful whether the Army could spare the men for such an attempt even if it was considered desirable …'.[14]

Meanwhile Fisher had a grander scheme for an attack in the Baltic, which he pushed harder after his return to the Admiralty in October 1914. It was based on an attack on Germany from the north. He compared it with Frederick the Great's campaign in the Seven Years' War, when he was invading France while threatened by Russia from the east. 'He knew that a blow in force from the Baltic could at any time prevent him from striking right and left, and it was in dread from this from Russia that he began by pressing us [the British] so hard to provide him with a covering fleet in that sea.'[15] Fisher wanted to land Russian troops on a ten-mile stretch of the Pomeranian coast only 90 miles from Berlin.[16] He planned to use up to 50,000 mines to make the North Sea uninhabitable to the Germans and thus prevent an invasion of Britain, though nothing like that number were available and Churchill suggested it was more like a lottery whether they would sink anything if sown indiscriminately.

It is difficult to believe that the Baltic scheme would have worked. Entry to the sea might have inspired a German invasion of Denmark which would have cut off most of the route. It would be very difficult to co-ordinate the efforts of the British navy and the Russian army, divided not only by culture and operational practice but by language and even alphabet. Landing on a hostile shore was far more difficult than Fisher allowed for, and it was not credible that the Germans would have left vital sectors of their coast undefended once the threat had arisen. Nevertheless Churchill did not criticise it severely, perhaps to retain the support of Fisher for his own schemes. Churchill wrote in December 1914: 'I am wholly with you about the Baltic. But you must close up this side first. You must take an island and block them in, *à la* Wilson; or you must break the canal or the locks, or you must cripple their fleet in a general action.'[17] Sir Arthur Wilson, highly respected as a tactician, stated on 10 December: 'I do not think we can do any good in the Baltic with any combined fleet of French and English such as we could make up even with the help of the Italians in the Mediterranean without reducing the North Sea fleet below the safe limit until we have found some means of greatly reducing the danger from submarines, or else of completely blocking the canal.'[18]

Churchill even allowed Fisher to order three more 'large light cruisers' which were intended to support the Baltic scheme. The *Glorious* and *Courageous* were armed with four 15-inch guns each, with the speed and armour of cruisers; they may have been intended to use their speed for protection and to bombard the German defences. The *Furious* was even stranger, with two 18-inch guns. Though he had consented to them, Churchill called them 'an old man's children'.[19] To others the three ships were 'the weird sisters' and no one could find any use for them in their original configuration until they were eventually converted to aircraft carriers.

★

Churchill's island plan, as he admitted, was descended from the one which had left him incredulous when Sir Arthur Wilson presented it at the CID in August 1911, but now it was better presented and planned and with different targets. He rejected any idea of taking the fortified island of Heligoland as 'the most difficult to take and miserably small when taken'. It focussed on two separate islands, Sylt and Borkum, which fulfilled four essential conditions.

(a) They cannot be attacked from the mainland, except across several miles of sand intersected by channels, the whole flooded twice daily by the tide. This means they cannot be attacked at all, except in boats and form the sea.
(b) They cannot be bombarded at any point by heavy howitzers of field guns.
(c) They contain deep water anchorages (6 to 8 fathoms) sheltered in all weathers, out of range of howitzers and field guns, and
(d) They are large enough to give ample elbow room for all our purposes once we have gained them.[20]

Sylt is seven to twelve miles off the coast of Schleswig Holstein, which Germany had taken from Denmark in 1864, and Churchill had studied it in some detail. It was nearly 23 miles long but only half a mile wide except in the middle. It was also dominated by dunes with about 3,500 inhabitants who mostly depended on fishing, though it was also a popular holiday resort. According to Churchill on 2 December, 'On the land side it is protected by 8,000 to 14,000 yards of sand covered twice daily by the tide. These sands, the neighbouring island of Rom and the mainland opposite Lister Deep for 6,000 yards inland, can be dominated by the fire of warships lying in Lister or Romer Deep. This fire will also prevent reinforcements being brought to the enemy from one part of the island to another.' He proposed to land a brigade of 4,000 infantry on the north of the island and to establish a destroyer, submarine and aircraft base from which the German coast could be harried and 'to maintain a regular observation and control upon the debouches of the Heligoland Bight, thus preventing any raid or invasion from putting to sea unperceived and without full warning'. Old battleships of the *Majestic* or *Royal Sovereign* classes were to bombard, with the three monitors closer inshore – though several days of calm and fair weather would be needed to get these craft across more than 300 miles of sea.[21]

By 3 January 1915 Churchill had an expanded and more detailed scheme to take Sylt by landing 12,000 infantry in flat-bottomed craft plated against rifle fire and armed with machine guns. Monitors would carry out the advance bombardment from shallow water, supported by cruisers further off, and that would silence the German batteries. Destroyers, mines and indicator nets would protect against submarines. The force would advance under cover of night and protected by smoke. Meanwhile a fleet of 40 submarines and 60 destroyers would keep the High Seas Fleet cooped up.[22]

The alternative island was Borkum, which was situated at the mouth of the River Ems leading to Emden. It was 5¾ miles long and 3½ broad and consisted of two parts joined artificially. It was largely sand dunes and most of the 3,100 inhabitants were seafarers and their families living in Borkum village, but the island was also a resort, attracting 20,000 summer visitors per year before the war. The ever-aggressive Keyes reported on 2 January 1915 that Borkum could not be 'commanded by [German] gun fire from the mainland or the island of Juist'. He presumed the approaches to Emden would be blocked up, and did not think 'the defence of Borkum from seaward would be a difficult matter provided a sufficient number of submarines, destroyers, trawlers and aircraft can be maintained there in an efficient condition'. He advocated a force of nine C- and nine E-class submarines with two depot ships. He planned to berth the ships in the Fischer Balje which he believed had recently been deepened. The eastern flank should be mined.[23]

Two days later Churchill wrote to Jellicoe that they should take advantage of the 'priceless information' from decoded messages while the advantage lasted:

But everything convinces me that that we must take Borkum as soon as full and careful preparation can be made. The possession of an oversea base quadruples our submarines making all our B and C boats available for service in German waters. It is the key not only to a satisfactory naval policy, but to future military action whether by the invasion of Schleswig Holstein or (better perhaps) Oldenburg. Troops for Borkum will be available: and although the capture is a difficult operation I am sure we ought to make the attempt, and am also confident that success will be obtained.[24]

He elaborated a week later:

Having taken the island in question, we must make it the most dreaded lair of submarines in the world, and also the centre of an active mining policy .... Once established there we should confront him with all the ugliest propositions. If he sends mine-sweepers out destroyers will sink them. If he sends transports covered by bombarding battleships, what more could our submarines ask? ... Our position there would be intolerable to him. He would have to come out to attack us not at any point he chose on our sparsely guarded coast, but where he would have to face a concentrated swarm of submarines.[25]

The island projects became an obsession. As Rear-Admiral Oliver tried to get some well-earned sleep after a long day in the War Room, Churchill would often look in and 'tell me how he would capture Borkum or Sylt. If I did not interrupt or ask questions he could capture Borkum in 20 minutes.' By 9 March Churchill had fixed a firm date for an operation and wrote to Jellicoe: 'the First Sea Lord is making extraordinary exertions to complete six monitors by May 1st, three 14-inch, two 15-inch, and one 12-inch. Allowing a fortnight to haul and veer on, the attack on Borkum should take place on or about the 15th of May ... in three days the capture will be complete; in six the new base will be established.'[26] But by that time Churchill was deeply embroiled in another campaign, and he would not be at the Admiralty much longer.

★

Churchill never completely dropped the Borkum and Sylt schemes. Even after the failure at the Dardanelles and his own dismissal from the Admiralty, he wrote detailed plans in July 1917 while out of office. If these were not practicable, he suggested artificial islands instead. 'A sufficient number of flat-bottomed barges or caissons made, not of steel but of concrete, should be prepared in the Humber, at Harwich and in the Wash, the Medway and Thames. ... on arrival at the buoys marking the island, sea-cocks would be opened and they would settle down on the bottom. ... by this means a torpedo and weather-proof harbour, like an atoll, would be created in the open sea, with regular pens for the destroyers and submarines, and launching platforms for aeroplanes.'[27]

However from his new office as Minister of Munitions he did not support the one apparently successful amphibious operation of the war, when his old protégé Roger Keyes raided Zeebrugge on 22 April 1918. It provided some cheer at the height of German advances on the Western Front, but did not completely block the harbour entrance. In any case, as Churchill argued, Ostend and Zeebrugge were not, as some argued, 'the source of submarine warfare' whose destruction was vital. 'As a matter of fact, these harbours ... have never been and never could be the main base of submarine warfare' but were merely 'serious annoyances'.[28]

CHAPTER 18

Work and Conflict

Churchill's ten months in charge of the wartime Admiralty, from August
1914 to May 1915, were perhaps the most active and intense of his life,
with the possible exception of 1940. He went well beyond the normal
scope of the Admiralty in setting up an air base at Dunkirk and directing naval and land warfare there, taking over the defence of London
against bombing, organising and to some extent commanding troops at
Antwerp, and initiating work which led to the development of the tank.
He was often absent from the office on trips to the Dunkirk base, to
try to relieve Antwerp, and at the Western Front – though there were
far fewer visits to naval bases. Despite all that he kept up his constant
stream of memos on every aspect of the navy and of the defence of the
country. Even Lord Fisher, no sluggard himself, wrote that 'His power
of work is absolutely amazing!'[1]

Churchill was in personal control. As he wrote: 'I accepted full
responsibility for bringing about successful results, and in that spirit I
exercised a close general supervision over everything that was done or
proposed. Further, I claimed and exercised an unlimited power of suggestion and initiative over the whole field, subject only to the approval
and agreement of the First Sea Lord on all operative orders.'[2] But to
start with at least, he did not expect the pressure of war to become
an excuse for shoddy administration. On the fourth day of the war he
asked Hood to inform the staff that '… the adoption of regular and
careful methods is enjoined in all departments. In particular thrift and

scrupulous attention to details are the mark of efficient administration in war.'[3] Though he had a strong hand in naval strategy, he tended to pay less attention to matters of material and personnel than in peace, perhaps because originally he believed that it would be a short war in which far-reaching changes would have no effect. He modified that view in May 1915 when he minuted the heads of departments that 'for the present it is assumed that the war will not end before the 31st December 1916' and that 'All Admiralty arrangements and plans should be prepared on this basis ...'.[4] But by then his time at the Admiralty was nearly over.

There were far fewer meetings of the main Admiralty Board after the war started, only three in the first six months of 1915 before Churchill left.[5] Sir Graham Greene, the permanent secretary, agreed that 'A Board is not the place nor the manner of conducting business such as that transacted between the First Sea Lord and the Chief of the staff, and if all members of the Board had to be consulted about orders to the fleet efficient executive action would be much impaired, while the administrative duties of the members of the Board would seriously suffer.'[6] Churchill put it far more strongly: 'To collect a set of petty potentates sitting round a table every one of whom has a right to record a minute of dissent, and apply that to the conduct of the operations of war, full of hazard and often turning out wrong ... would, I am sure, be absolutely an impossible way of working.'[7] The junior sea lords complained that they were 'too much set aside and not consulted enough'.[8] 'The sea lords are not the accepted advisers of the First Lord on naval war policy. They may not be and in many cases have not been informed of what that policy until after it has been embarked upon and even on technical matters within the scope of the departments under their individual superintendence First Lord can and does consult subordinates to the exclusion of the superintending members of the Board.'[9] To Churchill they were merely 'a reserve of naval opinion ... but they did not take part in the daily executive decisions'.[10]

Instead Churchill relied on his war group to make the major operational decisions. According to Greene, 'At the commencement of the war the First Lord arranged for daily meetings in the War Room over which he presided. The meetings comprised the First Sea Lord, the Second Sea Lord, the Chief of Staff and the Permanent Secretary. These meetings were held in the first place every morning and evening when the important events of the war were discussed and general orders determined.'[11]

Apart from Churchill himself, this inner circle was led by the First Sea Lord. The colourless Sir Francis Bridgeman had been retired from the post in December 1912, ostensibly due to ill health but also because he was not compatible with Churchill's style. His successor was Prince Louis of Battenberg, who had been born in Austria in 1854, a grandson of Queen Victoria and a member of the minor German royalty in Hesse. Determined on a sea career, he entered the Royal Navy as a cadet in 1868, two years before Germany was unified. His royal connections, his slight German accent and his intelligence attracted suspicion, but he rose through the ranks. He served as secretary to the predecessor of the CID and as director of naval intelligence before being appointed to command a cruiser squadron in 1905. He was Second Sea Lord from December 1911. He was a good administrator and he got on well with Churchill and understood his intentions, while offering sensible and constructive criticism – he was the only one of four First Sea Lords with whom Churchill could work well; he wrote of Battenberg: 'He was a thoroughly trained and accomplished Staff Officer, with a gift of clear and lucid statement and all that thoroughness and patient industry which we have never underestimated in the German race.' But by October Churchill was having doubts and was 'pouring his woes' into Asquith's ears; the latter thought that 'Battenberg will have to make as graceful a bow as he can to the British public'.[12] Fisher, who had everything to gain by Battenberg's retirement, wrote in October that the Prince was 'played out', and Churchill blamed him for exonerating Milne over the Goeben affair.[13]

Sir Frederick Hamilton was appointed Second Sea Lord on 28 July 1914 in succession to Jellicoe. He was well-connected; according to Fisher he was 'a bosom friend of the King, who calls him by his Christian name and who lends him a cottage at Sandringham ...'.[14]

He had his hands full with his regular job of mobilising, recruiting, training and deploying the navy's personnel during wartime, but he had recent sea experience as a squadron commander with the Home Fleet, and he attended the War Group as understudy to the First Sea Lord. This arrangement continued until 1917, when Wester Wemyss came in as Deputy First Sea Lord. Until then, Wemyss pointed out, 'should the First Sea Lord for any reason be absent from the Admiralty, the whole of the burden and responsibility of the war devolved automatically on the Second Sea Lord, whose duties in connection with personnel did not allow him sufficient time to discuss staff matters'.[15] This goes some way to explain failures in communication which led to the escape of the *Goeben* and the loss of Cradock's squadron off Cornel in 1914.

Henry Oliver was director of intelligence until October 1914, naval secretary for about three weeks, then chief of war staff from 7 November. 'Stern and sombre', he held the Churchillian view that 'if you never did anything except what the text-books bore you out in, you would never do anything in war, because you would always find a reason for not doing a thing somewhere'.[16] Sir Arthur Wilson wrote of him: 'He is a man of marvellous knowledge of almost all the branches of the navy, and has a most extraordinary power of working longer hours, I think, than anyone I have ever seen.'[17] Oliver would need that while working with Churchill, and certainly his whole life was devoted to the task. He wrote: 'I had the library in the First Lord's official house for my office with three windows looking out on the Horse Guards Parade. I had a camp bed in the corner and a tin bath. I went up to Churchill's bedroom as soon as I was dressed about 7.15 am. He would be sitting up in bed with a big cigar working at papers and telegrams.' In the evening, 'I went to bed generally about 12.30 and Churchill would often look in on his way to bed ...'.

At the centre of the tactical scheme was the War Room, a development of the one set up by Fisher in 1908 and revived for the 1912 manoeuvres. By 1914 the War Room itself was in a large former bedroom of Admiralty House with the chief of war staff in the library next door. The director of the operations division was in a smaller bedroom and the war registry, which was 'responsible for the correct issue of all telegraphic orders' in a medium-sized one.[18] It covered a far wider range of activities than ever before. 'From the middle of September onwards we began to be at our fullest strain. The great map of the world which covered one whole wall of the War Room now presented a remarkable experience. As many as twenty separate enterprises and undertakings dependent entirely upon sea power were proceeding simultaneously in different parts of the globe.'[19] At the start there was a problem with the security of the room, according to Oliver:

> Then I went to a big room near my office where there was an immense chart of the world covering the whole of one wall with pins and flags showing the positions of all ships. I would then shift the flags showing the places of any important movements to incorrect places. This was a necessity because Churchill and Fisher and other dignitaries brought in MPs and lords and cabinet ministers and bishops and all sorts of club gossips and editors etc. to see the map and an incorrect map impressed them just as much. I kept correct charts covered up in a chest in my office and when I was not in it or the chairwoman was dusting, the duty captain came in and kept watch.[20]

This had to stop. Churchill wrote: 'when the war broke out the War Group Room, where the operations were conducted from, was crowded by an enormous concourse of people who came in while others were working there: that our most secret plans and our dispositions of the fleet were on the wall, and all sorts of secret matters were being transacted and I took the very drastic action at the beginning of the war to cut down the number of persons who had access to that room'.[21] So, according to Cecil Lambert the Fourth Sea Lord, 'A list was put on the door in Mr Churchill's own handwriting of people who were allowed to go there and the names of the junior lords were crossed out and the names of the civil members of the board were crossed out.'[22]

From the War Room Churchill could enjoy the thrill of distant battle.

> There can be few purely mental experiences more charged with cold excitement than to follow, almost from minute to minute, the phases of a great naval action from the silent rooms of the Admiralty. Out on the blue water in the fighting

ships amid the stunning detonations of the cannonade, fractions of the event unfold themselves to the corporeal eye. ... But in Whitehall only the clock ticks, and quiet men enter with quick steps laying slips of pencilled paper before other men equally silent who draw lines and scribble calculations, and point with the finger or make brief subdued comments. Telegram succeeds telegram at a few minutes' interval as they are picked up and decoded, often in the wrong sequence, frequently of dubious import; and out of these a picture always flickering and changing rises in the mind, and imagination strikes out around it at every stage flashes of hope or fear.[23]

★

There was a growing campaign against Battenberg in the nation at large. Admiral Lord Charles Beresford, Fisher's implacable opponent, had to deny that he had suggested 'that the First Sea Lord cannot be trusted to maintain the interests of this country because of his German descent' in various clubs and other places.[24] But there was anti-German hysteria among the public – shops with German names were looted and families, including eventually the royals, changed their names. In October Churchill was aware of a newspaper campaign 'for raising suspicion against Prince Louis', backed he believed by Beresford and the editor of the *Morning Post*.[25] There were anonymous letters and by the end of the month Prince Louis had been 'driven to the painful conclusion that at this juncture my birth and parentage have the effect of impairing in some respects my usefulness on the Board of Admiralty' and offered his resignation.[26] Churchill was fulsome in his praise despite his doubts about Battenberg:

> The Navy of today, and still more the navy of tomorrow, bears the imprint of your work. The enormous impending influx of capital ships, the score of 32-knot cruisers, the destroyers and submarines unequalled in modern construction which are now coming to hand, are the results of labours which we have had in common, and in which the Board of Admiralty owes so much to your aid.[27]

Asquith regretted 'our poor blue-eyed German will have to go, and (as Winston says) he will be reinforced by two well-plucked chickens of 74 and 72'.[28] The first of these was Fisher, who had been advising Churchill since the start of the war; five days before it was declared he came to London and had 'some momentous conversations'. After that he 'constantly saw Mr Churchill'.[29] It was a difficult job to persuade the King to consent to his reappointment. According to his private secretary, 'The First Lord then suggested to His Majesty that Lord Fisher should be brought back to the Admiralty as successor to Prince Louis .... This proposal was a great surprise to the King who pointed out to Mr Churchill his objections to the appointment. Lord Fisher has not the confidence of the Navy: he is over 73 years of age. When First Sea Lord he no doubt did much for the Navy but he created a state of unrest and bad feeling among the officers of the service.' They went through a list of other candidates including Sir Hedworth Meux, Sir Henry Jackson and Sir Frederick Sturdee, but Churchill rejected them all.[30] The King insisted on taking the matter up with the Prime Minister before he approved it, which was about as far as a constitutional sovereign could reasonably go in such a matter. Asquith supported Churchill as he did not want his resignation, for he had 'a most intimate knowledge of the navy'.[31] On 29 October the King finally agreed as 'he could not ... oppose his minsters in this selection but felt it his duty to record his protest'.[32] Next day Churchill took Fisher round the War Room just as the situation in South America approached a crisis: 'I ... went over with him on the great map the positions and tasks of every vessel in our immense organisation. It took more than two hours.'[33]

The second of the 'chickens' was Sir Arthur Wilson, retired as First Sea Lord in 1912. At first Churchill suggested him as chief of staff, an irony in view of his opposition to the setting up of such a body.[34] Instead he came in with Fisher in an advisory capacity, though apparently he had had some role before that. Immediately after Battenberg's resignation he wrote: 'I think you had better leave me to go on working much as I am doing now, except that I should like to have a room set apart for me near the War Room, and a confidential clerk well acquainted with the different departments who could get me any information I want. I would then work simply as Fisher's slave to tackle any problems he likes to set me.'[35] Later he testified: 'It was my place to help the First Lord and First Sea Lord as much as I could ... Discussion went on from day to day of all these different schemes, and it was always a question of getting over difficulties which we saw in carrying out any of them.'[36] Churchill wrote to Jellicoe on 11 January 1915: 'Sir Arthur Wilson rules our councils in tactics and is incomparably superior to anyone I have seen.'[37]

At first Churchill and Fisher seemed to work well together, and Churchill wrote to Jellicoe in January 1915: 'The machine is working far better than it has ever worked before.'[38] Under Fisher the War Group meetings were suspended and replaced by more formal conferences which were summoned by the First Lord.[39] As well as Churchill and Fisher they were attended by Sir Arthur Wilson, the Chief of Staff, the Permanent Secretary and the Naval Secretary to the First Lord. – Sir Frederick Hamilton was no longer invited as Fisher suspected him of trying to undermine his reforms. According to Churchill, '… the War Group in its new form brought all our opinions more effectively into common stock and most of the proposals for the movement of ships'.[40] Sir Graham Greene testified: 'At these meetings a great variety of questions relating to the war were brought forward and discussed and decisions arrived at, many of which were embodied at the time in minutes dictated by the First Lord and concurred in by the First Sea Lord.'[41] This hints at the growing rift between the First Lord and the First Sea Lord. There were two huge egos in the same department, or as Greene put it, 'two very active and strong personalities in the position of First Lord and First Sea Lord'.[42] Churchill was not used to strong character in his chief adviser; Fisher was not used to a dynamic First Lord. For a time he tolerated his position due to the necessity of war: 'In the peace organisation I should say that my position with the First Lord as First Sea Lord was one of close communion. If I could not agree, I should say, "Well, I do not think it is a good thing for me to be here," and I should go away; but in war I should say to myself, "Now, look here; here is a very big thing going on and it does not do to have any quarrels or partings now. It is too big a business." And I should to a large extent sacrifice my views unless it led to anything disastrous.'[43]

Ostensibly the main cause of dispute was the Dardanelles Campaign. Fisher testified: 'Mr Churchill and I worked in absolute accord until it came to the question of the Dardanelles.'[44] But in addition there was what some called an 'objectionable change of practice' and Greene admitted that 'While Mr Churchill was First Lord of the Admiralty he would initiate orders to the fleet and consult the First Sea Lord afterwards.'[45] Greene hinted that from his long experience this was unusual. 'I think that very few First Lords would attempt to deal with the initiation of orders to the fleet, they would probably prefer to indicate their views on a point of policy and ask the First Sea Lord to give those instructions to the fleet.'[46] Fisher wrote: 'Winston has so monopolised all initiative in the Admiralty – and fires off such a multitude of purely departmental memos ... that my colleagues are no longer "superintending Lords" but only "the First Lord's Registry"!'[47] Churchill summed up the decline in the relationship: '... his letters were couched in an affectionate and paternal style. "My beloved Winston," they began, ending usually with a variation of "Yours to a cinder," "Yours till Hell freezes," or "Till charcoal sprouts." ... Alas, there was a day when Hell froze and charcoal sprouted and friendship was reduced to cinders; when "My beloved Winston" had given place to "First Lord: I can no longer be your colleague."'[48]

It was largely a question of initiative. In May 1915 Hamilton, Admiral Tudor, the Third Sea Lord, and Captain Lambert, the Fourth Sea Lord, supported Fisher and claimed that 'the present method of directing the distribution of the fleet, and the conduct of the war by which the orders for controlling movements and supplies appear to be largely taken out of the hands of the First Sea Lord'. Churchill replied that 'No order of the slightest consequence' was ever issued without Fisher's agreement, but the three sea lords were not satisfied: '... in most cases action has been initiated by yourself and referred to the First Sea Lord for concurrence. What we maintain is that all such orders should be initiated by the First Sea Lord and referred to you for criticism or concurrence.' Churchill did not accept this. 'Had I neglected to propose it in default of the First Sea Lord's initiative, injury would have resulted to vital interests. It is better that the First Sea Lord should make proposals, and the First Lord criticise them or concur. But no rule can be laid down.'[49]

Then Churchill was accused of a much more serious breach of etiquette over a signal to move ships from the Dardanelles to Taranto, marked 'First Lord to see after action.'[50] This allegedly was the last straw and the cause of Fisher's resignation after he had already withdrawn it several times. Lambert, the Fourth Sea Lord, claimed:

> When Lord Fisher had left, Mr Churchill sent for me. I was with him for several hours and he asked me if I would go over to Lord Fisher the next morning [Sunday] and endeavour to persuade him to come back. I was unwilling because I did not suppose I anything I could say would influence Lord Fisher, but as Mr Churchill put it to me in that way I went. Lord Fisher was very excited. He told me a long story which I cannot remember, but the gist of it was his annoyance at this particular telegram on which was written in Mr Churchill's handwriting, 'The First Lord to see after action.'[51]

Churchill denied this, but Fisher's resignation had already damaged him beyond repair and his position at the Admiralty was doomed.

CHAPTER 19

Forcing the Straits

On 17 August, a week after the *Goeben* and *Breslau* had reached Turkey, Asquith reported that at a Cabinet meeting 'Winston, in his most bellicose mood, is all for sending a torpedo flotilla through the Dardanelles – to threaten and if necessary sink the *Goeben* and her consort.' This was ruled out on the grounds that nothing should be done to antagonise Turkey.[1] But by the end of the month Churchill expected war and he arranged joint talks with the War Office to 'examine and work out a plan for the seizure by means of a Greek army of adequate strength or the Gallipoli peninsula, with a view to admitting a British fleet to the Sea of Marmora' – though Greece had not joined the war at this stage. Major-General Callwell of the War Office reported that any attack was likely to be 'an extremely difficult operation of war' and suggested 60,000 men would be needed.[2]

War was declared on 31 October and next day Churchill ordered the commander on the spot, Vice-Admiral Sackville Carden, to mount a 'demonstration' by shelling the outer forts from a range of 12,000 to 24,000 yards, with the ships keeping under way all the time.[3] It lasted for about ten minutes before the ships withdrew, and many considered it to be a mistake which would only alert the Turks. Churchill, however, defended it on the grounds that a squadron had been waiting in the area for months and 'It was natural that fire should be opened upon the enemy as it would be on the fronts of hostile armies', and that it was necessary to know the range of the Turkish guns – though probably not much could be learned in ten minutes of long-range fire as the enemy barely had time to respond.[4]

Apart from Churchill's desire to avenge the humiliation over the *Goeben* affair, there was much to be gained by a major attack and passage through the Dardanelles. It was believed that a fleet off Constantinople would threaten the city and force Turkey out of the war. It would make a link with Russia, allowing her to export huge quantities of grain to pay for the war and feed the west. The Russia armies were desperately short of supplies including rifles and that could be rectified from the industrial power of the west. It would impress wavering potential allies such as Greece and to a lesser extent Italy, and deter potential enemies such as Bulgaria. Through Rumania it would open up the Danube which would allow British sea power to penetrate the heart of Europe. Above all, it would lead away from the increasingly futile stalemate on the Western Front.

On 25 November Churchill tried to enlist Kitchener's interest when he told the War Council that 'the ideal method of defending Egypt was by an attack on the Gallipoli peninsula' – though it was 'a very difficult operation requiring a large force'. Kitchener only agreed that some kind of diversion against the Turks might be useful, but the time was not ripe.[5] Though Churchill had been accumulating transport in Egypt in case it was required for an expedition, he decided to put the idea aside for now.[6]

The situation changed on the second day of 1915 when a telegram arrived from the British ambassador in Petrograd, stating that the Russians were hard pressed in the Caucasus and would appreciate a diversion against Turkey. Kitchener agreed that 'the only place that a demonstration might have some effect in stopping reinforcements going east would be the Dardanelles'. Fisher also agreed with his usual emphasis: 'I CONSIDER THE ATTACK ON TURKEY HOLDS THE FIELD! But ONLY if it's IMMEDIATE! However it won't be!'[7] On the 4th, though writing more temperately, he went further: 'the naval advantages of the possession of Constantinople and the getting of wheat from the Black Sea are so overwhelming that I consider Colonel Hankey's plan for Turkish operations vital and imperative and very pressing'.[8] From this point the plans began to spiral towards a conclusion, with

Churchill usually at the centre. He was already thinking of much more than a demonstration, telegraphing Carden:

Do you consider the forcing of the Dardanelles by ships alone a practicable operation? It is assumed older battleships fitted with mine-bumpers would be used, preceded by colliers or other merchant craft and mine-bumpers and sweepers. Importance of results would justify severe loss.[9]

The admiral's reply was generally favourable. He thought that the Dardanelles could not be rushed but 'might be forced by extended operations with large number of ships'. Next day Churchill replied that these views were shared by 'high authorities here' – Jackson and Oliver but not, as it transpired, Fisher – and asked him what force would be needed. Carden's plan, drawn up by an up-and-coming captain of marines, William Godfrey, arrived on the 11th. It envisaged four stages over about a month – the 'total reduction of the defences at the entrance', the clearing of defences just inside the Straits, the clearing of the Chanak Narrows and the clearing of the minefield above that which would open the passage to the Sea of Marmara. Twelve battleships would be needed, including four with mine-bumpers, plus three battlecruisers, cruisers, destroyers and submarines. Frequent reconnaissance by seaplanes would be essential; there would be a large expenditure of ammunition. This, according to Churchill, 'made a great impression on everyone who saw it. It was in its details an entirely novel proposition.'[10]

Churchill reported to the War Council on the 13th: 'The sense of Admiral Carden's reply was that it was impossible to rush the Dardanelles, but … it might be possible to demolish the forts one by one.' Besides the three modern warships, he suggested pre-Dreadnoughts, some of which were on trade protection and others about to be scrapped to save on personnel.[11] Lloyd George liked it, Kitchener thought it was worth trying. With his long Middle East experience he was always wary of losing face with an obvious failure but that could be concealed: 'We could leave off the bombardment if it did not prove effective.'[12] Fisher and Wilson were strangely silent, apparently confused about their role under the authority of their minister. Fisher testified later: 'I did not think it would tend towards good relations between the First Lord and myself nor to the smooth working of the Board of Admiralty to raise objections in the War Council's discussions. My opinion being known to Mr Churchill in what I regarded as the proper constitutional way, I preferred thereafter to remain silent.' Wilson claimed: '... it was not my business to interfere, and if they decided on a plan all I had to do was to help them to the best of my ability'.[13] But the members of the council took this silence for assent. Asquith even thought of Churchill, Fisher and Wilson as 'the naval trinity' and did not seem to suspect their growing differences.[14] The meeting decided that 'the Admiralty should prepare for a naval expedition in February to bombard and take the Gallipoli Peninsula with Constantinople as its objective'. This was ambiguous: Asquith thought it was only ordering the Admiralty to get ready for the expedition; Churchill believed that it was an order to go ahead, and he proceeded accordingly.[15] He issued orders for concentrating the fleet, which he believed could not be delayed, and allocated ships to the task.[16]

★

Underlying all this was the question of whether modern armoured warships with long-range guns could take on fortifications on land. The navy knew the Dardanelles forts quite well; apart from passing warships the naval attaché often had a chance to see them from steamers going up and down the straits. Rear-Admiral Arthur Limpus served as naval adviser to the Turkish government up to 9 September 1914 and knew the area well. Fisher took a traditional view about forts: 'I was unable to give the Dardanelles proposal any welcome, for there was the Nelsonic dictum, "any sailor who attacked fort was a fool".'[17] But there were new factors. Modern warships were heavily armoured and were not vulnerable to red-hot shot which could set a wooden ship alight. They had much longer-range guns with explosive charges which could be devastating in the right conditions. Sir Arthur Wilson was more ambiguous than Fisher: 'It has been often proclaimed as a maxim, but I have always considered that there are many cases in which it was necessary that ships should undertake the bombardment of forts, and it has occurred in every war.'[18] 'In the old days the firing of ships was very inferior in accuracy to the firing of forts, and now by the improvement of rangefinders and telescope sights and all the applications of control, the accuracy of ships' firing has been practically the same as firing from the shore.'[19]

The only modern experience of guns against forts was from Belgium. Oliver agreed that 'high angle fire at Antwerp, Namur and Liege' had weighed on his mind. 'The Dardanelles forts were big forts with a good deal of masonry work. They were fairly good targets, and there was something tangible to shoot at. They were not modern forts. I thought that a large shell with a high explosive would have a considerable effect on them.'[20] Churchill remembered that in 1913 a model of a 9.2-inch gun was set up on the island of Colonsay and bombarded. He watched from the *Enchantress* while it was knocked out more quickly than expected.[21] He remembered his Belgian experience: 'I was in Antwerp at the time, and I was enormously struck by the sudden collapse of the morale of the Belgian army when they saw these forts, in which they had trusted, which they had been told throughout Europe by all the experts were impregnable, collapsing day after day, one after another, step by step. … their hearts were absolutely broken by the sudden collapse of these forts …'.[22] He did not mention how he had seen the Dervish forts demolished by naval gunnery during the Nile campaign, but perhaps that was at the back of his mind. But the Belgian experience was with land-based howitzers, not low-trajectory naval guns; the Colonsay experiment only showed it was possible to knock out an individual gun, not a fortress; and it would take a large amount of ammunition to knock them out one by one. As to ships, Admiral Bacon had had some success with the Dover Patrol and commented: 'You can sink a ship but not a fort. For success therefore, the ship should outrange the heavy guns in the fort.'[23] As with so many things in this war, the new technologies could only be fully tested in battle.

On the 15th Sir Henry Jackson completed his appraisal of the Carden scheme and wrote: 'Concur generally in his plans.' Later he would claim that he had only approved the attack on the outer forts, but that is not apparent from his comments, and Churchill believed he had approved the whole plan.[24] Fisher's doubts were clearly growing and on 25 January he pointed out: 'We play into Germany's hands if we risk fighting ships in any subsidiary operations such as coastal bombardments or the attack on fortified places without military co-operation … the sole justification of coastal bombardments and attacks by the fleet on fortified places, such as the contemplated prolonged bombardment of the Dardanelles first by our fleet, is to force a decision at sea …'.[25] He objected to any diversion from the Grand Fleet beyond the *Queen Elizabeth* as 'the battle cruiser action [Dogger Bank] showed very conclusively the absolute necessity the absolute necessity for a *big* preponderance of this type of ship …'.[26] Churchill noticed that 'During the weeks that followed [the January 13 meeting] I could see that Lord Fisher was increasingly worried about the Dardanelles situation. He reproached himself for having agreed to begin the operation. Now it was going to broaden out into a far larger and far longer undertaking than he had contemplated, his great wish was to put a stop to the whole thing.'[27] The two went to see Asquith before a meeting of the War Council on 28 January 'and gave tongue to their mutual grievances'. When the matter of the Dardanelles was brought up at the full meeting, Fisher replied that he 'had understood that this question would not be raised today' and that the Prime Minister was well aware of his views. He intended to resign and left the room to be followed by Kitchener, who persuaded him to return, but he said no more in the meeting.[28]

Kitchener had his own bombshell to deliver. Having stated at the January 28th meeting that there were absolutely no troops to spare, on 16 February he told an informal War Council meeting that the 29th Division, originally intended for the Western Front, was now free and could be sent out 'to be available in case of necessity to support the naval attack in the Dardanelles'. It might be ready to sail in nine or ten days. According to Hankey, the cabinet secretary, this was 'the all-important decision from which sprang the joint naval and military enterprise',[29] but the naval attack was already scheduled to begin before then.

*

Meanwhile the force was assembling in the Aegean. Vice-Admiral Sir Sackville Hamilton Carden was an undistinguished officer who had taken

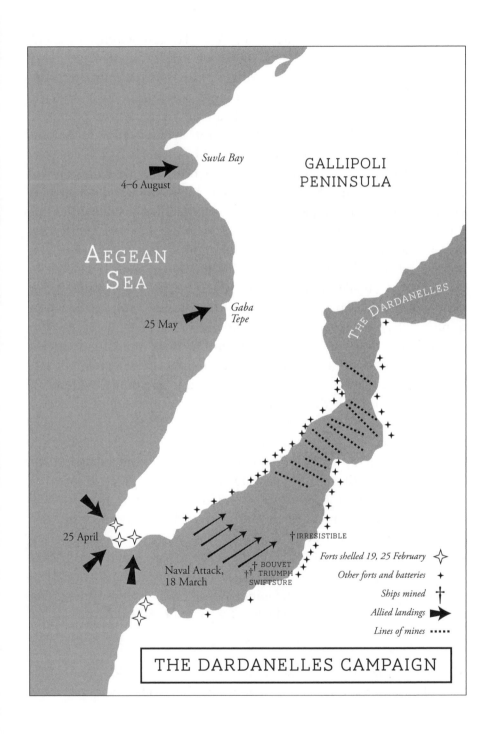

Suvla Bay

GALLIPOLI
PENINSULA

4–6 August

AEGEAN
SEA

THE DARDANELLES

Gaba
Tepe

25 May

25 April

†IRRESISTIBLE

Naval Attack,
18 March

†† BOUVET
† TRIUMPH
SWIFTSURE

Forts shelled 19, 25 February

Other forts and batteries

Ships mined

Allied landings

Lines of mines

THE DARDANELLES CAMPAIGN

up the eastern Mediterranean command by default when Troubridge was sent home after the *Goeben* affair. Keyes found him likeable and witty, but cold-hearted and without ambition. He was ageing at nearly 59, and 'read a novel and dozed' when crucial decisions had to be taken.[30] Perhaps as a balance to this, two of Churchill's favourite mavericks, Samson and Keyes, were to take part in the operation; Keyes predicted: 'We two outcasts will come into our own if the good God wills it.'[31] Keyes would leave the submarine service where he was frustrated by the lack of sea time and become chief of staff to Admiral Carden. Samson would take charge of the aircraft of the seaplane carrier *Ark Royal*, and eventually command the naval wing in the area.

In his more positive phase, Fisher had already offered the most powerful ship in the world for the operation, though she had only been completed in January and her crew had not yet trained with the mighty 15-inch guns. Fisher wrote to Oliver on the 12th: 'I have told Crease to find out from Percy Scott and the gunnery experts of anything to prevent *Queen Elizabeth* firing all her ammunition at the Dardanelles forts instead of uselessly into the ocean at Gibraltar. ... If this is practicable she could go straight there, hoist Carden's flag and go on with her gunnery exercises.'[32] Apart from that the fleet was to include the battlecruiser *Inflexible* which was being sent out to replace another which was already in the area, eight pre-Dreadnoughts with 12-inch guns, the old 'second class battleships' *Swiftsure* and *Triumph* with 10-inch guns, four light cruisers, 16 destroyers with a depot ship, a yacht and 21 trawlers for minesweeping, and six submarines.[33] To Admiral Wemyss they were 'vague ships brought together anyhow and anywhere ... they have never had a chance of being properly and quietly organised as a whole and ... consequently they have not got that invaluable asset of having worked together beforehand'.[34] The French would provide two battleships and supporting vessels. Also to be sent out was the pioneering aircraft carrier *Ark Royal*, converted from a tramp steamer to a 'seaplane carrying ship' as planned in the 1914 estimates. She carried six seaplanes in her hold, which could be craned out and launched from the water, and four landplanes which could take off from a bow ramp but could only land ashore, or in the sea, 'at considerable risk to the pilot and with practical certainty of seriously damaging – if not wrecking – the machine'.[35] Until she arrived, seaplanes were to be operated from cruisers, each carrying two which could be lowered over the side to take off from the water.

Though it was still considered a purely naval operation, some troops would be needed 'for any small landing operations which can be carried out under the fire of the ships' guns, such as destroying mining stations and fire observation stations'.[36] In the absence of army co-operation Churchill found them from his own resources. The Royal Marine brigade which Keyes persistently referred to as 'WC's own' was 'made up of pensioners of 40 to 50 – 12 year men of 32 to 40 – and boys of 19 to 22 – Kitchener's or Winston's. The officers are – many of them – schoolboys – clerks – volunteers – etc. – not much experience naturally. In fact it was the same tale as Antwerp.'[37]

The Greek island of Limnos (known as Lemnos) was selected as a base. It was 45 miles from the Straits and had a good natural harbour at Moúdros (Mudros) It was a delicate situation as Greece was still neutral and had to pretend that it was occupied against her will. Admiral Wester Wemyss was denied the title of governor on Foreign Office advice and became senior naval officer instead. According to Keyes he was 'a dear good fellow – and wonderful for the work. No-one could possibly be better – so tactful with our soldiers and the French – never put out, wonderful organiser.'[38]

The bombardment of the Dardanelles forts began on 19 February, as described by Keyes: 'We fired slowly and deliberately until about 4 pm, certain ships gradually getting in closer – hitting time after time. We were outside their range. Two big masonry forts with a number of heavy guns were very badly damaged, but two earth works containing two 9.2 –inch guns each – on opposite sides of the entrance – though hit time after time were still intact.'[39] The aeroplanes were a disappointment: '… the sea planes which we had relied on to give us information for the Queen Elizabeth's indirect fire managed nothing … They are gallant fellows, but they are not much use as their machines can only get up in flat calm and it takes ages to get to a safe height, if they get there at all.' And on the 9th, 'Unfortunately the light was bad, a succession of rain clouds; sea planes could do nothing from a safe height as the clouds were low, and we couldn't see to shoot or spot the fall of shots.'[40]

As they moved into the straits they had to sweep for mines and Keyes described the technique on 15 March: 'We sweep with two trawlers with a wire between them, the wire is kept at the correct depth by "kites". They sweep simply towing "fishes" with wire cutters which are kept out to cover a good area by "kites". It is very ingenious and very effective.' But the sweepers with their gear out could make little or no headway against the current of up to four knots, so they had to go through the minefield and then come down with the current.[41] Churchill later conceded that 'the force of minesweepers provided by the Admiralty was – it must be freely admitted – inadequate both in numbers and efficiency'.[42] But on 26 February he was confident and told the War Council: 'In three weeks' time Constantinople might be at our mercy.'[43]

On 16 March, on the eve of a major attack, Carden was taken ill and had to withdraw. Fisher later testified, 'I had a sort of feeling the thing was rather too much for Carden, to tell the truth.'[44] The responsibility fell on his second-in-command. Rear Admiral John Michael de Robeck was a natural leader and a sportsman with a gentlemanly manner. According to Keyes, 'the Admiral's great qualities are – first and foremost his magnetic personality. He inspires affection, confidence, and admiration in everyone who serves with him or under him [including] the soldiers [and] the French sailors and soldiers. He has a great eye for country, comes from his hunting experience I expect!'[45]

The main attack began at 1030 on 18 March, as soon as the light permitted. Keyes highlighted the problem of an attack with gunfire alone: '… at 4 pm we really had the forts beat – I mean their fire – but destroying big open forts like those is a very different matter and the odds against hitting a gun hard enough to put it out of action completely are enormous. You must land men to blow up every individual gun which has not been ruined by gun fire – our experience about 90%!!'[46] Fire from the shore was dangerous and Keyes reported: 'It is very obvious that all the defences are run by Germans. Their system is wonderfully good and they fire in salvoes.'[47] During the day they also saw the truth of Bacon's statement that 'You can sink a ship but not a fort.' Though at the time it was believed that the mines had been floated down, it was a line of mines stretched across the straits which sank the pre-Dreadnoughts *Irresistible* and *Ocean* and the French *Bouvet* while the battlecruiser *Inflexible* was damaged as was the French *Gaulois* – Churchill received the news next morning after visiting the trenches among the sand dunes of the Belgian coast and it did not take him long to see that 'no good result had been achieved'.[48] De Robeck sent an more positive addendum, perhaps inspired by Keyes and Godfrey. 'With the exception of ships lost and damaged, squadron is ready for immediate action, but the plan of attack must be reconsidered and means found to deal with floating mines.' Churchill remained confident; some losses had been allowed for and the loss of life was small, apart from the 600 crew of the *Bouvet*. 'I regarded the news only as the results of the first day's fighting. It never occurred to me for a moment that we should not go on within the limits of what we had decided to risk, until we had reached a decision one way or the other.'[49]

However, De Robeck met with Generals Hamilton and Birdwood and changed his mind in view of the prospect of army support coming along. He telegraphed the Admiralty: '… it seems in future destruction of guns will have to be carried out in face of strenuous and well prepared opposition. I do not think it a practicable operation to land a force adequate to undertake this service inside Dardanelles. General Hamilton concurs in this opinion. If the guns are not destroyed, any success of the fleet may be nullified by the straits closing up after the ships have passed through and loss of materiel will possibly be heavy, ships may not be available to keep the Dardanelles open.' Churchill received this with 'consternation' as he feared a long campaign.[50] He drafted a telegram suggesting De Robeck 'ought to persevere methodically but resolutely with the plan contained in your instructions … and that you should make all preparations to renew the attack begun on the 18th at the first favourable opportunity…'. Oliver supported this, but Jackson, Wilson and Fisher were opposed – the last stated that he had only agreed to proceed because it was recommended by the admiral on the spot, which was no longer the case. There was a heated meeting of the War Group in which Churchill 'pressed to the very utmost the duty and need of renewing the naval attack'. He found little support and took the case to the Prime Minster, who agreed but refused to overrule the admirals.

Churchill never ceased to believe that the naval attack was not far from success. After the war he collected reports from former enemies, including one from Enver Pasha, the Turkish minister of war. 'If the English had only the courage to rush more ships through the Dardanelles, they could have got to Constantinople; but their delay enabled us thoroughly to fortify the Peninsula ...'.[51] Keyes tended to agree, and was in 'torment ... to think of what could have and ought to have been achieved by the fleet'.[52] And failing that, thought Churchill, it might have been possible to end the affair there and then, as he testified in 1916: 'It appears incontrovertible that if we had stopped after the breaking off the naval attempt, the operation would have been of a small but highly profitable character ...'.[53] But instead the army and navy were committed to a very different and much larger operation in the area.

CHAPTER 20

Landing and Withdrawal

The Dardanelles operation was now to be expanded yet again, rather than abandoned. The army commander, who arrived just before the naval attack on 18 March, was General Sir Ian Hamilton. It was fifteen years since Churchill had reported on his march to the relief of Ladysmith, and at 63 he was old for a soldier. He and his staff were sent out in the light cruiser *Phaeton* and Churchill ordered her captain to 'embark as many seaplanes and aeroplanes, with their personnel, as can reach you before the time of sailing, and for which you have room. … Apart from the general and the senior officers, you need not trouble about cabins. Active service conditions must prevail, with officers sleeping on mattresses on deck or in hammocks.'[1]

It was the navy's duty to transport the army to the beaches and provide the craft to land them, but there is no sign that Churchill took much direct interest in the preparation. Horse boats were the only specialised craft and had been collected in Egypt since the operation began. Since horses could not be expected to jump over the side like soldiers, each had a ramp in the bows which could be lowered into the water. Much of the landing would be done by ships' boats – on 24 April the *Queen Elizabeth* went to Tenedos 'to get rid of our boats which are required for disembarkation'.[2] A ship of that size would carry about a dozen boats of various sizes, with three or four powered by steam. Each of these would tow a chain of unpowered boats across the sea and then embark men for the landing. Fisher had designed armoured lighters for his planned Baltic operations, but these did not arrive until later. The main innovation was the *River Clyde*, a converted merchant ship known as the 'wooden horse' in reference to the proximity to Troy, or 'the wreck' presumably because she was supposed to be grounded. 'In the ship's side great ports are cut. As soon as the crash comes and we grind ashore, these dragons teeth spring armed from the ports and race along a balcony to the stern of the vessel, there they pass forward along a steam hopper and thence over a bridge to dry land.' There was only one of them because, as Lieutenant-Commander Wedgwood told Churchill: '... it is an experiment, and only a First Lord makes experiments on a lordly scale'.[3]

There was no experience of what became known as 'combat loading', arranged so that the goods in each ship could be got out in the order required. Jack Churchill wrote on 3 April: 'the task of unloading so many ships is almost finished and re-embarking begins on the 5th. The delay has been very irksome, but it was absolutely essential. The ships were packed anyhow and a reshuffle was essential. It would have been fatal to have attempted anything, without having units completely self contained, and ready to disembark under any circumstances.'[4] Many of the ships had to be sent to Egypt to be re-stowed and the port of Mudros was not large enough. Hamilton's chief of staff testified: 'I do not think anybody could stow the ships properly, except the people who knew how the men were going to be taken off the ships. ... We took the different beaches, and saw how many men we would get on to them, and from that we worked it backwards on to the boats, on to the lighters, on to the ships and into the holds.'[5]

A substantial force of 50,000 men was built up in Egypt and at Lemnos, including the Royal Naval Division. There were 8,000 Australian and New Zealand troops training in Egypt for eventual transfer to France, but they were diverted for this operation. According to Kitchener they were 'very good soldiers and did not form part of the garrison of Egypt'.[6] Wemyss saw some of them on Lemnos and thought they were 'the most magnificent body of men I have ever seen'.[7] The 29th Division sent out from Britain was formed by combining various units withdrawn from the garrisons of the empire. They were regular British troops and began to arrive in Egypt from 7 April. While at Lemnos Rupert Brooke of the Royal Naval Division, the best known war poet and a friend of Churchill's secretary Eddie March, died and Churchill wrote an obituary for *The Times*: 'The thoughts to which he gave expression in the very few incomparable war sonnets which he has left behind will be shared by many thousands of young men moving resolutely and blithely forward into this, the hardest, the cruellest, and the least rewarded of all the wars that men have fought.'[8]

The *Ark Royal* arrived on station bringing Samson and his aircraft. According to Hamilton, 'Even more than in the fleet I find in the Air Service the profound conviction that, if they could only get in direct touch with Winston Churchill, all would be well. Their faith in the First Lord is, in every sense, *touching*. But they can't get the contact and they are thoroughly imbued with the idea that the Sea Lords are at best half-hearted; at the worst, actively antagonistic to us and to the whole of our enterprise.'[9] Samson was convinced that with a force of 30 two-seaters and 24 fighters 'he could take the peninsula all by himself and save us all a vast lot of trouble'.[10] Instead he had a miscellaneous collection of aircraft. One of them, a large seaplane, was equipped with a 250-watt radio set which could transmit (but not receive) to a range of 50 miles. Three lighter Sopwith seaplanes had smaller sets with ranges of up to ten miles. They had made some effort to study the progress the army had made on the Western Front with artillery spotting, though it was recognised that naval requirements were different.[11] Samson claimed some success with another aircraft: '... one of the Farman's has come back and reported that she spotted with great success, that the *Agamemnon* completely destroyed three out of four howitzers in a battery that had been annoying the fleet and landing place'.[12]

They could also operate from the shore, and Keyes's men worked to build an airfield, which Samson said was 'the best aerodrome he has ever had!!' More aircraft were sent out in crates and Keyes admired Samson 'after seeing him work in his aerodrome, and get into a machine pulled out of its packing cases, put together, and go skywards in a series of most appalling spirals ...'.[13] Samson was hard worked, writing on 2 May: 'We live in the air all day, and it is taking it out of our machines. ... We generally do a breakfast bomb attack. Lieutenant Butler has taken wonderful photographs of the German positions which have proved of great value to the army. ... We are giving them no rest with bombs. One of our machines got two 100 lb bombs in a divisional camp and blotted out over 18 tents and their occupants. They must have killed over 100 men.'[14]

★

Hamilton's orders forbade him to land on the Asian shore. He rejected the idea of cutting the neck of the peninsula at Bulair and decided that the main landing should be at Cape Helles covering the entrance to the Straits, where naval support would be available on two sides of a triangle. There would be a subsidiary landing further north on the western edge of the peninsula, to create a diversion and cut the main road to Cape Hellas. There were five landing beaches round the cape, lettered S to Y, and the northern landing, by Australian and New Zealand troops, was beach Z.

Churchill was well supplied with information from his brother Jack with the Naval Division, from Ian Hamilton, and others. Jack was on board the *Queen Elizabeth* as part of Hamilton's staff when the landing began on 25 April. On Y beach, 'Things seemed to be going well. Here was the weather – the one thing that even optimist feared – perfect, and three beaches out of six successfully accomplished. ... Clearly W party had also landed and made good considerable ground. ... Infantry were lying down all along the top of the cliff. A mass of wire entanglements could be seen in front of them.' But as they rounded Cape Helles, '... we could see the "Wooden horse" ... It soon became clear that all was not well here. The boat had done well and was piled up on the shore. The lighters formed a pier from her bows, but she was still full of men.'[15]

Josiah Wedgwood was on board with the RNAS Armoured Car Division and described the situation graphically:

> Five tows of five boats with some 30–40 in each came into V beach simultaneously with ourselves, and in ten minutes there were some 400 dead and wounded on

234 • CHURCHILL: WARRIOR

the beach and in the waters. Not more than 10% got safe to shore and took shelter under the sand edge. Some of the Munster Fusiliers tried to land from the *River Clyde* about 7 am, after some sort of a connection had been made with a spit of rock. Very few of them got safe to land, and General Napier and his brigade major were killed on the lighter. Thereafter the wounded cried out all day and for 36 hours – in every boat, lighter, hopper and all along the shore.[16]

They waited until dark to try again.

That night we landed the rest of the Munsters and the Hampshires (some 100 in all). The losses then were small. For three hours I stood on the end of the spit of what had been rock in two feet of water helping the heavily laden men to jump ashore on to submerged dead bodies and trying to persuade the wounded over whom they had to walk that we should soon get them aboard. This is what went on monotonously. 'Give me your rifle'; 'and your shovel'; 'your left hand'; 'jump wide'; 'it's all right, only kits'; 'keep clear of that man's legs, can't you'.[17]

Men were landed on all the beaches, but at great cost. There were huge casualties with around 19,000 men killed in the early stages of the campaign. The troops failed to advance inland so were held in a narrow strip by well-placed Turkish trenches. Churchill wrote: 'Sir Ian Hamilton's whole army was cramped and pinned down at two separate points on the Gallipoli Peninsula. His two main attacks, though joined by the sea, were otherwise quite disconnected with each other. None of the decisive positons on the Peninsula were in our hands. A continuous line of Turkish entrenchments stood between the British and Achi Baba ...'.[18] The defences were stiffened by German advisers led by General Liman von Sanders. Already there were accusations in the press of a 'gigantic and fatal blunder'. On 9 May De Robeck reported ominously: '... the army is checked .... This threatens a state of affairs similar to that in northern France.'[19] He suggested another attempt by sea on 13 May, but Churchill felt that the moment had passed and he gave his reasons to the War Council. The Italians had joined the war and would need some assistance from the Royal Navy; German submarines had arrived and were now a threat; and the attack was now primarily a military rather than a naval affair. Oliver summed up the situation as it was seen from the Admiralty: 'On March 18 the fleet was single, now it has a wife on shore.'[20]

Fisher threatened to resign unless the *Queen Elizabeth* was sent home to reinforce the Grand Fleet and match new German ships. Churchill acceded, but Kitchener was furious, claiming he had only agreed to the operation when told of the massive power of the *Queen Elizabeth's* guns, and that her withdrawal would be 'the first sign of the abandonment of the enterprise'.[21] Churchill promised the first two 14-inch monitors instead, followed by seven more. He told Fisher: 'When this large accession of force reaches the Vice-Admiral he should be able to spare a portion of his battleships for service in Home Waters ...'.[22] But it was no use. Fisher resigned again on the 15th. Asquith wrote: 'In the King's name, I order you at once to return to your post' but this time it was final.[23] This set off a chain of events which led to Churchill's resignation. With a parallel scandal over the supply of shells to the Western Front, Asquith needed to from a coalition government and Churchill was not acceptable to the Conservatives in his present post. Clementine wrote plaintively to Asquith:

> For nearly four years Winston has worked to master every detail of naval science. There is no man in this country who possesses equal knowledge, capacity and vigour. If he goes, the injury to Admiralty business will not be reparable in many months – if indeed it is ever made good during the war. Why do you want to part with Winston? unless indeed you have lost confidence in his work and ability? ...
>
> Winston may in your eyes and in those with whom he had had to work have faults but he has the supreme quality which I venture to say very few of your present and future cabinet possess, the power, the imagination, the deadliness to fight Germany.[24]

The Prime Minster dismissed this as 'the letter of a maniac'[25] and the change went ahead. According to Clementine, 'When he left the Admiralty he thought he was finished. I thought he would never get over the Dardanelles. I thought he would die of grief.'

★

Churchill was moved to the sinecure post of Chancellor of the Duchy of Lancaster, while Arthur Balfour became First Lord with Sir Henry Jackson as First Sea Lord. As he left the Admiralty 'in pain and sorrow',

Churchill wrote to Balfour warning him of the growing danger of submarine attack in the Dardanelles and concluded: 'Punishment must be doggedly borne.'[26] He was soon 'chafing desperately at having no work to do'[27] but he did not give up his interest in the campaign in Turkey. He was a member of the Dardanelles Committee which replaced the War Council, but he began to see events unfolding 'like a Greek tragedy'.[28] He denied that an attack on the Peninsula was as futile as one on the Western Front, where 'beyond the ground captured so dearly lies all the breadth of Flanders before even the Rhine can be reached ... but an advance of three or four miles in the Gallipoli Peninsula would produce strategic results of a decisive character'.[29] By 11 June he was advocating an attack on the neck at Bulair as the situation had changed. 'The flower of the Turkish army, all the Germans, the bulk of their artillery, is now massed around the Kilid Bahr plateau, and cutting them off would be decisive.' Kitchener rejected this on the grounds that the beaches were not suitable and the landing force would be exposed from two sides.[30] On the 18th Churchill was still optimistic that Constantinople could be taken before the end of the summer.[31]

In June, at the depth of his despair, Churchill began to paint. He was visited by Hazel Lavery, the wife of the painter Sir John. She told him: 'Painting! What are you hesitating about? Let me have the brush.' She delivered bold strokes on the canvas, and Churchill found that he 'never felt in awe of a canvas since'. He had discovered a means of escape from his difficulties. In July it was planned that he should visit the Dardanelles to 'secure for the Cabinet valuable information and suggestions in regard both to the future of the campaign and to our policy in that theatre of the war'. Kitchener was keen that he should produce an independent report, though he also admitted privately 'that he would not have been sorry to get rid of Winston for a while'. Believing he might come under Turkish shellfire Churchill wrote a final letter to Clementine, to be opened in the event of his death, saying farewell to his family; but Lord Curzon of the War Cabinet doubted 'as to the wisdom of sending a cabinet minister to the scene of war and as to the reception that public opinion might give to such an act'. He was joined by the Conservative leader Bonar Law and they went to Asquith to have it stopped.[32] On the spot, Keyes was relieved. 'He would like to be – Generalissimo – and will be an awful nuisance!'[33]

More troops were poured into the campaign and on 6 August another landing took place in Suvla Bay north of the Australian beach, now known as Anzac Cove. Fisher's new armoured lighters were now available and Keyes (who mistakenly thought they had been designed by Churchill) described them to his wife: 'They are rather wonderful, they have a heavy oil engine ... they hold 500 men – 40 or 50 horses – guns – carts, etc. or 150 tons of cargo.' He described their operation. 'Destroyer towing lighter – on approaching beach – lighter slipped, steamed in and ran up on the each, destroyer anchored as close as possible – picket boat followed lighter to take a line from lighter to destroyer in case lighter stuck to haul it off, the lighter took destroyer's 500 [men] and went in again.' However their RNVR officers were mostly 'quite unfit' for the position.[34] Again the troops failed to move inland and the stalemate was not broken. On 21 August Churchill wrote to Asquith and Balfour, 'Nearly 110,000 casualties have been sustained. An army nominally equivalent to 14 infantry divisions has been committed and is deeply, possibly inextricably, involved.'[35]

In September the Australian journalist Keith Murdoch (father of the media mogul) wrote an 8,000-word letter which made his name and defined the campaign in the eyes of many. He waxed lyrical about the Australian soldier, claiming 'It is only these fighting qualities, and the special capacity of the Australian physique to endure hardship, that keep the morale at Anzac good.' In contrast the British soldiers were 'merely a lot of childlike youths without strength to endure or brains to improve their conditions'. Above all he deplored the arrogant staff living in luxury at Mudros. He liked Hamilton personally but thought the campaign could only progress if he was replaced. There was no direct blame on Churchill, only that the naval attack 'failed mainly because London expected far too much from floating artillery' – and of course he had only indirect influence on the campaign by this time; but it was the beginning of a myth that he was personally responsible for the loss of thousands of fine young Australian lives.

Godfrey and Keyes devised a plan for a new naval assault, which envisaged a coordinated attack by battleships, cruisers and monitors on the forts, carefully planned minesweeping and aerial reconnaissance. Relations between the admiral and his chief of staff had broken down. De Robeck thought his chief of staff was 'the best and bravest fellow in the world and always for having a go; but having got you to do so, he will accuse you of being rash'. However he was tolerant enough to let Keyes take his plan to London to be considered. The plan 'would not lead to any result if we got through with a few ships. It most probably leads to a most colossal disaster!'[36] Keyes thought that 'De R as a fighting admiral ceased to exist on 18th March.'[37]

In London, Keyes visited the Admiralty with the plan, where Balfour treated him like a headmaster dealing with a schoolboy, having the attitude 'wait and see what will turn up'.[38] Keyes thought a meeting with Churchill might be embarrassing but failed to avoid it. He and his wife had dinner at the Churchills' house, when Winston was '*very, very* indiscreet'.[39] Churchill considered his plan to be 'remarkable for its audacity' but now he had even less power to order it – he was excluded from the new War Committee which replaced the Dardanelles Committee and met on 2 November. His days in office were numbered.[40]

Late in October General Munro was sent to the Dardanelles to assess the prospects. Writing later, Churchill was scathing of his efforts. He had already made up his mind before spending six hours ashore, and 'He came, he saw, he capitulated.' The official historian of the war challenged Churchill's assessment. Munro was by no means a man of 'fixed ideas and rapid decision ... six hours ashore was ample. What good could he do by wandering around more trenches when he could see all he wanted from the water.'[41] Churchill was serving on the Western Front by the time the final withdrawal was ordered, though as he wrote: 'I was not without information on the course of affairs from my friends ...'.[42] He wrote to Mrs Keyes: 'I could not have influenced this tragic event. ... We have fallen among thieves.'[43] It was feared that thousands of men might be lost in the evacuation, but it went quite smoothly. Suvla and Anzac were abandoned on the 18th to 20th December covered by an attack at Helles which cost 283 casualties. That beachhead was itself abandoned by 8 January.

It was never a true combined operation with the army, navy and air service in full accord and minute-by-minute contact. Even the Keyes/ Godfrey plan did not envisage much role for the army in the forcing of the straits. The version of 23 September devoted less than 50 words to 'Co-operation by [rather than with] the army.' They were to provide a diversionary attack and to try to prevent the movement of light guns to protect the minefields.[44] One of the messages of the Antwerp affair was ignored – the German bombardment of the forts succeeded only because infantry were ready to storm them, driving off the defenders and making it impossible to recapture them. Forcing the straits would probably require a series of landings along the shore in support of each bombardment, but differences between the army and navy ran too deep for that, and landing techniques and equipment were not developed enough. There was no constitutional way in which a general could be put in charge of an admiral or vice versa, so success largely depended on co-operation between the two. It was not that the leaders on the spot, Hamilton and De Robeck, did not get on, but they seemed to work to different rhythms; both were bound by decisions made in London and they therefore suffered from the tensions between Churchill and Kitchener.

The perennial and perhaps unanswerable question is, whose fault was the disaster? Churchill did not originate the project, but he pushed for it and it would probably not have happened without his drive. He placed too much faith in shore bombardment and aircraft, and he allowed the naval operation to go ahead without the army. But that was not disastrous, it was only when the army was embroiled on the peninsula that heavy casualties began to ensue. Heavy losses on landing can be put down to inexperience of modern amphibious warfare. The failure to advance, if anyone was culpable, was down to the army and not to the navy or Churchill. The cabinet hesitated in whether to reinforce or withdraw and save lives. The Report of the Dardanelles Commission largely blamed Kitchener, who was now dead, for persisting in the face of disaster, mainly to save face in the Middle East; but Churchill was also adamant that they should stay.

If any real blame did attach to Churchill, it was far less than what was found in the popular mind. According to his biographer Martin Gilbert, 'Churchill became the scapegoat for the failure at the Dardanelles, even for the period after his departure from the Admiralty, during which he was no longer responsible for the Navy, and even for the land war which was Kitchener's domain.'[45]

CHAPTER 21

In the Trenches

Churchill carried on in government for five months after leaving the Admiralty, in the sinecure office of Chancellor of the Duchy of Lancaster but with a seat in the War Council. When Asquith reorganised the government in October, Churchill resigned as he could not 'accept responsibility without power'. The natural course was for him to return to the army – he had told one of the officers of the *Enchantress* that his greatest regret in the event of war with Germany was that due to his official position he would be 'unable to take a fighting part and share the risks and dangers with the officers of the services'.[1] As early as 12 June the head of the army's Southern Command offered him the colonelcy of the second battalion of the Oxfordshire Hussars, but perhaps that was just a formality as he was the senior major. In any case he declined.[2] Now he was free to do that, but Captain Kincaid-Smith (a former Liberal MP and rebel who was now serving in the army) advised him not to back go to the Hussars: 'The cavalry are as you know, all sitting behind at St Omer, ... I should say do anything rather than join a unit in the cavalry corps – you would be bored to distraction in a week or so with this semi peace existence.'[3] His friend Captain Archibald Sinclair had a similar opinion: 'If there is a difficulty about a higher formation surely the command of a Kitchener battalion would be a better position than that of second in command of a yeomanry regiment which in common with the rest of the cavalry can only work dismounted? Why not get a battalion – no-one could object to that on any grounds? A Scotch one as you are a Scotch member for the Scotch divisions of the [Kitchener's?] armies (9th and 15th) have fairly eclipsed the others.'[4]

Churchill did indeed leave to join the yeomanry at St Omer on 18 November, but once in France different prospects opened to him. He was taken to General Headquarters, 'a fine chateau, with hot water, beds, champagne and all the conveniences'.[5] There, Sir John French offered him command of a brigade as Asquith had done, but Churchill told him that 'beforehand I must feel myself effectively the master of the conditions of trench warfare'[6] – for it was clearly very different from the conflicts had had seen in Cuba, India, Egypt and South Africa. He suggested a Guards regiment as 'the best school' and was sent to join the 2nd Battalion of the Grenadier Guards. His letters to his wife, combined with other sources, give us one of the best pictures of life on the Western Front, at least in a quiet period, for unlike many soldiers he was not too traumatised to talk frankly about it.

At first he was not welcome in the battalion, and the colonel later admitted that his coming 'was not a matter in which we were given any choice'.[7] He found himself in odd and untidy trenches which offended his Sandhurst traditions. 'The line of trenches – or rather breastworks we are now holding is built along the ruins of older lines taken from the Germans or built later by the Indians. The Guards are cleaning everything up and work day and night to strengthen the parapets and improve the shelter.' He found that 'the tradition and the system of the Guards asserts itself in hard work, smartness and soldierly behaviour'.[8] One day he was sent for to meet the corps commander and set out across the fields among stray bullets and shells, only to find that the meeting had been cancelled as the staff car could not get through. When he was away the dugout in which he was sitting had been destroyed by a shell – it was 'all chance and destiny'.[9] They left the line soon afterwards with the troops singing *Tipperary* and *The Farmer's Boy*, and Churchill was always keen on military singing. It was 'like getting to a jolly good tavern after a long day's hunting, wet and cold and hungry'. He had 'a glorious hot bath' in 'this abode of comfort'.[10] Back in the line in mid-December, he reported how ten grenadiers under a 'kid' of an officer had raided the enemy lines, 'beat the brains' out of two Germans and captured another one, though he had to keep quiet about how the officer had shot one of his own men by accident. The prisoner was well treated, 'petted' and given cigarettes and was apparently not unhappy that he was out of it.[11] He enjoyed his time with the Grenadiers; in 1933 he dedicated the first volume of his book on Marlborough to them, 'in memory of the courtesies and kindness shown to him by the regiment in the Great War'.[12]

That December 'Major the Right Honourable Winston S. Churchill' produced a paper on 'Variants of the Offensive' dated from 'General Headquarters, British Army in the Field'. It is no surprise that it was dedicated to means of attack, though not the frontal assault by unprotected troops. As well as his ideas on the tank which were already under development, he suggested shields carried by individual men or by small groups of up to 15, which might be pushed on a caterpillar track – but it is difficult to believe that he understood the forces involved. From his naval experience he suggested a torpedo net cutter to penetrate the barbed wire, and the use of trench guns. His Sandhurst training perhaps inspired his section on 'The Attack by the Spade'. It was already common to dig saps in front of the lines, but he wanted to do it on a more extensive scale with perhaps 300 saps in 30,000 yards and men working for ten days until they were within 70 yards of the enemy line, where his artillery could not be used. It was 'nothing more than the penultimate phase of a siege when the sap-heads are pushed into the fortress covered way and the counterscarp blown in: but it is a siege advance on a gigantic front'. In contrast to his later statements he was callous about casualties: 'Any operation on the western front is justified if we take at least a life for a life. The more this is done the sooner a decision will be reached.'

He went home on leave over Christmas and by the beginning of January it was becoming clear that he was to take command of the 6th Battalion of the Royal Scots Fusiliers, mainly made up of Ayrshire men including many miners, with a sprinkling of English. The RSF was a lowland regiment so did not wear the kilt. One of the officers,

Captain Gibb, imagined that Churchill might be sent to the Argyll and Sutherland Highlanders who did wear the kilt, and were used to handling celebrities after being written about in the best-seller, *The First Hundred Thousand*, by Ian Hay. The 6th RSF had suffered great losses in the Battle of Loos, the first to involve the bulk of the new armies, and the first in which the British deployed gas. 'Like all the rest of this Scottish division, it fought with the greatest gallantry in the big battle and was torn to pieces. More than half the men, and ¾ of the officers were shot, and these terrible gaps have been filled up by recruits of good quality, and quite young inexperienced officers.'[13] This allowed Churchill to bring in his friends Edward Spiers and Archibald Sinclair, whom he made second-in-command. The regiment was 'pathetic' – presumably meaning 'exciting pity, sympathy or sadness' rather than the modern sense which has overtones of 'contemptible'. The young officers were 'all small middle class Scotsmen – very brave and willing and intelligent: but of course all quite new to soldiering'.[14] He drilled the men – 'On the second day of Winston's tenure of office he gave orders that all the companies should parade in a certain slushy meadow, when he intended personally to inspect the work of each company and meet the officers and men in their official capacity.'[15] He found 'the regiment is full of life and strength and I believe I shall be a help to them'.[16]

Churchill attended a lecture on the Battle of Loos by Major-General 'Tom' Holland on 18 January, and it confirmed his worst fears: '… his tale was one of hopeless failure and sublime heroism of splendid Scottish soldiers shorn away in vain – with never the ghost of a chance of success. 6,000 killed and wounded out of 10,000 in this Scottish division alone. Alas alas. Afterwards they asked what was the lesson of the lecture. I restrained an impulse to reply "Don't do it again". But they will – I have no doubt.'[17] For the moment he only communicated this opinion to his wife, for open criticism of his superiors' tactics would be a serious offence for a serving officer. He was moved enough to mention the heroism of the Scottish Division in parliament a few months later, though he focussed on the Cameron Highlanders for some reason.[18]

On the 20th he inspected the section of line that his battalion was to take over and compared it with the one he had served in with the Guards: 'It is much the best bit of line I have yet seen all along the front. Incomparably better on every score than the sector where the Guards were. It is dry – the trenches are boarded and drained. The parapets are thick and bullet proof. The wire is good. The field of fire clear ...'. It was 'a jolly day'.[19]

Churchill was replacing a well-liked CO and it was ironic that Gibb would have preferred it if he had replaced the unpopular brigadier or the over-aggressive divisional commander. But soon he won them over, and 'materially altered the feelings of the officers towards him by this kindliness and by the first insight we gained into the wonderful genius of the man' – and this was written in 1924 when his general popularity was still very low. But when he asked his officers 'Do you like war?' they pretended not to hear. The troops 'seemed to be delighted with their new Colonel' and hoped that his influence might be used to sort out various personal problems with the army administration. They loved it when he spoke to them individually as one of the 'high heid yins'. His attitude to the men 'was not marred by that condescending *hauteur* which goes so far to frustrate the efforts of a number of our regular officers'. But he was tactless in comparing the RSF unfavourably with their rivals, the Gordon Highlanders.[20]

Churchill gave a dinner party for his officers to the accompaniment of bagpipes and 'recognized as many Englishmen do not, that the pipes are instruments capable of playing definite airs' and asked for *Bonnie Dundee* after his constituency – though to his wife he referred to the tunes as 'doleful dirges'. He described his three ties to Scotland – his constituency, his wife and his regiment, which was greeted with 'salvoes of cheering'.[21] According to Captain Gibb, he declared war on lice and, well prepared as usual, he gave a discourse on their 'origins, growth and nature'.[22] On 26 January, before moving up to the line, he gave advice to his officers which he compared to that of Polonius in *Hamlet*:

> Don't be careless about yourselves – on the other hand not too careful. Keep a special pair of boots to sleep in and only get them muddy in a real emergency. Use alcohol in moderation but don't have a great parade of bottles in your dugouts.

> Live well but do not flaunt it. Laugh a little, and teach your men to laugh – great
> good humour under fire – war is a game that is played with a smile. If you can't
> smile grin. If you can't grin keep out of the way till you can.[23]

Then, 'On a cold raw day in January the colonel and the company commanders with a few other important officers of the battalion moved out of the billeting area in a motor omnibus bound for the neighbourhood of Armentieres and Plugstreet' – arguably contradicting his wife's later assertion that Churchill had never been on a bus.[24] The latter place, a soldier's pronunciation of the Belgian village of Ploegsteert, was relatively peaceful with shops still open and the church tower still standing – though it was knocked down by shellfire a few days later.[25] The rest of the battalion arrived and they marched towards the trenches in columns of fours. They took over 1,000 yards of front 'with the utmost precision in under two hours. I don't think the Grenadiers ever did better.' He wrote to his wife, 'rest assured, there will be no part of the line from the Alps to the sea better guarded'.[26] Again Churchill revived the knowledge of fortification he had gained at Sandhurst 20 years ago. 'To see Winston giving a dissertation on the laying of sandbags …. You felt sure from his grasp of practice that he must have served apprentice to a bricklayer and a master-mason, while his theoretical knowledge rendered you certain that Wren would have been proud to sit at his feet …'. The officer he appointed 'master of works' had to 'devise shelters and scarps and counterscarps and dugouts and half-moons and ravelins'.[27] He devoted himself to the main tasks of a battalion in the line during a quiet period – 'the subjection and annoyance of the enemy and the improvement of the trenches'.[28]

The command of a battalion was the highest position in which an officer had regular contact with the men under him. It had a real identity within the regiment and often there was real affection for the colonel. The future Field-Marshal William Slim thought it was one of the four best commands alongside a platoon, when one was young, a division and an army – the battalion was 'a unit with a life of its own; whether it is good or bad depends on you alone; you have at last a real command'.[29] Churchill himself wrote: 'I am anxious to

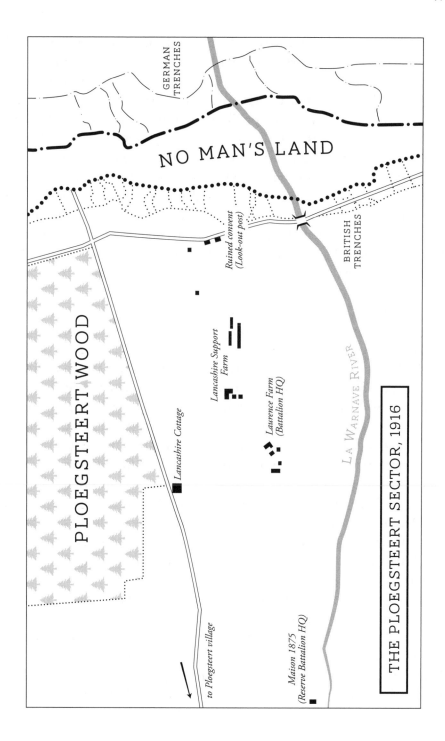

GERMAN TRENCHES

NO MAN'S LAND

BRITISH TRENCHES

Ruined convent
(Look-out post)

PLOEGSTEERT WOOD

Lancashire Support
Farm

Lancashire Cottage

Laurence Farm
(Battalion HQ)

LA WARNAVE RIVER

to Ploegsteert village

Maison 1875
(Reserve Battalion HQ)

THE PLOEGSTEERT SECTOR, 1916

make them feel their corporate identity and the sense of my personal control. A colonel is within his own sphere an autocrat who punishes and promotes and displaces at his discretion.'[30] A brigade included at least three battalions but the command was far more impersonal and distant. A division, another of Slim's favourites, consisted of about 20,000 men and was commanded by a major-general. It was perhaps a more interesting formation, the smallest one to combine all arms of cavalry, infantry and artillery. In another campaign it might have offered some opportunity for independent action, but not on the Western Front where it was still under the direct orders of the corps commander and the commander-in-chief. Nor is it likely that Churchill could have risen to an independent command on another front, much as he would have loved it. Even if he could have overcome the prejudice against him, his service on the Western Front would have been valueless. So it is difficult to see where his military ambition might lead, for he would have to rise through many grades to have any real influence and authority

He did take command of the brigade for a few days early in February but he did not enjoy it, partly because it was on a temporary basis. 'So I remain here in command. It is not a very satisfactory arrangement, as of course I am only a caretaker and cannot attempt to take a grip of the whole machine. I do the office work and have prepared myself to meet any emergency; but otherwise I wait about from hour to hour.'[31] But permanent promotion remained an illusion, especially after Sir Douglas Haig succeeded Sir John French as commander-in-chief on 18 December, and was far less sympathetic to Churchill's case. Despite French's recommendation and reports of Churchill's keenness, command was 'impossible until W had shown that he could bear responsibility in action as CO of a battalion'.[32]

Early in November Churchill had acquired a French *poilu* helmet or 'casque Adrian' which would protect his 'valuable cranium'. It made him look 'most martial ... like a Cromwellian' and he was photographed and portrayed wearing it. The British style helmet, reportedly based on even earlier warriors who had fought at Agincourt in 1415, was in the course of being issued at the time, and 500 had arrived at the 6th battalion by 24 January. At other times Churchill grudgingly accepted the Glengarry cap of the Scottish regiments, though he did not like it. When Sinclair was photographed in the standard peaked cap of the English regiments, it was regarded as the 'perfidy' of a 'false Scot', whereas Churchill's blue helmet became his trademark. Visiting the troops in the trenches at least three times a day, 'In wet weather he would appear in a complete outfit of waterproof stuff, including trousers or overalls, and with his French light-blue helmet he presented a remarkable and unusual figure.'[33]

The battalion alternated in the line, being relieved after six days and sent to a rear base which was still within the range of enemy shells; though Churchill claimed he preferred it in the trenches, 'where there is always something going on, and where one really is fighting in this great war for the triumph of right and reason'.[34] On 13 February he watched an air battle overhead with some misgivings – 'I was disgusted to watch one German aeroplane sailing about scornfully in the midst of 14 British …. As for our guns they fired hundreds of shells without lifting a feather of this hostile bird.'[35] In March he and Sinclair walked around the lines held by other battalions.

> The same conditions and features reproduce themselves in every section – shattered buildings, sandbag habitations, trenches heavily wired, shell holes, frequent graveyards with thickets of little crosses, wild rank growing grass, muddy roads, khaki soldiers – and so on for hundreds and hundreds of miles – on both sides …. Only a few rifle shots and the occasional bang of a gun broke the stillness of the evening.[36]

It occurred to him that he was now at the rank which he might have reached if he had stayed in the army. He wrote to Clementine: 'It seems almost to me as if my life in the great world was a dream, and I have been moving slowly forward in the army all these years from subaltern to colonel.'[37] Despite all the disappointments and hardships he continued to be upbeat in his letters, but one wonders how much it was forced. With the Guards he claimed everyone said he looked ten years younger and he 'had never been in better health and spirits'.[38] He was 'cool and indifferent in danger here'.[39] With his officers he reminisced about military life and regaled them with anecdotes about Fisher and leading politicians, as well as commenting freely on Antwerp and the Dardanelles; but he did not have a good word to say for Asquith and he was 'unenthusiastic' about Kitchener. The officers tolerated his tin bath, 'a thing like a great magnified soap-dish' which needed a great deal of hot water to fill it. But Churchill needed his bi-weekly bath even in the front line.

Regulations barred senior officers from taking part in raids and reconnaissance in no-man's-land, but in February he admitted to his wife: 'You cannot show yourself here by day, but in the bright moon-light it is possible to move about without danger (except from random bullets) and to gain a very clear impression. Archie [Sinclair] was a very good guide. We went out in front of our own parapet into the no man's land and prowled about looking at our wire and visiting our listening posts.' It was evidently not the first time, for he wrote: 'This is always exciting.' He was out with Sinclair again a week later. He paid attention to his men's raids across the lines, when patrols cut large sections of barbed wire and brought them back as trophies – however he deplored the bravado of one of the officers who fixed a union flag on the site, giving the Germans reason to be more vigilant. 'Can you imagine such a silly thing.'[40]

Corporal John McGuire described the experience of going on a raid with Churchill:

> I strapped on a revolver and two Mills bombs, and at midnight Winnie turned up with his adjutant. He wore his trench helmet, trench coat and Sam Browne belt with revolver. We topped the parapet and slipped through a gap known only to scouts. Ten yards further on I lay down on the second line of trench concertina wire enabling the other two to cross. From there we crawled on our stomachs across muddy ground punched with shell holes. Near the German lines we settled into a hole and listened to the Germans talking. After two hours we crawled home. This was the pattern for all our trips. While we were out our own side never fired, but the Germans, worried by the silence, sent up Verey lights and followed up with heavy machine gun strafing. I often thought we'd 'had it' but Churchill showed no fear. He would smile and say, 'They know I'm here, McGuire, they know I'm here.'[41]

There was no major British attack planned at this time, though late in February Churchill's leave was cancelled because a German offensive was expected, but it never happened. In January 1916 he claimed: 'I could not leave the army in the field for any position which did not give me an effective share in the direction of the war' – presumably in the War Cabinet.[42] But his service was interrupted when he was allowed leave to speak in debates in the House of Commons. Already he was being drawn back to political life at home where, with his varied war experience, he might make some contribution even from the back benches. The prospect of the publication of the Dardanelles papers which might clear his name was a further stimulus. Since several battalions of the RSF had been reduced by battle it was decided to merge the 6th and the 7th, and the colonel of the latter was the senior, which gave a pretext for relieving Churchill. On 6 May he gave a farewell dinner to his officers and told them 'that he had come to regard the young Scot as a most formidable fighting machine'. The adjutant represented the thinking of the others in saying 'what it had been to serve under him' and 'every man in the room felt Winston Churchill's leaving us as a real personal loss'.[43] The commanding officer of the battalion which succeeded him remarked: 'I went up to take over my little bit with Winston Churchill, who described himself as a cavalry soldier run to seed; all the same the service lost a good soldier when Winston took to politics.'[44] Churchill returned to what he called 'the bray of Parliaments'.[45] His short term at the front left him open to jibes, such as the one in *The Nation* in March 1919: 'after a few weeks of shivering in the trenches, Mr Churchill himself preferred to shine in the Senate'.[46]

One wonders what would have happened if Churchill had remained in command until the beginning of July, when the bloody Somme offensive began with the death of 20,000 men on the first day. Would he have been obliged to lead his men to their deaths in a battle which he knew to be futile? In August, after a month's fighting at the Somme and while still a backbencher, he sent a memorandum to F. E. Smith which was placed before the cabinet, claiming

> In personnel the results of the operation have been disastrous; in terrain they have been absolutely barren. And, although our brave troops ... are at the moment elated by the small advances made and the capture of prisoners and souvenirs, the ultimate moral effect will be disappointing. From every point of view, therefore,

the British offensive *per se* has been a great failure. With twenty times the shells, and five times the guns, and more than double the losses, the gains have but little exceeded those of Loos. And how as Loos viewed in retrospect?[47]

He was even more scathing when he wrote about the battle in *The World Crisis* in 1927: '… the campaign of 1916 on the Western Front was from beginning to end a welter of slaughter, which after the issue was determined left the British and French armies weaker in relation to the Germans when it opened, while the actual battle fronts were not appreciably altered. … The battlefields of the Somme were the graveyards of Kitchener's Army. The flower of that generous manhood … was shorn away for ever in 1916.'[48]

★

On 31 May 1916 the British and German fleets finally met in the North Sea in the Battle of Jutland, and all the virtues and faults of the Grand Fleet became evident. The gunnery of the Battle Cruiser Fleet was poor due to lack of training. Three of Fisher's beloved ships blew up with the loss of almost all hands, partly due to their thin skins, and partly to poor safety procedures. In another of Seymour's signalling errors, the mighty *Queen Elizabeths* of the Fifth Battle Squadron headed in the wrong direction at a crucial stage in the fight, reconnaissance work by the cruisers was poor but Jellicoe was nonetheless able to deploy his fleet in masterly fashion, 'crossing the T' of the enemy; though twice he exercised his option to 'decline to be so drawn' when the enemy turned away from him. As a result the High Seas Fleet inflicted heavy damage on the Grand Fleet but had to flee from the scene of the battle. The Germans had to give up any idea of trapping a section of the Grand Fleet and their great ships hardly left port again. It was a tactical defeat but a strategic victory for the British, but that was not how it was portrayed in the initial reports. The Germans proclaimed 'Great victory at sea', while the British communiqué concentrated on the losses and said nothing about the strategic effects. It fell to the back-bencher Churchill to correct this, when he called into the Admiralty to see the current First Lord of the Admiralty, A. J. Balfour. 'As I took a fairly cheerful view of what had occurred, it was suggested to me

that I might make a statement of a reassuring character to the public
…'.[49] In a message to the Press Bureau he concluded, not without an
element of self-justification,

> The hazy weather, the fall of night, and the retreat of the enemy, alone frustrated
> the persevering efforts of our brilliant commanders, Sir John Jellicoe and Sir
> David Beatty, to force a final decision. Although it was not possible to compel
> the German main fleet to accept battle, the conclusions reached are of extreme
> importance. … An accurate measure can be taken of the strength of the enemy,
> and his definite inferiority is freed from any element of uncertainty. The fast
> division 'Queen Elizabeth' seems to have vindicated all the hopes reposed in
> them.[50]

Jellicoe was less than pleased, complaining that '… we do take it as
rather trying that Mr Churchill should edit the Press Bureau summary
of the action before even my report on arrival at harbour has reached
the Admiralty'.[51]

Meanwhile Churchill continued in his role as a backbencher and was
known as 'Colonel Churchill' in official reports. He spent some time
giving evidence to the Dardanelles Commission and interrogating wit-
nesses, claiming 'that there was full authority; that there was a reasonable
prospect of success; that greater interests were not compromised; that
all possible care and forethought were exercised in the preparation; and
that vigour and determination were shown in the execution'. He was
relatively pleased when only one clause of the final report put any direct
blame on him, and he defended himself against that. In parliament he
defended his conduct at the Admiralty, for example when Sir Hedworth
Meux, one of the anti-Fisher officers he had rescued from obscurity,
claimed that the removal of Admiral Hood from the Dover command
was 'part of a policy of proscription pursued by Lord Fisher', and that
Battenberg had been allowed to bend the rules for his promotion to
admiral of the fleet. Some of Churchill's speeches were published as
The Fighting Line, in which he argued for better use of the manpower
resources, but did not raise the main point, that lives were being
expended needlessly in battle. However, after the United States entered
the war on 2 April 1917, he asked for a secret session of the house in
which he suggested that the army should not embark on any more

offensives until American resources became available, perhaps in nine months' time.[52] Lloyd George, now prime minister, refused to commit the government to this and the Third Battle of Ypres, or Passchendaele, was launched by General Haig on 31 July. By this time even Lloyd George had serious doubts but could not control the generals without damaging resignations. The battle would lead to nearly a quarter of a million British casualties, and Lloyd George later wrote: 'No soldier of any intelligence now defends this senseless campaign.'[53] The only hopeful spot was the Battle of Cambrai in November when 381 tanks broke through the enemy line and showed the possibilities of the new machine – but it was not supported and nothing material was gained. By that time Churchill was back in government and unable to make public comment.

The Ministry of Munitions

David Lloyd George became Prime Minister of a coalition government in December 1916. Churchill grew closer to him in the spring of
1917 and began to act as his unofficial adviser, visiting the front with
his support at the end of May. General Haig, the commander-in-chief,
offered no objections but made sure that the visit was carefully orchestrated. 'We saw the devastated regions, the battlefield of Verdun and the
Fille Morte sector in the Argonne in three successive days. There was no
danger – and hardly the sound of a gun.' He dined with various generals
and was perhaps a little jealous of his old friend Fayolle who had given
him the casque – he now commanded a force of 41 divisions. He dined
with General Pétain, a hero in this war and a villain in the next, who
'did not enter into any serious subjects' except the Salonika Campaign,
on which they differed.[1]

The question of Churchill's return to government arose and Lord
Esher believed that Lloyd George wanted him 'because he can strike
ideas into colour'.[2] There was now the possibility of founding an air
ministry and Churchill's friend, the South African General Smuts, recommended he accept it, as it 'offered great scope to his constructive
ability and initiative, and that with help from America our aerial effort
might yet become of decisive importance not only in the anti-submarine
campaign but also on the Western Front in the next twelve months'.[3] As
soon as rumours of return began to circulate, there was fierce opposition
especially from Conservatives. Admiral Lord Beresford, Fisher's most

prominent opponent, wrote to Andrew Bonar Law: 'I need not enu-merate to you the failure of Antwerp, Gallipoli, for which he is mainly responsible, the failure in administration of all his previous offices, the manner in which he turned the navy upside-down by his autocratic methods, and, with Fisher, ruled it with favouritism and espionage.'[4] Churchill was slightly shocked and told Hankey that he had 'no idea of the depth of public opinion against his return to public life', though he admitted he had been 'a bit above himself'.[5] On 17 July he took office as Minster of Munitions with a seat in the cabinet, but not in the crucial War Cabinet. Lord Derby, the Director General of Recruiting, believed that 'Winston Churchill is the great danger, because I cannot believe in his being content to simply run his own show and I am sure he will have a try to have a finger in the Admiralty and War Office pies.'[6] He was not far wrong.

★

Early in the war business leaders had initiated the slogan 'business as usual' for their commercial policy, though it was sometimes suggested that Churchill himself had coined it.[7] In any case it was soon obsolete as the war did not end by Christmas and a greater and greater propor-tion of national resources was sucked in. This came to a head in the spring of 1915 with the 'Shell scandal', a campaign orchestrated by the Northcliffe press which appeared to demonstrate that the troops at the front were being let down by lack of supplies. It was a parallel crisis to Fisher's resignation, and it helped force Asquith to accept a coalition with the Conservatives and Labour. The most dynamic figure still in a senior position in the government, Churchill's old ally David Lloyd George, founded the Ministry of Munitions and brought in businessmen to help run it. Initially it was mainly concerned with shell production and trench warfare supplies but soon it began to take over other military needs. It controlled the iron and steel, electrical and engineering industries and eventually had more than 250 government factories under its control. It had responsibilities for labour relations and preventing excessive profits. In December 1917 Churchill was convinced that the agitation for higher wages was due to the belief that enormous profits were being made, and suggested that the government took all of the excess profits, instead of just 80 per cent.[8] It employed more civilians than any other government department, with 65,000 in the ministry and a quarter of a million industrial workers. Nationalised industry, state control and limitations of profits might be seen as tendencies towards socialism, which was anathema to Gladstonian Liberals and especially the Conservatives, but it was defended on the grounds that the measures 'owed their inception not to any definite plan or policy of state monopoly but to the immediate stress of practical necessity'.[9]

According to Smuts, Munitions had become 'a somewhat routine department', but Churchill soon found scope for his energy and began to reform the unwieldy ministry.[10] 'The Minister of Munitions should be aided and advised by a council formally established. The time has come to interpose between more than fifty separate departments on one hand and the minster on the other, an organism which in the main will play a similar part and serve similar needs as the Board of Admiralty or Army Council.' In addition the ministry was to be divided into ten groups, 'classified as far as possible by kindred conditions'. He felt the need for a body of administrators to back up the businessmen. 'Experience shows the value for these purposes of a strong element of trained civil servants, thoroughly acquainted with official methods and inter-departmental relations.'[11] He ordered that 'A regular system of leave for the staff of the Munitions Ministry, and especially the higher branches, should be brought into existence.'[12] He suggested 'a luncheon club should be formed for the senior 60 or 70 officers of the Ministry. This would enable them to meet in twos or threes in *quiet* and agreeable surroundings daily. Everyone will get to know the other. "Shop" could be talked under good auspices.'[13]

His new job gave Churchill an overview of all the resources needed for the war, and he took the opportunity to criticise strategy. Derby was right about his interference; within ten days of taking office Churchill was telling Lord Curzon that there was no point in building more of the fast destroyers he himself had initiated. 'It is obvious that quite a different class of destroyer, much smaller and more humdrum, is required for submarine hunting far out of reach of all German surface ships.' Twenty-five knots would be 'quite sufficient for such a purpose'.[14] Though in theory he was not concerned with strategy, Churchill's control of labour and resources such as steel gave him an authority which he did not shrink from using. In August 1917 he wrote to one of his advisers: 'How many tanks, and of what patterns, are to be ready month by month in the next 12 months? By whom, and by what extent, have these programmes been approved? How much steel do they require? How much do they cost? How much skilled labour and unskilled do they require in these 12 months? What are the principal limiting factors in material and class of labour?'[15]

He clashed most strongly with Sir Eric Geddes, the current First Lord of the Admiralty, who complained: 'My fears as regards the Minister of Munitions are somewhat fortified by what has passed in conversation with him upon several occasions, and at recent meetings of the War Cabinet and Cabinet Committees. He has shewn that he contemplates an extension of his functions beyond what I have ever understood them to be, and an infringement of mine which I should view with great concern.'[16]

Churchill attempted to define his positon, conceding that 'the Ministry of Munitions has nothing to do with strategy and tactics' and 'he should express no official opinion on such subjects unless he is invited to be present as a minister of the crown at a meeting of the War Cabinet where such matters are raised, or is authorised by the Prime Minster to draw up a paper dealing with them', but on the other hand, 'in the sphere of *material*, the Minster of Munitions is entitled to review and examine the whole of our resources and to express his convictions as to the best use that can be made of them'. He was particularly concerned that 'At present the Admiralty claim a super priority upon all supplies ... even in regard to comparatively commonplace needs.'[17]

Certainly he still had strong views on how the navy should be run and supplied, and paradoxically his time at the Admiralty made him even more suspicious of their demands. He wrote in December 1917:

> ... every naval officer has been brought up with the feeling that it was his duty to do his utmost to screw as much out of the Treasury and the House of Commons

as possible. There was a great deal to be said for this in time of peace, and I myself profited enormously in wringing from Parliament and the Cabinet the necessary provisions. But it is no longer a question of extracting from peace-time indulgence or Treasury thrift the greatest possible supply for the upkeep of the Navy, but rather a question of draining the last drops of blood from the soldiers in the trenches and the last ounces of energy from the munitions factories.[18]

He went on: 'I am told that the construction of light cruisers of the largest kind, and battlecruisers, and the manufacture of heavy guns, is actually being proceeded with at the present time on a large scale …. It seems to me a very grievous thing that any warships other than for anti-submarine purposes, should be proceeded with at the present time.'[19]

Shells were the original priority of the ministry, and it was found that the Germans were using ones with false noses to give greater range. Churchill suggested ways of fitting existing British shells in response.[20] He advocated a much greater use of trench mortars and short-range artillery firing from trench to trench and supported increased production of the 6-inch howitzer.[21] In March 1918 he was suggesting a gas attack on a large scale and the next month he corresponded with General Rawlinson about which types to use, including the new mustard gas. Churchill believed that 'the Germans have very great difficulties in procuring the materials out of which good masks are made and are at a disadvantage in that respect'.[22] A new method had been adopted for the manufacture of rifle bullets, and the Germans claimed that they were in effect 'dum-dum' which had now been banned by the Hague Convention. Churchill denied this in the War Cabinet and suggested that if the Germans instituted reprisals, they should use counter-reprisals.[23]

★

The ministry had taken control of aircraft production early in 1917 and Churchill was well aware how much the picture had changed since his days with the Royal Naval Air Service. The number of aircraft in service in the Royal Flying Corps had expanded from 179 in August 1914 to 3,929 in January 1917; in the RNAS the figures were 93 and 1,567 respectively.[24] The pusher biplane was almost extinct and the monoplane was out of favour; the tractor biplane dominated the skies. The fighter aircraft had advanced since the development of the Constantinesco interrupter gear made it possible to fire through the propeller, and the most successful fighter of the war, the Sopwith Camel, entered service at the RNAS base at Dunkirk just as Churchill was taking up his new office.[25] It was a direct descendent of the Tabloids which he had known in 1914. Its main functions were to defend the homeland, now being attacked by twin-engined Gotha bombers as well as Zeppelins, and to gain air superiority over the Western Front – 1917 would see classic air battles against units such as the famous Richthofen Circus. The British, unlike the French and Germans, tended to emphasise team effort rather than individual brilliance, but 'aces' such as Mick Mannock and James McCudden gained a good deal of popular acclaim before their deaths in July 1918. The main purpose of air superiority was support for the army in the form of reconnaissance and spotting for artillery fire, but large-scale bombing of the trenches was advocated by Churchill's old friend General Barnes, who wrote from the front in November 1917: '… the winning or losing of this war (bar submarines) depends on one thing, and that is real supremacy in the air. … I am sure *bombing from the air* – now really only in its infancy – is going to make it *impossible* for the weaker side in the air to fight. … Last night we were bombed continuously with hundreds of bombs, and it fairly opened one's eyes, and mark you there is *no* protection possible.'[26]

Two-seater aircraft were developed for these purposes, including the excessively stable RE8, the classic Bristol Fighter and the DH9 bomber. At sea, most of the RNAS's aircraft operated from shore bases and the Short 184 was still the standard torpedo bomber, though being replaced. Aircraft were now being launched from the gun turrets of capital ships and cruisers although there was no means of recovering them. Squadron Commander Dunning landed on the converted foredeck of Fisher's eccentric battlecruiser *Furious*, but lost his life in the second attempt and it was clear that a carrier with a completely flat deck was needed – the first one, the *Argus*, was ordered to be converted from a liner late in 1916. Meanwhile Churchill was a strong advocate of bombing German industry using the Handley Page 0/400, developed from the machine Sueter had ordered in 1915. In September 1917 Churchill was confident that the 'immense programme of aeroplane construction' would be achieved.[27] But by March 1918 he was aware that it might be held up by shortage of machine guns, while engines were always a bottleneck. In August 1918 he complained: 'It would be disastrous if after having made for all these months immense preparations to bomb Germany … and having our organisation and plant prepared in all respects except one, the effort should be rendered abortive through lack of the last one, viz a comparatively small number of Liberty engines.'[28] Despite all the difficulties landplane production increased from 14,832 in 1917 to 30,782 in 1918.[29]

In the meantime, plans grew to form a new Air Ministry, on a par with the Admiralty and War Office and combining the aircraft of the army and navy. Surprisingly Beatty, now commander-in-chief of the Grand Fleet, accepted in August 1917 that the air services to the fleet 'could be performed from the naval point of view under an Air Ministry as they are under existing conditions'.[30] Churchill however 'anticipated no great difficulty in combining the principle of a uniform air service with the recognition of the special needs of the navy'.[31] It was finally formed on 1 April 1918 to take charge of the new Royal Air Force, and it took over Churchill's role in supplying aircraft.

Perhaps because he was now above inter-service rivalries, in October 1917 Churchill produced an extremely balanced and far-sighted paper on the future of air power. He described how there were no flanks in the land war, but Germany could exploit the situation by sea.

> If we take, on the one hand, the amount of national life-energy which the Germans have put into their submarine attack and compare it with the amount of national life-energy we are compelled to devote to meeting and overcoming that attack, it will be apparent what a fearfully profitable operation this attack on our communications has been to the enemy. Would it be an exaggeration to say that for one war-power unit Germany has applied to the submarine attack we have been forced to assign fifteen or twenty?

An attack on bases was even better than one on communications, though Churchill rejected the more extreme claims of the proponents of air power.

> It is improbable that any terrorization of the civil population which could be achieved by air attack could compel the government of a great nation to surrender. Familiarity with bombardment, a good system of dug-outs and shelters, a strong control by police and military authorities, should be sufficient to preserve the national fighting spirit unimpaired. ... Therefore our air offensive consistently be directed at striking at the bases and communications upon whose structure the fighting power of his armies and his fleets of the sea and of air depends. ... Any injury which comes to the civil population from this process of attack must be regarded as incidental and inevitable.

So far air attack had not been investigated fully because of the 'dominating and immediate interests of the army and the navy', and an air staff was needed to study it. He advocated specially trained 'bomb droppers' who would be the equivalent of naval gunlayers, so that bombs could be dropped in salvos as in naval warfare, and they should aim to 'straddle' the target. But first air supremacy had to be achieved: '... the primary objective of our air forces become plainly apparent, viz. the air bases of the enemy and the consequent destruction of his air fighting forces. All other objectives, however tempting, however necessary it may be to make provision for attacking some of them, must be regarded as subordinate to the primary purpose.' But once air superiority was won, bombing was not the only option. 'Considerable parties of soldiers could be conveyed by air to the neighbourhood of bridges or other important points, and, having overwhelmed the local guard, could *from the ground* effect a regular and permanent demolition.'

He also discussed land warfare, commenting: '... if one side discovered, developed, and perfected a definite method of advancing continuously, albeit it on a fairly limited front, a decisive defeat would be inflicted upon the other'.[32] He might have had cause to remember these words in 1940.

Churchill was also responsible for the safety of factories and workers during air raids, and in October 1917 he ordered that they should have dug-outs with overhead cover at least two layers deep 'with as wide an air space as possible in between the upper or detonating platform and the lower or actual roof'. Unless they were absolutely bomb-proof, they were to be divided to contain the blast. But they need not be perfect: 'Any shelter is better than none.' On a wider scale he wrote: 'I consider that, generally speaking, people are entitled to a safe shelter within reasonable distance of their homes or their work. I consider that in or near each street a house or houses should be prepared which affords reasonable security to the residents …'.[33]

★

The tank was of course one of Churchill's pet projects, and he believed that a year had been lost due to uncertainty about it.[34] A thousand had been ordered at the time of the Battle of the Somme, mostly Mark IVs which began delivery in April 1917. The Mark V, first tested in March that year, had a greatly improved driving system in contrast to the old one which needed the attention of four men. The first light tank, known as the Medium Mark A or the Whippet, was intended to exploit any breakthrough with a relatively high speed and it was first delivered in March 1918, in time to fight the German offensive. In April General Tudor wrote: 'I wish we had had some Whippets here: I have not believed in them, except originally as a great surprise used in large numbers. But I feel a few fast ones could have done great work here, especially if constructed to give good observation.'[35] Churchill wanted to expand the tank corps from 600–700 tanks and 18,000 men to a huge force of 10,000 tanks and 55,000 men, though of course he had to persuade the army and his cabinet colleagues of that.[36] An Anglo-American tank factory was started at Chateauroux in France, but Churchill came to regard it as 'an international scandal' and could not procure either the labour or the organisation to complete it.[37] He was not short of ideas and suggested tanks which could 'traverse the kind of inundations that are found on the Flanders Front' and imitation tanks which could serve to fool the enemy as well as training the infantry in co-operation with them.[38] He had a real one sent to his constituency in Dundee, describing it as 'This powerful weapon of war', 'a thoroughly British conception' which had 'proved on numerous occasions a method of saving lives and winning victories'.[39] He recognised that the Germans might develop anti-tank guns, but he advocated the use of smoke and darkness, and better tactical training with the infantry.[40] He now believed that the horse was obsolete in warfare and the cavalry should be mounted in tanks so that 'these splendid regiments' could be 'given a fair opportunity in the modern field'.[41]

By the end of 1917 Churchill was predicting: 'It looks as if the failure of the submarine attack as a decisive factor must leave the Germans no resource but a great offensive in the west. … I wish them joy of it … thank God our offensives are at an end.'[42] He visited the front as often as possible, and in May 1918 he suggested to Haig that he should have 'a permanent lodging' assigned to him.[43] He was allocated a chateau at Verchocq, 'very comfortable, simple and clean' with a bedroom containing 'fine and old' wood carved furniture.[44] He told Lloyd George: 'It is a very beautiful place, with the most lovely trees, and you might do far worse than spend a few days here.'[45] He continued to provide vivid accounts to his wife, who commented: 'How much better you describe things than the most brilliant newspaper correspondent. But I forget. You were one once.'[46]

In February he was at doing munitions business at Tramecourt: 'a fairly long day on ammunition, tanks and gas with the different people who supply', but he could not help but notice that he was close to the battlefield of Agincourt. By the 23rd he was much happier – 'I have been enjoying myself so much, and have had such very interesting days and pleasant evenings.' He had visited General Lipsett and General Barnes, his old companion in the 4th Hussars and Cuba. He had seen his old headquarters at Plug Street where the British trenches had moved forward about a mile and everything else was destroyed except a dugout which he had built and a convent he had drained. He worked with his shorthand writer and 'polished off two bags' before noon. In the afternoon he was moved on a visit to Ypres where thousands of British soldiers had lost their lives in three battles. He walked at least five hours each day, mostly on duckboard tracks, to view the sites whose names were known to the public only in newspaper reports: '… finally we got to Glencorse Wood and Polygon Wood. These consist of a few score of torn and splintered stumps only. But the view of the battle field is remarkable, Desolation reigns on every side. Litter, mud, the rusty wire and the pock-marked ground – Very few soldiers to be seen, mostly in "pill boxes" captured from the industrious Hun .... The Passchendaele Ridge was too far for us to reach but the whole immense area of slaughter was visible. ... Many of our friends and my contemporaries all perished here. Death seems as commonplace and as little alarming as to the undertaker.' He noticed that it was now possible to walk in the open without being fired on by snipers, and thought the Germans were 'so bored by the war, that they cannot even be bothered to kill a few passers by'. But the British continued to shoot at every opportunity, at least when Churchill was there.[47] Then he retired to the Ritz in Paris where he was 'amusing', according to the American writer Mary Borden.[48]

On 19 March Churchill was already on his fifth visit to France as Minster of Munitions and in a conference on tank production when Haig called him into his private room and showed him an enormous concentration of troops opposite the British sector of the front. He visited his old friend General Tudor, in charge of the 9th Division, and went into the trenches where 'a deathly and suspicious silence brooded over the whole front'. That night Tudor told him: 'It is certainly coming now. Trench raids this evening have identified no less than eight enemy battalions in a single half-mile of the front.' On 21 March he was in a chemical warfare conference when the Germans, deploying troops from the dormant Russian front, launched what Churchill called 'the greatest onslaught in the history of the world'.[49] He returned to London on the 23rd and visited the War Office to get the latest information. In the garden of Downing Street Lloyd George asked him about the prospects and he answered optimistically 'that every offensive lost its force as it proceeded. It was like throwing a bucket of water over the floor. It first rushed forward, then soaked forward, and finally stopped altogether until another bucket could be brought.' He helped to encourage the War Cabinet and suggested raising the age of conscription to 55. To General Sir Henry Wilson he was 'a real gem in a crisis, and reminded me of August 1914'.[50] He also urged the Prime Minister to take 50,000 men from the fleet, including most of the marines, and to extend conscription to Ireland.[51] But back home with his wife he spent his most anxious night of the war worrying about the crisis.[52] In the meantime he recognised his main responsibility was to keep the army supplied in the crisis. 'Everywhere the long-strained factories rejected the Easter breathing space which health required. One thought dominated the whole gigantic organisation. Guns, shells, rifles, ammunition, Maxim guns, Lewis guns, tanks, aeroplanes and 1,000 ancillaries were all gathered from our jealously hoarded reserves. Risks are relative, and I decided, without subsequent misadventure, to secure a month's supply of guns by omitting the usual firing tests.'[53]

*

Churchill went back to France on the 28th despite official discouragement and a message from Lloyd George 'to stick to Paris and not go directing strategy at the French GHQ'.[54] He was mildly encouraging in a telegram to Lloyd George, reporting: 'My impression was that the British Front was holding well in spite of continuous attack, but that the strain was great, the resources narrowing, and there was serious anxiety to know when and how the French will intervene in real force.'[55] He visited the Somme Montdidier front with Prime Minster Clemenceau, whom he compared with Fisher in style, but 'much more efficient'.[56] He reported that the French were doing everything they could but the Germans were very strong and could now shell the Amiens-Paris railway. At midnight on the 31st he reported that no serious attack had taken place that day, and on 1 April he asked the Prime Minister to come over to sort out differences between the British and French commanders. He did, and it was agreed to put General Foch in over all command as the situation began to stabilise.[57] Churchill was in Haig's headquarters on 29 April when there was near panic as it was reported that Mont Rouge and Mont Vidaigne had been taken. He headed out there but the French commander telephoned that it was all a mistake, nothing had happened.[58]

He flew back to France early in June, piloted by Lieutenant Cyril Patteson of the Royal Engineers, known as 'the canary'. The Germans were still only 45 miles from Paris and he endured an air raid in the city. A critical battle, a 'blunt trial of strength' was raging on the Montdidier-Noyon front and it seemed to be going well. He planned to fly back to Kenley aerodrome south of London.[59] In the meantime he had to fight against key men being drafted into the army. In July he wrote: 'Since the beginning of the year we have released no fewer than 100,000 men, nearly all of whom are skilled men, for military service. We have been deprived of all Grade I men of 19 to 20 without excepting even draughtsmen, men employed in making gauges, breech mechanisms, optical instruments and vital pivotal men.' He gave the example of the Glasgow optical firm of Barr and Stroud which was making an anti-aircraft height finder. Thirty men were about to be withdrawn which would postpone the introduction of this valuable instrument. Moreover 'men taken from industry after July will not reach the battle-front in time to influence the decision'.[60] Again he was hard on the navy, suggesting in March that '... the navy increased its complements after I left by 25% above the full approved war establishment. Their whole use of man power is luxurious. ... Fighting men are the need.'[61] In September he suggested sending sailors to the Western Front in an echo of the Royal Naval Division idea. 'There could be no better form for a naval contribution than to supply the men necessary to steer and manage, say, the last 2,000 British tanks to be completed before the battle.'[62]

★

Churchill flew out again in August, passing over the current family home at Lullenden south of London, where he urged his wife to take the children for safety from air raids. Wilson had announced to the War Cabinet that the British attack was about to open and the allied armies were advancing. Churchill was driven through Amiens and Villers Bretonneux, about 500 yards behind the lines which the Germans had held the day before. He rejoiced to see the tracks made by the 'invincible' tanks and to hear that Australian armoured cars had rushed through as soon as the enemy line was broken. He was beginning to believe that the tide had turned. He saw prisoners of war and from personal experience he sympathised with their 'miserable plight and dejection' though he was 'very glad to see them where they were'.[63] He still had to work and was 'cooped up in conferences hour after hour'. Representatives of the four major powers – Britain, France the USA and Italy – were meeting to co-ordinate munitions supplies and each had to take a smaller nation under its wing. Churchill commented ungraciously that Portugal was 'a rather dirty brat'.[64]

★

Churchill listened as General Sir Henry Wilson stood in front of a map in the cabinet room and outlined a battle plan in characteristic style. 'This morning, sir, a new battle. … This time it is we who have attacked. We have attacked with two armies – one British, one French. Sir Haig is in his train, Prime Minister, very uncomfortable, near the good city of Amiens. And Rawly [General Rawlinson] is in his left hand and Debeney in his right. Rawly is using five hundred tanks. It is a big battle, and we thought you would not like us to tell you about it beforehand.'[65] This time the tactics were right, the armies would break through and begin to push the Germans back to their frontier.

Churchill was back in France again in September despite Clementine's complaints that 'You have been away for nearly a month with your two visits – you bad vagrant.' She watched from St Margaret's Bay near Dover as his aircraft flew through a thunderstorm but 'the canary' was untroubled – he was 'much alarmed by motor cars and thinks them far more dangerous than aeroplanes'. And Churchill exulted that 'It gives me a feeling of tremendous conquest over space …'.[66] Once there, he was delighted that the soldiers received him 'with the broadest of grins and many a friendly shout and hand wave'. It was even better than the valuable estate he had recently inherited. He wrote to Clementine: 'The ruin of the countryside was complete. A broad belt of desert land stretches across the front in some places 30 miles wide without a tree that is not a blasted stump or a house that is not a heap of bricks. Everywhere pain and litter and squalor and the abomination of desolation. … Most of our dead are already buried, but a number of German blue grey bundles still lie about.'[67] On 26 September he was in Paris when he heard that Germany's ally Bulgaria had given in. He knew that the end of the war was in sight as the enemy powers collapsed one by one and Germany demanded peace. On a visit near the front, he did not realise how irregular the line was and came very close to the enemy near the village of Desselghem, with shells bursting 50 yards away.[68]

He was back in his office in Northumberland Avenue and looking out of a window as the Armistice took effect on the eleventh hour of 11 November 1918. The street was deserted as the first stroke of Big Ben rang out. 'Then from all sides men and women came scurrying into the street. ... The bells of London began to clash. Northumberland Avenue was now crowded with people in hundreds, nay, thousands, rushing hither and thither in a frantic manner, shouting and screaming with joy. ... Around me in our very headquarters, ... disorder had broken out. Doors banged. Feet clattered down corridors. Everyone rose from his desk and cast aside pen and paper. All bonds were broken.'[69]

PART III

Peace and War

CHAPTER 23

The Old Army and the New

A general election, the first since 1910, was called for 14 December 1918, and Churchill had a 'coupon' signed by Lloyd George and the Conservative leader Bonar Law saying that he supported the coalition – unlike Asquith's supporters and the rising Labour Party. He promised his voters in Dundee a choice 'between those sentiments of patriotism and comradeship which have won the war and those cowardly conceptions which at every stage have urged a dishonourable peace'.[1] His meetings were often rowdy but he won comfortably. Socialism was still a minority creed even in the moderate form adopted by the Labour Party that year, and it won only 59 seats compared with the coalition's 395, the Liberals' 163 and Sinn Fein's 73, which they would not take up.

As Lloyd George formed his new government, Churchill expected to get one of the service ministries, writing on 29 December: 'My heart is in the Admiralty. There I have long experience, and any claim that I may be granted in the public good will always rest on the fact that "The Fleet was ready".'[2] Sir Henry Wilson at the War Office had already heard that Churchill was to combine war and air and had his doubts about it.[3] Leopold Amery, the assistant secretary to the War Cabinet, reported that 'the army are terrified at the idea'.[4] On 9 January, however, Lloyd George offered Churchill 'the office of Secretary of State for War and Air', making it clear that there would only be one salary.[5] It was less clear whether it was considered as two separate jobs, or whether the air force was to be merged back into the other services. The next day Wilson asked him 'where the Admiralty came in' and he admitted 'Nowhere!' According to Lord Esher, the appointment was a gamble. It was 'mightily unpopular, but he possesses, as Macaulay said of Chatham, "an impetuous, adventurous and defying character"'.[6] Churchill would have preferred a combined Ministry of Defence (with himself in charge of course), with an under-secretary to head each service and another for supply. The issue came up in July 1919 and according to Sir Henry Wilson, Lloyd George 'put up all the objections he could think of but they were not very strong and in reality in the end, as he admitted to us later in the day, rested on the difficulty of getting Walter Long out of the Admiralty'.[7] For the moment Churchill had to be content without the Admiralty under his control.

Even so, no one else could run two departments at once, which was noticed in both of the ministries concerned. General Harington, the Deputy Chief of Imperial General Staff, remarked on 'his wonderful brain and capacity for work. How he got through it will always be a mystery to me. I used often to put twenty-five important papers in his box at about 8 p.m. and so did the other Army Councillors. They would all be back on our tables by 11 a.m. next morning with his decisions written in his own hand in red ink.'[8] And from the Air Ministry, Sir Hugh Trenchard wrote: 'It was possible to run a joint Secretary of State for War and Air in the case of Mr. Churchill with his enormous capacity for work and quick comprehension, at one reading, of the complicated questions that continually arise. But I am perfectly certain that no other man could have done this work without seriously handicapping the development of the air service and militating against economy ...'.[9]

Churchill's principal adviser at the War Office was Sir Henry Wilson, who had made such an impression at the Committee for Imperial Defence in 1911 and was now Chief of Imperial General Staff. He had spent almost all of his career in staff jobs, becoming Director of Military Operations and playing a key role in persuading the government to prepare an army to serve in his beloved France. According to the leading historian of the army of this period, he was 'one of Britain's most exuberant,

Gentleman-Cadet Spencer-Churchill around 1893, wearing a cap with the initials of the Royal Military College *Chronicle/Alamy Stock Photo*

Lieutenant Churchill in the elaborate uniform of a Hussar officer. *Keystone Pictures USA/Alamy Stock Photo*

Churchill as a war correspondent at Bloemfontein, South Africa, circa 1900. *Library of Congress*

Churchill (second from right) with Fisher on the way to a ship launch in 1911. *World History Archive/ Alamy Stock Photo*

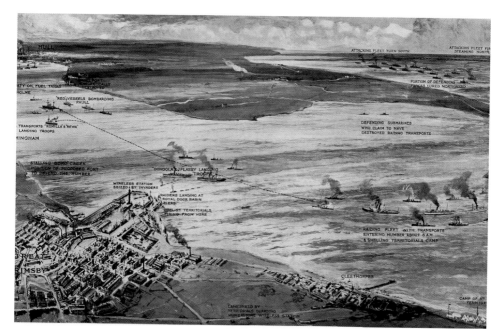

The public view of the 1913 manoeuvres, showing ships of the Red Fleet raiding the Humber estuary. © *Illustrated London News Ltd/ Mary Evans*

This cartoon of Asquith and Churchill on the yacht *Enchantress* is grossly unfair – far from relaxing, he was even more active than ever during the voyage. *Chronicle/Alamy Stock Photo*

UNDER HIS MASTER'S EYE.

SCENE—*Mediterranean, on board the Admiralty yacht " Enchantress."*

MR. WINSTON CHURCHILL. "ANY HOME NEWS?"

MR. ASQUITH. "HOW CAN THERE BE WITH YOU HERE?"

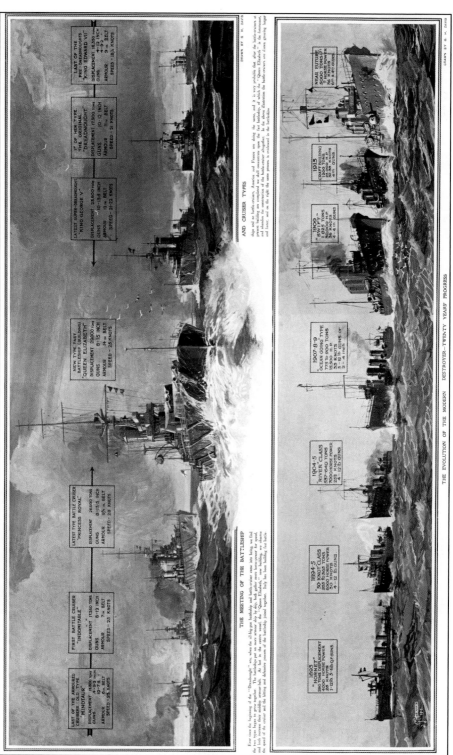

THE EVOLUTION OF THE MODERN DESTROYER—TWENTY YEARS' PROGRESS

The top half of this popular illustration shows the cruiser, battlecruiser and super-Dreadnought merging into the new Queen Elizabeth class of battleships. Below, new types of destroyer and cruiser types © *Illustrated London News Ltd/Mary Evans*

Churchill as Prime Minister, at his desk in the Map Room.
© *IWM (COL 30)*

Troops boarding the destroyer *Vanquisher* at the Mole at Dunkirk, during the evacuation.

The destroyer *Cossack* with her crew ready to board the prison ship *Altmark* in a neutral Norwegian fjord, February 1940. *Norman Wilkinson Estate/photo © National Maritime Museum, Greenwich, London*

Churchill at work in his special train, his usual means of making long journeys within Britain. © *IWM (H 10874)*

Winston Churchill inspecting a Cromwell tank of the Welsh Guards in Yorkshire, March 1944. © *IWM (H 37169)*

Churchill with the Chiefs of Staff in the garden of 10 Downing Street. Front row from left to right: Air Chief Marshal Sir Charles Portal, Field Marshal Sir Alan Brooke, Churchill, and Admiral of the Fleet Sir Andrew Cunningham. Back row, Major General L. C. Hollis, General Sir Hastings Ismay. © *IWM (H 41834)*

Churchill, full-length on the quarterdeck of HMS *Prince of Wales*, in which he travelled to the Atlantic Conference with Roosevelt in 1941. *Library of Congress*

Churchill comes ashore from a landing craft onto the east bank of the River Rhine in March 1945.
© IWM (BU 2249)

Crimean Conference: Prime Minister Winston Churchill, President Franklin D. Roosevelt, and Marshal Joseph Stalin at the palace in Yalta, where the Big Three met. *Library of Congress/U.S. Signal Corps*

Churchill on the balcony of Buckingham Palace with Princess Elizabeth (now Elizabeth II), King George VI, Queen Elizabeth and Princess Margaret on VE Day. May 1945. © IWM (MH 21835)

Churchill dressed for a flight with army officers, presumably at the Central Flying School. © *Illustrated London News Ltd/Mary Evans*

The Royal Naval Air Service raid the Friedrichshafen Zeppelin Sheds. © *Illustrated London News Ltd/Mary Evans*

An early anti-submarine boom at Scapa Flow, with floats slung between fishing boats.
© *IWM (SP 1053)*

The experimental tank Little Willie.

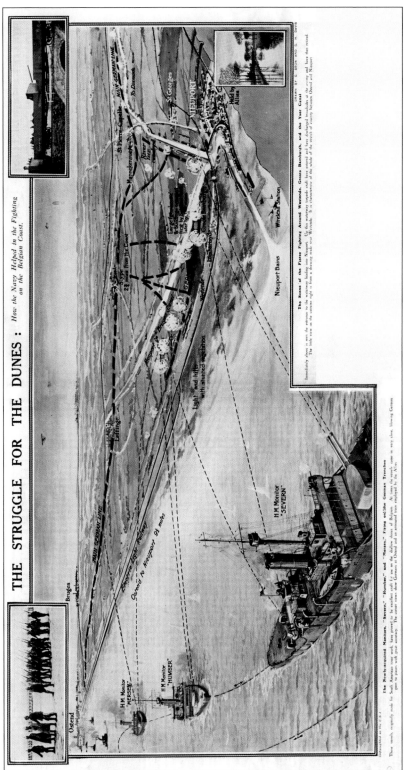

THE STRUGGLE FOR THE DUNES : How the Navy Helped in the Fighting on the Belgian Coast.

The monitors *Severn*, *Humber* and *Mersey* attacking German positions on the Belgian coast. © *Illustrated London News Ltd/Mary Evans*

The Track of Lusitania. W. L. Wyllie's painting does not fail to exploit the propaganda value of drowning civilians, women and children. *Chronicle/Alamy Stock Photo*

Also by Wyllie, this drawing shows the *Canopus* opening fire at Port Stanley to begin the Battle of the Falkland Islands. © *National Maritime Museum, Greenwich, London, Caird Collection*

Churchill in his office at the Admiralty, in consultation with Fisher during happier days. © *Illustrated London News Ltd/Mary Evans*

At 'V' beach on 25 April 1915, the steamer *River Clyde* lands British troops across pontoons under heavy fire. Many men were killed or wounded. *Chronicle/Alamy Stock Photo*

Churchill visiting General Fayolle at a French Army headquarters. He was presented with a French steel helmet which he continued to wear in the trenches even after British helmets had been issued. © *Mary Evans/Marx Memorial Library*

Minister of Munitions
Winston Churchill
inspects a production
line for heavy guns
during a visit to
Beardmore's Munitions
Works in Glasgow on
8 October 1918.
© *IWM (Q 84086)*

Churchill presents
the £10,000 *Daily
Mail* prize to Alcock
and Brown after their
pioneering flight across
the Atlantic.
© *The Royal
Aeronautical Society
(National Aerospace
Library)/Mary Evans
Picture Library*

A representation of
the night action in the
Battle of Jutland. The
German dreadnought
Nassau rams the
British destroyer
Spitfire. Both ships
survived. *Everett
Collection Historical/
Alamy Stock Photo*

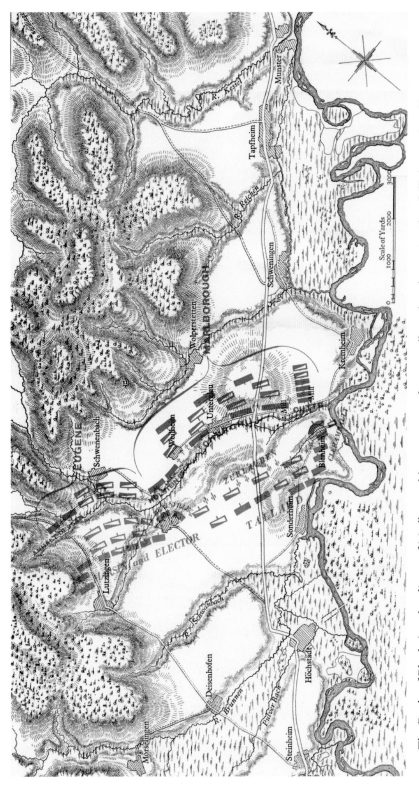

The Battle of Blenheim, the climax of Marlborough's career, one of many well-produced maps in Churchill's biography of his ancestor.

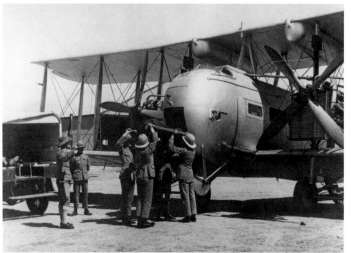

A Vickers Vernon
transport aircraft, based
on a bomber and fitted
with a bulbous fuselage,
is used to evacuate
wounded in Iraq.
© IWM (H(AM) 343)

A German air
delegation including
Feldmarschall
Ehrhard Milch is
shown Handley Page
Heyfords, the most
up to date bomber
in service, at RAF
Mildenhall, in October
1937.

A Light Tank Mk.VIA
of the 3rd King's Own
Hussars. © IWM
(ARMY TRAINING
6/6)

flamboyant, exotic, outspoken and even perhaps preposterous generals'.[10] He was a political general especially when his native northern Ireland was concerned, and a close adviser to Lloyd George who thought he had 'undoubtedly the nimblest intelligence amongst the soldiers of the highest degree'. Churchill had already felt 'the conceptions of war which I held ... received from him a keen and pregnant welcome' – though Wilson never believed that the final decision in the war could come anywhere but the Western Front. Churchill soon recognised his great responsibilities 'not only as supreme military adviser of the government but as executive officer responsible for the distribution of forces between various theatres ...'.[11]

★

There were enormous problems in the aftermath of war. Introducing the army estimates in March 1919 Churchill stated: 'The greater part of Europe and the greater part of Asia are plunged into varying degrees of disorder and anarchy ... the victorious allies, on whom there rests the responsibility for enabling the world to get to work again, are themselves exhausted in a very serious degree ...'.[12] In June 1920 Wilson warned of 'the extreme danger of his Majesty's Army being spread all over the world, strong nowhere, weak everywhere, and with no reserve to save a dangerous situation or to avert a coming danger'.[13] In France, a 'clearing up army' of about 120,000 men was needed to remove materials from the bases and guard prisoners. By the end of 1919 it had been reduced to 38,000, 18,000 of whom were exhuming bodies for reburial in neat rows in the Imperial War Graves cemeteries.[14] An Army of Occupation was necessary in Germany and forces were operating in different parts of Russia. The newly formed League of Nations 'mandated' various territories of the collapsed Turkish Empire to British control, all very difficult to govern. Palestine was seen as a buffer to Egypt but it was also affected by the Balfour Declaration offering it as national home to Jews – Churchill was ambivalent about Jews generally at this period, claiming that there were three groups – those who played a full part in the state where they lived, those who turned to Bolshevism, and Zionists. Of these he wrote: 'If, as may well happen, there should be created in our own lifetime by the banks of the Jordan a Jewish state under the protection of the British Crown which might well comprise three or four millions of Jews, an event will have happened in the history of the world which would from every point of view be beneficial and would be especially in harmony with the truest interests of the British Empire.'[15] But for the moment the army had to find a garrison of 9,000 British and 26,000 native troops to control the land, among the suspicious Arabs. Iraq, then usually known as Mesopotamia, was not considered valuable and Churchill wrote in February 1920: 'Apart from its importance as a link in the aerial route to India and the air defence of the Middle East, and apart from the military significance of the oil deposits, the General Staff are not pressing for the retention of Mesopotamia, or any part of it, on strategic grounds of Imperial security.' Persia was even less useful: 'Fancy spending the whole cost of a British Territorial Army on a weak and futile interference in the affairs of Persia!'[16] British forces would soon be withdrawn.

Nearer home there was a threat of revolution, and in January 1919 troops and tanks were deployed in Glasgow during a strike. The Irish revolt was even more serious and was tearing the army apart. The island required 80,000 troops in June 1921. The notorious Black and Tans, ex-army officers, carried out revenge attacks and Churchill did not entirely dissent. In November 1920 he advocated 'a policy of reprisals within strict limits and under strict control in certain districts in which it should be declared that conditions approximating to a state of war exist'.[17] But unlike in other campaigns, he made little or no attempt to direct military operations. B. L. Montgomery, the future field marshal, wrote that 'It developed into a murder campaign at which, in the end, soldiers became very skilful and more than held their own. But such a war is thoroughly bad for officers and men; it tends to lower their standards of decency and chivalry.'[18]

Early in 1919 the first task for the Minister of War was to demobilise most of the 3,350,000 British soldiers serving at the time of the Armistice. This had been planned since 1916, but the system was based entirely on the needs of the home economy – getting back skilled workers and preventing mass unemployment. It took no account of the needs of the army and the passionate wishes of most of the soldiers to get home as soon as possible. Apart from a small minority of regular soldiers with time on their engagements, the men were divided into five categories. At the top was the small group of 'demobilisers' whose services were needed in demobilising and transporting the others. After them were the 'pivotal men' whose work was considered essential in reviving civilian industry, and they too were to be released before general demobilisation began. Then there were the 'slip men' who had definite promises of employment and were to be released according to priorities drawn up by the Ministry of Labour, as general demobilisation started. Those in the fourth category had no definite jobs to go to but could be employed in industries which were regarded as important; and finally the 'non-slip' men did not fall into any of these categories. It was only within the groups that personal factors – married and family status, length of service, number of wounds and so on – were taken into account. Naturally men who had the shortest service were in closest touch with their former employers and might gain an advantage that way. The problem was compounded by an order that men who happened to be on leave might seek work and use that to their advantage. Moreover, fraud was often suspected.[19] In one battalion, by 30 January 1919, 'One officer and 365 other ranks, of whom 206 claimed to be miners, had been demobilised.'[20]

The injustice of the scheme was soon obvious to the troops. Early in January 1919 10,000 men at Folkestone refused to board ship to return to France, and there was a demonstration of 2,000 men at Dover. There was a mass meeting of 8,000 soldiers at Brighton on the 6th. The men were dissatisfied with the slow rate of demobilisation, and with the fear that they might be sent to Russia. Before taking office, according to Wilson, Churchill was 'full of fight and ideas. Wants to stop demobilisation altogether! Wants to bring home all reliable troops, ie household and other cavalry, yeomanry, county regiments etc.'[21] But soon he recognised the problems and wrote to Lloyd George: 'Situation in army causes great anxiety to all my advisers. A few more weeks on present lines and there will be nothing left but demoralised and angry mob.'[22]

By 14 January Churchill proposed to 'hold up demobilisation for all men who have not completed two years in France'. According to Wilson there was 'much to be said for his argument'.[23] Haig was recalled from France to confer with Churchill and Geddes in Churchill's office; it was agreed that all men who had joined since 1 January 1916 would be retained – they had either been conscripted or had mostly volunteered to avoid conscription. This, it was estimated, would produce 1,600,000 men, which was more than enough for the immediate tasks.[24] Churchill impressed the urgency on Lloyd George. 'At present the whole discipline of the army is being rotted – every platoon simultaneously – by the pulling out of people in ones and twos without any regard to what the ordinary man regards as fair play ... broadly speaking, I contemplate getting rid or three men out of four. The saving which will accrue from accelerating this process by even two months will more than pay the extra cost of rendering those who stop a contented and privileged class.'[25]

The scheme was announced in army orders on 29 January on Churchill's principle that 'if anyone has to stay, it must be those who are not the oldest, nor those who came the earliest, nor those who suffered the most'.[26] Those who had enlisted after the end of 1915, who were under 37 and had less than three wound stripes were to be retained, but they were allowed an increase of pay of at least 10/6 (52½ p) a week for a private. By 3 March he was able to tell the House of Commons: 'the plan has been well received and readily understood throughout the whole army. ... It has been followed by a great and sensible recovery of discipline and morale ...'.[27]

This raised another difficulty. As the law stood, conscripted men would have to be released soon after the peace treaty was ratified but the occupation of Germany was expected to last longer than that. Conscription had raised great passions in the general election and Lloyd George had promised not to renew the act once it had expired. Introducing a new bill, Churchill told parliament: 'Till I went to the War Office I was not acquainted with the fact that the whole of the

army fell to pieces on the ratification of the peace treaty.' He promised that conscription was not to become permanent and the bill was
passed with a large majority, but it remained unpopular. In September
Churchill postponed meetings in Dundee for fear of disruption, as
he had to be 'responsible for keeping so many people in the army
who wish to be free'.[28] But in fact the measure was barely needed
as the treaty was not ratified until January 1920, by which time only
150,000 conscripts were still serving.

*

An Army of Occupation was to be sent into Germany partly to enforce
the severe terms of the armistice and later the Treaty of Versailles.
Churchill wrote: 'I am quite sure that you will never get the Germans
to give up anything more than has actually been taken from them
unless you have effective forces at your disposal.'[29] He continued to
fear that 'Germany would get to work quietly producing munitions
and completing her plans, but she would only come into the open
when we and our present allies or associates began to quarrel … the
Republican Party in the United States was bent on disentangling their
country from Europe, one result of might be that one day they would
start competition in armaments.'[30] Under the armistice the allies were
to occupy Germany west of the Rhine, with a British force east of the
river occupying 30 kilometres around Cologne with the Americans in
Koblenz and the French around Frankfurt. British cavalry crossed the
Rhine on 12 December and the occupation was complete by the next
day. They would have to deal with the rival forces struggling for the
control of Germany, the communist Sparticists and the *Freikorps* largely
made up of discharged soldiers – though the main Spartacist revolt was
crushed in Berlin by 15 January, and the rival groups rarely clashed inside
the occupied zones.

For the army of occupation Churchill used 'Young Soldiers Battalions'
made up of young men aged 18 plus who had recently been called
up to their local regiments. Each group was formed into a company
and sent to join a Graduated Battalion organised in companies by age
group. Most of the regular NCOs had been discharged so they were

led by men who had gained their stripes at the front and knew little of peacetime discipline. The young men were not fully trained and lacked authority over the population. But the Germans were surprisingly tolerant of the British, perhaps because they wanted to drive a wedge between them and the French. The British Army of the Rhine started with more than 275,000 men and stood by in May 1919 in case the Germans revolted against the Peace Treaty. It was reduced to 50,000 by November 1921 and it remained in place until 1929, by which time it had already banned the performance of a play by the Hitler Youth as being 'slanderous and most prejudiced'.[31]

★

Churchill does not seem to have been very concerned when the Tsar of Russia was overthrown in March 1917 and replaced by a moderate socialist regime, nor with the 'October Revolution' of that year when the Bolsheviks under Vladimir Lenin and Leon Trotsky seized power with a far more extreme programme of world revolution. By the end of the year, however, he noticed with alarm that 'The collapse of Russia has released a large part of the German and Austrian armies in the Eastern Front.'[32] That was confirmed in March 1918 when the Treaty of Brest-Litovsk formally withdrew Russia from the war and ceded large territories to the Germans. After that he was obsessive about the threat to Bolshevism. Perhaps the key to his attitude is to be found in the quote from Lenin at the head of one of his chapters in *The World Crisis* – 'He is no socialist who will not sacrifice his fatherland for the triumph of the social revolution.'[33] This was anathema to Churchill, who thought little of party loyalty and changed his allegiances twice, but would never dream of betraying his country.

Soon several disconnected revolts were under way against the Bolsheviks. Soldiers of the Czech Legion, recruited to fight their Austro-Hungarian occupiers, were on a circuitous route home when they came into conflict with the Bolsheviks and accidentally found themselves in possession of the Trans-Siberian Railway. There were British forces in place to the north around Murmansk and Archangel and others supported the Cossacks under General Denikin to the south. Three months after Brest-Litovsk Churchill still wanted to 'reconstitute the fighting front against Germany in the east'. 'Surely now when Czech divisions are in possession of large sections of the Siberian Railway and in danger of being done to death by the treacherous Bolsheviks, some effort to rescue them can be made?'[34]

Just before the armistice Churchill suggested: 'We might have to build up the German Army, as it was important to get Germany on her legs again for fear of the spread of Bolshevism.'[35] The cabinet remained split over the issue as Churchill moved from Munitions to the War Office, where he had to defend the position of the troops already in Russia. On 27 January 1919 he wrote from Paris: 'We have very small forces (about 14,000) there. They are exerting great influence, particularly in Siberia, because they are thought to be the vanguard of Britain ... by giving the impression that Britain is behind them; whereas long ago Britain quitted the field.'[36] But early in February the cabinet decided that no reinforcements should be sent as 'there was considerable unrest in the army on the subject of Russia and ... the despatch of further troops might have serious results'. Churchill thought that the morale of the army was much improved from three weeks before but the others remained unconvinced.[37] The Bolsheviks were getting stronger every day. In the south, General Denikin's army had greatly deteriorated. General Krasnoff, the leader of the Don Cossacks, was discouraged, and believed the allies had thrown them over completely. The situation in Siberia was exactly the same. 'There was compete disheartenment everywhere.' Lloyd George replied that effective intervention might need a million men at least. Churchill 'did not suggest intervention on that scale, but we ought to try and keep alive the Russian forces which were attempting to make headway against the Bolsheviks'.[38] Churchill proposed a Russian Council to co-ordinate allied strategy, but the British cabinet remained undecided and other leaders were reluctant or opposed. Churchill was the only one to oppose Bolshevism consistently. His position was weakened yet more at the end of February when a British battalion mutinied in the North. London dockers had already refused to load the *Jolly George* with munitions for Russia. There were several naval mutinies connected with service in the Baltic, the First

Destroyer Flotilla refused to sail there and 87 men of the 6th Battalion of the Royal Marines were court martialled for insubordination and refusal of duty.[39] Eventually British troops were withdrawn and the Bolsheviks remained in power.

Churchill was to remain an implacable opponent of Bolshevism throughout the decades. When he published his *Great Contemporaries* in 1937 he had a good word for almost everyone – Douglas Haig was treated with sympathy despite the huge casualties in his 1916 and 1917 campaigns. The ex-Kaiser was partly excused by asking the question, 'What should I have done in his position?' Even Adolf Hitler, already known for tyranny and repression, might still 'go down in history as the man who restored honour and peace of mind to the Germanic nation and brought it ... to the forefront of the European family circle'. But Trotsky had no moral virtues, possessing 'the organising command of a Carnot, the cold detached intelligence of a Machiavelli, the mob oratory of a Cleon, the ferocity of Jack the Ripper ...'.[40]

★

Amidst all the post-war problems of Ireland, Russia, demobilisation and the mandates, it was necessary to create an army for the future, but there was no time, money or consensus for a coherent plan. In the spring of 1919 a Committee on the Organisation of the After War Army suggested a force of 20 divisions, which could fit out a small expeditionary force for colonial wars, but offered no radical solutions.[41] As well as financial stringency, a dominant factor from August 1919 was the 'ten year rule' which was drawn up by Sir Maurice Hankey and laid down that 'It should be assumed, for framing revised estimates, that the British Empire will not be engaged in any great war during the next ten years, and that no expeditionary force is required for this purpose ...'.[42]

Infantry had been the primary arm in the war and it would make up about half of the new army. The regimental system had been reinforced by the war. It allowed millions of civilians to be trained and be brought into the tradition of a particular regiment – a loyalty which many of them retained for the rest of their lives. This had perhaps been strengthened in Churchill's eyes by his experience with the Royal Scots Fusiliers. In June 1920 he spoke of 'the importance attached by soldiers to their uniforms', and by regiments to 'their regimental position'.[43] He referred to 'the unshakeable Cardwell system'.[44] He valued tradition more than ever. He reversed his earlier views on ceremonial dress and in February 1921 the guards at Buckingham Palace wore their traditional bearskins and red tunics again. Churchill was delighted with the crowd's reaction as they watched 'the splendid old pageant' – though like most British traditions it was largely Victorian.[45]

However, the Cardwell system had a serious flaw – the number of infantry battalions at home was based entirely on the number in the empire, with no regard to home defence or the need for an expeditionary force. In 1922, when Sir Eric Geddes proposed to reduce the number of battalions overseas and therefore those backing them up at home, a committee chaired by Churchill responded that the post-war army, like its pre-war counterpart, existed 'solely for the purpose of maintaining our foreign garrisons, of providing an adequate force to proceed to their relief or reinforcement and as an ultimate aid to the civil power'. They did not think 'that less than nine or ten battalions of Guards should stand available for the maintenance of order in the capital and seat of government, nor that 54 battalions of infantry are in excess of what might be required for similar purposes throughout Great Britain'.[46]

Churchill often took the artillery for granted. He was well aware of the effect of heavy guns on fortifications but, as he observed in 1917, 'artillery is so local in its action, so costly in its use, and so ponderous in its movement that the rate of advance has not hitherto led to any decisive strategic results'.[47] In January 1921 he asked why there were nearly a thousand more officers in the branch than at the start of the war. 'We are not likely to be engaged in any war for five years in which any large concentration of artillery will require to be used. The artillery should, therefore, be reduced in part to a nucleus basis.'[48]

The tank corps, formed into the Royal Tank Regiment in 1923, was always going to be far less glamorous and exciting than flying or cavalry. Tanks, especially the early models, were ugly machines and very early on they became emblems of oppression when they appeared in Glasgow in 1919, while armoured cars were regularly used against the rebels in Ireland. Perhaps the tank needed a Trenchard to put its case, but the nearest thing was J. F. C. Fuller, a tactical genius but a flawed character who supported many strange theories in his middle life, and Fascism in later years. He was a born maverick and a prolific writer, and indeed he resigned from the army when he was forbidden to publish. His ideas on tank warfare, and those of his associate Basil Liddell Hart, were taken up abroad by Charles de Gaulle and more ominously, by Heinz Guderian of the German army.

There was a contrary view, expressed by Major-General Sir Louis Jackson, that the tank was an aberration, conceived for the specialised task of crossing two or three hundred yards of no-man's-land. 'The tank proper was a freak. The circumstances which called it into existence were exceptional and are not likely to recur. If they do, they can be dealt with by other means.' Churchill, however, had no doubts about the possibilities. Perhaps he was thinking of innovative and highly mobile vehicles under development by Lieutenant-Colonel Philip Johnson when he wrote in October 1919: 'There is no comparison whatever between the best tank used in the war and this new model.' He pleaded with the Chancellor of the Exchequer to be allowed half a million pounds for technical development so that they could be proved. Well aware of conservatism and entrenched interests from his experiences in the last few years, 'I cannot hope to carry military opinion with me in the very drastic changes which I have in contemplation ... unless I am able to show these new weapons not as a mere experiment but as definite features in the military organisation. ... Unless these new tanks can be made and the military authorities impressed with their practical utility, it is hopeless to look for a speedy transition to a mechanical army.' He was a former cavalry officer but fully aware of the limitations of the horse. 'My plan is to do away with at least half the cavalry and substitute for them a much smaller number of these very fast tank units (which alone possess the swiftness of cavalry). But I shall never get military opinion to accept this, except under violent duress, unless and until it is possible to show the definite tactical results which can be achieved by the use of this new arm manoeuvring with the others.'[49] Development of the Johnson designs soon faltered and the Ordnance Department went for a less advanced light tank designed by Vickers.[50]

The financial authorities were not helpful; in May 1920 Churchill was refused the money for 78 specialist officers and wrote: 'If this decision is adhered to, it will not be possible to start the Tank Corps, consequently the experimental brigades, this year. Therefore all question of substituting modern mechanical methods for more man-power will be postponed for an additional twelve months at the very least. We cannot possibly reconstitute the Tank Corps except by use of officers who are already trained, and as these officers do not belong to the pre-war Regular Army, it is necessary to convert their temporary commissions into permanent commissions.'[51]

Churchill still favoured the armoured car, writing in June 1919: 'In the clearing up that remains to be done after the war, the armoured car will play a vital part. Instead of large forces of infantry, cavalry and heavy artillery maintained as garrisons, we require in many places smaller forces with machine guns in armoured cars which are very mobile and which can move into streets and villages and push out across deserts in suitable country and support civil and police administration. ... Everyone is crying out for armoured cars – India, Egypt, Mesopotamia, Denikin, Ireland, the Army of the Rhine.'[52]

★

Churchill continued to find time to play polo regularly, to the annoyance of Wilson: 'Winston said he would see about it tomorrow but he had to play polo!'[53] But that did not mean he had any illusions about the usefulness of cavalry in modern war; he wrote at the end of 1917: 'The cavalry myth is exploded at last ...'.[54] In February 1920 he told parliament: 'If anything had been proved by the war, it was that cavalry was less useful than we had previously thought.'[55] He was already proposing that 'these splendid regiments' (the cavalry) should be 'given a fair opportunity on the modern field'. He was pressing that they 'should be put by regiments into the tanks'.[56] He approached the issue differently in May 1920: 'There are 28 regiments of cavalry of the line, costing approximately £275,000 a year each. My proposal is to reduce these to 12, saving about £4,500,000, and to substitute temporarily an addition of 8,000 bayonets to the infantry of the line costing only about £800,000. It will later be possible to substitute for these bayonets the technical and mechanical units on which we are now experimenting ...'.[57]

As to the most decisive weapon of the war, since 1915 the heavy automatic weapons had been organised in the Machine Gun Corps so that their strength could be co-ordinated on the battlefield. A committee was appointed to consider 'the Provision of Officers for the After the War Machine Gun Corps'. It recommended three branches, for infantry, cavalry and motors. One officer even managed to blend the old and new armies by suggesting that officers for the cavalry section should 'go through all the elementary training as a cavalry recruit officer, riding school, square etc.', but that was never likely to happen.[58] In February 1920 Churchill told parliament: 'It was decided not to maintain a separate machine gun corps, but to put the machine gun units into the different battalions and squadrons, and that implies no diminution in the proportion of machine guns, but a different method of arranging them' – though the Corps was not abolished until 1923 after Churchill left the War Office.

The After War Committee of 1919 had not found the Territorial Army very useful, claiming that each unit contained 'men of unequal physical standards and widely differing ages' with 'no mechanism for expansion beyond units maintained in peace'. The great expansion during the war had by-passed the territorials, largely due to Kitchener's prejudices. Nevertheless it was planned to revive the force. Churchill spent a year discussing the subject 'with a great number of men, who from their experience were common to express an opinion'. He concluded that the old idea of a Territorial Force for home defence only was not practicable and recruits would be made aware that they might be called on to serve abroad or in the empire, but only with the consent of parliament, and they would be sent as units and not as individuals. Fourteen divisions were to be raised in this way.[59]

When Churchill left the War Office in January 1921 to become Secretary of State for the Colonies, he could claim that he had dealt with the worst of the army's post-war problems, especially demobilisation. But with limited time and budgets, and with no war looming to shake complacency, he could not claim any major reform. The historian of the period implies that the inter-war army 'remained firmly geared to the pace of regimental soldiering as an agreeable occupation rather than a demanding profession; and that many officers, so far from wishing to adapt to social and technological change, looked to the army as a haven where they could escape from them'.[60]

CHAPTER 24

Saving the Air Force

Churchill later explained Lloyd George's decision to appoint him joint Secretary of State for War and Air as '… the scale, size and cost of the Royal Air Force in the years immediately following the Great War would not be sufficiently large to justify the appointment of a separate Secretary of State'. If one was appointed to head a force which would be reduced to about 20,000 men, many other departments would demand equal status. 'To have a separate Air Minister and to include him in the Cabinet would create an anomalous position in regard to at least half a dozen other offices which for practical purposes have just as great a weight and importance …'.[1] One alternative was to have an air minister outside the cabinet, but that would clearly be a downgrading of the air force. Another, which was not far from Churchill's mind, was to form a ministry of defence to head all three services, but it was not to happen for now. Churchill was always clear that the RAF was to remain independent. On 8 February he wrote to Walter Long, the First Lord of the Admiralty: '… the fact that I hold the seals of two offices in no way implies the absorption of the Air Force into the Army. The arrangement is in principle temporary. It is of great convenience during the process of demobilisation that the Air Force and the Army can be guided step by step from one point of view.' A week later he wrote to his under-secretary that he would 'Resist strongly any proposal to remove any form of flying from control of Air Ministry.'[2]

The air forces that Churchill had known in 1912–15 had changed well beyond recognition. From 600 officers and men and 93 aircraft in August 1914, the RNAS had expanded to nearly 48,000 men and 2,741 aircraft by the end of 1917. The Royal Flying Corps was about double that size, and in April 1918 they were controversially merged to form the Royal Air Force, which had more than 291,000 men and 22,000 aircraft by the end of the war. Air power had proved its value – on the Western Front, the RFC and RNAS squadrons had suffered several ups and downs as new aircraft were introduced by both sides, but in the end they shot down 6,904 enemy aircraft for the loss of only 2,841 of their own. The tractor biplane was now almost universal. Eighty mph had been considered a good speed in 1914, now the Sopwith Snipe did 110. In 1912 Samson had been reluctant to carry a passenger 'owing to the sacrifice of petrol and the consequent reduction in the radius of action'. Now the Vickers Vimy could carry a bomb load of nearly 2,500 lbs. Ten years ago, interest in the air had been stimulated by Louis Bleriot's flight across the English Channel. In 1919 Churchill presented a *Daily Mail* cheque to the RAF officers Alcock and Brown for the first non-stop flight across the Atlantic.

With so many to choose from, only the best types were selected for the much reduced air force. The Sopwith Snipe was a development of the famous Camel, which in turn was descended from the Tabloid which Churchill had flown in 1914. The standard reconnaissance machine was the two-seater Bristol F2B, faster and far more manoeuvrable than the BE2s which Samson had favoured four years before. It was the most common type in the air force, with more than a thousand in total, including 360 on active service and 227 for training. The De Havilland 9a was the main light bomber and the second most prolific type. The four-engined Handley-Page V/1500 was dropped as being too expensive, so the main heavy bomber was the Vickers Vimy, though there were only 14 of them for training and 71 in reserve. Wartime stocks were still high; in all there were 840 landplanes in service, 806 for training and 1,765 in storage. There were 219 naval aircraft in service, 69 for training and 159 in reserve. They included the Sopwith Cuckoo torpedo bomber and various models of the three-seater Fairey III for reconnaissance duties. Flying boats were now well established and the Felixstowe F5 was the latest in a line developed in the east coast port. The only aircraft which Churchill might have recognised from his days in the Admiralty was the Avro 504 which had first flown in 1913; in its latest version, the 504K, it was the standard basic trainer of the RAF.[3]

*

On the recommendation of his predecessor Lord Weir, Churchill wanted Hugh Trenchard as the Chief of Air Staff and professional head of the Royal Air Force. He was a year older than Churchill, and the two had a great deal in common. Both failed entrance examinations in their early years and Trenchard got his army commission through the 'back door' of the militia. He was a cavalry officer skilled at polo, and the two first met during a hard-fought match in India in 1896.[4] After service in the South African War and Nigeria, Trenchard took up flying. Like Churchill he had difficulty as an older trainee, but he was able to concentrate and got through because of his 'enviable pluck and perseverance'.[5] When the war started he impressed Haig with his authority and his drive to produce better aircraft. He became head of the Royal Flying Corps in August 1915, as the German Fokker monoplane wreaked havoc and interrupted his policy of forward reconnaissance. He was already developing ideas about heavy bombing to destroy the enemy's industrial potential. When the new Royal Air Force was formed in April 1918 he was the natural though reluctant choice for its chief of staff, but he could not get on with his minister, the newspaper magnate Lord Rothermere, and resigned. He was sent to command the Independent Air Force being formed in France to bomb Germany, though privately he regarded it as a 'gigantic waste of effort and personnel'. Trenchard's rival, Sir Frederick Sykes, was already installed as Chief of Air Staff when Churchill took over, but he was persuaded to step aside and take charge of civil aviation under the same ministry. Trenchard took office on 9 February 1919, but by early March he had fallen ill during the influenza pandemic. He tendered his resignation, which Churchill refused to accept.[6]

Trenchard recovered and set his stamp on his service even more than Fisher did on his, and with more lasting effect, though in personality he was a complete contrast. His inarticulacy in speech or on paper was almost legendary. As he told the Royal Aeronautical Society in 1921, '... I am very bad at lecturing and words of more than two syllables give me some trouble'.[7] He told his personal assistant, the poet Maurice Baring: 'I can't write what I mean, I can't say what I mean, but I expect you to know what I mean.' Unlike Fisher, Trenchard tended to unite the new and beleaguered RAF. From the lowest ranks T. E. Lawrence wrote: 'The word Trenchard spells out confidence ... and by virtue of this pole-star of knowledge he steers through all the ingenuity and cleverness and hesitations of the little men who help or hinder him.'[8]

Churchill and Trenchard tended to complement one another, and no one was better than Churchill at putting Trenchard's thought into politically acceptable terms. While Churchill's mind was ranging over two services and several continents, Trenchard was dedicated to the new air force. Trenchard often suspected Churchill of lack of resolution in maintaining the existence of the air force. As he later said: 'Winston Churchill caused me more sleepless nights while he was in charge of the Air Ministry than any of his successors. His imagination was too strong for comfort and he tended to be too easily swayed by the last devil's advocate he happened to meet.'[9] This reflected the fact that as a politician Churchill had to be ready to make many manoeuvres and compromises, while Trenchard could remain single-minded. The two clashed most notably in September 1919 when the Trenchard went over to the War Office and burst into Churchill's room. There was a shouting match across the desk, until Churchill observed: 'You said something just now about the absurdity of trained airmen becoming mere chauffeurs for the army and navy. I like that, it's the best argument I've heard yet.'[10] He asked Trenchard to develop this into a paper, which became the basis of his arguments in cabinet. According to Trenchard there were two alternatives:

(1) To use the air simply as a means of conveyance, captained by chauffeurs, weighted by the army and navy personnel, to carry out reconnaissance for the army or navy, drop bombs at places specified by the immediately affecting local operations or observe for their artillery.

(2) To really make an air service which will encourage and develop airmanship, or better still, the air spirit, like the naval spirit, and make it a force that will profoundly alter the strategy of the future ....[11]

Sykes had prepared an ambitious scheme for a large peacetime force, but Trenchard was more realistic – he wanted a small but highly efficient service. The 'Trenchard Memorandum' of November 1919 was an 8,000-word document. It had a short preface by Churchill, announcing that it had been prepared under his direction. The main text took up his point about pilots not being mere chauffeurs. The RAF had been created to serve in a war which ended unexpectedly. Its personnel and buildings were nearly all temporary. Its aircraft were plentiful but often made obsolete by rapid progress. In a simile which probably owed much to the deeply religious and poetic Maurice Baring, it was compared to the prophet Jonah's gourd. 'The necessities of war created it in a night, but the economies of peace have to a large extent caused it to wither in a day, and we are now faced with the necessity of replacing it with a plant of a deeper root.'

The main part would be 'an Independent Force, together with the service personnel required to carry out aeronautical research'. There would be smaller parts trained to work with the navy and the army with the possibility, in a phrase which Trenchard later regretted, of 'these two small portions probably becoming, in the future, an arm of the older services'. Most of the force would be based overseas in India, Mesopotamia and Egypt, 'the Clapham junction of the air'. Only four squadrons were to be stationed at home. No major war was expected for some years so it was best to 'concentrate on providing for the needs of the moment as far as they can be foreseen and on laying the foundations of a highly-trained and efficient force which, though not capable of expansion in its present form, can be made to do so without any drastic alteration ...'. For co-operation with the army, one flight was eventually to be provided per division. For the navy, three aeroplane and two seaplane squadrons were to be built up. Airships were expensive but a station was to be kept up at Howden. Capital outlay was needed for permanent accommodation: '... the Air Force does not possess one single permanent barracks, and a large capital outlay on the provision of new buildings and the adaptation of the most suitable of the temporary buildings is inevitable during the first few years.' There was no mention of the actual landing surfaces; nearly all airfields in Britain would be grass until well into the Second World War.[12]

Trenchard claimed a success in setting up the Chiefs of Staff Committee with the heads of all three services, giving him an equality that was not reflected in budgets or prestige. As he said later, 'What I need is an official ring where I can face Wilson and Beatty as an equal. If they intend to destroy me, they'd have to do it under Queensberry rules.'[13] The committee was formally approved in 1923 and its members were tasked with 'considering and investigating the question of imperial defence as a whole, co-ordinating the functions and requirements of the navy, army and air force'. It was strengthened in 1926 and met monthly except during crises, but with Trenchard and Beatty across the table it was never going to be harmonious. Churchill wrote in 1926: '... the weakness of this body arises from the fact that, although they consider strategic and tactical problems from a general standpoint, each chief of staff regards himself as responsible only for his own particular service and as the champion of its interests .... We have in fact the meeting of three tribal chiefs, all working for the common victory, but allowing no inroad upon the vested interests of their tribe.'[14] Ironically this body, the scene of conflict in the 1920s, would later be used by Churchill to promote inter-service harmony.

Churchill also believed in a three-part air force and wrote to Wilson 'that not only should there be air officers, both permanent and temporary, but also a proportion of military officers and naval officers circulating through the air force'. Eventually, these young officers would 'acquire that influence in the army that would make their air force training really useful to the army'.[15] Trenchard wrote of the 'central portion' of the force, which was independent of the army and the navy, and claimed: '... we have to form the centre portion first, with the beginnings of the outside branches, which will grow in size and independence as we develop'.[16] In other words the main aim was the building up of an independent force, and the other services should wait until the financial situation improved.

The first draft of the Geddes cost-cutting report of 1921 suggested a devious and divisive way of reducing expenditure: 'If the navy and the army require further air units, we feel that they should be able to show reductions in their own provisions which would justify the supply of these units.'[17] This was rejected by Churchill's committee in February 1922. 'Apparently the intention was to force the army and navy to make further economies in order to secure the indispensable air services. ... We do not think it feasible to deprive the army and navy of all aviation. Such a course would mutilate both the services.'[18]

The issue was more important for the navy than for the army. Navigation was harder over the sea. Spotting for naval guns and dropping of torpedoes required specialised techniques; many naval aircraft would operate from carriers where their crews would live among naval personnel, and they would train in the difficult and dangerous techniques of deck take-off and landing. This was becoming increasingly urgent. The navy had built the first true 'flat-top' aircraft carrier, the *Argus*, in 1918 and tested landing techniques in the Firth of Forth before the war ended. It was followed by the *Eagle* which introduced the 'island' superstructure set off to one side, and the *Hermes*. When Fisher's eccentric battlecruisers, *Glorious, Courageous* and *Furious*, were converted to carriers they would carry 132 aircraft between them, trebling the air power of the fleet. Churchill continued to maintain that 'the Royal Air Force should be regarded as the parent service for all airmen in their capacity as airmen'.[19] But in 1922 a compromise was reached by which 70 per cent of naval pilots would be naval officers, and 100 per cent observers – a trade then unknown to the RAF. The naval pilots would hold dual rank in the RAF, and the air group of a carrier would be headed by an RAF wing commander. Aircraft on board would be maintained by RAF personnel but handled largely by the navy. It worked reasonably well on board ship, but in-fighting in Whitehall continued to restrict the development of naval aviation. From being world leader in 1918, the British began to fall behind the United States and Japan.

★

In 1919 a committee considered the terms for new officers, including the age of entry. According to Arthur Longmore, 'After comparing the relative merits of the early age, as adopted by the Navy, and that of the army in the case of Sandhurst and Woolwich, we decided in favour of the latter (17 to 19), which gave longer time to obtain the benefit of a public or secondary school education, as well as costing less to the state.'[20] The competition was not very close, the 13-year-old entry to the navy was a curiosity even among world navies, and learning to fly was an essential part of an air force officer's training; it is difficult to believe that could be attempted below the age of 16.

The Trenchard Memorandum assumed that all new officers in the RAF would be pilots, except for small numbers of accountants, chaplains and doctors. Churchill did not demur from this, perhaps because the rise of the observer in the RNAS had only begun after his time. During the war the RFC observer usually sat behind the pilot in a two-seater, navigating or rather map-reading over the trenches, recording what was observed, spotting for artillery, manning a Lewis gun and operating a radio or a camera. The RNAS's task of navigating over the sea was more difficult, and the observers were more carefully trained. All this experience was to be lost after the war, when any remaining observers were expected to train as pilots. By an order of January 1920, '... all pilots may in future be employed in any capacity as crew of an aircraft, i.e. as observers, gunners, photographers, etc. It should be noted that no provision is to be made for observers in the permanent Air Force, all officers are to be considered available for the duties of observers, etc.'[21]

To provide navigators, as well as engineers and other specialists, the naval practice was to be adopted. After some operational service, a permanent officer would go on for further training rather like naval officers who specialised in gunnery, torpedo, navigation and so on. But few of the courses actually took place, and these were often under-subscribed. Secondly, a pilot who was put on navigation duties regarded that as a demotion. Air force tradition demanded that the pilot was in command of the aircraft even if he was outranked by the navigator. There were very few posts for specialists above the rank of flight lieutenant, so they had little influence on policy and tended to neglect their specialisation when promoted.[22] These problems were never really rectified between the wars, and as a result the RAF's navigation was grossly inadequate in 1939.

It was suggested that air force officers might be trained in the existing army and navy colleges to save money, but Churchill was aware of their deficiencies. At Sandhurst he had found that the curriculum was too narrow, so 'our minds were not allowed to roam in working hours beyond a subaltern's range of vision'.[23] As to the navy, before the war he had found Osborne had 'a certain air of kindergarten', while at Dartmouth the course was 'so ambitious for boys of that age as to provoke doubts that it is thorough'. He supported the setting up of a new RAF College at Cranwell in Lincolnshire.

At a time when the army and navy gave regular officers the prospect of a career for life, Trenchard had a very different idea, for the air force needed a much higher proportion of junior officers, who could not remain on flying duties as they got older. 'I assumed that the air force would want 4,000 officers, then I worked out what promotion they would get. I found they would become squadron-leaders at about the age of fifty. ... That would have been fatal. We wanted not an older but a younger service than the army or navy. I then worked out the requirements until I reached a reasonable curve of promotion. I came to the conclusion roughly that it was necessary to divide the 4,000 officers by half in order to give a good curve of promotion to those officers who were permanent.' Trenchard proposed a system of short service, four years plus four in the reserve. This matched Churchill's early view that pilots could only remain effective for three to five years, and the first regulations were drawn up in October 1920.

The Trenchard Memorandum proclaimed: '... we must use every endeavour to eliminate flying accidents, both during training and subsequently. This end can only be secured by ensuring that the training of our mechanics in the multiplicity of trades necessitated by a highly technical service is as thorough as it can be made. The best way to do this is to enlist the bulk of our skilled ranks as boys and train them ourselves.'[24] He believed it would not be possible 'to draw the technical personnel of the Air Force solely from apprentices taken from the Trade Unions'.[25] Murray Sueter claimed that flying accidents had been fewer in the early days of the RNAS than the RFC, because of naval artisans, 'engineers of considerable skill'.[26] Churchill was well aware of this tradition and commented in June 1919: 'Here, again, the Navy affords much valuable experience. In their training establishments on the "Fisgard", etc., for producing the boy artificer, which is an indispensable element in a force so largely dependent upon mechanics.'[27] The circumstances, however, were very different. The navy needed to train a few score artificers a year, to keep watch in the engine rooms and carry out specialised maintenance. Trenchard envisaged that a large proportion of the non-flying staff of the air force would be ex-apprentices. Their training establishment at Halton was to be purpose-built and Churchill had to defend it against Geddes in 1922 as five-sixths of the money had already been spent.

Trenchard believed that airmen should be attached to squadrons 'which they can regard as their home, as the sailor does his ship, or the soldier his regiment'.[28] That was a little misleading; a sailor was only in a ship for a limited period of time while a soldier would probably serve his whole career in the same regiment. Churchill, also from an army background, agreed with this.

> C.A.S. [Chief of Air Staff] spoke to me some time ago about his wish to introduce something like the regimental system of the Army into the R.A.F. thus preserving the identities for the future of famous squadrons. With this I am heartily in accord. We must create definite units of a permanent character possessing their own esprit de corps with good strictly managed messes, the officers of which know each other, and where there is a strong public opinion on the question of behaviour. A ceaseless fluctuation of individuals cannot be allowed; the presumption of every officer should be that he will be working with the same lot of officers at any rate for several years to come.[29]

Churchill continued to learn to fly despite the long gap since his pre-war training, but on 18 July 1919 he had a near miss after taking off from Croydon. The aeroplane was about 90 feet off the ground when it side-slipped and crashed, and the pilot turned off the engine to prevent an explosion. Churchill was bruised but was able to attend a diner in the House of Commons that evening.[30] In 1925 he told Roger Keyes, after he too had a lucky escape: 'I gave up flying after my last crash, and although in your position I suppose it is occasionally a duty, I am sure it should not become a habit in a C-in-C.'[31]

From the start of the air force a new light blue uniform had been considered, but it was used only by a very small number of officers who were prepared to buy mess dress while the rest wore khaki. Light blue was never common for British uniforms and was associated more with comic opera. During Churchill's term it was replaced by a darker shade of blue which eventually became standard for most independent air forces throughout the world, though its origins remain obscure. Trenchard wanted to increase what he called the 'dining out power' of his officers, meaning that they should be accepted in upper-class society. Perhaps this is why a full-dress uniform was designed, with gold sleeve stripes. Longmore was on the clothing committee, but claimed 'we were not responsible for the full dress hat, the design of which started with the motif of a fur flying helmet and which developed into something quite unique and unsuited to the large majority of its wearers'. For formal and parade dress, all ranks wore a version of the army uniform with puttees and breeches, which perhaps reflected the influence of the cavalry but was pointless for pilots and mechanics. From his recruit training at Uxbridge T. E. Shaw – the name assumed by Churchill's friend Lawrence of Arabia – wrote: 'the RAF puttee is inelastic, with no give to fit it round the leg like Fox's puttees, which are the first purchase of an airman with twelve shillings to spare'.[32]

The question of separate rank titles for the air force had come up even before it was founded, and an imaginative scheme was suggested in 1917 – a colonel or naval captain would become a 'banneret', named after a leader of medieval knights; the highest ranks were to be held by 'ardians', which might be rendered from the Gaelic as 'chief bird'. According to the historian H. A. Jones, 'The translation detracts something from its dignity.' In any case it was never implemented. RAF officers, including those from the RNAS, took on army ranks for now.[33] In February 1919 Churchill told the First Lord of the Admiralty that he intended to 'de-militarise' the air force – that he planned to introduce new titles 'appropriate to a new service and a new element standing midway between the two parent services and catering for the needs of both'.[34] For once he was at odds with Trenchard, who believed that changing titles and traditions 'built up through four years of war' would be 'unpopular inside and outside the air service and would cause inevitable wasting of time'.[35]

Churchill outlined three principles in choosing the new titles – they should correspond to actual functions, they should be equivalent to those in the other services, and there should be no repetitions of words. The pilot officer was to be equivalent to a 2nd lieutenant. He was only responsible for flying his own machine, while the flying officer would have 'more experience of flying than a mere pilot'. Above that, 'The Flight Lieutenant commands his flight. The Squadron Leader leads a squadron. The Wing Commander commands a wing. The Group Captain is in charge of a group.' These reflected RNAS ranks, and air force officers were to wear exactly the same number of sleeve stripes as their naval equivalents. Churchill also favoured the use of the term 'air marshal' for senior officers.[36]

The proposals were sent to the King on 20 May and Churchill explained their purpose:

> ... the nomenclature of the officer ranks of the Royal Air Force ought not to remain the same as that of the Army. Such an arrangement is not satisfactory to either service. It suggests identities of organisation and outlook which do not now exist, and it will become increasingly anomalous, as the evolution of the Air Force proceeds on the lines determined by its own distinctive needs. ... in the course of years the new titles will become increasingly associated with the great deeds of the Force in the war and will help in the perpetuation of a great tradition.[37]

The King agreed with the titles, with the exception of the highest one, marshal of the air, asking, according to Trenchard, 'Don't you think it tends to poach a bit on the preserve of the Almighty? Why not simply Marshal of the Royal Air Force?'[38] In June Trenchard asked Churchill to sign a submission to the king: 'In place of "Marshal of the Air" substitute "Marshal of the Royal Air Force", and if this is not satisfactory ... the King should be called "Chief of the Royal Air Force" ...'. Churchill obliged, the title of Marshal of the Royal Air Force was accepted and Trenchard was the first holder in 1927.

As to the other air ranks, Churchill's scheme of air chief marshal, air marshal and air vice-marshal had the advantage that, since there was no air chief marshal for the moment, Trenchard would take on the title of air marshal which hinted at supreme authority. There were other objections; in the army field marshal was the highest rank, awarded for long and distinguished service. Mocked by Sir Henry Wilson, who did indeed hold that rank, Trenchard had one of his staff officers search the London Library for other uses of the term, which included provost-marshal, court-martial and the department store Marshall and Snelgrove.[39]

The new titles gave an air of modernity which would not be found in the army ranks of major and colonel, which were increasingly associated with retired officers writing angry letters to the newspapers – the term 'squadron leader' was a particularly fortunate choice.

Churchill remained at the Air Ministry even after he was transferred from the War Office to the Colonial Office in February in January 1921, and it was not until March 1922 that he was replaced as air minister by his cousin Frederick Guest. After their differences and doubts, Trenchard paid an unaccustomed and sincere tribute to Churchill at the end of his term in the ministry:

> I am perfectly certain that no other man that I have ever yet met could have done this work without seriously handicapping the development of the Air Service and also militating against economy, except Mr Churchill, and owing to his capability in doing this he has enormously assisted in the formation of the air service on a very economical basis.[40]

CHAPTER 25

A Role for the RAF

The armed forces had just begun to settle into some kind of post-war stability when two further shocks hit them. The first affected only the navy, as the Americans and Japanese began to plan new fleets for conflict with one another. Churchill was the first to anticipate this, and in May 1919 he wrote to Lloyd George: 'it is absolutely vital to persuade President Wilson not to start building new big ships'.[1] At a CID meeting in December 1920 Lloyd George argued that 'because we owed America £1,000,000,000, because she had a population of 100 million to our 40 million, because she was rich and we were poor, therefore we could not hope to keep command of the sea'.[2] The 'one power standard', which in effect meant equality with the United States, was now accepted as the main policy. This time it was a question of prestige rather than preparation for war – Japan was still an ally and open conflict with the USA was highly unlikely. Churchill was well aware that such a war could not end well: 'the United States is entirely self-contained and independent of a navy while we are dependent on four fifths of our food supplies on overseas markets'.[3] But if the Americans built more and more battleships in a race with Japan, the British would be left further behind unless they spent a great deal of money. As a committee under Churchill's chairmanship reported, '... this would have required the most rigorous efforts from us unless we were definitely to resign ourselves to the second or third place among naval powers. If this situation had arisen, no diminution in our naval effort would have been possible.'⁴ It would be a 'ghastly state of affairs' if Britain was drawn into such an arms race again.⁵ The only alternative was a conference of all the major powers to restrict warship building.

In the meantime Churchill joined the Bonar Law Committee on the future of the battleship in the face of the submarine and air power. He, along with Beatty and Long, the First Lord of the Admiralty, dissented from the report which suggested that the issue could not be decided either way. Churchill was clear that 'the Admiralty have made out an overwhelming case for the retention of the capital ship as the foundation of sea power in the period with which we now have to deal'. He discounted the threat from submarines. 'My feeling is that it is more probable that the submarine era will pass rather than that the battleship will pass. ... I think the picture of the improved capital ship able to locate by asdics any under-water craft within two or three thousand yards and to hurl an enormous depth charge with great accuracy to the point located is at least as probable as any other forecast which has been made.' As to the air threat, he did not accept all the theories of Trenchard. 'Obviously there is more future before an arm which is all-seeing than before an arm which is all-blind. ... But I do not feel that within the period with which we are concerned anyone could confidently rely on the Air Service to take the place of the British line of battle as the foundation of our safety and authority throughout the world.'⁶

Churchill was convinced that any conference on arms reduction would have more legitimacy if it took place in Washington rather than London, and it convened there in November 1921. The British and Americans were allowed equal tonnage of 500,000 in capital ships, Japan had 300,000 tons and France and Italy had 175,000 tons each. Older ships were to be scrapped to bring the tonnage down, while the conference took up Churchill's old idea of a 'naval holiday' – according to Roger Keyes, 'the naval holiday appeals to him so intensely because he originated the idea and suggested it before the war'.⁷ There would be no more capital ship building for the next ten years – Beatty objected on the grounds that Britain had already had a five-year holiday with no new construction since Jutland apart from the battlecruiser *Hood*, but he was overruled. An exception was made for ships already started, provided they did not exceed the limit of 35,000 tons and 16-inch guns. The design process for the *Rodney* and *Nelson* had already begun and they were built with three 16-inch turrets forward of the superstructure. To the educated they were the 'cherry trees' cut down by Washington. To the lower deck they were 'the ugly sisters' or 'the pair of boots'. But in many ways they followed the process which Churchill had encouraged ten years earlier, of heavier guns, high speed and stronger armour.

★

The next shock affected all three services. Sir Eric Geddes, former First Lord of the Admiralty and now Minister without Portfolio, was commissioned to find drastic cuts in all government departments. He found that three years after the armistice, despite 'a broken and exhausted Europe with no German menace', the armed forces had 'far greater fighting power, with a larger personnel, and greater preparations for war than at any stage in our history'. His first report, published in February 1922, recommended cuts of £75 million, of which £20 million was to come from the army, £21 million from the navy and £5½ million from the air force. The report was sceptical about the need for a separate air force, as no other nation had one, but it suggested that a unified Ministry of Defence, 'a co-ordinating authority ... responsible for that seeing each force plays its part and is allotted appropriate responsibility for carrying out various functions' would make its abolition unnecessary.[8]

The services were outraged, especially the Admiralty. Churchill was appointed to chair a cabinet committee to look into the cuts to the armed forces. In typical Churchillian style it recommended 'That the essential elements of fighting strength shall be maintained on such a scale as to ensure that we shall maintain the national security until we are able to achieve victory by bringing the full mobilised war power of the Empire into being.' On the other hand the peace establishments of the 'ancillary services' should be reduced to a nucleus – but of course the definition of ancillary services was always open to dispute.[9] It was too late to incorporate any cuts in the current estimates, so a sub-committee of the cabinet was set up under Churchill to consider the individual services in more detail. It was decided that no further cuts were needed in the air force and in fact it was to be expanded; the army was to be examined by Sir Alfred Mond and Stanley Baldwin, while Churchill took charge of the navy committee himself, assisted by two rear-admirals, two assistant secretaries from the Admiralty and representatives from the Treasury and the CID.[10]

Churchill had always been highly critical of the way the navy had been run since he left in May 1915. It is rare to find a page of the minutes of the committee without two or three questions being asked by him, and he sent the admirals and civil servants off to provide a plethora of facts and statistics. At the first meeting he asked what was still to be spent on new destroyers, the distribution of naval police, the need to convert a sloop for surveying, the cost of fuel, the use of gyro compasses taken out of old ships, the cost of electronic and fire control apparatus, the disposal of old craft, why the new battleships were being built in private yards rather than the Royal Dockyards, the need for a new armour-piercing shell and the reserve of small arms ammunition.[11] The naval officials produced satisfactory answers to most of Churchill's questions and the final report was quite favourable. The cut in the naval budget was halved.

★

With no credible enemy in Europe, the RAF had to find a role. In peacetime the navy had the job of protecting the nation's sea routes, but the aircraft of 1919 did not have nearly enough range to help much with that. The army was there to defend the empire in numerous outposts, and this task appealed to Churchill for the air force. In February 1919 he wrote to Long: '... the whole future garrisons of the British Empire have to be reviewed in the light of the war and the increased responsibilities cast upon us by our victory. It is desirable that in this review the disposition of the Air Forces and those of our garrisons should be regulated from a single standpoint ...'.[12]

Trenchard anticipated the idea of 'air control' in his memorandum of December 1919:

> Recent events have shown the value of aircraft in dealing with frontier troubles and it is not perhaps too much to hope that before long it may prove possible to regard the Royal Air Force units not as an addition to the military garrison but as a substitute for part of it. One great advantage of aircraft in this class of warfare approximating to police work is their power of acting at once. Aircraft can visit the scene of incipient unrest within a comparatively few hours of the receipt of news. To organise a military expedition even on a small scale takes time, and delay may result in the trouble spreading. The cost is also much greater, and very many more lives are involved.[13]

Muhammed Abdullah Hassan, known as the 'Mad Mullah' to the British, was a Jihadist and longstanding opponent of British rule in Somaliland. The idea of controlling the region from air had first occurred in the middle of 1914, when it was proposed by Lieutenant-Commander Boothby of the Admiralty Air Department. He ruled out the use of aeroplanes as they were too liable to engine failure, but suggested that airships might be used in co-operation with land forces.[14] The Great War intervened, but another expedition was prepared in early 1920. The *Ark Royal* arrived at Berbera with eight aircraft which began operations with the Somaliland Field Force, the Somaliland Camel Corps, the King's African Rifles and Indian troops. The Dervishes had no answer to the bombing campaign as their men and flocks were dispersed and their forts destroyed. A hospital aeroplane was used to ferry a sick officer to hospital, while messages were dropped to keep in contact with the troops on the ground. Group Captain Gordon reported: 'Opportunity was taken to test the theory that the moral effect of the new arm, with its power to carry out, without warning, a form of attack against which no counter measures could avail, would so disperse the Dervish following that troops would be enabled to capture the Mullah's forts and destroy his flock.'[15] They were successful, the Mullah fled and died soon afterwards. Churchill told parliament: 'We have had an example of the possibilities of the Air Force recently in the Somaliland campaign, which for a cost of about £30,000 achieved much more than we were able to do in one expedition before the war for an expenditure of over £2,500,000.'[16]

By August 1919 Churchill as War Minister was complaining about the enormous cost of controlling Mesopotamia, including 25,000 British troops, 80,000 Indians, 20,000 local levies and 13,000 followers.[17] As he stated later, 'Down in the desert near the scanty palm groves are established at the utmost cost and inconvenience the messes, regimental establishments, telegraph and signal stations, depots, dumps and headquarters of regiments, squadrons, batteries and battalions of British and Indian troops.'[18] In February 1920 he cited the example of Somaliland and told parliament: 'I propose to apply that principle to another field. I have directed that the chief of air staff to submit an alternative scheme for the control of Mesopotamia, the air force being the principal force or agency of control, while the military and naval forces on the ground would be an ancillary power.'[19] He suggested to Trenchard 'a series of defended areas in which air bases could be securely established. In these air bases, strong aerial forces could be maintained in safety and efficiency. An ample system of landing grounds judiciously selected would enable these air forces to operate in every part of the protectorate and to enforce control.' They would be strongly defended with blockhouses and pill boxes. The air force should 'possess the power to convey swiftly two or three companies of men to any threatened point', and he ordered 'the construction of special aeroplanes for this purpose' – the origin of the Vickers Vernon transport which used the wings and tail of the Vimy bomber but added a very bulbous fuselage. Churchill went on: 'If the air force were to undertake this task and submitted a practical scheme which commended itself to the cabinet, I should appoint an air officer to be commander-in-chief in Mesopotamia, and he would have under his orders the local ground and river forces. A flotilla on the river, certain organisations of armoured cars, and the necessary garrisons of ground troops to hold the defended areas and generally to assist in maintaining control would, of course, be essential.'[20]

Trenchard had completed a preliminary memorandum by 1 April and Churchill sent it on to General Haldane, his fellow would-be escapee in South Africa.[21] At first the general was sceptical but later wrote to Churchill's gratification: '... disturbances can be checked or prevented from arising by the speedy arrival of aircraft, and ... unless, which is improbable, rebellion were to arise in every corner at once, the sudden arrival of aeroplanes on several days should act as a preventative'.[22] Air Vice-Marshal Salmond was sent to the area to report and make plans. The message was reinforced in August when a column of 400 men was wiped out and from the army Wilson could only think of abandoning Persia or sending more troops in from India.[23]

Churchill gave up his War Office responsibilities for the Colonial Office in January 1921 but remained in charge at the Air Ministry, so he had a double interest in Mesopotamia. He and Lloyd George decided to hold a conference on Middle Eastern affairs in Cairo in March, at which Churchill met and admired T. E. Lawrence (of Arabia) and it was decided to go ahead with the air scheme. Feisal Ibn Hussein, Lawrence's former ally in the desert campaign, was elected king of Mesopotamia after the French had ejected him from Syria, and this gave some kind of legitimacy to the British protectorate. After many amendments, Trenchard described his plans to Churchill in June, partly based on his long colonial experience before the war:

> Ordinary policing duties would be undertaken by the Arab levies, supplemented by the regular system of what may be called 'air route marches', which would be provided for the frequent patrolling of certain areas as required by varying local conditions, the aeroplanes would land, sometimes with and sometimes without the political officers, and visit the local chief and even bring him in to Baghdad to see the chief political officer. This would correspond to route marches by infantry and, from the experience we have so far in Iraq, would be of substantial morale effect.
>
> If a tribe became restive in an area where there were no levies a demonstration by air would take place over its villages and a message would be dropped to tell the chief that hostile action against him would have to come in. This demonstration would be repeated three or four times and if the necessary offensive action from the air should be initiated, in the first instance by attacks on the enemy's flocks and cattle and then if he is still obdurate on his villages.

In August 1921 Churchill's successor as Secretary of State for War, Sir Laming Worthington-Evans, complained about the general principle of the scheme to the cabinet. The Air Ministry proposed 'the creation of both naval and military units in the shape of gunboats, armoured trains, supplies, signals, ordnance, medical, veterinary and similar services'. This might well have been due to Churchill's tendency to create units from the different elements under his own control, as had been seen with the RNAS not so long ago; but the army saw it as wasteful duplication in a time of economy. Furthermore, it was 'undesirable and uneconomic to allow the Air Force to depart from its present functions of an ancillary force'. He went on:

> ... the forces in Mesopotamia are intended to keep order and gradually to reconcile hostile tribes to a civilised rule. Punitive measures may have to be taken against disturbers of the peace; the only means at the disposal of the Air Force, and the means now in fact used, are the bombing of the women and children in the villages. If the Arab population realise that the peaceful control of Mesopotamia ultimately depends on our intention of bombing women and children, I am very doubtful if we shall gain that acquiescence of the fathers and husbands of Mesopotamia as a whole to which the Secretary for the Colonies looks forward. More probable is it that the new King, Feisal, will complain that he cannot expect loyal co-operation of the tribes so long as their women and children are done to death. He will probably be forced to call upon the Air Force to desist, and one it is realised that the Air Force can no longer use their only weapon their military value will be lost.[24]

Churchill replied forcefully that this was 'a gross exaggeration. Bombs are not thrown as bolts from the blue without warning. Aircraft can be used to make life intolerable for a village community by rendering the village unapproachable by day or night, by preventing the tilling of the ground, by burning ripe crops, by destroying their cattle.' The idea of a different service run by the RAF was also an exaggeration: 'The Air Force does not want a land army, it desires to control a few ancillary units, of technical types which it is well equipped to maintain.' He concluded: 'This is the real crux of the whole matter and the real reason for the War Office attitude ... the General Staff cannot reconcile themselves to the prospect of this new service bursting the bonds of subordination to its older sisters.' The cabinet supported Churchill but Worthington-Evans, 'while stating his intention loyally to carry out the decisions of the cabinet, asked that his dissent from this policy might be recorded'.[25]

The garrison of Mesopotamia was set at eight RAF squadrons, three armoured car companies, two armoured trains, four river gunboats, an Indian pack artillery battery, two battalions of British infantry and two Indian. Bombing was already going on before the RAF took control, and Churchill was not inclined to neglect humanity, even in a brutal business. In May 1921 he was outraged when he read a report on an air attack.

> The eight machines involved in the attack broke formation and attacked at different points the encampment simultaneously, causing a stampede among the animals. The tribesmen and their families were put in confusion many of whom ran into the lake making a good target for the machine guns.

He commented to Trenchard: 'To fire wilfully on women and children taking refuge in a lake is a disgraceful act, and I am surprised you do not order the officers responsible for it, to be tried by court martial. … Combatants are fair game and sometimes non-combatants get injured through their proximity to fighting troops, but this seems to be quite a different matter.'[26]

The military control of Mesopotamia (known increasingly as Iraq) was scheduled to be handed over formally to the RAF on 1 October 1922, but Churchill had other issues to deal with before that happened. He changed his attitude to the Irish rebellion in the spring of 1921, perhaps because his wife urged him to use his influence for 'some sort of moderation or at any rate justice in Ireland'. Lloyd George carried out the 'most complete and sudden … reversal of policy' and began to negotiate with the rebels. Churchill supported him after he was reassured that the naval base at Berehaven would be retained. He had the job of presenting the results to parliament. 'He spoke with great force and power and with equal skill and tact.'[27] It was not the end of the affair, the agreement to sever the six counties in the north from the new Irish Free State led to a bloody civil war. The Ulsterman Sir Henry Wilson was far from happy and regarded Lloyd George as a traitor for talking to Sinn Fein. He left the army to enter parliament in February 1922 but was assassinated by Irish republicans in June.

★

Meanwhile Turkey revived under the leadership of Mustapha Kemal, who had led forces against the allies in the Dardanelles. By the Treaty of Sevres at the end of the war the Dardanelles were a neutral zone and Greece was allowed parts of Asia Minor, but now the Turkish armies advanced against them. The British outpost at Chanak on the Dardanelles was threatened and Lloyd George and Churchill were ready for war. But no one else, even the Conservatives in the coalition, was ready for another struggle so soon after the armistice, and they had to back down. It was a fatal blow to Lloyd George's power, he resigned and in the election which followed Churchill was confined to bed after an appendix operation; his once despised temperance opponent, Edwin Scrymgeour, gained more than 35,000 votes, and Churchill came fourth in a two-member constituency. The Lloyd George party collapsed and Churchill famously wrote: '... in the twinkling of an eye I found myself without an office, without a seat, without a party and without an appendix'. His career would soon move in a different direction

★

In Iraq, the handover to RAF control happened at the worst possible moment. The Chanak affair was not fully settled and Iraq was subject to Turkish incursions from the north which also 'served to foment restlessness and to give moral support to intriguers and ill-disposed persons wherever their propaganda could obtain a foothold'. Ground troops had to be retained longer than expected, but the Turks were driven back during the next few months, Groups of sheiks also revolted in the Nasiriyah area and bombing and demonstration flights forced most of them to submit. There were more revolts, but 'In every instance air action was only necessary on a surprisingly limited scale.' By March 1923 it was reported that 'An ordinary outbreak of lawlessness in defiance of government could be rapidly, effectively and economically dealt with by means of air action.' Twenty-one officers and men had been killed in the last eight months of army control with 20 missing and 33 wounded. In eight months of RAF control nine were killed including three in aircraft accidents, and 21 were slightly wounded.[28]

Churchill soon had his doubts and wrote to Keyes: 'I hate Iraq. ... I wish we had never gone there ...'.[29] But the air control of Iraq was generally considered a success, though it only applied to selected parts of the country and the British left in 1931. Despite the RAF claims, it depended very much on co-operation with ground forces; and action in clear skies over a sparsely populated territory, against an enemy with no means of retaliation against aircraft, had no lasting lessons for the future of air power.

The World Crisis

With his long-established and well-honed skills as a writer and correspondent, it would have been surprising if Churchill had not written of his experiences in what was then known as the Great War. Of course it would be far wider and deeper than his accounts of Cuba, the North West Frontier, Egypt and South Africa – it was a much larger and more far-reaching war than any of these essentially local campaigns, and his own involvement was at a much higher level. He was to develop a unique concept, combining personal experience with broader history. In addition, he felt it necessary to explain his conduct on Antwerp, the Dardanelles and the intervention in Russia.

By the end of December 1920 he had already written his account of the Agadir Incident of 1911 and showed it to Sir Henry Wilson, now his colleague at the War Office, who was highly praised in it.[1] At first his aims were less than a general history, and in July 1921 he wrote to Admiral Jackson that he was grateful the he would help 'in the technical professional and historical accuracy of my book on the naval war'. He had already written a chapter on the Coronel-Falklands affair.[2] It began to expand, and in February 1922 he wrote to Clementine: 'Long talks with Thornton Butterworth about the size of the book. He is clear that the first volume must be one volume only and not two, but his reader thinks all the stuff so good that it is a pity to cut any of it out. I am not at all sure. I think much pruning is desirable, as well as some omissions to be supplied.'[3] He soon had lucrative contracts with British and American publishers.[4]

Writing was a gregarious rather than a solitary activity for Churchill. With the work's huge scope and other demands on his time, he employed expert consultants, research assistants and typists on a large scale; perhaps his long experience in government gave him some skill in deploying them. He described his technique in July 1921: 'My habit is to dictate in the first instance what I have in my mind on the subject and a body of argument which I believe is substantially true and in correct proportion.'[5] Churchill's early books were 'circulated in the form of draft chapters for the advice and criticism of friends and knowledgeable acquaintances. … Once the story had been written or "got off his chest" then he relied on others to do the checking and tidying up.'[6]

He had plenty of expert advice as the first volume progressed. By February 1922 Sir Grahame Greene, the former Permanent Secretary at the Admiralty, had 'made a number of wise notes'. Churchill showed a chapter to Keyes, who was 'a tremendous judge of what could or could not be done in attacking the island of Borkum'.[7] Later the admiral wrote: 'Bayly's, Aston's Borkum plan simply wasn't *war* under modern conditions.'[8] Sir Tennyson d'Eyncourt, the Director of Naval Construction, suggested a few small technical corrections.[9] Beatty commented on the Heligoland Bight action, and Trenchard wrote: '… the policy of flying aeroplanes off warships and carriers … was not so much neglected as action in that respect was appallingly dilatory …', which seems harsh since the RNAS was far ahead of the world in that respect.[10] But the volumes said surprisingly little about air power, just an account of Churchill's efforts against the Zeppelins in 1914–15, and nothing about its role in supporting the army on the Western Front. Churchill relied on Eddie Marsh for details, for example the exact German origins of Battenberg.[11] But in the end, according to Maurice Ashley who worked on *Marlborough*, 'at every stage in his historical writing Churchill did the bulk of the work himself; it was his own mind, his own method of presenting the facts, his own rhetorical prose style that shaped all his books. Nothing irritates those who worked for him more than to be introduced as one who wrote Churchill's books for him.'[12]

Work naturally accelerated after he lost office in November 1922. He was close to finishing the first volume by the end of January 1923 when he wrote from the Ritz in London: 'I have been working continuously on the book ... I think it will be finally off my hands by the time I leave on Sunday week.'[13] Suggested titles included 'Within the Storm', 'The World Crisis', and more obscurely 'The Meteor Flat'. 'Sea Power and the World Crisis' was also suggested, but that might have restricted the range. On the other hand, the editor of *The Times* proposed 'The Great Amphibian' which might have revealed something about how Churchill saw his role, but it was not favoured by the publishers.[14]

He relied heavily on official documents and that caused controversy as extracts were published in *The Times* at the beginning of 1923. Several Labour MPs raised the question in the House and the Prime Minister referred to the 'obligation upon ministers and officials not to disclose confidential state or official papers or information without the approval of His Majesty's government for the time being ...'.[15] But there already was a precedent. When Lord Esher published a very misleading account of Churchill's departure for Antwerp in 1914, Churchill was allowed to use official papers to vindicate his action. Since so many of Churchill's actions were controversial, this gave him a wide scope. Moreover he claimed with some exaggeration that 'practically every important naval and military authority and actor in these events has already told his story to the public, and in doing so has freely used confidential information'.[16] The first volume, dealing with 1911–14, came out in April and Churchill sent copies to many friends and acquaintances, including the Prince of Wales. It was well received by them and by reviewers, and Asquith thought that he was funding his house at Chartwell in Kent on the proceeds.[17]

The second volume, dealing with the Dardanelles, was the most crucial for clearing Churchill's reputation. It was, he wrote later, 'in the main a documentary justification of my own action'.[18] Firstly he had to show that the operation was worthwhile, which in some ways was the most difficult. It was not clear that forcing Turkey out of the war would have removed a 'prop' from Germany. True, the collapse of her eastern allies in 1918 triggered her demise, but her situation was far less critical in 1915. As to the sending of supplies to Russia, the western allies had no such surplus of their own at the time.[19] Next he had to prove that he had not been rash in pushing for the operation, for he was particularly stung by the conclusion of the official Australian historian and war correspondent C. E. W. Bean: 'So through Churchill's excess of imagination, a layman's ignorance of artillery, the fatal power of a young enthusiasm to convince older and slower brains, the tragedy of Gallipoli was born.' To this end his chapter on 'The Choice' is largely formed of documents, at the end of which he asserts: 'So far all opinion has been favourable. So far no voice has been raised and no argument advanced against it.'[20] But this conceals many doubts and hesitations among his naval advisers alone. Carden's reply had been ambivalent, Jackson had wanted to use troops and only Oliver was wholly in favour. Sir Arthur Wilson's statement that 'on general grounds he had not been much in favour of the policy' was not used by Churchill.[21]

The chapter on 'Second Thoughts and Final Decisions' is largely a criticism of Fisher for failing to offer consistent advice, and ends with Churchill's defence of going ahead without military support even when he knew it might be available later: 'What would have happened if I had taken Lord Fisher's advice and refused point-blank to take any action on the Dardanelles unless or until the War Office produced on their responsibility an adequate army to storm the Gallipoli Peninsula?' His answer is that the naval attack was necessary to force Kitchener's hand. 'I do not believe that anything less than those tremendous hopes, reinforced as they were by dire necessity, would have enabled Lord Kitchener to wrest an army from France and Flanders. In cold blood, it could never have been done.'[22] This leads to an attack on Kitchener's vacillation. The Secretary of State was a dictator within the War Office, a general in a civilian job with all his best subordinates in France and a general staff which offered only information rather than solid advice. He was over-stressed but unwilling to divest any of his powers, so lacked strategic vision. Churchill's view was largely endorsed by the Dardanelles Commission, though by that time Kitchener was not alive to defend himself.

Churchill was positive about the early stages of the naval attack: by 2 March the outer defences were destroyed, including about a fifth of the whole gun defence of the Straits. The fleet was able to enter safely up to six miles inside and there was 'the greatest satisfaction at the Admiralty, and I found myself in these days surrounded by smiling faces'. This of course ended with the failure of the attack on the 18th which he attributed largely to De Robeck's naval caution: '... these old ships were sacred. They had been the finest ships afloat in the days when he as a young officer had first set foot upon their decks. The discredit and even disgrace of casting away a ship was ingrained deeply by years of mental training and outlook.'[23] It was the only case, according to T. E. Lawrence, where his presentation lacked generosity, and Keyes thought it had hurt the old admiral, whom he still respected. The passage was omitted from the condensed edition of the work.[24] But apart from that, Churchill accepted Keyes's view that a little more persistence would have crushed the defences. This became a regular theme – what would have happened if the attack had gone on for longer and been better supported at each stage, and the troops had not been withdrawn?

Churchill did not spell out the lessons of the Dardanelles campaign, except to maintain that he was not at fault, so we are left to draw our own conclusions. One is the weakness of the command structure at the top. Asquith was an amiable but disengaged prime minister. Kitchener was a dictator in the War Office but vacillated fatally about whether to offer military support. The naval staff, despite Churchill's claims, did not offer solid and consistent advice, and the War Office staff was weak and committed to the Western Front. The commanders on the spot were undistinguished and were there mainly by chance. Amidst all this Churchill is a beacon of consistency and initiative, but he could not have carried it alone, and perhaps he should have recognised that sooner. A second lesson was that the army and navy should co-operate more effectively rather than just being present in the same space and operating to different rhythms, but it would require a great cultural shift to make that happen in the next war. A third lesson, not acknowledged by Churchill at the time, was that such an expedition needed detailed planning at all levels and could not be improvised or expanded *ad hoc* as time went on; but perhaps that was never really learned, as several affairs in the next war would show.

★

Though much of the work was based on his personal experience, it was his descriptions and evaluations of two key battles he had not witnessed that provided the most controversial points. The first was Jutland. Churchill was out of office at the time and in 1924 he wrote to Keyes: 'This is the first time I have ever read the story of the Battle of Jutland. I had only the vaguest idea what had taken place.'[25] By that time the affair had been well picked over, inside and outside the Admiralty. As First Sea Lord from 1917–19, Wester Wemyss commissioned Rear-Admiral J. E. T. Harper to write a 'narrative' of the battle. It was generally in favour of Jellicoe's caution and Beatty objected strongly to certain passages, including a suggestion that his flagship had turned through 360 degrees while pursuing the High Seas Fleet. When he became First Sea Lord in 1919 he refused to publish it, which only increased the controversy. Meanwhile the official historian, Sir Julian Corbett, supported Jellicoe. Beatty commissioned the brothers Captains A. C. and Kenneth Dewar to produce what was called a 'Staff Appreciation' of the battle. This came down firmly on the side of Beatty, so much so that Corbett dismissed it as 'a grotesque account' and 'a burlesque of history' while Harper called it 'an account which for inaccuracy and bias would be difficult to surpass' and claimed that Kenneth Dewar was heckled when he attempted to deliver it as a lecture to senior officers.[26] Even the Beatty Admiralty refused to distribute it as being highly divisive. When Madden, formerly Jellicoe's chief of staff, became First Sea Lord in 1928 he recalled all copies to be destroyed, though at least one survived in Beatty's possession.[27] Nevertheless this was one of the books Keyes sent to Churchill in August 1924, and he praised it as being 'admirable in its lucidity and … written with great and restrained power'.[28] Furthermore, in September 1926 'Beatty put Commander

Kenneth Dewar at my disposal, and I have been having some lively arguments with him.'[29]

Churchill's account of the battle was described by Maurice Ashley as 'so clear, so concise, and so persuasive' that 'I cannot believe that anyone who enjoys the reading of history can fail even now to be excited by [it]'.[30] But Ashley was wrong in suggesting that he was fair to Jellicoe. Churchill was perhaps constrained by the fact that he had appointed Jellicoe as well as Beatty to the command, but Jellicoe had spent much of Churchill's wartime administration at the Admiralty demanding that 'Every vessel that the northern harbours could contain must be placed at his disposal.'[31] In *The World Crisis* he was famously 'the only man who could lose the war in an afternoon', but is portrayed as being obsessively over-cautious. Conversely Churchill has hardly a bad word to say about Beatty. The first controversial point in the battle was the failure of the 5th Battle Squadron to get into action quickly. The Dewars only mentioned this in passing, but it was enough to upset their former commander Sir Hugh Evan-Thomas, who commented: 'the Admiral in command must be to blame if a signal is not made'.[32] Churchill went further, explaining why Beatty did not wait to concentrate his fleet; but he too said nothing about the signalling failure which led to the great battleships going off in the wrong direction and which could be attributed, as at Scarborough and Dogger Bank, to Beatty's flag lieutenant Seymour.

There was an even more controversial point as the High Seas Fleet approached Jellicoe's main force. The ships were still sailing in column before deploying into line of battle, a concept which was familiar to Churchill. 'The evolutions of cavalry in the days of shock tactics and those of a modern fleet resemble each other. Both approach in column and fight in line, and cavalry and fleet drill consist primarily in swift and well-executed changes from one formation to the other.'[33] But the essential difference was that the cavalry would turn so that each horse and rider would face the enemy for a charge; with the fleet, the ships were at right angles to the enemy to deploy their gun power for maximum effect, so it was essentially a defensive formation and useless if the enemy refused to fight. As soon as he had just enough information on the enemy's course, Jellicoe deployed on his port column, the furthest away from the enemy, which would allow him to 'cross his T' and concentrate a large amount of gun power on the German van. The Dewars and Churchill objected to this, pointing out that a deployment on the starboard side would bring the fleet much closer to the enemy with decisive effect. Jellicoe's supporters argued that this would have been highly dangerous and might have resulted in his own T being crossed. The Dewars and Churchill had a third alternative, to revive an almost forgotten order which would have allowed them to deploy on one of the centre columns, bringing them two or three miles closer to the enemy.

In any case Admiral Scheer turned away very skilfully but found himself cut off from his bases. He turned back to the eastward to be confronted with the might of the Grand Fleet yet again. He turned away and launched an attack by torpedo craft and battlecruisers, leading to the most controversial moment of all. According to the Dewar report, at this moment, 'According to all accepted ideas, Scheer's advance at 6.55 should have led to the annihilation of the High Seas Fleet. His battlecruisers, already severely damaged, were practically unsupported, within about 10,000 yards of a large portion of the British battle fleet; the 3rd Squadron was also in a very dangerous situation, and the 1st and 2nd Squadrons were not in a position to offer much help. Even the light conditions which prevented the Germans from seeing anything but the flash of their opponent's guns were in favour of the British.'[34] But instead, according to Churchill,

> Once more Jellicoe, obedient to his method, turned away from the torpedo stream …. Here at any rate was a moment when … it would have been quite easy to divide the British fleet with the 5th Battle Squadron leading the starboard division, and so take the enemy between two fires. But the British commander-in-chief was absorbed in avoiding the torpedo attack by turning away. The range opened, the fleets separated, and Scheer vanished again from Jellicoe's view – this time for ever.[35]

Yet again, according to this theory, the great power of Churchill's own, very expensive, *Queen Elizabeths* had been squandered. Contact was lost during the night and the battle was of course inconclusive.

Churchill was often accused of self-justification in his historical memoirs, but he could easily have taken the soft option and accepted that Jellicoe had done the best in the circumstances, and that decisive victory would not have changed the course of the war. Instead he laid himself open to criticism for appointing Jellicoe in the first place, and that was voiced by Lady Beatty. Her husband replied fairly that 'Everybody thought in those days that Jellicoe was the best admiral we had. He certainly was the cleverest ...', and for once he showed some gratitude to Churchill: 'He has been a good friend to me and has backed me many times under circumstances of great difficulty.'[36]

Churchill's account found much favour with the Beatty camp, and Walter Cowan, who had commanded the *Princess Royal* in the Battle Cruiser Fleet, wrote to Keyes in March 1927: 'I think that W Churchill's account and diagnosis of that miserable Jutland business are as fair and correct and level minded an effort as possibly be drawn up.'[37] But Admiral Sir Reginald Bacon, who had commanded the Dover Patrol before he was succeeded by Keyes, took a very different view. He had already published a passionate volume, *The Jutland Scandal*, about the failure to publish the Harper Report. In the 1933 edition he added a section refuting Churchill's arguments with a welter of facts and figures, and claiming that his chapters on Jutland were 'plausible to the casual reader' but 'historically unreliable, both because of the inaccuracy of many of the statements regarding the details of the fight, and also because of the deductions drawn from them by Mr Churchill'. Admiral Bacon regretted 'the belief that the surest way of belauding Lord Beatty lay in belittling Lord Jellicoe'.[38] Of course he was one of the strongest partisans himself, but there is an underlying point. Rather than pick over the disputed facts about a past battle and attribute blame, it might have been better to consider what the real lessons were, and what could be done in any future action. There is no doubt that the Dewars' ideas would have been impracticable in the real context of Jutland. It is inconceivable that Jellicoe would have executed them, and Beatty made no great changes in tactics after he took command of the Grand Fleet. None of the squadron commanders had been trained to act independently, as shown by Evan-Thomas's lack of initiative, and it would have required a huge cultural shift for the navy to operate as they suggested. But the Dewars' document had been written as a 'staff appreciation', not as history; it was intended 'for the use and instruction of staff officers' and was 'an endeavour in the light of fuller knowledge and careful analysis to deduce lessons for their future guidance and investigation'.[39] Taken in that context it ultimately had some success. Churchill concluded on a prescient note: '... a different doctrine, other methods and above all another spirit must animate our captains at sea, if and whenever the Navy is once again at war'.[40]

The navy was in danger of another schism like that induced by Fisher, and Churchill was taking sides in it. So far the public was greatly in favour of Beatty, who was handsome and charismatic and knew how to handle the press; he was also in office at the Admiralty, and according to Jellicoe the naval staff was now 'almost entirely composed ... of officers who were serving in the Battle-Cruiser Fleet at Jutland'.[41] Jellicoe, on the other hand, was self-effacing and was out of the country as Governor-General of New Zealand from 1920 to 1924. But in the end the conflict was a false one. Neither was a new Nelson – Jellicoe was too cautious, Beatty was too slapdash. Even a blend of the best qualities of the two would not have produced the answer, as neither did much to develop battle fleet tactics. The answer would come from elsewhere. Destroyers had played a 'purely passive role' at Jutland, according to Churchill[42] but in many ways they offered hope for the future of the Royal Navy. Andrew Cunningham, the greatest naval commander of the next war, was a destroyer officer and asserted that 'any captain will tell you that the best officers to be found in big ships have come from submarines and destroyers'. Most of the leading officers of the next war, including Cunningham himself, Max Horton, Bertram Ramsay, Bruce Fraser and Philip Vian, would indeed come from such a background.

But neither Keyes nor Kenneth Dewar would play any further part in tactical development. In a bizarre affair involving the bandmaster of the *Royal Oak* which he commanded, Dewar fell foul of Rear-Admiral Collard, a notorious bully. He and his executive officer were court martialled and dismissed from the ship. Churchill wrote: 'If officers of this distinction are to be punished with such severity for making a complaint absolutely justified in fact though irregular in form, what chance has an ordinary rating of having his grievances considered? Thus a safety valve indispensable to discipline is in danger of being choked.'[43] The affair reflected on Keyes's command of the Mediterranean Fleet and he came under fire for the great size of his staff and his preference for officers who played polo, which was not considered acceptable in a slightly more egalitarian age. He was not promoted to First Sea Lord, but entered parliament with the support of Churchill.

★

The next controversial point was the great Somme offensive of 1916. Churchill quibbled about the use of the term 'battle' in the circumstances. 'Operations consisting of detached episodes stretching over months and divided by intervals during which a series of entirely new situations are created, however great their scale, cannot be compared – to take some modern instances, with Blenheim, Rossbach, Austerlitz, Waterloo, Gettysburg, Sedan, the Marne or Tannenberg.'[44]

On 1 July 1916, after an intense bombardment lasting a week, tens of thousands of British and French troops mounted the parapets and began the attack. Churchill's account of the notorious first day relied heavily on the description by Matthäus Gerster from the German side. He related how the end of the long bombardment signalled the start of the attack, how they brought up machine guns from the dugouts and quickly mounted them, firing into the long lines of British infantry. Despite huge losses the lines continued to advance, for 'The British soldier ... has no lack of courage, and once his hand is set to the plough he is not easily turned from his purpose.' Then, according to Churchill, 'At several points the British who had survived the awful firestorm broke into the German trenches. They were nowhere strong enough to maintain their position; and by nine o'clock the whole of the troops who were still alive and unwounded were either back in their own front-line trenches, or sheltering in the shell-holes of no man's land, or cut off and desperately defending themselves in the German trenches.'[45]

With a total of 60,000 casualties including 20,000 killed, it was the bloodiest day in the history of the British army. Arthur Conan Doyle wrote of this section of *The World Crisis* in *The Times*: 'Kitchener's army had "received a worthy panegyric".' He had 'given an adequate appreciation of that glorious army of patriotic volunteers who gave themselves so ungrudgingly to their country's service'.[46] Others saw it as an anti-war statement, a reversal of the common view of Churchill as a warmonger – but that only expressed the duality of his thought, both fascinated and repelled by war.

In Churchill's account the battle continued as a desultory series of engagements until the tanks were uselessly thrown in on 15 September. It was the casualty figures which seemed most striking and damning, and they caused the most controversy. In August 1926, according to Thomas Jones, he was 'dictating Volume III of the World Crisis, and has been working out comparative figures of British and German casualties with the help of Professor Lindemann and the small boy' – his son Randolph.[47] He purported to show that British losses in the offensives of 1916 and 1917 were generally about twice those of the Germans. The figures were disputed by many historians but accepted by others;[48] they established the common view that the attacks were examples of futile mass slaughter. In the end Churchill's attitude to the Battle of the Somme was summed up in advance by his letter to Clementine in January 1916 about the lecture on Loos: '"Don't do it again." But they will – I have no doubt.'[49] And finally he wondered: '… how then is war to be waged? Are both sides to sit down with enormous armies year after year looking at each other, each convinced that whoever attacks will be the loser?'[50] Certainly this is how some of his colleagues would see the situation during the 'phoney war' of 1939–40.

Churchill tried very hard to be fair to Haig, and was full of praise for his qualifications and abilities. 'Alike in personal efficiency and professional credentials, Sir Douglas Haig was the first officer of the British army. He had obtained every qualification, gained every experience and served in every appointment requisite for the general command.'[51] Though he disagreed profoundly about his attacks in

1916 and 1917, Churchill admired his tactics in the last months of the war, and corresponded with him about it, writing, 'I do not seek to condemn individuals, but to establish certain impersonal views upon the war by sea and land.' It was all part of his learning. 'Even knowing what I did about the facts I have been astonished by my studies.'[52] Though he does not say so, the public adulation of Haig must have rankled with Churchill. Taking an extreme view in which Churchill was responsible for all the casualties of the Dardanelles, 114,000 at most could be laid at his door. Haig was responsible for three quarters of a million British and Commonwealth casualties at the Somme and Third Ypres, with less excuse for the second battle as he might have learned the lessons of the first. Yet Churchill was still under the shadow of the Dardanelles, and his narrow defeat in the Abbey Division of Westminster in 1924 was attributed to the affair.[53] Meanwhile Haig was regarded as the war's ultimate hero. He was made an earl and voted £100,000 by parliament, supplemented by a public subscription to buy his ancestral estate at Bemersyde in the Scottish borders. He was given the freedom of dozens of towns and cities. He created the British Legion and headed the charity for war veterans – the famous poppies sold for Armistice Day had the letters 'HF' for Haig Fund in their centre. It was only after his death in 1928 that his role was questioned by historians.

★

Churchill gave up his writing for a time on becoming Chancellor of the Exchequer in 1924, believing that his office precluded him from such work. By 1926 he found out that this was not so, he was only forbidden from journalism on current issues, so he decided to publish the first two volumes, followed by the third.[54] In December 1927 he decided on a fourth volume of 100,000 to 125,000 words, to be called *The Aftermath*.[55] James Scrymgeour-Wedderburn describes his work-life balance in September 1928. 'He works at bricklaying four hours a day, and lays 90 bricks an hour. ... He also spends a considerable time on a history of post-war Europe which he is writing. His ministerial work comes down from the Treasury every day, and he has to give some more hours to that. It is a marvel how much time he gives to his guests ...'.[56] Naturally this volume had much less on military strategy but offered his reasons for advocating the intervention in Russia.

Writing the books allowed Churchill to research deeply into areas he had not experienced personally, and helped him to review those he had participated in. He wrote to Beatty in November 1924: 'I live a good deal in those tremendous days.'[57] In the preface to *The Aftermath* he wrote:

> I have been surprised in writing of events with which this volume deals, to find the number of important affairs in which I was personally concerned which had utterly passed from my mind. In these years the press of business was extreme; developments succeeded each other in ceaseless transformation. ... It was only when I re-read the speeches, letters and memoranda of the time that these intense and exciting years live again for me.[58]

CHAPTER 27

An Iron Chancellor

After his defeat in Dundee, Churchill had the consolation of time to spend on his writing, and on developing (often with his own hands) his country house at Chartwell in Kent. In 1923 Stanley Baldwin, the new Prime Minister, called an unexpected general election because he wanted a mandate to introduce protection which he believed would allow him to reduce unemployment. This of course was Churchill's original reason for leaving the Tories and he sought a constituency to stand in, making the unfortunate choice of Leicester where he formed no relationships with the people and fought a lacklustre campaign, losing to a wealthy Labour Party candidate. His only consolation was that the electorate had given no mandate for protection.

Baldwin had thrown away a substantial parliamentary majority. Lloyd George and Asquith, in agreement for once, supported the formation of a minority Labour government under Ramsay Macdonald. Churchill disagreed violently; in January 1924 he wrote to *The Times*: 'The enthronement in office of a socialist government will be a serious misfortune such as has usually befallen great states only on the morrow of defeat in war.'[1] This was his break with the Liberal Party. Soon afterwards the Conservative member for the Abbey Division of Westminster died, leaving a constituency which included most of the West End of London, inhabited by the wealthy upper classes and very different from Dundee. He stood as an 'Independent Anti-Socialist' with the tacit support of many Conservative leaders, though they could not prevent an official party candidate standing against him. It was a far more stimulating campaign, with Churchill travelling round the West End in a coach with a trumpeter and deploying the chorus girls of Daly's Theatre; he lost by 43 votes.

He had been moving closer to the Conservatives for several years, perhaps since he first became a 'big navy man' more than a decade before. In March 1922 he was 'more Tory than the Tory ministers' in opposing recognition of the Bolshevik regime.[2] In June 1923 he described himself as 'what I have always been – a Tory Democrat' and claimed that only 'force of circumstance', including the question of tariff reform, had pushed him towards the Liberals nearly 20 years ago.[3] In the spring of 1924 he appeared at a huge Conservative rally in Liverpool, and began to seek a seat as a Conservative candidate. He was adopted for Epping, to the north-east of London, and the suburban voters provided a reliable Tory majority. When the Labour government fell at the end of the year, he was elected with a majority of more than 9,000. From this point he remained a member of the party until his death more than 40 years later, and on these grounds the Conservatives have claimed him as one of their own. Yet it can be argued that all his best work was done as a reforming Liberal minister, or a Conservative rebel, or as Prime Minister of a coalition; and in 1940 it was not the Conservatives who welcomed his elevation to the premiership.

Baldwin asked Churchill to join his government as Chancellor of the Exchequer. Churchill wanted to reply 'Will the bloody duck swim?' but instead answered with more dignity: 'This fulfils my ambition. ... I still have my father's robe as Chancellor.'[4] One leading Conservative commented: 'Winston's appointment is genius – you have hamstrung him ...'.[5] Certainly he was not the obvious candidate for the post – he knew little or nothing of economics or finance, he sometimes gambled compulsively and his own affairs were often in a mess. He would not leave the office with his reputation enhanced.

Nevertheless he was a reforming chancellor in many ways. He reduced the minimum pension age from 70 to 65, he reorganised the system of paying war debts to the United States and reformed the rating system of local government finance. But he returned to the Gold Standard at an unfavourable rate, which severely restricted credit, and he was opposed to any deficits in the budget while determined to cut taxes to restore the post-war economy. John Maynard Keynes followed up his *The Economic Consequences of the Peace* (about Versailles) with *The Economic Consequences of Mr Churchill*:

> Why did he do such a silly thing?
>
> Partly, perhaps, because he has no instinctive judgement to prevent him from making mistakes; partly because, lacking this instinctive judgement, he was deafened by all the clamorous voices of conventional finance; and most of all, because he was gravely misled by his experts.[6]

In addition Churchill alienated many with his typically combative conduct during the General Strike of 1926. Maurice Ashley, recently chairman of Oxford University Labour Club, almost turned down a post as his research assistant as 'To me Winston Churchill was the politician who ... had helped crush the General Strike. ... Churchill was not merely a Conservative, a turncoat from the milder Liberals, but a reactionary of the deepest dye.'[7]

★

As Chancellor Churchill had some kind of interest in every department of government, but he was driven to cut defence spending which formed the largest portion of the national budget apart from the servicing of debts. He was up against formidable teams in each of the service ministries. Beatty was all-powerful at the Admiralty, with his charm, his connections and his political skills. He was supported by the First Lord, William Bridgeman, whom Lloyd George described as on the one hand having 'engaging and childlike simplicity' while on the other being 'a wily Salopian'.[8] The Bridgeman–Beatty partnership was probably as close as any between any two holders of these offices.[9] Trenchard at the Air Ministry was even more domineering. His minister, Samuel Hoare, was the first full-time peacetime Air Minister to sit in the cabinet. He demonstrated his faith in the air by flying to India with his wife in 1927, at a time when long-distance flights were regarded as heroic. He was a clever and effective politician himself, but regarded Trenchard as a prophet. The army was less dramatic, headed by Laming Worthington-Evans as War Minister, who had already clashed with Churchill over air control. The Chief of Imperial General Staff from 1926 was General Sir George Milne, who started off with plans for reform but was soon bogged down in army conservatism.

Churchill was still particularly suspicious of naval demands, largely based on his personal experience. In August 1919 he wrote: 'I suffered from three years of naval finance before the war and every pound was fought with an extreme but at the same time a salutary ferocity.'[10] The Liberal MP Joseph Kenworthy, a former naval officer, wrote in 1927: 'A former big navy advocate, he is now the watchdog of the Treasury.'[11] But Churchill believed he had good reasons for the change as the navy wanted to indulge in several very expensive projects with no real enemy in sight. In November 1924 he told the cabinet: 'In view of the probable necessity for the development of a naval base at Singapore and the Admiralty desire for an increase in the cruiser programme ... some investigation was required as to the rate at which these projects could be undertaken consistently with our financial situation and the desirability from a political point of view of avoiding any increase in expenditure on armaments in the forthcoming financial year.'[12]

The great naval base at Singapore was a central part of the strategy against Japan, after Britain was forced to drop the alliance with her as part of the Washington negotiations. Back in 1904 Fisher had claimed that Britain possessed 'Five keys that lock up the world!' – the Cape, Alexandria, Gibraltar, Dover and Singapore. To him they were 'another proof that we belong to the ten lost tribes of Israel', but Churchill was much more pragmatic.[13] In 1921 the cabinet, including Churchill, had adopted a plan for an £10½ million base, but it was dropped by the Labour government, which enraged Churchill: 'They have flouted the Dominions. They have deprived the British navy of the power of defending Australia and New Zealand.'[14] He was less keen when the incoming Conservatives restored the programme in 1924, though he was never totally against it. His policy, as with building the air force and new cruisers, was to 'slow down the rate of expansion'.[15]

The plan depended on defending the base against Japanese attack until the main fleet was mobilised to be sent to the region, and this aroused great controversy. The army and navy favoured six or eight 15-inch land-based guns to counter the Japanese battleships, the air force wanted torpedo bombers. Churchill supported the latter, partly because of its flexibility: 'it is much better to have this cost represented in mobile air squadrons rather than tied up forever in one spot in two heavy batteries'. Moreover, from the Chancellor's point of view it did not involve immediate cost and fitted in with the long term plan for the base: 'if this work were completed in fifteen or twenty years, the air should play a far larger part in it than is now contemplated'.[16] Trenchard of course supported this view but was overruled, much to his regret. Churchill also drew up his ideas for the strategy of a war in the Far East, though it was well beyond his remit as Chancellor. He suggested a division of battlecruisers or fast battleships during a period of tension, which would harass the Japanese while the main fleet was sent from the Mediterranean. If war was declared, a 'preconceived programme of new construction' should be started which would include the preparation of a floating base including store ships, tankers, repair ships and all kinds of ancillaries 'capable of being moved forward point to point by selected anchorages with the movement of the battle fleet'.[17]

According to Churchill in July 1925, there was no question of 'mortal peril', which he defined as 'a physical assault so violent as to deprive Great Britain finally of the power to convert to war purposes the latent energy of the empire'.[18] Only two powers, Japan and the USA, had the capacity to threaten the British Empire on the seas. 'However foolish and disastrous such a war would be … We do not wish to put ourselves in the power of the United States. We cannot tell what they might do if at some future date they were in a position to give us orders about our policy, say, in India, or Egypt, or Canada …'.[19] In September 1928 he 'talked very freely' and claimed that the Americans were 'arrogant, fundamentally hostile to us, and that they wish to dominate world politics. … their "big navy talk" is a bluff which we ought to call … we ought to say firmly how large a navy we require, and that America must do the same.'[20]

As to Japan, he stated in March 1925:

> Everything really turns upon whether the cabinet wish the navy to be ready as soon as possible to put a superior battle fleet with all the ancillaries in the Pacific in case of a war with Japan. If this is the policy, I do not think that the Admiralty requirements are excessive. If we are to beat Japan in her own home waters and ward off France while our navy is at the other end of the world, and guard all the trade routes simultaneously through all the oceans and seas, even more, in my opinion, will be needed.[21]

But he did not think this at all likely, and wrote to Keyes a few weeks later:

> I do not believe Japan has any idea of attacking the British Empire, or that there is any danger of her doing so for at least a generation to come. … She would not, as in the case with Germany, have any chance of striking at the heart of the Empire and destroying its power to wage war. We should be put to great annoyance and expense, but in three or four years we should certainly sweep the Japanese from the seas and force them to make peace.[22]

★

Battleship construction was tightly controlled by the Washington Treaty, and in April 1925 Churchill even quibbled over the 'questionable policy' of adding anti-torpedo bulges to the *Queen Elizabeths*, though they were his favourite ships and bulging was one of his favourite policies. 'It is not only the expense incurred upon the ships … but the whole question of dock accommodation is affected thereby.'[23] The main battle now was over the number of cruisers. Their size was fixed by the Washington Treaty at 10,000 tons and 8-inch guns, but there was no agreement on the number. The Admiralty wanted a force of 70 to protect British interests over the seas, but the war-built light cruisers had only six 6-inch guns in single turrets and on 4,000–5,000 tons they were barely suitable for ocean operation. Even the six ships of the *Effingham* and *Emerald* classes, built in 1916–25, with seven 7.5-inch guns, were now considered obsolete – Beatty claimed that 'the advent of the 8-inch gun ship has made not only the 6-inch ship, but also the 7½-inch ship out of date, and if you pit a 7½ inch ship against an 8-inch ship you are courting disaster …'.[24] The Labour government of 1924 was pressurised by fear of unemployment into continuing with five new 8-inch cruisers of the *Kent* class. The opposition claimed the credit, however, and Clementine wrote: '… these silly Tories are probably now so pleased with Ramsay [Macdonald] over the five cruisers that they will not yet need your help in fighting Labour'.[25]

There is no better example of Churchill's habit of falling into the role he was playing at the time and using his enormous ability to pursue it, than the struggle over cruiser construction in the mid-1920s. According to the leading naval historian of the period:

> An interesting feature of Churchill's attack on the navy estimates for 1925–26 is that not only in tone and content but at times in the actual words used, it bears an extraordinary resemblance to Lloyd George's attack, as Chancellor of the Exchequer, on the estimates for 1913–14 … except that this time Japan had been substituted for Germany as the probable adversary.[26]

Churchill maintained friendly relations with Beatty and his ardent supporter Keyes. He wrote to Lady Keyes late in 1924: 'I feel that my duties as Chancellor of the Exchequer will leave me on the other side of the table to the Admiralty, at any rate during the unhealthy estimate season.'[27] Beatty wrote: 'That extraordinary fellow Winston had gone mad, economically mad, and no sacrifice is too great to achieve what in his short-sightedness is the panacea for all evils, to take one shilling off the income tax. … As we at the Admiralty are the principal spending department he attacks us with a virulence, and now proclaims that a navy is a quite unnecessary luxury.'[28] Clementine on the other hand urged: '… stand up to the Admiralty and don't be fascinated or flattered or cajoled by Beatty. I assure you, the country doesn't care two pins about him. … Beatty is a tight little screw and he will bargain with you and cheat you as though he were selling you a dud horse which I fear the navy is.'[29]

★

Naval estimates totalling £60½ million were finally presented in March 1925, with no new construction, but it was not a victory for Churchill as the question of new cruisers was left to a supplementary estimate after an investigation. There was a 'ding dong' battle in a committee chaired by Lord Birkenhead, and in July Beatty wrote to his wife: 'We have reached an impasse with the government on the cruiser question, and I do not see the way out. We have made our proposals as being the very lowest we can agree to, and they won't have them, with the result that somebody has got to give way completely and Willie Bridgeman is as firm as a rock. Therefore the whole of the Admiralty is with him *en bloc* and I suppose we shall have to go.'[30] But Bridgeman worked on the Prime Minister, persuading him that it would be easier to lose Churchill than him and Beatty and the rest of the Board of Admiralty. It was announced that four cruisers were to be laid down in 1925–26, and three more in the following year.

Churchill had been defeated, but he did not change his mind. In July 1927 he recalled the events of 1914–15:

> I have never accepted the 70 cruiser programme or the reasoning on which it stood, and the cabinet assent in 1925 was given only to an instalment of that programme up to 1929, large reductions being made by the Admiralty through an arbitrary extension of the life of cruisers. … There is no parity whatever in the tasks of defending trade and attacking trade. Less than ten German cruisers, loose in the great waters, were not destroyed till after several months of serious depredations by more than 100 British and allied vessels. I believe, therefore, that the safeguard of our food supply will be found not in multiplying cruisers beyond a certain point, but in instituting convoys.[31]

In 1927 a Geneva conference instituted the B class of cruiser, still with 8-inch guns but on a tonnage of 7,500 so that it had only six guns instead of eight. This led to further disputes and in October 1927 Churchill told the Prime Minister: 'My opening talk with the Admiralty revealed abysmal differences. I am proposing no cruisers in '27–'28 or '28–'29, and they want three B class in each of these years, with possibly a smaller type of B substituted in the second year.'[32] Churchill was sceptical: 'I cannot help seeing in imagination this B class cruiser, chosen in such indecent haste by the cabinet, caught alone in some distant ocean by a foreign ship of which she might have been the equal and after a gallant fight at needlessly unfair odds, sinking beneath the waves with all her crew.'[33]

Even after the dispute Keyes did not miss a chance to emphasise the unseaworthiness of the older cruisers, as Churchill sailed with him in the *Queen Elizabeth* in 1928: 'From this steady platform, looking at the destroyers and light cruisers plunging into heavy seas I am thankful that the former are no smaller ... and pray that our small C and D class cruisers ... may have reached their allotted span, for heaven help them if they have to fight cruisers of the type the United States, Japan, France and Italy are building.'[34]

Behind Churchill's scepticism was the fear that the new ships would be outmoded by the time any war came. He quoted Fisher:

> Build late, build fast,
> Each year better than the last.[35]

In February 1929 he pointed out that 'the 18 vessels that we now had on our hands would almost certainly be outclassed by the new American cruisers. This illustrated the mistake in building prematurely.'[36] He also noted that 'the Germans were building a new 10.000 ton vessel embodying novel features. By lightening weights and developing a very high horse-power per ton they had been able to design a very remarkable ship ... armed with 11-inch guns; it would have a greater radius of action than our battlecruisers, and would fire a greater weight of shell per minute than they.'[37] These were the 'pocket battleships'. Named the *Deutschland, Admiral Scheer* and *Admiral Graf Spee*, they were the largest allowed under the terms of the Treaty of Versailles but they found a gap which had not been expected, and they would cause concern in later years.

Comparatively little attention was paid to destroyers, which were not mentioned in the Washington Treaty. There was a large stock of wartime V and W classes, descendants of Churchill's M class of 1913–14. They were excellent ships in their day but now ageing. In July 1925 it was agreed that 'an annual construction of nine destroyers and six submarines, together with certain ancillary vessels, will be required'.[38] The annual order included a flotilla leader (instead of a light cruiser as in the past) and eight ships, beginning with *Codrington* and eight vessels of the A class launched in 1929. As more were launched in subsequent years, they would become the 'A to I' classes which would form the core of the navy's destroyer force at the beginning of the next war. Submarine construction progressed with the O and P classes launched in 1928–29. Anti-submarine vessels were revived when in October 1927 'Admiral Field spoke of the importance of beginning a few sloops of the Flower class at £100,000 apiece in the latter part of 1928 ...'.[39] These became the *Bridgewater* and *Sandwich*, developments of the Flower class of the last war, to be followed by four similar vessels; but in general anti-submarine warfare was neglected due to faith in the asdic as a means of detecting them.

★

Churchill was constantly aware of cost saving and expense. During a visit to Keyes in the Mediterranean Fleet in 1926 he worried about the dues on passing through the Corinth Canal: 'I have to look at these things very carefully.'[40] He examined other areas of naval expenditure and complained in November 1924: 'Practically every ship not in dockyard hands refitting is kept permanently manned with its full complement of active-service ratings. These complements have been largely increased *in the same ships* since 1914; for instance the approved war complement of the *Iron Duke* in 1914 was 885, the approved peace complement is now 1,089, and the super-war complement ... is 1,212.' There was little provision for reserves, but 'We are invited to live, perhaps for a quarter of a century of peace with our pistol at full-cock and our finger on the trigger.'[41]

The advantages of technology were not being exploited and in February 1927 he wrote to Bridgeman: '... the very fact that the navy has a better and more modern plant should enable reductions in the lower grades of personnel to be effected. The inconsistency lies with anyone who says: because we have better and more powerful weapons, we must have more men. Machine power within certain limits should be a substitute for man power ...'.[42]

In January 1928, in an attempt to cut the estimates to £56 million, he suggested 'that the scheme of anti-aircraft armament should be postponed for this year'.[43] He complained about 'an item in the Admiralty estimates for expenditure on an anti-aircraft weapon which ... had not yet been tested in concert with the Air Ministry, and the suggestion was made that before serious expenditure is incurred, the merits of this weapon should be discussed by the Committee of Imperial Defence'.[44] He refused to pay marriage allowances to naval officers to bring them into line with the army and RAF, which greatly annoyed Beatty.

★

From the army, General Philip Chetwode wrote to Churchill on his appointment to the Exchequer: 'Don't be too ferocious with the poor army – we are just beginning to get back to 1914 standards – in fact better in some respects ...'.[45] Churchill agreed that 'there was little, if any, room for reduction in the size of the army'.[46] In January 1925 he disagreed with an army proposal to sell old rifles: 'There is no greater security against vague and unmeasured dangers than a large store of rifles. ... We ought never to have less than two million rifles of all sorts and kinds in this country.'[47] He urged more flexibility in organisation, writing to Worthington-Evans in January 1927 during a crisis in China: 'The army are accustomed to think in divisions. They were the bricks out of which the Western Front was built ... But it does not follow that a division as constituted for the Western Front is the proper unit for the interests of China. What you want is to make up a "force" for China, fitted as accurately as possible to the work you think it may have to do ...'.[48]

Churchill did not forget the idea of mechanising the cavalry after he left the War Office. In 1928, his desire for economy caused him to demand that cavalry be either mechanised or abolished. That caused a shock in the War Office which leapt to the defence of the cavalry, and for the moment only the junior Hussar regiments, the 11th and 12th, were re-equipped with armoured cars. That year a committee on the future of the cavalry could only conclude that a new design of lance was needed.[49]

★

Despite his efforts to save the independent air force, Churchill had left the Air Ministry with a very weak home defence force. In 1923 Britain had 24 fighters, 12 bombers and 24 army co-operation machines, a total of 60; France had 300 fighters, 296 bombers and 596 army co-operation aircraft, a total of 868 or a superiority of 14 to 1. There was no real prospect of a war with France, but it highlighted how far the RAF at home had fallen behind. A plan was drawn up to increase the force to 642 aircraft by 1930, which also involved building and equipping new airfields and training the pilots and mechanics, while 400 of Trenchard's short service pilots were to be taken on. War with France was even less likely in 1925 after the Treaty of Locarno settled many differences. Hoare wrote: 'The relations between England and France are as friendly as they could be. Germany is altogether deprived of an air force, yet France continues to maintain an air strength more predominant than was ever her military strength under Napoleon or Louis XIV. Are we justified in remaining for many years in a position of such numerical inferiority in air strength?'[50] Churchill did not demur from the general principle of air expansion, but questioned the urgency. In November 1925 he agreed that 'some increase in the Royal Air Force must be faced in order to secure the safety of the country'.[51] He complained about 'the violent alterations in policy to which the air service had been subjected in the past'. Current plans stretched up to 1931; he suggested that might be extended to 1940.[52] This time he did not object to the foundation of the Royal Auxiliary Air Force of 'weekend flyers', perhaps because it was a cheap way of building up the force to its nominal strength.

His support for the independent air force was not unconditional, and in September 1925 he wrote to Hoare: 'Up to the present the Treasury view has been favourable to the maintenance of a separate air force, but you would be surprised to hear all the quarters in which misgivings are felt on the subject. My own view is strictly in favour of the air force on the merits, subject only to the query "can we afford it".'[53] This probably inspired Trenchard to write to him: 'I ask you to look at the service that has been formed and is growing up. Have you any idea of the spirit which obtains in the air force? Wherever you go, whether it is a Punch-and-Judy show or in grand opera, in the highest circles or the lowest, you will hear the opinion that the air force do better than anyone else. ... take the Hendon display; take flying generally; … the spirit animating the whole service …'.[54] The air force generally got off lightly and as the 1928 estimates were being prepared Churchill wrote: 'In view of the large economies already made in the air estimates, the Secretary of State for Air found it impossible to give a favourable reply to the further appeal made to him by the Chancellor of the Exchequer for still greater savings, and Mr Churchill felt he could not press the point.'[55]

Though air power had proved very useful on the Western Front for reconnaissance and spotting for guns, the army did not fight hard for control of army-co-operation squadrons, perhaps because they regarded that kind of war as an aberration and had no vision of air power in any other circumstances. That part of the air force was therefore neglected, as Hoare admitted in 1925. The RAF only had 48 army-co-operation aircraft and no plans to expand that number in parallel with the rest of the service; they were 'greatly inferior in number' to French machines and not suitable for a bombing attack on France.[56] It was very different for the navy, where Beatty fought strongly and skilfully with Trenchard over control of the Fleet Air Arm. Churchill however maintained his policy of 'unity of the air' as proclaimed in 1922.

Churchill's prejudice against airships continued, and in June 1926 Sir Samuel Hoare wrote: 'Winston, on the totally irrelevant evidence of the war, is still dead against airships and loses no time to dig at the programmes.'[57] The issue was disposed of in October 1930 when the airship R101 crashed in France killing 47 people, including the Labour Air Minister Lord Thomson and the Director of Civil Aviation. *John Bull* and the *Daily Telegraph* both turned down Churchill's articles on the disaster, the former because it already had a cheaper article.[58] Churchill was not disappointed when the government cancelled all airship projects,

An election was called for 30 May 1929 and Churchill retained his safe seat comfortably. This time Labour was now the largest single party with 287 seats compared with the Conservatives' 261 and the Liberals' 59. Ramsay Macdonald formed his second government and Churchill was out of office again.

CHAPTER 28

Marlborough

Now in his mid-fifties, Churchill seemed a figure from a bygone age. To Leopold Amery in August 1929 he was 'mid-Victorian, steeped in the politics of his father's period'.[1] Harold Nicolson wrote in January 1930: 'Incredibly aged ... An elder statesman. His spirits have also declined and he sighs that he has lost his old fighting power.'[2] The great depression of 1929 perhaps warned him of the dangers of economic prediction, for in 1927 he had stated: 'Again for the twentieth time let me repeat that the finances of the country after 1931 will be substantially stronger than they are at present.'[3] He lost heavily in the Wall Street Crash of 1929, he was injured while coming out of a taxi in New York, and while he was out of the country the Conservative Party decided to support a measure of self-government for India, which he opposed strongly. Most of the 1930s were to be dominated by near-bankruptcy (staved off by lucrative and prolific writing), poor health and political isolation, as the India issue made him appear more reactionary and out of touch than ever.

Churchill had not entirely said goodbye to *The World Crisis*. In 1930 he wrote two articles for *Collier's Magazine* for a series called 'Crucial Crises of the Great War', on the Russian assault on East Prussia and the Battle of Tannenberg in 1914. This led to further interest in a subject which was almost unknown in the west. He wrote: 'Although I lived and toiled through the war years in positions which gave a wide outlook and the best information, I was surprised to find how dim and often imperfect were the impressions I had sustained of the conflict between Russia and the two Teutonic Empires.'[4] It was an epic struggle involving millions of soldiers and it led to the downfall of the Austro-Hungarian and Russian empires with incalculable effects on history. It was fought over a vast front with a much more fluid kind of warfare, which appealed to Churchill. 'In the west the armies were too big for the country; in the east the country was too big for the armies. ... No large force on either side could advance far without intense and growing anxiety, lest some other powerful body were advancing swiftly from an unexpected angle and would suddenly manifest itself in unknown strength, marching upon the vital communications.'[5] It featured genuine battles in the old sense, such as Tannenberg, and heroes such as General François of the German Army, who disobeyed the orders of the more famous Ludendorff to win it; and it was linked to the Dardanelles Campaign which still obsessed Churchill.

He found out more about his *bête noir* Trotsky from his biography. 'The light which it throws upon the inner and subterranean workings of communism, and upon the mental processes of that formidable sect, is deeply interesting to the every student of modern politics.'[6] But surprisingly the finished book (titled *The World Crisis: The Eastern Front*, and published in 1931) dealt with the collapse of the Russian empire in only seven pages. All seemed well at the beginning of 1917, new regiments were being formed and the railway from Murmansk, built at great cost in human life, was ready to bring in supplies from the allies as it would do again in 1941–45. But the regime collapsed without any explanation given, except the effects of defeat in war, and 'cold, calculating, ruthless, patient, stirring all, demanding all, the world-wide organisation of international communism'.[7] Perhaps he felt he had dealt with the issue adequately in *The Aftermath*, but it leaves *The Eastern Front* looking truncated. Though it was an interesting exercise, it did not catch the public imagination. W. Lints Smith of *The Times* declined to serialise it, claiming 'our readers, we find, are responding less and less to war history even when it is being told by someone who writes at first hand'.[8] The publisher Butterworth reported: 'I am sorry to say that *The Eastern Front* has not done as well as we expected.'[9]

Almost as soon as he left office, Churchill began work on his autobiography up to the age of 25 when he entered parliament and ended his active military career. There was much discussion over the title; in the end *My Early Life* was favoured in Britain and *A Roving Commission*, Churchill's own favourite, in the United States. It was a contrast to *The Eastern Front* which had required an enormous amount of research – the new book was 'all in my head, or actually finished'.[10] He had about 70,000 words in articles already published and would add another 30,000 to 40,000 'so as to make a continuous homogeneous narrative'.[11] He wrote: 'I have tried, in each part of the quarter-century in which this tale lies, to show the point of view appropriate to my years, whether as a child, a schoolboy, a cadet, a subaltern, a war correspondent, or a youthful politician.'[12] Perhaps he carried this too far, if Stanley Baldwin's remark is to be believed. With his views on India, 'He has become once more the subaltern of hussars of '96.'[13] He might have used the opportunity to write more frankly about the deceased, such as Kitchener, but one review said: 'There is no bitterness or invective … such as the attack on the late Sir Charles Munro in *The World Crisis*.'[14] It gave him a chance to review his military life and see his campaigns in the context of what followed, and it is regarded as perhaps his best book.

At the same time he was looking at an 'abridgement' of the first three volumes of *The World Crisis*, though in practice it would be rather more than that – he wrote a brand new chapter on the Battle of the Marne of 1914, perhaps reflecting his interest, as expressed in *The Eastern Front*, in modern battles of movement. It was, he wrote, 'the greatest battle ever fought in the world', but at the same time 'It was less like a battle than any other ever fought. Comparatively few were killed or wounded.' He condensed the text of the rest of the work largely by reducing the number of documents, for he felt most of those on the Dardanelles were not needed any more. 'Although a good many technical memoranda have been excluded and some discussions abridged, no key document is omitted and the tale runs forward unbrokenly though the whole of this tremendous period.' He believed it had 'gained a good deal by concentration'.[15] He would also publish a collection of his essays,

Thoughts and Adventures, in September 1931, as well as a prodigious amount of journalism in newspapers and magazines.

*

Despite his exposure to the Marlborough tapestries at Blenheim Palace, Churchill was reluctant to begin a biography of his great ancestor when asked by publishers, for he had read Thomas Babington Macaulay's histories as a major part of his self-education as a subaltern. He attributed his conversion to a lunch with Lord Rosebery, who pressed him to write on 'Duke John' as he called him, who was 'a tremendous fellow'. Churchill raised the objection of the Camaret Bay letter which suggested treason, but the aged Rosebery hobbled along to his library to fetch a copy of Paget's *Examen*, which claimed that Marlborough had written the letter but did not send it until the news of the Brest expedition had already been revealed. Even so, that was 'a poor defence'. Later Churchill set his assistant to work and proved to his own satisfaction that the letter was actually a decoded message and was probably concocted. 'I have submitted them to very eminent lawyers, and have asked them to consider whether there are flaws in the arguments, and they have assured me that there is absolutely no ground whatever for fastening such an odious charge.'[16]

Churchill had been too busy to begin such a work while in office, but in 1929 he agreed with George Harrap to publish the life in two volumes.[17] He took on the young Oxford historian Maurice Ashley at £300 a year, whose main duty initially was to search the archives at nearby Blenheim. Churchill described his intention to him: '... my method will probably be not to attempt to "defend" or "vindicate" my subject, but to tell the tale with close adherence to chronology in such a way and in such proportions and with such emphasis as will produce in the mind of the reader the impression I wish to give.'[18] He wrote to Lord Camrose, the newspaper proprietor: '... you may be right in saying that the topical interest will not be so keen as was in the case of a war book. Nevertheless I have no doubt that I shall be able to tell this famous tale from a modern point of view in a way that will rivet attention.'[19] Interest in the period was already being fostered by the successive volumes of historian G. M. Trevelyan's *England in the Reign of Queen Anne*. Though Trevelyan was related to the now despised Macaulay, he wrote to Churchill in October 1930: 'Well now for the Great Duke! I can't tell you how much I am looking forward to it.'[20]

Ashley described Churchill's methods as used in this book – for they evolved over the years and differed according to the needs of the work in question. 'Churchill always preferred to get something down on paper and to fill in the gaps later. I always remember my astonishment to find myself listening to him dictating an introductory chapter about Marlborough before, as far as I could make out, he knew anything about him beyond the skeleton of his career as it was familiar to every school-boy. ... Brought up, as I had been, in the most rigorous atmosphere of Oxford historical research ... I found it difficult to envisage how anyone could start an important work of history without previously mastering all possible sources, comparing them and sorting out the wheat from the chaff.'[21] The method is perhaps more familiar in the age of the word processor and the search engine, so that an author does not need a large staff to make rapid progress.

According to Ashley, 'The duties of Churchill's research assistants were threefold; in the first place they were required to feed him with material. This meant not only the collection and marshalling of historical documents but the provision of all the books that he needed in order to write a given chapter. ... The second main duty ... was to make sympathetic and co-operative noises while Churchill dictated. They were required to sit by and if possible fill in the gaps in his knowledge. ... The third duty ... was to ferret out facts and get points checked.'[22] But they were not alone: 'On the *Marlborough* he had not only a principal research assistant but a military adviser and a naval adviser.'[23] For army affairs he used Brigadiers Sir James Edmonds, the head of the military branch of the historical section of the Committee of Imperial Defence, and R. P. Pakenham-Walsh, a staff officer at the War Office who had served in the Dardanelles. Churchill believed that Marlborough was 'an amphibious strategist' who had served with the navy early in his career (as many land officers did) at the Battle of Solebay and also 'first understood the importance of Mediterranean power'.[24] He believed that 'the naval strategy like all the great measures originated with the redoubtable John'. 'Unlike Napoleon and many other great military commanders, he never underrated the peculiar conditions and extra difficulties of the sea service and always assigned to naval officers their indispensable primacy upon the sea.'[25] With this in mind he approached Kenneth Dewar as his consultant. He in turn referred him to Commander J. H. Owen, who was preparing a history of the war at sea under Queen Anne. However he soon found that 'the naval part of "Marlborough" is reduced to much smaller dimensions than I first supposed' and therefore reduced payments to Owen.[26] In August 1933 he wrote to Ashley: 'I am doubtful whether it will be possible to incorporate any of Commander Owen's stuff.'[27] Nevertheless he maintained that 'British control in the Mediterranean which still endures, is the outcome of Marlborough's mind.'[28]

Churchill cast his net widely with his research. He received 420 letters on Marlborough in 1933, and wrote 308.[29] On receiving the historians' reports he would study them all day and 'after dinner and with his three secretaries working in shifts, he would walk up and down his long study dictating steadily as he walked. This often went on till the early hours of the morning'.[30] He preferred to use the printed word for corrections. 'The great advantage of working these large galley proofs is that one sees practically three pages of typescript at a glance. This enables the structure to be much more easily shaped. You must not however suppose that I attach any finality to the proofs, because they are printed. I always knock them about a great deal and incorporate the criticisms of many authorities who read them.'[31]

The great Georgian historian Lewis Namier wrote to him: 'You will remember what Gibbon said about the experiences of the captain of the Hampshire Grenadiers and the historian of the Roman Empire.' He urged him 'not to try to write history as other historians do, but do it in your own way'. This involved deploying his experience of government, but as a political historian Namier did not mention Churchill's knowledge of military affairs, which was equally important in the context.[32]

Macaulay became something of an obsession, though to Maurice Ashley '"exposing" Macaulay is like flogging a dead horse'.[33] In 1934 Namier wrote about Churchill's 'pre-occupation' with him: 'I have heard it said in Whig circles that you are forcing an open door in tilting against him.'[34] The playwright George Bernard Shaw wrote that his work was 'largely a protest against Macaulay' but was 'badly damaged in places by its Macaulayisms'.[35] On reading the first volume his old friend Violet Bonham-Carter (née Asquith) wrote that she could not love Marlborough and that 'It is easier to return Macaulay's ball than to serve Marlborough's.'[36]

The soldier-statesman was Churchill's ideal figure. Such a character was standard in earlier times, before a more specialised world began to draw the distinction between the two and impose a regular career pattern on military leaders. If Churchill had paid more attention to his classics at school he might have become aware of Themistocles, who quite literally risked ostracism by warning the Athenians of the dangers of Persian invasion, strained every nerve and broke a few rules to build up a great fleet, then led it in person and inspired the men the with his speeches before winning the Battle of Salamis in 480 BC and saving western civilisation, according to some opinions. Medieval kings were expected as a matter of course to lead their armies in battle as well as conduct the affairs of state, though only a few did both equally well. In more modern times, he had a great admiration for Napoleon Bonaparte, though he was aware that his system was not applicable to modern Britain. Napoleon's great adversary the Duke of Wellington also ventured into the political field, though with little success. But going back a century earlier, Churchill could find his own ancestor, whom he regarded as an ideal hero despite the flaws that others saw in him.

It would be difficult for him not to see parallels, for Marlborough was married to a powerful and intelligent wife and was a soldier-statesman of great tactical and political skill, who (in Churchill's eyes at least) was unfairly traduced and cast aside. And Marlborough was a man of initiative, not afraid to lead his army away from sterile fortress warfare in Flanders to fight on a different front to the east. It is not hard to see wishful thinking and prediction in his preface:

> Upon his person centred the union of nearly twenty confederate states. He held the grand Alliance together no less by his diplomacy than by his victories. He rode into action with the combinations of three-quarters of Europe in his

hand. His comprehension of war extended to all theatres, and his authority alone secured design and concerted action. He animated the war on sea no less than on land, and established till the present time the British naval supremacy in the Mediterranean. His eye ranged far across the oceans, and the foundations of British dominion in the New World and in Asia were strengthened as the result of his continental policy.[37]

He contrasted the commanders of the recent war with those of earlier days. Modern generals endured

> ... trials of mind and spirit working in calm surroundings, often beyond even the sound of the cannonade. There are no physical disturbances: there is no danger: there is no hurry. The generalissimo of an army of two million men, already for ten days in desperate battle, has little or nothing to do except keep himself fit and cool. His life is not different, except in its glory, from that of a painstaking, punctual public official, and far less agitating than that of a cabinet minister who must face an angry chamber on one hand or an offended party on the other. There is no need for the modern commander to wear boots and breeches: he will never ride a horse except for the purposes of health.

But in Marlborough's day

> ... the great commander proved in the day of battle that he possessed a combination of mental, moral, and physical properties adapted to an action which were so lifted above the common run as to seem almost godlike. His appearance, his piercing eye, his gestures, the tones of his voice – nay, the beat of his heart – diffused a harmony upon all around him. Every word he spoke was decisive. Victory often depended on whether he rode half a mile this way or that.[38]

This justified and reinforced his own habit of getting as close as possible to the front line, whether as subaltern, war correspondent or prime minister.

Descriptions of battles saw Churchill in his element – one can almost feel him settling into Marlborough's mind as he rode his horse among his troops. This was reinforced by a visit to the battlefields, and in August 1932 he wrote to his daughter Mary as they sailed from Dover to Calais, then travelled in Pakenham-Walsh's car through the Great War battlefields: 'After that I am going to motor across Europe from Brussels to the Danube in Bavaria along the line your great ancestor marched with a small English army and conquered all the foes as he met them.'[39] Next month he reported: 'The battlefields were wonderful. Pakenham-Walsh presented them admirably and I am able to re-people them with ghostly but glittering armies. A surprise was their great size. Ramillies, Oudenarde, and Blenheim all seemed to me bigger than Austerlitz or Gettysburg, and far bigger than Waterloo. The topography is practically unchanged – one could recognise all the well-known points and admire these masterly exhibitions of flexible moving action.'[40] He was excited to find a barn at Ramillies with the battle scars still visible, that the trenches at the Schellenberg were still there, and that there was still a bridge of boats where Marlborough's armies had crossed the Rhine.[41]

Marlborough's greatest single achievement was the Battle of Blenheim, which among other things gave the name to Churchill's birthplace. To win it he had to move away from the western front of the day, where British, Dutch and German armies tried to force their way through multiple lines of trenches and fortresses, and take his army to Bavaria – he was the prototype of the 'easterner' of the Great War. Technology plays its part in every modern war, and Churchill described how the English army had adopted the flintlock and the ring bayonet while the French were slowly converting from the matchlock and the plug bayonet. Marlborough exercised his men in firing by platoons rather than in lines to give greater flexibility. Though he had large numbers of cavalry he generally used infantry for the main attack, but co-ordination of all three arms was the key to success. And Marlborough's tactical flexibility, only possible because of his presence on the field, was essential. Churchill wrote to the historian Keith Feiling in 1932: 'Oudenarde is particularly astonishing for its continuous improvisation. But just look at the team he had – Cadogan, Eugene, Argyll, and old Overkirk, all so experienced and comprehending; like sheep-dogs perfectly trained, rounding up sheep under their unquestioningly-obeyed shepherd.'[42] But it was lack of political control which hampered the Duke. 'It is extraordinary how modern Marlborough's military conceptions were. He saw all that Napoleon saw, but being only a servant in a rigid age, instead of a sovereign in a molten one, he could only occasionally give effect to his genius. Napoleon could order, but Marlborough could never do more than persuade or cajole. It is hard to win battles on that basis.'[43]

Churchill could never have flourished in Marlborough's early career as a sycophantic courtier and diplomat. He wrote to Clementine: 'What a downy bird he was. He will always stoop to conquer. His long apprenticeship as a courtier had taught him to bow and scrape and put up with the second or third best if he could get no better. He had far less pride than the average man. This greatly helped his world schemes and in raising England to the heights she has never since lost.'[44] On the issue of loyalty, the notorious Camaret Bay was the key. Churchill's provisional conclusion, expressed in January 1933, was that Marlborough 'never intended to bring back James and run the risk of Popish deposition in England. ... Marlborough kept only his left hand on the Jacobites, and made them believe he was friendly to their plans, but his right hand punch was Anne.'[45] Churchill was not in any sense corrupt, though he sometimes pushed the boundaries of what he was allowed to do with the publication of official documents. He was in no way treasonable, indeed he might be accused of excessive loyalty to Edward VIII before he was forced to abdicate in 1936. He changed parties twice but was constantly loyal to his country. *Marlborough* eventually expanded from two volumes to four, for as Churchill wrote to Feiling, 'It is like climbing a hill where a new rise always comes in sight.'[46] The last volume was published in 1938, by which time Churchill was busy on other works, and in preparing for another war.

★

In January 1932 Churchill made a speech to an audience in Worcester, Massachusetts, in which he claimed that 'Co-operation of the two great English speaking nations is the only hope now to bring the world back to the pathway of peace and prosperity.' Of course his mother was American, and it as not the first time he had mentioned the theme, though the train had been interrupted by the naval rivalry of the 1920s and a general anti-British feeling in the United States. But this time, he thought, 'It certainly went extremely well. The people were almost reverential in their attitude,' and he used the lecture again.[47] In December that year he contracted with the publisher Cassell to write 400,000 words on *The History of the English Speaking Peoples*, to be completed by 1939, for a lump sum of £20,000. It gave him a chance to look well outside his normal time period, and he was fascinated when the archaeologist Mortimer Wheeler agreed with him that 'Britain was therefore still joined to Europe when the pyramids were a-building.'[48] But apart from that he did not enjoy it, and in December 1938 he wrote: 'It is very laborious and I resent it, and the pressure.'[49] Often he would have several different centuries in his mind at a time. On 9 July 1939 he was considering the American Civil War, the next day he sent off notes on Richard I from the twelfth century and John Wycliffe from the fourteenth, while corresponding with his old friend Archibald Sinclair about what to do in the event of the next war.

As the work progressed beyond the unfamiliar medieval period, he could see references from his own life as well as current politics. He warned the pro-Fascist Lord Rothermere that any understanding with Hitler to dominate Europe would be 'contrary to the whole of our history. We have on all occasions been the friend of the second strongest power in Europe and have never yielded ourselves to the strongest power. Thus Elizabeth resisted Philip II of Spain. Thus William III and Marlborough resisted Louis XIV. Thus Pitt resisted Napoleon and thus we all resisted William II of Germany.' He discovered the virtues of another great war leader, William Pitt the Elder, later Earl of Chatham, who led the country during the Seven Years' War. In his early days in parliament he was known as 'this terrible cornet of horse', which is not far from Asquith's dismissal of Churchill as 'an ex-lieutenant of Hussars'. As an orator Pitt could fill the public galleries of the house, and he was compared with Garrick the actor. He thought in terms of world policy and led Britain to perhaps its greatest victory of all time. He was 'a man who from a private station compelled a sluggish, all-powerful government to capitulate, and thereafter in four brilliant years gained the Seven Years' War and the building of "The First British Empire".'[50] Churchill was also interested in the American Civil War: 'Of all the wars that men have fought in their hard pilgrimage, none was more noble than the great Civil War in America nearly eighty years ago. Both sides fought with high conviction, and the war was long and hard.'[51] More generally, he took comfort in the belief that 'tyrannies cannot last long except among servile races'.[52] On 31 August 1939, as the next conflict was imminent, he wrote that 'It is a relief in times like these to escape into other centuries' – a delight which would not be allowed him for long. The work was almost complete, but publication was postponed for more than a decade and a half because of more pressing matters.[53]

CHAPTER 29

The Study of Air Power

Churchill was visiting Germany to research the Marlborough battlefields in the summer of 1932 when he met a Herr Hanftstaengl who claimed to be a friend of Adolf Hitler, the 'Führer' of the rising Nazi Party. A meeting between the two was planned, until Churchill asked 'Why is your chief so violent about the Jews?' and no more was heard of it.[1] Churchill already had doubts about Hitler and in 1930 Prince Bismarck of the German embassy had failed to reassure him: 'Hitler had admittedly declared he had no intention of waging a war of aggression; he, Churchill, however was convinced that Hitler or his followers would seize the first opportunity to resort to armed force.'[2] His old friend Sir Ian Hamilton wrote to him that year reporting the views of Dr Cuno of the Anglo-German Association on the desperation of the German people: '... out of 32 million people in Germany there were 29 million who were finding life just about intolerable ... they had resolved to sweep away the whole of the existing system of compromise. ... They were going to have a try at something entirely new and the whole question ... was whether the change would be to the right or to the left. ... They had got the swing to the right and he hoped that the responsibility of power would make this new government more moderate in action than it had been in words.'[3]

The Nazis took power at the end of January 1933 and six weeks later Churchill rejected the idea of trying to control the situation by further disarmament. 'In the present temper of Europe, can you ever expect that France would halve her air force and then reduce the residue by one third?' He went on: 'Not to have an adequate air force in the present state of the world is to compromise the foundations of national freedom and independence.' He suggested the abandonment of the ten-year rule for which he had largely been responsible, but was optimistic about British air power: 'There is no reason to suppose that we cannot make machines as good as any country. We have ... a particular vein of talent in air piloting in advance of that possessed by other countries.'[4] He returned to the ten-year theme on 7 February 1934: 'A new situation has been created, largely in the last few years ... largely, I fear, by rubbing this sore of the Disarmament Conference until it has become a cancer, and also by the sudden uprush of Nazi-ism in Germany, with the tremendous covert armaments which are proceeding there today.'[5]

★

As Churchill was aware, the Nazi regime was already creating an air force in secret, based on experience in civil aviation and the training of glider pilots under the Weimar Republic. In July 1934 he claimed that 'Germany has already, in violation of the Treaty, created a military air force which is now nearly two-thirds as strong as our present home air force.'[6] When Hitler formally announced the creation of the Luftwaffe in February 1935, it came as no surprise. The air weapon appeared to make Britain's situation more dangerous, as Churchill stated in February 1934: 'This cursed, hellish intervention and development of war from the air has revolutionised our position. We are not the same kind of country we used to be when we were an island, only 20 years ago.' Britain could no longer 'live under the shield of the navy' and needed an air force 'at least as strong as that of any power that can get at us'.[7] An air staff report of July 1938 went so far as to suggest that 'from the point of view of the security of the British Empire the invention of the aeroplane was a misfortune. ... continental air powers have been given a means of overcoming the advantages we enjoyed in the past through our possession of superior sea power.'[8]

The British public had a fear of air power which was largely fostered by air force officers, anxious to establish their own arms in times of national economy. The Italian Giulio Douhet led the way in 1921 with his theory that a force of bombers was virtually unstoppable and that it could bypass the traditional armed forces, bombing cities and destroying the people's will to resist. The only answer was a counter-force of bombers. Trenchard took this up on behalf of the RAF, though with more emphasis on military targets, claiming: 'It is not ... necessary for an air force, in order to defeat the enemy nation, to defeat its armed forces first. ... Air power can dispense with that intermediate step, can pass over the enemy's armies and navies, and penetrate the air defences and attack direct the centres of production, transportation and communication from which the enemy war effort is maintained.'[9] This differed from what Churchill had written in 1917, that the initial objective was the destruction of enemy air bases to gain supremacy.[10] The RAF based its research on a raid on Folkestone in 1917 which had caused panic among the population. This fear was augmented by Stanley Baldwin, who asserted in 1932: 'I think it is well for the man in the street to realise that there is no power on earth that can protect him from being bombed. Whatever people may tell him, the bomber will always get through. ... the only defence is in offence, which means that you have to kill more women and children more quickly than the enemy if you want to save yourselves.' The 1936 film *Things to Come*, based on an essay by H. G. Wells, described the collapse of civilisation in 'Everytown' following air raids; Wells even used the term 'The Second World War'. A report of December 1938 suggested that 6,000 tons of bombs might be dropped in the first week of a war, followed by 7,000 tons each week thereafter. This would lead to the destruction of 465,000 homes and damage to a further 5 million, out of a total of 14 million in the country.[11]

Churchill did not totally accept these views, which he saw as brutal as well as defeatist, and he followed his ideas of 1917. He tended to see the first strike by either side as aimed at strategic points, and in April 1938 he wrote in the *News of the World*: '... if both air forces are fairly equal, the one that concentrates on attacking military objectives, and breaking up the communications of the enemy armies, and beating the other air force both in in the air and in its nests, will soon have a great advantage over the side which just goes bombing and murdering the mass of the civil population in the hope of terrorising them into making peace'.[12] And if the worst came to the worst, as he wrote to a German correspondent in August 1938, 'It would be a great mistake to imagine that the slaughter of the civil population following upon air raids would prevent the British Empire from developing its full war power. ... the worse the air-slaughter at the beginning, the more inexpiable would be the war. Evidently, all the great nations engaged in the struggle, once started, would fight on for victory or death.'[13]

★

Meanwhile the Nazi regime became ever more threatening. In March 1933 the Reichstag gave total power to the Führer and soon there was a boycott of Jewish businesses. In June 1934 the leaders of one wing of the Nazi Party were summarily massacred, showing the ruthlessness and lawlessness of the regime. In 1935 the disarmament clauses of the Versailles Treaty were repudiated. The British government began its policy of 'appeasement', recognising that Germany had been hard done by in the treaty and some rectification was justified. In July the Anglo-German naval agreement allowed them to build up to 35 per cent of British strength, and to have U-boats. While German youth under Nazi domination relished the prospect of war and glory, the British public was largely pacifist. In the meantime Japan had invaded Manchuria in 1931, and Mussolini's Italy defied the League of Nations by invading Ethiopia in 1935.

British leaders were soon convinced of the need to build up the air force, largely for preventing war. 'Air parity' was defined as having a home air force equal to any 'within striking distance of these shores'. It was the equivalent of the naval one power standard, but it was far more difficult to measure. It was impossible to conceal a Dreadnought battleship, but aircraft were built under cover in numerous factories and dispersed round dozens of aerodromes. Moreover the strength at the start of a war was only one factor. Aircraft could be produced far more quickly than battleships and it was impossible to predict the numbers entering service after the factories entered full production. Sir Herbert Samuel saw this as a weak spot in Churchill's campaign and claimed that he wanted expansion 'utterly regardless of any question of what parity really means in terms of airplanes and other equipment, utterly regardless of any needs of the situation'.[14]

Churchill used contacts inside the administration to supply him with information, deploying it sparingly to avoid giving them away. Desmond Morton was head of the Committee of Imperial Defence's industrial intelligence centre. The two had first met when Churchill was Minister of Munitions and Morton was an aide-de-camp to Douglas Haig. Morton lived a mile from Chartwell and was a frequent visitor, helping Churchill with his literary work as well as providing him with data. In August 1934 Lord Rothermere of the *Daily Mail* produced wildly exaggerated figures which suggested Germany might have 20,000 aeroplanes by the end of 1935. Morton poured cold water on this, reporting someone who replied 'that even if model aeroplanes in the toy shops were added in, the figure of 20,000 would not be attained' and warned against 'gross or even ludicrous exaggeration'.[15]

Another informant was Ralph Wigram, a counsellor in the Foreign Office who was horrified by the Nazi menace. With the support of some of his superiors he leaked information to the press and Churchill. When he died at the end of 1936 Churchill described him as 'A bright steady flame burning in a broken lamp, which guided us towards safety and honour.'[16] For more technical advice Churchill relied on Squadron Leader (later Wing Commander) Charles Anderson, who first rang Chartwell from the Air Ministry in May 1936.[17] Maurice Hankey of the Cabinet Office disapproved: 'It shocks me not a little that high officers in disciplined forces should be in direct communication with a leading statesman who, though notoriously patriotic beyond criticism, is nevertheless in popular estimation regarded as a critic of the departments under whom these officers serve.'[18]

★

In July 1935 Churchill joined the Air Defence Research sub-committee of the Committee of Imperial Defence. It was intended to 'undertake the direction and control of research into, and experiments in connection with, new methods or the improvement of existing methods of defence against hostile aircraft'.[19] It was supplemented by a scientific committee under Henry Tizard, which at Churchill's insistence included his friend Professor Frederick Lindemann. This gave him access to a great variety of very interesting papers, but it tended to hamper him as many of them were highly secret and could not be raised in parliament. Hankey, the cabinet secretary, told the members of the committee that 'the notes of the air staff contain some very secret matter. While the notes do not name actual sources of supply of secret information, they necessarily disclose the fact that a great deal of the information on which the air staff paper is based comes from secret service sources.'[20]

Churchill prepared for his first meeting on 25 July 1935 with a paper written with the help of Lindemann, which he presented with 'much diffidence' – not a common word in the Churchill vocabulary. He expected a war against Germany with France and Belgium as allies. The early stages would be dominated by mobilisation, which the air forces would try to disrupt by bombing communications, railways and bridges. The enemy of course would do the same and 'thus any German aircraft used to commit acts of terror upon the British and French civil populations will be grudged and sparingly diverted'. However they might attempt to 'burn down London' and he could not rule out 'the ugly possibility that those in authority in Germany may believe that it would be possible to beat a nation to its knees in a very few months, or even weeks, by violent aerial mass-attack. The concept of psychological shock tactics has a great attraction for the German mind ... this might well lead it to commence hostilities with the air arm alone.' To prevent this he suggested unarmed but very fast aircraft with a top speed of at least of 350 mph. They would find the enemy over the North Sea and follow them to guide the main force of defending fighters. Known as lambs ('and everywhere that Mary went, the lamb was sure to go'), their main problem was to fix their own positions. He expected the enemy to attack in large formations, as only one skilled navigator was needed for each. Moreover 'By no means all pilots have sufficient firmness of purpose to fly across hostile territory .... If they fly in formation they will be observed should they fall out.'

As to destroying the enemy, he believed that hitting an aircraft was 'like shooting a flying duck with a pea rifle'. He favoured Lindemann's 'aerial mine-curtain': 'These curtains invisible to the naked eye descend slowly in echelons both in height and depth. Any hostile aircraft coming in contact with the wire drags the explosive charge upon itself like a whiplash, producing an explosion which would break a spar or flying wire or injure the fuselage. … With aeroplanes of roughly a 100-feet span, one would need approximately 10,000 such mines to bring down half the aeroplanes passing through a region ten miles broad and twelve hundred feet deep. Ten thousand of these half-pound mines would weigh little more than two tons, a weight well within the compass of a single aeroplane.'[21] The meeting decided that his ideas 'should be explored'.

Meanwhile the committee looked at other factors in defending the country. It considered the meteorological conditions for raids, looked at fire precautions, and experimented with the range of searchlights and the use of old ships as anti-aircraft batteries. Apart from sighting, the only method of detecting approaching aircraft was by sound, and large concrete concave 'mirrors' were placed at strategic points on the coast-line to reflect the noise; however a paper presented to the committee in May 1935 gave some worrying figures:

> At present, the necessary warning period is <u>in favourable circumstances</u> composed of three minutes for the collection and transmission of intelligence, appreciation and issue of orders; two minutes for aircraft previously 'standing by' to leave the ground; ten minutes to climb to, say, 20,000 [feet], with a further three minutes to allow the fighters successfully to engage the bombers before the objective is reached, making a total of 18 minutes. The ground speed of the modern bomber may be 300 mph, so the distance of first detection should be at least 100 miles from the area to be protected ….

The maximum range of sound detection was 20 miles in good conditions. 'The development of a means of detecting enemy aircraft at a range of 100 miles, of assessing their strength and of continuously plotting their position and height, irrespective of visibility conditions, is therefore of an immediate and vital importance that cannot be over-emphasised.'[22]

In the general election of 3 November 1935 the Conservatives won 385 seats, and with their supporters they had a total of 428 compared with 184 for the disparate opposition. Stanley Baldwin became prime minister again and Churchill was bitterly disappointed not to be offered a place in the new government – paradoxically he felt that the government's large majority made it less necessary to neutralise him.

★

Air power was on the eve of a technological revolution. Despite an image of modernity, air forces were rarely in the vanguard of change; they had limited budgets and favoured the manoeuvrability of the biplane. Meanwhile airlines in the United States and Germany were developing monoplane wings with internal strength so they did not have to rely on bracing one wing against another. They used all-metal construction with the skin as part of the structure, which allowed higher speed with more powerful engines. They had retractable undercarriages, and were fitted with flaps to be lowered on take-off and landing, and variable pitch propellers. In Britain the main agent for change came with the seaplanes developed by R. J. Mitchell to win the Schneider Trophy races, but the first modern British monoplane fighter, the Bristol 133, was unsuccessful and in 1934 the Air Ministry contracted for the Gloster Gladiator, whose only concession to the new age was its enclosed cockpit. After that change was rapid and several classic fighter designs emerged in 1934–36, including the Hawker Hurricane (still fabric covered on its rear surfaces), the Supermarine Spitfire descended from the Schneider Trophy seaplanes, and in Germany, the Messerschmitt 109. In five or six years speeds had risen from 174 mph of the Bristol Bulldog to 355 mph of the early Spitfire, and the British aircraft carried eight machine guns instead of two. Aircraft became rapidly obsolete unless they were capable of further development, and a rearmament programme begun too early was likely to saddle the air force with types that were positively dangerous in combat.

Bomber development was not far behind, and sometimes ahead of the fighters. In July 1935 it was reported that the most likely German bomber was the Junkers 52, a development of an airliner with a speed of only 167 mph. They were reported to be developing the twin-engined Heinkel which had a speed of 218 mph, with at least nine squadrons of dive bombers in service.[23] That year Churchill complained: 'One of our bombing squadrons is equipped with the Virginia, a machine of the 1923 pattern. Other squadrons are being re-equipped with the Heyford and Hendon type of design, which itself is seven years old.'[24] It was little better in November 1937 as the first generation of monoplanes came into service. They were 'forced to trust our immediate future to types such as the Blenheim, Battle, Wellesley, Harrow and Whitley whose suitability for the work required of them is at least doubtful', but due to lack of flexibility there was no choice but to put them into production.[25] For the moment, according to Churchill, 'Of the 123 squadrons of the metropolitan air force now formed more than half are still armed with obsolete types. In fact out of 1,500–1,700 machines at least 850 consist of Hinds, Harts, Heyfords, Gauntlets etc., the design of which are in most cases more than ten years old.'[26] Even the Wellington, by far the best of the bombers in prospect, was not without its problems and Anderson wrote in November 1938: '… there will be many difficulties with the new type of aircraft, as regards inability to bomb, bomb-racks, wireless etc.; again, it is regarded by the Air staff only as a stop-gap. The ideal bomber is yet to be designed, at present it is on the drawing board …'.[27]

The Air Defence Research Sub-Committee considered a plan to drop coal dust near the coast to obscure it by night, and this was taken seriously enough to test it.[28] Churchill had always valued the use of smoke screens in land warfare but it was reported that 'to put the smoke screen only on the area itself would do no more than define it', so an area at least nine times as great had to be covered. Another plan was to use a line of drifters across the North Sea to give warning of an approach, which was reminiscent of the patrol lines of cruisers and destroyers which Churchill had disposed of effectively in 1912. Pilotless aircraft were considered, with plans to explode them in the vicinity of the attackers. It was suggested that the newly invented television cameras might be fitted to aircraft so that details of an attacking force could be sent back to base. Searchlights were fitted to aircraft for night work, but the results were disappointing.

In June 1936, after Lindemann suggested that work on his aerial mines was going on in 'a peace time atmosphere', Churchill complained that after nearly a year nothing had been done. This greatly annoyed Tizard of the scientific committee: 'I take the strongest exception to a member of my committee, who has not succeeded in convincing his colleagues on scientific and technical questions, endeavouring to force his views through a member of [the Air Defence Research Committee] however distinguished.' In fact there had been experiments and several long discussions, but the scientific committee had decided 'as a whole (Professor Lindemann dissenting), further experiments on the nature and amount of explosive (though in progress) are not regarded as being of the highest priority'.[29] Lindemann was driven out in November 1936, largely due to conflict with Tizard. Churchill wrote: 'you are in my judgement losing one of the finest brains in the country, and a man whose chief thought for many years has been fixed on these problems'.[30] Churchill survived in 1938 only because Hankey wanted to avoid an open clash with him.[31]

One of Churchill's pet projects was the use of 'unrotated projectiles' or UPs – rockets which would be fired into the path of aircraft so that they would be entangled in their parachutes. Lindemann wanted to combine this with his aerial minefields. In June 1939 Churchill suggested another way of deploying the mines:

> The large numbers of obsolescent aircraft which will be available should enable one or two groups of fifty each to be stationed on the east Coast at the most likely interception points. They will operate only over the sea, and perhaps only on the return journey of the raiders. The raiders will go straight home along a line drawn from the point where they have been throwing their bombs to their departure bases, and give a fairly accurate interception ... I see this process as a most important means of talking toll.[32]

He wrote to the air minister that the invention 'may turn out to be as good as the tank or the anti-submarine methods' though he deleted the point that 'It has certainly had the same obstruction from the authorities.'[33]

Lindemann investigated the detection of aircraft by infra-red methods, but in July 1937 the scientific committee reported that 'it seems very improbable that a practicable solution of detecting one aircraft from another will be found' though the work was to continue.[34] By February 1936 the committee was already receiving reports of 'the early promise of the radio method for locating aircraft approaching the coast'. A chain of stations was being erected from Orford Ness in East Anglia to Dover, to protect the most vulnerable stretch. It was recommended that Robert Watson-Watt, currently employed part-time on the project, should be put in full-time charge of research.[35] From then on the committee received regular reports of progress. In July 1937

> Single aircraft or close formations approaching the Bawdsey station at heights above 10,000 feet can be located in plan at distances up to 80 miles, and on occasions up to 100 miles. At lower heights the range is reduced until, at 1,000 feet, it is in the order of 20 miles. Height can be estimated to within about 2,000 feet, and discrimination between single aircraft and a formation is possible. When located, aircraft can be followed to within about ten miles of the station.[36]

Churchill was still sceptical in June 1938, writing about the work of the ADR committee: 'it is a delusion to think that for the next two or three years there will be any substantial contribution to defence from this source'.[37] By April 1939 20 stations were in operation between Portsmouth and Scapa Flow, capable of detecting aircraft from 50 to 120 miles at 10,000 feet.[38] Churchill visited the RDF (as radar was then known) research station at Bawdsey in June 1939 and was impressed with 'the wonderful development'. He worried about their vulnerability and wanted to set up dummy stations, but settled for the use of smoke clouds to obscure them. He was still interested in his 'lambs' and felt that RDF would give them 'smelling-power' to meet the raiders out at sea. And he continued to press for his favourite idea, the mine curtain. He believed that the conventional attack of bombers from the rear was obsolete, for they might drop mines behind them. He suggested that 'hostile aircraft can only be engaged with certainty on parallel or near parallel courses'.[39] The Air Ministry had already flown the prototype of the Boulton Paul Defiant which was intended to deploy a four-gun turret to attack bombers from the side.

★

Churchill continued to press on the growing size of the Luftwaffe and British attempts to keep up and was critical of much of the information he received through the committee, though Wigram pointed out in

December 1935: '... it is idle to get into the discussion of these details with the Air Ministry. Each side can throw dust in the other's eyes until the day of reckoning comes. ... The discussion of first line strengths is therefore not only endless, but also meaningless. The real test, and the only real test, is the capacity to manufacture machines and to train pilots in an emergency.'[40]

In November 1935 Churchill questioned the official belief that the Germans now had 594 aircraft, a figure only obtained by 'some conventional classification of first line strength in vogue at the Air Ministry'. The authorities replied that it was impossible to give chapter and verse for their secret sources, but the figure included 'only the number of military aircraft maintained in commission in combatant units for the operation of which pilots are available without measures of mobilisation'. In June 1936 he got hold of figures prepared for a French senatorial commission, which the air staff claimed used different methods of counting the aircraft. A standard German squadron had nine aircraft with two or three more in immediate reserve; the French had counted these in the total, the British did not, and if that was taken into account the differences were small. Churchill replied that aircraft and pilots seemed to disappear from the figures: '... 1,200 machines and 1,114 pilots are unaccounted for. This would be amply sufficient to duplicate every one of the 88 squadrons now believed to have been identified. When we remember the fondness evinced by Germany in history for this particular form of surprise, and note the large number of machines and pilots which seem to have vanished into thin air and the hundred odd aerodromes which have been constructed, this possibility cannot be excluded.' The Air Ministry replied that it shared Churchill's apprehensions, but 'the execution of such a plan would not be in keeping with Germany's well-known love of method and organisation and would be contrary to the first and main principle of air force organisation'. By December 1936 the two sides were almost agreed that the Germans now had 4,040 military aircraft and 3,225 trained pilots, except that Churchill had made no allowance for items such as monthly wastage.[41]

The government replied to the growth of the Luftwaffe with a series of expansion plans of its own. Scheme A rather vaguely projected a total

THE STUDY OF AIR POWER • 363

of 960 first-line aircraft by March 1939, with no provision for reserves. Scheme C of 1935 matched German growth more closely, with plans for 1,512 aircraft by March 1937. This was soon overtaken by Plan F for 1,736 aircraft by 1939. These did nothing to deter Hitler, and Schemes H and J never came into operation before they were superseded by Scheme K for 2,305 aircraft by 1941, and Scheme L which accelerated the process with 2,373 by 1940. All these put emphasis on the bomber, which outnumbered the fighter by about two to one. Only Scheme M of 1938 called for 50 squadrons of 800 fighters, reflecting a growing recognition of their use. Fighter Command was established in 1936 to train and control them, 'shadow' factories were set up to produce them, and much greater numbers of Halton apprentices were taken on to service them – the number jumped from 638 in 1934 to 1,466 in 1935, and exceeded 2,000 by 1937. More airfields were needed, and it was now recognised that they should have hard surfaces rather than grass.[42]

Government figures on the expansion of the Luftwaffe were reasonably accurate, but the whole policy was based on a misconception. Certainly the founders of the force, including the flamboyant World War I fighter ace Hermann Goering, had followed the ambitious theories of airpower and hoped eventually for a strategic bomber force, but there were far more urgent needs. In the early stages it was feared that France and Poland might react as Germany rejected parts of the Treaty of Versailles, and defences were needed against that. It was only in 1937–38 that Germany began to regard Britain as a real threat. In the meantime experience in the Spanish Civil War showed the value of aircraft, especially dive bombers, in hitting targets accurately in support of the army. This led to a concentration on the type, not only on the single-engine and poorly performing Ju 87 'Stuka', but in the adaptation of twin-engine aircraft such as the much more effective Ju 88, leading to delays in production. The Luftwaffe did not neglect defence with its excellent fighter the Messerschmitt Bf 109, but it had no plans for an air attack on Britain, and was not equipped for it.[43]

When a German mission headed by General Erhard Milch visited RAF stations in October 1937, there was confusion about whether to deter them by showing the best equipment, or to keep it secret. On the one hand, Churchill wrote: 'A desperate effort is now being made to present a sham. A power-drive turret is to be shown, as if it was the kind of thing we are doing in a regular way. Ought it to be shown at all?' On the other hand, the visit 'threw into clear relief the exact state of the Royal Air Force as regards re-equipment, and the degree of preparedness for war ...'.[44]

In July 1936 Churchill gave his views on RAF personnel, informed by Anderson. The Cranwell entry, which would provide all-round officers and the commanders of the future, had not been expanded. The terms for the short service entry were not very attractive, the educational and physical standards of the entrants were low, and supplies from public schools had practically dried up: '... far more is needed than the art of flying. A background is needed either of inspiration or prolonged training or habit of command and obedience – preferably both.' Only 50 university entrants were commissioned each year, though there was great demand for places. Airmen pilots were being recruited to be given the rank of sergeant after training, but they were tending to displace the Halton apprentices who had behind them 'a considerable period of discipline, training and association with flying'. The new part-time Royal Air Force Volunteer Reserve only offered the rank of sergeant – 'this is not a time for class prejudice. I think we should choose the best, irrespective if they belong to the officer class or not.'[45]

On the old question of the all-pilot air force, in 1937 the RAF reintroduced the flying grade of observer. With the basic rank of corporal and with ground in addition to flying duties, most had neither the education nor the authority to act as main adviser to the pilot. At the end of the year it was decided to recruit observers direct from civilian life.[46] Churchill commented: '... pilots are little use without observers who navigate the aeroplanes and aim the bombs. To use pilots as observers is almost to halve your pilot strength. Is it true that the supply of observers is wholly insufficient in numbers and inadequate in quality? There is urgent need to institute a corps of observers drawn from persons of a high level of intelligence and education and given a permanent career.'[47] This was putting a finger on one of the great weaknesses of the RAF.

In September 1937 he wrote to Swinton, the Air Minister:

I visited the Biggin Hill aerodrome as you authorised, and was much interested in the demonstration which they gave of interception methods. I had not realised the vital important change which has been made effecting contact with the enemy from the ground, instead of leaving the squadron leader in the air to find them for himself. The officers assured me that provided 'Cuckoo' was accurate, the percentage of interception was extraordinarily high. This has greatly affected my thought on the subject, and I think of writing a short paper for our Committee on the tactical aspects, as far as they affect design.[48]

615 (County of Surrey) Squadron of the Royal Auxiliary Air Force was formed in June 1937 at Kenley south of London. Early in 1939, when it was equipped with biplane Gloster Gladiators and Gauntlets, Churchill was asked to become its honorary air commodore and soon accepted. Though he was colonel of several army regiments, including the 4th Hussars, he was never awarded any naval rank, and air commodore was the most senior rank he held. He was granted the right to wear wings by the King in 1942, perhaps on the precedent of his father George V, who had worn them but never actually flown – at least Churchill had tried. Churchill helped the squadron to buy town premises in Croydon and visited it in April 1939, being photographed making a rather ungainly exit from the cockpit of a Gauntlet, all of which confirmed his interest in the air.

CHAPTER 30

The Drift to War

Despite his concentration on air power, Churchill still had plenty of views on the army and navy, and did not hesitate to use his experience of past wars. As Italy prepared to invade Abyssinia in August 1935, a Mediterranean war seemed possible and Churchill offered advice to Sir Samuel Hoare, now First Lord of the Admiralty: '... be on your guard against the capital fault of letting diplomacy get ahead of naval preparedness. We took great pains about this in 1914.' 'Where are the fleets?', he asked, 'Are they in good order? Are they adequate? Are they capable of rapid and complete concentration? Have they been formally warned to take precautions? Remember you are putting extreme pressure on a dictator who may get into desperate straits.' He had a high view of the capability and strength of the Italian navy: '... you have not got half the strength of Italy in modern cruisers and destroyers, and still less in modern submarines'. There were rumours that the Royal Navy might evacuate the Mediterranean, which would leave Egypt and the Suez Canal exposed. Hoare replied tersely: 'You may rest assured that all the points you have mentioned have been and are being actively discussed.' But Churchill did not let the matter rest; he worried that the battleship *Barham* was not with the fleet and might have to cross the sea without an escort, and that the carrier *Glorious* was still at Malta which had practically no anti-aircraft defence. He did not want to withdraw to the Suez Canal or the Red Sea, but it was better than being 'Port Arthured' or besieged like the Russian Fleet in 1904. He hoped the main fleet, which he still referred to as the Grand Fleet, would be sent to the Mediterranean.[1] In September he had a discussion with retired Commander Maitland, who reassured him that the three commanders at home and in the Mediterranean – Chatfield, Roger Backhouse and William Fisher – were all ideally suited for their jobs and greatly liked in the navy. It was pointed out that the Italians had no aircraft carriers or big ships – the two battlecruisers they had laid down would not be ready for nearly two years.[2]

In 1935 it all came to nothing as the League of Nations failed to act. In March 1939, as a more general war was feared, Churchill was far more confident about the sea: 'Assuming Italy is hostile, which we may perhaps hope will not be the case, England's first battlefield is the Mediterranean. All plans for sealing up the ends must be discarded in favour of decisive victory there. Our forces alone should be sufficient to drive the Italian ships from the sea ... certainly within two months, possibly sooner.'[3]

★

The old issue of the control of the Fleet Air Arm surfaced again in the middle of the decade, and Keyes strongly supported transfer to the navy. In June 1936 he wrote to retired admiral Herbert Richmond: '... now I have enlisted Churchill in the fight – and hope you will join in with your gifted pen. We *won't* be beat.'[4] He had 'enlisted Churchill and Guest's help – not too easy, as they both took a hand in defeating us in 1922–3'.[5] In November Churchill wrote to J. A. Chamier, a retired air commodore: 'I wish at this stage to have the Fleet Air Arm under the control of the navy because I am anxious to see the aggregate air power of Britain increased as fast as possible, and I believe that the naval personnel, commissioned and other ranks, will be an important additional rivulet of supply. In addition I feel that the Air Ministry is overweighted at the present time and the gigantic expansion which is being attempted is failing alarmingly at many points.'[6]

In April 1937 Keyes believed that Churchill 'really is out to help us – but I think he feels he owes something to the RAF and wants to give them a little to "save face" ...'.[7] That month, partly reversing his position as air minister, Churchill wrote: 'It is impossible to resist an admiral's claim that he must have complete control of and confidence in the aircraft of the battle fleet, whether used for reconnaissance, gun-fire or air attack on a hostile fleet.' He was ambivalent about shore-based aircraft operating over the seas, repeating his assertion that 'This division does not depend upon the type of undercarriage of the aircraft, nor necessarily the base from which it is flown. It depends upon the function. Is it predominantly a naval function or not?' But otherwise

> The Admiralty should have plenary control and provide the entire personnel of the Fleet Air Arm. Officers, cadets, petty officers, artificers etc. of this force would be selected from the Royal Navy by the Admiralty. They would then acquire the art of flying and the management of aircraft in the RAF training schools, but after acquiring the necessary degree of proficiency as air chauffeurs and mechanics they would pass to shore establishments under the Admiralty, for their training in the Fleet Air Arm.[8]

Keyes later wrote to Chatfield, the First Sea Lord: 'Churchill's intervention in May 1936 was of great value.'[9]

But there was still an outstanding issue, and in May 1937 Chatfield wrote to Keyes, referring to the Minister for Co-ordination of Defence: 'the last meeting was on shore based aircraft which is really the only uncertain problem in Inskip's mind (I think)'.[10] In fact it was decided that shore-based maritime aircraft should remain as part of the RAF, and deployed by Coastal Command. Nevertheless Sir Cyril Newall, the Chief of Air Staff, was shocked by the news of the transfer, which he received on the way back from a fishing holiday in Norway. He wrote to Trenchard that he had been asked to address the annual Trafalgar Day dinner of the Navy League and respond to Churchill as the main speaker. He wondered whether to say anything about the issue but decided not to in view of the presence of reporters.[11]

★

When Civil War broke out in Spain in July 1936 Churchill was ambivalent – he did not want to see Italian and German strength grow in the country, but equally he feared the Soviet Union which supported the other side, and according to Harold Nicolson he was influenced by 'personal friendship with Spanish Grandees'.[12] In July 1937 he was worried about heavy guns being moved near Gibraltar. Not only could they bombard the port and anchorage, but combined with more mounted across the Straits in Spanish Morocco, they might 'constitute a menace to the free navigation of the Straits, that is to say the maximum discharges from the two sides would overlap each other, and vessels passing through the Straits might have to run the gauntlet of their fire'.[13] As to lessons from the air war, Desmond Morton thought they were very few. Nothing in that war, or Japan's attack on China, 'can in any way be taken as a precedent for what might happen in Europe between two countries who did not expect to own the property they were destroying, so soon as the war ended. Not one single air attack in Spain by either side can be shewn to have been an attempt to destroy morale. In fact both sides went out of their way to try and avoid killing civilians.'[14] But there was no mention of the tactical use of air power, from which the Germans learned a great deal.

★

In March 1938 the Nazis went beyond the boundaries of Germany and marched into Austria, forging an Anschluss or union with questionable claims of popular support. To Churchill it was a 'dastardly outrage'. He was apparently re-animated, and Harold Nicolson described him as 'this old battlehorse' with 'his tremendous radiating personality and his immense courage'. Soon he followed Marlborough's terminology in proposing a 'grand alliance' against aggression, but nothing was done.[15] Hitler's claim on the German-speaking Sudetenland of Czechoslovakia went even further – the border region contained all the defences of the new state, set up in 1919, and it had never been part of Germany. Churchill was pleased when the fleet was mobilised on the threat of war, and looked back to 1914 yet again. He wrote for the press that the current First Lord 'is to be congratulated upon having at last obtained authority to issue the necessary mobilisation orders to the fleet'. It was also the case that 'the main fighting strength of the fleet has been disposed of in the best possible manner', following 'the Admiralty tradition of being well in advance of the final moves of diplomacy'.[16] But this turned to rage and shame when Neville Chamberlain, Prime Minister since the retirement of Baldwin in 1937, made several visits to Munich to confer with Hitler and climb down humiliatingly, claiming 'It is peace for our time.' Much of the British press and public were ecstatic, but Churchill was depressed and enraged. 'Silent, mournful, abandoned, broken, Czechoslovakia recedes into the darkness,' he told the House. His stand was unpopular with the Conservatives and soon brought him into conflict with his constituency party in suburban Essex: '... we feel increasingly uneasy at Mr Churchill's growing hostility to the govern-ment, and to the prime minister in particular, at a time when unity is of vital importance'.[17]

Churchill attributed the debacle to fear of air power, writing in June 1939: 'The main reason why Herr Hitler has been able to overawe France and England while he has been breaking his treaties and overrunning his weaker neighbours is the fears, or perhaps it would be truer to say the uncertainties, about the power of the air arm. The French know where they are about the army. The British are very clear upon the navy. But the air belongs to what Bismarck called "the imponderabilia".' By now he was becoming far more confident himself. The French regarded air attack as 'a somewhat less efficient and more widely ranging form of artillery' while the Royal Air Force was at last becoming stronger and should be ready to meet an attack by 1940.[18]

The great historic argument over the Munich settlement is whether a more determined stand would have worked. It could perhaps have deterred Hitler without a war. If war did come, what were the relative strengths? British air defences were still weak, but on the other hand the German bomber force was not nearly as formidable as it was believed to be. The French, Czechs and British had a great superiority in numbers, including tanks, for the Germans had not yet built up that arm and had not gone far with the development of Blitzkrieg which would be their main advantage. But to save Czechoslovakia, Britain and especially France would have had to take the offensive on the Western Front, which neither was psychologically prepared to do.

Though Japan's invasion of China had been conducted with great brutality since 1931, in March 1939 Churchill was not seriously worried about a threat from Japan, even in combination with Germany and Italy. Singapore was safe for 'a fortress of this character with cannon which can hold any fleet at arm's length only requires an adequate garrison and supplies of food and ammunition, preferably for a year'. He was certain that the Japanese would not risk an attack 2,000 miles from their homeland, for they were 'an extremely sensible people'.[19] Chatfield agreed that 'we must take some risk in the Far East while we are settling the Mediterranean, but I very much doubt whether the Mediterranean problem will be settled in two or three months'.[20]

★

As the Washington Treaty and its successor the London Treaty of 1930 expired in 1936, the British began to plan for a new generation of capital ships. They hoped to agree a limit of 35,000 tons with Italy and Japan, and for a maximum of 14-inch guns. They had to start the design for new ships before the next treaty was agreed, and in the event it never was, so they were left with ships with an unusual calibre of main armament, smaller even than the 15-inch which Churchill had approved 20 years before – though with modern design they could make up much of the difference. Churchill was not happy with this in May 1937: ' … there was a case that you could not afford the delays entailed in redesigning the first two battleships, and that the action of the other countries was uncertain. But if quite soon we know that the United States, Japan, Germany and Italy, or most of them, are laying down vessels with 16-inch guns, I am sure ours will be considered undergunned and will be consequently written down as factors of naval strength by all other countries.'[21] The following month he was still hopeful of changing the design to use 16-inch guns in triple turrets, as indeed the United States would do, and wanted to have 'the designs for the larger guns and turrets completed without delay'.[22] But it was too late; the 14-inch design was far advanced. The Admiralty planned to increase the fire power by using twelve of the new guns in quadruple turrets, but that caused stability problems and one was replaced with a twin turret thus reducing the armament to ten guns. Other problems would emerge with the design, which Churchill would become aware of through personal experience. However he was aware that the old ideas of battleship tactics no longer applied, writing in January 1938: 'At the present time, no other power in Europe, except the British, can attempt to form a line of battle, nor indeed all the powers in Europe together.'[23]

On cruisers, Churchill believed that the three-funnel 8-inch gunships he had reluctantly financed in the 1920s were already becoming obsolete and were 'certainly inferior in strength and stiffness to the great batch of later American 8-inch vessels'. More worryingly, it was suggested that the Germans were building large cruisers which would use all the best features, and might emulate the feats of the *Emden* in the last war. The current trend in the Royal Navy was to build 6-inch cruisers which Churchill presumed would be for 'attendance on the battle fleet' – but 'it will be a long time before any power, except the United States and Japan, can draw out a line of battle …'. With the increased use of aircraft for fleet reconnaissance, he felt that small or weakly armed cruisers were a waste of money – 'What is all-important is to be able to kill when found.'[24] However he accepted the need for the new *Dido* class of light cruisers with only 5.25-inch guns; they were 'justified on the two main grounds, first of releasing larger cruisers for the trade routes, and second in its anti-aircraft value'.[25]

Asdic was a system which used a ping and echo to detect a submarine underwater. It had been developed towards the end of the Great War and gave the navy confidence that the submarine was no longer a major threat – the anti-submarine branch was happy to have its work recognised, while the gunnery branch, still all-powerful, did not want money diverted from its own activities. Churchill went along with this, and was further convinced by a visit to the anti-submarine research station at Portland in June 1938. He wrote to Chatfield: 'What surprised me was the clarity and force of the indications. I had imagined something almost imperceptible, certainly vague and doubtful. I never imagined I should hear one of these creatures asking to be destroyed, both orally and literally.'[26] And in March 1939 he concluded: 'The submarine has been mastered, thanks very largely to Lord Chatfield's long efforts at the Admiralty. It should be quite controllable in the outer seas, and certainly in the Mediterranean. There will be losses, but nothing to affect the scale of events.' At the same time he was confident that warships could be protected against air attack: 'In my opinion, given with great humility (because these things are very difficult to judge) an air attack upon British warships, armed and protected as they now are, will not prevent the full exercise of their superior sea power.'[27]

★

Though the navy had its budget increased from £50 million in 1933 to £81 million in 1937, and the RAF went from £19.6 million to £56.5 million in the same period, the army was left behind in the rearmament programme as it was assumed that the war could be fought by sea and in the air. It was only in 1936 that its budget began to increase substantially, from £39.7 million to £44.6 million, then £54.8, £77.9 and finally £121.4 million in 1939, as plans for an expeditionary force in Europe were drawn up after the Munich crisis. There was a certain amount of modernisation as the Lewis machine gun was replaced by the lighter and more mobile Bren which would become the weapon of each infantry section. In June 1938 Churchill complained: 'Of one battalion it is said there are only five Bren guns out of forty, and one anti-tank rifle out of twenty-four. The rest are represented, or were a month ago by coloured rags on sticks.'[28] At the end of 1938 Churchill enquired how quickly the infantry were being equipped with anti-tank rifles and the Bren, and was told that 50 Brens were to be issued per battalion, and 20 anti-tank rifles.[29]

According to Churchill the arguments about naval control of the Fleet Air Arm did not apply to army co-operation aircraft, which took off from aerodromes like others, and which were involved 'in an affair of co-operation only', while naval aircraft were 'an integral part of modern naval operations'.[30] In fact the air force view was that 'neither in attack nor in defence should bomber aircraft be used on the battlefield itself, save in exceptional circumstances'.[31]

The policy of conversion to armour was eventually adopted, and when Churchill's old regiment finally went over in 1935 he told the sergeants' mess: 'Whatever be the weapons which are given to the 4th Hussars, the regiment will play the same tune on them and will carry the same old traditions, whether it be the sabre and wheel into line for the charge, whether it is as mounted infantry, as rifle-armed cavalry or, as you now are, a mechanised unit.'[32] In May 1937 Churchill was sent a paper by Sir Cyril Deverell, the current Chief of Imperial General Staff, outlining the procedure for converting the remaining regiments. The first step was the removal of all horses as they would distract from mechanised training. Secondly they would carry out a year's training on wheeled vehicles, followed by tracked vehicles, then tactical training on older light tanks, and finally the issue of the complete peace establishment of light tanks. It was hoped that this would be completed by the summer of 1938.[33] Churchill replied that he had long urged this step but complained: 'It is very disheartening for ... the 4th Hussars to be a whole year without horses or mechanised vehicles except for training.' He disclaimed knowledge of later tank design, but presumably he knew that they were now divided into slow-moving heavily armoured 'infantry' tanks and lighter 'cruisers'. He was concerned that there was no medium tank in production, able to cross trenches.[34] In later years practice was still affected by the conversion of the cavalry and General Brooke wrote: 'a large gap ... existed in the relations between the extremists of the Tank Corps and the cavalry. ... The cavalry naturally resented deeply losing their horses, giving up their mounted role and becoming dungaree mechanics.'[35]

★

Land anti-aircraft guns were left in the hands of the army, but in June 1937 Churchill received advice from a retired expert, Colonel Henry Hill, that 'there had been no perceptible improvement in AA shooting as judged from the effect on the target in the past seven years with the present service equipment. The rate of fire is slow, the accuracy is poor.'[36] A year later he described the situation as a 'horrid scandal'. There was 'a total absence of defence, apart from the RAF, for our cities and vulnerable points'. Old re-lined 3-inch guns were 'better than nothing' but no substitute for the newer 3.7-inch – but only a dozen or so were available. The design of the carriage for the 4.7 inch gun was still not completed and the balloon barrage was on a small scale. Since the RAF was only a third of the size of the Luftwaffe, the position looked bleak.[37]

But in any case, in June 1939 Lindemann advised that 'anti-aircraft guns are useless in defending large areas' – they were valuable only for the defence of warships and small targets.[38] The idea of parachute troops was not yet well known, but Churchill might have gone back to his prediction of 1917 that 'Considerable parties of soldiers could be conveyed by air to the neighbourhood of bridges or other important points, and, having overwhelmed the local guard, could *from the ground* effect a regular and permanent demolition.' He had heard of exercises landing men by aeroplane in Germany to attack munitions works, bridges and other targets. He wondered if 'a few score of determined men could create havoc and very likely return to their aeroplanes and take off again without serious loss'. The Air Minister reassured him that modern bombers and troop carriers required prepared runways for landing, and that there were very few suitable places beside key vulnerable points. However he did raise the possibility that 'the demolition party would, in such circumstances be landed by parachute rather than by troop-carrying aircraft'.[39]

Churchill was confident about the British ability to survive air attack and was not 'favourably impressed' by a scheme for shelters put forward by a Russian architect: 'It appears to be inspired by a wish to exaggerate the dangers of air attack and to emphasize the futility of basement protection in the interests of some particular scheme with which you are associated.'[40] In March 1939 he told the Commons: 'Personally, I believe that the weapon of air terror cuts both ways, and I believe also, that it cannot in any case be decisive against the life of a brave and free people.'[41] And in June he wrote an article for the *News of the World* entitled 'Bombs Don't Scare us Now'.

Churchill continued to press for a ministry of defence. In March 1936 Baldwin appointed Sir Thomas Inskip as Minister for Co-ordination of Defence – not an actual defence minister with real power, but only to chair joint meetings in the absence of the prime minster and to recommend and cajole, while the three service ministries remained untouched. Moreover he was a lawyer with no service experience apart from some war service, which Baldwin perhaps regarded as an advantage as he was less likely to be accused of bias. In that sense he was the opposite of Churchill, who was largely free of bias because of his deep inside knowledge of all three services, and his commitment to each at different times. Churchill was not impressed, and Lindemann remarked: 'It is the most cynical thing that has been done since Caligula appointed his horse as consul.'[42]

Nevertheless Churchill sent Inskip a memorandum advocating a ministry of supply as a successor to the Ministry of Munitions. He complained that 'the existing office of the Minister for the Co-ordination of Defence comprises unrelated and wrongly grouped functions'. He recommended that 'The service departments prescribe in general technical terms their need in type, quality and quantity, and the supply organisation executes these in a manner best calculated to serve its customers.'[43] Government officials saw many difficulties, especially after he published an amended version in The Times in May 1938, mainly because he was dissatisfied with the progress of traditional departments, and in May 1938 he complained of the 'monstrous and cumbersome organisation' of army re-equipment, run by the Master General of the Ordnance, his old adversary from the early tank days. He wanted a ministry of supply instead to inject more urgency.[44] He appeared to be suggesting that the Admiralty would retain control of ship design and naval stores, and it seemed likely that the Air Ministry would demand the same rights over aircraft production. Colonel Ismay of the Committee of Imperial Defence was asked to draft a reply and did so reluctantly, as 'a staff officer has no option but to follow with absolute loyalty the directions of those who bear the ultimate responsibility'.[45] He could not see how such an operation could work in peacetime without the direct control of industry which had been applied in war. There was 'no intermediate stage' between 'full war control with compulsory powers' and 'the normal peace-time method of voluntary co-operation with industry'; in the circumstances it was 'difficult to see where Mr Churchill's proposal leads us'. It was proposed in the House of Lords that month, seconded by Trenchard, but voted down.

Any hope of lasting peace was shattered in March 1939 when the Germans, breaking the Munich agreement, marched into the remainder of Czechoslovakia. Churchill looked to the Baltic as a possible way of getting at Germany, reviving the ideas of Fisher in 1914. He was well aware that Britain now had the supremacy in surface ships over Germany that he and Fisher had craved in 1914–15, and he looked the same way as Fisher had done then: 'To Germany the command of the Baltic is vital. Scandinavian supplies, Swedish ore, and above all protection against Russian descents on the long, undefended northern coast-line of Germany ... make it imperative for Germany to dominate the Baltic.' Submarines and cruisers and perhaps a pocket battleship might be sent out as raiders, but the main task of the German navy would be to defend the sea. An air attack on the Kiel Canal would render 'that side door useless'. However, 'the one great naval offensive against Germany is the Baltic. If, for instance, we had today a superior fleet in the Baltic, one might almost say for certain that Germany would not declare war' – though that would not be possible until the Mediterranean was cleared.[46]

In August 1939 Churchill embarked on a three-day tour of the great French defences known as the Maginot Line, and one report suggests he was impressed with what he saw. He concluded: 'The French front cannot be surprised. It cannot be broken at any point except by an effort which would be enormously costly in life and would take so much time that the general situation would be transformed while it as in progress. ... the flanks of the front, however, rest upon two small neutral states.'[47] He was silent during the journey through the French cornfields until he remarked: 'Before the harvest is gathered in – we shall be at war.'[48] He was unlikely to agree with Neville Chamberlain's view, as expressed to his sister that July: 'That is what Winston and Co never seem to realise. You don't need offensive forces sufficient to win a smashing victory. What you want are defensive forces sufficiently strong to make it impossible for the other side to win except at such cost as to make it not worth while.'[49]

The USSR and Germany signed a non-aggression pact in August, and Britain guaranteed assistance to Poland. War loomed on 1 September when the Germans and Soviets invaded that country and Britain and France issued an ultimatum. Air raid sirens sounded in London soon after war started formally at 11 am on 3 September, and there were many who feared 'the ugly possibility that those in authority in Germany may believe that it would be possible to beat a nation to its knees in a very few months, or even weeks, by violent aerial mass-attack', as Churchill had believed possible. According to his bodyguard, Inspector Thompson, he went down to the basement under his flat in Morpeth Mansions with a bottle of brandy, then rushed up to the roof when the all clear sounded – it was a false alarm and no aircraft were seen. He attended a debate in the House of Commons, and then Thompson accompanied him to Downing Street to see Chamberlain. Expecting to be appointed to another sinecure office, he emerged saying 'It's the Admiralty. That's a lot better than I thought.'[50]

CHAPTER 31

Winston is Back

The famous signal 'Winston is back' was sent out to the fleet as Churchill took office – though no actual copy of it survives, and it was never made clear whether it was a celebration or a warning. Churchill arrived at the Admiralty at seven that evening and the poignancy of the occasion did not escape him: 'So it was that I came again to the room I had quitted in pain and sorrow almost exactly a quarter of a century before ... I had, as the reader may be aware, a considerable knowledge of the Admiralty and the Royal Navy.' He sat again in the First Lord's chair in the board room, and replied emotionally to the First Sea Lord's welcome, that 'there we would be many difficulties ahead but together we would overcome them'.[1]

The team around him was headed by Admiral Sir Dudley Pound, who had become First Sea Lord only because of the premature death of other candidates. According to Admiral John Godfrey, who know him well, he was 'clever and able but not accomplished'. 'A tremendous worker, he was unable to relax into any sort of humorous guise. He was soon out of his depth if you got away from service topics and, although he was a dedicated man, his dedication had a horizon which did not include worldliness, human relations, international politics, or the effect of his words (always kindly meant) and deeds upon others.'[2] In general he got on well with Churchill, who remarked: '... the First Sea Lord and I were one'.[3] Pound himself wrote: 'I have the greatest admiration for WSC, and his good qualities are such, and his desire to hit the enemy so overwhelming that I feel one must hesitate in turning down any of his proposals.'[4]

Though Churchill was nearly 65 his energy was as great as ever. His wife wrote: 'Winston works night and day – he is well thank God and gets tired only if he does not get his eight hours sleep – he does not need it at a stretch but if he does not get that mount in the 24 hours then he is weary.'[5] Geoffrey Shakespeare, the Financial and Parliamentary Secretary, wrote of him: 'If he finished dictation by 2 am, he usually wanted to visit the War Room to study the positions of the warships on the oceans of the world. It was very difficult to get him to bed.'[6]

Maps were important to Churchill – he perhaps learned their value from Hamley's *Operations of War* at Sandhurst and he had used them extensively in the last war. He had insisted on a high standard of plans and diagrams in both *The World Crisis* and *Marlborough*. On 4 September Commander Richard Pim of the Ulster Division of the RNVR was called to the Admiralty and Churchill gave him 48 hours to set up a map room in Admiralty House in a familiar site: 'The First Lord, who had utilised these rooms prior to and during the First World War, knew exactly what he wanted … it was not long before the library was transformed into the Upper War Room, the title by which it was to be known during the years of hostilities.' Pim went on: 'I called on the Hydrographer of the Navy and asked him to get all the maps and charts I required delivered and painted in contrasting colours by the next day …'. After the allotted period he was satisfied – 'efficient lighting installed and each ship shown by a symbol on a special pin pushed into the coloured maps and much more information besides'. Churchill called in on his way to bed, remarking 'Very good, very good … but the maps will all have to be replaced. When you know me better you will know that I only paint in pastel shades, and these strong colours under the lamps would give me and you a headache.'[7] The room was soon in regular use. Two naval watch-keeping officers were always present, along with a military officer. 'Our main duty was to plot accurately the position of every British and Allied warship in the world, and also the position of all known enemy surface ships and U-boats … Every convoy was plotted – its escort, speed and number of ships shown. In addition, the position of every British, allied and neutral merchant vessel at sea and in port was shown.' Pim reported: 'The positions were plotted from signals which came in day and night in a continuous stream and reached me after being decoded elsewhere. ... If any signal of importance arrived, a very few moments would elapse before he arrived in the War Room and was in complete possession of all the facts. I had always heard that he was an indefatigable worker and there is no other word to describe his activities.'[8] The upper floors of Admiralty House provided a very comfortable flat, the lower rooms were used for official dinner parties, and bedrooms were available for the First Sea Lord and Vice Chief of Naval Staff, with doors leading directly off the War Room.

★

For the second time in almost exactly a quarter of a century Churchill found himself in charge of the Royal Navy as a great war broke out, but there were essential differences. In the first place, it was not an immediate attack by sea that was feared, but one by air. Secondly, this navy was not of Churchill's creation, or at least only remotely so. This was especially true in the case of ships, and Churchill did not think much of the collection he was endowed with: 'All the constructive genius and commanding reputation of the Royal Navy has been besmirched and crippled by treaty restrictions for twenty years.'[9] As to the largest ships, he was concerned about the 14-inch guns of the *King George V* class under construction. He still wanted 16-inch gun battleships, but recognised it would not be possible to design and build them before the end of 1941, so they were postponed, and never appeared.[10] He found that there were four spare 15-inch gun turrets and ordered that they be used for a new battleship, which emerged only after the war as the *Vanguard*. But apart from that he had to make do with the *King George Vs*, or *KGVs*, as the only fast, modern battleships in prospect. Two of them were to be named *Jellicoe* and *Beatty* but Churchill objected that 'in spite of the distinction of these officers, it is better to look at the past, where all is mellow. ... it is undesirable to choose names of eminent officers so recently deceased that the controversies in which they played their part are still living issues in the fleet.'[11] He followed this with a minute to Pound (who had served under Jellicoe at Jutland) in which he described the admiral as 'of a timorous and pessimistic disposition' and listed his failures, including the inadequacies of shells, three missed opportunities at Jutland, and the reluctance to use convoys.[12] The ships were re-named *Anson* and *Howe*.

He asked about 'limiting factors' in the completion of the *King George V* class ships − 'I suppose as usual the gun-mountings.'[13] He was quite right, but in fact the problem was longer term than that, as he would find out later. He wanted to hurry them on as he feared Germany's new fast battleship might be ready first. 'The *Bismarck* is running her neck and neck, and the appearance of the *Bismarck* before *KGV* could affect the whole strategy of the navy. The enemy would possess a unit which could not be caught by any ship she could not kill.'[14] Early in 1940 he suggested: 'If the two-gun turret is a cause of serious delay, would it not be better, having regard to our other strength in capital ships, to seal it up and mount a dummy turret in its place?'[15] He also suggested she might be commissioned before her electric wiring was completed and sent to Plymouth as a bluff.[16]

No new monitors had been built since the war, and Churchill found that the surviving ones were in poor condition. He ordered two new ones, the *Roberts* and *Abercrombie* based on the *Erebus* class but with increased anti-aircraft protection, with a view to supporting the army in Flanders as in the last war; but that was irrelevant by the time they were completed in 1941–43.[17]

In carriers, the navy suffered from two disadvantages. First, the long and debilitating struggle for control of the Fleet Air Arm had inhibited development. But even before that particular rot set in, the navy suffered from being a pioneer, and all its carriers except one were early experiments, or conversions from other ships. The old *Argus* of 1918 was very small by modern standards but Churchill wanted aircraft to be specially designed 'as these can be made much quicker than a new aircraft carrier'.[18] The *Eagle* was the first with the characteristic island superstructure while the *Hermes* of 1919 was the first to be built as such from the keel up, but was very small at 11,000 tons. Larger and faster ships were found by converting Fisher's eccentric battlecruisers, the *Courageous, Glorious* and *Furious*, and they provided much experience in operating aircraft. The only new one was the *Ark Royal*, which was completed at the end of 1938 to carry 60 aircraft in two hangar decks; she would become one of the most famous ships in the navy, largely because of spurious German claims to have sunk her. Three ships of the *Illustrious* class were under construction. They followed the *Ark Royal* design but were fitted with armoured decks which reduced the hangar space and the aircraft complement to 33. The *Indomitable* was launched by Mrs Churchill in May 1940. Three more had been ordered to compromise designs to retain the armour but carry more aircraft.

Cruisers were of particular concern to Churchill. He still favoured the 8-inch ships over the new *Fiji* class with twelve 6-inch, and told Pound: 'The idea of two *Fijis* fighting an 8-inch cruiser will never come off! All experience shows that a cluster of weak ships will not fight a strong one.'[19] On the contrary he wanted a class of 14,000-ton cruisers with 9.2-inch guns to overpower the German 8-inch ships.[20] Otherwise, speed in construction was important and it was agreed at the end of September: 'The following cruisers have been ordered: Six *Dido* class, estimated to cost £11,300,000, and two *Fiji* class, estimated to cost £500,000. The First Lord expressed some reluctance to agree to so large a programme of cruisers, on the ground … that they would not be available for some considerable time …'. The *Fijis* were to be cancelled, or at least not built in the Royal Dockyards, but eventually they reappeared.[21]

Destroyers were to become the most important single class of surface ship. Though 187 were available in October 1939, Churchill wrote: 'that is the great problem for us – to find destroyers for the many needs'.[22] He was shocked in mid-September when Admiral Forbes took him out of Scapa in the *Nelson* without a destroyer escort and he was told: '… that is what we should like; but we haven't got the destroyers to carry out any such rule'.[23] He recognised that destroyer captains needed to be allowed a good deal of initiative: 'They should be encouraged to use their ships with wartime freedom, and should feel they will not be considered guilty of unprofessional conduct if they have done their best …'.[24]

The destroyer force was still dominated by the V and W classes of 1917–19 and the A to I classes which had originated during Churchill's term at the Treasury. In 1936 there was concern about large Japanese destroyers and the Tribal class was designed, with eight 4.7-inch guns instead of four – they would become the elite ships of the navy and see hard and dangerous service. But they were expensive and were followed by slightly smaller 'intermediate' ships with six guns. Even so, Churchill was sceptical about them: 'Destroyers of 1,650 tons almost amount to small cruisers. These unarmoured vessels with nearly 200 men on board become ... a prize and target for a U-boat in themselves. ... What we require are larger numbers of smaller vessels more quickly delivered.'[25] He also wrote: 'Having regard to the U-boat menace ... the type of destroyer to be constructed must aim at numbers and celerity of construction rather than size and power. It ought to be possible to design destroyers which can be completed in under a year, in which case 50 should be begun forthwith.'[26]

Several classes of sloop had been built between the wars for convoy escort, though not in great numbers. By 1939 the main effort was with small, cheap destroyers of 1,000 tons with four 4-inch guns. Names were important to Churchill: 'I do not see any advantage in calling these ships Fast Escort Vessels. They are in fact, destroyers of the medium size in every respect, and their prime function is to destroy U-boats.'[27] He suggested UBD for U-boat destroyer, but eventually they became escort destroyers, of the Hunt class. Their original design was flawed because a junior constructor miscalculated their stability and they had to be modified; and four guns were not necessary in anti-submarine warfare. Another, cheaper type was based on the design of whale-catchers, and they were known as 'whalers' until Churchill objected that this was 'an entire misnomer, they are not going catch whales'.[28] Designed originally for North Sea operation, they became the corvettes of the Flower class.

★

Churchill was not satisfied with the pace of the shipbuilding programme; perhaps he missed Fisher's combination of drive and inside knowledge. Early in October 1939 he was 'shocked to see the lag in the

1936 programme in battleships' and wanted 'a supreme effort' to finish the *KGV* and *Prince of Wales*. The carrier *Illustrious* was five months late and the others were even worse – 'All these ships will be wanted to take part in the war and not merely to sail the seas – perhaps under the German flag – after it is over.' There were just as many problems with cruisers and destroyers: 'We have at this moment to distinguish carefully between running an industry or a profession, and winning the war.' Only ships which would be finished by the end of 1941 should be given priority.[29] He wanted all the *KGVs* by the summer of 1941; by February he had decided to ask for no new aircraft carriers and wanted 'to sacrifice the entire aircraft-carrier, cruiser and light cruiser construction (except light cruisers already approved by the treasury since the war) in order to provide for the capital ship long-term programme and make possible the largest developments of the anti-U-boat and anti-mining flotillas'.[30]

He was not satisfied with the quality of the Fleet Air Arm, which had barely had time to reorganise itself after the transfer from the RAF. He complained at the end of September: 'neither in the quality of machines, nor in the organisation, nor in general spirit do I find the strength and efficiency which are needed'.[31] There was a particular problem with the obsolescence of many of the aircraft:

> When some years ago the Fleet Air Arm was being discussed, the speed of carrier-borne aircraft and shore-based aircraft was not unequal; but since then the shore-based development has been such as to make it impossible for carrier-borne aircraft to compete with shore-based. This left the Fleet Air Arm the most important duties of reconnaissance in the ocean spaces, of spotting during an action with surface ships and launching torpedo seaplane attacks upon them. However, there are very few surface ships of the enemy, and one can only consider the possible break-out of a German raider or fast battleship as potential targets. Provision must be made for this; but certainly it does not justify anything like this immense expenditure.

He recommended that the personnel should take over some of the duties of RAF Coastal Command in operating patrols.[32] By February 1940 he was planning for the Fleet Air Arm to take over Hurricane fighters for the defence of Scapa, and encouraged Admiral Royle's proposal 'for adapting a certain number of Spitfires to fly off carriers'.[33]

Again he rejected the use of airships. In September 1939 he told Murray Sueter: 'Except for the useful patrolling work of the little blimps around the harbours, they were not otherwise of much military value. Today the Admiralty possess no airships, but in view of their small offensive value against submarines, and their extreme vulnerability to attacks from enemy aircraft and from the anti-aircraft armament of U-boats, there is no need to deplore our deficiency in this respect.'[34] But one wonders if a fleet of radar-equipped airships, operating well beyond the range of enemy fighters, might have closed the 'air gap' in the middle of the Atlantic and saved him from his only real worry.

★

The initial mobilisation of the navy included the calling up of reservists, who numbered 73,000, and about 62,500 of them had been mobilised by the end of 1939. Beyond that the expansion of the navy in the early stages of the war was far less rapid than that of the army or air force, largely because sailors were useless without ships to put them in. A growth from 235,000 to 310,000 men was planned in the first instance, and it was not difficult to find them with the aid of conscription. The policies of 1939–40 set precedents which would allow a much greater, and largely unforeseen, expansion later in the war.

Traditional officer training would continue for regulars, though Churchill was no happier with the standard of Dartmouth cadets than he had been in 1914: 'I could not help being unfavourably struck with the aspect of the Dartmouth cadets whom I saw marching by the other day.'[35] As to his own creation, the Special Entry Scheme, it had survived though not flourished during the peace, being augmented in 1936 as more rapid expansion became necessary. Churchill was concerned that three candidates who had done well in the examination had been turned down as unsuitable – one was the son of a chief petty officer, another of a merchant navy engineer, and the third had a slight Cockney accent. He wrote: 'One has to be particularly careful that class prejudice does not enter into these decisions ...'.[36] Always an advocate of promotion for the lower deck, he was shocked to discover that only 15 per year had been commissioned in each of the last five years, and wanted this increased to at least 75.[37] As to regular engineer officers, he complained about the length of the course at Keyham near Plymouth, with 250 young men spending three years and eight months there.[38] He wrote to the engineer-in-chief: 'too much emphasis must not be placed upon the maintenance of the navy after the war. If we lose the war, we shall not be allowed to have a navy at all. A certain compromise has therefore to be made between peace courses designed to fit young men for their after-life in the navy, and the effective use of all our energies to prevent defeat.'[39] He was outraged to discover that skilled men from the artisan branches had no path to commissioned rank. Referring to Hitler's alleged employment as a house painter, he asserted: 'Apparently there is no difficulty about painters rising in Germany!'[40]

But Dartmouth, Keyham and Special Entry would not suffice to fuel the great bulk of the naval expansion, which would need men of many different classes and age groups, and not necessarily those committed to a naval career. In October 1939 Churchill told parliament how the 'abnormal needs' would be dealt with: 'First, for temporary officers our main reserve and source will be the Royal Naval Volunteer Supplementary Reserve, who will be given commissions in the Royal Naval Volunteer Reserve and called up in batches for training.' These were amateur yachtsmen who had enrolled after the scheme was set up in 1936, but naturally their numbers were limited. 'Secondly, a number of candidates recommended by university recruiting boards or otherwise, as suitable for commissions, will be accepted' – but that was never a major source. 'Thirdly, promotion to commissioned rank from the Royal Naval Reserve ratings, or from the successive age groups called up under the National Service Act for hostilities only, will be open on lines similar to those now in force for the promotion of permanent ratings from the lower deck.'[41] It was this last group, made up largely of men of good education who had been conscripted into the navy, who would make up the great bulk of temporary officers as the navy expanded beyond any predictions. He compared the new type of officer favourably with the Dartmouth entry: 'I was enormously impressed with the candidates for commissions from the ranks whom I saw drilling and being trained on the parade ground at Portsmouth. They were, of course, much older, but a far finer looking type.'[42]

The navy was determined to maintain peacetime systems for entry of boys for continuous service of 12 years with the fleet, and special service entry of adults for five years with the fleet and seven in the reserves. Churchill supported the custom of sending the boys to sea even in wartime. 'It has always been the practice and tradition of the navy to have a certain proportion of boys afloat in peace or war. The boys have all volunteered, and we have no intention whatever of turning them off their ships.'[43] Other recruits, whether conscripts or volunteers, would be recruited for 'hostilities only'.

At the start of the war general conscription was brought in, with young men called up by age group at intervals. At first the Admiralty was unsure if it really needed it, and one officer wrote in October 1939: 'the navy got through the 1914–18 war without any recourse to conscription, but in deference to the government plan for an orderly method of utilising the manpower of the country was willing to adopt the conscription system'.[44] In any case, men outside the age groups were able to volunteer. Churchill objected to the first draft of an order on this, as it suggested 'that we prefer the conscripts, which is not the case. Our policy should be to take all the volunteers who offer themselves, who are not in reserved occupations, etc., and then make up the deficiency by selected men who have been called up and indicated a preference for the navy.'[45] Each conscript was allowed to indicate a preference for the navy or air force rather than the army. The RAF was the most popular of the services at this stage, and the army the least popular with the folk memory of the Western Front. The navy was expanding more slowly and could afford to turn down about two-thirds of those who applied, so it had a high standard of entrant.[46]

★

Naval bases were a recurring problem from the past, as the defences of Scapa Flow had been abandoned at the end of the last war. Churchill travelled there on 15 September. Most of the fleet was taking refuge in Loch Ewe and there was more *déjà vu* when Admiral Forbes took him there in the *Nelson*: 'My thoughts went back a quarter of a century to that other September when I had last visited Sir John Jellicoe and his captain in this very bay, and found them with their long lines of battle-ships and cruisers drawn out at anchor, a prey to the same uncertainties as now afflicted us.'[47] This time air attack was also a serious concern, but he objected to find that it was intended to 'lock up three regiments of AA artillery, etc., (comprising 6,200 men) for the whole war in Scapa. Scapa is no longer the base of the Grand Fleet, but only of three or four principal vessels.'[48] But the actual attack did not come from the air. At 1.30 in the morning of 14 October the R-class battleship *Royal Oak* was struck by four torpedoes from *U-47*, which had penetrated through a gap in the sunken blockships in Holm Sound. In all 833 men were lost. Churchill had to admit to the War Cabinet: '... certain representations had been made by the local naval authorities in the early part of the year as to the Scapa defences, but it had not been considered necessary to take steps to improve them'.[49]

The fleet was now going to the Clyde, which was 30 hours sailing from the North Sea. Churchill objected and wrote to Pound: '... the moment he arrives in the Clyde his whereabouts will be known to the Germans. There are plenty of Irish traitors in the Glasgow area; telephone communication with Ireland is, I believe, unrestricted; there is a German ambassador in Dublin.'[50] Moreover it had 'a long dangerous approach' and was poorly protected by anti-aircraft guns, balloons and fighters.[51] He intended to have the battleships in two watches, 'of which one would always be at sea in the northern approaches'. It was 'physically impossible' to make Scapa safe before February. The battlecruisers *Hood, Repulse* and *Renown* were to be sent into the 'broad waters' and possibly based at Halifax in Nova Scotia.[52]

A week after the start of the war Churchill had told the Prime Minister: 'I do not feel the assurances which I gave on Admiralty authority in 1914 and 1915 against the danger of oversea invasion have in any way lapsed. On the contrary, as the Germans cannot form a line of battle to fight a general action, and have a much weaker navy, they seem to be more valid than ever.'[53] But at the end of October he felt obliged to dispose his forces to meet a sudden raid, though at the time it was not possible to station heavy forces on the east coast. Instead 35 destroyers at Harwich and four cruisers at Rosyth would provide the initial protection.[54] The navy should not be driven out of the North Sea and 'no base on the west coast can be accepted except for a brief and unexpected interval. *Nelson* and *Rodney*, the "Captains of the Gate", must take their stations at Rosyth, and fight it out there when not at sea. *Warspite* and *Valiant* are available to replace casualties. ... Every effort should be made to make Rosyth the strongest defended war-harbour in the world.'[55] A conference at Loch Ewe on the 31st decided that the defences of Scapa were to be increased, that the Loch itself, known as Port A, was to be maintained, and that Rosyth was to be the main operational base.[56] Churchill visited the Flow in December to look at some dummy ships he had ordered as decoys. He noticed that seagulls did not cluster round them, and ordered food to be thrown from them occasionally to attract them.[57]

★

Churchill did not give up his interest in the other services, legitimised to a certain extent by his inclusion in the Land Forces Committee. This recommended building up an army of 55 divisions, with 20 ready after a year, and construction of 2,550 aircraft a month to reach parity with Germany after 18 months. All the financial and industrial implications of the programmes were considered, and Churchill complained that a soldier appeared to cost five or six times as much as in 1918. However he agreed that it would not conflict with his own requirements, because 'Our naval demands would probably be less than in the last war', while the force of 55 divisions was less than the 100 of 1918, and the population of the country was larger than it had been then.[58] In general Churchill was keen to offer help to the other services; in September 1939 he offered cordite, shells and spare guns to the army.[59] Perhaps he was looking forward to the future when he would have control of them all, and indeed some were already talking of him as prime minister. In the meantime, at the beginning of April 1940 he was to preside over a committee of the service ministers in addition to his duties at the Admiralty.[60] On the committee, the army pointed out that an enemy advance through Belgium and the Netherlands could only be stemmed 'by air action against the German columns, either while they are concentrating in Germany or as soon as possible after they have advanced into the Low Countries'. But it was 'most unlikely' that special aircraft for the purpose would be available by the spring of 1940, and Churchill remembered the Sopwith Salamander of 1918, designed for trench attack but soon known as the 'flying coffin'.[61] The army was offered only the obsolescent Blenheims and Battles, which would remain under RAF control.

Churchill did not abandon the idea of the unrotated projectile and aerial mines. On 11 November he told the air minister: 'the development of the mine is of deep interest to the navy, not only for the discharge from an aeroplane in defence of naval bases, but also because of the study we are making of firing it from guns, rocket apparatus, or the large size chemical mortars, as a protection against a low dive-bombing attack'.[62] In his memoirs he claimed it was 'a stop-gap necessitated by our grievous shortage of short-range weapons', but that does not reflect his interest in the subject at the time.[63]

CHAPTER 32

The Navy at War

The expression 'phoney war' was soon in use to describe the lack of activity on the Western Front and in the air, but it was never applicable at sea. In the first afternoon of the war the liner *Athenia* of 15,000 tons, carrying 1,100 passengers, was sunk by *U-30* whose captain believed she was an armed merchant cruiser. A convoy system was set up immediately, though ships at sea were of course still unescorted and Churchill told parliament that 65,000 tons of shipping had been lost in the first week of the war, reducing to 46,000 in the second, 21,000 in the third and less than 6,000 over the next two weeks.

★

The regular officers of the navy were mostly products of the training system which Churchill had criticised so heavily during his first term at the Admiralty, yet at the top level at least, there was a remarkably high standard of commander. At the head was Admiral Andrew Cunningham, closely followed by Bertram Ramsay and Max Horton, with Bruce Fraser, Philip Vian and James Somerville not far behind. Cunningham, Horton, Ramsay and Somerville had all entered the navy before the Selborne Scheme started and perhaps they had not suffered so much from the cramming. Some of them had served in the empire, including the South African War, before Fisher recalled the ships, and they had had chances to use their initiative. According to Cunningham, '… any captain will tell you that the best officers to be found in big ships have come from submarines and destroyers'. Cunningham himself had joined his first one in 1903, Horton had made his name as a submarine commander in the last war, Fraser had also served in destroyers, and Vian took command of a flotilla relatively late in his career. Ramsay, on the other hand, had been trained as the kind of staff officer that Churchill wanted. But not all of these commanders had flourished in peacetime. Ramsay had to be recalled from retirement, Somerville had retired due to ill health, and Horton was in the backwater of the Reserve Fleet. In the early stages of the war, less distinguished men were in command of the main fleets.

The Jutland controversy had died down somewhat after the deaths of Jellicoe and Beatty in 1935. Now tactical studies looked to the future rather than the past, and encouraged individual initiative in the age of air power and submarines, even in a fleet action. The 1937 report of the Tactical School at Portsmouth shows how far tactics had moved on since the rigidity of the Jellicoe days. The instructors were concerned with realism, for example whether the maximum speeds of foreign ships were really accurate. In contrast with the Grand Fleet Orders in which battleship fought battleship, cruiser fought cruiser and so on, they tried out massed destroyer attacks and suggested that a few of the attackers should come in to very close range. They exercised with light forces only, unsupported by heavy ships, including a battle between the British and Italians 'in a realistic setting'. They produced standardised war game 'sets' for use in other bases, and they were not afraid to question the established instructions, which did not 'meet all requirements'. The Battle Instructions were 'subject to piecemeal corrections over a long period', giving an impression of being out of date and losing the confidence of the officers. They suggested they might be renamed 'Fighting Instructions' to represent the new reality, and the term 'main force' instead of 'battle fleet' should be used. They took air reconnaissance into account, and wanted to delete the obsolete concept of the 'fleet submarine' from the vocabulary.[1] All this would bear fruit in the next eight years.

★

As always Churchill was not content with a defensive policy and looked towards Fisher's old idea of the Baltic. It was more practicable with the lack of German capital ships, but also more dangerous with the possibilities of submarine and air attack, which of course did not deter Churchill. In September 1939 Lord Chatfield, once Beatty's flag captain and now Minister for the Co-Ordination of Defence, told the Supreme War Council of the allies: 'It was impossible to say anything definite at this stage regarding the possibilities of naval action in the Baltic. If we could destroy the German capital ships, it might be then, but not until then, advisable to take a risk with some of our own.' Submarines had been deployed in the area in the last war, but they could not refuel without the support of Russia.[2]

Churchill, however, already had Plan 'Catherine' which owed a good deal to Fisher and for which 'special tools must be constructed'. This involved fitting at least two old R-class battleships with enormous caissons on each side to increase their breadth to 140 feet, which would protect against torpedoes and mines as well as reducing their draft. The deck armour would be increased to protect against bombing. They would be accompanied, perhaps, by three 8-inch and two 6-inch cruisers, two flotillas of destroyers, and submarines. They would force their way into the sea by day or night and from there they would isolate Germany by intercepting supplies of iron ore from Sweden. It was 'the supreme naval offensive open to the Royal Navy'.[3] By 21 September, in an echo of the Dardanelles, he suggested that the *Queen Elizabeth* might be added as she would not be ready for fleet service until next August and this would be 'no derogation from naval strength'. She already had strong deck armour but it should be 'reconsidered from the point of view of air attack'.[4] He recognised that political conditions might change by the time the project was ready, but wanted to load a metaphorical gun, which 'could be fired or not as circumstances require in the spring. If the gun is not prepared and loaded, no such option will be open.' But for the moment he did not want the idea to go to the over-cautious cabinet.[5] Confiding in Pound, he wanted the ships to be 'tortoises' – 'Do not worry about the look of the ship. Pull the super-imposed turrets out of them. ... They must bristle with AA and they must swim or float wherever they please.'[6] But by the end of October he was still vague about the purpose of the operation. One object might be 'the support of the Scandinavian and Finnish nations should their independence be threatened. Or, if Russia were to join the allies, to assist the Russian fleet to carry on an aggressive campaign in the Southern Baltic against the common enemy. Other situations can be envisaged'[7] – though this time there was no mention on an attack on Berlin. Another possibility was to reduce pressure elsewhere: 'The entry of the Baltic, for instance, would soon bring the raiders home and give us measureless relief.'[8] By mid-November it was clear that the work on the ships would not be finished by January, so the working up for the operation was postponed until the end of March.[9] In December Pound wrote that it was 'a great gamble, even if there were adequate fighter protection for the fleet, and if Russia were on our side and we had the use of Russian bases'.[10] But finally on 15 January 1940 he reluctantly conceded that 'the operation we outlined in the autumn will not be practicable this year. We have not yet obtained sufficient mastery over U-boats, mines and raiders to enable us to fit the many smaller vessels required for their special duties.'[11]

'Rhine mines', code-named 'Royal Marine' was a plan to attack German trade on the great river. Some mines would be launched from the French part of the river, and Lindemann suggested discharging them from sewers into the stream to let them drift down, at the rate of one per minute on the first night of the operation. Others would be dropped from aircraft, though only close to the full moon. Some of these, however, could be fitted with delayed action fuses and lie on the bottom. Others would be dropped in still waters such as canals, and more in estuaries. Churchill was shown an example in December. According to an Admiralty civil servant, 'It was like a circular cake tin, with horizontal antennae, and a vertical spike in the middle. [Major Jefferis] invited the First Lord to prod the spike, which he did, with a cautious forefinger. There was a small flash at the base of the spike and a small explosion. Churchill grunted, but did not comment; I do not think he was much amused.'[12] Five thousand mines were to be prepared for the first attack, with a total of 20,000 on order. German barges up to 350 feet long would be damaged by the campaign, along with tugs driven by paddles, which were 'very suitable from our point of view'. After chairing a

396 • CHURCHILL: WARRIOR

meeting in mid-January 1940, Churchill directed 'that all steps were to proceed at the highest priority, and any hitches to be reported'.[13]

Another recurring problem was the presence of German raiders on the high seas at the beginning of the war, though there were fewer this time. The powerful battlecruisers *Scharnhorst* and *Gneisenau* sank the armed merchant cruiser *Rawalpindi* on 23 November. By the beginning of October the navy was hunting a ship believed to be the 'pocket battleship' *Admiral Scheer*, which had been sighted off Pernambuco, Brazil, and was being chased by a group including the battlecruiser *Renown* and the carrier *Ark Royal*. By mid-December she was identified as the *Graf Spee*, and she was attacked by three cruisers. An example of the 'very remarkable ship' with 11-inch guns which Churchill had feared so much in February 1929 was defeated by a force of three cruisers including the *Exeter*, the second of the 'B-class' cruisers which Churchill had envisioned 'sinking beneath the waves with all her crew' against superior enemy forces, and two small 6-inch cruisers which were able to drive her into neutral Montevideo after the *Exeter* was damaged. Churchill contrasted 'the offensive spirit shown by Commodore Harwood with the lack of enterprise shown in somewhat similar circumstances in the last war when the *Goeben* was allowed to escape'.[14] There was jubilation when the *Spee* sailed out of the harbour to be scuttled by her crew. Churchill was pleased that it allowed the *Renown* and the *Ark Royal* to come home, and more than pleased with a much-needed victory after the loss of the *Courageous* and *Royal Oak*. He commented that the *Exeter* had suffered for 'tremendous fire', and her survival reflected 'high credit on the constructor's department that she should have been able to stand up to such a prolonged and severe battering'.[15] When she returned to Plymouth after repair in the Falkland Islands, crowds lined up to cheer her and Churchill addressed her crew, who 'came like a flash of light and colour' in a dark and depressing winter, 'carrying with it an encouragement to all who are fighting'.[16]

By mid-September the Admiralty was aware that 'M bombs' or magnetic mines could be dropped from the air and set off by a ship's magnetic field. In November a minefield in the Thames estuary was believed to consist of these weapons and they sank or damaged three ships. Churchill held a meeting on the dangers in his room on 20 November, and the following day the cruiser *Belfast* was almost sunk by one in the Firth of Forth; the battleship *Nelson* was damaged at Loch Ewe early in December and it was increasingly urgent to find an answer to the threat. An answer was already on the way. On 23 November Lieutenant-Commander J. G. D. Ouvry recovered an intact magnetic mine off Shoeburyness in Essex and countermeasures could be devised using a fleet of specially equipped sweepers and by 'desgaussing' ships, or reducing their magnetic field. It diverted much effort and was not the war-winning weapon its inventors had hoped. Churchill congratulated 'all those concerned in dealing with magnetic mines on the success which has so far been achieved'.[17]

As to the submarine threat, on the second day of war Churchill decreed that 'To avoid confusion, German submarines are always to be described officially as U-boats in all official papers and communiqués' and later this would be extended to all enemy submarines.[18] He reminisced: 'It is a strange experience to me to sit in the Admiralty again, after a quarter of a century, and to find myself moving over the same course, against the same enemy, and in the same months of the year. But it gives me an opportunity of making comparisons which, perhaps, no one else could make, and I see how much greater are the advantages we possess today in coping with the U-boat than we did in the first U-boat campaign 25 years ago.'[19] There was disaster on 17 September when the aircraft carrier *Courageous*, with only a weak destroyer escort, was sunk by *U-29* 330 miles west of Land's End, almost exactly 25 years after the three cruisers were lost in 1914, though in this case 687 men out of 1,200 were picked up. The shortage of destroyers caused Churchill to consider the possibility of getting older ones from the United States – 'even if we could only secure 20 of their old vessels, they would be of great assistance to us'.[20]

Convoys were instituted as soon as the war started, and in November Churchill suggested dividing them into fast and slow groups.[21] Important ones, especially those carrying large numbers of troops, were covered by battleships to protect against raiders such as the *Scharnhorst*. At first Churchill was sceptical about attempts to send fast ships such as Atlantic

liners without convoy, and at the end of September he commented of
the Cunarder *Aquitania*, 'We must not offer the enemy easy scoops.' She
was 'too fast to move in convoy' but he questioned whether it was 'sufficient to counterbalance the loss of such a fine ship'.[22] But experience
soon showed that such liners, with speeds of 30 knots or more, were
almost immune to submarine attack, and Churchill would use this to his
advantage later in the war. For less glamorous ships it was much slower
and more dangerous as Churchill told parliament: 'such is the U-boat
war – hard, widespread and bitter, a war of groping and drowning, a
war of ambuscade and stratagem, a war of science and seamanship'.[23]
Aggressive as always, he wanted to attack the U-boats rather than just
defend convoys: 'Nothing can be more important in the anti-submarine
war than to try to obtain an independent flotilla which could work like
a cavalry division ...'.[24] But with the shortage of escorts it would be
several years before such a force could be organised.

German claims of success in sinking British ships were greatly exaggerated, and on 8 November Churchill amused parliament by stating:
'... we should be quite content to engage the entire German navy, using
only the vessels which at one time or another they have declared they
have destroyed'.[25] But his own claims about U-boat sinkings were also
exaggerated, and brought him into conflict with Rear-Admiral John
Godfrey, the chief of naval intelligence. Godfrey employed Commander
Ian Fleming of the RNVR as his personal assistant and later became
the model for 'M' in the James Bond novels, which he hated. There
were petty disputes between Churchill and Godfrey. Churchill queried
the methods of reporting intelligence: 'In view of the urgent need for
economy even in comparatively small matters such as staff and paper, I
should like some reassurance that this weekly summary, admirable as it
is in quality, is fulfilling a real need in the Admiralty.'[26] More seriously,
when Pound claimed that 30 U-boats had been sunk by the end of
1939 and Churchill claimed 40 (leaving only 32 still in service), Godfrey
believed that the figure was only nine, and it was later confirmed as ten.
Godfrey wrote that he was disappointed with himself for not putting the
case for nine more effectively to Pound and deplored the fact that Pound
was 'infected' with the idea which 'regarded intelligence as a flexible

commodity'. The affair strengthened his resolve 'that intelligence reports emanating from the Admiralty should not be wishful'.

Nevertheless the U-boat threat was under control for the moment. By the end of May 1940, 23 U-boats had been sunk for the loss of 215 merchant ships and two warships. According to the navy staff history, 'From the enemy's point of view this was not too favourable an exchange rate and was in fact sufficiently adverse to result in a steady reduction in the strength of the U-boat fleet owing to its initial small size and to the tardiness with which a replacement and expansion was put in hand. For us too it was an unfavourable rate. If it were kept up by an expanding U-boat fleet, the shipping losses would become crippling.'[27]

★

On 19 September 1939 Churchill told the cabinet of the passage of Swedish iron ore from the Norwegian port of Narvik to Germany. In summer it passed through the Baltic, but when that sea froze it went to the neutral port, and the supply ships passed among the Norwegian islands and territorial waters to Germany. Since nine million tons of ore were essential in the production of Germany's war materials, it was important to stop it and he recommended laying minefields.[28] In November he rejected a plan to land a force at Narvik, but persisted with the mining scheme.[29] Since the Soviet Union was now at war with Finland, he thought 'it would be to our advantage if the trend of events in Scandinavia brought it about that Norway and Sweden were forced into war with Russia. We would then be able to gain a foothold in Scandinavia with the object of helping them ...'.[30]

On 15 December he put forward two proposals; one for a barrage across the North Sea to the Norwegian coast, as had been done with American support in the last war but would take time to implement; the other was for mining in Norwegian waters to drive shipping outside the 3-mile limit where it could be examined by the Royal Navy.[31] On 1 January the cabinet, at Churchill's insistence, was considering a much wider scheme, 'a daring offensive ... which they think might bring Germany to her knees but which also, to my mind, is dangerously reminiscent of the Gallipoli plan', according to the Prime Minister's

Secretary John Colville.[32] The idea of landing a force near Narvik was on the agenda again, and Trenchard was to be asked to make a plan to base fighters there, while destroyers and submarines would be used in support.[33] Churchill considered that a German invasion was unlikely as 'it would not be an opportune moment, from the point of view of world opinion, to invade Norway at a time when she was protesting against our action'. However if they did he would be glad.

> Norway would make a protest at our action. A German reaction might then follow, possibly in the form of an invasion. The effect of this would be vexatious but would in no way be decisive. On the other hand it would open the way to our next action, which would be the occupation of the northern ore fields. The Norwegians would undoubtedly resist a German invasion which would be a violation incomparably greater than the violation of territorial waters of which we would be guilty. Thus, by interrupting the trade from Narvik we should be paving the way to the major project if it appeared, later, to be in our interests to carry it out.[34]

On 19 January 1940 the War Cabinet approved plans for the despatch of a force to Narvik for the occupation of ports in southern Norway and for a force to help defend southern Sweden.[35] Churchill was impatient as always and on 21 January he complained: 'we had now been considering the proposal to stop the Narvik traffic for some six weeks, and so far we had taken no action'; so far 'we had let the initiative rest with Germany' in the conduct of the war.[36] It was 'very painful to watch during the last two months the endless procession of German oreships down the Norwegian territorial waters'.[37]

There was further impetus in mid-February when the *Graf Spee*'s storeship *Altmark*, carrying nearly 300 merchant ship prisoners, tried to get home by Norwegian waters and was found in Jossingfjord. Churchill ordered Captain Vian of the destroyer *Cossack*: 'You should board the *Altmark*, liberate the prisoners and take possession of the ship pending further instructions. If Norwegian torpedo-boat interferes you should warn her to stand off. If she fires on you, you should not reply unless attack is serious, in which case you should defend yourself using no more force than is necessary, and ceasing fire when she desists.' Admiral Forbes, the commander-in-chief of the Home Fleet, later complained that this order had been sent over his head.[38] Vian's men boarded without interference and an officer cried to the men imprisoned in the hold, 'Come up – the navy's here!' to be met with loud cheers. The Norwegian government protested even though they were in the wrong in allowing an auxiliary warship carrying prisoners to operate in their territorial waters, but Churchill was relieved that shots had not been fired between them. He even urged moderation, saying that their attitude was not an excuse for a landing, but the minelaying operation was still valid. At the end of February the Prime Minister took soundings among the opposition parties concerning the minelaying proposal, but Clement Atlee of the Labour Party 'doubted whether we should gain any advantage sufficient to outweigh the moral disadvantages we should incur'.[39]

The Germans were already planning their own strike on Norway, though Admiral Raeder warned Hitler that 'the operation itself is contrary to all principles in the theory of naval warfare. According to this theory, it could be carried out by us only if we had naval supremacy.'[40] But by 6 April the six divisions required for the operation were being embarked in six groups, protected by the battlecruisers *Scharnhorst* and *Gneisenau* and the heavy cruiser *Hipper* as well as light cruisers, destroyers and U-boats, supported by 800 fighters and bombers and 200 transport aircraft. They were to land in the ports of Oslo, Kristiansand, Egersund and Bergen in the south, Trondheim in the centre of the country and Narvik in the north, while the army would march into Denmark.

British intelligence failed to spot what was happening. The different services – army, navy, air force and Foreign Office – were rivals and reluctant to share their sources. There were reports from the British Embassy in Stockholm, from a secret Foreign Office source in Germany, from the American Ambassador in Copenhagen and from photo reconnaissance, all pointing to an invasion to the north.[41] An Admiralty intelligence report of 7 April suggested that 'Hitler is reported from Copenhagen to have ordered the unostentatious movement of one division by ten ships by night to land at Narvik with simultaneous occupation of Jutland' but this was dismissed as being 'of doubtful value'.[42] The British admirals agreed with Raeder's assessment and did not believe that that such an attack was possible. When Admiral Forbes knew that that the German forces were at sea, he took the Home Fleet north-east to prevent them entering the Atlantic and thus missed the landings in the south of Norway. Troops had been embarked in four cruisers at Rosyth but were disembarked and the ships were ordered to join the fleet – though Churchill's later claim that this had been agreed with Forbes does not bear examination.[43] Men had also been embarked in troopships on the Clyde but their naval escort sailed without them.

At first Churchill was jubilant after hearing about the German landings, claiming 'our failure to destroy the German fleet up to the present is only due to the bad visibility and rough weather, while if the German ships fly for home ports, they will leave their garrisons exposed to our expeditionary forces'.[44] The forces which had landed were 'potential prizes for us'.[45] But apparently he was overworking, for his secretary Eric Seal wrote on 9 April: 'I was very worried about Winston, who was knocked right out last night. I had to manoeuvre him to bed; he has had a good night, and this morning is in wonderful fighting spirit.'[46] He seemed a little more cautious when he told Pound: 'The Germans have succeeded in occupying all the ports on the Norwegian coast, including Narvik, and large scale operations will be required to turn them out of any of them. Norwegian neutrality and our respect for it have made it impossible to prevent this ruthless coup.'[47] On the 10th a force of destroyers attacked the Germans in Narvik. Two destroyers were sunk on each side, but the German ones were bigger and their overall destroyer force was much smaller, and in addition they lost several transports. However the British might have been even more successful if they had been ordered to wait for the battlecruiser *Renown* to join them. The cruiser *Königsberg* was sunk by naval aircraft at Bergen, and on the 11th Churchill deployed his knowledge of history, telling parliament: 'I consider that Hitler's action in invading Scandinavia is as great a strategic and political error as that which was committed by Napoleon in 1807 or 1808, when he invaded Spain.'[48] The King was of similar view and congratulated Churchill on 'the splendid way in which, under your direction, the navy is countering the German move against Scandinavia'.[49] Then on the 14th Admiral Whitworth in the

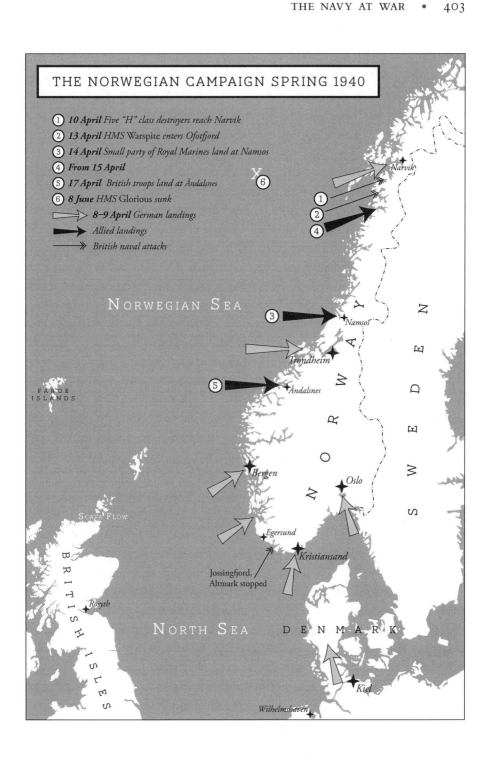

THE NORWEGIAN CAMPAIGN SPRING 1940

① *10 April* Five "H" class destroyers reach Narvik
② *13 April* HMS Warspite *enters Ofotfjord*
③ *14 April* Small party of Royal Marines land at Namsos
④ *From 15 April*
⑤ *17 April* British troops land at Åndalsnes
⑥ *8 June* HMS Glorious *sunk*
8–9 April German landings
Allied landings
British naval attacks

NORWEGIAN SEA

FAROE
ISLANDS

Narvik

X ⑥

①
②
④

③ Namsos

Trondheim

⑤ Åndalsnes

NORWAY

SWEDEN

Bergen

Oslo

SCAPA FLOW

Egersund

Jossingfjord,
Altmark stopped

Kristiansand

BRITISH ISLES

Rosyth

NORTH SEA

DENMARK

Kiel

Wilhelmshaven

venerable *Warspite*, now fitted with anti-torpedo bulges, entered the fjord with nine destroyers and sank eight German destroyers, most of the enemy's force in these ships. The Prime Minister 'expressed the congratulations of the War Cabinet to the First Lord of the Admiralty and the First Sea Lord for the brilliant operation carried out at Narvik the previous day'.[50]

The idea of British landings was revived and Whitworth was ordered to prepare for one at Narvik against his better judgement – a poorly equipped and untrained military force had already left the Clyde with the code name Rupert. Churchill dithered about supporting another landing at Trondheim to support the Norwegians in the south, though it soon became clear that a double expedition was beyond the resources available. Sixty-seven-year-old Admiral of the Fleet, the Earl of Cork and Orrery, was in charge of the naval force, independent of Forbes, while Major-General Mackesy was in command of the army. The two sailed in different ships and did not meet until they were off the Norwegian coast, when they disagreed about how to proceed. On the 15th the troops for Rupert were disembarked in the vicinity of Narvik but could not advance because they had no equipment to help them through the thick snow. On the next days the forces for Operation Maurice landed near Trondheim but were even less well equipped; in an echo of the Dardanelles, the ships had not been combat loaded.

Despite everything, the operation might conceivably have succeeded had it not been for air power. The Germans had the use of shore airfields and more than 700 aircraft. The theatre was 800 miles from RAF bases, while the navy could only deploy three aircraft carriers, the *Ark Royal*, *Glorious* and *Furious*, with a total of 120 aircraft – mostly the biplane Swordfish, which was a very successful torpedo bomber when not faced with enemy air cover but had a top speed of only 139 mph, and the Blackburn Skua, which tried unsuccessfully to combine the dive bomber with the fighter – it had its moment of glory with the sinking of the *Königsberg*, but it was already obsolete with a top speed of 225 mph. Mauriceforce was evacuated at the beginning of May and the ships were attacked for the first time by the deadly Stuka dive bomber with the loss of two destroyers. The attempt on Narvik continued.

Even in the impersonal pages of the Official History, Captain S. W. Roskill is critical, relying on 'Personal knowledge and experience of officers of OIC':

> Mr Churchill used, during critical periods in naval operations, to spend long hours in the Admiralty Operational Intelligence Centre and the tendency for him to assume direct control therefrom is easily to be understood. Many of the signals sent during such periods bear the unmistakeable imprint of his language and personality and, admirable though their purpose and intention were, it now appears plain that they sometimes confused the conduct of operations and increased the difficulties of the Commander-in-Chief.[51]

In a rare admission of error, Churchill later wrote: 'Looking back on this affair, I consider that the Admiralty kept too close a control upon the Commander-in-Chief, and after learning his original intention to force the passage into Bergen we should have confined ourselves to sending information.'[52]

The comparison with the Dardanelles occurred to many in authority, but paradoxically it had the opposite effect on Churchill's career. A momentous House of Commons debate beginning on 7 May started as a criticism of the action in Norway, which left Churchill highly vulnerable, but soon turned to the general conduct of the war and a motion of censure on the government. This tested his loyalty to Chamberlain to the full, but he defended his chief. Keyes wore his uniform to denounce the government, while Leo Amery used the Cromwellian injunction which might have appealed to Churchill in other circumstances: 'Depart, I say, and let us have done with you. In the name of God, go!' The Labour Party refused to enter a coalition with Chamberlain as leader, and after Lord Halifax was ruled out, Churchill became Prime Minister. Clementine told her husband, 'Had it not been for your years of exile etc., repeated warnings re the German peril, Norway might have ruined you.' Winston himself wrote, but did not publish: 'it was a marvel – I really do not know how – I survived and maintained my position in public esteem while all the blame was thrown on poor Mr Chamberlain'.[53] He recalled: 'I felt as if I was walking with destiny, and that my past life had been but a preparation for this hour and for this trial. ... I thought I knew a good deal about it all, and I was sure I should not fail.'[54] His resolution would soon be tested to the full as German forces began their assault on the Netherlands and Belgium.

PART IV

Finest Hour and After

CHAPTER 33

Finest Hour

No British prime minister has ever taken power during such a grave crisis as that of 10 May 1940, as the Norwegian operation faltered. Early that morning 136 German divisions invaded the Netherlands, Belgium and Luxemburg, exceeding the scope and violence of their operation in 1914. Rotterdam was heavily bombed, paratroopers seized key bridges and the pivotal Belgian fort of Eben-Emael was overrun by glider-borne troops. All this was happening while Churchill was still appointing ministers. On 12 May Hankey wrote of 'complete chaos', and that 'The Dictator, instead of dictating, was engaged in a sordid wrangle with the politicians of the left about the secondary offices.'[1] It was 14 May when Captain Berkeley of the War Cabinet Secretariat wrote: 'Winston has a government.'[2]

For the moment there was not much that government could do; the British Expeditionary Force (BEF) was under French command and by pre-arranged plan it began to advance into Belgium to attempt to occupy a line running north to south through Namur and Antwerp to Amsterdam. Relations between the allies were not good, the Belgian border guards hesitated about allowing the troops through, and progress was slow. Once in, the nine British, 30 French and 22 Belgian divisions outnumbered the 30 German divisions in the country, but lack of co-operation and fierce attacks by the Luftwaffe turned the scale in the enemy's favour.

The sensational invasion of three neutral countries and the innovative use of bombers, gliders and paratroopers deflected attention from an even more dangerous movement. The French army had always regarded the Ardennes as impassable by tanks, and indeed there was a huge traffic jam as more than 40,000 vehicles of Panzergruppe Kleist made their way through, but there was no air strike on these sitting targets. It was the opposite of the conventional allied view of the German army. Hitler was very hesitant about the advance and twice ordered it to halt, once with drastic consequences. Initiative rested with the commanders of all ranks – Generals Guderian and Rommel both disobeyed direct orders, while junior officers and even in one case a sergeant exploited chances to advance.[3]

Churchill correctly assessed the situation to the War Cabinet on the 13th: '... the Germans might either be launching their great land attack with the object of trying to defeat the Franco-British, or they might content themselves with making contact along the line which the allied armies had taken up in Belgium, and with consolidating their position in Holland preparatory to their great attack on this country'.[4] In fact the Germans had started out with the more limited of these aims, but would soon see a great opportunity opening before them. That day Guderian's forces made their breakthrough at Sedan, the site of the French defeat of 1870. General Ironside, Chief of Imperial General Staff, told the War Cabinet that 'mechanised forces could not be stabilised. The Germans had so far only used mechanised forces and we would inevitably be able to compel these forces to retire unless the Germans moved their main army forward.'[5] At first Churchill was not worried, perhaps he remembered the German breakthrough of March 1918 when he had believed an offensive 'was like throwing a bucket of water over the floor. It first rushed forward, then soaked forward, and finally stopped altogether until another bucket could be brought.' So he commented on the 14th: 'The enemy's break through on a comparatively narrow front would be difficult to sustain, as the forts on the flanks should be able to hold firm, and the Maginot Line itself was self-contained.'[6]

But soon the messages from France became ever more alarming. On the morning of 15 May Churchill was rung at 8.30 by the Premier Paul Reynaud who was 'considerably shaken' and expected an attack on Paris. He demanded more assistance from Britain. Churchill tried to reassure him that the penetration was on a narrow front, but he could not send any more men in time for the present battle. Reynaud had already asked for ten more fighter squadrons to augment those already in France. Churchill announced his intention of going to France himself to stiffen resistance,[7] but the Germans had made a deep penetration and on the 16th Churchill told the War Cabinet that he 'took an extremely grave view of the news'.[8] Four fighter squadrons were to be sent to France, where the German bombers and dive bombers had 'destroyed the French morale to such an extent that the German troops had been able to advance almost without the loss of a man'. They would be taken from the north of Scotland, and Churchill suggested the defence of the fleet at Scapa might be left to anti-aircraft guns, or the fleet might move to the Clyde.

That afternoon he flew to France in a De Havilland Flamingo aircraft and Ismay reported that as soon as they landed at Le Bourget 'it was obvious that the situation was far more critical than we had suspected. The officers who met us said that the Germans were expected in Paris in a few days at most. With the memory of 1914–18 in our minds, none of us could believe it.'[9] Churchill told the inter-allied Supreme War Council 'that certain pre-war prophets had been proved wrong as the offensive was coming into its own again'. He wrote later: 'A heavy onrush of armoured vehicles was advancing with unheard-of speed towards Amiens and Arras, with the intention, apparently, of reaching the coast at Abbeville. Alternatively they might make for Paris.'[10] General Gamelin, the French chief of staff, commented: 'The difference between 1918 and now … was that then infantry met infantry whenever a break occurred. We were now, he said, at the period of the melee. In order to meet such an attack as the present we needed armoured fighting vehicles to meet armoured fighting vehicles.'[11] Churchill declined to send out any more fighters, claiming that 'the British only had 39 squadrons of fighters for the protection of England. These were the life of the country and guarded our vitals from attack. We must conserve them.'[12] Gamelin explained the situation and Churchill asked 'Where is the strategic reserve?' and then, in what he admitted was 'indifferent' French, 'Où est la masse de manoeuvre?' Gamelin answered 'Aucune' (there is none) and, Churchill reported, 'There was another long pause.' He was aware that Guderian's tanks were taking a risk in advancing to the coast without the support of infantry and a counterattack could well move into the gap and cut them off; but there was nothing to do it with. He went on: 'Outside in the garden of the Quai d'Orsay clouds of smoke arose from large bonfires, and I saw from the window venerable officials pushing wheel-barrows of archives onto them. Already therefore the evacuation of Paris was being prepared.'[13]

In London there was a cabinet meeting to discuss a 'terrifying' telegram received from Churchill in Paris, and it was agreed to send six Hurricane squadrons to bomb the crossings of the River Meuse. Ismay conveyed the message to Reynaud in his flat, and next morning Churchill breakfasted in the British Embassy before flying back. He reported: 'There was no doubt that the 9th French army had sustained a heavy defeat.' Meanwhile Lord Gort, the British commander-in-chief in France, offered two alternatives – 'to attempt to join hands with the French force in the south by moving towards Amiens', which he regarded as 'impracticable unless the French army attacked from the south', or to 'break away from the French and Belgian armies and form a bridgehead round the Channel ports'.[14] Churchill, however, was still optimistic and wanted the BEF to move south to the Amiens line as 'the last chance of retrieving the situation'. On the 19th, recalling 1918 again, he told parliament that 'We may look with confidence to the stabilization of the front in France,' but a British counter-attack at Arras failed and on the 21st Churchill was depressed and planned to fly out again to make the point that 'it is no use concentrating on the destruction of German motorised columns which have already penetrated far into France, but that we must withstand the main German advance and ourselves attack'.

On the 22nd he flew out again, against the advice of the chiefs of staff. The German thrust was now heading westward so Paris was not under immediate threat, and there were changes in the French government and the army to increase resolution. Churchill had more confidence in the new French commander, Weygand, and the idea for an attack to the south of Belgium was approved. It was recognised that the Channel ports of Boulogne, Calais and Dunkirk had to be held for supply lines and possible withdrawal. When he returned to London he was 'almost in buoyant spirits'.[15] He told the War Cabinet: 'If General Weygand's plan succeeded, it would mean the release of 35 allied divisions from their present serious predicament. If it failed, it would be necessary to make a fresh plan with the object of saving and bringing back to this country as many of our best troops and weapons with as little loss as possible.'[16] But by the 23rd it was clear that the German panzers had reached Abbeville on the Somme and were about to attack Boulogne, so the forces in Belgium were cut off. Churchill had to reassure the House of Commons that no peace terms would be contemplated without the agreement of the French.

Around this time Captain Pim heard him discuss the effect of modern warfare.

> He recalled the tactics which would have been employed in other wars had this breakthrough been made by cavalry – the counter part of tanks in those days – how the policy would have been to allow them to go through, then to close the gap, cut them off and deal with them with our own cavalry. 'But', he said, 'there is this difference today. This new type of cavalry is heavily armoured and you say you have nothing to counter it. … We cannot leave our army to be slaughtered or to surrender – no, never that! We must get out and provide them anew with the necessary weapons to deal with the enemy.'
>
> Facing the map showing the situation the Prime Minister went on to say that we must put our artillery in the rearguard and fight the enemy wherever they were most and our men must battle through to the coast at Dunkirk. When they got there the navy would get them out.[17]

On the 23rd Churchill was behind a message to Reynaud – 'Salvation of these armies can only be obtained by immediate execution of Weygand's plan. I demand that French commanders in north and south and Belgian GHQ be given the most stringent orders to carry this out and turn defeat into victory.'[18] But it was not done. Boulogne was evacuated on the night of 23/24 May and Churchill asked 'why Gort gave up Arras, and what actually he is doing with the rest of his army? Is he still persevering with Weygand's plan, or has he become largely stationary?'[19] Soon attention began to focus on Calais, which Churchill was determined to hold though it was besieged. A rumour of evacuation was 'surely madness' and he wanted Gort to counter-attack. On the 27th he sent a message to him:

> At this solemn moment I cannot help sending you my good wishes. No one can tell how it will go. But anything is better than being cooped up and starved out. I venture these few remarks. First cannon ought to kill tanks and they may as well be lost doing that as any other way. … very likely the enemy tanks attacking Calais are tired and anyhow busy in Calais. A column directed on Calais while it

is still holding out might have a good chance. Perhaps they will be less formidable when attacked themselves. ... Presumably the troops know they are fighting their way home to Blighty. Never was there such a spur for fighting.[20]

The German tanks began to penetrate, but Churchill ordered 'that this force must fight it out in the town and endeavour to engage the Germans in street fighting, which they would be very anxious to avoid if possible'.[21]

Already plans for evacuation were being prepared and Churchill told the Defence Committee that Gort should take his army north 'in battle order, under strong rearguards, striking at all forces between himself and the sea'. The navy should prepare for evacuation, 'not only at the ports but on the beaches' and the RAF should strive to 'dominate the air above the area involved'.[22] The War Cabinet began to discuss what would happen if France were to drop out of the war, and the chiefs of staff were to consider 'What are the prospects of our continuing the war alone against Germany and probably Italy. Can the navy and air force hold out reasonable hopes of preventing serious invasion, and could the forces gathered in this island cope with raids involving detachments not greater than 10,000 men' – a real risk if the army was destroyed or captured in France.[23] Things got worse at four in the morning of the 28th when the Belgian army surrendered despite the entreaties of Roger Keyes, leaving a huge gap in the line. It had been 'completely demoralised by incessant bombing from large numbers of German aircraft'.[24] But Britain rallied and Lees-Smith, the Labour spokesman in parliament, stated: 'Whatever he may have to tell us in the next few days or weeks or months, we have not yet touched the fringe of the resolution of this country.'[25]

Meanwhile the evacuation from Dunkirk, Operation Dynamo, began. At first Churchill was cautious, on the 28th he suggested 'We should certainly be able to get 50,000 away. If we could get 100,000 away that would be a magnificent performance.'[26] At a cabinet meeting he announced 'quite casually', 'Of course, whatever happens at Dunkirk, we shall fight on.' The ministers were inspired: 'Quite a number seemed to jump up and come running to my chair, shouting and patting me on the back.'[27]

Luck was on his side for the first time. Though Calais had finally fallen, Dunkirk held out and Hitler mysteriously ordered his armies to stop their advance on the port, possibly because he wanted to give the Luftwaffe, which was more closely associated with the Nazis, a share of the glory of destroying the British army. Though many on the beaches felt a lack of air support, in fact the RAF was operating further inshore to prevent more serious attack. The weather was calm, and British sailors of all kinds were mobilised to send a fleet of 'little ships' across the Channel – though most of the rescue work was done by naval destroyers. Churchill was determined that French troops should be evacuated too and on the 29th, in the first known use of his famous 'Action this day' tag, he stated: 'It is essential that the French should share in such evacuations from Dunkirk as may be possible. Nor must they be dependent only upon their own shipping resources.'[28] In the end 338,226 troops were evacuated, including 139,097 French; but 1.7 million French soldiers were left behind. Privately Churchill had figures drawn up showing how this dwarfed the evacuation of the Dardanelles; publicly he was prepared to make the best of a unique moment of national unity. On 4 June, in perhaps the most famous of his many speeches, he paid tribute to the operation but warned that 'Wars are not won by evacuations' and went on 'We shall fight in France, we shall fight on the seas and oceans, we shall fight with growing strength and growing confidence in the air, we shall defend our island whatever the cost may be.'[29]

★

Meanwhile, in anticipation of a possible raid or invasion by sea or air, an amateur fighting force, the Local Defence Volunteers, was founded. Churchill was not happy with the name, for he was never a fan of the word 'defence' even if applied to older men and untried youths who could have done little else. After inspecting various units on 26 June he wrote to Eden: 'I don't think much of the name "Local Defence Volunteers" for your large new force. The word "local" is uninspiring. Mr. Herbert Morrison suggested to me to-day the title "Civic Guard". But I think "Home Guard" would be better.'[30] Thousands of armbands had already been printed with the letters LDV, but Churchill insisted that the name be changed.

The campaign in Norway was finally abandoned to spare resources for a more urgent campaign and the aircraft carrier *Glorious* was lost on

8 June, largely due to her old-fashioned captain allowing her to close with the battlecruisers *Scharnhorst* and *Gneisenau*.

However, as his famous speech and the withdrawal of French forces showed, Churchill was far from believing that the war in France was over. On 31 May, as the evacuation of Dunkirk was nearing completion, he and his party flew to Paris again in two Flamingos escorted by nine Hurricanes. At a meeting of the Supreme War Council he claimed that

> ... the Germans were being very hard pressed. In spite of their great successes they had, behind the technical troops largely responsible for the recent advance, an army which was very far from the standard of 1914. ... If the allies could hold out through the summer, Britain would emerge as a most important factor. In the meantime, she would do what she could to help, but her contribution would be limited for some time; it was useless to send out troops without weapons.[31]

By all accounts it was an inspiring performance, and Churchill went home to order that the paintings in the National Gallery should be buried in caves rather than sent abroad, and that no plans should be made for the evacuation of the Royal Family. 'I believe we shall make them rue the day they try to invade our island. No such discussion can be permitted.'[32] On 2 June he ordered Ismay: 'The BEF in France must immediately be reconstituted, otherwise the French will not continue the war. Even if Paris is lost, they must be adjured to continue a gigantic guerrilla.' He wanted to hold out in the Brittany peninsula until a new army could be developed.[33] He made plans to send three British divisions including the Canadians, plus two more evacuated from Narvik, plus the equivalent of five French divisions from Dunkirk.[34] In the event he decided against sending the Canadians, but the 51st and 52nd Divisions were embarked for France.

On 11 June he set off for Paris again to 'survey the situation with unclouded eyes'. Most of the French army had been trapped in Belgium and the rest was being harried by the invincible panzers. Weygand was now in despair, saying 'There is nothing to prevent the enemy reaching Paris. We are fighting on our last line and it has been breached.' Churchill was flushed and focussed on a junior war minster at the table, Charles De Gaulle, apparently seeing some qualities that were not present in the others.[35] Weygand was cautious about the Brittany plan, claiming that 'Brittany had no industries whatever and the French forces in the redoubt would be wholly dependent upon the United Kingdom. Meanwhile there could be no doubt that the Germans would revenge themselves by systematically destroying every town, village and factory in the occupied parts of France. It was, therefore, a most grievous prospect to contemplate.'[36] After the meeting he told Churchill that the Germans had a hundred divisions to spare to invade England and asked Churchill what he would do. The Prime Minister replied modestly that he was 'no military expert' but he was advised that 'the best method of dealing with the German invasion of the island of Britain was to drown as many as possible on the way over and knock the others on the head as they crawled ashore'. Weygand echoed his countryman Napoleon's opinion that the English Channel was 'a mere ditch' which would be 'crossed as soon as someone has the courage to attempt it', but also stated from a very different point of view: 'You have a very good anti-tank trap in the Channel.'[37]

Churchill was not long back in London when he was asked by telephone to go to Tours where the French government had been evacuated. It was feared that the French were about to give in, and were honouring Reynaud's promise to consult Churchill beforehand. On arrival at the airport on the 13th it was found to have been bombed the night before and there was no welcoming party. A car was commandeered to take them to the Prefecture, where French ministers arrived after a few hours. They reported that the French army was at its last gasp and it would be necessary to plead for an armistice. Reynaud wanted 'definite proof that America would come in with sufficient speed and force'. That was wildly optimistic in the circumstances, but the British delegation agreed to telegraph President Roosevelt anyway. Churchill hoped that France would carry on, 'fighting south of Paris down to the sea and, if need be, from North Africa'. He went on: 'At all events England would fight on. She had not and would not alter her resolve: no terms, no surrender, the alternatives for her were death or victory.' General Spears remembered how Lloyd George had often asked for an adjournment during the negotiations for the Versailles Treaty and the party convened in the garden, so they followed suit. Beaverbrook then summed up their general opinion. 'We shall gain a little time and see how these Frenchmen sort themselves out. We are doing no good here. In fact, listening to these declarations of Reynaud's only does harm. Let's get along home.'[38]

They were not back in London for long. On the 14th Weygand stated that organised resistance had come to an end. The new expeditionary force under General Brooke was no longer to consider itself under French command but was to get ready to withdraw. The Prime Minster called Brooke by telephone and asked what he was going to do with the 52nd division and Brooke replied that it had been sent out to support the French but that 'it was impossible to make a corpse feel, and that the French army was, to all intents and purposes, dead'. Churchill suggested there was a gap in front of him, but Brooke argued that it would be 'the throwing away of good troops with no hope of achieving any results'. After a long argument which brought Brooke close to exhaustion, Churchill conceded: 'All right, I agree with you.'[39] It was the first argument between the two, but far from the last. The withdrawal began and nearly 200,000 troops were evacuated, but not before the *Lancastria*, with 5,800 servicemen on board, was sunk in the Loire estuary with the loss of 3,000 lives – the worst British maritime disaster of all time.

Still Churchill was not finished; that day he planned to sail to Concarneau in southern Brittany to meet Reynaud and talk about the terms of surrender, which might be too harsh to accept. He wanted to confront the French with the proposition that there would be no release from the obligation not to surrender separately 'unless the French fleet is sailed to British ports', and he offered 'an indissoluble Anglo-French union' while the French fought from their North African colonies.[40] The party was already in a train at Waterloo to take them to Southampton to join a cruiser when the news arrived that the government had changed in France and the trip was cancelled. Even Churchill had to accept that the 'Battle of France' was over.

Churchill had already made several key, world-changing decisions during the first seven weeks of his premiership. He was probably right in refusing to send more fighters to France, and there is evidence that the French did not employ their own aircraft effectively. His decision to return troops to Western France was based on incurable optimism and is perhaps more difficult to justify. Even morally it was a failure, as the public mind has tended to believe ever since that the British participation in the campaign ended with the retreat from Dunkirk. But now the French had accepted deliberately humiliating terms from the Germans, for Hitler's character had been formed as a blinded soldier in the last armistice. This included signing the armistice in the very railway carriage on the same site where the Germans had surrendered in 1918. There was no guarantee on the French fleet. A long month ago, on 17 May, 'the War Cabinet had been faced with the gravest decision that a British cabinet ever had to take' when it refused to send more fighters.[41] But now Churchill had to make an even more difficult decision, perhaps the most difficult of any British prime minister.

★

Though Churchill coined the phrase 'finest hour' to describe the expected conduct of the British people in 1940–41, it might be argued that his own finest hour came just before that. For the first time, perhaps since his days at the Admiralty before the First World War, he was both in command of the situation and not making any major mistakes. It was not just his implacable decision to fight on; it is doubtful if any other individual could have combined the political and military skills that were necessary in the great crisis.

Churchill had written to Ismay on 18 May as the German advance proceeded: 'I do not feel that we have enough trustworthy troops in this country, in view of the very large numbers that may be landed in air-carriers preceded by parachutists. I do not consider this danger is imminent at the present time, as the great battle in France has yet to be decided.'[42] It echoed his prediction of 1917, that 'Considerable parties of soldiers could be conveyed by air to the neighbourhood of bridges or other important points, and, having overwhelmed the local guard, could *from the ground* effect a regular and permanent demolition.' But later he became more sceptical about the possibilities of invasion, telling the House of Commons in June: '… it seems to me that as far as seaborne invasion on a great scale is concerned, we are far more capable of meeting it to-day than we were at many points in the last war and during the early months of this war ...'.[43] Next month he told his staff that he hoped 'to drown the bulk of them in the salt sea'.[44] But he also recognised the moral value of the threat and on 12 July he told them that 'the great invasion scare ... is serving a most useful purpose: it is well on the way to providing us with the finest offensive army we have ever possessed and it is keeping every man and woman turned to a high pitch or readiness. He does not wish the scare to abate therefore, and though personally he doubts whether invasion is a serious menace he intends to give that impression, and to talk about long and dangerous vigils, etc., when he broadcasts on Sunday.'[45] On 12 August he told his staff 'that he is feeling more confident than two months ago. Our defences on this island have been immensely improved'.[46] However during a critical point in September when time and tides seemed suitable for an attempt his private secretary reported: 'The PM seems more apprehensive than I had realised about the possibility of invasion in the immediate future and he keeps on ringing up the Admiralty to ask about weather in the Channel.'[47] Admiral Sir Charles Forbes was as sceptical as Churchill and wrote on 4 June: 'there is little likelihood of the enemy being able to or being so confident as to try to invade England, Scotland or Wales by sea',[48] though he did not rule out an attempt on Ireland. He argued that there was no point in weakening the Home Fleet to counter it.

★

As early as 11 June Lord Hankey reported on the problems that would ensue if France was knocked out: '... where the French government takes asylum outside France, no difficulty should arise about securing the removal of the French fleet from ports in France to British ports or French colonies', but on the other hand '... it is practically certain that as a condition of an armistice the enemy would demand the surrender of the French fleet. If it were withdrawn in advance it is possible that France might be exposed to great sufferings until it was returned, and in those circumstances there would be great pressure on the French navy to return. In these circumstances the First Sea Lord thinks it would be better if the French fleet were sunk before that emergency arises ...'. Churchill ordered 'that the matter must be watched by someone from day to day who has access to Darlan and Reynaud'.[49]

By 24 June it was reported via Admiral Sir Dudley North that the French would not hand over their fleet in any circumstances, though Churchill was sceptical about that.[50] Next day he told the House of Commons: 'What our relations will be with the Bordeaux [later Vichy] government, I cannot tell. They have delivered themselves over to the enemy and lie wholly in his power.'[51] The First Sea Lord did not doubt the good faith of the French Admiral Darlan but pointed out to his commanders-in-chief that 'under the armistices now signed with Germany and Italy, French naval vessels have to be demobilised and disarmed under German and Italian control, ie to be handed over as fighting units to Germany and Italy'.[52]

Churchill was most concerned about the battleships *Richelieu* and *Jean Bart*, stating: 'If these fell into the hands of the Germans, they would have a very formidable line of battle when the *Bismarck* was commissioned next August' and would be faced by only the *Nelson*, *Rodney* and a few older battleships.[53] But the *Jean Bart* left Brest for Casablanca and the *Richelieu* for Dakar. On 27 June Pound told the War Cabinet: 'The real question at issue was what to do as regards the French ships at Oran.' One possibility would be to mine them in, but he suggested a much more decisive and final action. A force of four capital ships and the carrier *Ark Royal* could be assembled by 3 July and arrive off the North African port to offer three possibilities – to let the ships be demilitarised under British control, to sail to British ports, or to be bombarded unless they were scuttled within three hours. This was approved by Churchill and the War Cabinet, and two days later he stated that the first option was 'infinitely preferable, and should be supplemented by a promise to repatriate the crews, to restore the ships at the peace, and to pay full compensation for any loss or damage during the war'. If that was rejected the second demand should be made, and only if that failed would the drastic action of sinking be implemented.[54] The operation off Oran was duly begun, and on the day the War Cabinet was impatiently awaiting news from Admiral Somerville in charge of Force H. According to

John Colville, Churchill was 'walking up and down saying "terrible, terrible"', while Dill said that 'he had never seen anything comparable: the two nations who were fighting for civilisation had turned and rent each other while the barbarians sat back and laughed'.[55] After the not unexpected rejection of his other proposals Somerville opened fire at 5.55 in the evening of 3 July and at 11 the War Cabinet was told that 'All the French warships had been put out of action with the exception of one ship of the *Strasbourg* class which had succeeded in breaking out.'[56]

The enormous strain was beginning to tell on the Prime Minister. Early in June John Colville reported that he was 'in an impatient frame of mind' and angry with both Pound and Eden.[57] Later in the month, Clementine was concerned about his attitude to his subordinates. She wrote to him:

> I hope you will forgive me if I tell you something that I feel you ought to know.
>
> One of the men in your entourage (a devoted friend) has been to me and told me that there is a danger of your being generally disliked by your colleagues and subordinates because of your rough sarcastic and overbearing manner. ... If an idea is suggested (say at a conference) you are supposed to be so contemptuous that presently no ideas, good or bad, will be forthcoming. I was astonished & upset because in all these years I have been accustomed to all those who have worked with & under you loving you – I said this and was told 'No doubt it's the strain.'
>
> ... with this terrific power you must combine urbanity, kindness and if possible Olympian calm ... I cannot bear that those who serve the country and yourself should not love you as well as admire and respect you.[58]

She tore it up then pasted it together again and handed it to him. It appeared to work, there were no more complaints, but Churchill was never an easy man to work with.

CHAPTER 34

War Leader

By the middle of July Churchill's mood had greatly improved, as had the war situation. On the 10th the RAF claimed 12 confirmed enemy aircraft 'killed' and 17 probables – the next four days were 'the most glorious in the history of the RAF'. According to John Colville he was 'more cheerful than at any time since he took office'.[1] Broadcasting to the nation on the 14th, he came close to hinting that Britain was better without allies. 'We are fighting *by* ourselves alone. We are not fighting *for* ourselves alone. … we await undismayed the impending assault. Perhaps it will come tonight. Perhaps it will come next week. Perhaps it will never come.'[2] By the 27th he was 'bubbling with infectious gaiety' over dinner at Chequers.[3]

The immediate crisis was over, and Churchill's style of government began to settle into a pattern. He came to the task with a unique and unrepeatable experience. As well as heading all three services at different times, he had been the first to organise the air defence of a great city, he had planned strategic bombing raids, he had played a part in the invention of the armoured car and the tank which were now dominating the battlefield, he had opposed the first U-boat campaign, he had ordered battleships which were still valuable 25 years later, he had seen the Western Front at first hand, and he had even predicted an offensive by airborne troops. He had studied and criticised every major aspect and action of the last war and tried to learn lessons from them. He had studied the history of war through his great ancestor, and begun to appreciate the role of war in history though writing the *English Speaking Peoples*.

There was no doubt about his dominant position as Prime Minister, even if he did not always get his own way. All three main parties in parliament supported him, and virtually the whole nation was solidly behind the war effort. Despite occasional mild revolts and poorly supported motions of censure or no confidence, parliament gave the government almost everything it wanted. It could impose conscription on the population, including women, direct labour into particular industries and factories, intern aliens and suspected persons, ration food and clothing and impose all kinds of restrictions on the population. To fight the war it could raise taxes at a far higher level than ever before. Churchill enjoyed an unprecedented power over the country that earlier war leaders such as the Pitts could only have dreamed of. He was an ardent monarchist, though he had a strange admiration for Oliver Cromwell and regretted that German bombing had destroyed the 'best bit' of the House of Commons, where Cromwell had signed Charles II's death warrant.[4] He was casual in his treatment of the King, often postponing meetings or arriving late for them, but he wrote: 'I valued as a signal honour the gracious intimacy which I, as first minister, was treated, for which I suppose there has been no precedent since the days of Queen Anne and Marlborough during his years of power.'[5]

Born into the ruling classes at the height of the British Empire, Churchill had enormous self-confidence. He had been proved right about the Nazi threat (though not about self-government for India, his other campaign of the 1930s). He had an enormous capacity for work and knew every detail of the war effort, but left domestic affairs largely to Sir John Anderson, a former civil servant, and the Labour members of the coalition. His oratory was almost a weapon of war in itself – the American journalist Ed Murrow wrote that he 'mobilized the English language and sent it into battle'.[6] He had a far greater capacity for the ringing phrase than his most apposite predecessor Pitt the Elder: 'I have nothing to offer but blood, toil, tears and sweat'; 'This was their finest hour'; and 'Never in the field of human conflict was so much owed by so many to so few.'

Though he was fighting to preserve democracy, according to General Sir Alan Brooke 'One of his first acts ... was virtually to convert that democracy into a dictatorship! Granted that he still was responsible to parliament, and granted that he still formed part of a cabinet; yet his personality was such, and the power he acquired adequate, to place him in a position where both parliament and cabinet were only minor inconveniences to be humoured occasionally, but which he held in the palm of his hand, able to swing both of them at his pleasure.'[7]

Churchill used a very large staff – according to one of them he sometimes travelled with 'a retinue that Cardinal Wolsey might have envied'. He had political associates such as Anthony Eden and Lord Beaverbrook (whom many regarded as an evil influence). At a slightly lower level he had his Minister of Information, Brendan Bracken, and his scientific adviser, 'Prof' Lindemann. As Minister of Defence he employed three of the ablest soldiers of the day, General 'Pug' Ismay, Brigadier Leslie Hollis and Colonel Ian Jacob. As Prime Minister he was assisted by three or four very competent private secretaries, graduates of the best universities. According to one of them, John Colville, 'there was never a day or night when at least one Private Secretary was not with Winston Churchill – that is to say capable of being physically present at his desk or at his bed-side within a couple of minutes, or on the same train, ship, aircraft or car and able to comply with any request, reasonable or not, on the telephone or in person'. Commander C. R. 'Tommy' Thompson followed him from the Admiralty as an aide-de-camp and accompanied him on every trip, as did his long-serving bodyguard, Inspector Walter Thompson of Scotland Yard. Churchill deployed teams of typists to take down his ideas and write his memos and speeches.

In July 1940 he decreed: 'I do not accept any responsibility for matters relating to national defence, on which I am alleged to have given decisions, unless they are recorded in writing.'[8] As to the material sent to him, he demanded that reports be in 'short, crisp paragraphs and that detailed arguments should be set out in appendices'.[9] Though the prose style in his books was often quite wordy, he demanded brevity in wartime, complaining about telegrams which were 'long essays'.[10] He often asked for a report 'on one sheet of paper' and was equally keen on speed – 'Action this day' tags formed part of the office equipment. Colville described his working day in 1940 while he was still living at the Admiralty:

> He has a boxful of papers left outside his room each night and works through this in bed in the morning, dictating to a shorthand-writer, and generally does not get up and dress till quite late. About 11 he comes over to No 10 for the daily Cabinet meeting, which lasts till about 12. There is much coming and going of ministers and chiefs of staff etc. for this. ... Then the PM returns to Admiralty House for lunch and rest, usually working in Downing Street (or having another meeting of ministers there or in the House of Commons) from about 4.30 until dinner time. He dines in Admiralty House and sees a succession of ministers until bed time not much before midnight and maybe a good deal later.[11]

He would maintain this punishing schedule unless interrupted by travel or illness.

★

Right from taking office as Prime Minister in May 1940, Churchill made sure that the three services would co-operate far better than they had done in the last war. He finally had himself appointed Minister of Defence, though in a sense that was a sham. He had no legal power beyond what was already vested in the three service ministries, and there was no actual ministry – only a small staff of about a dozen officers plus clerks and typists. It would have been almost meaningless if he had not been prime minister as well, but it gave him a moral authority to interfere in service matters, which a prime minister would not normally have done, and he used it to the full. The First Lord of the Admiralty, the Secretary of State of War and the Secretary of State for Air were not members of the War Cabinet and were relatively minor political figures, apart from Anthony Eden. Churchill confined them to political and administrative duties and dealt directly with the chiefs of staff on strategy. Lord Reith commented disapprovingly: 'The three service ministers are Sinclair, Eden and Alexander. This is obviously so that Churchill can ignore them more or less and deal direct with the chiefs of staff.'[12] In a sense it was a development of his structure at the Admiralty in 1914–15, in that the administration was separated from the conduct of the war, with Churchill playing a leading part in the latter.

WAR LEADER • 427

This could lead to confusion and resentment. Admiral Godfrey claimed that 'In originating these telegrams to naval, military and air Cs-in-C abroad, Mr Churchill rang the changes on Prime Minister, Minister of Defence, Chiefs of Staff and Admiralty so that the recipient was sometimes not sure if his own service chief agreed with the contents. ... Churchill must have known what he was doing and that a sense of loyalty and deference to a more senior officer's opinion ...would exact obedience to an order from the First Sea Lord and might provoke an argument if it originated from the Prime Minister.'[13]

Hastings Ismay was a displaced cavalryman and polo player like Churchill and a star student at the Staff College in 1923. He joined the staff at the CID and learned his way round Whitehall. Churchill came to know him well when he was charged with co-ordinating defence early in 1940 and he transferred him to the Ministry as his chief of staff. In August 1940 he ordered Ismay: 'All important naval, air and military telegrams should come to the Defence Office immediately. They should be sifted by your staff, and anything of interest or importance marked to me.'[14] At the end of September he began to receive the decoded 'Enigma' messages which were marked 'Only to be opened by the Prime Minister in Person.'[15] Leslie Hollis was a Royal Marine, Ismay's deputy and alter ego, who had served at Jutland and in the plans division of the Admiralty before joining the secretariat of the CID. Ian Jacob was the son of a field marshal, and an engineer officer who had hardly ever commanded troops but served in many staff posts and inevitably, the CID. These three provided Churchill with sound professional advice for the rest of the war.

Churchill had close contact with the chiefs of staff of all three services, meeting them collectively almost daily. At the start of the war the Chief of the Imperial General Staff was General Sir Edmund Ironside, a huge 60-year-old Scot and one of the army's most thoughtful officers. When appointed he had no experience in the political affairs of Whitehall. He did not do well in dealing with the Norwegian and French campaigns. On 25 May, as Dunkirk was being evacuated, he saw that the post of commander-in-chief home forces was likely to be the centre of the army's next battle. It was 'An honour to me and a new and most important job, one more to my liking than C.I.G.S. in every way.'[16] His successor as CIGS was Sir John Dill, who had the manner of a perfect English gentlemen though he had been brought up in Northern Ireland. He was 'lamb-like, a mild-looking scholarly old fellow ... Slow moving, looks every year of his age (59).'[17] He had been a very efficient staff officer and a lecturer but had seen very little regimental service. He was embarrassed at Chequers in July 1940 when it was pointed out that his figures for the issue of equipment to divisions did not match the reality.[18] His health was slowly declining, perhaps because of aplastic anaemia. He was not good at dealing with Churchill's quick brain and often thought of the perfect reply when it was too late. Churchill called him 'Dilly-Dally'; Dill himself was said to be 'very fed up with Churchill' by the end of November.[19]

He was replaced by General Sir Alan Brooke, who distinguished himself in the French campaign, as recognised by Churchill: 'His record stood high. Not only had he fought the decisive flank-battle near Ypres during the retirement to Dunkirk, but he had acquitted himself with singular firmness and dexterity, in circumstances of unimaginable difficulty and confusion, when in command of the new forces we had sent to France during the first three weeks of June.'[20] On his return he was put in command of the Southern District and Churchill was impressed with him during a visit in mid-July. He was appointed commander-in-chief of the home forces two days later in place of Ironside. Brooke was highly efficient: '... without question the dominating personality, very shrewd, decisive, expresses himself well in a high strong voice'.[21] His diaries show a far more sensitive and self-doubting man, finding relief in his family and in bird-watching. He was not optimistic on his appointment as CIGS: 'If it was peace time I should love to try it, but in war the responsibility is almost overwhelming. The consequences of failures and mistakes are a nightmare to think about.'[22] He remained formidable in the role, often critical of Churchill and making acerbic remarks on him in his diaries, but he was an essential feature in the running of the war.

Churchill retained Pound as First Sea Lord, even when the admiral's health began to decline and he was increasingly seen sleeping during COS meetings and only waking when the navy was mentioned – which arguably undermined the purpose of making the three chiefs jointly responsible for operations. It is something of a mystery why Churchill kept him on even after the disaster of Convoy PQ 17. Perhaps he liked a familiar face and a pliant personality, perhaps he felt that things were going well enough on the whole. But it was not simply that Churchill needed 'yes men' around him; he had already appointed the outspoken Brooke as CIGS. Pound died in October 1943. Churchill had apparently dreamed of appointing Lord Louis Mountbatten to the post, though the promotion of one so young and junior would be unthinkable in naval circles.[23] Then he turned to Admiral Sir Bruce Fraser, the commander-in-chief of the Home Fleet, but he declined as he knew that Sir Andrew Cunningham had a far better claim. Cunningham had fought a glorious campaign in the Mediterranean (though he had a tendency to treat the naval war as separate from the land, and to underestimate air power). He went to Washington as head of the Admiralty delegation, then returned to the Mediterranean to command the landings in North Africa. He had the strength of character to stand up to Churchill, but by this time most of the key decisions had been made, and both men were approaching exhaustion.

Sir Cyril Newall was a surprise appointment as Chief of Air Staff in 1937. He had learned to fly in the army in 1911 but preferred ground administration to leadership in the air. He assisted the development of the Hurricane and Spitfire fighters, but he knew very little about modern tactics. He had no charisma, preferring to stay in his office in the Air Ministry and retreating to an underground shelter at night. In October 1940 he was replaced by Sir Charles 'Peter' Portal, one of the more intellectual air marshals, having studied law before going to the Western Front. He was a major in command of a squadron by 1917 at the age of 24, and he flew more than 900 operational missions. In peacetime as Air Member for Personnel he oversaw the great expansion programme. He became head of Bomber Command a week before the invasion of Norway and set more realistic targets for the offensive, while planning better navigation and the use of radio aids. Churchill was impressed with his efficiency and promoted him to replace the inadequate Newall. Portal too rarely visited air stations, but he had great administrative competence and force of personality. He was an austere man and, according to Colville, 'quiet, unforthcoming and not easy to converse with, he was shrewd in his judgement and seldom averse to risk and adventure'.[24] But he was typical of the air force of his day in that he favoured the bombing offensive above all else.

In November 1940 it was reported that 'The COS, at any rate, are quite subservient and wholly engaged in ways and means.'[25] But Churchill did not normally override the chiefs of staff. According to the not unbiased opinion of Keyes (quoting Lloyd George), '"The iron of Gallipoli entered his soul" and since [Fisher] walked out and broke him, he has feared to challenge his professional advisers.'[26] Captain Basil Liddell Hart went further: 'It is astonishing to find how often he failed to get his views accepted by the chiefs of staff, even when his views were most clearly right' and he had 'a deference to officialdom, that ran counter to the popular picture of his dominating personality'.[27] But both of these were resentful outsiders, and the situation looked very different to Brooke, the most articulate and by far the most revealing of the wartime chiefs of staff: 'Winston never had the slightest doubt that he had inherited all the military genius from his great ancestor Marlborough.'[28]

★

Churchill continued to use the Upper War Room in Admiralty House even after he moved into Downing Street, as the two buildings were adjacent. According to Pim, 'the scope of the upper war room was greatly widened to cover military and air operations as well'. Pim saw the First Lord A. V. Alexander each morning at 8 before going to Downing Street to report to Churchill on current events 'no longer confined now to naval matters but embracing also all the latest War Office, Air Ministry and Ministry of Home Security news, the latter mostly about air raid damage'. Meetings were often held in the Upper War Room, 'usually when the subject was a naval one and these were attended by the chiefs of the services'.

Churchill even took the War Room on his travels, with Pim setting up a simplified version in the ship he was travelling in, or the house where he was staying. The writer H. V. Morton was impressed with it on the *Prince of Wales* during the voyage to meet Roosevelt in August 1941:

> They had taken over an office in the ship for the purpose. An enormous map of the Atlantic Ocean occupied one wall. It was lit by strip lights. The opposite wall bore large maps of the Russian front. The officers in charge were busily engaged all day in filing war cables and marking up the maps to correspond with them. ... Most impressive to see were the great convoys crossing the Atlantic, sixty or seventy little red ships escorted by grey ships lying in a wide space of open water.[29]

According to Churchill, the conference at Yalta in 1945 was 'the zenith of the Map Room's career' when Roosevelt and Stalin came in for half an hour to discuss world strategy.[30]

In October 1943 Pim set up another war room in the underground Cabinet War Rooms, known as the No 10 Annexe, following the example of Roosevelt who had such a room in the White House: '... admission to this room was strictly limited and it was therefore possible to show the very fullest and most secret particulars. ... Military news was looked after by the colonels from the Upper War Room and air information was brought down from the Air Ministry War Room by Section Officer Lyttleton and put on our large scale maps. It was thus possible to follow the progress of long distance raids and to know the results as soon as they became available.' It was known as the Defence Map Room by the Prime Minister's orders. It came in useful when Churchill was exhausted after his illness in Morocco: 'Probably to avoid fatigue the Defence Map Room which was situated but a few paces from his bedroom and study, was used more frequently for meetings especially in the evenings. Thus the Prime Minister avoided having to go across to Downing Street.'[31]

★

One of the most important jobs of the wartime prime minister was to allocate resources between the three services and industry. As Ismay put it, 'Churchill, as Prime Minister and Minister of Defence, bore the primary responsibility for ensuring that all available resources in shipping, man-power, equipment, oil, and the rest were apportioned between the home front and the various theatres of war, in the best interests of the war effort as a whole ...'.[32] The limiting factor was not money. The peacetime system of control which Churchill had applied strictly in the 1920s was abandoned and as First Lord Churchill told the House of Commons in 1940: 'It will not be necessary to consult the Treasury merely because a proposed service may involve an excess on the vote or subhead concerned' – a freedom which also applied to the other services in wartime. Instead it was manpower, which term included women joining the ATS, WRNS and WAAF and working in factories. Again his experience made him sceptical of his former department, and he commented in August 1942: 'The Admiralty always want not only to win the game, but to go to bed with the ace.'[33]

The services each put forward their own demands for men. More than 96,000 joined the RAF from the declaration of war to the end of 1939, and more than 276,000 in 1940. It was not hard to attract volunteers and many joined early to avoid conscription and have a better choice of service. As to conscripts, almost twice as many chose the RAF as the navy during most of 1940, rising to three times by the end of the year.[34] The RAF was largely able to pick and choose its men, and most of them were highly motivated.

The demands of the navy were usually met for the first three years of the war. In September 1940 it wanted to recruit 145,755 men and 13,000 women up to the end of 1941, at an average of nearly 10,000 entrants per month.[35] In mid-1941 it was allowed 110,000 men and 11,000 women recruits until June 1942, almost the same rate of increase.[36] The army on the other hand was subjected to a ceiling on Churchill's orders – originally 2,195,000 men in February 1941, increased to 2,374,800 in 1942.[37] In September 1941 Churchill demanded an increase in the bomber programme, and 850,000 more workers were needed to produce them. He was sceptical about introducing conscription for the women's services in December 1941, but it could also be used to compel them to work as civilians in the defence industries, including aircraft manufacture, so many of them were directed that way.

By May 1942 the manpower resources of the country were almost exhausted. Ernest Bevin, the Minister of Labour, wrote: 'we have now deployed our main forces and drawn heavily upon the Reserves'. Use of resources had already gone further than it had in 1918, after four years of war.[38] In November that year the armed forces asked for 1,600,000 more men and women for the following year, while industry needed more than a million – but only 1,600,000 were available for all the country's needs. Sir John Anderson wrote: 'A gap of this magnitude cannot be closed by the familiar process of trimming the demands and stretching the supply.'[39] The danger of imminent invasion had ended with the German attack on Russia in June 1941 and Churchill believed that 'the greatest danger we now face is the U-boat peril'. He wanted to give priority to replacing lost merchant shipping, but Alexander persuaded him that it was better to maintain warship building to protect the merchantmen. The navy was given 85 per cent of the resources it wanted, while the army and RAF demands were cut by half.[40] This pleased the Admiralty: 'The most important event of the year in this connection is the decision of the Cabinet to allow a largely increased number of recruits from the depleted manpower resources of the country. This will involve a record entry, and will impose a severe strain on our resources for training and accommodation.'[41] But Churchill warned for the future: 'The manpower and raw materials shortage makes it absolutely imperative to ensure that the requirements of the Service Departments are not in excess of needs.'[42]

Nineteen forty-four was expected to be the crucial year of the war, when northern Europe would be invaded. In October 1943 the Admiralty put in a huge demand for 247,000 men and 41,500 women – 104,000 for new ships coming into service as the naval building programme began to bear fruit, 10,000 more for landing craft for the invasion, and 37,000 for the expansion of the Fleet Air Arm, mainly to fight the Japanese. Wastage was anticipated at 53,000 men and nearly 15,000 new officers were needed.[43] Churchill was beginning to fear that a long-drawn-out conflict would exhaust the nation and wrote in November:

> The problem is no longer one of closing a gap between supply and requirements. Our manpower is now fully mobilised for the war effort. We cannot add to the total; on the contrary, it is already dwindling. All we can do is to make within that total such changes as the strategy of the war demands. If we had to carry on the war against Germany and Japan for several more years, the scale of our war effort in terms of manpower would have to decrease progressively.[44]

It was assumed that Germany would be defeated by the end of 1944, after which the British naval effort would build up to fight Japan. But resources were short and large-scale British participation in the Pacific was gradually cut down. Maximum effort would still be needed for the invasion of Europe but, as Churchill pointed out, the other demands on the navy were reducing.

> The question arises, why does the Admiralty require more men in 1944 than in 1943, observing that the new facts are:
> (a) The decisive defeat of the U-boats, largely through the air assistance
> (b) The surrender of the Italian Fleet
> (c) The accession of the *Richelieu* and many French units to active service
> (d) The establishment by the United States of two-to-one strength over the Japanese in the Pacific
> (e) The immobilisation for a good many months to come of the *Tirpitz*, the only hostile capital ship in the western world (unless the new German carrier is ready)[45]

The navy's allocation was drastically reduced to 40,000 men. The Admiralty protested that it would need 67,200 even with minimum effort in the Pacific. This would still involve cuts – half a dozen battleships, one old aircraft carrier, 13 cruisers and 20 destroyers would have to be reduced to the reserve, or to training ships. There would be no resources to man seven light fleet aircraft carriers which were completed for the war against Japan.[46]

According to Ismay, 'He never ceased to cry out against the inordinate "tail" which modern armies required. "When I was a soldier," he would say, "infantry used to walk and cavalry used to ride. But now the infantry require motor-cars, and even the tanks have horse-boxes to take them to battle."'[47] In 1944 Churchill complained: 'probably not one in four or five men who wear the King's uniform even hear a bullet whistle, or are likely to hear one. The vast majority run no more risk than the civil population of southern England.'[48] He had a particular down on the RAF Regiment, founded in 1941 to defend airfields such as the attack on Maleme in Crete, but generally composed of older and less fit men. He objected to their use of the very rank titles he had established: 'Is it not very absurd that the officers of this ground service should be called pilot officers, flight-lieutenants, etc., when they have never flown and are never going to fly?'[49] In 1944 he demanded: 'The largest possible block of the RAF Regiment should be scraped off the airfields and incorporated in the general pool of infantry of the army.'[50]

★

Churchill the Prime Minister was as hands-on as he had been in the previous war, making regular visits to factories, training bases and even operational areas. The first was to the coast defences only nine days after the cancellation of his final trip to France, and he thanked General Ironside for enabling him 'to obtain a comprehensive general view of the coastal measures of all three services'. Nineteen forty-one was his busiest year in that respect, uninterrupted by major illness and with only two overseas visits. The first of his 25 United Kingdom visits to military sites was to the gunnery range at Shoeburyness in Kent on 3 January for a demonstration of the '3-inch land service projector', a variation on his unrotated projectile. In mid-January, after visiting Scapa Flow, he went to Glasgow to see the Rescue and Demolition Depot and a first aid post of the Civil Defence Services. On his fourth trip early in February he inspected his old regiment the Royal Scots Fusiliers in Essex. In the middle of the month he visited the 2nd Armoured Brigade and saw 'cruiser tanks of an armoured brigade manoeuvring across open, hilly country and supported by the motor battalion which forms part of the brigade and by the 25-pounder guns of the Royal Horse Artillery'. In April after a visit to Czech troops at Leamington, the exiled President Beneš 'expatiated on the Prime Minister's grasp of the fundamentals of this war. Above all, he praised his power of inspiring others, his constancy to his ideals, and his prescience.' His support during the Munich Crisis was not forgotten, and 'It would be difficult to exaggerate the implicit trust which every Czechoslovak patriot places in the British Prime Minister whose name today is honoured in the remotest villages of the protectorate and of Slovenia.' Churchill saw further demonstrations of his unrotated projectile twice at Weybourne. In September he saw the new Crusader tanks in the Nuffield Works at Cowley, Oxford. In November he was in Liverpool to see Western Approaches Headquarters, followed by a visit to the aircraft carrier *Indomitable* which his wife had launched a year earlier. He was introduced to the senior officers, the arrester gear and catapult were demonstrated to him, and he was shown the recreation space and soda fountain before he and his wife were given drinks in the wardroom.[51]

On one occasion he was delighted when a soldier in the rear rank remarked 'He's a pugnacious looking b...' during an inspection.[52] But not everyone was pleased to see him, a former miner in the crew of the battleship *Ramillies* perhaps remembered the general strike and said 'in a voice full of venom', 'There goes the bastard, back to his bloody brandy.'[53] He continually questioned the use and issue of resources. When a Young Soldiers Battalion was sent to Chartwell to guard him during a visit in May 1942, he asked about its equipment and found 'They were short of Bren Gun Carriers and very short of Brens' and that two different marks of rifle were being used.[54]

The trips were meticulously organised by his naval aide Commander Thompson. Allied government officials and officers were often included, along with Commonwealth prime ministers. They covered all three services, though he visited the RAF less than the others. Factory visits might have varied results. The management of Hepworth and Grandage of Bradford, manufacturers of pistons, piston rings, gudgeon pins and liners, were so delighted that they commissioned a special booklet. The shop stewards of the De Havilland aircraft works, on the other hand, presented the Prime Minister with a petition demanding the opening of the second front, and urging him to get rid of 'certain reactionary pro-Fascist people in high places who want to make a deal with Hitler'. The press was often annoyed about not being invited, but there were security considerations which prevented that. Local mayors were equally indignant, but visits could not be announced in advance.

Churchill usually travelled long and medium distances by train, but the Southern Railway quibbled about the cost of tickets, while the London, Midland and Scottish provided a private train for use in his northern visits. This was a mobile hotel, office and communications centre. Rather than sleep in a hotel which would need guarding, Churchill often spent the night in a railway siding and the train moved into a tunnel if an air raid threatened. A special communication system which could be hooked up to a telephone line when the train was stationary allowed instant communication with London. The MP and diarist 'Chips' Channon wrote during one trip: 'How luxuriously the PM lives, a most lavish lunch and a grand train.'[55]

Churchill still hankered to come under fire, 'to hear the whistle of bullets all round' as he had done more than 40 years ago, and he was not satisfied with taking risks by exposing himself during air raids. He planned to be on board the cruiser *Belfast* for the Normandy landings. Ismay was horrified, 'not so much at the risk involved, but at the prospect of the Prime Minister being cut off from communication with the outside world when critical and immediate decisions might have to be taken'. Eventually he was dissuaded by a letter from the King: 'I ask you ... not to let your personal wishes ... lead you to depart from your own high standard of duty to the State.'[56] However he did manage to get ashore on the Normandy beaches on D-Day plus six. In March 1945 he took an opportunity to urinate on the Siegfried line, the famous German defence, and on a visit later in the month he was warned that 'there are snipers in front of you, they are shelling both sides of the bridge, and now they have started shelling the road behind you'. According to Brooke, 'the look on Winston's face was just like that of a small boy being called away from his sandcastles on the beach by his nurse!'[57]

CHAPTER 35

War on Land

The army that Churchill had under him in 1940 was superficially less familiar than the other services. That summer it was still reeling from the effects of Dunkirk as well as pre-war reforms. From 1937 temporary officers were to be recruited from men who had served for some time in the ranks. Leslie Hore-Belisha, the Secretary for War, described the new meritocratic force:

> In this Army the star is within every private soldier's reach. No one, however humble or exalted his birth, need be afraid that his military virtues will remain unrecognised. More important, no one, who wished to serve in the Army need consider his status minimised by starting on the bottom rung of the ladder.[1]

But this did not take account of the existing officers mainly from upper middle and upper class backgrounds, or faults in the selection process which favoured men from these backgrounds for promotion, for the regular army was still more class-bound than almost any other part of British society. According to the leading historian of the desert war:

> Although the army of a twentieth century social democracy and a first-class industrial power, it was nevertheless spiritually a peasant levy led by the gentry and aristocracy. ... Few poor men of great ability chose the army as a rewarding outlet for their talents – pay for all ranks was less than an income. ... Men of great ability did of course make their careers in the army, but because it was a tradition in their caste and because they enjoyed private means. Therefore in a true sense most regular officers of the British army were amateurs as well as gentlemen.[2]

There were just over a million and a half soldiers in the United Kingdom in July 1940, not counting women and Commonwealth troops, but they were disorganised and demoralised by their recent experiences. When General Brooke took over the Southern Command in July, he found 'Untrained men, no arms, no transport, and no equipment. And yet there are masses of men in uniform in this country but they are mostly untrained, why I cannot think after 10 months of war.'[3]

The glorious red and dark-blue tunics of Churchill's youth had been put aside in wartime to be replaced by uncompromisingly functional 'battledress', based on a mechanic's overall. Buttons were hidden and needed no polishing and it was far less attractive than the 'service dress' of the last war. Only the colour, khaki, was familiar to Churchill as it had been adopted in India towards the end of the previous century. It was claimed that 'Men can look smart in battle dress if it is worn correctly and the necessary trouble is taken', but the same source had to admit that 'a slovenly man can look like a tramp'.[4] A character in the film *The Way Ahead* of 1943 claimed that it made him feel like a convict.

According to Hastings Ismay, Churchill 'venerated tradition but hated convention'.[5] The regimental system of the infantry and cavalry was particularly venerated (though like many British traditions it dated from only the last quarter of the nineteenth century). This was reflected in Churchill's interest in his old regiment, the 4th Hussars. In October 1941 it had recently been evacuated from Greece after having more than 400 officers and men taken prisoner and the loss of all its tanks. As it gradually rebuilt its strength in Egypt, one officer at least was heartened by the news that Churchill had been appointed their colonel: 'Hope, pride and self-confidence could be seen in the bearing of all ranks and was heard in their voices. The regiment was not forgotten. It would be supported and succoured by the great man to whom all the world was looking.' He was deeply disturbed in July 1944 to find that the Oxfordshire Hussars, in which he was also a colonel, was being used for drafts for the 21st Army Group which meant 'that it can never serve as a fighting unit, and will disappear in all but name'.[6]

The pre-war army reforms allowed only essential badges indicating rank and trade. The War Office relented in September 1940 and allowed 'arm of service' stripes across the upper sleeve, scarlet for infantry, yellow for the

RASC and blue for the Royal Engineers.[7] Regimental distinctions were
still banned, mainly for security reasons but perhaps also because Whitehall
thought a more homogeneous army would be easier to administer. With
troops abroad, it would be far simpler if men could be transferred from
one regiment to another to fill vacancies. Churchill accepted this reluctantly, writing in 1942: 'Of course in the stress of world war it may be
necessary to post men to units different from those which they joined
or from those which represent the part of the country from which they
come. This process must be kept to a minimum.' He wanted 'to invest
all combatant units with a clear sense of individual characteristics and
distinction'. Regimental badges, in the form of shoulder 'flashes' with the
regiment's name, were creeping back, largely paid for out of regimental
funds. In 1942 the Army Council issued an order forbidding them with
the conclusion: 'This decision is final and no further applications will
be submitted.' Churchill found out about it during an inspection of the
53rd Division on 20 November 1942 and was furious about the potential
'stripping off of the badges'. He ordered a reversal of the policy.

The War Office objected that the issue was 'one of discipline', that
a strongly worded Army Council Instruction could not be withdrawn
without loss of face. Churchill replied that 'The War Office frequently
make mistakes which entail alterations of policy.' Furthermore it should
not have been passed by the military members alone, it was 'exactly one
of those cases which affect morale and nationalist and territorial feelings,
in which the parliamentary ministers should have been consulted'. He
suggested that the adjutant-general, in charge of army personnel, was
an artillery officer who did not understand these things. He did not
mention that his chief, Sir Alan Brooke, was also an artilleryman. The
matter caused Churchill to dictate several long memoranda, and write at
least one letter by hand. He offered the War Minister a special meeting
of the Cabinet to consider the matter, but the order was withdrawn and
all ranks below full colonel were to wear regimental distinctions on their
shoulders as soon as they could be produced.[8]

★

In view of this personal role in its early development and in the conversion of cavalry regiments, followed by the dramatic effect of German

machines in the Fall of France, it is not surprising that Churchill took a personal interest in the tank. He had to admit, however, that the German success came as a surprise and wrote later: 'Not having had access to official information for so many years, I did not comprehend the violence of the revolution effected since the last war by the incursion of as mass of fast-moving armour. I knew about it, but it had not altered my inward convictions as it should have done.'[9] This puzzled Captain Basil Liddell Hart, one of the prophets of armoured warfare, who wrote that Churchill 'had often heard, and also read, the views of Fuller and myself about the potentialities of mechanized warfare'.[10]

Since nearly all of the army's heavy equipment was left behind with the withdrawal from Dunkirk, there were only about a hundred modern tanks in Britain in June 1940. Churchill called a meeting on 11 June to consider the tank production programme: 'those under production at the time were of a type which had proved in battle in France to be too weak to stand up to the German tank guns'. The manufacture of more tanks was a priority and he ordered 500 or 600 more in addition to current programmes. But tanks were not as urgent as aircraft. In August he told Beaverbrook: 'If it came to a choice between hampering air production or tank production, I would sacrifice the tank.'[11] In October 1940 he was confident enough about the situation at home to order that 'the armoured fighting vehicles of the 2nd Armoured Division might now be withdrawn to be prepared for operating in the Middle East',[12] beginning a row with the Admiralty about whether the convoy carrying them should pass through the Mediterranean or go round the Cape of Good Hope, putting them out of service for weeks.

The next question was the types and quality of tanks. In July he told the Defence Committee that 'the choice which had to be made was not between a good tank and a better one, but between a fairly good tank and no tank at all'.[13] Light tanks were obsolete except for a type that was being developed for transport by air, for use in difficult country and on combined operations. One cruiser tank, the Covenanter, which appeared in the summer of 1940, was so unreliable that it never saw active service. The Crusader was a little better and saw action in the desert war from the middle of 1941. The Cromwell was reasonably reliable and was fast, but crews tended to prefer the American Grant and later the Sherman. The specification for a new type of infantry tank, the A22, was considered at a meeting on 20 June 1940, and a month later 'the General Staff expressed themselves entirely in favour of the project. Work proceeded with the utmost enthusiasm.' At a meeting in February 1941, 'The Prime Minister said that priority in delivery to the troops, and in provision of all kinds of weapons and equipment, should be accorded to the A22, in view of its superiority over all other models.'[14] But this would lead to trouble which attracted notice in the House of Commons. There were many teething troubles before the tank was fully ready.

In the spring of 1941 Churchill was concerned enough about tanks to bring together various interested parties: 'I am particularly anxious that all officers attending the meeting should be encouraged to send in their suggestions as to the points which should be discussed, and to express their individual views with complete freedom. I contemplate in fact a "Tank Parliament".'[15] At the first meeting on 5 May he announced: 'Reviewing the progress of events since the last war, and the experiences of the present day, when we saw large armies paralysed by comparatively small forces of armoured fighting vehicles, it was evident that our tank programme was a matter of the greatest importance.' He wanted to develop the A22 as the standard tank for 1941, but was aware that it might be obsolete by 1943. He wanted to build up a force of 25 armoured divisions instead of the 15 already planned. Tank production had been set aside due to the need to concentrate resources on the aircraft industry, and the Secretary for War proposed that 'a similar effort should now be directed towards the production of tanks'. There was discussion on the best form of organisation, whether in brigade groups or in larger divisions. In practice flexibility would prove the key to success, according to one officer: 'It was not until our third battle in Normandy that we got it right, and that was an organisation of complete flexibility. At the shortest notice the organisation could be altered from an armoured brigade and an infantry brigade to two mixed brigades, each of two armoured regiments, and two infantry battalions and artillery as required.'[16] General Brooke found it 'a useful meeting, as it brought those responsible for the production of tanks in close contact with those responsible for commanding them in action'. He pressed for more attention to spare parts, but 'Winston always disliked the idea of the provision of spares, everything in the front window'.[17] The Tank Parliament held six more meetings over the next few months, considering such matters as army-air co-operation, the transport of tanks by air, the development of tank and anti-tank weapons, production schedules, and Anglo-American co-operation. The last recorded one was on 23 July when Churchill pointed out that 'it was evident we should require even larger guns for our tanks in late 1942 and 1943. This would mean a heavier tank.' Though the meetings allowed strong characters like Brooke and Hobart to express their views forcefully, there was little consensus and the idea seems to have been dropped.

Originally tanks were known by mark and model numbers, but as always Churchill preferred names, writing in June 1941: '... it would be far better to give names to the various marks of tank. These ... would avoid the confusing titles by marks and numbers. ... it is evident that a real need for it exists, because the [Infantry] Tank, Mark I is widely known as the Matilda, and one of the other infantry tanks is called the Valentine.' And, as he commented coyly, 'A 22 has an alias, I think'[18] – it was already known informally as the Churchill. It was never clear whether that was a reference to the Prime Minister himself or his distinguished ancestor, but in either case Churchill took a special interest in its service; in September 1942 he asked for reports on them from the divisions to which they had been issued: 'Do not let it be known that the report is for me, as I simply want to know how the tank is viewed by the troops.' Comments from the 21st and 25th Tank Brigades suggested that it was 'definitely a superior type of fighting vehicle' to the Matilda and Valentine, on account of its better armament and armour, better obstacle performance, greater radius of action and ammunition capacity and more space for the crew.[19] Though the infantry tank was not suitable for war in the desert, which was often fast-moving, Churchill ordered a few to be sent to North Africa, from where it was reported: 'A lot of trouble has been experienced and the amount of sand thrown up which lodges in the interior of the tank is such that ... this model is unlikely to be entirely successful in that part of the world.'[20] Eventually it proved

444 • CHURCHILL: WARRIOR

an effective weapon in the European campaign, though by the time it landed in Normandy it was on the verge of obsolescence and many were used for support roles as ARVEs (assault vehicles Royal Engineers).[21]

One of the core problems of British tank design was the type of gun to be fitted, which was barely mentioned in the Tank Parliament. Perhaps it was because, as an Army Training Memorandum of January 1944 put it, 'There had been ... a tendency in the past to look upon the crushing power of the tank, rather than its fire power, as its chief weapon.'[22] As early as January 1940 Churchill had suggested using anti-aircraft guns in the anti-tank role, as the Germans did very effectively with the 88mm, but the suggestion 'had been considered before but rejected'.[23] The 2-pounder was the main gun available early in the war, and was ordered to be fitted to the early Churchills. The 6-pounder had been developed just before the war without the consent of the General Staff, who declared 'there was no need for the gun' and only accepted it in February 1941.[24] It was intended as the main armament for the Churchill as soon as it was available. On April 1942 the Prime Minister had to consider whether to upgrade existing 2-pounder Churchills but concluded that 'the argument for leaving the 1185 unimproved and making the best use of them and their 2-pounder guns, and going ahead full speed on the new type, seems overwhelming'.[25] After the successful use of American Sherman tanks armed with 75mm guns in the Battle of Alamein, the War Office decided to adopt it as standard for future British tanks. This was questioned in the cabinet in April and May 1943 with Lindemann (by then Lord Cherwell) advocating the 95mm howitzer and the Director of Artillery a flat-trajectory weapon such as the 17-pounder of 76.2mm. Churchill decided that 30 per cent of British tanks should mount the Sherman type gun, now classified as the 77mm; 20 per cent should have the 95mm howitzer, and the remaining 50 per cent should stay with the existing 6-pounder or 57mm until some of them could be converted or replaced.[26] But the British did not produce a truly successful tank to match the later Panzer models and the Russian T34 until the Centurion entered service just as the war ended.

With the sidelining of J. F. C. Fuller, the leader of Brooke's 'extremists of the Tank Corps' was Major-General Percy Hobart, who had approached Churchill back in 1936 and warned him 'of the terrible neglect to make the tanks and even decide upon the models'.[27] He had been retired in March 1940 before Churchill became Prime Minister and served as a corporal in the Home Guard until Churchill called him to Chequers in October. To John Colville he was 'an erratic genius' and therefore likely to appeal to the Prime Minister.[28] Churchill went further when he wrote to Dill: 'The catalogue of General Hobart's qualities and defects ... might almost exactly have been attributed to most of the great commanders in British history. ... Cromwell, Wolfe, Clive, Gordon and in a different sphere Lawrence, all had very close resemblance to the characteristics assembled in para 2.'[29] But Hobart's idea of an independent tank army, with himself as chief of staff on a level with Brooke, Portal and Pound, was rejected and he found a role as commander of the 79th Armoured Division developing specialist armoured vehicles to destroy fortifications and surmount obstacles in an assault. These were often based on the Churchill tank and included the Crocodile with a flame thrower, the AVRE or Assault Vehicle Royal Engineers, with a large, low velocity gun for destroying bunkers, the Bobbin for laying a track, as well as assault bridges, 'swimming' tanks for beach landing and beach armoured recovery vehicles. All would play a part in the Normandy invasion, some more effectively than others.

★

For four years between the Fall of France and the invasion of Normandy, the only place where British soldiers were in long-term contact with the enemy was in North Africa and the Mediterranean. In some ways it was an ideal war, with wide spaces for much of the region, a small population and the possibility of support by sea. There is a suspicion that in an ideal world Churchill would have liked to take command himself, and certainly he took a great interest in it, sending numerous messages which often annoyed the commanders on the spot. Ismay advised General Auchinleck after his appointment: '[Churchill] made a practice of bombarding commanders with telegrams on every kind of topic, many of which might seem irrelevant and superfluous. I begged Auchinleck not to allow himself to be irritated by these never-ending

446 • CHURCHILL: WARRIOR

messages, but to remember that Churchill, as Prime Minister and Minister of Defence, bore the primary responsibility for ensuring that all available resources ... were apportioned ... in the best interests of the war effort as a whole. Was it not reasonable that he should wish to know exactly how all these resources were being used before deciding the allotment to be given to this or that theatre?'[30]

When Italy opened the campaign by declaring war in June 1940, the commander-in-chief in the Middle East was General Archibald Wavell, another intellectual soldier. He had wide responsibilities including Sudan, Somaliland and Palestine, but the main focus was in North Africa, where troops under General Richard O'Connor had a spectacular advance into Libya, taking 125,000 Italian prisoners. It was largely political consid-erations which caused Churchill to order part of the Middle East army to go to the relief of Greece in 1941, which does not in itself invalidate the decision. As early as November 1940 he told the War Cabinet: 'If Greece was overwhelmed, it would be said that in spite of our guarantee we had allowed one more small ally to be swallowed up.'[31] Later he was swayed by a telegram from Anthony Eden in Cairo who claimed that 'Collapse of Greece without further effort on our part to save her by intervention on land ... would be the greatest calamity' and would also lead to the loss of Yugoslavia. 'No doubt our prestige will suffer if we are ignominiously ejected, but in any event to have fought and suffered in Greece would be less damaging than to have left Greece to her fate.' Always mindful of American opinion, Churchill told Roosevelt: 'we have felt it our duty to stand by the Greeks. ... We are therefore sending the greater part of the Army of the Nile to Greece, and are reinforcing to the utmost possible in the air.'[32] But they were indeed 'ignominiously ejected' from Greece and then from Crete, though that was a pyrrhic victory for the Germans. The navy's prestige was boosted by a second Dunkirk in Crete while that of the army suffered. British forces were overstretched by land, sea and air, while German units, far more formidable than the demoralized, badly led and ill-equipped Italians, landed in North Africa. If that was not enough they were led by Lieutenant-General Erwin Rommel, a military genius on the level of Churchill's heroes Marlborough and Napoleon. A few weeks later the

British lost their most effective field commander when O'Connor was captured by a German patrol.

Mostly the desert generals were able to put off Churchill's orders for premature attack, but Wavell gave way with Operation Battleaxe, an attack on Halfaya, in June 1940. The British forces were badly organised, intelligence was weak and the newly arrived tanks had constant mechanical troubles. The Germans used their 88mm gun, conceived as an anti-aircraft weapon but now used in an anti-tank role, with devastating effect. Churchill decided to replace Wavell. Churchill had not had much regard for Claude Auchinleck after his participation in the Norway campaign, until he showed determination and skill in putting down a rebellion in Iraq while he was commander-in-chief in India. In June 1941 Churchill had him change places with Wavell, but after taking up the post in Egypt Auchinleck flatly refused to begin an early offensive. He and Churchill shared some interests. The general referred to Churchill's 'stored knowledge of the history of war, and of war itself' but warned him against believing too rigidly: 'These are no new lessons − they are as old as time itself.' On his side Churchill drafted a plan for attack in the desert based on Napoleon's tactics at Austerlitz, though it is not clear if he sent it.[33] Auchinleck scored an impressive victory in advancing again into Cyrenaica late in 1941, rallying the troops by flying up to the front after a near disaster. He refused to fly to London to put the case against further attack to the War Cabinet but was ordered to begin by 1 June. However Rommel began his attack before that, driving the British and Commonwealth troops back to Egypt. Auchinleck's greatest fault was perhaps in his judgement of character, and he allowed the inexperienced General Ritchie to take command in the field. Churchill was visiting Roosevelt in June 1942: 'When ... I went into the President's room, I was greatly shocked to be confronted with a report that Tobruk had fallen. I found the news difficult to believe, but a few minutes later my own telegram, forwarded from London, arrived.'[34] Auchinleck's days were numbered. He organized a successful defence at Alam el Halfa, 'the first Battle of Alamein', and prevented Rommel advancing to Alexandria, but that did not exonerate him in Churchill's eyes. None of the generals Churchill replaced was a bad commander, though perhaps lacking in the unbridled aggression that Churchill favoured.

During a visit to Cairo Churchill chose a new leader of the 8th Army, the main fighting force in the desert. Lieutenant-General William 'Strafer' Gott had risen from the command of a battalion at the beginning of the war to lead the 13th Corps, and all his promotions had been earned in battle. But his aircraft was shot down and he was killed on the way to Cairo, and Churchill turned to General Bernard Montgomery, a far less likeable man. 'If he is as disagreeable to those about him he is also disagreeable to the enemy,' he wrote to Clementine. As commander-in-chief in the Middle East, he appointed Harold Alexander. Montgomery, partly through a campaign of self-publicity, restored the morale and confidence of the 8th Army and began to receive new supplies, including American Grant and Sherman tanks, while Rommel was increasingly inhibited by lack of fuel as the Royal Navy and RAF cut his supply lines. Montgomery attacked at El Alamein on 23 October and by 4 November, after much rethinking of tactics, he had broken through. Rommel was in retreat, but there was much criticism of Montgomery's failure to pursue. Churchill famously managed expectations, proclaiming: 'It is not even the beginning of the end. But perhaps it is the end of the beginning.' But his later assessment was more sweeping. 'It in fact marked the turning of the "Hinge of Fate". It may almost be said, "Before Alamein we never had a victory. After Alamein we never had a defeat."'[35] With the landings in French North Africa, it became an Anglo-American campaign and General Eisenhower was put in overall command to eventually drive the enemy out of North Africa.

★

For all his interest and experience, Churchill did not tackle the basic flaws in the British army which would hinder its performance after it returned to northern Europe in 1944. Beside the long-standing problems with class and amateurism, there was a serious lack of initiative among junior officers and NCOs, who stuck rigidly to plans and were at a loss when changes had to be made. Churchill was not unaware of this. In October 1940 there was a discussion with Dill and others about 'the British army and its lack of good officers' in which it was concluded: 'The present trouble was that officers were admirably versed in weapon training but had little stimulus to use their imagination and look at military problems with a broad view.'[36] The army's selection boards for finding junior officers were highly praised in the press as a step towards a more egalitarian army, but Churchill thought that 'the commanding officer of a battalion or tank unit is the best judge, and if he is not a good judge he is scarcely fit for his position'. He distrusted psychologists, who he maintained were 'capable of doing an immense amount of harm with what may easily degenerate into charlatanry'.[37] Though he had commented on the treatment of American officer cadets at West Point in 1895 and criticised the training of naval cadets in 1912–14, he never visited the Officer Cadet Training Units where young men were trained, according to some accounts, to become 'perfect private soldiers' rather than leaders and tacticians.[38]

There was still little true co-operation between infantry and tanks, and most problems were solved by heavy artillery. Churchill perhaps supported this practice in March 1942 when he asked: 'Surely the way to silence machine gun posts is to bring up some guns and silence them.'[39] An Army Training Memorandum of June 1944 described the problem under the heading 'Not the Universal Panacea' and went on: 'The use and power of massed artillery fire is now so well appreciated throughout the army that there is, perhaps, a tendency to use concentrations on all occasions, to the exclusion of accurate ranging and deliberate shoots by batteries, troops, and even single guns.'[40] Churchill paid great attention to the training of pilots and troops for amphibious warfare, but surprisingly little to the training of army units and officers. The problem went very deep; the flaw of the regimental system was that the different types of unit trained separately, and the results were often uneven. The infantry often included the men who were rejected for employment elsewhere; according to Major-General Utterson-Kelso they were 'the legitimate dumping ground for the lowest forms of military life'.[41]

The tanks were still divided between the Royal Tank Regiment proper and the ex-cavalrymen, who retained their old attitudes. There were reports of 'the Hussars charging into the Jerry tanks, sitting on top of their turrets more or less with their whips out' looking 'like the run-up to the first fence at a point-to-point'.[42] Early in 1942 Auchinleck had warned Churchill in one of his regular letters: 'closer and absolutely continuous association of the three arms ... cannot be avoided, however much precedent and tradition may say against it', though he tended to blame the tank officers for tending to 'segregate the armoured corps from the army, and to say that the handling of armoured formations is so technical and delicate a business that the ordinary commander cannot hope to cope with it'. But, he told Churchill, 'we were ... in common with many others, led astray by the idea that the tank was omnipotent' whereas co-operation was the key to the Germans' success.[43] Some lessons were learned, but reports from the fighting in the desert and in Italy were not circulated adequately among the troops. After they resumed the land war with the invasion of Normandy in June 1944, the British and Canadian forces took more than a month to capture Caen, which was one of the objectives for the first day. The conduct of British troops came in for much criticism. Leigh-Mallory, the air commander, claimed that the army's vision was bounded 'by the nearest hedge or stream'. One brigadier reported: 'We were always very aware of the doctrine, "Let metal do it rather than flesh." The morale of our troops depended on this.' And Liddell Hart commented: 'Time after time we were checked or even induced to withdraw by boldly handled packets of Germans of greatly inferior strength. But for our air superiority, which hampered the Germans at every turn, the results would have been much worse. Our forces seem to have had too little initiative in infiltration, and also too little determination ... that was particularly marked in the armoured formations.'[44]

By 1944 Churchill was becoming increasingly tired and he had less formal control over the armies in France than over a purely British army, especially since the Americans now provided three-quarters of the troops. His influence was lessened further after Eisenhower took personal command of land forces on 1 September, but Churchill continued to follow and try to influence progress for the remaining months of the European war. He and the British high command had little faith in Eisenhower's tactical skill. Montgomery tended to favour concentration of forces in a single advance and was supported by Churchill, who also wanted to push for his old stomping ground of Antwerp, as the allies were still dependent on the Arromanches Mulberry Harbour and distant Cherbourg for their supplies. Montgomery's next plan was a 'daring stroke, by far the greatest operation of its kind yet attempted', according to Churchill. The plan was to capture several crossings of the Rhine and its tributaries, but it was famously 'a bridge too far' and failed at Arnhem. Churchill concluded: 'Had we been more fortunate in the weather, which turned against us at critical moments and restricted our mastery in the air, it is probable we should have succeeded.'[45] But the failure meant a longer war in which British resources would be increasingly drained. When the Germans counter-attacked though the old area of the Ardennes and put the Americans on the back foot, Churchill claimed that 'Montgomery's comments and predictions beforehand have in every way been borne out'.[46] When the time came to cross the Rhine, Churchill was not concerned. He remembered his reading of Hamley's *Operations of War* at Sandhurst, in which Napoleon's retreat through the Champagne district in 1814 showed that 'a river running parallel to the line of advance is a much more dangerous feature than one which lies squarely athwart it' – though he admitted that air superiority was also very helpful in this case.[47] As the end neared for Nazi Germany with the Soviet and western allies' advances, he suggested that Montgomery should take Lübeck to prevent the Soviets entering Denmark.[48]

CHAPTER 36

War at Sea

Churchill was of course already familiar with the navy when he became Prime Minister. His four years at the Admiralty from 1911 to 1915 were a distant if happy memory, but he had just completed another eight months heading the service. On the surface it had changed less than the *others*. Its men continued to wear the dark blue uniforms based on Victorian patterns (though on active operations most sailors wore far more functional dress) and it still had grey-painted ships in the form of battleships, cruisers, destroyers, escort vessels, submarines and smaller craft. Only the aircraft carrier was a major new type since Churchill had left in 1915.

It was the spirit of the navy that had changed most since 1916, and it was in line with Churchill's criticism of the conduct at Jutland as expressed in *The World Crisis*, though there is no evidence that had any direct effect. Admiral Cunningham described tactics at the Battle of Matapan in March 1941, when three Italian cruisers and one destroyer were sunk and a battleship damaged:

> ... it followed almost exactly the lines of the battles we used to fight out at the table of the Tactical School at Portsmouth, a tribute to the nature and of the studies and the instruction we received there. First we had the contact of long-range reconnaissance aircraft; then the exact positioning of the enemy relative to our own fleet by the Fleet Air Arm aircraft from the carrier, and the informative and accurate reports of their trained observers. Next the carrier's striking force of torpedo bombers went in to the attack. ... Meanwhile the cruisers, spread on a line of bearing, pushed in to locate the enemy's battle fleet, and finally the heavy ships themselves came into action.[1]

As it turned out Matapan was the only action in the war with multiple capital ships and cruisers on both sides, but the techniques show how much had been learned about tactics since the dark days of Jutland.

Churchill did not sack admirals as easily as he did generals, and perhaps he kept Sir Dudley Pound on too long as his health declined. The one major dismissal involved Sir Dudley North, the commander-in-chief at Gibraltar, whom some thought had spent too much time before the war in social duties such as running the royal yachts. There was confusion about his responsibilities; normally a fleet or a command had a clear geographical base, including his at Gibraltar, but Force H, a group of capital ships, aircraft carriers and supporting ships was also based there and the command structure was unclear. When a French force of cruisers and destroyers reached the Straits in June 1940, intelligence had not been passed on to North and he had little initiative so they escaped, forcing the abandonment of an operation against the French colony of Dakar. Churchill remembered Troubridge and the *Goeben* affair and concluded: 'It is evident that Admiral Dudley North has not got to the root of the matter in him, and I should be very glad to see you replace him by a more resolute and clear-sighted officer.'[2] North did not accept this and campaigned vigorously until he was largely vindicated in the late 1950s.

★

The Germans had no battlefleet as such, but their raiders were at least as dangerous as in the last war. When the great battleship *Bismarck* broke out from Norway in May 1941, Churchill followed her progress with concern and interest. When the popular but flawed battlecruiser *Hood* was sunk by her, Churchill was at Chequers and was reported to be 'very gloomy' at the cabinet next day. After that, according to Pim, 'The Prime Minister spent most of that night in the Upper War Room and when told two torpedo aircraft from *Ark Royal* had hit *Bismarck* amidships, remarked "Hit him hard; he ain't got no friends." The Prime Minister was never in finer form than during a naval engagement and he followed closely every stage of the action.' Pim describes the scene around the long blue clothed table: 'all movement round the room was made with a minimum of noise so that the First Sea Lord could discuss

454 • CHURCHILL: WARRIOR

the situation with the Prime Minister and the members of the board without raising their voices'.[3] Churchill was not present when the ship was finally hounded and sunk, but his secretary John Martin was in the official box in the House of Commons when he was handed a note to that effect: 'I passed it forward to him and he rose again to announce it. Great jubilation.'[4] Perhaps he took some pleasure that it was the torpedo bomber which he had sponsored a quarter of a century before that saved the day.

★

Churchill's interest in ship design tended to focus on the larger end, perhaps reflecting his experience in the last war when the battleship was king of the seas. His dislike of the *King George V* class battleships was perhaps increased when he visited the name ship at Rosyth in October 1940 and almost got stuck in one of the hatches.[5] When the former First Sea Lord and Minister for the Co-ordination of Defence, Lord Chatfield, criticised the lack of new capital ship building in the House of Lords in February 1942, Churchill was 'not prepared to leave Chatfield unanswered'. The great new 45,000 ton battleships *Lion* and *Temeraire* were not being proceeded with 'as the construction effort has been concentrated on vessels likely to reach the line earlier', and they were never finished. The *King George V* class, which Churchill alleged Chatfield had been responsible for, were 'of course most useful ships, and we are very glad to have them as they come out', but they could have been much better with a 15-inch or 16-inch gun instead of the 14-inch.[6] He was speaking from personal experience, for he had recently crossed the Atlantic in the *Prince of Wales* and *Duke of York*. In the former ship in August 1941, he had to move out of his cabin in the stern because of excessive vibration. He complained about the provision of aircraft hangars and catapults amidships which interrupted the armoured 'citadel': 'Although it must have looked very progressive to be able to fly two aeroplanes off a battleship, the price paid in the rest of the design was altogether excessive.' Her gun turrets, designed to an over-ambitious specification, had already failed during the action with the *Bismarck* in May, and in an exercise on the way back Y turret, manned by the Royal Marines, was hampered because of failure to follow procedure. The *Duke of York* crossed in December 1941 and another design fault became apparent – the Admiralty of the time had demanded the guns be able to fire directly forward so the bows were kept low, which did not help in rough weather. The party was subjected to eight days of 'the dull pounding of the great seas on the ship's ribs' and Lord Beaverbrook refused to countenance a return voyage in 'that submarine the *Duke of York*'.[7]

It was an exaggerated faith in the battleship, combined with British fear of the German giants *Bismarck* and *Tirpitz*, which led to one of the great naval disasters. Churchill was aware of the danger of a war with Japan, though in July 1940 Pound believed that 'This country was not in a position to take on more than one war at a time.'[8] In the event of war he wanted to send the battlecruiser *Hood* to Singapore with two old R-class battleships, three 8-inch cruisers and a dozen long-range destroyers.[9] He believed that the *Hood* would be a deterrent, and tended to believe that the presence of British battleships in the region would have the same effect as the great German ships did in the Atlantic, tying up large amounts of resources. The *Hood* had been lost by November 1941, but Churchill told the Defence Committee: 'We had before us the example of the battleship *Tirpitz*, which now compelled us to keep on guard a force three times her weight in addition to the United States forces patrolling the Atlantic. The presence of one modern capital ship in Far Eastern waters could be calculated to have a similar effect on the Japanese naval authorities, and therefore on Japanese foreign policy.'[10] The battlecruiser *Repulse* was already there, and he proposed to reinforce her with the *Prince of Wales*. This did not find favour with the Admiralty, represented by Alexander and Admiral Sir Tom Phillips, the Vice Chief of Naval staff, as Pound was away. Phillips wrote to Pound: 'The First Lord and I defended the position as well as we could, but the Prime Minister led the other members of the Defence Committee to the conclusion that it was desirable to send the *Prince of Wales* to join the *Repulse* and go to Singapore as soon as possible.'[11] Churchill, who was said to be 'scathing in his comments on the Admiralty attitude to the matter', agreed not to take a final decision without consulting

Pound, who thought that only a larger and better balanced force should be sent, if at all. The only aircraft carrier available to join the force, the *Indomitable*, ran aground off Jamaica and was out of service. Churchill eventually browbeat Pound into sending the *Prince of Wales* to Cape Town and then on to Singapore.

As commander of the force, Pound chose the same Sir Tom Phillips who had opposed the plan but was due for sea time after two years at the Admiralty. He was an intelligent man, whom Churchill described as 'a great friend of mine, and one of our ablest admirals', but he had no appreciation of air power. Churchill was greatly excited in December 1941 when the attack on Pearl Harbor brought the United States into the war, and wrote later: 'No American will think it wrong of me if I proclaim that to have the United States at our side was to me the greatest joy. ... Being saturated and satiated with emotion and sensation, I went to bed and slept the sleep of the saved and thankful.' Clearly the deterrent had failed, but it was not Churchill who ordered Phillips to put to sea without air support. The *Prince of Wales* and *Repulse* were battered by waves of Japanese bombers and torpedo bombers and sunk. Churchill heard the news: 'In all the war I never received a more direct shock. The reader of these pages will realize how many efforts, hopes, and plans foundered with these two ships.'[12] But it was even worse two months later when Singapore itself fell, a severe and fatal blow to British prestige in the East. Churchill had been surprised to learn that there were no defences to the north of the island where the Japanese attacked. The 15-inch guns which had been the subject of controversy in the 1920 could only fire to seaward.[13]

Britain's stock of aircraft carriers was reduced by the loss of the *Courageous* in 1939, the *Glorious* off Norway in 1940 and the highly publicised *Ark Royal* in November 1941. Though carriers provided much needed victories at Taranto and against the *Bismarck*, Churchill's interest in them was spasmodic; however his visit to the *Indomitable* in September 1941 stimulated it. He was mostly concerned with the six armoured carriers of that type, each of which he hoped would become 'the most efficient possible unit if given suitable aircraft'.[14] Their stature was perhaps increased when the Americans asked for two carriers to support the war in the Pacific as they had no armoured carriers and their fleet was depleted at the end of 1942.[15] At one stage there was even an idea to convert the battleship *Vanguard*, which was being built slowly on Clydeside, into an armoured aircraft carrier, but it was rejected. Churchill tended to dismiss merchant ship conversions to operate low-performance aircraft in the Battle of the Atlantic, and later escort carriers built to American design, as 'improvised carriers' which, he believed, did not stand 'on the same level'. There were also unarmoured light fleet or 'intermediate' carriers under construction by the end of the war, but very few were finished on time.

Churchill had perhaps been more right than he knew in his criticism of cruiser design, as the 8-inch gun turret continued to have mechanical problems. In wartime the *Suffolk* and *Norfolk* which were fitted with it distinguished themselves by shadowing the *Bismarck*, but the class suffered heavy losses against the Japanese. But in any case 1939–45 was not a cruiser's war, in the sense that 1914–18 had been a battleship's war. The destroyer was the most flexible type of warship, and they took part in almost every operation. The American observer Joseph Wellings noted in 1941 that they were 'always on the go'.[16] They fought hard and 154 were lost during the war, more than the total number in commission at the beginning. From the first day of the war production concentrated on the ships of the Emergency War Programme. Churchill approved of the speed of production instead of high quality: 'I am all for building destroyers, and I do not mind how large they are, or how great their endurance, *provided* that they can be constructed in 15 months. This should be taken as the absolute limit, to which everything else must be made to conform. We were making destroyers which took three years to build, everyone thinking himself very clever in adding one improvement after another.' He was not concerned about endurance, but that would lead to problems when destroyers had to leave convoys as their fuel threatened to run out. He believed that the corvettes, formerly known as whalers, had the range and endurance for mid-Atlantic work, but for the moment he was unaware of their problems with stability.[17]

Churchill was delighted in August 1940 when President Roosevelt agreed to provide 50 old US destroyers in exchange for the lease of naval

458 • CHURCHILL: WARRIOR

bases, but that was a political gesture as much as anything else. To the War Cabinet he considered that it was 'certainly not a neutral action', though he played that down in public. The ships, he said, would be 'of enormous value to the Admiralty',[18] though that was not borne out in practice. They had been built for the US navy at the end of the last war but hardly used by them, and they proved very unstable in the Atlantic. The most famous was the *Campbeltown*, ex USS *Buchanan*, which was expended in ramming the dock gates at St Nazaire in 1942.

The submarine was a weapon of aggression, which appealed to Churchill, but it was never likely to be a war-winning weapon for the British, in contrast to the Germans. The question of naming rather than numbering them first arose in June 1940, but in December 1942 Churchill was 'still grieved to see our submarines described as P212 etc.' Giving them names was 'with the feelings of the officers and men who risk their lives in these vessels. Not even to give them names is derogatory to their devotion and sacrifice'. The names were to be chosen by the crews, but the problem was that those being built were of the S-, T- and U-classes and had to have names with these initials, though many of the most apt ones had already been taken up by destroyers. Churchill objected to 'Truculent' and 'Trespasser' but supported 'Tutenkhamen', while names like *Trenchant* and *Taciturn* were eventually adopted.[19]

★

In August 1940 Churchill was still unduly optimistic about the U-boat war, claiming that far more than the official Admiralty figure of 25 had been sunk – the actual number was 27.[20] But by the end of the month he was talking privately about 'the startling shipping losses in the North-Western Approaches, where lay the seeds of something that "might be mortal" if allowed to get out of hand'.[21] On 5 November he told the House of Commons that the sinkings in the Atlantic were 'more serious than the air raids' and he constantly queried the shortage of destroyers in actual service, for they were needed both for the main fleets and for anti-submarine work.[22] The 50 destroyers sent from the USA in exchange for the use of naval bases were a disappointment, though he had to be tactful in expressing this to Roosevelt. They were not being kept out of service due to manning difficulties but because of 'the necessity for carrying out considerable dockyard work to fit them for service in the arduous conditions of the north-western approaches'.[23] His concern increased with the loss of eight merchant ships in a Halifax convoy in 2 December.[24] Reviving his antipathy to mines from the last war, he blocked an Admiralty proposal to lay 'an underwater carpet of dynamite' three miles wide and 60 miles long in the North Channel off Ireland.[25] Another old scheme, the descendant of the Q-ship, failed and he ordered disguised ships to be taken off these duties in December. Churchill claimed to have taken the initiative in setting up a new command. In July 1940 the campaign in the Atlantic was still controlled by the Commander-in-Chief, Plymouth. He asked: 'Ought not a new command of the first order to be created in the Clyde ...?'[26] Western Approaches Command was set up in Liverpool under Admiral Sir Percy Noble in February 1941.

On 6 March 1941 the air offensive against the British cities was beginning to falter and the threat of invasion had receded. Churchill could see that there was only one method of attack left to Germany and declared: 'In view of various Germans statements, we must assume that the Battle of the Atlantic has begun.' He and others had already extended the term 'battle' to include Britain and France, but this was going even further – a campaign which would last until the end of the war over millions of square miles of ocean. Later he wrote: 'The only thing that ever really frightened me during the war was the U-boat peril.'[27] In a sense he was paying for his two mistakes about the U-boat in the past, in overestimating both the effect of Asdic and the number of enemy casualties.

Characteristically his answer was to attack. 'We must take the offensive against the U-boat and the Focke Wulf [long-range aircraft] whenever and wherever we can. The U-boat at sea must be hunted, the U-boat in the building yard or in dock must be bombed. The Focke Wulf, and other bombers employed against our shipping, must be attacked in the air and in their nests.' Ships were to be fitted with catapults to launch fighters, the strength of Coastal Command (such as it was) was to be concentrated on the north-western approaches, escort vessels including the American destroyers were to be hurried forward, it was to be considered whether merchant ships with speeds of 12 to 13 knots could proceed independently, the navy was to be given priority in anti-aircraft weapons (including the UP), and measures were to be taken to defend and improve the efficiency of the ports.[28]

For Germany the Battle of the Atlantic involved the navy and ship-builders with desultory participation by the Luftwaffe. For Britain it involved the whole of society, for losses of ships carrying particular goods might be felt in the shops and factories. In 1917 Churchill had asked: 'Would it be an exaggeration to say that for one war-power unit Germany has applied to the submarine attack we have been forced to assign fifteen or twenty?'[29] The factor was not likely to be much less in 1941. As well as the navy, air force and merchant shipping, the campaign could be affected by speed of unloading and turnaround of ships, the building of replacements for lost tonnage, the use of extemporised ports after London was effectively closed, and the more efficient use of goods and materials, controlled by the rationing and allocation of resources as well as development of techniques. Clearly it involved co-operation and decisions at the very highest level. The Battle of the Atlantic Committee grew out of the Import Executive, which had two meetings in February 1941, before being renamed and expanded. Its first meeting on the 19 March was held in Downing Street, chaired by Churchill himself and composed of the three service ministers and the ministers of supply, air-craft production, transport, labour and food. It was attended by the chiefs of staff or their deputies, the commander-in-chief of Coastal Command, the controller of merchant shipbuilding and repairs, Professor Lindemann, and various other staff and civil service officers. Its membership became quite flexible and later attendees included Roosevelt's representative Averell Harriman and Admiral Stark of the US Navy. It met weekly or fortnightly under Churchill's chairmanship, except when he was away, when it was usually chaired by the minister of aircraft production. The agenda of the fifth meeting in April 1941 included subjects such as the use of pneumatic welders in the Bristol area, fire-fighting on the Clyde and 'crew questions', as well as more military issues such as aerodromes in Iceland, the supply of Catalina aircraft, and one of Churchill's favourites, the fitting of ships with catapult aircraft.[30] In contrast to some other committees, Churchill's own interventions, whether as Prime Minister or Minister of Defence, were quite rare and brief. At the first meeting he merely emphasised the need to reduce the turnaround time for shipping. On 26 March he sought to make sure that enough barges and coasters were available at the west coast ports in case one was put out of action, commented on improvements in the rate of discharge of bulk cargoes, and suggested that cargo liners might bring more imports if they gave up carrying exports. On 22 October he supported an idea for net defence against torpedo attack, and later he commented on awards to merchant seamen.[31] But despite his relatively restrained comments, there is no doubt that Churchill's character and knowledge played a large part in coordinating and galvanising the campaign. Again he combined humour with an eye for detail, as reported by Pim: 'During the months of March and April [1941] the attacks on our convoys became extremely heavy and the Prime Minister often discussed the situation with the naval staff in the Upper War Room. Often I was questioned about the cargo of some torpedoed ship – in one instance it was carrying a cargo of eggs.' On learning this Churchill commented: 'This is serious, it represents one egg for every second person in Great Britain.'[32]

The greatest single convoy disaster came with PQ 17, on its way to Russia in July 1942, as Dudley Pound misinterpreted Ultra intelligence and believed that the *Tirpitz* was out. He ordered the escort to retreat and the convoy to scatter, much to the horror of the officers and crews concerned. Churchill was not consulted about this, though his claim that he knew nothing about it until after the war must be questioned – Pound reported it to the cabinet on 1 August, the day before Churchill flew to Cairo, so perhaps he was uncharacteristically inattentive.[33]

On 4 November 1942, as the campaign approached a climax, Churchill told the committee: '… we must expect to have to face a larger number of U-boats in 1943, operating in all the oceans and moving from one area to another. To meet this, we should provide much stronger escorts for our convoys.' This would be met in practice by the commissioning of new ships, including the River class frigates which had been designed after the start of the campaign, specifically for service in the Atlantic.

They would be equipped with new weapons such as the Hedgehog which could throw projectiles ahead of the ship, and later the Squid anti-submarine mortar. But this discussion led on to the most controversial matter in the campaign, the use of aircraft over the ocean. Most sinkings were now in the 'air gap' in the centre of the Atlantic, where Coastal Command's Sunderland flying boats and other aircraft could not reach with any time for patrol. Churchill commented that 'more aircraft would be required, but he was most anxious that his should not be achieved at the expense of our night-bombing effort against Germany. He was strongly opposed to converting Lancasters for ocean work, and he thought that a number of United States aircraft, unsuitable for night-bombing, might be made available for the protection of sea communications.' The First Lord of the Admiralty also suggested another plan: 'we should seriously consider converting, by special priority, about 12 merchant ships to enable them to carry four to five Swordfish each'. One wonders if a force of radar-equipped airships would have solved the problem, and they could have proved their worth despite Churchill's disdain.[34]

These plans were eventually implemented, but not before the campaign became more serious than ever. When the group (now renamed the Anti-U-Boat Warfare Committee) met in Downing Street on 17 March 1943, the latest statistics were already out of date and they were given 'details of the heavy losses that had occurred in the North Atlantic during the last three days, which were not included in the statement under review'. Convoys HX 229 and SC 122 were under severe attack and lost 30 ships between them – 72 ships were lost that month. But at the same meeting Admiral Sir Max Horton, the dynamic commander of Western Approaches, reported on a war game to decide whether it was best to employ the new aircraft carriers alongside support groups of destroyers or in separate units – for enough ships were now becoming available to adopt Churchill's old idea of 'an independent flotilla which could work like a cavalry division'.[35] In this case he commented that a large number of destroyers would be needed to create separate forces, but conceded that 'the tactical employment of these ships was a matter for

Admiralty decision, and he was only anxious that the available limited resources should be employed to the best advantage'.

And soon the tide began to turn as three successive convoys – ONS 5, HX 237 and SC 130 – fought through large concentrations of U-boats with minimal losses. Churchill was at sea in the *Queen Mary* as the critical battles were fought, but kept in touch via the travelling Map Room, and Pim commented: 'There is something very fascinating in watching such a picture which portrays as faithfully as possible the varying fortunes of the Battle of the Atlantic, especially when … the month of May had been the most successful month in the war against the U-boat, evidence of which could be seen reflected daily on our charts.'[36] The U-boat threat never went away during the war but was greatly reduced, allowing a massive build-up of men and munitions in Britain for the invasion of Europe.

CHAPTER 37

Air Power in Operation

The air force that Churchill took over in 1940 still wore the blue-grey
uniforms and had the same rank structure that he had set up, but it
was very different in other ways. Bomber squadrons were headed by
wing commanders rather than squadron leaders, and a group captain
was likely to command an air station rather than a group, which was
led by an air vice-marshal. The pilots were led into battle by squadron
leaders and wing commanders, which sounded far more dynamic and
modern than majors and colonels, who were associated with living in
the past. In contrast to the puttees and stiff collar of T. E. Lawrence's
day, all ranks now wore trousers and tunics with open necks, or the
increasingly ubiquitous battledress as used by the army. The service was
beginning to recognize the importance of non-pilot aircrew such as
observers, radio operators and gunners, and all of them were promoted
to at least sergeant in April 1940. Despite Trenchard's desire for 'din-
ing-out power', it had a much more demotic image than the other
services. Churchill's left-wing nephew Esmond Romilly volunteered for
it to avoid 'the interminable drilling, mastery of neatness, submission
to all kinds of meaningless routines administered by a legion of officer
class petty tyrants that he anticipated in a war which was basically run
by English Tories'.[1]

As to ground crews, many more skilled men than Halton could produce
were needed, to cope with greater sophistication as well as the increasing
numbers of aircraft. This could be done by increasing the number of

specialised trades, which needed shorter training. In June 1940 alone, 29 new trades were added to the list, including link trainer instructor, radio mechanic, grinder and meteorologist.[2] Perhaps the most obvious difference from the Churchill/Trenchard force was in its distribution. The force of 1920 had neglected home defence almost completely and the great majority of its active squadrons were based in the empire. By 1940 it tended to concentrate almost obsessively on home defence and strategic bombing to the exclusion of everything else.

On 18 June 1940, reluctantly accepting defeat across the Channel, Churchill told the House of Commons: 'What General Weygand called the "Battle of France" is over. I expect that the Battle of Britain is about to begin.' It was a way of minimising the defeat. At the time he was thinking about the threat of invasion and the prospect of paratroops and panzers on British soil, but in the event the phrase came to mean something different, and it changed slightly over the months. At the end of August he spoke to the War Cabinet about the 'battle for Great Britain' and early in September it was 'the 1940 Air Battle of Britain'.[3]

It was the air battles over southern England, perhaps more than anything else, which established Churchill's historical reputation as a great war leader; yet his approach to them was far less hands-on than in many other campaigns. It was not lack of technical knowledge which inhibited him, for that never stopped him in any other field. Perhaps he regarded the campaign as purely defensive, and he was certainly thinking about all sorts of offensive strategy during these months. But a fast-moving air campaign of this nature was also far more difficult to follow in detail in the War Room, which did not have the large and specially trained staff of a fighter headquarters. Churchill made a habit of visiting these, and was deeply impressed with the operations room of No 11 Group in September 1940, using a system developed by Dowding in the last few years:

> The Group Operations Room was like a small theatre, about sixty feet across, and with two storeys. We took our seats in the Dress Circle. Below us was the large-scale map table, around which perhaps twenty highly-trained young men and women, with their telephone assistants, were assembled. Opposite to us, covering the entire wall, where the theatre curtain would be, was a gigantic

blackboard divided into six columns with electric bulbs, for the six fighter stations, each with their squadrons having a sub-column of its own, and also divided by lateral lines. Thus the lowest row of bulbs showed as they were lighted the squadrons which were 'Standing By' at two minutes notice, the next row those at 'Readiness', five minutes, then at 'Available', twenty minutes, then those which had taken off, the next row those which had reported having seen the enemy, the next – with red lights – those which were in action, and the top row those which were returning home. On the left-hand side, in a kind of glass stage-box, were the four or five officers whose duty it was to weigh and measure the information received from our Observer Corps. Radar was still in its infancy, but it gave warning of raids approaching our coast, and the observers, with field glasses and portable telephones, were our main source of information about raiders flying overland. Thousands of messages were therefore received during an action.[4]

These required 'several roomfuls of experienced people' to sift them. This was a reference to the Filter Room at Fighter Command Headquarters in Bentley Priory in north-west London, where contradictory data from many sources was assessed before being passed on to the control rooms. An Air Ministry minute stated: 'the accuracy of filtering is of vital importance. At only one point in the whole vast network of the radar system does the information collected and forwarded by the radar chain assume a tangible form on which fighter action can be taken.' The Filter Room had only recently become fully efficient with the recruitment of specially trained officers, usually scientists or mathematicians.[5] Churchill's Upper War Room in Whitehall would not have been able to handle that kind of data. Perhaps he remembered the more primitive days of 1917, when the anti-aircraft guns were controlled by telephone from the War Office; or the raid of May 1915 when Zeppelin LZ38 dropped 120 bombs across east London, and only one of fifteen aircraft sent out made any contact but did no damage.

During that visit Churchill uncharacteristically 'watched in silence' until he asked a question. On a visit to Fighter Command headquarters on 31 August he 'found it very instructive to watch the officers of the Fighter Command deploying their forces and building up a front at the threatened points', but there is no sign that he attempted to direct operations.[6] He also visited 615 Squadron as honorary air commodore, as reported by John Colville: 'Winston was arrayed in RAF uniform which, curiously enough, suited him well. We inspected the men and machines in pouring rain, watched twelve Hurricanes take off for patrol and went to see the operations room from which the activities of all aircraft in the area are directed.'[7]

Instead of intervening directly on operations, Churchill took much interest in how the RAF was using its resources. At that moment the greatest shortage was in trained pilots. On 18 July he complained about figures showing that only three in ten pilots were with operational squadrons: 'Thus more pilots are employed giving or receiving instruction than are actually serving on operations.'[8] On 26 August he delayed a scheme to train aircrews in Canada and South Africa even though the skies over Britain were increasingly crowded and dangerous: 'Until the issue of the battle becomes clear it would not be right to separate any large portion of our reserve of pilots or of potentially operational machines from the fighting strength of the RAF in this country.'[9] He deplored 'the tendency of every station commander ... to keep as much in his hands as possible'.[10] Fifty more airfields were needed in addition to 75 already under construction, and he hoped that large numbers of diggers and concrete mixers could be released soon from the construction of coastal defences.[11]

★

The RAF had advantages in its fighter aircraft, the Hurricane and the superb Spitfire. Both of them, unlike most contemporary bombers, had been conceived at the right moment and were capable of further development. Their eight-machine-gun armament, however, had less range and destructive power than the 20mm cannon used by the Germans, and British pilots were not well trained in gunnery. But the biggest single advantage was in the use of Radio Direction Finding or RDF, as radar was then known. Following the trial station at Bawdsey which Churchill had seen in 1939, the 'chain home' series of 20 stations had been set up after being accelerated by the Munich crisis. A dozen more stations of the 'Chain Home Low' were opened by July 1940 to detect low-flying aircraft. But the radar chain only operated outwards, which concerned Churchill. Once the aircraft had crossed the coast they could only be followed visually by members of the part-time Observer Corps, who had 'done splendid work, but in cloudy weather like yesterday and today, they have the greatest difficulty in functioning accurately'. He pressed for more stations to be set up inland as soon as possible.[12]

In the first phase, which began around 23 June, the German attack was mainly on convoys in the English Channel. On 10 July Churchill was shocked to find that Archibald Sinclair intended to let Sir Hugh Dowding's term as commander-in-chief of Fighter Command expire and wrote: 'I have greatly admired the whole of his work in the Fighter Command, and especially in resisting the clamour for numerous air-raid warnings, and the immense pressure to dissipate the fighter strength during the great French battle. In fact he has my full confidence.'[13] Among other achievements Dowding had set up the control system that Churchill was so impressed with, and he was allowed to stay; later John Colville assessed him as 'splendid: he stands up to the PM ... and is the very antithesis of the complacency with which so many Englishmen are afflicted'.[14] On 10 July the enemy raided the South Wales docks and Churchill was ecstatic with the result, believing the enemy had lost at the rate of five to one.[15] And on 11 August he believed that fighters had shot down 70 enemy aircraft over the Channel, though it was difficult to verify claims for kills over the sea. To Colville 'He expatiated on the debt we owed to our airmen and claimed that the life of the country depended on their intrepid spirit. What a slender thread, he exclaimed, his voice tremulous with emotion, the greatest of things can hang by!'[16]

The second and perhaps the most crucial phase began around the second week of August when the Germans began to attack airfields and aircraft factories, hoping to eliminate Fighter Command in preparation for an invasion. On 15 August Churchill was at Fighter Command headquarters at Stanmore to watch 'the greatest and most successful air battle of all'. The Germans had launched attacks against targets all over England, hoping to saturate the defences. An attack across the North Sea towards Sunderland was heavily defeated and in all the Luftwaffe lost 75 aircraft (though not 'well over a hundred' as Churchill believed), with more damaged, forcing a rethink of tactics. But their campaign against airfields was taking its toll. On visiting Manston near the tip of

Kent, Churchill was distressed to find that bomb craters on the landing areas had not yet been cleared.[17] Later he complained that damaged hangars had been left unrepaired at several key airfields.[18] He addressed the House of Commons on 20 August with one of his most famous speeches, praising the 'brilliant actions' of the fighter pilots: 'Never in the field of human conflict was so much owed by so many to so few.' He was annoyed by American correspondents who tended to underestimate enemy losses – 'they will find out quite soon enough when the German attack is plainly shown to be repulsed'.[19]

On 19 August Churchill complained that there had been several air raid warnings over London in the last few days, but no actual air fighting had taken place there.[20] On the 24th some aircraft jettisoned their bombs over the city and the RAF felt justified in retaliating with a raid on Berlin on 25–26 August, which did more psychological than material damage. The Germans, annoyed by this, did indeed switch the attack to London. It was a historic mistake; the raids on airfields and aircraft factories were beginning to bear fruit, and moreover the range of the German fighters only allowed them a few minutes over London. After the first major raid on 7 September, Churchill visited the scene of the damage in the East End and Ismay recalled what had happened as he visited the site of an air raid shelter in which 40 people had been killed: 'The place was full of people searching for their lost belongings when you arrived. They stormed you, as you got out of the car with cries of "It was good of you to come Winnie. We thought you'd come. We can take it. Give it 'em back." It was a most moving scene, you broke down completely and I nearly did, and as I was trying to get to you through the press of bodies, I heard an old woman say, "You see, he really cares, he's crying."'[21]

A week later Churchill left Chequers to visit the headquarters of No 11 Fighter Group which was charged with the defence of south-east England including London, and witnessed what turned out to be the climax of the battle. After a quiet start, red bulbs showed that most of the squadrons were airborne, and Air Vice-Marshal Park asked Dowding for assistance from another group. Churchill, echoing his question to Gamelin three months earlier, asked Park, 'What reserves have we?' and looked grave when he was told 'There are none.' But already the battle was won, the bombers were withdrawing and no new attack developed. Churchill went back to Chequers and, according to Ismay, said: 'Don't speak to me; I have never been so moved.'[22] He slept longer than usual, from 4.30 until 8. When he awoke his secretary John Martin told him, among generally bad news, that the RAF had shot down 183 planes for the loss of fewer than 40. In fact the Germans had lost 58 aircraft, but it was a victory nevertheless.

After the 20th the main threat was the night bomber attack on London, which was not difficult to find from bases in France, and to begin with there was no real means of stopping it. For Churchill personally it gave him a chance to experience the hazards of war. He continued to live in London, moving to the underground Cabinet War Rooms in the most dangerous periods. He visited Chequers at weekends, though he was aware that the Luftwaffe might target him there. Commenting that he did not object to chance 'but feels it a mistake to be the victim of design', he took up an offer to use Ditchley Park when conditions made a raid likely.

On 7 October the Night Air Defence Committee began to meet under Churchill's chairmanship. It included representatives of the services and ministries involved, but the most prominent members were Dowding as head of Fighter Command, until he was superseded by Sholto Douglas; Sir Frederick Pile of the army's Anti-Aircraft Command which manned the guns; and Robert Watson-Watt, the inventor of radar, though Lindemann was also present. Churchill was comparatively silent, though he usually concluded the meeting with a series of orders. Over the next few months it looked at numerous ideas. Churchill naturally pushed his own favourites, the rockets and mines, and the project was codenamed 'Mutton'. After many delays it was tried on the night of 19 April with no apparent result. Sholto Douglas explained to him on 20 April:

> I have an idea that you think I am not really trying with 'Mutton'. This is not the case. I do believe that on fine nights there is a better chance of getting down Huns with Beaufighters plus AI; and in such conditions, when there is competition between Beaufighters and 'Mutton' for [Ground Controlled Interception]

facilities, I have ruled that the Beaufighters must have preference. On the other hand, in non-moonlight periods or in bad weather when there is a stream of enemy aircraft coming in, I think that 'Mutton' may prove to be more profitable.

Experiments with one squadron were inconclusive, and finally Douglas pointed out that a Beaufigher squadron operating from the same airfield had shot down 40 enemy aircraft while Mutton claimed one, plus five probables. Other schemes included 'cats-eye' fighters, single seaters in which the pilot relied on his own vision; Albino or free barrage balloons as suggested by the Admiralty, which could only be used in ideal weather conditions and had a tendency to drift into enemy territory; Turbinlite or airborne searchlights; and intruder operations over the enemy airfields.[23]

From the first meeting of the committee, however, the real solution was clear and only had to be developed. Lindemann's infra-red beams were set aside and radar was to be developed as fast as possible. The fixed stations had proved invaluable in the daylight Battle of Britain, but at night they could only guide an aircraft to the general area of the target. Part of the answer was to be found in directing the fighters more closely to the enemy aircraft, known as ground controlled interception and codenamed Jessie, and stations were set up during the next few months. This was to be supplemented by Airborne Interception or AI radar, fitted to the aircraft itself. As early as June 1940 Robert Watson Watt had sent a report for the Prime Minister, and Ismay arranged for a 'plain language version of it' to be produced by Lindemann for Churchill's consumption. It stated that 'Using RDF methods alone at night, only very skilled men will be able to exploit AI at the present stage of development.' Another problem was that the current night fighter, the obsolete Blenheim, was too slow to overtake the enemy. The new and faster Bristol Beaufighter still had its teething troubles, as Lindemann reported to Churchill: 'It now appears that despite an extra 30 miles an hour the Beaufighter has proved no more successful than the Blenheim. In consequence of this the view is at last gaining ground that the failure to make interceptions with AI is due not to lack of speed but to the fact that the enemy becomes aware that he is being pursued and jinks away.'

Watson Watt was right about the difficulties of operating the early set; C. F. Rawnsley described his introduction to it in his squadron:

> A low buzzing sound came from somewhere in the depths of the equipment. On each tube there appeared a luminous green line, horizontal on one tube and vertical on the other. These, Cape explained, were what were called time traces. He twiddled one of the knobs, and across the lines little diamonds of light came into being. These represented the echoes ... from the target in front. ... The distance from one end of the trace would tell us the range of the target. ... We were going to have to juggle around with a lot of blips, deducing from their appearance the various ranges and bearing, and so interpret the position and movement of the target.[24]

At last on the night of 12–13 December a successful interception took place and it was reported to Churchill: 'The enemy aircraft was seen to turn almost vertical with left wing down and to enter in a steep dive. The pilot followed him down to 6,000 feet' – but in fact the aircraft was not destroyed. By that time there were 57 Beaufighters with the squadrons compared with 85 Blenheims.[25]

As the defences slowly developed, London endured its Blitz throughout the winter of 1940–41, as did other cities such as Liverpool and Coventry. The night offensive came to an end in May 1941, partly because the German aircraft were needed to attack the Soviet Union, but the new methods had played a key part. On 12 May Douglas stated that 'AI, assisted by CGI, was the most profitable means of night interception. For this reason everything possible should be done to accelerate the provision of Beaufighters for use in night fighting.' Churchill decreed that this should be implemented.[26]

Churchill turned to the Night Air Defence Committee yet again in March 1943, believing that 'we must be prepared to meet a heavier scale of enemy air attack on this country since, he believed, such a course was being forced upon the Germans by our own energetic and successful air offensive'.[27] But this only came to the 'Baedeker' raids against provincial towns of little strategic importance, which began in April.

The Battle of Britain and the Blitz were the ultimate vindication for Churchill's policy of maintaining the independent air force in 1919 – otherwise the nation might have been saddled with the old policy of naval aircraft meeting the enemy over the sea and the army fighting them over the land. But they were unique battles, paralleled only by the allied air offensives against Germany and Japan, in which the defenders were the losers – though not entirely because of air power in either case.

★

General Brooke claimed that 'every operation we were engaged in was a "combined" one' involving all the services, but that was less true of the bomber offensive against Germany in which only the RAF was involved, alongside Commonwealth and allied air forces. In May 1940 Churchill was still convinced that it was far better to bomb military targets when he told the War Cabinet: 'In attacking this country they would find it far more profitable to concentrate on specific military targets.'[28] But he had not forgotten his aim to attack Germany and in July 1940, when the Fall of France was hardly completed, he contrasted the situation with 1914 and told Beaverbrook:

> The blockade is broken and Hitler has Asia and probably Africa to draw from. Should he be repulsed here or not try invasion, he will recoil eastward, and we have nothing to stop him. But there is one thing that will bring him back and bring him down, and that is an absolutely devastating, exterminating attack by very heavy bombers from this country upon the Nazi homeland.[29]

But it was not so simple. On 13/14 August eleven out of twelve Blenheims were lost over Holland and daylight raids were generally catastrophic, so night bombing was the only alternative.[30] Churchill claimed in a memorandum of September 1940: 'The navy can lose us the war, but only the air force can win it. Therefore, our supreme effort must be to gain overwhelming mastery in the air. Fighters are our salvation, but the bombers alone can provide the means of victory. We must therefore develop the power to carry an ever-increasing volume of explosives to Germany, so as to pulverize her entire industry and scientific structure on which the war effort and economic life of the enemy depends ...'.[31]

At the end of August Churchill asserted: 'The reason why our aircraft are able to bomb Germany accurately by night is because they have superior navigational training.'[32] This was wildly optimistic; RAF navigational training was still very backward, partly because the Churchill/ Trenchard Air Ministry had dispensed with observers – the grade was only re-established in 1937 but had low status to start with. There was some attempt to use astro-navigation techniques but that was difficult at speed, and there was no specialised navigation branch until 1942, by which time radio aids were coming into use.

There were plenty of other signs that a bomber offensive would not be easy. On 5 September, just before the major bombing of London began, Churchill observed: 'How very differently this air attack which is now raging has turned out from what we imagined it would be before the war. More than 150,000 beds have stood open and, thank God, empty in our war hospitals for a whole year. … So far as the air attack is concerned, up to the present we have found it far less severe than what we prepared ourselves to endure and what we are still ready, if necessary, to endure.'[33] On 8 October he told the House of Commons: 'On that particular Thursday night 180 persons were killed in London as a result of 251 tons of bombs. That is to say, it took one ton of bombs to kill three quarters of a person … therefore, the deadliness of the attack in this war appears to be only one-thirteenth of that of 1914–18.'[34]

Later Sir Arthur Harris used the 8 July memorandum as justification for his indiscriminate bombing campaign, but at the time Churchill was not thinking of war against civilians – he still tended to believe, as in 1917, that 'It is improbable that any terrorization of the civil population which could be achieved by air attack would compel the government of a great nation to surrender.' In contrast to the 'indiscriminate bombing by night of our built-up areas' into which the Germans had 'relapsed', he told parliament: 'We should be foolish to shift off those military targets which the skill of our navigators enable us to find with a great measure of success' and that 'Our object must be to inflict the maximum harm on her war-making capacity. That is the only object that we shall pursue.'[35] But after the Luftwaffe made a devastating raid on Coventry on 14 November he ordered Operation Abigail, for 'the most destructive possible bombing attack against a selected German town'. Two hundred aircraft were to be involved, though no attack up to then had used more than 80. It was to be a town 'of some industrial importance' and Mannheim was chosen out of a shortlist of four. It took place on the night of 16/17 December, but the city centre was largely undamaged and seven bombers were lost against 43 German civilians. Churchill was undeterred, writing on 30 December: 'We must ... increase our bomb deliveries on Germany, and it appears that some of the types and patterns most adapted to this are not coming forward as we had hoped.'[36] The year ended with 'the most serious and precise of many melancholy reports we are having of our air bombing' from the US naval attaché in Berlin who claimed that raids had done 'little damage'.[37]

Lindemann commissioned a report on bombing accuracy by a Mr Butt of the War Cabinet Secretariat and the results, produced in August 1941, were devastating – an analysis of photographs taken from nearly 350 aircraft showed that only one bomb in three fell within five miles of the target. Lindemann told Churchill: 'however inaccurate the figures may be, they are sufficiently striking to emphasise the supreme importance of improving our navigational methods'. Churchill commented to Portal that this was 'a very serious paper, and seems to require your most urgent attention'.[38] By October Churchill had begun to moderate his expectations and wrote to Portal:

> The Air Staff would make a mistake to put their claim too high. Before the war we were greatly misled by the pictures they painted of the destruction that would be wrought by air raids. This is illustrated by the fact that 750,000 beds were actually provided for air raid casualties, never more than 6,000 being required. The picture of air destruction was so exaggerated that it depressed the statesmen responsible for the pre-war policy, and played a definite part in the desertion of Czechoslovakia in August 1938. Again, the Air Staff, after the war had begun, taught us sedulously to believe that, if the enemy acquired the Low Countries, to say nothing of France, our position would be impossible owing to the air attacks. However, by not paying too much attention to such ideas, we have found quite a good means of keeping going.

He concluded that 'he is an unwise man who thinks there is any certain method of winning this war, or indeed any other war between equals in strength. The only plan is to persevere.'[39]

It was increasingly clear that precision night bombing was not an option, so the only alternative left, apart from abandoning the idea altogether, was mass bombing of cities. By September there was a plan for a force of 4,000 bombers which Churchill endorsed with a certain amount of scepticism, warning Portal: 'Even if all the towns of Germany were rendered largely uninhabitable or even that war industry could not be carried on, it does not follow that the military control would be weakened or even that war industry could not be carried on …'.[40]

The picture changed at the beginning of 1942 when Air Chief Marshal Sir Arthur Harris was appointed to head Bomber Command. He was a dedicated, uncompromising and ruthless character – qualities which appealed to Churchill, though he never warmed to the man personally. Like Trenchard, Harris was inarticulate and used an academic, Harry Weldon of Magdalen College Oxford, to express his thoughts. He was dedicated to area bombing and dismissed all attempts to single out individual targets or industries as 'panaceas'. New aircraft were becoming available with the four-engined Stirling, Halifax and especially the Lancaster replacing the Wellington as the mainstay of the force. Navigational accuracy began to improve with radio and radar aids such as GEE, Loran and H2S. By 1945 95 per cent of aircraft were dropping their bombs within three miles of the aiming point, though it was still not precision bombing except for occasional specialised raids. On 30 May 1942 a force of a thousand bombers, gathered only by emptying the training bases, pounded Cologne with great psychological effect. It was followed by equally large raids on Essen and Bremen, though none of them did huge damage and the training programme had to be reinstated. Even so, Churchill was still ambivalent about the offensive at the end of 1942:

> In the days when we were fighting alone, we answered the question 'How are you going to win the war?' by saying. 'We will shatter Germany by bombing.' Since then the enormous injuries inflicted on the German army by the Russians, and the accession of the manpower and munitions of the United States, have rendered other possibilities open. … We must regard the bomber offensive against Germany at least as a feature in breaking her war-will second only to the largest military operations which can be conducted on the continent until that war-will is broken.[41]

However, he used the campaign to justify his reluctance to set up a second front, telling Stalin in April 1942: 'I must emphasize that our bombing of Germany will increase in scale month by month' and sending him photographs of wrecked cities – though the dictator was not impressed.[42]

At the Casablanca Conference in January 1943 the Americans agreed to use their Eighth Air Force for daylight bombing of Germany in addition to the British effort. In March 1943 Bomber Command began the Battle of the Ruhr with attacks on Germany's industrial heartland, which also happened to be reasonably close to British bases. It had some success, as even those most sceptical about the bombing campaign conceded: 'Reading contemporary accounts, there can be no doubt that the Battle of the Ruhr marked a turning point in the history of the German war economy, which has been grossly underestimated by post-war accounts.'[43] That summer Churchill dismissed fears that the use of 'window', metal strips dropped from aircraft to block the radar, would be taken up by the Germans and used against the allies, with the words, 'Let us open the window!' The result was a devastating raid on Hamburg in July, which caused a firestorm and destroyed large areas of the city for the loss of twelve bombers out of 728. Harris claimed in August: 'We are on the verge of a final showdown in the bombing war, and the next few months will be vital.' In November he wrote to Churchill listing 19 cities already destroyed, and claimed: 'We can wreck Berlin from end to end if the USAAF will come in on it.'[44] In fact the American Army Air Force did not agree but the Berlin offensive went ahead anyway with Churchill's support, giving relief to the industries of the Ruhr but making little contribution to the war effort. In attacks on Berlin and other cities the RAF lost more than a thousand aircraft from November 1943 to March 1944. After that the bombers were switched to targets in preparation for the Normandy invasion, despite protests from Harris.

The offensive resumed in September with more success, partly because the American daylight bombers were now escorted by Mustang fighters which challenged the Luftwaffe and gave air superiority. As the war approached its end it was clear that Harris, built up by the press as the uncompromising hero of the campaign, was out of control. Portal began to have increasing doubts about area bombing, wondering 'whether the magnetism of the remaining German cities has not in the past tended as much to deflect our bombers from their primary objectives as the tactical and weather difficulties'. Harris replied strongly: 'It has always been my custom to leave no stone unturned to get my views across, but when the decision is made I carry it out to the best of my ability. I am sorry that you should doubt this.' The controversy became so intense that the writers of the post-war official history were banned from publishing the letters, but Harris had his way.[45] Churchill was drawn in after the controversial attack on Dresden on 13 February. He wrote at the end of March: 'It seems to me that the moment has come when the question of bombing of German cities simply for the sake of increasing the terror, though under other pretexts, should be reviewed,' though he later toned this down under pressure from the airmen.

Supporters of the air offensive claimed that it was an alternative to the Battles of the Somme and Ypres, but it led to the deaths of 55,573 airmen, mostly highly intelligent, trained and motivated young men who might have become leaders of the future. It tended to undermine the allies' moral case with indiscriminate attacks on civilian areas. It took up between seven per cent and a third of British effort, according to which figures one accepts, and most historians believe it was an overall failure. Churchill distanced himself from the campaign after the war, refusing a medal for the aircrews and a peerage for Harris. He had good reasons for going ahead with the bombing in the early stages and slightly less good ones for continuing it, but he too failed to control 'Bomber' Harris and must take some of the blame for the campaign's faults.

CHAPTER 38

Air Support

The Trenchard Memorandum which Churchill had endorsed in 1919 stated that smaller parts of the RAF would be trained to work with the navy and the army with the possibility of 'these two small portions probably becoming, in the future, an arm of the older services'. That in a sense happened with the transfer of the Fleet Air Arm in 1937, much against the will of the RAF, but shore-based naval aircraft, including flying boats, remained part of the RAF's Coastal Command, while army co-operation was a smaller and much neglected command within the RAF.

On 13 May 1941 at the second meeting of the Tank Parliament, Sir Alan Brooke, then Commander-in-Chief of home forces, raised the question of air co-operation with the army, and he was not ruled out of order even though it had no connection with the title of the meeting. He wanted 'bomber and reconnaissance aircraft working in close co-operation with armoured divisions, in a manner which had been so successfully exemplified by the Germans'. Churchill replied that 'no-one could disagree on the principle that the army, and particularly the armoured divisions, must have air forces working in the closest coop-eration with them. The question at issue was one of quantity, and of the impingement of army requirements on other programmes.' At the time the return to continental land warfare was far from certain, and the main role of the army was still defence against invasion. For the RAF, Portal commented that air power was of little use in defensive operations: 'there was little time to preconcert the close support of units by air squadrons, and it would generally be more advantageous to the latter to operate against targets in the rear of the enemy's advance'. Brooke 'became a bit heated and attacked the Air Ministry strongly, as regards recent attitude towards army co-operation'. Churchill commented 'that this strategic bombing of ports, ships, beaches, etc. could not be regarded in the same light as close support of armoured formations' which 'would be moving forward perhaps over ground partly occupied by the enemy, and would need immediate air support under their own control'. Brooke wrote: 'PM backed me strongly and meeting was a great success!'[1] However, after viewing a bomber squadron carrying out an army co-operation exercise in July 1941, he commented: 'Good progress had been made, but I was more convinced than ever that we cannot expect real close co-operation from bomber squadrons suddenly swinging from an independent role to that of close cooperation with the army.'[2]

At the 13 May meeting Portal agreed that the low-performance Lysanders at present in army co-operation service were inadequate and proposed to use American Curtiss Tomahawks, whose low service ceiling made them unsuitable as fighters. Churchill asked why only three squadrons were to be equipped with them though there were many more in the country. He demanded at least 14 army-co-operation squadrons, some with Tomahawks and some with Blenheims. Meanwhile American dive bombers, the Vultee Vengeance and the Brewster Bermuda, were eagerly awaited to fill the role of the Luftwaffe's Stuka in the French campaign. Both, as it turned out, were of very moderate performance. The Bermuda, with a top speed of 284 mph and a very short range, was never employed on operations; the Vengeance had a speed of 279 mph but proved very useful in the jungles of Borneo where fighter opposition was unlikely. Salvation was found in another failed fighter. The design of the Hawker Typhoon was begun as early as 1937 as a successor to the Hurricane, with much greater armament and engine power. It was not given priority and after it first flew in 1941 it suffered from horrific teething troubles. One of its test pilots was awarded the George Medal for avoiding a crash, the tail had a tendency to detach itself, and pilots suffered from carbon monoxide poisoning in in the cockpit. When these had been sorted out, it was found that the Typhoon's performance was poor above 20,000 feet, so it was allocated to the army co-operation role.[3] But the Typhoon was not a dive bomber and no such aircraft entered service on the allied side in Europe. Instead a different means was found for attacking tanks, bridges and strong points.

In April 1942 Brooke still found the going difficult: 'I became involved in a heavy discussion with the [Secretary of State] for Air. I should have liked to have told him even more plainly that he was deliberately speaking untruths! However, the PM backed me up, and rubbed into Sinclair the necessity for devoting more love and affection to those air forces destined for army requirements.'[4] Tactics had been developed in the North African War partly by Sir Arthur Longmore, one of the first naval fliers and now an Air Marshal. According to General O'Connor, who led the success-ful advance late in 1940: 'In [the enemy's] recent retreat from Tobruk you gave his ground troops no rest, bombing their concentrations, and carrying out low-flying attacks on their [motor transport] columns. In addition to the above you have co-operated to the full in carrying out many requests for special bombardments, reconnaissance and protection against enemy action …'.[5] But Churchill was far less appreciative: 'ACM Longmore has shown himself very unappreciative of the immense efforts we are making to support him and to increase his forces. At every stage throughout this Libyan affair we have had to press him forward beyond his judgement or inclination …'.[6] Longmore was succeeded by his deputy, Air Marshal Arthur Tedder, one of the most educated of his rank and service, who had constant disputes with Churchill which he usually won, and who had a greater vision of inter-service co-operation than most of his contemporaries. He developed a close relationship with General Eisenhower which continued for the rest of the war, becoming the General's 'aviation lobe', as Churchill put it.[7]

A manual was issued by General Alexander in 1943, though it spent a great deal of space on the need for air superiority, which the air force was expected to contest anyway. It was followed by a more general manual produced by the general and air staffs in July that year, beginning with the rather Churchillian injunction: '"United we stand, divided we fall." Victory can only be won by the combined action of all services acting in complete unison.' It went on, 'The conception has long since passed that "army co-operation" merely envisages the employment of a few specialist squadrons to assist a land force for a particular operation. The three fighting services now operate as a combined force, the commanders of the three services controlling their own forces and co-ordinating their action in accordance with a combined plan.' It outlined the value of air power in its range and flexibility and the role of the air force in photographic and visual reconnaissance and attack by machine gun and cannon, by low level bombing and by dive bombing – though at this stage there was no mention of rockets. It emphasised the need for the army to keep the air force informed of its positions. It was rather vague, promising 'A series of pamphlets dealing with this subject is in preparation, and will be issued shortly,' but it was a considerable advance on the attitudes and tactics of 1941. The great material change came when the 2nd Tactical Air Force was formed in the summer of 1943 by transferring light and medium bombers from Bomber Command. Soon it was equipped with a mixture of Tempests, Mosquitos, Spitfires, Mustangs, Boston light bombers and Auster light reconnaissance aircraft.

Lindemann's UP rocket found another use, largely unnoticed by Churchill. It was Dowding who suggested, in June 1940, that it might be adapted to be carried by a Beaufighter and set to explode in the middle of a bomber formation and disrupt it. Tests were held in Wales but were inconclusive. By March 1941 Lindemann was suggesting another use: 'The general idea is to fly the Beaufighter on to the enemy aeroplane by AI methods, and then, without actually sighting the enemy, to fire the UP, the shell of which would be fitted with a radio fuse and would detonated on passing the target aircraft.' Again tests were inconclusive, but the idea of fitting the rocket under the wings of aircraft had been found practicable.[8] By June 1941 there was a clear need for a method of attacking tanks from the air and it was found that the recoil of a 40mm cannon would have been too great. At the same time the Fleet Air Arm wanted an anti-ship weapon for use against surfaced submarines. Reports from Russia suggested that rockets could be used effectively against tanks, but there was no time to develop a completely new weapon, so the designers turned to the 3-inch unrotated projectile which needed only minor modifications for the new uses. It was fitted with a 25 lb armour-piercing shot, with a 60 lb shot for use against seaborne targets. 'Projectors' or launching rails were designed for fitting under aircraft wings, each loaded with four missiles so that the aircraft could normally carry eight. In November 1942 it was fitted to Swordfish and Hudson aircraft and tested in attacking a submarine. It was found that it could penetrate the hull with a 25 lb charge, that five out of 14 attacks resulted in hits, and that this would improve with practice.[9] The rocket, originally designed to attack aircraft from the ground or sea, had turned the tables and was most successful in aerial attack on surface targets. Thus Churchill's favourite anti-aircraft weapon, never fully used in its original purpose, was deployed decisively in land and sea war.[10]

★

Though he had been almost the founding father of the Royal Naval Air Service and had followed the progress of its successor the Fleet Air Arm though two decades (not always on the same side of the controversy), Churchill was deeply dissatisfied with its progress at the beginning of November 1940. He claimed that it was not expanding properly and that the navy was not making the best use of it.[11] Most of his doubts were removed on the 11th when Swordfish biplane aircraft from HMS *Illustrious* and *Eagle* launched a torpedo attack on Italian ships in Taranto Harbour, seriously damaging several ships. It was a much needed success in a bleak period and Churchill hailed it as 'a crippling blow at the Italian fleet'.[12] The torpedo hit which crippled the *Bismarck* in May 1941 was perhaps a lucky strike, but it only made up for plenty of bad luck during that campaign.

The Fleet Air Arm's most obvious problem was the lack of modern aircraft. The venerable Swordfish was the star of both Taranto and the *Bismarck* operations; its intended replacements, the Albacore and Barracuda, were obsolescent by the time they entered service, so it soldiered on. For fighters, at the beginning of the war the navy had to rely on the Fulmar, a version of the Fairey Battle which suffered disastrous losses in France in 1940. The navy was pinning its hopes on the Firebrand and Firefly, which in fact would not be ready until 1943 and 1944, in small numbers. One solution was to convert RAF fighters for naval use, but when Churchill visited the *Indomitable* at Liverpool in September 1941 he was 'astonished to learn that the handful of Hurricanes to be allotted to this vital war unit were only of the lower type, Hurricane one'. He wanted 'only the finest aeroplanes that can do the work to go into all aircraft carriers'.[13] This stimulated much debate and the Ministry of Aircraft Production commented: 'The position regarding the modification of up-to-date RAF fighters for carrier operation is – Hurricane II and Spitfire (any Mark) can be fitted with arrester hook and ATOG spools now, if the Admiralty could extract from the Air Ministry the necessary aeroplanes to be modified.' The official was 'fully alive to the urgency of getting the best procurable fighters for the fleet. The difficulty is to obtain the necessary diversions from the RAF, having committed ourselves, some time ago, to the naval types – Firebrand and Firefly. .... If the PM will say, "give the best fighters to the fleet rather than send them elsewhere" – the matter would be settled very quickly. Unfortunately, "elsewhere" at the moment, had priority over the navy.'[14]

Nevertheless a naval version of the Spitfire, the Seafire, was produced and the First Lord of the Admiralty credited Churchill with it, referring in December 1941 to 'the prospective supply of 200 Spitfires, which you yourself were instrumental in obtaining for us from the Royal Air Force subsequent to your visit to HMS *Indomitable*'. Churchill went further, even agreeing that 'In principle, I am prepared to help you to get all that you require for the armoured carriers, even in priority over the bomber programme.' But the Seafire was not entirely successful as a carrier aircraft. The Admiralty pointed out that as its wings could not be made to fold it could not be used in the small lifts of the *Illustrious* class carriers and took up a great deal of space in the others; that its small endurance meant frequent landings and take-offs, during which the carrier had to turn into the wind, and it did not carry all the radio equipment needed for flights over the sea. In the long run the navy found it more efficient to use American aircraft such as the Grumman Martlet, though supply was dependent on their production priorities.[15]

In July 1943 Churchill turned on the Fleet Air Arm again, asserting: 'it is rather a pregnant fact that out of 45,000 officers and ratings ... only thirty have been killed, or are missing, or have been taken prisoners during the three months ending April 30. I am very glad of course that they have not suffered, but the whole question of the scale of the Fleet Air Arm is raised by this clear proof of how very rarely it is brought into contact with the enemy.' It was a remarkably cruel and incomplete way of assessing the effectiveness of the force, which spent much of its effort hunting U-boats in the Atlantic when it was not involved in major and highly dangerous operations; but it was not a passing indiscretion, he was proud enough to print it in his memoirs.[16]

★

Churchill had opposed the splitting off of Coastal Command from the RAF in 1937, but by November 1940 he believed that with the expansion of the air force, it 'would not ... seriously harm them and might improve operational control', though he feared a duplication of training. The problem was compounded in December when Trenchard threatened to raise the matter in the House of Lords, claiming 'that it was proposed to break up the RAF into separate air services', while Sinclair, the Secretary of State, warned Churchill that opinion in the RAF was 'very strong' on the subject.[17] Lord Beaverbrook and the First Lord favoured transfer, but Churchill commented 'that it might have been desirable, if he had been starting afresh in peacetime, to make the great change proposed. It would be disastrous at the present moment to tear a large fragment from the Royal Air Force', though he supported the transfer of operational control to the Admiralty.[18] This did not solve the problem that the command was under-resourced.

On 1 November 1940 Coastal Command had seven flying boat squadrons, four of Short Sunderlands and the others of obsolete Lerwicks and Stranraers. It had a mixed bag of 22 squadrons of 402 landplanes, including a few Spitfires for photo reconnaissance, American Lockheed Hudsons and obsolescent Ansons, Whitleys, and Blenheims.[19] In October Churchill asked 'why the aircraft and crews available for operations in Coastal Command were so few in relation to the total initial equipment of operationally fit squadrons'. The Air Minister replied that there was only one Operational Training Unit but meanwhile the command had taken on larger aircraft which needed increased crews, who had to be trained at squadron level.[20] But by December even Alexander, the First Lord of the Admiralty, was advocating a reduction – he wanted to send the officers and men of two squadrons to the Middle East as reserve crews for the aircraft carriers, arguing that 'We have at the moment the grandest opportunity of passing these personnel direct through the Mediterranean …'. Churchill could see problems developing nearer home and replied: 'I hope this may be held up for the time being. The gravest danger is in the North Western approaches and we cannot spare the promised aid which the Coastal Command are expecting.'[21]

As with army-co-operation, Coastal Command was offered American aircraft which the RAF regarded as unsuitable in their early versions. In July 1941 Churchill asked Portal why Flying Fortresses and Liberators were not being used in the bombing of Germany as the Americans expected. 'Mr Hopkins has been asking me about their use, and seemed to be recording an American impression that they were lying idle because we had no crews wherewith to man them.' Portal replied that the Liberator I was 'unsuitable for bombing Germany either by night or day. It lacks adequate defensive armament, self-sealing tanks, armour, flame damping equipment etc. It must therefore be used in the Atlantic, where opposition from the air is unlikely.'[22] As to the Flying Fortress, it was intended as a high-flying day bomber over Germany but proved ineffective in that role and the remaining nine were given to Coastal Command. Meanwhile some of the twin-engine bombers, Wellingtons and Whitleys were transferred from Bomber Command as larger aircraft came into service. All this had some effect and by October 1941 Alexander was able to tell Churchill 'beyond all doubt that the close approaches to the United Kingdom have been made perilous to enemy submarines, and in these waters our close range aircraft have been able to exercise adequate supervision'. But the problem remained in the mid-Atlantic. At this stage even Portal was helpful, agreeing with the First Lord that Wellingtons and Whitleys should not be diverted from Coastal Command until flying boats were available to replace them as 'The loss to Coastal Command would be considerable, but the gain to Bomber Command relatively small.'[23]

This began to change early in 1942 as the bomber offensive was stepped up, and Alexander chose a bad time to ask for an increase in Coastal Command. He needed air support in three campaigns – in the Indian Ocean where it was feared that the Japanese would soon attack shipping, in the middle of the Atlantic and in the Bay of Biscay, to attack U-boats leaving and returning to their French bases. He pointed out 'The acute shortage of shipping tonnage will be the principal factor limiting the allied war effort during 1942. The Germans are building U-boats at the rate of 20 a month, and this figure is expected to reach 24 a month shortly. The importance of strengthening our offensive against the U-boat is therefore very great. With recent technical developments such as [air to surface vessel radar], searchlights in [general reconnaissance] aircraft, torpex depth charges with shallow settings and 100 lb torpex filled contact bombs, better results can now be expected when attacking U-boats.' He asked for 6½ Wellington squadrons and 81 Fortresses or Liberators as they became available. Portal's reply was well calculated to meet Churchill's prejudices in favour of the bombing offensive and against purely defensive action:

> The transfer of bomber squadrons without the necessary modification would be a dispersion of our bombing resources in an attempt to contribute defensively to the control of communications over immense areas of ocean where targets are uncertain, fleeting and difficult to hit. Their efforts in this direction would be largely wasted. It remains the considered view of the Air Staff that squadrons of Bomber Command could best contribute to the weakening of the U-boat offensive by offensive action against the principal industrial areas of German within our range, including the main naval industries and dockyards. To divert them to an uneconomical defensive role would be unsound at any time. It would be doubly so now when we are about to launch a bombing offensive ....[24]

By this time Air to Surface Vessel or ASV radar was becoming increasingly common, and it changed the picture with its ability to detect a surfaced U-boat at might. As Portal had hinted, it would take time to fit any aircraft with ASV and they would be almost useless without it. Churchill was torn between two campaigns and merely commented: 'Pray review this ...'. Cherwell found other reasons to deny any more aircraft, suggesting that crews might be 'double-banked' to get twice as much use from the existing aircraft. This did not find favour with the Air Ministry, who presumably recoiled at the extra training effort needed. Instead Portal drew attention to the maintenance problems with the squadrons and suggested an improvement might increase operational efficiency. In July Churchill turned down a further request for aircraft on the grounds that, on Lindemann's figures, squadrons of 20 machines were flying only 30 hours a day, and better maintenance was needed: 'Until everything possible has been done in this direction there can be no case for transferring additional squadrons from Bomber to Coastal Command.'[25]

Meanwhile the Japanese offensive in the Indian Ocean did not develop as fast as feared, while the Bay of Biscay campaign was of dubious value; at the same time, the U-boat offensive was now concentrated on the gap in American defences off her east coast, where the British were not invited to intervene. It was August before the U-boats retuned to mid-Atlantic to do great damage to shipping. In the meantime Churchill had ruled that eight long-range Liberators could be transferred to Coastal Command, and eventually more of these were found. At the end of 1943 Churchill referred to 'The decisive defeat of the U-boats, largely through the air assistance.'[26] That was not the whole story: increased numbers of escorts eventually allowed the formation of mobile support groups, largely on the lines that Churchill had suggested in 1941. Air support came in two forms, carrier-based and shore-based, but Churchill did not mention how difficult it had been to persuade him to allocate enough resources to it.

CHAPTER 39

Combined Operations

Churchill set up a powerful inter-service organisation, Combined Operations, within weeks of the Fall of France. In characteristic fashion it was focussed entirely on renewing the attack on the enemy. The chiefs of staff appointed the Adjutant General of the Royal Marines to head it, but Churchill wanted something 'far more extensive than is at present foreseen'[1] and took on his old colleague and adversary, Admiral of the Fleet Sir Roger Keyes, who at least had character and aggressive spirit, with experience of both the Dardanelles and Zeebrugge. According to John Colville, however, he was given the job 'out of loyalty and affection and in so doing has angered the younger men in the navy'.[2] To General Sir Alan Brooke 'The title "Chief of Combined Operations" was also badly chosen, since every operation we were engaged in was a "combined" one. It was certainly not intended that he should direct combined strategy – his job was to evolve the technique, policy and equipment for the employment of the three services in combined operations to effect landings against opposition.'[3]

Though most British wars had involved amphibious operations, the practice had been neglected between the wars. The failure of the Dardanelles campaign had cast its shadow and in any case it was assumed that the next war would be fought by sea and air. When it was decided to expand the army in 1937, the war was to be fought in alliance with France. But in 1938 the possibility of war with Japan caused the setting up of the Inter-Service Training and Development Centre which produced the assault landing craft, later known as the LCA under the American system of designation. It could be launched from the lifeboat davits of a converted passenger ship and land a platoon under combat conditions. It was first used to land the French Foreign Legion at Narvik in 1940, then to withdraw troops from Dunkirk, after which it was involved in all the major European amphibious operations. There already were a few vessels to carry these craft – the liners *Glenearn, Glenroy* and *Glengyle* had been taken up for Churchill's abortive operations in the Baltic and were being converted to landing ships, infantry, to carry troops and a dozen LCAs. They were soon joined by Belgian ferries, and all the British LSIs (infantry landing ships) used during the war originated as merchant ships.

A modern landing, apart from a brief commando raid, was not likely to succeed unless it could bring heavy armour with it, and at the end of June 1940 Churchill asked for tank landing craft to be designed. On 9 August 1940 he wrote to Ismay: 'Get me a further report about the designs and types of vessels to transport armoured vehicles by sea and land on beaches.'[4] The original LCT was capable of carrying three tanks of 40 tons, the largest then envisaged, and landing them in 2 ft 6 ins of water. It was designed for operations as far as the west coast of France. The first was delivered in November and began a line of development.[5] But still Churchill was not satisfied, for as one of the designers put it: 'The first LCT had hardly completed its trials [when] the Prime Minister demanded ships that could land tanks ... on beaches anywhere in the world. The problem was difficult physically because of the obvious fact that we should have to have an ocean-going ship of limited draught; it was difficult psychologically because it seemed certain that any ships so used would need to be written off after the first assault.'[6] This was the landing ship tank, which could carry up to 18 tanks across the ocean and land them on a beach. They were the beginning of a bewildering series of ships and craft that were to evolve over the next four years. Some were to carry personnel, some vehicles, while others were support craft which might provide gunfire, control and communications, culinary services and many other functions. Minor landing craft like the LCAs were carried into action by landing ships such as the Glens. Major landing craft such as LCTs could make the whole journey themselves, while landing ships, apart from the LSTs (landing ship, tank) were designed to carry and launch minor landing craft. But despite the progress, the shortage of landing craft was always a brake on operations at least until 1944.

As to the crews, Churchill was cautious about keeping large numbers in readiness and minuted in November 1942: 'No doubt there must be a nucleus of skilled personnel to handle them and keep the engines in order. They do not have to be kept up however like a fleet or flotilla, as they are only needed for a special operation, and if all goes well, only for the preliminary stages of that.'[7] But under Mountbatten the numbers of men in landing craft crews would expand greatly and in practice they were kept in service as one invasion followed another from Torch onwards. Churchill tended to underestimate the skills needed, but they would become evident when they moved to the tidal waters off Normandy.

★

The use of term 'commando' is attributed to Lieutenant-Colonel D. W. Clarke, an aide to General Dill who had been an infant during the siege of Ladysmith and had heard many stories about the daring of the Boer commandos. He 'produced the outline of a scheme .... The men for this type of irregular warfare should, he suggested, be formed into units to be known as Commandos ... Nor was the historical parallel far-fetched. After the victories of Roberts and Kitchener had scattered the Boer army, the guerrilla tactics of its individual units (which were styled "Commandos") ... prevented decisive victory. ... His ideas were accepted; so also, with some hesitation, was the name Commando.'[8] Whatever hesitation he encountered in the War Office, there was none from Churchill when he took the idea to him on 6 June. The Prime Minister was perhaps influenced by his admiration for these units 40 years before and by his friendship with Field Marshal Smuts, who had led some of them. The term originally referred to a unit rather than an individual. They were of about 600 men, essentially the equivalent of infantry battalions without the administrative and logistic tail. As to weapons, they were lightly armed, but not too lightly. Churchill complained at the end of September 1940 of No 7 Commando at Felixstowe: 'It has no Bren guns, no anti-tank rifles, and though it has some Tommy guns, they have no ammunition.'[9] The novelist Evelyn Waugh, serving with the Royal Marines, had to drop rank to join the commandos but wrote to his wife: 'You need have no misgivings about my prestige. Everyone in the army is competing feverishly to get into a commando and it is more glorious to be a subaltern here than a captain in the RM Brigade.'[10] Apart from the success of the units, the term gained a glamour and currency well beyond its original meaning. Even if Churchill did not originate that use of the term, he certainly publicised it.

On 25 August 1940 Churchill wrote to Eden the War Secretary: 'I feel the Germans have been right, both in the last war and in this, in the use they have made of storm troops. In 1918 the infiltrations which were so deadly to us were by storm troops and the final defence of Germany rested mainly upon brilliantly posted and valiantly fought machine gun nests. The defeat of France was accomplished by an incredibly small number of highly equipped elite while the dull mass of the German army came on behind ...'. Any campaign of 1941 would depend on 'surprise landings of lightly equipped, nimble forces accustomed to work like packs of hounds instead of being moved about in the ponderous manner which is appropriate to the regular formations'. When accused of failing to implement this policy, Eden countered effectively: 'If I seem to you to be violently opposed to the storm troop principle, it is only because I do not want the greater part of the British Army to become a dull dead mass.'[11]

Churchill had his way, though the commandos did not flourish to start with. Three of them were grouped into Layforce under Brigadier Robert Laycock and sent on the long voyage to the Middle East early in 1941. They lost 600 men out of 2,000 in the defence of Crete and were disbanded; however another commando force was reconstituted for service in the Mediterranean.[12] But Churchill maintained his interest and in August 1942 proclaimed: 'It must be most clearly understood that the policy of [His Majesty's government] is to maintain and develop the Commando organization with the utmost energy and to make sure that the wastage and losses are replaced by good quality men.'[13]

★

In 1940–41 Churchill generally thought the war would be won by bombing and that the function of Combined Operations was to organise increasingly large raids on the enemy coast. In July 1940 Keyes was reported to be 'studying the whole subject of medium raids, ie not less than five nor more than ten thousand men. Two or three of these might be brought off on the French coast during the winter.'[14] By the end of August he was far more ambitious, suggesting 'the capture of Oslo and the consequent undoing of Hitler's first great achievement; the invasion of it by sea'; or the cutting off of the Cherbourg peninsula 'and, most attractive of all, a landing in the Low Countries followed by the seizure of the Ruhr, or at any rate North German territory'. He envisaged forces of 100,000–120,000 men being used.[15] More moderately, Churchill told the Tank Parliament in May 1941: 'if we could land at various places in the enemy's enormous coast line really powerful forces of tanks, we could reckon on the uprising populations to assist us'.[16] By July 1941 he was advocating to Roosevelt 'the simultaneous landing of say 15,000 tanks from specially fitted ocean-going ships on the beaches of three or four countries ripe for revolt'.[17] These highly ambitious plans crystallised into Operation Sledgehammer, which had American support and was defined as 'the establishment of a bridgehead on the continent in the event of a crack in German morale'. It involved landing three lightly equipped infantry brigade groups, three tank battalions and three commandos around the port of Le Havre, with the support of paratroopers, hundreds of ships, twelve bomber squadrons and more than 600 fighters. The Chiefs of Staff warned in August 1942 that 'our plan is only suitable for these conditions of German demoralisation, as we have contemplated risks that would be unacceptable in any less favourable circumstances'.[18]

In fact the only raid which approached that scale was on Dieppe on 19 August 1942, when 5,000 Canadians, 1,000 British commandos and a tank brigade landed. It was a disaster: 60 per cent of the men were killed or captured, and losses at sea and in the air were also heavy. Having sacrificed dominion troops in a fruitless venture, Churchill might have faced the same dislike as in Australia after Gallipoli, had his prestige not been so high by this time. German propaganda made a great deal of it, suggesting that it was a failed invasion. In retrospect Churchill asked a series of questions, including: 'Who made the military plans, and who approved them?', 'Did the General Staff check the plan?', and 'What were the reasons for using tanks in a frontal assault off the beaches by the casino instead of landing them a few miles up the coast and entering the town from the back?' He commented: 'At first sight it would appear to a layman very much out of accord with the accepted principles of war to attack the strongly fortified town without first securing the cliffs on either side ...'.[19] Mountbatten, who had recently taken over in Combined Operations, claimed that important lessons had been learned. The most important one was that it would be almost impossible to capture a Channel port, and this stimulated the development of artificial harbours. It also ended the concept of the large-scale raid, and from then on landing operations consisted of short, sharp commando attacks, or full-scale invasions in which the force would stay there until ultimate victory.

Otherwise, raids on the enemy coasts were small scale. In 1941 a raid was planned on the Lofoten Islands off Norway, partly to destroy a fish oil factory believed to be a major source of vitamin A. Churchill queried its effect on one of his pet projects and was assured that 'The chiefs of staff do not consider that the operation is likely to stir up the Norwegian coast or lead to reinforcements of German forces in the peninsula. They are able to reassure you that there is no intention to land anywhere on the mainland.' The raid took place, but German reprisals were so savage that the Norwegian government in exile begged them not to repeat it. Mass risings, whether supported by large-scale raids or not, were part of the Churchill dream, and he set up the Special Operations Executive or SOE to support them. Resistance movements in Western Europe had some value in sabotage and intelligence, but had not the scope, training or weaponry to organise a full-scale rising, while German ruthlessness tended to keep them suppressed and isolated.

★

Like most people, Churchill was impressed with the performance of the German paratroopers in Holland and Belgium and indeed he had suggested something similar in his paper of October 1917: 'Considerable parties of soldiers could be conveyed by air to the neighbourhood of bridges or other important points.' He did not mention parachutes but the aircraft of that time could usually land in fields; it was different for the much more powerful machines of 1940. On 22 June, just as France signed the armistice with Germany, he called for 'a corps of at least 5,000 parachute troops, including a proportion of Australians, New Zealanders and Canadians, together with some trustworthy people from Norway and France'. There was some confusion about the numbers: in April 1941 when he was told that 500 were now ready he commented, 'I said 5,000,' and was told that was the eventual aim, but limitations of equipment made it impossible for now.[20] The Air Staff put the problem down to the lack of suitable aircraft. The type used for training was the Whitley, a failed bomber, but it could carry only eight passengers and they had to exit though a narrow hole in the floor at great risk of being trapped. They exited so slowly that they might be spread over a wide area on landing. The Douglas DC3 or Dakota had been developed as a civilian airliner and offered far better possibilities with its side door, but at the moment there were only four of them and they were needed elsewhere. Eventually over 1,900 of them would be supplied to the RAF.

Crete was invaded by German paratroopers in May 1941 and Churchill was even more anxious. On the 27th he dictated a memo: 'This a sad story ... I feel myself greatly to blame for allowing myself to be overborne by the resistances which were offered.' The Air Staff, always resentful of any diversion from the bombing campaign, had commented in August that 'dropping troops from the air by parachute is a clumsy and obsolescent method. ... The Germans made excellent use of their parachute troops in the Low Countries by exploiting surprise, and by virtue of the fact that they had practically no opposition. But it seems to us at least possible that this may be the last time that parachute troops are used on a serious scale in major operations.' This was a red rag to Churchill, who remarked: 'One can see how wrongly based these resistances are … in the light of what is happening in Crete, and may soon be happening in Cyprus and in Syria.'[21]

The Air Staff tended to favour the glider over the parachute, and this found support from Churchill. In September 1940 he commented: 'Of course if the glider scheme is better than parachutes, we should pursue it, but is it being seriously taken up? Are we not in danger of being fobbed off with one doubtful and experimental policy and losing the other which has already been proved?'[22] By May 1941 a dozen eight-seat gliders were under construction, a 25-seat model was progressing, and the design of one to carry a light tank was in progress. These became the Horsa and the Hamilcar, which were used in the Normandy invasion of 1944. But there was more truth in the Air Staff assessment than Churchill allowed. Hitler drew the opposite conclusion from the Crete affair, seeing it as an expensive diversion, and it was the last German airborne attack. The success of the paratroopers in Normandy in 1944 was questionable, and they failed at Arnhem later that year.

★

Keyes had been haranguing Churchill ever since the trip to Loch Ewe in 1914, and he did not stop now. He had no regard for Dudley Pound, who had once been his flag captain and chief of staff, and relations with the Admiralty were poor. Churchill was already becoming 'bored with his importunity' by December 1940.[23] He often had occasion to rebuke Keyes, for example in January 1941: 'You and your commandos will have to obey orders like other people. And that is all there is to be said about it.'[24] His long, rambling letters did not fit in with Churchill's desire for brevity. He set up a separate headquarters in Richmond Terrace opposite Downing Street and established the force of commandos as well as a training base at Inveraray in Scotland. His favourite operation was one to attack the Italian island of Pantelleria.

Churchill, always a fan of island adventures, supported this, but it did not meet with the approval of the chiefs of staff or the Commander-in-Chief of the Mediterranean, who thought it would be impossible to hold. Keyes's role was downgraded in September 1941 and Churchill had him relieved.

Keyes's successor was Lord Louis Mountbatten, the son of Battenberg the former First Sea Lord of 1914. He was fresh from the command of a destroyer which was lightly fictionalised by Noel Coward for the film *In Which we Serve*. Even Churchill hinted that he was rash, commenting when Mountbatten wanted to take command of an aircraft carrier: 'You fool! The best thing you can hope to do there is to repeat your last achievement and get yourself sunk.' He had a rapid promotion from captain to acting vice-admiral. According to Brooke, 'His appointment ... was excellent and he certainly played a remarkable role as the driving force and mainspring of this organisation. Without his energy and drive it would never have reached the high standards it achieved.'[25] His diplomacy and charm contrasted with Keyes's stridency and he was far better at getting what he wanted, including a voice on the Chiefs of Staff Committee. During his time Combined Operations expanded from 22 landing ships to 113, from 509 landing craft and barges to 3,979, and from 4,970 trained naval personnel to 38,209.[26] When Mountbatten left for the Far East Churchill appointed Robert Laycock, who had led the commandos since their early days. He had a far lower profile than his predecessors, but by that time the issue had moved on as the biggest project of all began to take shape. It was never expected that the head of Combined Operations would command in the field, but it provided the trained personnel for the invasion of France in 1944.

★

Ever since the eighteenth century British amphibious operations had been dogged by bad relations between army and naval commanders, and at that time there was no legal mechanism for putting one in charge of the other. The problem had of course been highlighted at the Dardanelles, when the two services often seemed to be moving to different rhythms, and it was compounded by the use of air power over land and sea. In March 1926 Churchill advocated closer integration of the services:

> One of the earliest tasks of the joint defence committee, ministers and experts together, would be to call into being a joint staff training organisation to create near the summit a band of officers of general attainments and habits of thought and also to create a staff college or system of study for officers of the middle rank to secure a more deeply laid foundation in the future. All this is an essential preliminary of a joint general staff.
>
> There is nothing starting or untried in this conception. Infantry, artillery and cavalry officers, proud of their own arms and with the stamp of these areas imprinted on them by their earlier training, nevertheless are considered equally qualified to direct armies composed of all three arms and of many others.[27]

A further step was to appoint a supreme commander over all three services for a particular theatre or operation, which Churchill tried to do, in unpropitious circumstances, in Norway in April 1940: 'In order to ensure concerted action in operations to capture Narvik His Majesty's Government has decided that absolute command should be vested in one officer. Admiral of the Fleet Lord Cork as senior officer will in consequence assume command forthwith of all forces committed to this task.'[28] But Churchill later admitted that 'naval officers, even when granted the fullest authority, are chary of giving orders to the army about purely military matters. This would be even more true if the positions were reversed.'[29]

The lack of a supreme commander to defend against invasion seriously worried Brooke in 1940:

> ... there was no form of combined command over the three services. And yet their roles were ultimately locked together. Who was deciding the claims between the employment of destroyers against hostile landing craft, as opposed to anti-submarine operations on the Western Approaches? Who would decide between the conflicting calls of the Army for bombers to attack beaches, as opposed to the Navy wanting them for attacks on hostile fleets? ... It was a highly dangerous organization; had an invasion developed I fear that Churchill would have attempted as Defence Minister to co-ordinate the actions of these various commands. This would have been wrong and highly dangerous, with his impulsive nature and tendency to arrive at decisions through a process of intuition, as opposed to 'logical' approach. Heaven knows where he might have led us.[30]

Churchill of course was always a military commander *manqué*, so that was not unlikely. Brooke also saw the possibility of the three chiefs of staff taking joint command during an invasion, but that was no more encouraging, as he attended a meeting on 8 September: 'It reminds me of the tea party in *Alice in Wonderland*, with Dill as Alice, Portal as the Hatter, and Dudley Pound as the Dormouse.' It is difficult to see how 'Dilly-dally', the narcoleptic Pound and the inadequate Newall could have found the dynamism and daring to lead the defence.

The invasion did not come and instead emphasis shifted to the war in the Mediterranean. In February 1942 it was suggested that 'General Auchinleck to be supreme commander over the three services in his command, navy, army and air'.[31] This would not have fitted well with the highly competent Admiral Cunningham, who was fighting a war of his own with the Italian fleet as well as supporting the army in Greece and Crete, and it was not implemented. Nevertheless in March Churchill was 'Increasingly impressed with the disadvantages of the present system of having naval, army, and air force officers equally represented at all points and on all combined subjects ... we should move in the direction of appointing supreme commanders in particular areas and for special tasks.'[32] The chiefs of staff had slight differences when asked; Pound wanted a commander-in-chief 'exercising joint command. Preferably under chairmanship of minister of state (eg the present system in the Middle East).' Brooke was emphatic that the supreme commander 'should seldom, if ever, exercise direct command of his own service' while Portal went further, stating 'Supreme Commander should not exercise tactical control of any forces'. Churchill resolved this in a memo of 4 April 1942, concluding: 'There is no risk of an officer selected for his all-round experience and qualities thrusting himself into the tactical details of a service other than his own. On the contrary, the danger is in the direction of undue diffidence leading to the paralysis and negation which are so much criticised in our operations.'[33] Mountbatten could not be accused of 'undue diffidence', which is perhaps why he was appointed supreme commander in South-East Asia in October 1943. But Churchill rejected Sir Stafford Cripps's idea of a single commander for the Battle of the Atlantic on the grounds that it was too broad: 'Anti-U-boat warfare affects every command afloat and ashore and every branch of the Admiralty. Such an organisation as you propose would cut across all existing arrangements and disturb all existing loyalties.'[34] Brooke, having declined command in the desert war in 1942, believed Churchill had three times promised him the supreme command of the invasion of France, but in August 1943 Churchill broke the news that for political reasons it would go to Eisenhower. Brooke was 'swamped by a dark cloud of despair'.[35]

★

The first permanent invasions, as distinct from raids, were in French colonial territories where the opposition was likely to be light or non-existent. An attempt on Dakar in 1940 was abandoned largely because of the escape of the French cruisers, but it also showed that organisation for such an affair was still primitive – at last Churchill was beginning to see that such operations could not be improvised and needed long and detailed planning. The only long-range operation was to take Madagascar in May 1942, in order to forestall the Japanese setting up a submarine base in the harbour of Diego Suarez, though Churchill was aware that 'The rest of the enormous island was of less strategic importance.'[36] Churchill supported the invasion of French North Africa, Operation Torch, as an alternative to a premature invasion of northern Europe or American withdrawal to the Pacific. He originally hoped it might be accompanied by Jupiter, the invasion of northern Norway to ensure the sea route to Russia, but that did not find American support. The landings took place in November 1942 and Churchill deemed the assault phase 'a brilliant success' by which 'the fall of Algiers and Casablanca had been obtained cheaply' though only with Free French support and little resistance.[37]

Churchill's Mediterranean strategy was never fixed and only emerged slowly. He was typically reluctant to create the 'second front' demanded by popular opinion and invade the enemy directly in northern Europe, going into his strongest point and perhaps creating a new western front. Instead he persuaded Stalin (temporarily at least) that western forces should go for the 'soft underbelly' of the Axis by invading though the Mediterranean. At Casablanca in January 1943 he persuaded the Americans to back this strategy as soon as the Germans and Italians were cleared from North Africa. This led to landings in Sicily and mainland Italy which were opposed to varying degrees, and provided experience for the largest of all, code-named Overlord. There is little doubt that Churchill was right to decline to attack northern France in 1942, when few American resources were available. It remains controversial whether it could have been done in 1943, if resources, especially landing craft, had not been diverted to Sicily and Italy. But in any case Italy was not the 'soft underbelly' that Churchill had predicted and the offensive there ground to a halt against German resistance. The invasion of northern France was inevitable.

★

Churchill claimed to have been the inspiration for artificial harbours with his minute of May 1942, and certainly it must have stimulated debate – 'They must float up and down with the tide. The anchor problem must be answered. ... Let me have the best solution worked out. Don't argue the matter. The difficulties will argue for themselves.'[38] In a sense it harked back to his ideas for an artificial island in the North Sea in 1917, made up of 'flat-bottomed barges or caissons made, not of steel but of concrete'. The failure of the Dieppe raid made it clear that a port could not be captured intact in time, and several schemes were under consideration by August 1943. There was the bubble breakwater and the 'Lilo' breakwater, for it was found that 'a quilted canvas bag, inflated by air at low pressure and ballasted to float so that the greater portion is below the surface, damps out waves'. Churchill queried its abandonment in October, asking for photographs. There were more conventional floating piers and sunken blockships, which had been used for different reasons at Scapa Flow since 1914. But in practice the main breakwaters would be made of concrete and known as Phoenixes. Churchill kept a close eye on production; in January 1944 he was 'Disturbed by recent reports about the Mulberry position' (as the harbour project was code-named). He was also concerned about the blockships, for 'the total loss of such a large number of ships was a very serious matter'.

His son-in-law Duncan Sandys arranged for him to visit some Phoenix units in East India Docks, London, in April, and anxiety increased as D-day approached, but the harbours were ready.[39]

Though he had little operational control over the invasion, Churchill devoted the first few days of June to it. On the 1st the King visited the War Room and 'The Prime Minister explained how it was proposed the landing should be effected and the parts to be played by the navy, army and air force respectively', while Admiral Ramsay gave details of naval build-up. This was partly to deflect Churchill from his plan to witness the invasion on board HMS *Belfast*. The invasion was set for the 5th, and the day before, according to Pim, Churchill and Montgomery 'visited huge masses of men embarking in the ships to take them across the French coast'. The party went into a naval motor launch to take them down Southampton Water: 'During the whole of this cruise we were passing ship after ship of an armada the size of which is hard to contemplate all ready for the signal which would direct their course towards the French coast.' They went to Eisenhower's headquarters in the hills above Portsmouth, but the signal to start did not come that day as the winds were likely to be too strong. Churchill and his party went back to London, and it was Eisenhower who made the critical decision to exploit a gap in the bad weather and land on the morning of the 6th.

During the night of 5/6 June, according to Pim, 'three times during the night the Prime Minister came in to get the very latest information'.[40] On the morning of the 6th the allied armies stormed ashore in Normandy, having been preceded by paratroopers and glider troops, which Churchill had developed. The shore bombarding force included the old battleships *Warspite* and *Ramillies* which Churchill had ordered, as well as the monitors *Roberts* and *Erebus*. Commandos landed to secure the flanks. The landing craft themselves were manned by British and Americans in roughly equal numbers, but nearly four-fifths of the crews of the supporting warships were British. After their naval training under Keyes and Mountbatten, most of the British landing craft crews found the right spots on the beaches, unlike many of the Americans. 'Swimming tanks' as developed by Hobart largely failed in the bad weather, so the first to land as part of the main force on the British and Canadian beaches were the special tanks, 'Hobart's funnies'. Some of the infantry were carried in the Glen ships which Churchill had originally procured for the navy, and the later waves of tanks came in LSTs. Soon the troops ashore would be supported by rockets, in the design of which, largely unwittingly, Churchill had played a part; and construction would begin soon on the Mulberry harbours which he had encouraged. Though he had been reluctant to start the invasion of north-west Europe, and though his control over the operation was far less complete or direct than he might have wished, he had reason to take personal pride in the force which landed.

A storm on 19–20 June damaged the British artificial harbour, Mulberry B at Arromanches, and especially the American Mulberry A at Omaha Beach. Churchill pressed for their restoration, ordering additional blockships as the matter was 'especially urgent'.[41] But in fact the American Mulberry was never completely repaired; it was found that much simpler 'Gooseberries', created simply by blockships, were adequate for the purpose. As with many of the D-day inventions, the simplest solution was found to be the best.

In some ways the Normandy landings were a supreme triumph against great difficulties and ultimately they were the culmination of much of Churchill's philosophy as well as deploying quite a few of his ideas. They were perhaps a counterpoint to the failure at the Dardanelles, but they showed that such an operation needed a clear command structure and meticulous planning, and perhaps worked better by allowing the men on the spot to make the key decisions without political interference.

Conclusion

On 8 May 1945 the war with Germany came to an end, and this time Churchill was not sitting anonymously in his office as in 1918. He appeared on the balcony of Buckingham Palace before a huge crowd, standing between the King and Queen and their two daughters (Elizabeth wearing her khaki ATS uniform). There was 'a great outburst of cheering which continued for at least five minutes'. He waved his cigar to the crowd then left in his car, to be cheered again on the way out. It was perhaps the climax of his career. He had successfully directed the war but was well aware that there was another one still to be concluded against Japan, though he would not have the opportunity to conduct it. A general election was called and on the morning of the 26 July, after the votes of servicemen had been flown in from around the world and counted, he settled in the basement of No 10 where Captain Pim had set up a version of the map room to plot the results – for Churchill had a habit, unfortunate in the circumstances, of seeing the election as an extension of the war.

> Every constituency in the British Isles was shown including the name of the existing member and the party to which he belonged, and as the results came in the new position was indicated in a space left opposite the constituency. I also had a score board on another wall, on the lines of an American tennis tournament court, and this showed from minute to minute the gains and losses of each respective party. ...
>
> We had a staff of eight on duty all day, and there was not one moment for several hours when they could relax. ... With the exception of half an hour for

> lunch, the Prime Minister never left us all day. ... By lunchtime many members of the government had fallen. ... This, indeed, was democracy for which we had been fighting for six long years.

The Conservatives and their allies had 213 members, the Liberals had 12, and other parties had 22. Labour had 393 and a majority of 146 over all parties – by far its best result so far.

Churchill the Conservative leader was never popular electorally; when he did regain the premiership in 1951 in the third election since the end of the German war, he had a majority of seats but only a minority of the popular vote. Apart from the setting up of the National Health Service by the Labour Government, which the British still love passionately despite its faults, one advantage of Churchill's defeat in 1945 was that he had time to write *The Second World War*, his six-volume account of the conflict and his own part in it, in the style established in *The World Crisis*. According to Professor David Reynolds who has made the most detailed and critical study of it, it is 'a vast and intricate work'. He goes on: 'The most enduring image from the memoirs is of Churchill as leader. He was trying to shift perceptions of himself from the man of words to the man of deeds – to balance the war speeches that, through broadcasts, records and texts, had become his public persona. The documents he prints at such length in the chapters and the appendices show an omnipresent, almost omniscient, leader.'[1] It infuriated Brooke, now Lord Alanbrooke, who published his own diaries as a counterblast to what he saw as Churchill's egoism and insensitivity, though with some of the most critical passages edited out. The controversy over Churchill's exact role began and continues to this day.

★

Hardly anyone would dispute that Churchill played a vital role in preventing a deal with the Germans in 1940, and in rallying morale then and for the rest of the war. Beyond that, some have argued that his influence was largely negative, with his overbearing manner and his constant interventions. Perhaps the most damaging, from the inside at least, was Brooke's comment that 'He know no details, he has only got half the picture in his mind, talks absurdities and makes my bold boil to listen to his nonsense.'

Later he admitted that his criticism was 'unnecessarily harsh' and 'written at a moment of exasperation', but his diaries are full of comments which are only slightly milder.[2] But it was this creative tension which produced the best results. Admiral Godfrey wrote: 'The proper conduct of the war demanded that Mr Churchill would remain in power and that those around him should be the sort of people he could work with, who could work with him and who would retrain his wasteful and time-consuming plans without being flung out of office. This was not an easy balance to achieve, as after 1941 all the available energy and brain power of the country had been absorbed in the machinery of war.'[3]

In 1940 Churchill proclaimed: 'If the British Commonwealth and its Empire lasts for a thousand years, men will still say, "This was their finest hour."' If his mission was to defend and restore the British Empire, then he was a failure. The Fall of Singapore damaged its prestige irreparably and helped fuel the rise of nationalist movements. By the time he died in 1965, nearly all the colonies had become independent. But he did qualify it with the word 'Commonwealth' which survives to this day. As to the second part of the quotation, many people do believe that 'This was their finest hour.' In his authoritative and dispassionate assessment of Britain's military effectiveness, Williamson Murray states that 'with Churchill in control the system worked with extraordinary efficiency. With his drive, bureaucratic sense, and intellectual strength Churchill hammered his advisers and the system into effectively allocating and utilizing resources and making timely decisions.' Murray might have added Churchill's military knowledge to the list of qualities, and indeed he hints that his predecessors failed because they 'had lacked a depth of knowledge on military and strategic matters'.[4]

The achievement can only be seen in the context of what was happening in the other warring nations. Britain and the United States were the only countries to maintain full 360-degree effort over several theatres of war. Germany had no aircraft carriers, crude landing craft and fought entirely in Europe, the Atlantic and the Mediterranean, while Italy was confined entirely to the inland sea with inferior equipment. Japan deployed carriers to full effect in the Pacific, but her armoured forces were primitive, the country had no radar, and there was no question of a strategic bombing offensive. The Soviet Union was preoccupied with the land war against Germany and had only a small navy and a tactical air force. Britain on the other hand fought in the Europe and South-East Asia, in the Atlantic, Pacific and Indian Oceans and deployed every kind of weapons system except, towards the end, pilotless bombs and guided missiles like the Germans. But Britain had far fewer resources than the United States in personnel, finance and material goods so it was a great strain to fight on so many fronts and with so many different techniques. And under Churchill the British economy and society was more mobilised for war than any other, with the possible exception of the Soviet Union.

Williamson Murray also wrote:

> The military performance of Britain in the Second World War provides any number of important points. In many respects it was truly outstanding. Its mobilisation and resource allocation was the best of any combatant in the war; its conduct of strategy and it ability to co-operate with allies in an effective fashion were also excellent. Interservice cooperation, particularly in combined operations, made major contributions to the winning of the war, and the conduct of intelligence and incorporation of both technical and 'Ultra' information into the war effort was outstanding.[5]

With the possible exception of intelligence, all these factors were deeply influenced by Churchill. His role as arbiter between the needs of the different services and industry depended very much on his inside knowledge of their affairs, gained by his time at the three service ministries and in Munitions. This experience gave him a justified scepticism, particularly when he remembered the tricks he had used to augment the naval budget in 1911–14. Co-operation with allies was another of his key interests, and depended a great deal on his knowledge of the world and its history. He failed in his attempts to persuade France to fight on in 1940, but his diplomacy and his frequent travels reinforced Roosevelt's tendency to give priority to the European war over the Pacific, though at the time many Americans thought that Japan was the main enemy. Anglo-American co-operation was one of the most notable features of the war.

Churchill's success in fostering inter-service co-operation might seem limited, in view of the controversies over coastal command and army co-operation, but in the end these problems were solved, making major contributions to victory. The success of Churchill's combined approach can best be measured against the practice in other countries. Only in the other two maritime powers, the United States and Japan, were the army and navy regarded as approximately equal, though neither country had a fully independent air service. In the United States naval aviation was a powerful force in its own right, with high-performance fighters like the Hellcat and Corsair as well as long-range aircraft such as the PBY Catalina. More than 83,000 aircraft were built for it during the war, and at its peak it had nearly 431,000 personnel. The USA had no immediate need for fighter defence, but its heavy bombers were part of the Army Air Force. Officially that was subject to the Secretary for War, but in fact it had a good deal of independence, and it was even more sensitive than the RAF about using its aircraft for the direct support of ground operations. It learned a great deal from observing British tactics in North Africa, and the XIX Tactical Air Force played a key part in the Normandy campaign.

In the Pacific the Americans had two separate drives towards Japan. The northerly and most direct one was led by Admiral Nimitz for the navy and was the famous 'island hopping' campaign across the central Pacific. Since the navy had its own marine corps which was half a million strong at its peak, as well as strong forces of carrier-borne and land-based aircraft, there was minimal need for army support. The southern drive, led towards the Philippines by General MacArthur of the army, was widely seen as political, following MacArthur's highly publicised promise 'I shall return' after the evacuation of the Philippines in 1942. Though he relied on naval support in the form of carriers and landing craft, he had a separate command answering only to Washington. The USA did develop a strong force of landing craft for the European war, often in co-operation with the British and with Churchill's personal intervention. But in the key landing in Normandy in 1944, four-fifths of the crews and supporting ships were British and Canadian.

The Japanese had no independent air force and the army and navy fought separate wars, the army in China and the navy in the Pacific. They came together in Tokyo to compete fiercely for funding. The army practically controlled the state and was not subjected to criticism from any quarter. It had easy successes against the divided Chinese, while the navy had spectacular coups against the Americans and British in the early stages, but soon the faults began to show. When the services did have to come together, as the in the Guadalcanal campaign of 1942, the results were disastrous, according to an American account: 'The Imperial army and navy, which were supposed to be co-operating in the Guadalcanal campaign, not only failed to coordinate planning but worked together, if at all, with ill-concealed hostility.'[6]

General Brooke, later Lord Alanbrooke, accompanied Churchill on many of his overseas travels and had a chance to see other leaders at work. He wrote of Roosevelt and his relations with the Chief of Staff of the army: 'The President had no military knowledge and was fully aware of this fact and consequently relied on Marshall and listened to Marshall's advice. Marshall never seemed to have any difficulty in countering any wildish plans which the President might put forward.'[7] Brooke envied this, but there were weaknesses in the Roosevelt leadership, even before his health declined seriously in 1945. Certainly the President did not delve deeply into the affairs of the military as Churchill did, but according to the constitution he was commander-in-chief of the armed forces and he tended to take this seriously. With vast resources, their allocation was never quite such a serious matter as it was in Britain, and the war fronts were some distance away. Roosevelt generally did allow the chiefs of staff to take the initiative and only overruled them if it did not suit his purposes. He did do this on occasion, especially in the approval for Operation Torch, and later at Casablanca when he was convinced by Churchill's plans for a Mediterranean offensive, and adopted the policy of 'unconditional surrender' off his own bat.[8]

Stalin presented almost the opposite picture. Brooke 'rapidly grew to appreciate the fact that he had a military brain of the very highest order. Never once in any of his statements did he make a strategic error, nor did he ever fail to appreciate the implications of a situation with a quick and unerring eye.'[9] Brooke also saw the much darker side of Stalin in his 'unpleasantly cold, crafty, dead face' and was aware that he had executed many of his generals in 1937–38, a much worse fate than Churchill's occasional sacking of his. Stalin's war leadership is usually divided into three phases. In the first one he was shocked and paralysed by the Nazi invasion in contravention of the pact with Hitler, though Churchill had warned him it was coming. After that he rallied the nation and like Churchill looked back at the tactics of the wars he had experienced – in this case the tight discipline and political control of the Russian Civil War of 1918–21. He controlled his commanders too rigidly and had little understanding of tank warfare. In the second phase, with the German assault on Stalingrad, he appointed Marshal Zhukov as his deputy with other highly competent generals alongside him. Now 'decision making would be made on a more collegiate basis and disagreement with the dictator would be tolerated' – which was not unlike Churchill's system. In the final phase, after the Battle of Kursk in 1943, he matured into 'a real military commander', according to Zhukov, and this is when Brooke reported on him. He took control of the central front himself and relished the victory.[10]

Of course Brooke did not have a chance to see Adolf Hitler at work, but he really was a 'dictator' in far more senses than Brooke had used the term about Churchill. Hitler too thought he was a military genius, with far less justification than Churchill – his only military service was four years on the Western Front when he did not rise above the rank of gefreiter, the equivalent of private first class – he was never a corporal and leader of men as many accounts suggest. The invasion of France, perhaps his greatest single success, was carried out without his authority and largely against his will, though he did not hesitate to claim the credit for it later.[11] His insight, however, was enough to convince at least one distinguished commander. After a meeting in 1943 Admiral Karl Dönitz commented with apparent sincerity:

> The enormous strength which the Fuehrer radiates, his unwavering confidence, and his far-sighted appraisal of the Italian situation have made it very clear in these days that we are all very insignificant in comparison with the Fuehrer, and that our knowledge and the picture we get from our limited vantage are fragmentary. Anyone who believes he can do better than the Fuehrer is silly.[12]

But unlike Churchill, Hitler did indeed surround himself with sycophants and became enraged if his orders were questioned or disobeyed, however impossible they might be. Military leaders were kept at arm's length, and Hitler did not have a Brooke, Cunningham, Portal or Ismay close enough to him to provide sound military advice and stand up to his wilder ideas. His system of government was described as 'near anarchy of competing fiefdoms' in which his subordinates were expected vaguely to 'work towards the Fuehrer'.[13] Early in the war many of the key policies – U-boat warfare on merchant shipping, Blitzkrieg tactics in France, and the bombing of London – were initiated by accident or by relatively junior officers and adopted as general policy. Later, as the armies were driven back, Hitler issued peremptory orders to hold out in impossible positions, notably at Stalingrad. The early wartime policy of leaving the decisions to those on the spot was progressively undermined.

In these terms, Brooke had reason to be thankful he was working with Churchill. As one historian put it: 'the most notable aspect of the machine for the direction of Britain's war was that it was better ordered than that of any other belligerent, notably including those of German and later the US. A cynic might suggest that Churchill created a system to protect himself from his own excesses. In a remarkable degree, this was successful.'[14]

With hindsight there is no doubt that many of Churchill's ideas were misguided. If he is often seen backing the wrong horse, for example on unrotated projectiles or ever-increasing commando raids, it is only because the breed was constantly evolving and the rules of the race were constantly changing. But in running the war it was not the individual ideas which counted, but his effect on the situation as a whole. By the end of the war Churchill had an excellent team of clever and sometimes brilliant officers under him as the chiefs of staff, but despite their contact over several years, none of them showed any sign of transcending his own service – unlike say Mountbatten, Tedder, Ismay and his colleagues at the Ministry of Defence. It was only Churchill's leadership and knowledge that prevented the Chiefs of Staff Committee, and therefore the British war effort, from descending into incoherence. It is often said, and supported by letters and minutes of meetings, that only the chiefs of staff and the officers of the Ministry of Defence prevented Churchill from embarking on many rash ventures. That rather misses the point; his advisers *were* there and despite Brooke's comments, he was not really a dictator like Adolf Hitler – in the end he would nearly always listen to reason. But very often it was Churchill who produced the ideas about running the war, for the chiefs of staff, even Brooke and Cunningham, were burdened with work, blinkered by sectional interests, and sometimes short of imagination. They were far more than the 'tribal chiefs' that Churchill had described in 1936, but without Churchill the committee was no more than the sum of the parts.

The Prime Minister who directed the British war effort for five years was still in a sense the boy who had played with toy soldiers. In 1943 he reminisced to Brooke, of all people, about how when his nurse took him to Hyde Park he longed to get back to them.[15] In the following year Brooke compared him to 'a small boy being called away from his sandcastles'. Churchill was still the subaltern of Hussars, anxious to come under fire and lead his men into battle. He was still the advocate who 'surpassed in that direction the ablest of lawyers and would make a weak case appear exceeding strong' as feared by Jellicoe. He was still the would-be pilot, and when flying as a passenger he often insisted on taking the controls, to the horror of his fighter escort. He was still the First Lord of the Admiralty, the Secretary of State for War, the Secretary of State for Air and the Minister of Munitions as he had been in 1911–21, and in effect he ran three of these departments throughout the Second World War, by-passing their nominal heads on matters of strategy and tactics. He was the innovator who had promoted the idea of the tank and hoped to do the same with the unrotated projectile. (But he was not, perhaps, the Chancellor of the Exchequer who had been so strict about service budgets in 1924–29.) He was the historian who had gained much insight 'not only in taking part in the previous world war but also in writing about it' and was already thinking what he would write about his one.[16] He was the backbench critic of the 1930s who constantly questioned the figures put before him. In his mind he was Marlborough, whether or not he had inherited his military genius; perhaps he was also Pitt the Elder with his world view of empire, and Napoleon with his unique grasp of both political leadership and military tactics. Chance (or fate) had given a unique opportunity for all these characters, combined in one quick-thinking and hard-working brain, to leave a permanent stamp on the largest war in history, and on the world order which followed it.

Notes

Introduction

1 Martin Gilbert, ed., *The Churchill War Papers*, vol. 3, London, 2001, p. 555.

2 John Colville, *The Fringes of Power, 1939–1955*, London, 1985, p. 366.

3 Lord Moran, *Winston Churchill: The Struggle for Survival, 1940–65*, London, 1966, p. 123.

4 A. G. Gardner, *Prophets, Priests and Kings*, London, 1908, pp. 108, 106.

5 Winston Churchill, *Thoughts and Adventures*, London, 1932, pp. 130–31.

6 Roy Jenkins, *Churchill*, London, 2001, p. 40.

7 Martin S. Gilbert, ed., *Winston S. Churchill, Companion*, vol. 5, part 1, London, 1979, p. 672.

8 Martin S. Gilbert, *The Churchill War Papers*, vol. 1, London, 1993, p. 63.

9 Maurice Ashley, *Churchill as Historian*, London, 1968, p. 20.

10 Winston Churchill, *The Second World War*, vol. 1, *The Gathering Storm*, London, 1965, p. 601.

1. Becoming a Soldier

1 Winston Churchill, *My Early Life*, reprinted London, 2002, p. 1.

2 Ibid., p. 76.

3 Randolph S. Churchill, in Gilbert, ed., *Winston S. Churchill, Companion*, vol. 1, part 1, London, 1967, p. 78.

4 Churchill, *My Early Life*, p. 10.

5 John G. Garratt, *Model Soldiers: A Collector's Guide*, London, 1959, passim.

6 Churchill, *My Early Life*, pp. 19–20.

7 Ibid., pp. 20–21.

8 Gilbert, ed., *Winston S. Churchill, Companion*, vol. 1, part 1, p. 166.

9 Ibid., p. 173.

10 Ibid., pp. 180–81.

11 Gilbert, ed., *Winston S. Churchill, Companion*, vol. 1, part 1, p. 189.

12 Ibid., p. 190.

13 Churchill, *My Early Life*, pp. 20–21.

14 Ibid., p. 20.

15 Ibid., pp. 28–9.

16 Randolph S. Churchill, *Winston S. Churchill: Youth, 1874–1900*, London, 1966, pp. 206–07.

17 Gilbert, ed., *Winston S. Churchill, Companion*, vol. 1, part 1, p. 463.
18 Randolph Churchill, *Churchill: Youth*, p. 213.
19 Gilbert, ed., *Winston S. Churchill, Companion*, vol. 1, part 1, p. 540.
20 Karl August Eduard Friedrich Hohenlohe-Ingelfingen Kraft, *Letters on Cavalry* ..., trans. N. L. Walford, Woolwich, 1889, p. 9.
21 Winston S. Churchill, *The Second World War*, vol. 6, *Triumph and Tragedy*, London, 1954, p. 361.
22 Gilbert, ed., *Winston S. Churchill, Companion*, vol. 1, part 1, p. 550.
23 G. Philips, *Text Book on Fortification etc, for the Use of the Royal Military College, Sandhurst*, London, 1877 edition, pp. 47–48.
24 Gilbert, ed., *Winston S. Churchill, Companion*, vol. 1, part 1, p. 464.
25 Cornelius Francis Clery, *Minor Tactics*, London, 1880, pp. 111, 145.
26 Edward M. Spiers, *The Late Victorian Army, 1868–1902*, Manchester, c 1992, p. 104.
27 T. H. Holding, *Uniforms of the British Army, Navy and Court*, London, 1894, p. 32.
28 Douglas S. Russell, *Winston Churchill, Soldier*, London, 2005, p. 60.
29 Gilbert, ed., *Winston S. Churchill, Companion*, vol. 1, part 1, p. 478.
30 Ibid., pp. 433–34.
31 Winston S. Churchill, *The Story of the Malakand Field Force*, 1897, reprinted 2005, p. 207.
32 *Hansard*, vol. 523, 1 February 1954, cols 39–113.
33 Gilbert, ed., *Winston S. Churchill, Companion*, vol. 1, part 1, pp. 625–62.
34 Kraft, *Letters on Cavalry*, pp. 7–8.
35 *Royal United Services Institute Journal*, vol. XLV, July 1901, p. 842.
36 Churchill, *My Early Life*, p. 63.
37 Ibid., pp. 101, 116–17.
38 Randolph Churchill, *Churchill: Youth*, p. 325.
39 Gilbert, ed., *Winston S. Churchill, Companion*, vol. 1, part 1, p. 477.

2. Wars and Words

1 Churchill, *My Early Life*, p. 74.
2 Gilbert, ed., *Winston S. Churchill, Companion*, vol. 1, part 1, p. 599.
3 Churchill, *My Early Life*, p. 79.
4 *Companion*, vol. 1, part 1, p. 620.
5 Ibid., p. 610.
6 Ibid., p. 620.
7 Ibid., p. 609.
8 Winston S. Churchill, *The Second World War*, vol. 5, *Closing the Ring*, London 1966, p. 607.
9 Churchill, *My Early Life*, p. 105.
10 Churchill, *My Early Life*, pp. 105–06.
11 Gilbert, ed., *Winston S. Churchill, Companion*, vol. 1 part 2, p. 725.
12 Randolph Churchill, *Churchill: Youth*, p. 320.
13 Randolph S. Churchill, in Gilbert, ed., *Winston S. Churchill, Companion*, vol. 1, part 2, 1896–1900, London, 1967, p. 791.
14 Churchill, *Malakand Field Force*, p. 63.
15 Ibid.
16 Ibid., pp. 63–64.
17 Gilbert, ed., *Winston S. Churchill, Companion*, vol. 1, part 2, p. 780.
18 Ibid., pp. 781, 783.
19 Ibid., p. 786.
20 Churchill, *Malakand Field Force*, p. 203.

21 Gilbert, ed., *Winston S. Churchill, Companion*, vol. 1, part 2, p. 791.
22 Churchill, *Malakand Field Force*, p. 96.
23 Ibid., p. 122.
24 Gilbert, ed., *Winston S. Churchill, Companion*, vol. 1, part 2, pp. 796–97.
25 Ibid., p. 799.
26 Ibid., p. 811.
27 Churchill, *Malakand Field Force*, p. 199.
28 Gilbert, ed., *Winston S. Churchill, Companion*, vol. 1, part 2, p. 839.
29 Churchill, *Malakand Field Force*, p. 85.
30 Gilbert, ed., *Winston S. Churchill, Companion*, vol. 1, part 2, p. 802.
31 Churchill, *Malakand Field Force*, p. 38.
32 Ibid., p. 196.
33 Ibid., p. 205.
34 Ibid., p. 185.
35 Ibid., p. 182.
36 Gilbert, ed., *Winston S. Churchill, Companion*, vol. 1, part 2, p. 835.
37 Ibid., p. 813.
38 Ibid., p. 808.
39 Ibid., p. 836.
40 Ibid., p. 893.
41 Ibid., p. 891.
42 Ibid., p. 913.
43 Ibid., p. 822.
44 Churchill, *My Early Life*, p. 161.
45 Ibid., p. 163.
46 Gilbert, ed., *Winston S. Churchill, Companion*, vol. 1, part 2, p. 952.
47 Ibid., p. 957.
48 Ibid., p. 968.
49 Ibid., p. 970.
50 Winston S. Churchill, *The River War*, 1899, reprinted London, 1973, p. 263.
51 Churchill, *My Early Life*, p. 188.
52 Randolph Churchill, *Churchill: Youth*, p. 418.
53 Churchill, *My Early Life*, p. 190.
54 Randolph Churchill, *Churchill: Youth*, p. 418.
55 Jenkins, *Churchill*, p. 40.
56 Randolph Churchill, *Churchill: Youth*, p. 418.
57 Ibid., p. 424.
58 Churchill, *My Early Life*, p. 194.
59 Randolph Churchill, *Churchill: Youth*, p. 442.
60 Gilbert, ed., *Winston S. Churchill, Companion*, vol. 1, part 2, p. 999.
61 David Scott Daniell, *4th Hussar*, Aldershot, 1959, p. 346.
62 Quoted in Russell, *Winston Churchill, Soldier*, p. 243.

3. South African Springboard

1 Gilbert, ed., *Winston S. Churchill, Companion*, vol. 1, part 2, p. 1055.
2 Churchill, *My Early Life*, p. 231.
3 Ibid., pp. 233–34.
4 Winston S. Churchill, 'Some Impressions of the War in South Africa', *Royal United Services Institute Journal*, July 1901, p. 846.
5 Winston S. Churchill, *Frontiers and Wars*, London, 1962, p. 370.
6 Churchill, *My Early Life*, p. 242.
7 Ibid., p. 256.
8 Ibid., p. 306.
9 Thomas Pakenham, *The Boer War*, London, 1979, p. 304.
10 Ibid., p. 366.
11 Winston S. Churchill, *Ian Hamilton's March*, London, 1900, p. 234.
12 Winston S. Churchill, *Thoughts and Adventures*, p. 549.
13 'Some Impressions of the War in South Africa', *Journal of the Royal United Service Institute*, vol. 45, July–December 1901, pp. 835–48.

14 Ibid.
15 Churchill, *My Early Life*, p. 363.
16 Mary Soames, ed., *Speaking for Themselves*, 1998, reprinted London, 1999, p. 23.
17 Gilbert, ed., *Winston S. Churchill, Companion*, vol. 1, part 2, p. 754.
18 Gilbert, ed., *Winston S. Churchill, Companion*, vol. 2, part 3, p. 1608.
19 Churchill, *Thoughts and Adventures*, pp. 76–77.
20 Ibid., p. 81.
21 Churchill, *Thoughts and Adventures*, pp. 75–83.
22 Soames, ed., *Speaking for Themselves*, p. 23.

4. Ruling the Navy

1 Martin Gilbert, ed., *Winston S. Churchill, Companion*, vol. 5, part 2, London, 1981, p. 503.
2 Companion, vol. 1, part 2, p. 709.
3 *Hansard*, series 4, vol. 122, 13 May 1903, col. 730.
4 Martin Gilbert, ed., *Winston S. Churchill, Companion*, vol. 3, part 2, London, 1972, p. 928.
5 National Archives, CAB 2/22.
6 Martin Gilbert, ed., *Winston S. Churchill, Companion*, vol. 5, part 3, London, 1982, p. 27.
7 Violet Bonham Carter, *Winston Churchill as I Knew Him*, London, 1965, p. 236.
8 Winston S. Churchill, *The World Crisis*, vol. 1, reprinted London 2015, p. 62.
9 J. A. Fisher, *Memories*, London, 1919, pp. 23, 24, 275, 273.
10 Barry Domvile, *By and Large*, London, 1936, pp. 35–38.
11 Lady Wester Wemyss, *Life and Letters of Lord Wester Wemyss*, London, 1935, p. 99.
12 Churchill, *World Crisis*, vol. 1, p. 48.
13 Ibid., p. 50.
14 Martin Gilbert, ed., *Winston S Churchill, Companion*, vol. 2, part 3, London, 1969, p. 1545.
15 Naval Estimates, 1912, p. 10.
16 National Archives, ADM 186/861.
17 Ernle Chatfield, *The Navy and Defence*, London, 1942, p. 98.
18 Churchill, *World Crisis*, vol. 1, p. 56.
19 Sir Dudley de Chair, *The Sea is Strong*, London, 1961, p. 149.
20 Martin Gilbert, ed., *Winston S. Churchill, Companion*, vol. 2, part 2, London, 1969, p. 1335.
21 Admiralty, *Official Procedure and Rules*, 1913, p. 48.
22 Martin Gilbert, ed., *Winston S. Churchill, Companion*, vol. 2, part 3, London, 1969, pp. 1656–57.
23 Martin Gilbert, *Churchill: A Life*, London, 1992, p. 186.
24 Quoted in Nicholas Lambert, 'Strategic Command and Control for Maneuver Warfare: Creation of the Royal Navy's War Room System 1905–1915', *Journal of Military History*, vol. 69, 2005, p. 365.
25 National Archives, CAB 1/31.
26 Gilbert, ed., *Winston S. Churchill, Companion*, vol. 2, part 2, pp. 1312–16.
27 Ibid., p. 1367.
28 National Archives, CAB 1/33.
29 Gilbert, ed., *Winston S. Churchill, Companion*, 1969, pp. 1486–92.
30 National Archives, ADM 234/434.
31 Kenneth Dewar, *The Navy from Within*, London, 1939, pp. 152–53.

32 Ibid., pp. 153–54.
33 Churchill College, Cambridge, CHAR 13/22B f 213.
34 Gilbert, ed., *Winston S. Churchill, Companion*, vol. 2, part 3, p. 1770.
35 National Archives, ADM 116/862.
36 Churchill College, Cambridge, CHAR 13/26 34–36.
37 National Archives, ADM 1/8377/120.
38 *Naval Review*, 1924, pp. 454–58.
39 Dewar, *The Navy from Within*, p. 143.

5. Strategy and Tactics

1 Matthew Johnson, 'The Liberal Party and the Navy League in Britain before the Great War', *20th Century British History*, 2011, passim.
2 Gilbert, ed., *Winston S. Churchill, Companion* vol. 2, part 2, pp. 1360–61.
3 Bernard Huldermann, *Albert Ballin*, London, 1922, p. 146.
4 Churchill, *World Crisis*, vol. 1, p. 77.
5 Gilbert, ed., *Winston S. Churchill, Companion*, vol. 2, part 3, pp. 1504–05, 1525–26.
6 Gilbert, ed., *Winston S. Churchill, Companion*, vol. 2, part 3, p. 1504.
7 *Hansard*, series 5, vol. 35, 18 March 1922, col. 1555.
8 Adam W. Kirkaldy, *British Shipping*, London, 1914, p. 582.
9 Gilbert, ed., *Winston S. Churchill, Companion*, vol. 2, part 3, p. 1549.
10 Nicholas Lambert, *Sir John Fisher's Naval Revolution*, Columbia, South Carolina, 2002, p. 253.
11 Ibid., p. 263.
12 Ibid., p. 264.
13 National Archives, ADM 116/3381.
14 National Archives, ADM 116/1176A.
15 National Archives, ADM 116/3381.

16 Gilbert, ed., *Winston S. Churchill, Companion*, vol. 2, part 3, p. 1614.
17 Lambert, *Strategic Command and Control for Maneuver Warfare*, p. 385.
18 National Archives, ADM 116/1176A.
19 National Archives, ADM 116/8273.
20 Lambert, *Sir John Fisher's Naval Revolution*, p. 264.
21 Martin Gilbert, ed., *Winston S. Churchill, Companion*, vol. 4, part 1, p. 79.
22 Navy Records Society, vol. 128, 1989, *The Beatty Papers*, vol. 1, pp. 75–76.
23 Navy Records Society, vol. 108, 1966, *The Jellicoe Papers*, vol. 2, p. 29.
24 National Archives, ADM 53/63025.
25 National Archives, ADM 116/1169.
26 Henry Baynham, *Men from the Dreadnoughts*, London, 1976, p. 146.
27 National Maritime Museum, OLV/14.
28 Ibid.
29 Jon Sumida, *In Defence of Naval Supremacy*, London, 1993; John Brooks, *Dreadnought Gunnery and the Battle of Jutland*, Abingdon, 2005, passim.

6. Churchill at Work

1 Admiralty, *Official Procedure and Rules*, p. 4.
2 Domvile, *By and Large*, p. 14.
3 Navy Records Society, *Jellicoe Papers*, vol. 1, p. 27.
4 Ibid., p. 28.
5 Sir Richard Vesey Hamilton, *Naval Administration*, London, 1896, pp. 164–65.
6 National Archives, CAB 1/32.
7 Gilbert, ed., *Winston S. Churchill, Companion*, vol. 2, part 3, pp. 1527–28.
8 *Hansard*, series 5, vol. 41, 22 July 1912, cols 838–50.

9 National Archives, CAB 37/114/11.
10 National Archives, CAB/1/32.
11 *Hansard*, vol. 50, 26 March 1913, cols 1790–1.
12 Gilbert, ed., *Winston S. Churchill, Companion*, vol. 2, part 3, pp. 1796–98.
13 Gilbert, ed., *Winston S. Churchill, Companion*, vol. 2, part 2, pp. 1372–73; *Hansard*, vol. 35, 5 March 1912, col. 197.
14 Soames, ed., *Speaking for Themselves*, p. 62.
15 Bonham Carter, *Winston Churchill*, p. 263; Navy Records Society, *Beatty Papers* vol. 1, p. 45.
16 Bonham Carter, *Winston Churchill*, p. 254.
17 Joseph Bonnici, *The Malta Grand Harbour and its Dockyard*, Malta, 1994, p. 192.
18 Bonham Carter, *Winston Churchill*, p. 269.
19 Gilbert, ed., *Winston S. Churchill, Companion*, vol. 2, part 3, pp. 1582–83.
20 Ibid., p. 1639.
21 Marinell Ash, *This Noble Harbour*, Edinburgh, 1991, pp. 191–92.
22 Julian Thompson, *The Imperial War Museum Book of the War at Sea, 1914–18*, London, 2005, p. 41.
23 Gilbert, ed., *Winston S. Churchill, Companion*, vol. 2, part 3, pp. 1551, 1723.
24 Navy Records Society, *Beatty Papers*, vol. 1, pp. 35, 46.
25 Bonham Carter, *Winston Churchill*, p. 262.
26 Violet Bonham-Carter, *Winston Churchill as I Knew Him*, London, 1965, p. 273.
27 Gilbert, ed., *Winston S. Churchill, Companion*, vol. 2, part 3, pp. 1818–73.

7. Personnel

1 National Archives, ADM 116/682, esp. pp. 168–91.
2 Ibid., p. 66.
3 Ibid., p. 30.
4 Ibid., p. 191.
5 National Archives, ADM 116/1288.
6 *Naval Review*, 1913, pp. 181, 281.
7 National Archives, ADM 116/682 p. 133.
8 National Archives, ADM 116/1288.
9 National Archives, ADM 1/8370/65.
10 Ibid.
11 Lionel Yexley, *The Inner Life of the Navy*, London, 1908, p. 288.
12 Baynham, *Men from the Dreadnoughts*, p. 128.
13 *Naval Review*, 1913, p. 159.
14 'Clinker Knocker', *'Aye, Aye, Sir'*, London, nd, p. 96.
15 *Brassey's Naval Annual*, 1913, p. 430.
16 Quoted in Anthony Carew, *The Lower Deck of the Royal Navy*, Manchester, 1981, pp. 68–69.
17 Gilbert, ed., *Winston S. Churchill, Companion*, vol. 2, part 3, p. 1645.
18 National Archives, ADM 116/1182.
19 *The Fleet Annual and Naval Year Book*, 1913, p. iii.

8. Matériel

1 Sir Eustace Tennyson d'Eyncourt, *A Shipbuilders Yarn*, London, 1948, p. 72.
2 Churchill, *World Crisis*, vol. 1, p. 83.

3   Tennyson d'Eyncourt, *Shipbuilder's Yarn*, p. 59.

4   Norman Friedman, *The British Battleship, 1906–1914*, Barnsley, 2015, p. 45.

5   Gilbert, ed., *Winston S. Churchill, Companion*, vol. 2, part 2, p. 1329.

6   Churchill, *World Crisis*, vol. 1, p. 83.

7   Ibid., pp. 84–86.

8   Navy Records Society, *Beatty Papers*, vol. 1, p. 171.

9   *Hansard*, vol. 35, 18 March 1912, col. 1560.

10 Navy Records Society, vol. 103, *The Fisher Papers*, vol. 1, 1960, p. 81.

11 Gilbert, ed., *Winston S. Churchill, Companion*, vol. 2, part 3, p. 1929.

12 National Archives, ADM 116/1208.

13 Baynham, *Men from the Dreadnoughts*, p. 118.

14 National Archives, ADM 116/1208.

15 Churchill, *World Crisis*, vol. 1, p. 85n.

16 Ibid., p. 91.

17 Ibid., p. 92.

18 Ibid., p. 93.

19 Gilbert, ed., *Winston S. Churchill, Companion*, vol. 2, part 3, p. 1527.

20 Churchill, *World Crisis*, vol. 1, p. 95.

21 Churchill, *World Crisis*, vol. 1, p. 91.

22 Martin Gilbert, ed., *Winston S. Churchill, Companion*, vol. 4, part 1, London, 1977, p. 113.

23 Navy Records Society, vol. 142, *The Submarine Service*, 2001, p. 235.

24 Ibid., pp. 227, 232.

25 *Hansard*, vol. 59, 17 March 1914, col. 1914.

26 Gilbert, ed., *Winston S. Churchill, Companion*, vol. 2, part 3, p. 1538.

27 *Hansard*, series 5, vol. 51, 31 March 1913, col. 89.

9. The Naval Air Service

1   Charles H. Gibbs-Smith, *The Rebirth of European Aviation*, London, 1976, p. 280.

2   Gilbert, ed., *Winston S. Churchill, Companion*, vol. 2, part 3, p. 1875.

3   National Archives, AIR 1/2311/221.

4   R. D. Layman, *To Ascend from a Floating Base*, np, 1979, pp. 149–50.

5   Sir Arthur Longmore, *From Sea to Sky*, London, 1946, p. 21.

6   Navy Records Society, vol. 113, *Documents Relating to the Naval Air Service*, vol. 1, 1969, p. 26.

7   National Archives, AIR 1/724/76/2.

8   Quoted in *Brassey's Naval Annual* 1912, p. 376.

9   Gilbert, ed., *Winston S. Churchill, Companion*, vol. 2, part 3, p. 1875.

10 Murray F. Sueter, *Airmen or Noahs*, London, 1928, p. 181.

11 Ibid., p. 76.

12 Churchill, *Thoughts and Adventures*, p. 181.

13 National Maritime Museum, JRR/10.

14 Gilbert, ed., *Winston S. Churchill, Companion*, vol. 2, part 3, pp. 1550–51.

15 Ibid., pp. 1875–76.

16 National Archives, AIR 1/2496.

17 Navy Records Society, *Documents Relating to the Naval Air Service*, p. 26.

18 Gilbert, ed., *Winston S. Churchill, Companion*, vol. 2, part 3, p. 1882.

19 Churchill College, Cambridge, CHAR 13/22B.

20 Churchill College, Cambridge, CHAR 13/6B.

21 Gilbert, ed., *Winston S. Churchill, Companion*, vol. 2, part 3, p. 1904.

22 Navy Records Society, *Documents Relating to the Naval Air Service*, p. 115.
23 Ibid., pp. 158–59.
24 Gilbert, ed., *Winston S. Churchill, Companion*, vol. 2, part 3, p. 1914.
25 Navy Records Society, *Documents Relating to the Naval Air Service*, p. 162.
26 Ibid., p. 114.
27 Ibid., p. 139.
28 Gilbert, ed., *Winston S. Churchill, Companion*, vol. 2 part 3, p. 1914.
29 Sueter, *Airmen or Noahs*, p. 241n.
30 Gilbert, ed., *Winston S. Churchill, Companion*, vol. 2, part 3, p. 1913.
31 Navy Records Society, *Documents Relating to the Naval Air Service*, p. 72.
32 Ibid., p. 153.
33 Ibid., p. 157.
34 Gilbert, ed., *Winston S. Churchill, Companion*, vol. 2, part 3, p. 1880.
35 Ibid., p. 1900.
36 Longmore, *From Sea to Sky*, p. 30.
37 Martin Gilbert, ed., *Winston S. Churchill, Companion*, vol. 5, part 3, London, 1982, p. 1168.
38 Gilbert, ed., *Winston S. Churchill, Companion*, vol. 2, part 3, pp. 1883–84.
39 Soames, ed., *Speaking for Themselves*, p. 80.
40 Ibid., p. 82.
41 Gilbert, ed., *Winston S. Churchill, Companion*, vol. 2 part 3, p. 1889.
42 Gilbert, ed., *Winston S. Churchill, Companion*, vol. 2, part 3, pp. 1899–90.
43 Ibid., p. 1891.
44 National Archives, AIR 1/824/204/5/71.
45 Gilbert, ed., *Winston S. Churchill, Companion*, vol. 2, part 3, pp. 1891–92.
46 Soames, ed., *Speaking for Themselves*, p. 87.
47 Ibid., pp. 90–92.
48 Gilbert, ed., *Winston S. Churchill, Companion*, vol. 2, part 3, p. 1921.
49 Andrew Boyle, *Trenchard*, London, 1962, p. 107.

10. The Aircraft

1 Phillip Jarrett, *Frank McClean*, Barnsley, 2011, p. 69.
2 C. H. Barnes, *Shorts Aircraft since 1900*, London, revised 1989, passim.
3 National Archives CAB 16/16.
4 Gilbert, ed., *Winston S. Churchill, Companion*, vol. 2, part 3, p. 1884.
5 Barnes, *Shorts Aircraft since 1900*, pp. 77–78.
6 Ibid., pp. 54, 58–62.
7 National Archives, AIR 1/2496.
8 *Hansard*, series 5, vol. 55, 17 July 1913, col. 1501.
9 Navy Records Society, *Documents Relating to the Naval Air Service*, p. 72.
10 Ibid., p. 151.
11 Sueter, *Airmen or Noahs*, p. 49.
12 Navy Records Society, *Documents Relating to the Naval Air Service*, p. 118.
13 Gilbert, ed., *Winston S. Churchill, Companion*, vol. 2, part 3, p. 1913.
14 Bruce Robertson, *Sopwith, the Man and the Aircraft*, Letchworth, 1970, pp. 37–38, 174, 211.
15 Layman, *To Ascend from a Floating Base*, p. 208; Barnes, *Shorts Aircraft*, p. 92.
16 Sueter, *Airman or Noahs*, p. 49.
17 Longmore, *From Sea to Sky*, p. 36.
18 National Archives, AIR 1/2311/221/26.

19 Navy Records Society, *Documents Relating to the Naval Air Service*, p. 80.

20 Norman Friedman, *British Carrier Aviation*, London, 1988, pp. 23, 28–29.

21 National Archives, AIR 1/8331.

22 Navy Records Society, *Documents Relating to the Naval Air Service*, p. 40.

23 Sueter, *Airmen or Noahs*, p. 117.

24 Gilbert, ed., *Winston S. Churchill, Companion*, vol. 2, part 3, pp. 1887–89.

25 Navy Records Society, *Documents Relating to the Naval Air Service*, p. 134.

26 Longmore, *From Sea to Sky*, pp. 28–30.

27 Navy Records Society, *Documents Relating to the Naval Air Service*, p. 108.

28 Ibid., p. 95.

29 Ibid., p. 113.

30 Ibid., p. 119.

31 Ibid., pp. 143–44.

32 Ibid., p. 116.

33 Ibid., p. 123.

34 Ibid., p. 139.

35 Ibid., p. 139.

36 Gilbert, ed., *Winston S. Churchill, Companion*, vol. 1, part 3, p. 284.

11. The North Sea War

1 Soames, ed., *Speaking for Themselves*, p. 96.

2 Churchill, *World Crisis*, vol. 1, p. 166.

3 Soames, ed., *Speaking for Themselves*, p. 162.

4 Gilbert, ed., *Winston S. Churchill, Companion*, vol. 4, part 1, p. 448.

5 'Clinker Knocker', *Aye, Aye, Sir*, London, nd, p. 133.

6 Gilbert, ed., *Winston S. Churchill, Companion*, vol. 3, part 1, p. 230.

7 Admiral Jellicoe, *The Grand Fleet, 1914–1916*, London, 1919, p. 3.

8 Gilbert, ed., *Winston S. Churchill, Companion*, vol. 2, part 3, p. 1950.

9 Navy Records Society, *Jellicoe Papers*, vol. 1, p. 38.

10 Navy Records Society, *Beatty Papers*, vol. 1, p. 79.

11 Navy Records Society, *Jellicoe Papers*, vol. 1 pp. 41–42.

12 Soames, ed., *Speaking for Themselves*, pp. 99–100.

13 Winston S. Churchill, *The World Crisis 1911–1918*, abridged and revised edition, 1931, reprinted London, 2005, p. 601.

14 Chatfield, *The Navy and Defence*, p. 101.

15 Churchill, *World Crisis*, vol. 1, p. 241.

16 Quoted in Brian Lavery, *Shield of Empire*, Edinburgh, 2007, p. 224.

17 Churchill, *World Crisis*, vol. 1, p. 182.

18 Navy Records Society, *Jellicoe Papers*, vol. 1, p. 49.

19 Navy Records Society, *Jellicoe Papers*, vol. 1, p. 75.

20 Ibid., p. 76.

21 Ibid., p. 15.

22 Quoted in B. Lavery, *Shield of Empire*, Edinburgh, 2007, p. 204.

23 Jellicoe, *The Grand Fleet*, London, 1919, p. 29.

24 Gilbert, ed., *Winston S. Churchill, Companion*, vol. 3, part 1, pp. 197–202.

25 Navy Records Society, vol. 117, 1972, *The Keyes Papers*, vol. 1, pp. 24–27.

26 Churchill, *Thoughts and Adventures*, pp. 89–95.
27 Quoted in Lavery, *Shield of Empire*, p. 210.
28 Navy Records Society, *Jellicoe Papers*, vol. 1, p. 94.
29 Ibid., p. 102.
30 Ibid., p. 88.
31 Ibid., p. 117.
32 Gilbert, ed., *Winston S. Churchill, Companion*, vol. 3, part 1, p. 298.
33 Ibid., p. 64.
34 Robin Prior, *Churchill's World Crisis as History*, London, c. 1983, pp. 17–18.
35 Navy Records Society, *Jellicoe Papers*, vol. 1, pp. 71–73.
36 Ibid., p. 115.
37 Ibid., p. 93.
38 Ibid., p. 128.
39 Ibid., pp. 143–44.
40 National Maritime Museum, OLV/14.
41 Prior, *Churchill's World Crisis as History*, p. 22.
42 Churchill, *World Crisis*, vol. 1, p. 372.
43 Navy Records Society, *Jellicoe Papers*, vol. 1, p. 113.
44 Churchill, *World Crisis*, vol. 1, pp. 372–73.
45 Gilbert, ed., *Winston S. Churchill, Companion*, vol. 3, part 1, p. 381.
46 Churchill College, Cambridge, CHAR 13/46/14.
47 Churchill, *The World Crisis*, abridged edition, p. 335.
48 Ibid., p. 346.
49 Ibid., p. 347.
50 Navy Records Society, *Jellicoe Papers*, vol. 1, p. 128.
51 Martin Gilbert, ed., *Winston S. Churchill, Companion*, vol. 5, part 1, London, 1979, p. 243.

12. Antwerp

1 Gilbert, ed., *Winston S. Churchill, Companion*, vol. 3, part 1, p. 122.
2 Ibid., p. 97.
3 Ibid., p. 98.
4 Dewar, *The Navy from Within*, p. 141.
5 Gilbert, ed., *Winston S. Churchill, Companion*, vol. 3, part 1, p. 178.
6 Lavery, *Shield of Empire*, p. 202.
7 National Archives, CAB 45/158.
8 Gilbert, ed., *Winston S. Churchill, Companion*, vol. 3, part 1, p. 54.
9 Ibid., p. 124.
10 National Archives, CAB 45/158.
11 Ibid.
12 Ibid.
13 Ibid.
14 Ibid.
15 Ibid.
16 Gilbert, ed., *Winston S. Churchill, Companion*, vol. 3, part 1, p. 152.
17 National Archives, CAB 45/158.
18 *Companion*, vol. 3, part 1, p. 16 and n.
19 Ibid., p. 163n.
20 National Archives, ADM 1/8397/362.
21 Churchill, *World Crisis*, vol. 1, pp. 275–76.
22 National Archives, CAB 45/158.
23 Gilbert, ed., *Winston S. Churchill, Companion*, vol. 3, part 1, p. 169.
24 Churchill, *World Crisis*, vol. 1 p. 281.
25 National Archives, CAB 45/158.
26 Gilbert, ed., *Winston S. Churchill, Companion*, vol. 3, part 1, p. 179.
27 National Archives, CAB 45/158.
28 J. E. Edmonds, *Military Operations in France and Belgium*, vol. 2, London, 1924, p. 63n.
29 Gilbert, ed., *Winston S. Churchill, Companion*, vol. 3, part 1, pp. 178, 192.

30 Churchill, *World Crisis*, vol. 1, p. 275.
31 Gilbert, ed., *Winston S. Churchill, Companion*, vol. 3, part 1, pp. 177–78.
32 Ibid., p. 193.
33 National Archives, CAB 45/158.
34 Ibid., pp. 188–89.
35 Churchill, *World Crisis*, vol. 1, pp. 283–84.

13. Defence and Attack in the Air

1 Gilbert, ed., *Winston S. Churchill, Companion*, vol. 3, part 1, p. 244.
2 Navy Records Society, *Documents Relating to the Naval Air Service*, pp. 183–84.
3 Ibid., p. 182.
4 Ibid., pp. 181–82, 172.
5 Churchill, *World Crisis*, vol. 1, p. 234.
6 Gilbert, ed., *Winston S. Churchill, Companion*, vol. 3, part 1, pp. 74–75.
7 Gilbert, ed., *Winston S. Churchill, Companion*, vol. 2, part 3, p. 129.
8 Gilbert, ed., *Winston S. Churchill, Companion*, vol. 3, part 1, p. 143.
9 Navy Records Society, *Documents Relating to the Naval Air Service*, pp. 173–74, 170–71.
10 Ibid., p. 178.
11 Ibid., p. 170.
12 Ibid., pp. 182–83.
13 Henry D. Capper, *Aft from the Hawsehole*, London, nd, pp. 194–210.
14 Gilbert, ed., *Winston S. Churchill, Companion*, vol. 3, part 1, p. 153.
15 Navy Records Society, *Documents Relating to the Naval Air Service*, pp. 188–89.
16 Ibid., p. 191.
17 Gilbert, ed., *Winston S. Churchill, Companion*, vol. 3, part 1, p. 483.
18 Ibid., p. 140.
19 Ibid., p. 98.
20 Navy Records Society, *Documents Relating to the Naval Air Service*, p. 180.
21 Gilbert, ed., *Winston S. Churchill, Companion*, vol. 3, part 1, p. 194.
22 Ibid., p. 275.
23 Ibid., p. 294.
24 Ibid., p. 336.
25 Navy Records Society, *Documents Relating to the Naval Air Service*, pp. 199–201.
26 Ibid., p. 260.
27 Ibid., p. 205.
28 Gilbert, ed., *Winston S. Churchill, Companion*, vol. 3, part 1, p. 807.
29 Layman, *To Ascend from a Floating Base*, p. 245.
30 Navy Records Society, *Documents Relating to the Naval Air Service*, p. 209.
31 Ibid., p. 217.

14. Armoured Car and Tank

1 Churchill, *World Crisis*, vol. 2.
2 Gilbert, ed., *Winston S. Churchill, Companion*, vol. 3, part 1, p. 88.
3 Samson, *Fights and Flights*, pp. 47, 49, 54, 153.
4 Gilbert, ed., *Winston S. Churchill, Companion*, vol. 3, part 1, p. 264.
5 David Fletcher, *War Cars*, London, 1987.
6 Ernest D. Swinton, *Eyewitness*, London, 1932, p. 80.
7 Ibid., p. 31.
8 Ibid., p. 12.
9 Ibid., p. 60.
10 Gilbert, ed., *Winston S. Churchill, Companion*, vol. 3, part 1, pp. 377–78.
11 Albert G. Stern, *Tanks, 1914–18: The Log-book of a Pioneer*, London, 1919, pp. 8–10, plate facing p. 17.

12 National Archives, MUN 5/210.
13 Swinton, *Eyewitness*, p. 140.
14 Churchill, *World Crisis*, vol. 2, p. 79.
15 pp. 20–21.
16 Ibid., p. 23.
17 Ibid., p. 24.
18 Swinton, *Eyewitness*, p. 141.
19 Stern, *Tanks*, p. 39.
20 Swinton, *Eyewitness*, pp. 116–17.
21 Stern, *Tanks*, p. 26.
22 Swinton, *Eyewitness*, p. 81.
23 Stern, *Tanks*, p. 41.
24 Swinton, *Eyewitness*, p. 158.
25 Stern, *Tanks*, p. 58.
26 Ibid., pp. 58–59.
27 Gilbert, ed., *Winston S. Churchill, Companion*, vol. 3, part 2, p. 1431.

15. The Underwater War

1 Gilbert, ed., *Winston S. Churchill, Companion*, vol. 4, part 1, p. 50.
2 Ibid., p. 246.
3 Gilbert, ed., *Winston S. Churchill, Companion*, vol. 3, part 1, p. 222.
4 Churchill, *World Crisis* vol. 1, pp. 418–20.
5 Gilbert, ed., *Winston S. Churchill, Companion*, vol. 4, part 1, p. 323.
6 Ibid., p. 372.
7 Ibid., pp. 161–62.
8 Winston S Churchill, *The World Crisis*, vol. 2, reprinted London, 2015, p. 281.
9 Navy Records Society, *Keyes Papers*, vol. 1, p. 79.
10 Churchill, *World Crisis*, vol. 2, p. 282.
11 Navy Records Society, *The Submarine Service*, pp. 290–91.
12 Gilbert, ed., *Winston S. Churchill, Companion*, vol. 4, part 1, p. 215.
13 Prior, *Churchill's World Crisis as History*, p. 19.

14 Gilbert, ed., *Winston S. Churchill, Companion*, vol. 3, part 1, pp. 127–28.
15 Gilbert, ed., *Winston S. Churchill, Companion*, vol. 4, part 1, p. 490.
16 Ibid., p. 604.
17 Ibid., p. 491.
18 Ibid., p. 619.
19 Ibid., p. 501.
20 Churchill, *Thoughts and Adventures*, p. 125.
21 Norman Friedman, *Naval Weapons of World War One*, Barnsley, 2011, pp. 388–90.
22 Willem Hackman, *Seek and Strike*, London, 1984, p. 23.
23 Navy Records Society, *Beatty Papers*, vol. 1, p. 264.
24 Churchill, *World Crisis*, vol. 2, p. 291.
25 Churchill College, Cambridge, CHAR 13/50.
26 Gilbert, ed., *Winston S. Churchill, Companion*, vol. 4, part 1, p. 701.
27 Churchill, *World Crisis*, vol. 2, pp. 290–91.
28 Alan G. Jamieson, 'Martyr or Pirate? The Case of Captain Fryatt in the Great War', *Mariner's Mirror*, vol. 85, part 2, May 1999.
29 Churchill, *World Crisis*, vol. 2, p. 335.
30 Ibid., p. 334.
31 Winston S. Churchill, *The World Crisis*, vol. 3, reprinted London, 2015, p. 263.
32 Churchill, *Thoughts and Adventures*, p. 136.

16. The Rest of the World

1 Martin Gilbert, ed., *Winston S. Churchill, Companion*, vol. 4, part 2, 1977, p. 1322.
2 Gilbert, ed., *Winston S. Churchill, Companion*, vol. 3, part 1, p. 33.

3   Churchill, *World Crisis*, vol. 1, pp. 156–58.
4   Churchill, *World Crisis*, vol. 1 pp. 157–59.
5   Ibid., p. 175.
6   National Archives, ADM 156/76, para 457.
7   Gilbert, ed., *Winston S. Churchill, Companion*, vol. 3, part 1, p. 35.
8   Dan van der Vat, *The Ship that Changed the World*, London, c. 1985, p. 167.
9   Churchill, *World Crisis, 1911–1918*, abridged edition, p. 136.
10 Van der Vat, *The Ship that Changed the World*, p. 169.
11 National Archives, ADM 156/110.
12 Churchill, *World Crisis*, vol. 1, p. 207.
13 National Archives, CAB 37/136/2.
14 National Archives, ADM 137/1022.
15 Churchill, *World Crisis* vol. 1, pp. 328–30.
16 Ibid., pp. 330–31.
17 Churchill, *World Crisis*, vol. 1, p. 331.
18 Gilbert, ed., *Winston S. Churchill, Companion*, vol. 3, part 1, p. 252.
19 Ibid., p. 250.
20 Churchill, *World Crisis*, vol. 1, p. 343.
21 Ibid., p. 337.
22 Ibid., p. 338.
23 Churchill, *World Crisis, 1911–1918*, abridged edition, p. 241.
24 Ibid., p. 243.
25 Churchill, *World Crisis*, vol. 1, p. 346.
26 Gilbert, ed., *Winston S. Churchill, Companion*, vol. 3, part 1, pp. 300–01.
27 Ibid., p. 302.
28 Ibid., p. 496.

17. Plans for Attack

1   Gilbert, ed., *Winston S. Churchill, Companion*, vol. 3, part 1, pp. 24–26.
2   Ibid., pp. 45–46.

3   Ian Buxton, *Big Gun Monitors*, revised edition, Barnsley, 2012, pp. 92–94.
4   Gilbert, ed., *Winston S. Churchill, Companion*, vol. 3, part 1, p. 195.
5   Ibid., p. 219.
6   Churchill, *World Crisis*, vol. 1, p. 297.
7   Julian S. Corbett, *History of the Great War, Naval Operations*, vol. 1, London, 1920, pp. 216–34.
8   Ibid., p. 225.
9   Edmonds, *Military Operations, France and Belgium*, vol. 2, p. 300.
10 Buxton, *Big Gun Monitors*, passim.
11 Gilbert, ed., *Winston S. Churchill, Companion*, vol. 3, part 1, p. 312.
12 Ibid., pp. 407–09.
13 Sir Lewis Bayly, *Pull Together*, London, 1939, pp. 152–53.
14 Navy Records Society, *Jellicoe Papers*, vol. 1, pp. 36, 40–41.
15 Gilbert, ed., *Winston S. Churchill, Companion*, vol. 3, part 1, p. 285.
16 Sir Reginald Bacon, *The Life of Lord Fisher of Kilverstone*, London, 1929, vol. 2, p. 183.
17 Churchill, *World Crisis*, vol. 2, p. 433.
18 Gilbert, ed., *Winston S. Churchill, Companion* vol. 3, part 1, p. 304.
19 Churchill, *World Crisis*, vol. 1, p. 365.
20 Gilbert, ed., *Winston S. Churchill, Companion*, vol. 4, part 1, p. 85.
21 Gilbert, ed., *Winston S. Churchill, Companion*, vol. 3, part 1, pp. 292–94.
22 Ibid., p. 365.
23 Navy Records Society, *Keyes Papers*, vol. 1, pp. 69–70.
24 Navy Records Society, *Jellicoe Papers*, vol. 1, p. 119.
25 Ibid., p. 123.
26 Ibid., p. 150.
27 Gilbert, ed., *Winston S. Churchill, Companion*, vol. 4, part 1, p. 91.

28 Gilbert, ed., *Winston S. Churchill, Companion*, vol. 3, part 1, pp. 331–32.

18. Work and Conflict

1 Gilbert, ed., *Winston S. Churchill, Companion*, vol. 3, part 1, p. 319.
2 Churchill, *World Crisis*, vol. 1, p. 170.
3 Gilbert, ed., *Winston S. Churchill, Companion*, vol. 4, part 1, p. 22.
4 Gilbert, ed., *Winston S. Churchill, Companion*, vol. 3, part 1, p. 862.
5 *The Dardanelles Commission Minutes of Evidence*, National Archives CAB 19, para 5053.
6 Ibid., para 5071.
7 Ibid., para 5415.
8 Ibid., para 3862.
9 Ibid., para 3007.
10 Ibid., para 3042.
11 Ibid., para 3046.
12 Gilbert, ed., *Winston S. Churchill, Companion*, vol. 3, part 1, p. 206.
13 Prior, *Churchill's World Crisis as History*, p. 14n.
14 Arthur J. Marder, *Fear God and Dread Nought*, London, 1959, pp. 505–06.
15 Wemyss, *Life and Letters of Lord Wester Wemyss*, p. 363.
16 *The Dardanelles Commission Evidence*, para 5203.
17 Ibid., para 4702.
18 National Archives, ADM 234/434, App M, *Dardanelles Commission*, para 3046.
19 Churchill, *World Crisis*, vol. 1, p. 208.
20 National Maritime Museum, OLV/11, pp. 137–38.
21 *Dardanelles Commission Evidence*, para 5105.
22 Ibid., para 4112.
23 Churchill, *World Crisis*, abridged edition, pp. 335–36.

24 Gilbert, ed., *Winston S. Churchill, Companion*, vol. 3, part 1, pp. 68–70.
25 Ibid., p. 202.
26 Ibid., p. 226.
27 Ibid., p. 230.
28 Ibid., p. 220.
29 *Dardanelles Commission Evidence*, para 3055–56.
30 Gilbert, ed., *Winston S. Churchill, Companion*, vol. 3, part 1, p. 221.
31 Ibid., p. 225.
32 Gilbert, ed., *Winston S. Churchill, Companion*, vol. 3, part 1, p. 232.
33 Churchill, *World Crisis*, abridged edition, p. 234.
34 Gilbert, ed., *Winston S. Churchill, Companion*, vol. 3, part 1, p. 221.
35 Gilbert, ed., *Winston S. Churchill, Companion*, vol. 4, part 1, p. 233.
36 *Dardanelles Commission Evidence*, para 4757.
37 Navy Records Society, *Jellicoe Papers*, vol. 1, p. 124.
38 Ibid., p. 124.
39 *Dardanelles Commission Evidence*, para 3046.
40 Ibid., para p 163.
41 Ibid., para 3046.
42 Ibid., para DC 5125.
43 Ibid., para 3058.
44 Ibid., para 3089.
45 Ibid., para 3047.
46 Ibid., para 3048.
47 Gilbert, ed., *Winston S. Churchill, Companion*, vol. 3, part 1, p. 319.
48 Quoted in Roy Jenkins, *Churchill*, p. 217.
49 Gilbert, ed., *Winston S. Churchill, Companion*, vol. 3, part 2, pp. 896–97, 899, 902, 907.
50 *Dardanelles Commission Evidence*, para 4117.
51 Ibid., para 4119.

19. Forcing the Straits

1 Gilbert, ed., *Winston S. Churchill, Companion*, vol. 3, part 1, p. 40.
2 Ibid., pp. 75, 81–82.
3 Ibid., p. 243.
4 Churchill, *World Crisis*, abridged edition, p. 283.
5 Gilbert, ed., *Winston S. Churchill, Companion*, vol. 3, part 1, pp. 278–79.
6 Ibid., p. 283; *The First Report of the Dardanelles Commission*, vol. 1, Guildford, 2000, p. 53.
7 Gilbert, ed., *Winston S. Churchill, Companion*, vol. 3, part 1, pp. 361, 367.
8 Ibid., p. 372.
9 Churchill, *World Crisis*, vol. 2, pp. 97–98.
10 *First Report of the Dardanelles Commission*, vol. 1, p. 64.
11 Gilbert, ed., *Winston S. Churchill, Companion*, vol. 3, part 1, pp. 405–06, 409.
12 Ibid., p. 410.
13 *Dardanelles Commission Evidence*, paras 3089, 1963.
14 Gilbert, ed., *Winston S. Churchill, Companion*, vol. 3, part 1, p. 412.
15 *First Report of the Dardanelles Commission*, vol. 1, pp. 78–79.
16 Gilbert, ed., *Winston S. Churchill, Companion*, vol. 3, part 1, p. 413.
17 *Dardanelles Commission Evidence*, para 3089.
18 Ibid., para 4660.
19 Ibid., para 4660.
20 Ibid., para 1868.
21 Ibid., para 4689.
22 Ibid., para 5369.
23 Ibid., para 4973.
24 Churchill, *World Crisis*, vol. 2, pp. 115–18.
25 Gilbert, ed., *Winston S. Churchill, Companion*, vol. 3, part 1, p. 453.
26 Ibid., p. 460.
27 *First Report of the Dardanelles Commission*, vol. 1, p. 95.
28 Gilbert, ed., *Winston S. Churchill, Companion*, vol. 3, part 1, pp. 462–63.
29 *First Report of the Dardanelles Commission*, vol. 1, p. 112.
30 Navy Records Society, *Keyes Papers*, vol. 1, p. 153.
31 Ibid., p. 122.
32 *Dardanelles Commission Evidence*, para 5151.
33 Gilbert, ed., *Winston S. Churchill, Companion*, vol. 3, part 1, pp. 479–80.
34 Wemyss, *Life and Letters of Lord Wester Wemyss*, p. 227.
35 Navy Records Society, *Documents Relating to the Naval Air Service*, p. 202.
36 Gilbert, ed., *Winston S. Churchill, Companion*, vol. 3, part 1, p. 480.
37 Navy Records Society, *Keyes Papers*, vol. 1, pp. 100–01.
38 Ibid., p. 121.
39 Ibid., p. 91.
40 Ibid., pp. 103, 104.
41 Ibid., pp. 105–06.
42 Churchill, *World Crisis*, vol. 2, p. 261.
43 Gilbert, ed., *Winston S. Churchill, Companion*, vol. 3, part 1, p. 569.
44 *Dardanelles Commission Evidence*, para 3089.
45 Navy Records Society, *Keyes Papers*, vol. 1, p. 154.
46 Ibid., p. 113.
47 Ibid., p. 111.
48 Churchill, *World Crisis*, vol. 2, p. 229.
49 Ibid., p. 230.
50 Ibid., p. 233.
51 Ibid., p. 264.

52 Navy Records Society, *Keyes Papers*, vol. 1, p. 381.
53 *Dardanelles Commission Evidence*, p. 324.

20. Landing and Withdrawal

1 Gilbert, ed., *Winston S. Churchill, Companion*, vol. 3, part 1, p. 686.
2 Navy Records Society, *Keyes Papers*, vol. 1, p. 127.
3 Gilbert, ed., *Winston S. Churchill, Companion*, vol. 3, part 1, p. 825.
4 Ibid., p. 766.
5 Prior, *Churchill's World Crisis as History*, p. 120.
6 Gilbert, ed., *Winston S. Churchill, Companion*, vol. 3, part 1, p. 571.
7 Wemyss, *Life and Letters of Lord Wester Wemyss*, p. 205.
8 Gilbert, ed., *Winston S. Churchill, Companion*, vol. 3, part 1, p. 814.
9 Sir Ian Hamilton, *Gallipoli Diary*, London, 1920, p. 112.
10 Ibid., p. 111.
11 Navy Records Society, *Documents Relating to the Naval Air Service*, p. 203.
12 Ibid., p. 205.
13 Navy Records Society, *Keyes Papers*, vol. 1, pp. 121–2.
14 Navy Records Society, *Documents Relating to the Naval Air Service*, pp. 205–06.
15 Gilbert, ed., *Winston S. Churchill, Companion*, vol. 3, part 1, pp. 819–20.
16 Ibid., p. 826.
17 Ibid.
18 Churchill, *World Crisis*, abridged edition, p. 442.
19 Gilbert, ed., *Winston S. Churchill, Companion*, vol. 3, part 2, p. 855.

20 Ibid., p. 451.
21 Gilbert, ed., *Winston S. Churchill, Companion*, vol. 3, part 2, pp. 876–77.
22 Ibid., p. 886.
23 Ibid., p. 888.
24 Ibid., p. 921.
25 Ibid., p. 932.
26 Ibid., pp. 946–47.
27 Ibid., p. 1191.
28 Ibid., p. 976.
29 Ibid., p. 982.
30 Ibid., pp. 1003, 1009.
31 Ibid., p. 1040.
32 Ibid., pp. 1095–103.
33 Navy Records Society, *Keyes Papers*, vol. 1, p. 163.
34 Ibid., pp. 178–79.
35 Gilbert, ed., *Winston S. Churchill, Companion*, vol. 3, part 2, p. 1151.
36 Navy Records Society, *Keyes Papers*, vol. 1, p. 232.
37 Ibid., p. 293.
38 Ibid., p. 220.
39 Ibid., p. 228.
40 Churchill, *World Crisis*, abridged edition, pp. 528–30.
41 Prior, *Churchill's World Crisis as History*, p. 176.
42 Churchill, *World Crisis*, abridged edition, p. 535.
43 Navy Records Society, *Keyes Papers*, vol. 1, p. 283.
44 Ibid., p. 200.
45 Gilbert, *Churchill: A Life*, p. 328.

21. In the Trenches

1 Gilbert, ed., *Winston S. Churchill, Companion*, vol. 3, part 2, p. 1278.
2 Ibid., p. 1017.
3 Ibid., p. 1263.
4 Ibid, pp. 1263, 1270.

5   Soames, ed., *Speaking for Themselves*, p. 113.
6   Ibid.
7   Ibid., p. 124.
8   Ibid., p. 116–17.
9   Ibid., p. 119.
10 Ibid., pp. 120, 125.
11 Ibid., p. 133.
12 Martin Gilbert, ed., *Winston S. Churchill, Companion*, vol. 5, part 2, London, 1981, p. 639n.
13 Soames, ed., *Speaking for Themselves*, p. 145.
14 Ibid., p. 148.
15 Captain X [A. D. Gibb], *With Winston Churchill at the Front* Glasgow, 1934, p. 30.
16 Ibid.
17 Soames, ed., *Speaking for Themselves*, pp. 155–56.
18 W. S. Churchill, *The Fighting Line*, London, 1916, pp. 27–28.
19 Soames, ed., *Speaking for Themselves*, p. 157.
20 [Gibb], *Winston Churchill at the Front*, pp. 7–10, 24, 60–61.
21 Ibid., p. 43.
22 Ibid., p. 22.
23 Soames, ed., *Speaking for Themselves*, pp. 163–64.
24 [Gibb], *Winston Churchill at the Front*, p. 48.
25 Ibid., p. 51.
26 Soames, ed., *Speaking for Themselves*, p. 162.
27 [Gibb], *Winston Churchill at the Front*, pp. 60, 62.
28 General staff, *Notes for Infantry Officers*, March 1916.
29 Sir William Slim, *Defeat into Victory*, London, 1956, p. 3.
30 Soames, ed., *Speaking for Themselves*, p. 148.
31 Ibid., p. 171.
32 Sir Douglas Haig, *War Diaries and Letters*, London, 2005, p. 117.
33 [Gibb], *Winston Churchill at the Front*, p. 59.
34 Soames, ed., *Speaking for Themselves*, p. 165.
35 Ibid., p. 175.
36 Ibid., p. 191.
37 Ibid., p. 175.
38 Ibid., p. 127.
39 Ibid., p. 195.
40 Soames, ed., *Speaking for Themselves*, p. 176.
41 *Royal Scots Fusiliers Magazine*, quoted in *Britain at War*, June 2016, p. 7.
42 Soames, ed., *Speaking for Themselves*, p. 143.
43 [Gibb], *Winston Churchill at the Front*, pp. 108–09.
44 W. D. Croft, *Three Years With the 9th (Scottish) Division*, London, 1919, p. 27.
45 Soames, ed., *Speaking for Themselves*, p. 196.
46 *The Nation*, 15 March 1919.
47 Martin Gilbert, ed., *Winston S. Churchill, Companion*, vol. 5, part 1, London, 1979, p. 1538.
48 Churchill, *World Crisis*, abridged edition, p. 668.
49 Gilbert, ed., *Winston S. Churchill, Companion*, vol. 5, part 1, p. 80.
50 Gilbert, ed., *Winston S. Churchill, Companion*, vol. 3, part 2, p. 1512.
51 Navy Records Society, *Jellicoe Papers*, vol. 1, p. 273.
52 Gilbert, ed., *Winston S. Churchill, Companion*, vol. 4, part 1, p. 60.
53 David Lloyd George, *War Memoirs*, vol. 4, London, 1935, pp. xix–xx.

22. The Ministry of Munitions

1 Gilbert, ed., *Winston S. Churchill, Companion*, vol. 4, part 1, pp. 61–63.
2 Ibid., p. 64.
3 Ibid., p. 69.
4 Ibid., p. 67.
5 Ibid., p. 108.
6 Ibid, p. 107.
7 Arthur Marwick, *The Deluge*, London, 1967, p. 39.
8 Gilbert, ed., *Winston S. Churchill, Companion*, vol. 4, part 1, p. 217.
9 Marwick, *The Deluge*, p. 178.
10 Gilbert, ed., *Winston S. Churchill, Companion*, vol. 4, part 1, p. 69.
11 Ibid., pp. 137–38.
12 Ibid., p. 111.
13 Ibid., p. 191.
14 Ibid., p. 114.
15 Ibid., p. 123.
16 Ibid., p. 134.
17 Ibid., pp. 140–41.
18 Ibid., p. 212.
19 Ibid., p. 213.
20 Ibid., pp. 371–72.
21 Ibid., p. 131.
22 Ibid., pp. 266, 304.
23 Ibid., pp. 348–49.
24 National Archives, AIR 1/718/29/7.
25 Owen Thetford, *British Naval Aircraft*, London, 1991, p. 314.
26 Gilbert, ed., *Winston S. Churchill, Companion*, vol. 4, part 1, p. 186.
27 Ibid., p. 164.
28 Ibid., pp. 263, 377.
29 Great Britain, *Ministry of Munitions*, vol. 12, 1922, p. 173.
30 Navy Records Society, *Documents Relating to the Naval Air Service*, p. 521.
31 Gilbert, ed., *Winston S. Churchill, Companion*, vol. 4, part 1, p. 145.
32 National Archives, CAB 24/30.
33 Gilbert, ed., *Winston S. Churchill, Companion*, vol. 4, part 1, pp. 169–70.
34 Ibid., p. 174.
35 Ibid., p. 307.
36 Ibid., p. 389.
37 Ibid., p. 375.
38 Ibid., pp. 159, 401.
39 Ibid., p. 237.
40 Ibid., p. 390.
41 Ibid., p. 223.
42 Ibid., p. 222.
43 Ibid., p. 311.
44 Soames, ed., *Speaking for Themselves*, pp. 208–09.
45 Gilbert, ed., *Winston S. Churchill, Companion*, vol. 4, part 1, p. 371.
46 Soames, ed., *Speaking for Themselves*, pp. 212.
47 Ibid., pp. 204–06.
48 Gilbert, ed., *Winston S. Churchill, Companion*, vol. 4, part 1, p. 254.
49 Churchill, *World Crisis*, abridged edition, pp. 766–69.
50 Gilbert, ed., *Winston S. Churchill, Companion*, vol. 4, part 1, p. 275.
51 Ibid., p. 276.
52 Churchill, *World Crisis*, abridged edition, p. 776.
53 Ibid., p. 778.
54 Gilbert, ed., *Winston S. Churchill, Companion*, vol. 4, part 1, p. 282.
55 Ibid., p. 283.
56 Soames, ed., *Speaking for Themselves*, p. 206.
57 Gilbert, ed., *Winston S. Churchill, Companion*, vol. 4, part 1, pp. 293–97.
58 Churchill, *World Crisis*, abridged edition, p. 788.
59 Soames, ed., *Speaking for Themselves*, p. 207.
60 Gilbert, ed., *Winston S. Churchill, Companion*, vol. 4, part 1, pp. 343–47.

61 Ibid., p. 290.
62 Ibid., p. 385.
63 Soames, ed., *Speaking for Themselves*, p. 209.
64 Ibid., pp. 211–12.
65 Churchill, *World Crisis*, abridged edition, p. 761.
66 Soames, ed., *Speaking for Themselves*, pp. 216, 213.
67 Gilbert, ed., *Winston S. Churchill, Companion*, vol. 4, part 1, p. 393.
68 Ibid., p. 404.
69 Churchill, *World Crisis*, abridged edition, p. 840.

23. The Old Army and the New

1 Gilbert, ed., *Winston S. Churchill, Companion*, vol. 4, part 1, p. 435.
2 Ibid., p. 448.
3 Ibid., p. 443.
4 Ibid., p. 448.
5 Ibid., p. 450.
6 Ibid., p. 458.
7 Ibid., pp. 734, 739, 744.
8 General Charles ('Tim') Harington, *Tim Harington Looks Back*, London, 1940, p. 84.
9 Andrew Boyle, *Trenchard*, London, 1962, p. 379.
10 Brian Bond, *British Military Policy between the Two World Wars*, Oxford, 1980, p. 28.
11 Gilbert, ed., *Winston S. Churchill, Companion*, vol. 4, part 1, p. 710.
12 Ibid., p. 565n.
13 Bond, *British Military Policy*, p. 30.
14 J. E. Edmonds, *The Occupation of the Rhineland*, London, 1943, pp. 148–57.
15 Gilbert, ed., *Winston S. Churchill, Companion*, vol. 4, part 1, p. 1029.

16 Ibid., pp. 1032–33.
17 Gilbert, ed., *Winston S. Churchill, Companion*, vol. 4, part 2, p. 1230.
18 B. L. Montgomery, *Memoirs*, London, 1958, pp. 39–40.
19 Stephen Richards Graubard, 'Military Demobilization in Great Britain', *Journal of Military History*, 1947, pp. 297–311.
20 J. C. Dunn, *The War the Infantry Knew*, 1988, p. 574.
21 Gilbert, ed., *Winston S. Churchill, Companion*, vol. 4, part 1, p. 451.
22 Gilbert, ed., *Winston S. Churchill, Companion*, vol. 4, part 2, p. 469.
23 Gilbert, ed., *Winston S. Churchill, Companion*, vol. 4, part 1, p. 452.
24 Ibid., p. 459.
25 Ibid., p. 462.
26 Winston S. Churchill, *The World Crisis: The Aftermath*, London, 1929, p. 46.
27 *Hansard*, vol. 113, 3 March 1919, cols 73–74.
28 Gilbert, ed., *Winston S. Churchill, Companion*, vol. 4, part 2, p. 847.
29 Ibid., p. 495.
30 Gilbert, ed., *Winston S. Churchill, Companion*, vol. 4, part 1, p. 558.
31 Edmonds, *Occupation of the Rhineland*, pp. 91, 145–46, 158–61, 164–65, 120.
32 Gilbert, ed., *Winston S. Churchill, Companion*, vol. 4, part 1, p. 224.
33 Churchill, *World Crisis: The Aftermath*, p. 70.
34 Gilbert, ed., *Winston S. Churchill, Companion*, vol. 4, part 1, p. 332.
35 Ibid., p. 412.
36 Ibid., p. 486.
37 Ibid., pp. 515–16.
38 Ibid., pp. 521–22.

39 Anthony Carew, *The Lower Deck of the Royal Navy*, Manchester, 1981, pp. 212–13.

40 Winston S. Churchill, *Great Contemporaries*, London, 1937, pp. 200–01.

41 Bond, *British Military Policy*, p. 23.

42 Ibid., p. 24.

43 *Hansard*, vol. 130, 23 June 1923, col. 2332.

44 *Hansard*, vol. 125, 23 February 1920, cols 1354.

45 Gilbert, ed., *Winston S. Churchill, Companion*, vol. 4, part 2, p. 1355.

46 National Archives, CAB 27/168.

47 National Archives, CAB 24/30.

48 Gilbert, ed., *Winston S. Churchill, Companion*, vol. 4, part 2, p. 1293.

49 Ibid., pp. 942–3.

50 B. H. Liddell Hart, *The Tanks*, vol. 1, London, 1959, pp. 216–19.

51 Gilbert, ed., *Winston S. Churchill, Companion*, vol. 4, part 2, p. 1086.

52 Gilbert, ed., *Winston S. Churchill, Companion*, vol. 4, part 1, p. 709.

53 Gilbert, ed., *Winston S. Churchill, Companion*, vol. 4, part 2, pp. 1107, 1118.

54 Gilbert, ed., *Winston S. Churchill, Companion*, vol. 4, part 1, p. 222.

55 *Hansard*, vol. 125, 23 February 1920, col. 1354.

56 Gilbert, ed., *Winston S. Churchill, Companion*, vol. 4, part 1, p. 222.

57 Gilbert, ed., *Winston S. Churchill, Companion*, vol. 4, part 2, p. 1087.

58 National Archives, WO 33/3112.

59 Gilbert, ed., *Winston S. Churchill, Companion*, vol. 4, part 2, pp. 1017–19.

60 Q. M. Howard in *Royal United Services Journal*, February 1966, quoted in Bond, *British Military Policy*, p. 35.

24. Saving the Air Force

1 Gilbert, ed., *Winston S. Churchill, Companion*, vol. 4, part 1, pp. 563–64.

2 Ibid., pp. 529–30.

3 National Archives, AIR 8/41.

4 Boyle, *Trenchard*, p. 36.

5 Ibid., p. 101.

6 Gilbert, ed., *Winston S. Churchill, Companion*, vol. 4, part 1, p. 562.

7 National Archives, AIR 1/717/29/7.

8 H. Montgomery Hyde, *British Air Policy Between the Wars*, London, c. 1976, p. 57.

9 Boyle, *Trenchard*, p. 345.

10 Ibid., p. 342.

11 Ibid., p. 343.

12 Quoted in full in Ian M. Philpott, *The Royal Air Force*, Barnsley, 2005, vol. 1 pp. 423–26.

13 Boyle, *Trenchard*, p. 348.

14 Gilbert, ed., *Winston S. Churchill, Companion*, vol. 5, part 1, p. 673.

15 Gilbert, ed., *Winston S. Churchill, Companion*, vol. 4, part 2, pp. 1092–93.

16 Navy Records Society, vol. 132, 1993, *The Beatty Papers*, vol. 2, p. 83.

17 National Archives, AIR 8/41.

18 National Archives, CAB 27/168.

19 Navy Records Society, *Beatty Papers*, vol. 2, p. 212.

20 Longmore, *From Sea to Sky*, p. 85.

21 C. G. Jefford, *Observers and Navigators*, Shrewsbury, 2001, p. 106.

22 Ibid., pp. 106, 111.

23 Churchill, *My Early Life*, pp. 43–44.

24 Para 4, quoted in Ian M. Philpott, *The Royal Air Force*, vol. 1, Barnsley, 2005, pp. 423–26.

25 National Archives, CAB 27/168.

26 Sueter, *Airmen or Noahs*, p. 153.

27 Churchill College, Cambridge, CHAR 16/1.

28 Philpott, *Royal Air Force*, vol. 1, p. 425.
29 Churchill College, Cambridge, CHAR 16/1.
30 Gilbert, ed., *Winston S. Churchill, Companion*, vol. 4, part 2, p. 749.
31 Navy Records Society, vol. 121, 1980, *The Keyes Papers*, vol. 2, p. 149.
32 T. E. Lawrence, *The Mint*, London, 1955, p. 70.
33 H. A. Jones, *The War in the Air*, vol. 6, London, 1937, p. 25.
34 Churchill College, Cambridge, CHAR 16/1.
35 Boyle, *Trenchard*, p. 332.
36 National Archives, AIR 1/9/15/1/33.
37 Ibid.
38 Boyle, *Trenchard*, p. 338.
39 Ibid.
40 Gilbert, ed., *Winston S. Churchill, Companion*, vol. 4, part 2, p. 1341.

25. A Role for the RAF

1 Navy Records Society, *Beatty Papers*, vol. 2, p. 35.
2 Gilbert, ed., *Winston S. Churchill, Companion*, vol. 4, part 2, p. 1265.
3 National Archives, AIR 8/41.
4 Ibid.
5 Gilbert, ed., *Winston S. Churchill, Companion*, vol. 3, part 4, p. 1479.
6 Navy Records Society, *Beatty Papers*, vol. 2, p. 157.
7 Navy Records Society, *Keyes Papers*, vol. 2, p. 67.
8 National Archives, AIR 8/41.
9 Ibid.
10 National Archives, CAB 27/168.
11 Ibid.
12 Montgomery Hyde, *Air Policy Between the Wars*, p. 51.

13 National Archives, AIR 1/17.
14 National Archives, AIR 1/625/17/6.
15 National Archives, AIR 20/590.
16 *Hansard*, vol. 125, 23 February 1920, col. 1355.
17 Gilbert, ed., *Winston S. Churchill, Companion*, vol. 4, part 2, p. 828.
18 Ibid., p. 1079.
19 *Hansard*, vol. 125, 23 February 1920, col. 1354.
20 Gilbert, ed., *Winston S. Churchill, Companion*, vol. 4, part 2, pp. 1044–46.
21 Ibid., p. 1063.
22 National Archives, AIR 2/1522.
23 Gilbert, ed., *Winston S. Churchill, Companion*, vol. 4, part 2, pp. 1158–59.
24 National Archives, AIR 2/1522.
25 Ibid.
26 Ibid., pp. 1480, 1560.
27 Gilbert, ed., *Winston S. Churchill, Companion*, vol. 4, part 3, p. 1691.
28 Ian M. Philpott, *The Royal Air* Force, vol. 1, *The Trenchard Years*, Barnsley, 2005, pp. 428–29.
29 Navy Records Society, *Keyes Papers*, vol. 2, p. 163.

26. The World Crisis

1 Gilbert, ed., *Winston S. Churchill, Companion*, vol. 4, part 2, p. 1276.
2 Gilbert, ed., *Winston S. Churchill, Companion*, vol. 4, part 3, p. 1562.
3 Ibid., p. 1752.
4 Ibid., p. 2014.
5 Ibid., p. 1562.
6 Ashley, *Churchill as Historian*, p. 25.
7 Gilbert, ed., *Winston S. Churchill, Companion*, vol. 4, part 3, p. 1767.
8 Gilbert, ed., *Winston S. Churchill, Companion,* vol. 5, part 1, p. 886.

9 Ibid., p. 4.

10 Ibid., p. 6.

11 Ibid., p. 17.

12 Ashley, *Churchill as Historian*, pp. 25–26.

13 Gilbert, ed., *Winston S. Churchill, Companion*, vol. 5, part 1, p. 18.

14 Ibid., pp. 22, 25.

15 Ibid., p. 30n.

16 Ibid., pp. 32, 34, 37.

17 Ibid., p. 44.

18 Martin Gilbert, ed., *Winston S Churchill, Companion*, vol. 5, part 2, 1981, p. 160.

19 A. J. P. Taylor, *English History, 1914–1945*, Oxford, 1975, pp. 22–25.

20 Churchill, *The World Crisis*, abridged edition, p. 329.

21 Prior, *Churchill's World Crisis as History*, pp. 73, 77.

22 Churchill, *World Crisis*, abridged edition, p. 358.

23 Prior, *Churchill's World Crisis as History*, p. 110.

24 Gilbert, ed., *Winston S. Churchill, Companion*, vol. 5, part 1, p. 1447; Navy Records Society, *Keyes Papers*, vol. 2, p. 243.

25 Navy Records Society, *Keyes Papers*, vol. 2, p. 104.

26 Navy Records Society, vol. 111, 1968, *The Jellicoe Papers*, vol. 2, pp. 414–15, 482.

27 National Maritime Museum, BTY/22/9.

28 Navy Records Society, *Keyes Papers*, vol. 2, p. 104.

29 Ibid., p. 190.

30 Ashley, *Churchill as Historian*, p. 90.

31 Churchill, *World Crisis*, abridged edition, p. 603.

32 Navy Records Society, *Beatty Papers*, vol. 2, p. 473.

33 Churchill, *World Crisis*, abridged edition, p. 622.

34 Churchill, *World Crisis*, vol. 3, pp. 105–06.

35 Churchill, *World Crisis*, abridged edition, p. 635.

36 Gilbert, ed., *Winston S. Churchill, Companion*, vol. 5, part 1, p. 503.

37 Navy Records Society, *Keyes Papers*, vol. 2, p. 210.

38 Reginald Bacon, *The Jutland Scandal*, reprinted Barnsley, 2015, p. xiv.

39 National Maritime Museum, BTY/22/9/ p. 11.

40 Churchill, *World Crisis*, abridged edition, p. 601.

41 Navy Records Society, *Beatty Papers*, vol. 2, p. 471.

42 Churchill, *World Crisis*, abridged edition, p. 602.

43 Gilbert, ed., *Winston S. Churchill, Companion*, vol. 5, part 1, p. 1250.

44 Churchill, *World Crisis*, abridged edition, p. 553.

45 Ibid., pp. 658–60.

46 Gilbert, ed., *Winston S. Churchill, Companion*, vol. 5, part 1, p. 938.

47 Ibid., p. 746.

48 Prior, *Churchill's World Crisis as History*, pp. 210–30.

49 Soames, ed., *Speaking for Themselves*, pp. 155–56.

50 Churchill, *World Crisis*, abridged edition, p. 565.

51 Ibid., p. 652.

52 Gilbert, ed., *Winston S. Churchill, Companion*, vol. 5, part 1, p. 884.

53 Ibid., p. 126.

54 Ibid., p. 741.

55 Ibid., p. 1123.

56 Ibid., p. 1340.

57 Ibid., p. 243.

58 Churchill, *The World Crisis: The Aftermath*, p. 9.

27. An Iron Chancellor

1 Gilbert, ed., *Winston S. Churchill, Companion*, vol. 5, part 1, p. 94.
2 Gilbert, ed., *Winston S. Churchill, Companion*, vol. 4, part 3, p. 1814.
3 Gilbert, ed., *Winston S. Churchill, Companion*, vol. 5, part 1, p. 48.
4 Gilbert, *Churchill, a Life,* p. 465.
5 Gilbert, ed., *Winston S. Churchill, Companion*, vol. 5, part 1, p. 235.
6 J. M. Keynes, *The Economic Consequences of Mr Churchill*, London, 1925, p. 10.
7 Ashley, *Churchill as Historian*, p. 2.
8 *Hansard*, vol. 203, 14 March 1927, col. 1675.
9 Navy Records Society, *Documents Relating to the Naval Air Service*, p. 451.
10 Gilbert, ed., *Winston S. Churchill, Companion*, vol. 4, part 2, p. 783.
11 Gilbert, ed., *Winston S. Churchill, Companion*, vol. 5, part 1, p. 1040.
12 Ibid., p. 261.
13 Navy Records Society, *Fisher Papers*, vol. 1, p. 161.
14 Gilbert, ed., *Winston S. Churchill, Companion*, vol. 5, part 1, p. 216.
15 Ibid., p. 291.
16 Ibid., p. 300.
17 Ibid., p. 451.
18 Ibid., p. 383.
19 Ibid., p. 1033.
20 Ibid., p. 1342.
21 Ibid., p. 426.
22 Navy Records Society, *Keyes Papers*, vol. 2, p. 111.
23 Gilbert, ed., *Winston S. Churchill, Companion*, vol. 5, part 1, p. 453.
24 Navy Records Society, *Beatty Papers*, vol. 2, p. 301.
25 Gilbert, ed., *Winston S. Churchill, Companion*, vol. 5, part 1, p. 112.
26 Navy Records Society, *Documents Relating to the Naval Air Service*, p. 446.
27 Navy Records Society, *Keyes Papers*, vol. 2, p. 107.
28 Navy Records Society, *Beatty Papers*, vol. 2, p. 277.
29 Gilbert, ed., *Winston S. Churchill, Companion*, vol. 5, part 1, pp. 428–29.
30 Ibid., p. 503.
31 Ibid., p. 1031.
32 Ibid., p. 1062.
33 Ibid., p. 1103.
34 Navy Records Society, *Keyes Papers*, vol. 2, p. 239.
35 Gilbert, ed., *Winston S. Churchill, Companion*, vol. 5, part 1, p. 900.
36 Ibid., p. 1422.
37 Ibid., p. 1422.
38 Ibid., p. 517.
39 Ibid., p. 1077.
40 Navy Records Society, *Keyes Papers*, vol. 2, p. 199.
41 Gilbert, ed., *Winston S. Churchill, Companion*, vol. 5, part 1, p. 366.
42 Ibid., p. 936.
43 Ibid., p. 1184.
44 Ibid., p. 1209.
45 Ibid., p. 243.
46 Ibid., p. 261.
47 Ibid., pp. 344–45.
48 Ibid., p. 921.
49 National Archives, WO 32/2842.
50 National Archives, AIR 19/23.
51 Gilbert, ed., *Winston S. Churchill, Companion*, vol. 5, part 1, p. 261.
52 Ibid., p. 596.
53 Ibid., p. 548.
54 Ibid., p. 554.

55 Ibid., p. 1209.
56 National Archives, AIR 19/23.
57 Gilbert, ed., *Winston S. Churchill, Companion*, vol. 5, part 1, p. 732.
58 Gilbert, ed., *Winston S. Churchill, Companion*, vol. 5, part 2, p. 189.

28. Marlborough

1 Gilbert, ed., *Winston S. Churchill, Companion*, vol. 5, part 2, p. 36.
2 Ibid., p. 136.
3 Gilbert, ed., *Winston S. Churchill, Companion*, vol. 5, part 1, p. 1120.
4 Winston S. Churchill, *The World Crisis: The Eastern Front*, London, 1931, p. 7.
5 Ibid., p. 83.
6 Gilbert, ed., *Winston S. Churchill, Companion*, vol. 5, part 2, p. 161.
7 Churchill, *The Eastern Front*, p. 350.
8 Gilbert, ed., *Winston S. Churchill, Companion*, vol. 5, part 2, p. 331.
9 Ibid., p. 374.
10 Ibid., p. 150.
11 Ibid., p. 152.
12 Churchill, *My Early Life*, p. ix.
13 Gilbert, ed., *Winston S. Churchill, Companion*, vol. 5, part 2, p. 222.
14 Ibid., p. 200n.
15 Ibid., pp. 162–63.
16 Ibid., pp. 658–59.
17 Ibid., p. 2.
18 Ibid., p. 18.
19 Ibid., pp. 26–27.
20 Ibid., p. 207.
21 Ashley, *Churchill as Historian*, p. 23.
22 Ibid., pp. 26–28.
23 Ibid., p. 31.
24 Gilbert, ed., *Winston S. Churchill, Companion*, vol. 5, part 2, p. 700.
25 Ibid., p. 75.
26 Ibid., p. 240.

27 Ibid., p. 639.
28 Ibid., p. 700.
29 Ibid., p. 515.
30 Gilbert, ed., *Winston S. Churchill, Companion*, vol. 5, part 3, p. 1096.
31 Gilbert, ed., *Winston S. Churchill, Companion*, vol. 5, part 2, p. 453.
32 Ibid., p. 721.
33 Ibid., p. 15n.
34 Ibid., p. 720.
35 Ibid., p. 784.
36 Ibid., p. 614.
37 Winston S. Churchill, *Marlborough, His Life and Times*, London, 1947, p. 15.
38 Ibid., pp. 570–71.
39 Gilbert, ed., *Winston S. Churchill, Companion*, vol. 5, part 2, p. 469.
40 Ashley, *Churchill as Historian*, p. 235.
41 Gilbert, ed., *Winston S. Churchill, Companion*, vol. 5, part 2, pp. 474, 478.
42 Ibid., p. 475.
43 Ibid., p. 697.
44 Ibid., p. 983.
45 Ibid., p. 517.
46 Ibid., p. 521.
47 Ibid., p. 395.
48 Gilbert, ed., *Winston S. Churchill, Companion*, vol. 5, part 3, p. 1359.
49 Ibid., p. 1316.
50 Martin S. Gilbert, ed., *The Churchill War Papers*, vol. 1, London, 1993, p. 68.
51 Ibid., p. 195.
52 Ibid., p. 69n.
53 Gilbert, ed., *Winston S. Churchill, Companion*, vol. 5, part 3, p. 1601.

29. The Study of Air Power

1 Churchill, *The Second World War*, vol. 1, *The Gathering Storm*, p. 75.
2 Gilbert, ed., *Winston S. Churchill, Companion*, vol. 5, part 2, p. 197.

3 Ibid., pp. 208–09.
4 Ibid., p. 548.
5 Gilbert, ed., *Winston S. Churchill, Companion*, vol. 5, part 3, p. 718n.
6 Gilbert, ed., *Winston S. Churchill, Companion*, vol. 5, part 2, p. 834n.
7 Ibid., p. 718n.
8 National Archives, AIR 8/43.
9 Norman Longmate, *The Bombers*, London, 1983, pp. 41–43.
10 Jones, *The War in the Air*, vol. 6, Appendices, p. 21.
11 Williamson Murray, *The Luftwaffe, 1933–45*, Washington, 1996, p. 330.
12 Gilbert, ed., *Winston S. Churchill, Companion*, vol. 5, part 3, p. 968n.
13 Ibid., p. 1121.
14 Gilbert, ed., *Winston S. Churchill, Companion*, vol. 5, part 2, p. 826.
15 Ibid., pp. 836, 839, 846, 849–50.
16 Gilbert, ed., *Winston S. Churchill, Companion*, vol. 5, part 3, p. 523.
17 Ibid., p. 164.
18 Ibid., p. 803.
19 National Archives, CAB 16/133.
20 Ibid.
21 Gilbert, ed., *Winston S. Churchill, Companion*, vol. 5, part 2, pp. 1215–24.
22 National Archives, CAB 16/133.
23 Ibid.
24 Gilbert, ed., *Winston S. Churchill, Companion*, vol. 5, part 2, p. 1159.
25 Gilbert, ed., *Winston S. Churchill, Companion*, vol. 5, part 3, p. 840.
26 Ibid., p. 932.
27 Ibid., pp. 1278–79.
28 National Archives, CAB 16/134.
29 National Archives, CAB 16/133.
30 Gilbert, ed., *Winston S. Churchill, Companion*, vol. 5, part 3, p. 419.
31 Ibid., p. 1067.
32 National Archives, CAB 16/134.

33 Gilbert, ed., *Winston S. Churchill, Companion*, vol. 5, part 3, p. 1410.
34 National Archives, CAB 16/133.
35 Ibid.
36 Ibid.
37 Gilbert, ed., *Winston S. Churchill, Companion*, vol. 5, part 3, p. 1054.
38 National Archives, CAB 16/134.
39 Gilbert, ed., *Winston S. Churchill, Companion*, vol. 5, part 3, p. 933.
40 Gilbert, ed., *Winston S. Churchill, Companion*, vol. 5, part 2, p. 1356.
41 National Archives, CAB 16/133–34.
42 Philpott, *The Royal Air Force*, vol. 2, pp. 44–46, 69–73.
43 Murray, *Luftwaffe*, pp. 3–21.
44 Gilbert, ed., *Winston S. Churchill, Companion*, vol. 5, part 3, pp. 798, 837.
45 Ibid., pp. 269–71.
46 Jefford, *Observers and Navigators*, pp. 121–22, 128.
47 Gilbert, ed., *Winston S. Churchill, Companion*, vol. 5, part 3, pp. 269–71.
48 Ibid., p. 703.

30. The Drift to War

1 Gilbert, ed., *Winston S. Churchill, Companion*, vol. 5, part 2, pp. 1248–51.
2 Ibid., p. 1262–63.
3 Gilbert, ed., *Winston S. Churchill, Companion*, vol. 5, part 3, p. 1414.
4 Navy Records Society, *Keyes Papers*, vol. 2, p. 32.
5 Ibid., p. 369.
6 Gilbert, ed., *Winston S. Churchill, Companion*, vol. 5, part 3, p. 419.
7 Navy Records Society, *Keyes Papers*, vol. 2, p. 366.
8 Gilbert, ed., *Winston S. Churchill, Companion*, vol. 5, part 3, p. 646.

9 Navy Records Society, *Keyes Papers*, vol. 2, p. 369.
10 Ibid.
11 National Archives, AIR 8/223.
12 Gilbert, ed., *Winston S. Churchill, Companion*, vol. 5, part 3, p. 940.
13 Ibid., p. 783.
14 Ibid., p. 1425.
15 Ibid., pp. 934, 942, 953.
16 Ibid., p. 1186.
17 Ibid., p. 1239.
18 Ibid., p. 1537.
19 Ibid., p. 1414–16.
20 Ibid., p. 1421.
21 Ibid., p. 665.
22 Ibid., p. 697.
23 Ibid., p. 885.
24 Ibid., p. 667.
25 Ibid., p. 698.
26 Ibid., p. 1065.
27 Ibid., p. 1414.
28 Ibid., p. 1053–54.
29 Ibid., p. 1300.
30 Navy Records Society, *Keyes Papers*, vol. 2, p. 369.
31 Murray, *Luftwaffe*, p. 329.
32 Daniell, *4th Hussar*, p. 291.
33 Gilbert, ed., *Winston S. Churchill, Companion*, vol. 5, part 3, p. 684n.
34 Ibid., pp. 695–96.
35 Peter Beale, *Death by Design*, Stroud, 1998, p. 31.
36 Gilbert, ed., *Winston S. Churchill, Companion*, vol. 5, part 3, p. 711.
37 Ibid., p. 1052–54.
38 Ibid., p. 1512.
39 Ibid., pp. 1321–22, 1588.
40 Ibid., p. 1399.
41 Ibid., p. 1425n.
42 Ibid., p. 75n.
43 Churchill, *The Second World War*, vol. 1, *The Gathering Storm*, p. 611.
44 Gilbert, ed., *Winston S. Churchill, Companion*, vol. 5, part 3, p. 1052 n.
45 Lord Ismay, *Memoirs*, London, 1960, p. 84.
46 Gilbert, ed., *Winston S. Churchill, Companion*, vol. 5, part 3, p. 1416.
47 Ibid., p. 1594.
48 Ibid., p. 1592.
49 Ibid., p. 1573.
50 Ibid., pp. 1609–11.

31. Winston is Back

1 Gilbert, ed., *Churchill War Papers*, vol. 1, pp. 6–8.
2 National Maritime Museum, GOD/177, p. 303.
3 Gilbert, ed., *Churchill War Papers*, vol. 1, p. 325.
4 Ibid., p. 665.
5 Ibid., p. 128.
6 Ibid., p. 154.
7 Ibid., p. 42.
8 Ibid., p. 200.
9 Ibid., p. 47.
10 Ibid., p. 113.
11 Ibid., p. 373.
12 Ibid., p. 762.
13 Ibid., p. 223.
14 Ibid., p. 451.
15 Ibid., p. 701.
16 Ibid., pp. 681, 702.
17 Buxton, *Big Gun Monitors*, pp. 176ff.
18 Gilbert, ed., *Churchill War Papers*, vol. 1, p. 133.
19 Ibid., p. 74.
20 Ibid., p. 38.
21 Ibid., p. 167.
22 Ibid., p. 156.
23 Ibid., p. 105.
24 Ibid., p. 142.

25 Ibid., p. 736.
26 Ibid., p. 57.
27 Ibid., p. 499.
28 Ibid., p. 802.
29 Ibid., p. 223–24.
30 Ibid., p. 741–43.
31 Ibid., p. 175.
32 Ibid., p. 661.
33 Ibid., pp. 770–71.
34 Ibid., p. 163.
35 Ibid., p. 800.
36 Ibid., pp. 405, 730.
37 Ibid., p. 169.
38 Ibid., p. 178.
39 Ibid., p. 219.
40 Ibid.
41 Ibid., p. 204.
42 Ibid., p. 800.
43 Ibid., p. 283.
44 Brian Lavery, *Hostilities Only*, London, 2004, p. 29.
45 National Archives, ADM 1/10088.
46 Lavery, *Hostilities Only*, pp. 30ff.
47 Gilbert, ed., *Churchill War Papers*, vol. 1, p. 105.
48 Ibid., p. 125.
49 Ibid., p. 305.
50 Ibid., p. 309.
51 Ibid., pp. 365, 315.
52 Ibid., p. 313.
53 Ibid., pp. 61–62.
54 Ibid., p. 306.
55 Ibid., p. 312.
56 Ibid., pp. 319–20.
57 Ibid., pp. 482–83.
58 National Archives, CAB 66/1.
59 Ibid., p. 177.
60 Ibid., p. 955.
61 Ibid., p. 284.
62 Ibid., p. 356.
63 Winston S. Churchill, *The Second World War*, vol. 1, *The Gathering Storm*, London, 1965, p. 594.

32. The Navy at War

1 National Archives, ADM 116/6364.
2 Gilbert, ed., *Churchill War Papers*, vol. 1, p. 78.
3 Ibid., pp. 83–84.
4 Ibid., pp. 136–37.
5 Ibid., p. 235.
6 Ibid., pp. 274–75.
7 Ibid., pp. 310–11.
8 Ibid., p. 497.
9 Ibid., p. 414.
10 Ibid., p. 590.
11 Ibid., p. 644.
12 Ibid., p. 545.
13 Ibid., pp. 647–50.
14 Ibid., p. 508.
15 Ibid., p. 530.
16 Ibid., p. 765.
17 Ibid., p. 633.
18 Ibid., p. 18.
19 Ibid., p. 155.
20 Ibid., p. 110.
21 Ibid., p. 355.
22 Ibid., pp. 177, 183.
23 Ibid., p. 158.
24 Ibid., p. 397.
25 Ibid., p. 341.
26 Ibid., p. 232.
27 Navy Records Society, vol. 137, 1997, *The Defeat of the Enemy Attack upon Shipping*, p. 56.
28 Gilbert, ed., *Churchill War Papers*, vol. 1, pp. 120–21.
29 Ibid., p. 432.
30 Ibid., p. 492.
31 National Archives, CAB 65/2.
32 Gilbert, ed., *Churchill War Papers*, vol. 1, p. 593.
33 National Archives, ADM 205/4.
34 National Archives, CAB 65/11.
35 National Archives, CAB 66/5.
36 National Archives, CAB 65/11.

37 National Archives, CAB 66/5.
38 National Archives, CAB 65/6, Roskill 1 152.
39 National Archives, CAB 65/5.
40 Jak P. Mallmann Showell, ed., *Fuehrer Conferences on Naval Affairs*, London, 2005, p. 86.
41 Correlli Barnett, *Engage the Enemy More Closely*, London, 1991, p. 105.
42 Gilbert, ed., *Churchill War Papers*, vol. 1, p. 977.
43 S. W. Roskill, *The War at Sea*, vol. 1, London, 1954, p. 161.
44 John Colville, *The Fringes of Power*, London, 1985, p. 99.
45 National Archives, CAB 65/6.
46 Gilbert, ed., *Churchill War Papers*, vol. 1, p. 999.
47 National Archives, ADM 116/4471.
48 *Hansard*, vol. 359, 11 April 1940, col. 747.
49 Gilbert, ed., *Churchill War Papers*, vol. 1, p. 1037.
50 National Archives, CAB 65/6.
51 Roskill, *The War at Sea*, vol. 1, p. 202.
52 Churchill, *The Gathering Storm*, pp. 536–37.
53 David Reynolds, *In Command of History*, London, 2004, p. 126.
54 Churchill, *The Gathering Storm*, p. 601.

33. Finest Hour

1 Martin Gilbert, ed., *Churchill War Papers*, vol. 2, 1994, pp. 14–15.
2 Ibid., p. 30.
3 Karl-Heinz Frieser, *The Blitzkrieg Legend*, Annapolis, 2005, passim.
4 National Archives, CAB 65/7.
5 Gilbert, ed., *Churchill War Papers*, vol. 2, p. 27.
6 National Archives, CAB 65/7.
7 National Archives, CAB 79/4.
8 National Archives, CAB 99/3.
9 Gilbert, ed., *Churchill War Papers*, vol. 2, pp. 53–54.
10 Winston S. Churchill, *The Second World War*, vol. 2, *Their Finest Hour*, London, 1967, p. 42.
11 Gilbert, ed., *Churchill War Papers*, vol. 2, p. 56.
12 National Archives, CAB 99/3.
13 Churchill, *Their Finest Hour*, p. 42.
14 National Archives, PREM 188/6.
15 Gilbert, ed., *Churchill War Papers*, vol. 2, p. 116.
16 National Archives, CAB 65/7.
17 Public Record Office of Northern Ireland, *Reminiscences of Sir Richard Pim*, T3620, p. 80.
18 National Archives, PREM 3/188/6.
19 Ibid.
20 Ibid.
21 National Archives, CAB 69/1.
22 Ibid.
23 National Archives, CAB 65/13.
24 National Archives, CAB 65/7.
25 *Hansard*, vol. 361, 28 May 1940, col. 422.
26 Hugh Dalton, *Second World War Diary*, London, 1986, quoted in Gilbert, ed., *Churchill War Papers*, vol. 2, p. 182.
27 Churchill, *Their Finest Hour*, p. 88.
28 National Archives, PREM 3/188/6.
29 *Hansard*, vol. 361, 4 June 1940, col. 796.
30 Gilbert, ed., *Churchill War Papers*, vol. 2, p. 422.
31 National Archives, CAB 99/3.
32 National Archives, PREM 7/2.
33 Gilbert, ed., *Churchill War Papers*, vol. 2, p. 227.

34 National Archives, CAB 65/13.
35 Edward Spears, *Assignment to Catastrophe*, London, 1954, pp. 143–45.
36 National Archives, CAB 99/3.
37 Gilbert, ed., *Churchill War Papers*, vol. 2, p. 297.
38 Spears, *Assignment to Catastrophe*, pp. 213–14.
39 Alan Brooke, *War Diaries*, London, 2001, p. 81.
40 Churchill, *Their Finest Hour*, p. 186.
41 National Archives, CAB 65/7.
42 Gilbert, ed., *Churchill War Papers*, vol. 2, p. 76.
43 Ibid., p. 363.
44 Ibid., p. 478.
45 Ibid., p. 511.
46 Ibid., p. 656.
47 Ibid., p. 851.
48 National Archives, ADM 1/10566.
49 National Archives, PREM 3/188/2.
50 National Archives, CAB 65/13.
51 *Hansard*, vol. 362, 25 June 1940, col. 302.
52 National Archives, PREM 3/179/4.
53 National Archives, CAB 65/7.
54 National Archives, PREM 3/179/1.
55 Colville, *Fringes of Power*, p. 183.
56 National Archives, CAB 69/1.
57 Colville, *Fringes of Power*, p. 150.
58 Soames, ed., *Speaking for Themselves*, p. 454.

34. War Leader

1 Colville, *Fringes of Power*, pp. 194–95.
2 *The Times*, 15 July 1940.
3 Gilbert, ed., *Churchill War Papers*, vol. 2, p. 580.
4 Ibid., p. 1204.
5 Churchill, *Their Finest Hour*, p. 794.
6 Edward R. Murrow, *In Search of Light*, New York, 1967, p. 237.
7 Brooke, *War Diaries*, p. 170.
8 National Archives, PREM 4/68/9.
9 Gilbert, ed., *Churchill War Papers*, vol. 2, pp. 636–37.
10 Ibid., p. 1041.
11 Ibid., pp. 225–26.
12 Gilbert, ed., *Churchill War Papers*, vol. 2, p. 13.
13 National Maritime Museum, GOD/177.
14 *Churchill War Papers*, vol. 2, p. 637.
15 National Archives, PREM 4/80/3.
16 Sir Edmond Ironside, *Diaries, 1937–40*, London, 1962, p. 335.
17 Charles Carrington, *Soldier at Bomber Command*, London, 1987, p. 28.
18 Gilbert, ed., *Churchill War Papers*, vol. 2, pp. 580–81.
19 Ibid., p. 1158.
20 Ibid., pp. 531–32.
21 Carrington, *Soldier at Bomber Command*, p. 28.
22 Brooke, *War Diaries*, p. 199.
23 Philip Ziegler, *Mountbatten*, London, 1985, p. 175.
24 Colville, *Fringes of Power*, pp. 762–63.
25 Gilbert, ed., *Churchill War Papers*, vol. 2, p. 1079.
26 Navy Records Society, vol. 122, 1981, *The Keyes Papers*, vol. 3, p. 172.
27 *Encounter*, April 1966, p. 21.
28 Brooke, *War Diaries*, p. 273.
29 Brian Lavery, *Churchill Goes to War*, London, 2008, p. 42.
30 Public Record Office of Northern Ireland, Reminiscences of Sir Richard Pike, T3630, p. 190.
31 Ibid., p. 162.
32 Ismay, *Memoirs*, p. 270.

33 Winston S. Churchill, *The Second World War*, vol. 4, *The Hinge of Fate*, London, 1966, p. 788.
34 H. M. D. Parker, *Manpower*, London, 1957, pp. 485, 488.
35 Ibid., p. 103.
36 Ibid., p. 162.
37 Ibid., pp. 106–7.
38 Michael Howard, *Grand Strategy*, vol. IV, *September 1942 – August 1943*, London, 1972, p. 5.
39 Ibid., p. 6.
40 Ibid., p. 7.
41 National Archives, ADM 1/12133.
42 National Archives, CAB 66/31.
43 National Archives, ADM 116/5345.
44 John Ehrman, *Grand Strategy*, vol. V, *August 1943 – September 1944*, London, 1956, p. 44.
45 W. S. Churchill, *The Second World War*, vol. V, *Closing the Ring*, London, 1952, p. 595.
46 National Archives, ADM 116/5345.
47 Ismay, *Memoirs*, p. 270.
48 National Archives, WO 205/118.
49 Churchill, *Hinge of Fate*, pp. 802–03.
50 Churchill, *Closing the Ring*, p. 620.
51 National Archives, PREM 3/38/1, 2.
52 Paul Freyberg, *Bernard Freyberg VC*, London, 1991, p. 230.
53 Lavery, *Churchill Goes to War*, p. 62.
54 Churchill, *Hinge of Fate*, p. 774.
55 Quoted in Lavery, *Churchill Goes to War*, p. 22.
56 Brian Lavery, *The Last Big Gun*, Oxford, 2015, pp. 197–99.
57 Brooke, *War Diaries*, pp. 676–77.

35. War on Land

1 Jeremy A. Crang, *The British Army and the People's War, 1939–1945*, Manchester, 2000, p. 23.
2 Correlli Barnett, *The Desert Generals*, London, 1960, p. 99.
3 Brooke, *War Diaries*, p. 90.
4 *Army Training Memorandum no 35*, August 1940, p. 4.
5 Ismay, *Memoirs*, p. 270.
6 Winston S. Churchill, *The Second World War*, vol. 6, *Triumph and Tragedy*, London, 1954, p. 597.
7 Brian L. Davis, *British Army Uniforms and Insignia of World War Two*, London, 1983.
8 National Archives, PREM 3/54/7.
9 Churchill, *Their Finest Hour*, pp. 39–40.
10 *Encounter*, April 1966, p. 16.
11 Gilbert, ed., *Churchill War Papers*, vol. 2, p. 637.
12 Ibid., p. 900.
13 National Archives, CAB 70/1.
14 National Archives, PREM 3/482/2.
15 National Archives, CAB 86/1.
16 Beale, *Death by Design*, p. 34.
17 Brooke, *War Diaries*, pp. 155–56.
18 Gilbert, ed., *Churchill War Papers*, vol. 2, p. 862.
19 National Archives, PREM 3/427/5.
20 Ibid.
21 Beale, *Death by Design*, p. 65.
22 *Army Training Memorandum no 47*, January 1944, p. 38.
23 Beale, *Death by Design*, p. 110.
24 National Archives, PREM 3/482/2.
25 National Archives, PREM 3/427/5.
26 Beale, *Death by Design*, p. 97.
27 Gilbert, ed., *Churchill War Papers*, vol. 2, p. 942 and n.
28 Colville, *Fringes of Power*, p. 262.
29 Gilbert, ed., *Churchill War Papers*, vol. 2, p. 962.
30 Ismay, *Memoirs*, p. 271.
31 Gilbert, ed., *Churchill War Papers*, vol. 2, p. 1037.

32 Winston S. Churchill, *The Second World War*, vol. 2, *The Grand Alliance*, London, 1966, pp. 93, 97.
33 King's College London, Alanbrooke Papers, 6/2/12.
34 Churchill, *Hinge of Fate*, p. 361.
35 Ibid., p. 541.
36 Colville, *Fringes of Power*, p. 273.
37 Churchill, *Hinge of Fate*, pp. 811, 815.
38 Timothy Harrison Place, *Military Training in the British Army, 1940–1944*, London, 2000; Crang, *The British Army and the People's War*, passim
39 Churchill, *Hinge of Fate*, p. 755.
40 *Army Training Memorandum no 49*, June 1944, p. 7.
41 Place, *Military Training in the British Army*, p. 42.
42 Robert Crisp, *Brazen Chariots*, London, 1959, p. 32.
43 King's College London, The Alanbrooke Papers, 6/2/12.
44 Quoted in Max Hastings, *Overlord*, pp. 172, 179–80.
45 Churchill, *Triumph and Tragedy*, pp. 173–74.
46 Ibid., p. 233.
47 Ibid., p. 361.
48 Ibid., p. 597.

36. War at Sea

1 A. B. Cunningham, *A Sailor's Odyssey*, London, 1956, p. 260.
2 Gilbert, ed., *Churchill War Papers*, vol. 2, p. 552.
3 Pim, *Reminiscences*, p. 97.
4 John Martin, *Downing Street, the War Years*, London, 1991, p. 50.
5 Colville, *Fringes of Power*, p. 274.
6 National Archives, PREM 3/324/16.
7 Lavery, *Churchill Goes to War*, pp. 31, 45, 63–64, 83, 96.
8 National Archives, CAB 65/14.
9 Gilbert, ed., *Churchill War Papers*, vol. 2, p. 597.
10 National Archives, CAB 69/2.
11 Gilbert, ed., *Churchill War Papers*, vol. 2, p. 1346.
12 Churchill, *The Grand Alliance*, p. 551.
13 Churchill, *The Hinge of Fate*, pp. 42–43.
14 National Archives, PREM 3/171/3.
15 National Archives, PREM 3/163/1.
16 Joseph Wellings, *On His Majesty's Service*, ed. John Hattendorf, Newport, RI, 1983, p. 75.
17 National Archives, ADM 205/5.
18 National Archives, CAB 55/8.
19 National Archives, PREM 3/324/20.
20 Gilbert, ed., *Churchill War Papers*, vol. 2, p. 684.
21 Colville, *Fringes of Power*, p. 232.
22 *Hansard*, vol. 365, 5 November 1940, col. 1243.
23 National Archives, PREM 3/462/1.
24 Gilbert, ed., *Churchill War Papers*, vol. 2, p. 1175.
25 Churchill, *Their Finest Hour*, p. 536.
26 Gilbert, ed., *Churchill War Papers*, vol. 2, p. 609.
27 Churchill, *Their Finest Hour*, p. 259.
28 Gilbert, ed., *Churchill War Papers*, vol. 2, pp. 315–16.
29 H. A. Jones, *The War in the Air*, vol. 6, Appendices, p. 19.
30 National Archives, CAB 86/1.
31 Ibid.
32 Pim, *Reminiscences*, p. 96.
33 Robin Brodhurst, *Churchill's Anchor*, Barnsley, 2000, pp. 238–49.
34 National Archives CAB 86/1.
35 Gilbert, ed., *Churchill War Papers*, vol. 2, p. 397.
36 Pim, *Reminiscences*, p. 133.

37. Air Power in Operation

1 Jessica Mitford, *Hons and Rebels*, reprinted London, 1982, p. 218.
2 Air Ministry Order 433/1940.
3 National Archives, CAB 65/14, 65/9.
4 Churchill, *Their Finest Hour*, pp. 193–94.
5 Andy Saunders, *Battle of Britain, RAF Operations Manual*, Yeovil, 2015.
6 National Archives, CAB 65/9.
7 Colville, *Fringes of Power*, p. 191.
8 Gilbert, ed., *Churchill War Papers*, vol. 2, p. 547.
9 National Archives, CAB 66/11.
10 Gilbert, ed., *Churchill War Papers*, vol. 2, p. 721.
11 Ibid., p. 725.
12 Ibid., p. 818.
13 Ibid., p. 499.
14 Colville, *Fringes of Power*, p. 235.
15 Ibid., p. 194.
16 Gilbert, ed., *Churchill War Papers*, vol. 2, p. 651.
17 Ibid., p. 740.
18 Ibid., p. 787.
19 Ibid., p. 701.
20 National Archives, CAB 65/8.
21 Winston G. Ramsey, ed., *The Blitz Then and Now*, London, 1988, vol. 2, p. 65.
22 Ismay, *Memoirs*, p. 180.
23 National Archives, CAB 81/22.
24 C. F. Rawnsley and Robert Wright, *Night Fighter*, Manchester, 1998, p. 39.
25 National Archives, PREM 3/22/5.
26 National Archives, AIR 16/524.
27 National Archives, AIR 16/525.
28 National Archives, CAB 65/7.
29 Gilbert, ed., *Churchill War Papers*, vol. 2, pp. 492–93.
30 National Archives, CAB 65/8.
31 National Archives, CAB 66/11.
32 Gilbert, ed., *Churchill War Papers*, vol. 2, p. 732.
33 *Hansard*, vol. 365, 5 September 1940, col. 41.
34 *Hansard*, vol. 365, 8 October 1940, col. 290.
35 Ibid., col. 293.
36 Gilbert, ed., *Churchill War Papers*, vol. 2, p. 1304.
37 National Archives, CAB 120/300.
38 Noble Frankland and Sir Charles Webster, *The Strategic Air Offensive against Germany*, London, 1961, vol. 1, pp. 178–80.
39 Gilbert, ed., *Churchill War Papers*, vol. 2, p. 1313.
40 Max Hastings, *Bomber Command*, London, 1979, p. 142.
41 Ibid., p. 140.
42 Ibid., p. 212.
43 Adam Tooze, *The Wages of Destruction*, London, 2006, p. 597.
44 Hastings, *Bomber Command*, p. 306.
45 Ibid., pp. 399–401; Noble Frankland, *History at War*, London, 1998.

38. Air Support

1 National Archives, CAB 86/1; Brooke, *War Diaries*, p. 157.
2 Brooke, *War Diaries*, p. 172.
3 Francis K. Mason, *Hawker Aircraft Since 1920*, London, 1991, pp. 55–59, 316–28.
4 Brooke, *War Diaries*, p. 253.
5 Longmore, *From Sea to Sky*, p. 260.
6 Gilbert, ed., *Churchill War Papers*, vol. 2, p. 250.
7 Vincent Orange, *Tedder: Quietly in Command*, London, 2004, p. 254 and passim.

8   National Archives, AIR 2/5146.
9   National Archives, AIR 2/5386.
10 National Archives, AVIA 46/287.
11 National Archives, CAB 69/1.
12 *Hansard*, vol. 117, 13 November 1940, col. 700.
13 Gilbert, ed., *Churchill War Papers*, vol. 3, pp. 1285–86.
14 National Archives, PREM 3/17/3.
15 National Archives, PREM 3/171/3.
16 W. S. Churchill, *The Second World War*, vol. V, *Closing the Ring*, London, 1952, p. 576.
17 National Archives, PREM 3.171/2.
18 National Archives, CAB 69/1.
19 Air Historical Branch, *The RAF in Maritime War*, vol. 2, app. 1.
20 National Archives, PREM 3/97/2.
21 Ibid.
22 Ibid.
23 Ibid.
24 National Archives, PREM 3/97/1.
25 Ibid.
26 Churchill, *Closing the Ring*, London, 1952, p. 595.

39. Combined Operations

1   Gilbert, ed., *Churchill War Papers*, vol. 2, p. 489.
2   Colville, *Fringes of Power*, p. 234.
3   Brooke, *War Diaries*, p. 236.
4   Gilbert, ed., *Churchill War Papers*, vol. 2, p. 638.
5   R. Baker et al., *British Warship Design in World War II*, London, 1983, p. 181.
6   Ibid., p. 19.
7   Churchill, *The Hinge of Fate*, pp. 804–05.
8   *Combined Operations* (Min. of Information), 1943, vol. I, p. 11.

9   National Archives, PREM 3/103/1.
10 Martin Stannard, *Evelyn Waugh, No Abiding City*, London, 1993, p. 23.
11 National Archives, PREM 3/103/1.
12 Kings College, Alanbrooke 6/2/11.
13 National Archives, PREM 3/256.
14 Gilbert, ed., *Churchill War Papers*, vol. 2, p. 559.
15 Colville, *Fringes of Power*, p. 233.
16 National Archives, CAB 86/1.
17 Martin Gilbert, ed., *Churchill War Papers*, vol. 3, London, 2000, p. 1355.
18 National Archives, PREM 3/333/1.
19 National Archives, PREM 3/256.
20 National Archives, PREM 3/32/1.
21 Churchill, *The Second World War*, vol. 3, *The Grand Alliance*, p. 683.
22 Gilbert, ed., *Churchill War Papers*, vol. 2, p. 755.
23 Colville, *Fringes of Power*, p. 316.
24 Navy Records Society, *Keyes Papers*, vol. 3, p. 142.
25 Brooke, *War Diaries*, p. 236.
26 Ziegler, *Mountbatten*, p. 206.
27 Gilbert, ed., *Winston S. Churchill, Companion*, vol. 5, part 1, p. 674.
28 National Archives, ADM 199/1929.
29 Churchill, *The Gathering Storm*, p. 571.
30 Brooke, *War Diaries*, p. 96.
31 Churchill, *The Hinge of Fate*, p. 753.
32 Ibid., pp. 754–55.
33 National Archives, PREM 3/119/5.
34 Churchill, *The Hinge of Fate*, pp. 809–10.
35 Brooke, *War Diaries*, pp. 441–42.
36 Churchill, *The Hinge of Fate*, p. 199.
37 Ibid., p. 564.
38 National Archives, PREM 3/216/1.
39 National Archives, PREM 3/216/7.
40 Pim, *Reminiscences*, p. 170.
41 National Archives, PREM 3/216/7.

Conclusion

1 Reynolds, *In Command of History*, p. 504.
2 Brooke, *War Diaries*, pp. 590–91.
3 National Maritime Museum, GOD/177.
4 Alan R. Millet, ed., *Military Effectiveness*, vol. 3, *The Second World War*, London, 1988, pp. 92–93.
5 Ibid., p. 129.
6 E. B. Potter, *The Great Sea War*, London, 1960, p. 276.
7 Brooke, *War Diaries*, p. 272.
8 William Emerson, 'Franklin Roosevelt as Commander-in-Chief in World War II', *Military Affairs*, 1958–59, pp. 181–207.
9 Brooke, *War Diaries*, p. 483.
10 Clive Pearson, 'Stalin as War Leader', *History Review*, December 2008.
11 Frieser, *The Blitzkrieg Legend*, passim.
12 *Fuehrer Conferences on Naval Affairs*, London, 2005, p. 360.
13 Ian Kershaw, *Hitler, 1939–45*, London, 2000, p. 314.
14 Max Hastings, *Finest Years: Churchill as Warlord*, London, 2009, p. 148.
15 Brooke, *War Diaries*, p. 458.
16 Ashley, *Churchill as Historian*, p. 20.

Bibliography

Manuscripts

National Archives
Prime Minister's papers, PREM
Cabinet papers, CAB
Air Ministry and other papers relating to aviation, AIR
Admiralty papers, ADM
Combined Operations papers, DEFE
Army papers, WO
Ministry of Munitions, MUN

Churchill College, Cambridge
CHAR series contains Churchill's official papers. Many are reproduced the Companion
   series cited below.

National Maritime Museum
George Ballard, NAI/2/29
Sir David Beatty, BTY
Henry Oliver, OLV

Public Record Office of Northern Ireland
Reminiscences of Sir Richard Pim, T3620

King's College London
Alanbrooke Papers, GB0099

Books

Churchill's Autobiographical and Biographical/Historical Writings
In approximate chronological order for the period described.
Winston S. Churchill, *My Early Life*, 1930, reprinted London, 2002
Winston S. Churchill, *The Story of the Malakand Field Force*, 1897, reprinted np, 2005
Winston S. Churchill, *The River War*, 1899, reprinted London, 1973
Winston S. Churchill, *Frontiers and Wars*, London, 1962
Mary Soames, ed., *Speaking for Themselves*, 1998, reprinted London, 1999
Winston S. Churchill, *The World Crisis*
vol. 1, *1911–1918*, 1923, reprinted London 2015
vol. 2, *1915*, 1923, reprinted London, 2005
vol. 3, *1916–18*, 1927, reprinted London, 1995
vol. 4, *The Aftermath*, London, 1929
Winston S. Churchill, *The World Crisis 1911–1918*, abridged and revised edition, 1931, reprinted London, 2005
Winston S. Churchill, *Thoughts and Adventures*, London, 1932
Winston S. Churchill, *The Second World War*
vol. 1, *The Gathering Storm*, London, 1948, reprinted 1965
vol. 2, *Their Finest Hour*, London, 1949, reprinted 1967
vol. 3, *The Grand Alliance*, London, 1950, reprinted 1966
vol. 4, *The Hinge of Fate*, London, 1951, reprinted 1966
vol. 5, *Closing the Ring*, London, 1951, reprinted 1966
vol. 6, *Triumph and Tragedy*, London, 1954, reprinted 1954

Criticisms of Churchill's Writings
Maurice Ashley, *Churchill as Historian*, London, 1968
Robin Prior, *Churchill's World Crisis as History*, London, *c.* 1983
David Reynolds, *In Command of History*, London, 2004

Other Writings by Churchill
Winston S. Churchill, *The Fighting Line*, London, 1916
Winston S. Churchill, *Great Contemporaries*, London, 1937
Winston S. Churchill, *The World Crisis: The Eastern Front*, London, 1931
Winston S. Churchill, *Marlborough, His Life and Times*, reprinted in 2 vols, London, 1947

Churchill Biography
Randolph S. Churchill, *Winston S. Churchill*, vol. 1, *Youth, 1874–1900*, London, 1966
Randolph S. Churchill and Martin Gilbert, *Winston S. Churchill*, vol. 2, *Young Statesman*, London, 1967
Carlo D'Este, *Warlord: A Life of Churchill at War, 1874–1945*, London, 2009

Martin Gilbert, *Winston S. Churchill*, vol. 3, *1914–1916*, London, 1971
vol. 4, *1916–1922*, London, 1975
vol. 5, *1922–1939*, London, 1976
vol. 6, *Finest Hour*, London 1983
vol. 7, *Road to Victory*, London, 1986
Martin Gilbert, *Churchill, a Life*, London, 2001
Max Hastings, *Finest Years: Churchill as Warlord*, London, 2009
Roy Jenkins, *Churchill*, London, 2002
Brian Lavery, *Churchill Goes to War*, London, 2008
Douglas S. Russell, *Winston Churchill, Soldier*, London, 2005

Companion Volumes

Randolph Churchill, ed., *Winston S. Churchill, Companion*
vol. 1, part 1, *1874–96*, London, 1967
vol. 1, part 2, *1896–1900*, London, 1967
Martin Gilbert, ed., *Winston S. Churchill, Companion*
vol. 2, part 1, *1901–1907*, London, 1969
vol. 2, part 2, *1907–1911*, London, 1969
vol. 2, part 3, *1911–1914*, London, 1969
vol. 3, part 1, *July 1914–April 1918*, London, 1972
vol. 3, part 2, *May 1915–December 1916*, London, 1972
vol. 4, part 1, *January 1917–June 1919*, London, 1977
vol. 4, part 2, *July 1919–March 1921*, London 1977
vol. 4, part 3, *April 1921–November 1922*, London 1977
vol. 5, part 1, *The Exchequer Years, 1922–1929*, London, 1979
vol. 5, part 2, The *Wilderness Years, 1929–1935*, London, 1981
vol. 5, part 3, *The Coming of War, 1936–1939*, London, 1982
Martin Gilbert, ed., *The Churchill War Papers*
vol. 1, *At the Admiralty*, London, 1993
vol. 2, *Never Surrender*, London, 1994
vol. 3, *The Ever-Widening War*, London, 2000

Other Autobiographies and Diaries

Sir Lewis Bayly, *Pull Together*, London, 1939
Violet Bonham Carter, *Winston Churchill as I Knew Him*, London, 1965
Alan Brooke, *War Diaries*, London, 2001
Henry D. Capper, *Aft from the Hawsehole*, London, nd
Charles Carrington, *Soldier at Bomber Command*, London, 1987
Ernle Chatfield, *The Navy and Defence*, London, 1942
'Clinker Knocker', *'Aye, Aye, Sir'*, London, nd
John Colville, *The Fringes of Power*, London, 1985
A. B. Cunningham, *A Sailor's Odyssey*, London, 1956

Hugh Dalton, *Second World War Diary*, London, 1986
Sir Dudley de Chair, *The Sea is Strong*, London, 1961
Barry Domvile, *By and Large*, London, 1936
Kenneth Dewar, *The Navy from Within*, London, 1939
J. A. Fisher, *Memories*, London, 1919
Noble Frankland, *History at War*, London, 1998
Sir Douglas Haig, *War Diaries and Letters*, London, 2005
General Charles ('Tim') Harington, *Tim Harington Looks Back*, London, 1940
Bernard Huldermann, *Albert Ballin*, London, 1922
Sir Edmond Ironside, *Diaries, 1937–40*, London, 1962
Lord Ismay, *Memoirs*, London, 1960
David Lloyd George, *War Memoirs*, 6 vols, London, 1933–36
Sir Arthur Longmore, *From Sea to Sky*, London, 1946
John Martin, *Downing Street, the War Years*, London, 1991
Jessica Mitford, *Hons and Rebels*, reprinted London, 1982
B. L. Montgomery, *Memoirs*, London, 1958
Edward R. Murrow, *In Search of Light*, New York, 1967
Charles R. Samson, *Fights and Flights*, London, 1930
Sir William Slim, *Defeat into Victory*, London, 1956
Edward Spears, *Assignment to Catastrophe*, London, 1954
Albert G. Stern, *Tanks, 1914–18: The Log-book of a Pioneer*, London, 1919
Murray F. Sueter, *Airmen or Noahs*, London, 1928
Ernest D. Swinton, *Eyewitness*, London, 1932
Sir Eustace Tennyson d'Eyncourt, *A Shipbuilder's Yarn*, London, 1948
Lady Wester Wemyss, *Life and Letters of Lord Wester Wemyss*, London, 1935

Collections of Documents

Navy Records Society, vol. 103, *The Fisher Papers*, vol. 1, 1960
Navy Records Society, vol. 108, *The Jellicoe Papers*, vol. 1, 1966
Navy Records Society, vol. 111, *The Jellicoe Papers*, vol. 2. 1968
Navy Records Society, vol. 113, *Documents Relating to the Naval Air Service*, vol. 1, 1969
Navy Records Society, vol. 117, *The Keyes Papers*, vol. 1. 1972
Navy Records Society, vol. 121, *The Keyes Papers*, vol. 2, 1980
Navy Records Society, vol. 122, *The Keyes Papers*, vol. 3, 1981
Navy Records Society, vol. 128, *The Beatty Papers*, vol. 1, 1989
Navy Records Society, vol. 132, *The Beatty Papers*, vol. 2, 199?,
Navy Records Society, vol. 142, *The Submarine Service*, 2001
Navy Records Society, vol. 137, *The Defeat of the Enemy Attack upon Shipping*, 1997

Biographies

Sir Reginald Bacon, *The Life of Lord Fisher of Kilverstone*, London, 1929, vol. 2
Arthur J. Marder, *Fear God and Dread Nought* [Fisher] London, 1959

Ian Kershaw, *Hitler, 1939–45*, London, 2000
Robin Brodhurst, *Churchill's Anchor* [Pound] Barnsley, 2000
Paul Freyberg, *Bernard Freyberg VC*, London, 1991
Phillip Jarrett, *Frank McClean*, Barnsley, 2011
Philip Ziegler, *Mountbatten*, London, 1985
Andrew Boyle, *Trenchard*, London, 1962
Martin Stannard, *Evelyn Waugh, No Abiding City*, London, 1993

General and Economic History

Angus Calder, *The People's War*, reprinted London, 1982
David Cannadine, *In Churchill's Shadow*, London, 2002
J. M. Keynes, *The Economic Consequences of Mr Churchill*, London, 1925
Adam W. Kirkaldy, *British Shipping*, London, 1914
Norman Longmate, *The Bombers*, London, 1983
Arthur Marwick, *The Deluge*, London, 1967
Alan R. Millet, ed., *Military Effectiveness*, vol. 3, *The Second World War*, London, 1988
C. L. Mowat, *Britain Between the Wars*, reprinted London, 1987
A. J. P. Taylor, *English History, 1914–1945*, Oxford, 1975
Adam Tooze, *The Wages of Destruction*, London, 2006

Official Histories

Julian S. Corbett, *History of the Great War, Naval Operations*, vol. 1, London, 1920
J. E. Edmonds, *Military Operations, France and Belgium*, vol. 2, London, 1924
J. E. Edmonds, *The Occupation of the Rhineland*, London, 1943
John Ehrman, *Grand Strategy*, vol. V, *August 1943 – September 1944*, London, 1956
Great Britain, *Ministry of Munitions*, vol. 12, 1922
Michael Howard, *Grand Strategy*, vol. IV, *September 1942 – August 1943*, London, 1972
H. M. D. Parker, *Manpower*, London, 1957
S. W. Roskill, *The War at Sea*, 3 vols, London, 1954–61

Naval History

Admiralty, *Official Procedure and Rules*, 1913
Marinell Ash, *This Noble Harbour*, Edinburgh, 1991
Reginald Bacon, *The Jutland Scandal*, reprinted Barnsley, 2015
R. Baker et al., *British Warship Design in World War II*, London, 1983
Correlli Barnett, *Engage the Enemy More Closely*, London, 1991
Henry Baynham, *Men from the Dreadnoughts*, London, 1976
John Brooks, *Dreadnought Gunnery and the Battle of Jutland*, Abingdon, 2005
Ian Buxton, *Big Gun Monitors*, revised edition, Barnsley, 2012
Anthony Carew, *The Lower Deck of the Royal Navy*, Manchester, 1981
Norman Friedman, *British Carrier Aviation*, London, 1988

Norman Friedman, *Naval Weapons of World War One*, Barnsley, 2011
Norman Friedman, *The British Battleship, 1906–1914*, Barnsley, 2015
Andrew Gordon, *The Rules of the Game*, London, 1996
Willem Hackman, *Seek and Strike*, London, 1984
Sir John Jellicoe, *The Grand Fleet, 1914–1916*, London, 1919
Nicholas Lambert, *Sir John Fisher's Naval Revolution*, Columbia, South Carolina, 2002
Brian Lavery, *Hostilities Only*, Greenwich, 2004
Brian Lavery, *Shield of Empire*, Edinburgh, 2007
Brian Lavery, *The Last Big Gun*, Oxford, 2015
E. B. Potter, *The Great Sea War*, London, 1960
Jon Sumida, *In Defence of Naval Supremacy*, London, 1993
Jak P. Mallmann Showell, ed., *Fuehrer Conferences on Naval Affairs*, London, 2005
Dan van der Vat, *The Ship that Changed the World*, London, c. 1985
Sir Richard Vesey Hamilton, Naval Administration, London, 1896
Joseph Wellings, *On His Majesty's Service*, ed. John Hattendorf, Newport, RI, 1983
Lionel Yexley, *The Inner Life of the Navy*, London, 1908

Military History

Army Training Memorandum, published in 2 vols by Military Library Research Service Ltd, np, nd
Correlli Barnett, *The Desert Generals*, London, 1960
Peter Beale, *Death by Design*, Stroud, 1998
Brian Bond, *British Military Policy between the Two World Wars*, Oxford, 1980
Cornelius Francis Clery, *Minor Tactics*, London, 1880
Jeremy A. Crang, *The British Army and the People's War, 1939–1945*, Manchester, 2000
Robert Crisp, *Brazen Chariots*, London, 1959
W. D. Croft, *Three Years With the 9th (Scottish) Division*, London, 1919
David Scott Daniell, *4th Hussar*, Aldershot, 1959
Brian L. Davis, *British Army Uniforms and Insignia of World War Two*, London, 1983
J. C. Dunn, *The War the Infantry Knew*, 1988
Karl-Heinz Frieser, *The Blitzkrieg Legend*, Annapolis, 2005
General staff, *Notes for Infantry Officers*, March 1916
Captain X [A. D. Gibb], *With Winston Churchill at the Front* Glasgow, 1934
Timothy Harrison Place, *Military Training in the British Army, 1940–1944*, London, 2000
T. H. Holding, *Uniforms of the British Army, Navy and Court*, London, 1894
Karl August Eduard Friedrich Hohenlohe-Ingelfingen Kraft, *Letters on Cavalry ...*, trans. N. L. Walford, Woolwich, 1889
B. H. Liddell Hart, *The Tanks*, vol. 1, London, 1959
Thomas Pakenham, *The Boer War*, London, 1979
G. Philips, *Text Book on Fortification etc, for the Use of the Royal Military College, Sandhurst*, London, 1877

Royal Scots Fusiliers Magazine, quoted in *Britain at War*, June 2016
Edward M. Spiers, *The Late Victorian Army, 1868–1902*, Manchester, c 1992

Aviation History

Air Historical Branch, *The RAF in Maritime War*
C. H. Barnes, *Shorts Aircraft since 1900*, London, revised 1989
Charles H. Gibbs-Smith, *The Rebirth of European Aviation*, London, 1976
Max Hastings, *Bomber Command*, London, 1979
C. G. Jefford, *Observers and Navigators*, Shrewsbury, 2001
H. A. Jones, *The War in the Air*, vol. 6, London, 1937
T. E. Lawrence, *The Mint*, London, 1955
R. D. Layman, *To Ascend from a Floating Base*, np, 1979
Norman Longmate, *The Bombers*, London, 1983
Francis K. Mason, *Hawker Aircraft Since 1920*, London, 1991
H. Montgomery Hyde, *British Air Policy Between the Wars*, London, c. 1976
Williamson Murray, *The Luftwaffe, 1933–45*, Washington, 1996
Ian M. Philpott, *The Royal Air Force*, Barnsley, 2005
Winston G. Ramsey, ed., *The Blitz Then and Now*, London, 1988
C. F. Rawnsley and Robert Wright, *Night Fighter*, Manchester, 1998
Bruce Robertson, *Sopwith, the Man and the Aircraft*, Letchworth, 1970
Andy Saunders, *Battle of Britain, RAF Operations Manual*, Yeovil, 2015
Owen Thetford, *British Naval Aircraft*, London, 1991

Combined Operations

The Dardanelles Commission Minutes of Evidence, National Archives CAB 19
The First Report of the Dardanelles Commission, vol. 1, Guildford, 2000
Bernard Fergusson, *The Watery Maze*, London, 1961
Max Hastings, *Overlord*, London, 1984
Ministry of Information, *Combined Operations* 1943

Parliamentary Debates

Hansard is the official record of parliamentary debates. It is cited in the order, volume
    number, date, and column (not page) number

Articles and Journals

Winston S. Churchill, 'Some Impressions of the War in South Africa', *Royal United
    Services Institute Journal*, July 1901
William Emerson, 'Franklin Roosevelt as Commander-in-Chief in World War II',
    Military Affairs, 1958–59, pp. 181–207

Stephen Richards Graubard, 'Military Demobilization in Great Britain', *Journal of Military History*, 1947, pp. 297–311

Q. M. Howard in *Royal United Services Journal*, February 1966, quoted in Bond, *British Military Policy*, p. 35

Alan G. Jamieson, 'Martyr or Pirate? The Case of Captain Fryatt in the Great War', *Mariner's Mirror*, vol. 85, part 2, May 1999

Matthew Johnson, 'The Liberal Party and the Navy League in Britain before the Great War', *20th Century British History*, 2011

Nicholas Lambert, 'Strategic Command and Control for Maneuver Warfare: Creation of the Royal Navy's War Room System 1905–1915', *Journal of Military History*, vol. 69, 2005

Clive Pearson, 'Stalin as War Leader', *History Review*, December 2008

Naval Review, 1924

Brassey's Naval Annual, 1911–14

The Fleet Annual and Naval Year Book, 1913

Navy League Journal, 1912–13

Index